Warman's
COUNTRY
ANTIQUES & COLLECTIBLES

DANA GEHMAN MORYKAN
HARRY L. RINKER

Wallace-Homestead Book Company
Radnor, Pennsylvania

Volumes in the Encyclopedia of Antiques and Collectibles

Harry L. Rinker, Series Editor

Warman's Americana & Collectibles, 5th Edition,
edited by Harry L. Rinker

Warman's Country Antiques & Collectibles,
by Dana Gehman Morykan and Harry L. Rinker

Warman's English & Continental Pottery & Porcelain, 2nd Edition,
by Susan and Al Bagdade

Warman's Oriental Antiques,
by Gloria and Robert Mascarelli

Copyright © 1992 by Rinker Enterprises, Inc.

Published in Radnor, Pennsylvania 19089, by Wallace-Homestead, a division of Chilton Book Company

Manufactured in the United States of America

Library of Congress Cataloging-in-Publication Data
Morykan, Dana Gehman.
    Warman's country antiques & collectibles / Dana Gehman Morykan and
Harry L. Rinker.—1st ed.
       p.   cm.—(Encyclopedia of antiques and collectibles)
    Includes bibliographical references and index.
    ISBN 0-87069-625-4 (pbk.)
    1. Antiques—United States.   I. Rinker, Harry L.   II. Title.
III. Series.
NK805.M67   1992
745.1'0973—dc20   91-50681
                                                            CIP

1 2 3 4 5 6 7 8 9 0   1 0 9 8 7 6 5 4 3 2

CONTENTS

1990s COUNTRY

Country is a style that is both permanent and evolutionary. Country in the 1970s differed radically from its pre–World War II counterpart. Country in the 1990s contrasts sharply with Country in the 1970s. In the last fifteen years Country has passed through youthful exuberance, adolescence, and early adulthood. As the 1990s begins, Country has matured. It now must define its role as an adult.

Prior to World War II—in fact through the 1950s—American Country and early American were synonymous. A Country kitchen or den contained a large open-hearth fireplace with a wood-carved mantel, spider–legged cast iron cooking utensils, trestle table, spinning wheel, and appropriate accessories. Living rooms consisted of a mix of semi–formal Chippendale and Federal pieces with an occasional rustic piece, e.g., a table–chair, thrown in for good measure.

In the 1960s Country and early American diverged. There were several reasons for the divorce.

First, early American is an East Coast style, with a heavy New England presence. Collectors sought a style with a greater national emphasis. The heartland of America became the regional base for Country of the 1970s and later.

Second, Country collectors wanted a style which reflected nineteenth century—not eighteenth century—rural America. The vast majority of America's pioneer roots rest in the nineteenth and early twentieth centuries.

Third, early American pieces became expensive. Instead of tens of dollars, it required hundreds and thousands of dollars to buy key objects.

This trend continued through the 1970s and 1980s. The key to Country is its affordability. Country is a total look—period settings, not accent pieces.

Contemporary Country owes its birth to two major events: (1) the preparation and celebration of America's Bicentennial and (2) the social activism of the 1960s. Both reexamined America's past and came to similar conclusions. America's spirit rested not with our colonial ancestors, but in the perseverance and "can–do" attitude of nineteenth-century America, best exemplified in rural areas and small towns scattered across the country.

The decision to focus the celebration of America's Bicentennial on the local rather than national level was the catalyst that launched contemporary Country. America would celebrate all of its history, not just the 150-year period leading up to the American Revolution. America discovered itself and its "folk" along the way.

It should come as no surprise that Country and folk art evolved at the same time. There is a kinship between the two. However, where folk art is aesthetic (at least that is what its collectors and dealers would have one believe), Country is utilitarian. Both celebrate life, particularly the life of the "average" American. Where folk art emphasizes the individual, Country adds the tempering element of community.

A return to nature and revival of the handcraft technologies of the eighteenth and nineteenth centuries were the elements within the social activism of the 1960s that allowed contemporary Country to evolve. Country is closely linked to the colors and seasons of nature. Its roots are in the earth. It is a modernized version of the American myth.

The revival of handcraft technology was a reaction to mass production, look–alike goods found in most discount and department stores. The products of the handcraft revivalist allowed for individual expression, while at the same time creating a strong sense of the past. Since handcrafted goods often copied period pieces, they made Country affordable.

One final element is needed to explain the arrival and successful growth of contemporary Country: the interior decorator. Several museum exhibits in the early 1970s, most notably "The Flowering of American Folk Art," demonstrated the decorative potentials of Country. By the late 1970s Country was the dominant American decorating style—all thanks to interior decorators.

Country enjoyed a youthful exuberance during the 1970s and early 1980s. The style was free and open to a vast amount of interpretation. Country was eclectic. There was no emphasis on period, i.e., everything in a room had to be from a fixed historical time period. Country was what anyone wanted to make it.

During Country's adolescence in the 1980s, it became more narrowly defined and, in many ways, restricted. There was a literature explosion. Individuals wrote design books and price guides. Over a half–dozen magazines devoted exclusively to Country began. Specialized Country antique shows were held throughout the country. While this marked a growing maturity on the part of Country, it also corralled Country, i.e., fenced it in, so to speak. Youthful exuberance was replaced by established norms.

The late 1970s and early 1980s saw Country prices skyrocket. Many items doubled, tripled, or quadrupled in value in a relatively short period of time. As prices rose beyond the pocketbook in a number of categories, e.g., early decorated stoneware, Country collectors constantly scrambled to develop new and affordable collecting areas. Country was hot, not just in one sector, but across the board.

In the late 1980s, Country cooled. In no way should this be interpreted to mean that people turned away from Country. Far from it. Country remains the most popular design style in America. What it does signify is that the Country market became stable in price and settled into traditional approaches with which everyone is comfortable.

1990s Country is mature Country. It is evolving, but at a much slower pace than in the 1980s. Country of the 1970s and 1980s was "American" Country. 1990s Country has begun to explore the rural or peasant lifestyles of foreign lands, particularly Europe, with strong emphasis on England, France, and the Scandinavian countries. The approach is a highly romanticized one. Lacking a proper chronological and geographical understanding of European Country, collectors tend to mix countries and historical periods.

Country has gone formal. Instead of the pioneer look that dominated the 1970s and 1980s, Country of the 1990s favors the look of the prosperous farmer and small town merchant. Country is now equated with success, not struggle. Country of the 1990s stresses the finer things found in the Country household.

Many claim the current Victorian decorating craze has replaced Country. Not true! More and more Victorian collectors are realizing that the vernacular oak furniture and accompanying accessories represent a far greater number of Victorians than do the Renaissance Revival urban pieces. In truth, there is Victorian Country.

Country of the 1990s is comfortable Country. The look is well defined; it can be trusted. Collectors and designers blend period and handcrafted revival pieces with relative ease. More and more individuals are rediscovering the joys of making things themselves. The settled appearance of Country offers a welcome home to the Yuppie looking for an escape from the fast track pace of the 1980s.

Period pieces sell within narrow price ranges. The speculative Country prices of the 1980s ended with the 1990–1991 recession and the decline of the Yuppie era. At long last, collectors can buy Country with a high degree of confidence.

Despite its newfound comfortableness, Country still has a great deal of growing and maturing ahead. Material of the first half of the twentieth century needs to be incorporated into the look. Collectors must begin to explore Country at leisure, one of the most neglected aspects of Country collecting. It is time to end the divorce between Country and folk art. Folk art must be de–aestheticized and made part of popular culture, both in terms of interpretation and price.

Finally, Country must resist the temptation of trendiness. It deserves to be around forever.

INTRODUCTION

Welcome to *Warman's Country Antiques & Collectibles*, a volume in the Warman Encyclopedia of Antiques and Collectibles Series. While this volume contains all the traditional Warman features—category introductions featuring history, references, periodicals, collectors' clubs, museums, and reproduction alerts and detailed, accurate listings—it also represents a significant departure from our established format.

First, the book focuses on a "style" rather than group of objects. *Warman's Country Antiques & Collectibles* is one of two style books that will be part of the Warman Encyclopedia series. The other will focus on Victoriana.

Second, because Country marries period pieces with contemporary reproductions and copycats, you will find a listing of contemporary craftspersons and manufacturers in the category introductions. Initial reaction to this innovation has been extremely positive.

COUNTRY

For the purpose of this book, Country is defined as any objects that were part of nineteenth- and early twentieth-century rural life. The agrarian community included farms and villages. Objects from both are included in this book. This book is more than just a price guide to "farm" collectibles.

Country is part of Americana. Its objects reflect how a major portion of our country's population lived. This book documents a part of their legacy.

However, limiting Country just to American objects in the 1990s is shortsighted. In the 1980s Country collectors expanded their horizons and discovered English Country and French Country. You will find categories relating to each of these movements throughout the book.

There is a strong link between Country and folk art. Many so–called folk art items originated in rural America. Many Country categories, e.g., quilts, have been appropriated by folk art collectors and made part of their movement. This book is concerned only about the objects themselves. If an object is Country in origin, it belongs in this book. Hence, you will find a fair amount of "folk art" within these pages.

Throughout the 1970s and early 1980s collectors, dealers, and decorators stressed the informal, generic side of Country. In the mid-1980s they discovered that Country had a formal side. *Warman's Country Antiques & Collectibles* has carefully blended the formal and informal. As a result, some categories and listings will challenge your understanding of what does and does not constitute Country.

Finally, each of us defines Country differently. In a way this reflects the diversity and independent frame of mind that is so much a part of Country. This first edition of *Warman's Country Antiques & Collectibles* reflects how the authors currently view Country from their perspective. As Country continues to mature, so will the views of the authors and the presentation of subsequent editions.

FINDING COUNTRY

Country is everywhere. You will find objects that are part of Country at virtually every craft show, flea market, mall, shop, or show that you visit. This is due in part to Country's modern eclecticism and its dualistic nature—formal and informal.

In the past two decades a number of "Country" shows and flea markets have developed that have a strong Country emphasis. The following list will help you locate them. Because some of the show dates shift, the list is organized by promoter. Check with the promoter for the exact dates of their next Country event.

Jim Burk (3012 Miller Road, Washington Boro, PA 17582). Check the dates for his shows held at Dutch Town & Country Inn on Route 30 east of Lancaster, PA, and at the York County Fairgrounds, York, PA.

Ronald Cox (9411 East 141st Street, Fishers, IA 46038). Cox's Hoosier Antiques Exposition is held at the Indiana State Fairgrounds, Indianapolis, IN, in early April and mid-October each year.

Humberstone Management (1510 N. Hoyne, Chicago, IL 60622). The Sandwich Antiques Market is held at The Fairgrounds, Sandwich, IL, one Sunday each month between May and October.

Crutcher–Keighley (PO Box 1267, Hamilton, MT 59840). Antiques Show & Sale, Indiana State Fairgrounds, Indianapolis, IN, held in mid-April and mid-October.

Bruce Knight (PO Box 2429, Springfield, OH 45501). The Springfield Antiques Show & Flea Market is held at the Clark County Fairgrounds, Springfield, OH, the third weekend of the month, year around, excluding July. The December market is held the second weekend of the month.

Britton Knowles (PO Box 6606, South Bend, IN 46660). The Amish Heartland show is held three times a year at the Elkhart County Fairgrounds, Goshen, IN.

Richard E. Kramer (427 Midvale Avenue, St. Louis, MO 63130). Kramer's Heart of Country show held at the Opryland Hotel in Nashville, TN, in early spring each year is the bellwether Country Show in America. Also check out Home in Indiana held in Indianapolis in early fall.

Mrs. J. L. Robinson (PO Box 549, St. Charles, IL 60174). Kane County Antiques Flea Market is held at the Kane County Fairgrounds, St. Charles, IL, the first Sunday of every month and the preceding Saturday.

Sha–Dor Shows (PO Box 1400, Rockville, MD 20850). American Classic Antiques Show & Sale held at D.C. Armory, Washington, DC, in mid-May.

As you can see from the above list, Indianapolis, Indiana, is the real "heart" of Country. Almost every weekend there is a show either in Indianapolis or within a few miles distance that has a strong Country appeal. Malls in the surrounding area also heavily emphasize Country.

There are many regional Country shows, e.g., the American Country Antiques Show held in Windsor Locks, Connecticut, or the Zoar Antiques Show in Zoar, Ohio. Some communities such as New Oxford, Pennsylvania, and Fairhaven, Ohio, turn their entire town into an outdoor antiques festival one or more times a year. All these shows and antiques festivals are advertised in the leading trade papers. Attend as many as possible.

Do not overlook contemporary craft shows. State and regional craft shows abound. Check with your local Council of the Arts to determine the date and location of the shows nearest you. Many have become specialized, e.g., the Mid–Atlantic Quilt Festival held each year in late winter.

Finally, one auction house deserves special mention: Garth's Auctions, Inc. (PO Box 369, Delaware, OH 43015). No one offers a finer selection of Country on a regular basis. An annual subscription to his catalogs is a must for any serious Country collector.

ORGANIZATION OF THIS BOOK

General Approach: Warman's has never been wed to tradition. *Warman's Country Antiques & Collectibles* is an excellent case in point. Country is a *style*. It demands a different approach from the straight alphabetical listing of categories found in *Warman's Antiques and Their Prices* or *Warman's Americana & Collectibles*.

After careful consideration, we decided to treat Country topically. In order to do this, a twofold approach was used for the major categories. One group focuses on general collecting topics, e.g., furniture; the second concentrates on a phase of agrarian life, e.g., the barn. The key was to develop a presentation that corresponds with how *you* collect and deal with Country.

This approach is possible because of our commitment to a strong index. The index ties the book together. Used properly, it will lead you to the correct location for the Country item that you are seeking.

History: Here we discuss the category, describe how the object was made, who are or were the leading manufacturers, and variations of form and style. In many instances a chronology for the objects is established.

Whenever possible, we place the object in a social context—how it was used, for what purposes, etc. We also delve into how the objects are used within a Country setting. An object's decorative use is just as much a part of its history as its utilitarian use.

Where appropriate, we have added some collecting hints. We note where cross category collecting and outside factors are critical in pricing. There are hints on where best to find some of the objects.

References: A few general references are listed to encourage collectors to learn more about their objects. Included are author, title, most recent edition, publisher (if published by a small firm or individual, we have indicated "published by author"), and a date of publication.

Finding these books may present a problem. The antiques and collectibles field is blessed with a dedicated core of book dealers who stock these specialized publications. You may find them at flea markets, antiques shows, and through their advertisements in leading publications in the field. Many dealers publish annual or semi–annual catalogs. Ask to be put on their mailing lists. Books go out–of–print quickly, yet many books printed over twenty–five years ago remain the standard work in a field. Also, haunt used book dealers for reference material.

Collectors' Clubs: Collectors' clubs add vitality to any collecting field. Their publications and conventions produce knowledge which often cannot be found anywhere else. Many of these clubs are short-lived; others are so strong that they have regional and local chapters. Support those clubs that match your collecting interest.

Periodicals: The Country field is served by a wealth of general and specific publications. You need to be aware of the following:

American Country Collectibles, GCR Publishing Group, 1700 Broadway, New York, NY 10019.
Country, Reiman Publications, 5400 S. 60th Street, Greendale, WI 53129.
Country Accents, GCR Publishing Group, 1700 Broadway, New York, NY 10019.
Country Collectibles, Harris Publications, 1115 Broadway, New York, NY 10010.
Country Decorator, GCR Publishing Group, 1700 Broadway, New York, NY 10019.
Country Folk Art, 8393 East Holly Road, Holly, MI 48442.
Country Home, Meredith Corporation, 1716 Locust Street, New York, NY 10019.
Country Living, Hearst Corporation, 224 West 57th Street, New York, NY 10019.
Country Sampler, Sampler Publications, 707 Kautz Road, St. Charles, IL 60174.
Country Victorian Accents, GCR Publishing Company, 1700 Broadway, New York, NY 10019.
Country Woman, Reiman Publications, 5400 South 60th Street, Greendale, WI 53129.

Early American Life, Cowles Magazines, PO Box 8200, Harrisburg, PA 17105.
Farm and Ranch Living, Reiman Publications, 5400 South 60th Street, Greendale, WI 53129.

Articles about Country and Country collectibles are featured regularly in most trade newspapers. Two papers deserve special mention:

Antique Week, PO Box 90, Knightstown, IN 46148.
Maine Antique Digest, PO Box 358, Waldoboro, ME 04572.

Regional papers from New England, the Middle Atlantic, and the Midwest stress Country more heavily than regional papers from other parts of the country. You will find a complete list of these papers in David J. Maloney, Jr.'s *Collector's Information Clearinghouse Antiques & Collectibles Resource Directory* (Wallace–Homestead Book Company, 1992).

Museums: The best way to study a specific field is to see as many documented examples as possible. For this reason, we have listed museums where significant collections of collectibles are on display. We especially recommend visiting state and regional farm museums.

Reproduction Alert: Reproductions (exact copies) and copycats (stylistic copies) are a major concern. Unfortunately, many of these items are unmarked. Newness of appearance is often the best clue to spotting them. Where "Reproduction Alert" appears, a watchful eye should be kept within the entire category.

Reproductions are only one aspect of the problem. Outright fakes (objects deliberately meant to deceive) are another. Be especially alert for fakes in categories where Country and folk art come together.

Reproduction Craftspersons and Manufacturers: Not everyone can afford period pieces; not everyone wants period pieces. When achieving the "look" is the principal concern, reproductions and copycat items are perfectly acceptable.

Warman's Country Antiques & Collectibles is the first price guide to list contemporary craftspersons and manufacturers side by side with period material. We have done so because we believe these objects can just as effectively provide the Country look as period examples. Further, many are so well made that they will survive and become the collectibles of tomorrow and the antiques of the future.

We gathered the names of craftspersons and manufacturers from existing literature in the field. Some we know personally. Others we do not. None paid to have their name or business listed. Before buying from any, we urge you to inspect their merchandise personally and compare their products and prices with others offering similar products.

Listings: We have attempted to make the listings descriptive enough so the specific object can be identified. Most guides limit their descriptions to one line. Not those with the name *Warman's* in the title. We have placed emphasis on those items which are actively being sold in the marketplace. Nevertheless, some harder–to–find objects are included in order to demonstrate the market spread.

Because of the multifaceted nature of the antiques and collectibles field, category overlap will occur within the volumes in the Warman's Encyclopedia of Antiques and Collectibles. When this does happen, all new listings will be provided, with a few minor exceptions.

PRICE NOTES

Most prices within Country categories are relatively stable. This is why we use a one price system. When necessary, we will use ranges. But, as you will find in using this book, this is a rarity.

Our pricing is based on an object being in very good condition. If otherwise, we note this in our description. It would be ideal to suggest that mint, or unused, examples of all objects do exist. Objects from the past were used, whether they be glass, china, dolls, or toys. Because of this use, some normal wear must be expected. Furthermore, if the original box is important in establishing a price, it is assumed that the box is present with the article.

As the number of special interest collectors grows, a single object may appeal to more than one buyer, each of whom has their own "price" in mind. In preparing prices for this guide we look at the object within the category being considered and price it as though an individual who collects actively within that category is buying it.

Some Country objects have regional interest. However, a national price consensus has formed as a result of the publication of specialized price guides, collectors' club newsletters, and magazines and newspapers. Regional pricing is discounted in favor of the more general national consensus.

RESEARCH

Collectors of Country deserve credit for their attention to scholarship and the skill by which they have assembled their collections. This book attests to how strong and encompassing the Country market has become through their efforts.

We obtain our prices from many key sources: dealers, publications, auctions, collectors, and field work. The generosity with which dealers have given advice is a credit to the field. Everyone recognizes the need for a guide that is specific and has accurate prices. We study newspapers, magazines, newsletters, and other publications in the collectibles and antiques field. All of them are critical in understanding what is available in the market. Special recognition must be given to those collectors' club newsletters and magazines which discuss prices.

Our staff is constantly in the field—from Massachusetts to Florida, Pennsylvania to California. We utilize a Board of Advisors that provides regional as well as specialized information. Each *Warman's* title incorporates information from hundreds of auction catalogs generously furnished by the firms listed in the Auction House section. Finally, private collectors have worked closely with us, sharing their knowledge of price trends and developments unique to their specialties.

BUYER'S GUIDE, NOT SELLER'S GUIDE

Warman's Country Antiques & Collectibles is designed to be a buyer's guide, a guide to what you would have to pay to purchase an object on the open market from a dealer or collector. *It is not a seller's guide to prices.* People frequently make this mistake and are deceiving themselves by doing so.

If you have an object in this book and wish to sell it, you should expect to receive approximately 35 to 40 percent of the values listed. If the object cannot be resold quickly, expect to receive even less. The truth is simple. Knowing to whom to sell an object is worth 50 percent or more of its value. Buyers are very specialized; dealers work for years to assemble a list of collectors who will pay top dollar for an item.

Examine your piece as objectively as possible. If it is something from your childhood, try to step back from the personal memories in evaluating its condition. As an antiques appraiser, I spend a great deal of my time telling people their treasures are not "gold," but items readily available in the marketplace.

In respect to buying and selling, a simple philosophy is that a good purchase occurs when both the buyer and seller are happy with the price. Don't look back. Hindsight has little value in the collectibles field. Given time, things tend to balance out.

COMMENTS INVITED

Warman's Country Antiques & Collectibles is a major effort to deal with a complex field. Our readers are encouraged to send their comments and suggestions to Rinker Enterprises, PO Box 248, Zionsville, PA 18092.

STATE OF THE MARKET

Overall, Country is stable. This means that within most Country categories objects are selling this year for about what they sold last year. Price movement is within a plus or minus five percent range. Any price growth that occurs is gradual.

Do not interpret this to mean that Country objects are not selling. If this were the case, there would be no need for this book. Vigorous buying and selling often occurs within a stable market. Objects do change hands. What is missing from the market is sudden, rapid price increases.

A stable market has pluses and minuses. The pluses include a strong sense of confidence in the prices for pieces being offered, a more deliberate and slower–paced interaction between buyers and sellers, and a market dominated primarily by collectors who are in it for the long term. The negatives are the lack of a sense of excitement within the market and an inability to sell the low and middle range pieces quickly. Quality pieces sell regardless of the state of a market.

It is difficult to talk about Country as a single market in the 1990s. Country has become fragmented. There is American Country, English Country, and French Country; Victorian Country and Twentieth-Century Country; Midwest Country and Western Country. Many Country categories, e.g., stoneware, have developed a life of their own. One has to look at Country's individual parts to fully understand how the market is moving.

Country "animal" collectibles are gaining in popularity. Any advertising, from country store to gasoline station, that has a farm or farm animal motif is rising in value. The cow is the favored animal of the moment. What's next? Chickens? How else can you explain the strong prices within the stoneware market for chicken feeders?

Recycling is nothing new in rural America. This is reflected in the current market by the strong prices being realized for old tools. Many of these are being bought for use, not collectibility.

As one type of item within a category becomes pricey, another steps in to take its place among collectors who buy in the lower price ranges. Fiesta and Fiesta copycats along with Russel Wright dinnerware experienced major price increases in the 1980s. As a result, Bauer, Blue Ridge, Coors, Crooksville, Franciscan, and Stangl wares are attracting more and more interest. Another reason for this is that many of the patterns from these companies feature brilliantly colored floral and fruit patterns on earth tone backgrounds.

The popularity of many textile forms continues. However, emphasis is shifting from nineteenth-century examples to pieces made from the 1920s through the 1940s. One example is the price increase in Sunbonnet and Double Wedding Ring quilts. New collecting categories also are emerging. Crocheted items are doing well. Needlework decoration on a wide variety of textiles from the 1920s, ranging from tablecloths to guest towels, is in the "discovery" stage.

Nineteenth-century stoneware is spotty. Blue and white stoneware in the more commonly found patterns, white patterned ironstone, and spongeware have decreased slightly in value. Yellowware is fighting to hold its own. Mocha, with its random pattern designs ranging from seaweed to earthworm, realizes strong prices both on the auction block and at antiques shows.

Painted, wooden-handled kitchen utensils from the first half of the twentieth century have declined sharply in value. There are several explanations. First, the Country kitchen lost its pre–eminent place in a Country decorating scheme to the living room and bedroom. Second, the entire kitchen collectibles market cooled. Third, the market was flooded with examples for sale, and more survived than collectors realized. Painted, wooden-handled kitchen utensils that are selling are being bought largely for use.

Wire bird cages and "folk art" bird houses continue to command top dollar despite a market overwhelmed with large numbers of reproductions, copycats, fantasy items, and fakes. The trend has continued long enough that it is safe to predict a decline in value and interest in the immediate future.

Holiday collectibles, especially Christmas objects, have always been a vital part of Country. Halloween and Easter are challenging Christmas as the most popular of the holiday collectibles. The growing popularity of Easter collectibles has led to a strong interest by a number of collectors in rabbit collectibles.

If one did not know the circumstances involved, one might be persuaded that Shaker is the "hottest" regional Country collectible. A number of record prices have been set recently for Shaker furniture. The reason is that the Shaker market has been hyped to a number of nouveau riche celebrities who have been manipulated into paying far in excess of what the market warrants. Segments of the Shaker market in which they are not buying are flat. A truly strong market shows strength across the board. There are going to be some surprised individuals in five to ten years when they lose interest in their pieces and attempt to sell them.

The big 1991–1992 news is that the recession hit the Country market. Midwest dealers, flea markets, malls, shops, and shows who constitute the heart of Country seemed immune from the economic problems that were rampant in the trade along the East Coast in 1990–1991. No longer. The recession has hit the Midwest antiques and collectibles business full force.

The chief problem with the antiques and collectibles phase of the recession is that too many people see only the negatives. There are many positives to the picture. First, merchandise is affordable. Prices are coming down in many cases. Second, dealers are willing to negotiate more than ever. Third, many dealers are selling the best items from their private collections in an effort to generate operating capital. Some masterpiece items are available in the current market at very affordable prices. Finally, dealers are beginning to pay attention to the collector because they realize that collectors constitute the true backbone of the antiques and collectibles market. Decorators are fickle friends, delighted to tap into our market when there are profits to be made but totally unwilling to lend their support in hard times.

There is no question that Country will be around forever. It is the most important market segment next to the antiques and collectibles themselves. At the moment, Country is resting, waiting to a return to the glories it enjoyed in the mid-1970s. It will happen.

Meanwhile, enjoy the quiet of Country.

AUCTION HOUSES

The following auction houses cooperate with Rinker Enterprises, Inc., by providing catalogs of their auctions and price lists. This information is used to prepare *Warman's Antiques and Their Prices*, volumes in the Warman's Encyclopedia of Antiques and Collectibles, such as *Warman's Country Antiques & Collectibles*, and other Wallace–Homestead Book Company publications. This support is most appreciated.

Sanford Alderfer Auction
  Company
501 Fairgrounds Rd.
Hatfield, PA 19440
(215) 368-5477

Al Anderson
P. O. Box 644
Troy, OH 45373
(513) 339-0850

W. Graham Arader III
1000 Boxwood Court
King of Prussia, PA 19406
(215) 825-6570

Ark Antiques
Box 3133
New Haven, CT 06515
(203) 387-3754

Arthur Auctioneering
R. D. 2
Hughesville, PA 17737
(717) 584-3697

Noel Barrett Antiques and
  Auctions Ltd.
P. O. Box 1001
Carversville, PA 18913
(215) 297-5109

Robert F. Batchelder
1 West Butler Avenue
Ambler, PA 19002
(215) 643-1430

Biders Antiques, Inc.
241 South Union Street
Lawrence, MA 01843
(508) 688-4347

Richard A. Bourne Co.,
  Inc.
Corporation St.
P. O. Box 141
Hyannis Port, MA 02647
(508) 775-0797

Butterfield's
220 San Bruno Ave.
San Francisco, CA 94103
(415) 861-7500

Christie's
502 Park Avenue
New York, NY 10022
(212) 546-1000

Christie's East
219 E. 67th St.
New York, NY 10021
(212) 606-0400

Christmas Morning
1850 Crown Rd. Suite
  1111
Dallas, TX 75234
(817) 236-1155

Marvin Cohen Auctions
Box 425, Routes 20 & 22
New Lebanon, NY 12125
(518) 794-9333

Collector's Auction Services
P. O. Box 13732
Seneca, PA 16346
(814) 677-6070

Marlin G. Denlinger
RR 3, Box 3775
Morrisville, VT 05661
(802) 888-2774

William Doyle Galleries,
  Inc.
175 E. 87th St.
New York, NY 10128
(212) 427-2730

Early Auction Co.
123 Main St.
Milford, OH 45150
(513) 831-4833

Ken Farmer Realty &
  Auction Co.
1122 Norwood St.
Radford, VA 24141
(703) 639-0939

Fine Arts Co. of
  Philadelphia, Inc.
1808 Chestnut St.
Philadelphia, PA 19103
(215) 563-9275

Ron Fox
F. T. S. Inc.
416 Throop St.
N. Babylon, NY 11704
(516) 669-7232

William A. Fox Auctions,
  Inc.
676 Morris Ave.
Springfield, NJ 07081
(201)467-2366

Garth's Auction, Inc.
2690 Stratford Rd.
P. O. Box 369
Delaware, OH 43015
(614) 362-4771 or
  369-5085

Glass-Works Auctions
P. O. Box 187-102
Jefferson St.
East Greenville, PA 18041
(215) 679-5849

Grandma's Trunk
The Millards
P. O. Box 404
Northport, NI 49670
(616) 386-5351

Guerney's
136 East 73rd St.
New York, NY 10021
(212) 794-2280

Hake's Americana and
Collectibles
P. O. Box 1444
York, PA 17405
(717) 848-1333

Harmer Rooke
Numismatists, Inc.
3 East 57th St.
New York, NY 10022
(212) 751-4122

Hart Galleries
2311 Westheimer
Houston, TX 77098
(713) 524-2979 or
523-7389

Norman C. Heckler &
Company
Bradford Corner RD.
Woodstock Valley, CT
06282
(203) 974-1634

Leslie Hindman, Inc.
215 West Ohio St.
Chicago, IL 60610
(312) 670-0010

Michael Ivankovich
Antiques
P. O. Box 2458
Doylestown, PA 18901
(215) 345-6094

James D. Julia, Inc.
P. O. Box 830
Fairfield, ME 04937
(207) 453-7904

Charles E. Kirtley
P. O. Box 2273
Elizabeth City, NC 27906
(919) 335-1262

Les Paul's
2615 Magnolia St., Suite A
Oakland, CA 94607
(415) 832-2615

Howard Lowery
3818 W. Magnolia Blvd.
Burbank, CA 91505
(818) 972-9080

Alex G. Malloy, Inc.
P. O. Box 38
South Salem, NY 10590
(203) 438-0396

Martin Auctioneers, Inc.
Larry L. Martin
P. O. Box 477
Intercourse, PA 17534
(717) 768-8108

Robert Merry Auction
Company
5501 Milburn Road
St. Louis, MO 63129
(314) 487-3992

Mid-Hudson Auction
Galleries
One Idlewild Ave.
Cornwall-On-Hudson, NY
12520
(214) 534-7828

Milwaukee Auction
Galleries
318 N. Water
Milwaukee, WI 53202
(414) 271-1105

Neal Alford Company
4139 Magazine St.
New Orleans, LA 70115
(504) 899-5329

New England Auction
Gallery
Box 2273
W. Peabody, MA 01960
(508) 535-3140

New Hampshire Book
Auctions
Woodbury Rd.
Weare, NH 03281
(603) 529-1700

Nostalgia Publications, Inc.
21 South Lake Dr.
Hackensack, NJ 07601
(201) 488-4536

Pettigrew Auction
Company
1645 South Tejon St.
Colorado Springs, CO
80906
(719) 633-7963

Postcards International
P. O. Box 2930
New Haven, CT
06515-0030
(203) 865-0814

David Rago Arts & Crafts
P. O. Box 3592 Station E
Trenton, NJ 08629
(609) 585-2546

Lloyd Ralston Toys
173 Post Road
Fairfield, CT 06432
(203) 255-1233 or
366-3399

Renzel's Auction Service
P. O. Box 222
Emigsville, PA 17318
(717) 764-6412

R. Niel & Elaine Reynolds
Box 133
Waterford, VA 22190
(703) 882-3574

Roan Bros. Auction Gallery
R.D. 3, Box 118
Cogan Station, PA 17728
(717) 494-0170

Robert W. Skinner Inc.
Bolton Gallery
357 Main St.
Bolton, MA 01740
(508) 779-6241

Smith House Toy Sales
26 Adlington Rd.
Eliot, ME 03903
(207) 439-4614

Sotheby's
1334 York Avenue
New York, NY 10021
(212) 606-7000

Stanton's Auctioneers &
    Realtors
144 South Main St.
Vermontville, MI 49096
(517) 726-0181

Swann Galleries, Inc.
104 E. 25th St.
New York, NY 10010
(212) 254-4710

Theriault's
P. O. Box 151
Annapolis, MD 21401
(301) 224-3655

Western Glass Auctions
1288 W. 11th St., Suite
    #230
Tracy, CA 95376
(209) 832-4527

Winter Associates
21 Cooke St. Box 823
Plainville, CT 06062
(203) 793-0288

Wolf's Auction Gallery
13015 Larchmere Blvd.
Shaker Heights, OH 44120
(216) 231-3888

Woody Auction
Douglass, KS 67039
(316) 746-2694

ACKNOWLEDGMENTS

The gestation period for most books is considerably longer than that for a human. Somehow this does seem right. Children last a lot longer than most books.

The seed for *Warman's Country Antiques & Collectibles* was planted when *Warman's Americana & Collectibles* was developed for Warman Publishing Company in the early 1980s as part of a projected series entitled the Warman Encyclopedia of Antiques and Collectibles. Alas, this initial seed failed to germinate.

When Wallace–Homestead, a division of Chilton Books, acquired Warman Publishing, the idea for a Warman Encyclopedia series was replanted. Ronald A. Hoxter, Senior Vice President of Book Publishing, and Neil Levin, Director of Sales and Marketing, recognized the harvest that was possible. Their foresight and support was critical to this rebirth.

After an almost eight-year hiatus, I was developing a new Warman title. Since I view the Warman titles which I edit and author as extensions of my family, the concept of becoming a proud papa once again was a little overwhelming. However, it is impossible to be just a little pregnant. Thus, once the seed was planted, I had no choice but to allow the project to mature.

Warman's Country Antiques & Collectibles happened because of the strong support cast that has grown over the years—"The Rinkettes" (my office staff without whom nothing would be accomplished); advisors, collectors, dealers, and friends who shared their advice willingly and freely; auction houses, mail auctions, and direct sale dealers who provide their catalogs and lists; staff members of trade newspapers and periodicals who shared their thoughts; and, a new group of individuals from the craft community. Thank you one and all.

The only way that Rinker Enterprises, Inc., can accomplish the large number of projects that it does is to assign staff members to specific tasks. Dana Morykan was in charge of Country. Because of the major role that she played, her name appears along with mine as author, a credit well deserved.

Dana especially wishes to thank Aldine Gehman, her mother, whose example has been the basis for all her endeavors. Next her husband, Ray, who introduced her to auctions and the love of collecting. Finally, her children, who with their father, provided the constant support that made this undertaking such a pleasurable experience.

I found becoming a papa once again a rather enjoyable experience. I think I will do it again. I trust you will find this and my future children as useful as you have *Warman's Antiques and Their Prices* and *Warman's Americana & Collectibles*.

Without you, the readers and users of these books, all these efforts would be for naught. As a result, my final thanks are reserved for *you*.

PO Box 248
Zionsville, PA 18092
Dana Gehman Morykan and Harry L. Rinker
February 1992

ABBREVIATIONS

The following are standard abbreviations which we have used throughout this edition of **Warman's Country Antiques & Collectibles**.

adv	=	advertisement	l =	length
C	=	century	litho =	lithograph
c	=	circa	mkd =	marked
cov	=	cover	orig =	original
d	=	diameter	pcs =	pieces
dec	=	decorated	pr =	pair
emb	=	embossed	rect =	rectangular
ftd	=	footed	sgd =	signed
ground	=	background	SP =	silver plated
h	=	height	sq =	square
hp	=	hand painted	w =	width
imp	=	impressed	# =	numbered

COUNTRY BARN

If the Country kitchen is the farm's social center, the barn is the farm's work center. The barn and its supporting structures differ from region to region. Great bank barns are the dominant barn type in Pennsylvania. The lower level housed the animals, the upper level provided equipment storage and the lofts and attached silo stored feed. Support buildings—e.g., corn cribs, chicken houses, and storage sheds—completed the farm setting.

Much of farm labor is seasonal in nature and requires specific equipment designed for the task. In many instances, equipment usage is limited to a few days or weeks. As a result, farm equipment spends most of its time in storage, so plenty of space is a must.

Like most individuals, farmers tend to fill up space when it is available. Space makes savers. Farmers and individuals in rural communities are driven to saving by two key philosophies: (1) It's too good to throw out, and (2) I never know when I will need it. If it still works, save it. Best to keep it around in case the new one breaks. If it does not work, but can be repaired easily, save it anyway. It will get fixed the next time work is slow. It is primarily for these reasons that corners and lofts of barns are treasure troves for the Country collector.

The Country barn and outbuildings required continual maintenance, usually drawing the farmer's attention outside the planting and harvesting seasons. An individual farmer's worth in the community was judged on three key points—how he maintained his buildings, equipment, and animals. The condition of the barn was a fair assessment of the value of the farm.

The barn also had a developmental and social role. It was a gigantic playground, often an amusement park, for farm youngsters. The hay loft could be a medieval castle one moment, a frontier fort the next. Sneaking behind the barn was a common means of escaping the watchful eyes of parents.

No farm youngster needs a school course on sex education. One learns at a very early age the role of the bull, rooster, and serum injection. The privacy of the barn provides a haven for young lovers. Little wonder there is a strong tradition in rural America of shotgun weddings.

Removing the equipment from the barn created a social hall for functions ranging from an extended family meal to a hoedown. Social gatherings were extremely important in rural America, where the nearest neighbor may be a quarter to half a mile down the road.

Farm museums take pride in their period barn recreations. Since almost every state has one or more farm museums, locating an example should not prove difficult. The fun is to visit a Midwest farm museum shortly after visiting a New England farm museum. One quickly develops an appreciation for the development and differences in farm technology over time and as American agriculture moved west.

References: Joan and David Hagan, *The Farm: An American Living Portrait*, Schiffer Publishing, 1990; Lar Hothem, *Collecting Farm Antiques: Identification and Values*, Books Americana, 1982; R. Douglas Hurt, *Agricultural Technology in the Twentieth Century*, Sunflower University Press, 1991; Stanley Schuler, *American Barns: In A Class by Themselves*, Schiffer Publishing.

Reproduction Manufacturers: Cumberland General Store, Rte 3, Crossville, TN 38555; McClanahan Country, 217 Rockwell Rd, Wilmington, NC 28405.

ANIMAL RELATED

History: When one thinks farm, one thinks animals. Even grain farmers keep a few animals. The domestication of animals and development of agriculture were two of the most important steps in the evolution of humankind.

During the twentieth century many of the hand tasks associated with animals were mechanized. Two transitions that I witnessed as a young boy were the switching of a dairy farm from hand milking to mechanical milking and a chicken farm from nests to individual wire cages. The Country collector is not fascinated by these "new-fangled" devices. They prefer a simpler(?) time when there was one-to-one contact between farmer and animal. The image is highly myth oriented, but it persists.

Collectors focus on three types of animal related objects: (1) those used in the care and feeding of animals, (2) those involved in the use of the animal, and (3) those linked to an animal's food value. In almost every instance, the collector wants an object that shows signs of wear, but yet is in good enough condition to display.

The care and feeding category ranges from grain scoops to chicken feeds. Look for objects that contain elaborate stenciling, decoration, and manufacturer information, and/or have an unusual form. Do not overlook veterinary products. The "Veterinary Collectibles" category in *Warman's Americana & Collectibles, Fifth Edition* will introduce you to the possibilities.

Animals paid for their keep by working or producing a salable product; in some instances, both. The popularity of animal working gear is craze oriented. One year ox yokes are in vogue, another year animal harnesses prove popular. Many of these objects do not display well, making this material the least popular of the animal related collectibles.

The most popular category is items involved with processing animal products or involving the butchering of animals. Hog scrappers, milking stools, sheep shears, and egg crates are just a few of the popular items found in most Country decorating schemes. A single type of object is often found in dozens of variations, creating the opportunity for an unusual specialized collection.

Since many individuals utilizing a Country decor did not grow up in a farming environment, it is not unusual to find objects whose use is uncertain among the items displayed. These "what's-its" make excellent conversation pieces.

Few Country collectors attempt to recreate a barn or equipment shed environment. Instead, animal related items are used indoors and out primarily as decorative accents. A set of harnesses makes an attractive wall display. A stoneware chicken feeder finds a welcome home among a display of stoneware crocks and jugs. A pig carrier with a piece of glass on top functions well as a coffee table. A cast iron scalding kettle serves in the front yard as a planter.

The use of animal related objects in interior and exterior decorating is due in part to the image that they convey of hard but highly productive work. Metal objects develop a dark, smooth patina; wood implements have a weathered, worn-smooth look. They evoke a strong sense of the unending commitment that a farmer must make.

Reproduction Manufacturers: *Egg Crates—* American Country House, P. O. Box 317, Davison, MI 48432; *Sleigh Bells—*Conewago Junction, 805 Oxford Rd, New Oxford, PA 17350.

Bovine

Branding Iron, 21" l, wrought iron, "D"	25.00
Cowbell, 5" h, sheet iron, handmade, unmarked, orig leather strap	22.50
Cream Separator, painted tin body, wooden legs, window, brass spigot	60.00
Milk Pail, 8 quart, tin, wire handle	60.00
Milk Skimmer, punched tin, hanging loop, c1800	28.00
Milking Stool, 14" h, oak, three legs	48.00
Ox Muzzle, 10" h, plaited wood strips	50.00

Equine

Feeding Box, 13 x 17 x 8", wood	18.00
Harness Strap, 10" l, leather, four decorative brasses	40.00
Hoof Knife, iron, impressed horse outline, Heller, 1890–1900	20.00
Singletree, 14½" l, wood and iron	28.00
Tether, 20 lbs	35.00
Tether Weight, cast iron, 18 lbs, hemispheric	35.00

Hog

Scalding Kettle, 17 x 27", cast iron, handles	350.00
Scraper, 6½" h, tin, circular blade	18.00
Trough, 3½' l, two–sided	25.00

Ovine

Goat Yoke, single, wood, bentwood bow	10.00
Sheep Bell, 3½" h, brass, iron clapper	30.00
Sheep Shears, 13¾" l, stamped with crown, mkd "Cast Steel, W P Ward"	20.00

Branding Iron, wrought iron, 16½" l, $42.00.

Milking Stool, hickory, 10½" h, 13½" l, $50.00.

Egg Shipping Crate, wooden, marked "Gardiner Egg Carrier, made by New England Box Co., Boston, Mass.," metal spring type egg holders, hinged, 13¾" h, 10¼" w, $195.00.

Poultry

Chicken Catcher, wire, wooden handle	**40.00**
Chicken Feeder, tin	**12.00**
Egg Candler, 8" h, tin, kerosene burner, mica window	**20.00**
Egg Shipping Crate, 14 x 28", cardboard egg holders inside, Bangor, ME	**25.00**
Incubator, 39" h, wood cabinet . . .	**75.00**
Nest Egg, 2⅞" d, white milk glass . . .	**45.00**
Nesting Box, 14½" h, wood	**15.00**
Turkey Bell, 1¼" d, cast brass	**25.00**

LIGHTNING ROD BALLS AND PENDANTS

History: Lightning rod balls and pendants are the ornamental portion of lightning rod systems typically found on the roofs of barns and rural houses from the 1840s to 1930s. The glass balls and pendants served only aesthetic purposes and did not contribute to the operation of the lightning rod system.

Glass balls ranged in color from the common white milk glass and blue milk glass to clear glass.

Some clear glass has turned shades of sun colored amethyst (SCA) through exposure to the sun. Other colors include shades of amber, cobalt, green, and red to the rarer colors of pink, orange, yellow, and marbleized slag. Mercury colored balls were created by silvering the interior surface of balls of different colors to produce silver, gold, cobalt, red, and green mercury colors. Lightning rod balls were colored using several different glass making techniques—flashing, casing, and solid colors.

There are thirty–four standard shapes or styles of lightning rod balls:

Burgoon, round, covered with rows of dots and dashes, also called "Dot and Dash" ball, scarce.

Chestnut, 4" irregular shaped ball, resembles two ornate glass doorknobs attached face to face, 10 colors, fairly common.

D & S, 10-sided ball resembling Japanese lantern, letters D & S in a diamond in one panel, "Patent Pending" on two lower panels, 15 colors, manufactured exclusively for Dodd and Struthers of Windsor, Ontario, Canada, common.

Diddie Blitzen, 3¾" paneled ball, resembles two lamp shades placed bottom to bottom, embossed letters "DIDDIE BLITZEN" in the panels, 9 colors, fairly common.

Doorknob, 4" ball, resembles two antique ornate glass doorknobs placed face to face with indented equator, 11 colors plus slag glass, fairly common.

Ear of Corn, ovoid ball, panels that resemble kernels of corn on a cob, 6 colors, also known as "Harrisburg" ball because so many found in the Pennsylvania area, hard to find.

Electra Cone, 5" ball, resembles two funnels with tire bulge at equator of ball, letters "ELECTRA" at bulge, 10 colors, The Electra Protection Co. had offices in Chicago and Cresco, IA, fairly common.

Electra Round, raised letters "ELECTRA" at equator of ball, 11 colors, moderately available.

Hawkeye, resembles a hot air balloon, intaglio poinsettia on the upper portion of canopy, indentations running vertically to form stem, embossed letters "HAWKEYE" found in indentations, 10 colors, made by Hawkeye Lightning Rod Co. of Cedar Rapids, IA, moderately available.

JFG, 3¾", resembles bottom portion of an hourglass, raised letters "JFG" found on equator, 3 colors, made by Julius F. Gooetz, WI, scarce.

K–Ball, round, 4½", raised initial "K" found at base of the top collar, 9 colors, moderately available.

Maher, 5", detailed ball with raised swirls interrupted with a flat band at equator, "MAHER MANUFACTURING CO., PRESTON, IOWA" on band, 6 colors, difficult to find.

Mast, 5" d, raised swirls from pole to pole, emblem at equator on one side, embossed "Trade MAST Mark Reg US Pat Off," 6 colors, credited to Mast Lightning Rod Co., Ohio, scarce.

Moon & Star, 4½", intaglio of moon and stars over the entire surface, 13 colors, very common.

National, Belted, 5", shaped with a raised band at equator with letters "NATIONAL," 6 colors, made by National Cable and Manufacturing Co., Michigan, hard to find.

National, Round, 4½", raised letters "NATIONAL" on equator, 7 colors, moderately available.

Onion, 3½", shaped like natural onion, vertical indentations originating at necks of ball, 3 colors, non–capped ball used exclusively by the Burkett Lightning Rod Co., Ohio, scarce.

Patent '77, 3½", 4", and 5" d, "PAT'D 77" at equator, sometimes lettering was ghosted, 3 or 4 colors, scarce.

Patent '78, 4", "PAT'D 78" at equator, sometimes lettering was ghosted, 3 or 4 colors, scarce.

Plain, Round, 3", 3½", 4", and 4½" d (most common), 30 colors known, common.

Pleat, Pointed, 3½", 4½", 5", and 5½" d, vertical pleats, 6 colors, moderately available.

Pleated, Round, 4½", vertical pleats that have rounded edges, 7 colors, made by J. Barnett Co., Riverside, IA, also known as "Barnett" ball, moderately available.

Quilt, Flat, 5", quilt effect created with lateral incised lines forming flat diamonds, 13 colors, distributed by G. E. Thompson Lightning Rod Co., Owatonna, MN, moderately available.

Quilt, Raised, 5", quilt effect created with lateral incised lines forming raised diamonds, 4 colors, offered by Kretzer Co., St. Louis, Missouri, moderately available.

R.H.F., 5", raised daisy-like petals with the initials "R," "H," or "F" found in each of three daisy pattern centers, 6 colors, manufactured by Reyburn Hunter Foy Company, Cincinnati, OH, scarce.

Ribbed, Grape, round, equator of raised circles (grapes), raised panels going to each pole, 10 colors, made by several different companies, common.

Ribbed, Horizontal, 3½", resembling two flowerpots attached top to top with staircase type concentric circles, 8 colors, known among collectors as "Peewee," moderately available.

S Company, elongated, 5" l, 4" d, window-like panel indentations, running vertically at the equator, "S. Co." found in diamond at top of ball, 8 colors, made by Struthers Company, Peoria, IL, moderately available.

Shinn, Belted, resembles two petal bowls facing opening to opening, connected by large bulging equator with raised letters "W. C. SHINN MFG CO.," 8 colors, hard to find.

Shinn, System, 4", "SHINN SYSTEM" embossed at equator, 7 colors, moderately available.

S L R Co., 4½", long necks (collars) with large letters "SLR CO." found on equator, many balls found only with ghosts of the letters, used without metal caps, found in several colors, made by Security Lightning Rod Co., Burlington, WI, scarce.

Staircase, 4", heavy ceramic ball, staircase top and bottom, wide straight panel at equator, 2 colors, common.

Swirl, 5", raised swirls running pole to pole, 9 colors, moderately available.

Thompson, 4½", sharply ribbed ball, raised triangular equator, "GEO. E. THOMPSON LIGHTNING ROD CO., EST 1910" found on equator, 5 colors, ball still in production as reproduction.

Some of these lighting rod balls were made exclusively by a single glassmaker, while others were made by several. The Maher Company made the first lighting rod ball in the 1840s. Hawkeye Lightning Rod Company, Cedar Rapids, IA, introduced the Hawkeye ball in the 1940s.

Lightning rod balls have necks or collars at both ends, usually protected by a copper, brass, aluminum, or steel cap. Old necks or collars generally have an irregular or jagged edge, whereas reproduction balls generally have a ground edge. Roofers often replace missing or damaged balls with a modern day plastic ball with a ribbed horizontal pattern.

The value of a lightning rod ball depends on design, color, locality, and condition. Obviously, the scarcer patterns are more valuable and higher in price. Since some lightning rod balls closely resemble lamp parts whose collars often are ground, it is best to avoid any ball that has a ground or etched collar.

The white milk glass balls and the blue milk glass balls are the most common and usually the least expensive. Prices escalate by color beginning with sun colored amethyst, amber, and red. The rare colors of orange, pink, and yellow are at the top of the scale. Mercury balls are higher priced than the clear versions from which they were made.

Pendants were generally installed in sets of four, one dangling from each of the arms extending from a lightning rod. A metal hook or loop attached to a metal cap held the pendant in place. Rust and the elements often caused hook or cap to fail, resulting in the loss of a pendant. Cold weather could crack a pendant if water worked its way inside.

Pendants measure $5\frac{1}{2}$" high including cap and hook, $4\frac{1}{2}$" not including cap and hook. They are approximately 3" wide and teardrop in shape. Collectors prefer pendants in mint condition. Loss of the metal loop fastened to the cap or the cap itself reduces value.

References: Mike Brunner and Rod Krupka, *The Complete Book Of Lightning Rod Balls*, published by authors (available from Rod Krupka, 2615 Echo Lane, Ortonville, MI 48462), 1989; Dale Frazier, *Lightning Rod Ball Collector's Guide*, published by author, 1973.

Periodical: *The Crown Point*, 2615 Echo Lane, Ortonville, MI 48462.

Reproduction Alert: Reproductions of the Thompson ball have been found in five colors—white milk glass, amber, cobalt, blue-green, and red. Reports also have been received that some of the rarer colored balls recently have been reproduced using period molds.

Balls

Chestnut, silver mercury, $4\frac{1}{8}$" h, 4" w, Goshen, IN **95.00**

Diddie Blitzen, white milk glass, $4\frac{1}{8}$" h, $3\frac{3}{4}$" w, emb "Diddie Blitzen Rods" **12.00**

D & S Co, amber, $5\frac{1}{4}$" h, $3\frac{3}{4}$" w, 10–sided, emb "D & S" and "Patent Pending," Dodd & Struthers Co, Windsor, Ontario, Canada **25.00**

Doorknob, swirled slag, $4\frac{1}{4}$" h, 4" w, West Dodd Co **140.00**

Ear of Corn, vaseline, $4\frac{1}{8}$" h, $2\frac{7}{8}$" w, Harrisburg, PA. **125.00**

Electra, cone shape, red, $5\frac{3}{8}$" h, $4\frac{5}{8}$" w, emb "Electra," Electra Protection Co, Chicago, IL. **80.00**

Hawkeye, rust orange milk glass, $5\frac{1}{8}$" h, $4\frac{3}{8}$" w, Hawkeye Lightning Rod Co, Cedar Rapids, IA **250.00**

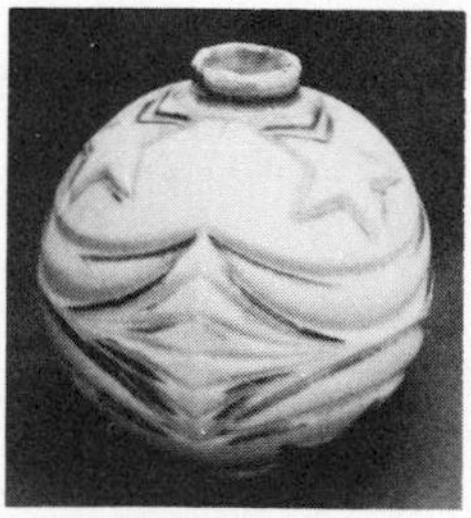

Moon and Star, flashed blue over white milk glass, $5\frac{1}{8}$" h, $4\frac{3}{8}$" w, $18.00.

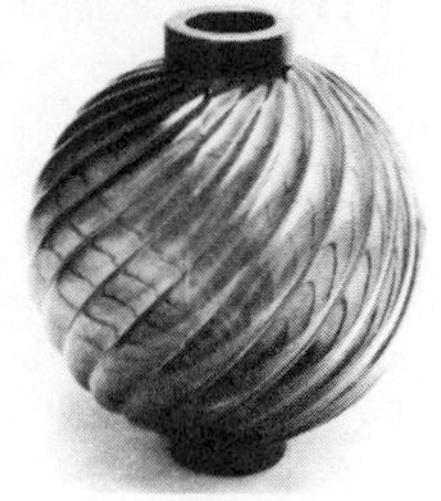

Swirl, amber, $42.00.

JFG, blue milk glass, $3\frac{7}{8}$" h, $3\frac{3}{8}$" w, emb "PAT," Julius F Goetz Mfg Co, Hartford, WI **25.00**

K Ball, flashed red, $5\frac{1}{8}$" h, $4\frac{1}{2}$" w, emb "K" **75.00**

Maher, amber, $5\frac{1}{4}$" h, $4\frac{3}{8}$" w, emb "Maher Mfg Co, Preston, IA" . . . **200.00**

Moon and Star, flashed blue over white milk glass, $5\frac{1}{8}$" h, $4\frac{3}{8}$" w, quarter moons and five pointed stars pattern **18.00**

National, round, sun colored amethyst, $5\frac{1}{4}$" h, $4\frac{1}{2}$" w, National Cable and Mfg Co, Niles, MI **28.00**

Onion, cobalt, $4\frac{1}{8}$" h, $3\frac{3}{8}$" w, Burkett Lightning Rod Co, Fremont, OH **225.00**

Plain, round, root-beer amber, $5\frac{1}{8}$" h, $4\frac{1}{2}$" w, ground ends **40.00**

Plastiball, plastic, transparent, snap together halves **3.00**

Pleat, pointed, white milk glass, $5\frac{1}{8}$" h, $4\frac{3}{8}$" w **12.00**

Quilt, raised, gold mercury, $5\frac{1}{2}$" h, 5" w, emb "Kretzer Brand Trade Mark," Kretzer Co, St Louis, MO **160.00**

Ribbed Grape, gray–green, $5\frac{1}{8}$" h, $4\frac{3}{8}$" w, National Lightning Protection Co **75.00**

Shinn, belted, sun colored amethyst, $5\frac{1}{8}$" h, $4\frac{1}{4}$" w, emb "W.C. Shinn, Lincoln Neb" **25.00**

Staircase, cobalt, $3\frac{7}{8}$" h, $3\frac{7}{8}$" w, ceramic, National Lightning Protection Co, St Louis, MO. **12.00**

Thompson, teal, emb "Geo E Thompson Lightning Rod Co, Est 1910," Owatonna, MN **10.00**

Pendants

Acorn, cobalt **150.00**

Flat Quilt, gray–green **450.00**

Hawkeye, amber. **380.00**

Paneled, silver mercury **115.00**

Plain, flashed red. **95.00**

Ribbed and Paneled, white milk glass **75.00**

Unembossed S Co, blue milk glass **160.00**

MILK BOTTLES

History: Hervey Thatcher is recognized as the father of the glass milk bottle. By the early 1880s glass milk bottles appeared in New York and New Jersey. A. V. Whiteman had a milk bottle patent as early as 1880. Patents reveal much about early milk bottle shape and manufacture. Not all patentees were manufacturers. Many individuals engaged others to produce bottles under their patents.

The golden age of the glass milk bottle is 1910 to 1950. Leading manufacturers include Lamb Glass Co. (Mt. Vernon, Ohio), Liberty Glass Co. (Sapulpa, Oklahoma), Owens–Illinois Glass Co. (Toledo, Ohio), and Thatcher Glass Co. (New York).

Milk bottles can be found in the following sizes: gill (quarter pint), half pint, 10 ounces (third quart), pint, quart, half gallon (two quart), and gallon.

Paper cartons first appeared in the early 1920s and 1930s and achieved popularity after 1950. The late 1950s witnessed the arrival of the plastic bottle. A few dairies still use glass bottles today, but the era has essentially ended.

Many factors influence the price: condition of the bottle, who is selling, the part of the country in which the sale is transacted, and the amount of desire a buyer has for the bottle. Every bottle does not have universal appeal. A sale of a bottle in one area does not mean that it would bring the same amount in another locale. For example, a rare Vermont pyro pint would be looked upon as only another "pint" in Texas.

A painted milk can, often with a regional folk art design, is a commonly used Country decorative accent. When used on the farm, milk cans had little or no decoration. "Folk Art" milk can painters pay between five and ten dollars for a plain can depending on size and condition. There are milk can collectors, but their number is few, thus keeping prices low.

References: Don Lord, *California Milks*, published by author; John Tutton, *Udder Delight*, published by author.

Periodical: *The Milk Route*, 4 Ox Bow Road, Westport, CT 06880.

Museums: The Farmers Museum, Cooperstown, NY; Southwest Dairy Museum, Arlington, TX; Billings Farm Museum, Woodstock, VT.

Half Pint, embossed, round	
Green Meadow Farm, Helena, MT	**26.00**
Grocers Milk Co, 296 Isabella St, Oak Dell	**14.00**
Milk for Health, Inc, Louisville, KY	**14.00**
Sibley Farms, Spencer, MA	**24.00**
Half Pint, pyroglazed	
Brookview Dairy, Bourbonnais, IL, round, orange	**14.00**

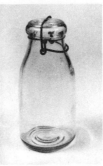

Pint, clear, blown, wire bail, lid, emb "Pat. A. For," $12.50.

Korter Pasteurized Milk, Moscow, ID, square squat bottle, yellow	**16.00**
Standard Dairy, Wallace, ID, round, red	**22.00**
Tri–City Dairy, Durand, WI, round, orange	**12.00**
Pint, embossed, round	
Arizona Creamery, Phoenix Store, Pasteurized, triple V neck treatment	**24.00**
FA Sacchi, Marshfield, OR	**18.00**
French Bros–Bauer Co, Cincinnati, OH, full fluting	**22.00**
Jersey Milk, Cream & Butter Co, Oakland, CA	**28.00**
Meadow Brook Farm, GA Porter, Bedford, NH, large letter "P" in slug plate	**28.00**
Wood County Dairymen, Parkersburg, WV, WC logo on base of bottle	**16.00**
Pint, pyroglazed, tall, round	
AR Perley's Jersey Milk, Richford, VT, same both sides	**12.00**
Butler Dairy, Willimatic, CT, "Call Butlers for the Best" and milkman illus on reverse, green	**16.00**
Lueck Dairy, Liverpool, NY, "Quality & Service," comic cow illus on reverse, orange	**16.00**
Seegers Dairy, Inc, Merrill, WI, Dairy Guild logo and "Dairy Foods of Excellence" on reverse, red	**14.00**
Stransdale Farms Products, Savanna, IL, "Grade A Pasteurized Milk" on reverse, black	**18.00**
Windale Farms, Galena, OH, dairy farm illus in background, orange	**12.00**
Quart, cream top, embossed, round	
Meadow Gold Silver Seal	**22.00**
Otto Milk Co, Pittsburgh, PA	**14.00**
Rainiers Dairies, Bridgeton, NJ	**24.00**

**Quart, clear, emb "Producer's Milk Co.,"
c1915, 9½" h, $15.00.**

Quart, cream top, pyroglazed, round
   Indiana Dairy Co, Indiana, PA, large
   Golden Guernsey Seal and logo
   on reverse, black **24.00**
   Mayflower Milk, "Fresh from the
   Farm," dairy farm illus, "Homog-
   enized Milk from the Dairy Coop-
   erative Association," woman with
   glass of milk and inscription "I'll
   say it tastes better" on reverse, red   **28.00**
Quart, embossed, tall, round
   Copper Country Cheese Co–Op,
   Dollar Bay, MI, swirled neck. . . .   **22.00**
   Dairy Products Container Co, De-
   troit, MI, swirl neck, "3" emb on
   shoulders **28.00**
   Ellis Dairy, Columbus, MS **28.00**
   Federal Prison Industries, Inc, La
   Tuna, TX **55.00**
   Medosweet Dairies, Inc, Tacoma,
   WA, ribbed body **32.00**
   Pure Gold Dairy, Paola, KS **26.00**
   Woods Cash & Carry Milk Depots,
   "All Over Lincoln" **18.00**
Quart, pyroglazed, tall, round
   Farm Dairy, Mullan, ID, red **26.00**
   Foster Hughs Dairy Products, Inc, St
   Joseph, MO, "Enjoy F–H Cottage
   Cheese," black **18.00**
   Hanks Bros–Wenepanin Farms, East
   Long Meadow, MA, same both
   sides, orange **16.00**
   Jersey Dairy, pasteurized milk,
   phone 616, Bozeman, MT, glass
   of milk and plate of sandwiches
   illus on reverse, "Ask for Jersey
   Chocolate Milk," blue **38.00**
   Judevines Pasteurized Milk,
   Douglas, WY, large Golden
   Guernsey logo on reverse, orange   **34.00**
   McGough Dairy, Burns, OR, outline
   of cow in shield on both sides,
   green **32.00**

Mountain Dairy, Grade A, Tucson,
   AZ, phone 1211, same both sides,
   maroon and brown **55.00**
Snowflake Pasteurized Milk, phone
   216, Cleburne, TX, same both
   sides, blue **35.00**
Sorges Milk, Manitowoc, WI, "Try
   Banquet Ice Cream from Sorges,"
   black **24.00**
Sundial Dairy Co–Op, Missoula,
   MT, baby illus on reverse, green   **48.00**
Winnebago Farms Dairy, Fond Du
   Lac, WI, orange **18.00**

MILK CANS

Cream, lid, impressed brass plate,
   Elkin's Dairy, bail handle, 4 qts,
   7" d, 10" h **20.00**
Milk
   Marked, brass nameplate showing
   name of shipper, 10 gallon **18.00**
   Unmarked, 10 gallon **10.00**

SCALES

History: Prior to 1900 the simple balance scale
commonly was used for measuring weights.
Since then scales have become more sophisti-
cated in design and more accurate. A variety of
styles and types include beam, platform, postal,
and pharmaceutical.
   Scales were used throughout the farm. Platform
scales weighed feed both for sale and use. Hanging scales were used to sell produce at roadside
stands and from farm wagons. Grading scales
were a necessity if eggs were sold.

Collectors' Club: International Society of Antique
Scale Collectors, 111 N Canal St, Chicago, IL
60606.

Reproduction Manufacturer: Sturbridge Yankee
Workshop, Blueberry Rd, Westbrook, ME 04092.

Balance
   Chatillon, #2, 0 to 50 lbs, pat Jan
   26, 1892 . . . .   **35.00**
   PS & T Warranted, 0 to 50 lbs, brass
   front, pat July 8, 1889 . . . .   **25.00**
Butcher, Standard Computing, enamel   **75.00**
Dairy
   Chatillon, 0 to 120 lbs, brass front   **85.00**
   Pelouze, white enamel on brass . . .   **65.00**
Egg Grading
   Jiffyway, brass **90.00**
   Oak Manufacturing Co **12.00**
Feed, red and white checked top, blue
   and cream bottom, metal pan,
   "Purina Feed Saver and Cow Culler"
   adv **85.00**

Egg Grading, Farm Master, red ground, black, yellow, and red letters, $35.00.

Spring, Chatillion Improved, New York patent Dec. 10, 1867, brass, $48.00.

Grain
Fairbanks, bushel, brass	**275.00**
Ohaus, brass	**250.00**
Winchester, bushel, brass, hanging	**200.00**

Spring Balance
Forschner, brass, hanging	**65.00**
Hanson Viking, #8910, 1 to 100 lbs, steel, painted green	**35.00**

TOOLS AND EQUIPMENT

History: The self–reliant aspect of agrarian life required that its members were builders, mechanics, and providers all rolled into one. Farmers and homesteaders were generalists, capable of performing many specialized tasks. In addition, the urgency of time and the state of finances often required "doing things yourself now."

As a result, most rural households and farms contained a wide variety of equipment and tools. Much of the equipment was specialized, designed to perform a specific task, such as a corn dryer or stitching horse. Tools were used to keep the equipment in repair, e.g., a hoopsetter or oilstone; or by the individual to perform a task, e.g., ax or saw.

Equipment and tools are one of the four principal criteria by which others judged individuals in the agrarian environment. The other three are land, buildings, and stock. Most equipment and tools were designed to last for generations, provided they received adequate care and proper use. On most farmsteads, the vast majority of equipment and tools will have been acquired through the secondary market, i.e., passed down through the family or purchased at a farm auction.

Initially farm tools and equipment were made by local craftsmen—the blacksmith, wheelwright, or the farmer himself. Product designs varied greatly. In a large number of instances, the reason a specific tool or piece of equipment was made has been lost. Many collections contain one or more of these "what's–its."

The industrial age and the "golden age" of American agriculture go hand in hand. By 1880–1900 manufacturers' saw the farm market as an important source of sales. Farmers demanded quality products capable of withstanding hard use. While Stanley is the most recognized and collected manufacturer, collectors have not ignored the thousands of other firms who concentrated on making equipment and tools for the agrarian community.

In the 1940s urban growth began to draw attention away from the rural areas and consolidation of farms took place. Bigger machinery was developed. Post–World War II farm tools and equipment are just beginning to attract the attention of collectors.

Within the Country community, equipment and tools serve primarily as furniture pieces and wall hangings. Few pieces are displayed in context. Decorators like pieces made wholly or partially of wood with signs of heavy use.

Tool collectors are a breed unto themselves. Although they are found at country auctions, they do much of their trading and buying through the mail, via phone, or at specialized shows and meets. Regional and state collectors' clubs include the Mid–West Tool Collectors Association (808 Fairway Drive, Columbia, MO 65201) and the Ohio Tool Collectors Association (PO Box 261, London, OH 43140).

References: Ronald S. Barlow, *The Antique Tool Collector's Guide to Value, Third Edition*, Windmill Publishing Company, 1991; Lar Hothem, *Collecting Farm Antiques: Identification and Values*, Books Americana, 1982; Kathryn McNerney, *Antique Tools, Our American Heritage*, Collector Books, 1979, 1988 value update; R. A. Salaman, *Dictionary of Tools*, Charles Scribner's Sons, 1974; John Walter, *Antique & Collectible Stanley Tools: A Guide to Identity and Value*, Tool Merchants, 1990.

Periodical: *The Fine Tool Journal*, RD 2, Box 245B, Pittsford, VT 05763.

Collectors' Clubs: Cast Iron Seat Collectors Association, RFD #2, Box 40, Le Center, MN 56057; Early American Industries Association, P O Box

2128 Empire State Plaza Station, Albany, NY 12220.

Museums: Bucks County Historical Society, Mercer Museum, Doylestown, PA; Pennsylvania Farm Museum, Landis Valley, PA; Shelburne Museum, Shelburne, VT.

Reproduction Craftspersons: Connie Carlton, Shaving Horse Crafts, 1049 Rice Rd, Lawrenceburg, KY 10342; Kevin Riddle, Mountainman Woodshop, P O Box 40, Eagle Rock, VA 24085.

Reproduction Manufacturer: Conewago Junction, 805 Oxford Rd, New Oxford, PA 17350.

Adze, polled lip, curved handle, 25" l	**75.00**
Apple Picker	
Wire Cage, long wood handle	**25.00**
Wood, three pronged, 54" l, NH. . .	**175.00**
Broad Axe	
B Laurent, Little Falls, NH, maker-marked blade, $8\frac{1}{2}$ x $9\frac{3}{8}$", wooden handle	**60.00**
New Orleans pattern, handmade, orig handle, PA	**85.00**
Broom, splint, 39" l	**110.00**
Bucksaw, wood frame, rigid blade, factory made	**20.00**
Butteris, hoof trimmer, forged iron, wood shoulder brace, c1850	**35.00**
Cobbler's Bench, 45", two drawers, leather seat, primitive	**850.00**
Corn Dryer, wrought iron	**15.00**
Corn Husking Peg, hand carved, 5" l, c1900	**30.00**
Corn Planter, marked "Acme"	**30.00**
Corn Sheller, wood case, iron gears, hand crank, 34" h, orig red wash, PA	**60.00**
Cradle Scythe, wood, metal blade, four finger bowl, one nib and handle	**125.00**
Cranberry Scoop, 18 fingers, wood and tin, factory made, early 20th C	**215.00**
Drawknife, 8" hand forged blade, reverse curve handles	**30.00**
Farrier's Nail Box, wood, metal base and handle	**40.00**
Feed Trough, cast iron, 36" l	**30.00**
Felling Axe, one piece iron, center fold, hand forged, hammer–welded blade, Kelly Handmade	**75.00**

Fence Stretcher, iron	**18.00**
Firkin, stave construction, iron bands, $13\frac{1}{2}$" h, refinished	**115.00**
Froe, cooper's, iron, partial stamped label, $15\frac{1}{2}$" l	**75.00**
Grain Cradle, four fingers, 41"	**60.00**
Grain Scoop, wood, hand carved, 38"	**75.00**
Grain Shock Tyer, wood and iron	**65.00**
Grain Shovel, one piece, wood, open D handle, 36" l, c1800	**200.00**
Grubbing Axe, two head, hand forged, c1850	**30.00**
Harrow, arrow shape, wood frame, iron spikes, mule–pulled	**30.00**
Hayfork, metal prongs, wood fork and handle, impressed maker's initials, PA	**135.00**
Hayfork, wood, handmade, primitive, 55" l, 1820–1870	**120.00**
Hay Rake, wood, 48" l	**35.00**
Hoe, hand forged iron blade, wooden handle, 60" l	**20.00**
Hoof Rasp, double ended, slanting sides, factory made	**15.00**
Hoopsetter, wood, concave base, handmade	**45.00**
Husking Tool, leather palm guard, shoestring laces.	**10.00**
Ice Tongs, wrought iron, double handle, 26" l	**45.00**
Leather Punch, hollow pins, brass base, 9" l	**15.00**
Mallet, carpenter's, burl	**35.00**
Mortising Axe, hand forged, 16" l handle, early 19th C	**150.00**
Mortising Gauge, cherry and brass, factory made.	**55.00**
Mowing Scythe, wood handle, metal blade	**32.00**
Oilstone	
Blacksmith, rect, walnut box	**25.00**
Scythe sharpening, 3 x 7", wood case and lid, AK.	**18.00**
Plane	
Block, double end, Winchester No. W130.	**80.00**
Gutter, wooden, $2\frac{1}{4}$ x $9\frac{3}{4}$", Parker & Son.	**45.00**

Broad Axe, cast steel, marked "Wm Beatty & Son, Chester," $23\frac{1}{2}$" l, $45.00.

Plane, molding, c1875, $18.00.

Molding, 9" l, Gladwin, Boston, No. 5½	25.00
Plow, joiner's plane, adjustable, cherry, brass fittings, eight blades	100.00
Rabbet, maple, wide eye, handmade	20.00
Post Hole Digger, clamshell shovels, double wooden handles	35.00
Pruning Hook, pole handle, lever operated	25.00
Pulley Block, cypress, iron hardware, wooden inside wheel	30.00
Pump, cast iron, c1900	55.00
Rake, wood, twelve prongs, three graduating semi–circle braces, 77" l, c1850	130.00
Reaping Hook, handheld, hand forged blade, wooden handle, sgd, c1870	90.00
Rip Saw, #10, finishing, factory made	18.00
Sap Spout, wood, carved	5.00
Sausage Grinder, wooden, iron crank and hardware, 7 x 12"	45.00
Seed Dryer, chestnut frame, pine spindles, 21 x 43"	75.00
Seeder, tin tube, cotton seed bag, shoulder strap, 18"	65.00
Shovel, cast iron blade, wood handle	25.00
Sickle, iron blade, wood handle, 21" l	18.00
Spade Drag, wood, 7' l handle	25.00
Spading Fork, four triangular tines	12.00
Spoke Shave, Stanley No. 66	10.00
Stitching Horse, hickory, wood screw vise, mortised, handmade, c1840	145.00
Tin Shears, open jaw, hand forged	20.00
Traveler	
Land Measure, wood, 38" d, clacker counts rods, center pin	28.00
Wheel Gauge, sheet tin, handmade, 11" l, 18th C	55.00
Vice, 30½" h, leather worker's, pine, dovetailed jaws, foot pedal, old finish	225.00

Tool Chest, mixed woods, fitted interior, 41" l, 25" d, 25½" h, $950.00.

Wagon Jack, wood and iron, sliding grip, handmade, New England	80.00
Wedge, log splitter, iron	15.00
Weed Cutter, wooden frame, metal blade, branded "Patented Lively Ladd Weed Cutter, August 10, 1926," 38" l	25.00
Wheelbarrow, wood, iron wheel and braces, removable sides, sgd	75.00
Winnow Sieve, wood, punched tin sieve	100.00
Woodworker's Shave, arched handles, alternating light and dark woods, 12¼" l, 4¾" h, c1900	220.00
Yankee Axe, double head, c1850	38.00

WEATHER VANES

History: A weather vane indicates wind direction. The earliest known examples were found on late 17th century structures in the Boston area. The vanes were handcrafted of wood, copper, or tin. By the last half of the 19th century, weather vanes adorned farms and houses throughout the nation. Mass-produced vanes of cast iron, copper, and sheet metal were sold through mail order catalogs or at country stores.

In addition to being functional, weather vanes were decorative. Popular forms include horses, Indians, leaping stags, and patriotic emblems. Church vanes were often in the form of a fish or cock. Buildings in coastal towns featured ships or sea creatures. Occasionally a vane doubled as a trade sign.

The champion vane is the rooster. In fact, the term weathercock is synonymous with weather vane. The styles and patterns are endless. Weathering can affect the same vane differently. For this reason, patina is a critical element in collecting vanes.

The two principal forms are silhouette and three-dimensional vanes. Silhouette vanes are extremely fragile. Most examples have been repaired with some form of reinforcing strap.

Sportsmen and others frequently used weathervanes for target practice. Bullet holes decrease the value of a vane. Filled holes usually can be detected with a black light.

References: Robert Bishop and Patricia Coblentz, *A Gallery of American Weathervanes and Whirligigs*, E. P. Dutton, 1981; Ken Fitzgerald, *Weathervanes and Whirligigs*, Clarkson N. Potter, 1967.

Reproduction Manufacturers: American Folklore, 330 W Pleasant, Freeport, IL 61032; The Antique Hardware Store, 43 Bridge St, Frenchtown, NJ 08825; Cape Cod Cupola Co, Inc, 78 State Rd, Rte 6, North Dartmouth, MA 02747; Country Cupolas, Main St, East Conway, NH

04037; Knot in Vane, 805 N 11th St, DeKalb, IL 60115; Lemee's Fireplace Equipment, 815 Bedford St, Bridgewater, MA 02324; Ricyn Country Collectables, P O Box 577, Twisp, WA 98856; Town and Country, Main St, East Conway, NH 04037; Unfinished Business, P O Box 246, Wingate, NC 28174.

Reproduction Alert: Reproductions of early models are being aged, and sold as originals. Check provenance and get a written guarantee from any seller.

In the early 1980s the market was flooded with silhouette vanes manufactured in Haiti. These vanes are made from old drums and lack the proper supporting strapwork of an older vane.

Airplane, copper, single propeller, extended landing gear, rod mounting, 25" l, 20th C **775.00**
Angel Gabriel, copper, molded, gilt, 30½" l, attributed to Cushing & White, Waltham, MA, late 19th C **1,750.00**
Arrow, sheet copper, gilded, 58" l, pierced geometric dec, late 19th C **750.00**
Banner, iron directional arrow, copper openwork scroll design, bullet hole in tail, 16¼" h, 30" l, late 19th C . . . **995.00**
Bull, copper and zinc, full-bodied, 25½" l **3,000.00**
Child and Pony Cart, copper, molded, gilded, full round figures, shaggy mane and tail pony, pulling little girl in two-wheeled cart, shaped sheet metal finial mounting, 35" h, 25" w, J L Mott Ironworks, NY, c1893 . . . . **33,000.00**
Cow, copper and zinc, molded, standing, rising horns, copper ears, molded eyes, solid tail, 13½" h, 24" l, late 19th C **3,575.00**
Distillery Factory, National Distillery Products Company, copper and zinc, painted, flat silhouette, pipes and tanks, initials "NDPC" at right,

Cow, silhouette, sheet metal, rod standard mounting, directionals, 16" l, $550.00.

arrow shaped rod mounting, 26" h, 37" l, early 20th C **2,100.00**
Dove, sheet iron, painted and gilded, folk art design, 23" h, c1860. . . . . . **2,860.00**
Eagle, copper and zinc, molded, full-bodied, cast zinc head, wings extended, standing on sphere, 36" l, A L Jewell Co, Waltham, MA **8,000.00**
Fish
Molded, copper, hollow, detailed scales and fins, 38" l, c1900 . . . . **5,390.00**
Silhouette, sheet copper, dorsal fins and tail, drilled eye hole, cut mouth, rod standard mounting on driftwood steeple base, 33½" h, 11½" l, 19th C **1,430.00**
Fox, running, copper, molded and incised eye and paw, rod mounting, 15¾" h, 31" l, 19th C **9,900.00**
Foxhound, running, copper, molded, swell-bodied figure, rod mounting, 11½" h, 29" l, c1883. . . . . **8,250.00**
Gamecock, copper and zinc, molded, gilded, standing on arrow, 22" h . . . **2,000.00**
Goddess of Liberty, copper and zinc, molded, swell-bodied figure, wearing Phrygian cap, five-point stars impressed on sash, full-skirted swaying skirt, holding standard with diamond-shaped finial, rod mounting with ball point zinc finial and arrow feather tail, directionals, 39" h, 32" w, attributed to Cushing and White, Waltham, MA, c1870. . **33,000.00**
Goose, flying, plywood core and wings, laminated body, painted, 42" l. **1,250.00**
Grasshopper, copper, molded, gilded, 16¼" h, 41½" l, 19th C. **4,675.00**
Griffin, sheet copper, silhouette, rod mounting with ball and tulips finials, directionals, traces of orig gilding, 43" h, 26½" w, early 20th C. **2,750.00**
Hand and Hatchet, pine, carved, painted, full round, realistic hand, red painted and gathered sleeve detail, holding short handled hatchet, traces of orig polychrome, 23½" h, 26" l, c1850 . . . . **4,675.00**
Horse
Flying, copper, molded, swell-bodied figure, tucked forelegs, extended rear legs, leaping over large sphere, sheet copper ears, ridged mane and tail, drilled eye hole, molded wood base, 27" h, 30" l, A L Jewell & Co, MA, 1875-1900. . . . . **46,200.00**
Index, copper and zinc, molded, gilded, swell-bodied, molded zinc fore-quarters and mane, copper legs and ears, molded

Horse, cast iron, Black Hawk, sgd "Harris & Co," 26" w, $6,500.00.

copper hind quarters, repousse sheet copper tail, wrought iron rod mounting, 19" h, 25" l, J Howard & Co, West Bridgewater, MA, 1875–1900 . . . . **24,200.00**

Miniature, copper, molded, hollow, twisted and scrolled iron directional arrow, 6" h, 24" l, late 19th C **1,265.00**

Percheron, copper, molded, swell–bodied, wearing blinders, incised mane and tail, trotting position, rod mounting, 51" h, 40½" l, 1875–1900. . . . . **30,800.00**

Running, Colonel Patchen, copper and zinc, molded, gilded, 30" l, 21" h, late 19th C. **1,100.00**

Horse and Rider

Copper and Zinc, molded, gilded, swell–bodied, prancing horse, stylized cast zinc rider with incised eye and hair detail wearing low–brimmed peaked cap, cut sheet copper fringed tail, 24½" h, 26" l, A L Jewell Co, Waltham, MA, mid 19th C **8,800.00**

Pine, carved, painted, single plank, rider wearing top hat, black, 17½" h, 35" l, mid 19th C **2,750.00**

Horse and Sulky, copper and zinc, molded, gilded, swell–bodied horse, orig bridle, reins, and fittings, cast zinc driver, two–wheeled sulky, 17¼" h, 34" l, 1875–1900 . . . **16,500.00**

Hunter, standing, copper, molded, holding rifle, wearing cap and jacket, island shape base, 29½" h, 47" l, 19th C. **8,250.00**

Indian

Mashamoquet, copper, molded, swell–bodied figure, Indian chief, shaggy pony tail, short skirt, repousse detail, drawing bow and arrow, standing on arrow headed

rod on abstract rockwork, 35" h, 37" l, c1850 . . . . **7,975.00**

Massasoit, copper, molded, gilded, swell–bodied figure, three–feathered headdress, quiver and arrows, short feather–trimmed skirt and leggings, holding bow and arrow, tubular rod mounting, 31" h, 19" w, MA, 1875–1900 . . **13,200.00**

Warrior on Horseback, zinc, cut and molded, silhouette figure, scalloped headdress, holding molded bow with twisted wire bow string, flat horse with molded neck, punchmark outlining, rod mounting, 27½" h, 35½" l, 19th C. **6,600.00**

Logger, sheet metal, silhouette, man pushing three logs, traces of orig paint, 28" h, 35" l, 19th C **1,100.00**

Mermaid, sheet iron, painted, gilded, pointing finger, pedestal mounting, 40¼" h, 19th C. **7,500.00**

Peacock, sheet iron, painted, scalloped tail, standing on arrow directional, one side yellow, one side white, 26½" h, 32" l, 19th C **1,430.00**

Pheasant, copper, molded, painted, brown body, cut crown feathers and split tail feathers, yellow double neck ring, wrought iron rod mounting, 9" h, 16" l, 19th C. **2,750.00**

Plow, copper and cast zinc, rod mounting, black metal base, 52 x 23", c1860 . . . . **5,500.00**

Quill Pen, copper, molded, polychrome painted, yellow, repousse feathers, rod mounting, black metal base, 33" l, 19th C. **9,900.00**

Rooster

Running, sheet metal, molded, gilded, stylized, swell–bodied figure, repousse linear tail feather detail, 17½" h, 19½" l, 19th C **6,050.00**

Rooster, copper, molded, wooden base, 21½" h, 22" l, $2,500.00.

Standing, pine, carved, painted, single plank, wrought iron reinforcement, stylized, sawtooth comb, elaborately pierced and bushy tail with relief carved details, green painted pine steeple base mounting, 15" h, 19½" l, Joseph Lombard, Bridgton, ME, late 19th C   **4,675.00**

Standing, sheet copper, molded, stylized, silhouette figure, smooth, swell–bodied, scalloped comb and wattle, pierced almond shaped eye, full sawtooth cut tail, no legs, 18½" h, 21¼" l, 19th C . . .   **5,225.00**

Sloop, copper, molded, full round hull, sheet copper sails hung from bowsprit and main mast, flying pennant and burgee, oval brass sternboard plate impressed with maker's name and location, 44" h, 50" l, Cushing & White, Waltham, MA, c1869 . . . .   **20,900.00**

Stag, leaping, copper, polychrome painted, yellow, cast zinc antlers, rockwork and vegetation, rod with orb mounting, 26½" h, 32" l, 19th C **18,700.00**

COUNTRY STORE

The country store is the heart of rural America. Its functions are manifold: supplies, equipment, drugstore, post office, bank, accounting and bookkeeping services, meeting place, transportation center, information source, and social arbiter. Although the famed "general" store has gradually been replaced by shopping centers and mini–malls, most Americans still have fond memories of spending time around a potbelly wood stove.

One's first country store image is generally the vivid advertising, from broadsides to products, that graced the counters, shelves, and walls. The countertop equipment is remembered next, followed by promotional giveaways, some failing to survive because they were consumable. These are recapturable memories. The individuals, smells, clutter, and grime that were a part of the setting are in the distant past. Most museums and private collection recreations are much too clean and orderly.

Recreating a complete turn–of–the–century country store has been a popular goal of collectors and museums since the 1920s. It was common to buy the entire contents of a country store that was going out of business as a collection base. The advertising craze that started in the 1970s put an end to this practice. Sellers quickly realized that they could obtain far more for their objects by selling them one at a time, rather than in a lot. Rapidly escalating prices, especially for store equipment, makes recreating a complete turn–of–the–century store in the 1990s a very expensive proposition.

For this reason, collectors have begun to focus on recreating Depression era and post–World War II country stores, recognizing that they were very different from their early 1900s counterpart. This corresponds with the newfound interest at farm museums in mid–twentieth century farming technology and life.

References: Douglas Congdon–Martin with Robert Biondi, *Country Store Collectibles*, Schiffer Publishing, 1990; Douglas Congdon–Martin with Bob Biondi, *More Country Store Antiques*, Schiffer Publishing, 1991; Don & Carol Raycraft, *Collector's Guide to Country Store Antiques*, Collector Books, 1987, 1990 value update.

ADVERTISING

History: The earliest advertising in America is found in colonial newspapers and printed broadsides. A large number of the advertisements are rural in nature, often accompanied by a farm-related vignette. Rural newspapers were in place by the early nineteenth century.

By the mid–nineteenth century manufacturers began to examine how a product was packaged. They recognized that the package could convey a message and serve as a source of identification, thus selling more product. The package logo also could be used effectively in pictorial advertising.

The advent of the high speed, lithograph printing press led to regional and national magazines, resulting in new advertising markets. The lithograph press also brought the element of vivid colors into the advertising spectrum.

Although the "general" store remained a strong force in rural and small town America into the 1950s, it changed with the times. Specialized departments were created. Some product lines branched off as individual stores. The amount and variety of products increased significantly, as did the advertising to go with them.

By 1880 advertising premiums, such as calendars and thermometers, arrived upon the scene. Country store merchants were especially fond of these giveaways. Die–cut point of purchase displays, wall clocks, and signs were introduced and quickly found their way on to walls and shelves.

Advertising continued to respond to changing opportunities and times. The advertising character developed in the early 1900s. By the 1950s the star endorser was established firmly as an advertising vehicle. Advertising became a big business as specialized firms, many headquartered in New York City, developed to meet manufacturers' needs. Today television programs frequently command well over $100,000.00 a minute for commercial air time.

Many factors affect the price of an advertising collectible: the product and its manufacturer, the objects or persons used in the advertisement, the period and aesthetics of design, the designer and/or illustrator, and the form the advertisement takes. Add to this the continued use of advertising material as decorative elements in bars, restaurants, and other public places. The interior decorator purchases at a very different price level than the collector.

In truth, almost every advertising item is sought by a specialized collector in one or more collectible areas. The result is a divergence in pricing, with the price quoted to an advertising collector usually lower than that to a specialized collector, a category into which country store advertising collectors fall.

References: Jim Cope, *Old Advertising*, Great American Publishing Co., 1980; Robert Joy, *The Trade Card in Nineteenth–Century America*, University of Missouri Press, 1987; Ray Klug, *Antique Advertising Encyclopedia*, Schiffer Publishing, 1978, updated price guide; Ray Klug, *Antique Advertising Encyclopedia, First Edition*, Schiffer Publishing, 1985; Ralph and Terry Kovel, *Kovel's Advertising Collectibles Price List*, Crown Publishers, 1986; Douglas Congdon–Martin, *Antique Advertising: America for Sale*, Schiffer Publishing, 1991.

Collectors' Clubs: Antique Advertising Association, P O Box 1121, Morton Grove, IL 60053; The Ephemera Society of America, P O Box 37, Schoharie, NY 12157; Tin Container Collectors' Association, P O Box 440101, Aurora, CA 80014.

Periodicals: *P.A.C.*, National Association of Paper and Advertising Collectibles, P O Box 500, Mt. Joy, PA 17552; *P.C.M.* (Paper Collectors' Marketplace), P O Box 128, Scandinavia, WI 54977.

Reproduction Manufacturers: Design Workshop, P O Box 236, West Barnstable, MA 02668; Lace Wood 'N Tin Tyme, 6496 Summerton, Shepherd, MI 48883.

Reproduction Alert

Calendars
  1889, E L McClain Mfg Co, Success Horse Collars, paper, $15\frac{1}{2}$ x $20\frac{1}{2}''$, horse sitting at desk, writing testimonial **412.00**
  1896
    Best Baking Co Milk Bread, cardboard, family at dinner table, 12 x $14\frac{1}{2}''$ **350.00**
    Judge Cigars, cardboard, woman inspecting three men wearing signs, 15 x $9\frac{3}{4}''$ **110.00**
  1897, Winchester Repeating Arms Co, paper, hunter with horse, aiming at deer in distance **650.00**
  1898
    New Process Gas Range, paper, $14\frac{1}{2}$ x $22\frac{1}{2}''$, cook holding loaf of bread, full pad **220.00**
    Old Conemauch Whiskey, cardboard, two boys, $9\frac{3}{4}$ x $17\frac{1}{2}''$. . . . **95.00**
  1899, Listers Animal Bone Fertilizers, 13 x 23", woman holding wheat, farm scene background, factory overprint on full pad **138.00**
  1900, Austin Powder Co, paper, $21\frac{1}{2}$ x 38". **1,200.00**
  1902, Green's August Flower, cardboard, man smoking cigarette, holding umbrella, "For Indigestion and Torpid Liver," $9\frac{3}{4}$ x $15\frac{3}{4}''$ **300.00**
  1902, J W Kenney Park Brewery, paper, young girl illus, 15 x 20". . . . **450.00**
  1903, A & P Tea Company, cardboard, 10 x $13\frac{3}{4}''$, shopkeeper, customers, and products illus, full pad. **110.00**
  1904, Singer Sewing Machines, $16\frac{1}{4}$ x $20\frac{1}{2}''$, Indian on diecut animal skin **85.00**
  1905, Grand Union Tea Co, four little girls, 29 x $9\frac{1}{2}''$. **275.00**
  1906, Fleischmann's Yeast, cardboard, $10\frac{1}{4}$ x $14\frac{1}{4}''$, horse drawn wagon, July through Dec pad . . . **121.00**
  1907, Peters Cartridge Co, hunter holding two geese, 20 x $34\frac{1}{2}''$. . . . **1,250.00**
  1910
    Empire Cream Separator **350.00**

Calendar, Compliments of Fike Brothers Eglon Roller Mills, Eglon, WV, 1910, F. A. Schneider printer, 14 x 22¼", $35.00.

Orange County Brewery, paper, woman wearing large hat, holding bouquet of roses, 28 x 15" **450.00**

1911, Eagle Brewing Co, paper, Curtiss flight, 23½ x 29½" **1,250.00**

1912, Cold Spring Brewing Co, paper, infant pouring from bottle into shell held by young girl, 14 x 20" **550.00**

1913, Johnston Harvester Co, two gentlemen talking **95.00**

1917, De Laval Cream Separators, 12 x 23", girl and collie dog illus, full pad **330.00**

1919
    Coca–Cola, young woman holding bottle, 14½ x 32½" **425.00**
    Cream City Sash & Door Co, cardboard, 11¾ x 16¼", elves riding loaded wagon past factory, full pad **550.00**
    Lambertville Rubber Footwear, paper, girl wearing sailor suit, 28½ x 41", full pad **235.00**

1922, C M Conant Co Pumps, 16¾ x 47¼", product illus, full pad **110.00**

1932, American Stores, paper, colonial man and woman holding 13-star flag, full pad **55.00**

1936, Nehi, paper, 11½ x 23½", girl's portrait illus, full pad lists historical events **198.00**

Clock
    Alox Shoe Laces, tin display, clock and mirror inserts, 14½ x 4¾ x 11¾" **100.00**
    Anton's Bitters, brass and tin, figural pocket watch, face printed "Time for Anton's Bitters," 9" h, 1870–1900................... **175.00**
    Black Cat Shoe Dressing, tin, hissing black cat standing on shoe polish tins..................... **4,500.00**
    Bull Durham, windup, bull illus at center, 6" h **1,200.00**
    Calumet Baking Powder, wood case, 35" h, regulator, reverse glass panel, calendar **495.00**
    Chief Bonus Tea, regulator, wood case, Indian wearing turban, Baird **2,750.00**
    Coca–Cola, figural bottle shape, "Drink Bottled Coca-Cola 'So Easily Served' " **475.00**
    Dam–I–Ana Benedictine Invigorator, bronze, figural, nude Greek figures pointing to bottle, 12" h, 9" w, 1900–1920 .... **1,050.00**
    Erie Hollow Ware, metal, skillet shape, 10 x 14 x 2½" **450.00**
    Fitu Corset, regulator, wood case, 40" h **2,500.00**
    Garfield Tea, wood case, black, gold lettering, "Cures Constipation/Restores the Complexion," Baird **2,000.00**
    General Electric Refrigerator, metal, figural Monitor–Top model, 5¼ x 9"..................... **175.00**
    Liberty Flour, wood case, tin face, electric, Statue of Liberty illus at center, 15¼" sq **350.00**
    Lucky Strike Tobacco, regulator ... **825.00**
    None Such Mince Meat Pumpkin and Squash, cardboard, pumpkin shape, tin hands, 9½" d **575.00**
    Olymp Root Compound, metal, figural, large bottle flanked by two

Clock, wall, Freed's Jewelry, Pittston, PA, $500.00.

cherubs standing beneath wreath encircled clock face, emb "Try Olymp Root Compound–Olymp Root Co, Louisville, KY," 13" h, 1890–1910 . . . .   **995.00**

Reed's Tonic, wood case, miniature grandfather clock, black and white, impressed dec, orig back label reads "This clock is presented by . . . to their customers . . . ," 18½ x 7 x 2½", 1860–1900 . . . . . .   **1,430.00**

Sauer's Flavoring Extracts, wall clock, wood case **1,000.00**

Simmons Liver Regulator, brass, figural horseshoe, emb "Take Simmons Liver Regulator In Time," 6" h, 1880–1890 . . . . . .   **295.00**

Sines Syrup, tin and brass, round, ftd, face printed "Sines Syrup for Coughs & Colds, 25 Cts at All Druggists/Pat Apl 12th 1881," 4" d **325.00**

Stanton's Pain Relief, bronze, emb, statue, bottle on eagle and shield pedestal, "For Internal and External Use/B E McGale Sole Proprietor, Montreal" on front, "Regent MFC Co, Chicago" on reverse, 14½" h, 1900–1920 . . . .   **1,320.00**

Vanner & Prest's Molliscorum Harness Oil, regulator, Baird Clock Company, Plattsburg, NY, 1890s   **525.00**

Display

Adams Pepsin Gum, tin, 16 x 2½ x 12¼", dispenses 5¢ chiclets and stick gum **220.00**

Adams Spearmint Gum, tin box, 6¾ x 6 x 4¾", striped, hinged lid, product illus **150.00**

American Gold Eagle Coffee, papier mache, figural eagle, wings spread, gold **650.00**

Dispenser, Blue–Jay Corn Plasters, 6 x 5¾ x 13½", tin litho, A.M.D. Co., $395.00.

Beech–Chewing Gum, tin stand, 15" h, marquis, girl holding 5¢ gum package, pedestal **360.00**

Beech–Nut Candy, tin dispenser, 9¾ x 11½", three tiered **105.00**

Boston Garters, tin box, 14½ x 13", man wearing garter illus **170.00**

Brownie Laundry Wax, cardboard box, 9½ x 5¾", glass front, slant top, paper label, Palmer Cox Brownies illus **28.00**

Buster Brown Shoes, diecut metal shoe rack, Buster Brown holding shoe platform above head, 15 x 8"   **750.00**

Chief Two Moon Bitter Oil, cardboard standup, 52" l, 39½" h, three sections, Indian and waterfall center illus **165.00**

Coca–Cola, steel stand, 16" d, 56" h, "Take Home a Carton/ 25¢," holds six cartons **110.00**

Detmer Woolens, cardboard box, 29 x 21", three lid illus **82.00**

Dr Daniel's, cardboard standup, 40" l, 23" h, veterinary illus both sides **605.00**

Fairbank's Gold Dust Washing Powder, cardboard standup, 14½ x 13", trademark twins flank product package **550.00**

Feen–A–Mint Laxatives, tin box, 7½ x 16¼", woman holding laxative and open package illus, oval mirror inset at top **175.00**

Frank Miller's Peerless Blacking, wood box, 11 x 3", Uncle Sam shaving label illus **385.00**

Gem Mops, metal, diecut, janitor holding mop handle, bucket, "Take Home a Dozen," 15 x 23½"   **1,200.00**

General Grocery, tin standup, 22" l, 14" h, three-dimensional grocery store, miniature sample size cardboard boxes on shelves **330.00**

Hartwell Handles, tin box, 14½" l, 8" h, holds wooden tool handles   **50.00**

Helmar Cigarettes, diecut cardboard standup, 20½ x 29", cowgirl on horseback lighting cigarette for cowboy, product package in foreground **138.00**

Hoyt's But–A–Kiss Candy, 18½ x 10½ x 8", figural railroad boxcar **605.00**

Junket Desserts, diecut cardboard standup, 13¼ x 8½ x 5", three dimensional, interior dining room scene, girls eating Junket desserts, cook standing in background . . .   **300.00**

Ked's Shoes, diecut cardboard standup, two children on gymnastics equipment, 9 x 16" **75.00**

Kraeuter Tools, diecut metal, pliers shaped, 36 x 10" **1,000.00**

KRO Rat Poison, diecut cardboard standup, smiling dog, "It Can't Kill Me/K–R–O Kills Rats Only," $19\frac{1}{4}$ x 32"................. **225.00**

Old Grist Mill Dog Bread, cardboard standup, mechanical, 36" l, 26" h, cat pops up behind product package, flanked by two nodding bulldogs **300.00**

Planters Peanut Bars, litho tin box, $4\frac{3}{4}$ x 12", diecut, Mr Peanut figure at top, holds 5¢ Jumbo Peanut Block bars................. **1,430.00**

Sen–Sen Breath Mints, diecut tin dispenser, 6 x $6\frac{3}{4}$", Sen–Sen sweetheart illus **160.00**

Smith Brothers Cough Drops, tin dispenser, $10\frac{1}{2}$" h, vertical louvers, hinged top, product illus....... **170.00**

Solarine Metal Polish, cardboard, figural, crescent moon, smiling face, holding product bottle between tips of moon, "We Shine For All," $5\frac{1}{2}$ x 6" **90.00**

Vaseline Preparations, tin box, $7\frac{1}{2}$ x 16", tubes mounted on front, hinged door............... **110.00**

Wedding Bell Coffee, cardboard standup, $27\frac{1}{2}$ x $16\frac{1}{2}$", diecut, seasonal illus, "Serve Cold When Hot/Serve Hot When Cold" **220.00**

West Electric Hair Curlers and Barrettes, tin dispenser, 9" h, hinged slant lid, product illus ... **55.00**

Wiss Scissors, diecut metal standup, figural scissors, 36 x 12" **1,000.00**

Wrigley's Gum, tin standup, 14 x $13\frac{1}{2}$", diecut, figural trademark Wrigley man, celluloid head, holding four gum boxes **605.00**

Poster

Adriance Buckeye Harvesting Machinery, paper, barefoot farm girl, horse drawn farm equipment vignettes, $20\frac{1}{2}$ x 28", 1897 .... **385.00**

Barnum & Bailey Circus, clown portrait, dark blue ground, "Felix and 99 Other Famous Clowns," 27 x 41", Central Printing and Illinois Litho,c1933 .... **60.00**

Damschinsky's Liquid Hair Dye, strands of dyed and natural hair, $13\frac{3}{4}$ x $18\frac{1}{2}$", ... **66.00**

D M Ferry & Co Seeds, canvas, vegetables in foreground, city street in background, $32\frac{1}{2}$ x $22\frac{7}{8}$", framed, c1900............. **1,800.00**

Granite Iron Ware, paper, woman carrying milking pail, cow, "For Kitchen and Table Use," $12\frac{1}{2}$ x 28", ... **575.00**

Harvard Pure Malt Beverages, building, beer bottle columns, beacon

Poster, The Hambletonian Stallion, Oswego Prince, breeding broadside, c1881, $14\frac{1}{16}$ x $20\frac{1}{2}$", $120.00.

sending out Harvard Brewing Co message, 9 x 14", framed, c1901 **160.00**

International Stock Food, paper, pig eating corn, $21\frac{1}{2}$ x 28"......... **143.00**

Jacob Hoffman Brewing Co, glass of beer, cigar stand, floral bouquet, $21\frac{1}{2}$ x $31\frac{1}{2}$", J Ottman Litho Co, c1900................... **30.00**

Kendall's Spavin Cure, woman feeding medicine to horse, two dogs and girl watching, 22 x 28" **275.00**

Lean Manufacturing Co, paper, horse, ox, and camel–drawn harrows, $21\frac{1}{4}$ x $27\frac{1}{2}$"............. **330.00**

Magic Yeast, boy giving root beer to globe–headed man, "Use Magic Yeast for Root Beer," 16 x 20", c1909................... **400.00**

Marlin Repeating Rifles and Shotguns, hunter in background, two ducks falling in water in foreground, "The Gun for the Man Who Knows," $16\frac{1}{4}$ x $24\frac{3}{4}$" **200.00**

Ragged Edge Cigars, cardboard, product package illus, 11 x $14\frac{3}{4}$" **35.00**

Ringling Bros Barnum & Bailey Circus, attacking lion and tiger, red, blue, black, brown, and orange, yellow ground, 28 x 44", 1950s **85.00**

Sandwich Baling Presses, paper, farm machinery, 24 x 29" **105.00**

Satin Skin Cream, woman's head, yellow ground, 28 x 41", 1903 .. **150.00**

Shamrock Tobacco, canvas, seated man holding knife and tobacco, "Plug Smoking–10¢ a Cut," 17 x 23", c1900 .... **190.00**

UMC Cartridges, hunter shooting at charging bear, "In a Tight Place, Shoot UMC Cartridges," 16 x $24\frac{1}{2}$", c1900.............. **170.00**

Waterman's Ideal Fountain Pen, paper, Uncle Sam at Treaty of Portsmouth, $41\frac{1}{2}$ x $19\frac{1}{2}$", early 1900s .. **2,530.00**

W B Cyclist Corsets, paper, women wearing corsets, playing sports, "Recommended by Leading Physicians & Modistes," $16\frac{1}{2}$ x $22\frac{1}{2}$", J P Ottmann Lith Co, c1895 ..... **660.00**

Salesman's Sample

Cash Register, R C Allen, dated 1958.................... **25.00**

Clothes Wringer, American Wringer Company, iron and wood, $10\frac{1}{2}$" l **150.00**

Coffin and Fault, 21" l, 18" h, cast white metal crank up fault, wooden coffin stamped "Clark" **330.00**

Farm Gate, wood, $32\frac{3}{4}$" l, 19" h, swings open **415.00**

Fence, galvanized wire, paper label, U S Poultry, 4" roll **35.00**

Food Grinder, J P Co, 3" **35.00**

Harrow, iron and wood, $7\frac{1}{2}$" l, horse–drawn............. **95.00**

Hitching Post, cast iron, jockey, $10\frac{1}{2}$" h................... **450.00**

Plow, wood, wrought iron fittings, horse–drawn, 26" l **400.00**

Porch Swing, wood, 16" l........ **125.00**

Pump, cast iron and bronze, wood base, painted, 30" h.......... **120.00**

Stock Pen, wood, folding, case, 24" l, pat Sept 29, 1891 .... **150.00**

Threshing Machine, wood and galvanized metal, cast iron mounts, 13".................... **425.00**

Windmill, aluminum, brass, and metal, 30" h **2,500.00**

Sign

Allen & Ginter Tobacco, paper, birds of the tropics, $21\frac{1}{2}$ x $28\frac{1}{2}$", c1900.................. **375.00**

American Stock Food, paper, Uncle Sam at barnyard, feeding horse **425.00**

Armour's Veribest Beans, tin, $24\frac{1}{2}$ x $14\frac{1}{4}$" **1,325.00**

Salesman's Sample, hay fork, wood and metal, three prongs, $18\frac{1}{2}$" l, $175.00.

Sign, Davis Carriage Mfg Co., Petersburg, VA, 7 x 20", $185.00.

Aunt Jemima's Pancake Flour, cardboard, diecut, Aunt Jemima on swing, 8 x $17\frac{1}{2}$"............. **300.00**

Barker's Horse and Cattle Powder, paper over canvas, 30 x 24", animals running from train illus **220.00**

Beech-Nut Peanut Butter, cardboard, "For Kids & Grown–ups," $24\frac{1}{2}$ x $14\frac{1}{2}$", framed **125.00**

Ben–Hur Horse Blankets, tin, 20 x $16\frac{1}{2}$", self-framed, horse looking at store window display **960.00**

Bon–Ton Corset, cardboard, maid tying corset of woman standing before mirror, $13\frac{1}{2}$ x 18", 1881... **600.00**

Campbell's Horse Foot Remedy, James B Campbell Co, Chicago, IL, cardboard, $18\frac{3}{4}$ x $21\frac{1}{4}$" **250.00**

Capewell Horsenail Co, paper, family at dinner table, horse reaching through door and being hand fed by mother, "One of the Family," 19 x 25", frame, c1910........ **215.00**

Ceresota Flour, paper, boy slicing bread loaf, "Always the Same," $16\frac{1}{2}$ x $21\frac{1}{2}$" **325.00**

Challenge Tobacco, cardboard, knight on horse, "All America Chews The Challenge/Spicer's Best Tobacco," $15\frac{1}{2}$ x $20\frac{1}{2}$", c1900 **800.00**

Cherry Blossom Soda, diecut tin, $11\frac{1}{2}$ x $6\frac{1}{2}$", boy and girl drinking soda, two sided **190.00**

Cherry Sparkle Soda, tin, emb, caricature boy holding soda bottle, $13\frac{1}{4}$ x 6", c1915 .... **175.00**

Coca–Cola

1939, $29\frac{3}{4}$ x $49\frac{1}{2}$", bathing beauty sitting on diving board, drinking Coke, "Drink Coca–Cola, Delicious and Refreshing".... **140.00**

1949, $40\frac{1}{2}$ x 26", woman wearing white dress, drinking Coke, "Coca–Cola, Refreshing," emb medallion on orig frame **165.00**

Colt Firearms Co, paper, cowboy on horseback, 23 x 27", c1890 .... **1,250.00**

Cow Brand Baking Soda, cardboard, three tigers, $14\frac{1}{2}$ x $11\frac{1}{4}$", 1915.... **85.00**

Joyce Cridland Co, jack stands, tin, man fixing flat on old touring bus,

"A Trip in Grief/But See/'Our Jack'/Brings Quick Relief," $13\frac{1}{2}$ x $9\frac{1}{4}''$, c1910 . . . . **575.00**

Dixon's Stove Polish, paper, young girl and dog, $10\frac{1}{4}$ x 20" **375.00**

Dr Dewitt's Household Remedies, cardboard, $30\frac{1}{4}$ x $24\frac{1}{4}''$, country store interior, vignettes illustrate cures, printed by Equitable Lith and Eng Co **2,860.00**

Ebbert Co, wagons, tin, 25 x 37", self-framed, c1902 . . . . **1,600.00**

Empire Mills Flour, heavy paper, flour sack and silhouette of state of Ohio, "Use Ohio Flour," 40 x 25"   **90.00**

Empress Chocolates, celluloid, 14 x 18", empress wearing crown and robe, printed by Whitehead and Hoag Co, c1906 . . . . **300.00**

Ferris Waists, tin, $16\frac{1}{2}$ x $22\frac{1}{2}''$ oval, two girls wearing corsets, self-framed **330.00**

D M Ferry & Company Seeds, paper, man sitting outside shack, $22\frac{1}{2}$ x 32", 1907 . . . . **340.00**

Five Brothers Plug, tin, five black bears around oversized product illus, "Toothsome as Honey," 16 x 16" **1,000.00**

Gold Coin Stock Food Co, paper, horse pulling surrey, "Gold Coin Stock Tonics and Remedies are the Best," $35\frac{1}{2}$ x $29\frac{3}{4}''$ **275.00**

Gold Dust Washing Powder, cardboard, Gold Dust twins sitting on pile of gold coins, $7\frac{1}{2}$ x $10\frac{1}{2}''$ **50.00**

Gold Seal Boots, tin, $13\frac{1}{2}$ x $19\frac{1}{2}''$, emb rubber boots illus, "For Sale Here," American Art Works **215.00**

Golden Loaf Flour, tin, no illus, "Use 'Golden Loaf' Flour," $48\frac{1}{2}$ x $13\frac{1}{2}''$, frame **30.00**

Granger Pipe Tobacco, cardboard, $29\frac{1}{4}$ x 45", young boy and black butler illus, product in foreground, "Your Daddy will sure like that" **110.00**

Heinz, paper, round, pickle center, "Pure Food Products/estd 1869/ 57 Varieties," 17" d **30.00**

Hill's Coffee, paper, 26 x 26", 1898 US Navy ships illus, "Remember the Maine" **110.00**

Hires Root Beer, tin, man holding bottle, "Drink Hires/It hits the Spot/Try a bottle and you'll buy a case," 9 x 18", 1914 . . . . **475.00**

International Stock Foods, paper, $20\frac{3}{4}$ x $26\frac{1}{2}''$, farmer feeding calves   **110.00**

J P Coats Spool Cotton, paper over plaster, $21\frac{1}{2}$ x $18\frac{1}{2}''$, "Gulliver and the Lilliputians" illus **248.00**

Sign, Dog Chains & Leads, The George Lawrence Co., Portland, OR, metal, tan, red, and black letters, $7\frac{1}{8}''$ sq, $25.00.

Kellogg's Cereals, canvas, woman holding quart of milk, reaching for box of cereal, "Morning Noon and Night for every taste," $18\frac{1}{2}$ x 29" **450.00**

Kellogg's Toasted Wheat Biscuit, heavy cardboard, boy eating breakfast, holding product package, "Gee! But It's Good," 30 x 40" **525.00**

CP Kimball & Co Carriage Builders, reverse on glass, horse drawn carriage, 24 x 33", 1890s **2,100.00**

Kirkoline Washing Powder, paper, roll–down, brass bound top and bottom edges, little girl looking in mirror, soap suds dripping on furniture **1,600.00**

Lice & Mites, cardboard, chicken illus, "Rid Your Fowls of Lice & Mites," $8\frac{1}{2}$ x 12", c1910 . . . . **30.00**

Maumee Coal, tin, emb, Indian wearing feathered headband, "Cleaner, Hotter, Better" on feathers, $14\frac{1}{4}$ x 16" **175.00**

L Miller & Sons Tobacco, tin, cigar box on draped American flag, "Society Smoke," 13 x $13\frac{1}{2}''$, c1900 . . . . **300.00**

M J Maher Dry Goods, paper, cartoon illus, man kicking boy, "Something New/Bargains at M J Maher's," $32\frac{1}{2}$ x 45", 1862 . . . . . **125.00**

Monarch Poultry Feeds, wood, figural, crowing rooster, 34 x 22" . . **750.00**

Napoleon Flour, cardboard, 16" d, round, Napoleon portrait illus . . . **105.00**

Nature's Remedy, wood frame, glass panels, 17 x $23\frac{1}{2}$ x $11\frac{1}{2}''$, wedge shaped, chipped and reverse painted mirror backed panels, lighted, hanging **880.00**

Neal's Carriage Paint, $20\frac{1}{4}$ x $14\frac{1}{4}''$, caricature people riding horse–

Sign, Kraft, "I Get The Milk Bank Boost From Kraylets," pig shaped, metal, 11¾" h, 18½" l, $115.00.

drawn wagon, racing past man driving mud cart **385.00**

New Way Large Bale Hay Press, paper, 24 x 18", horse team and product illus **140.00**

New York Enamel Paint Co, cardboard, 25¾ x 20¾", before and after house illus **495.00**

Nine–O'Clock Washing Tea, tin, 13¾ x 13", emb, woman pointing to grandfather clock, large product package in foreground, printed by Tuscarora Adv Co **300.00**

Nye's National Self-Dumping Rake, paper, 15½ x 12½", product illus, printed by Milton Bradley Co Lith **138.00**

Pacific Coast Borax Co, tin, selfframed, mule team illus, 32¾ x 23", 1896 . . . . **1,375.00**

Perfection Cigarettes, cardboard, 20½ x 27", girl wearing large red hat, orig frame **440.00**

Pillsbury Flour, paper, 18 x 24", eagle atop flour barrel, dock scenes, factory insert, "For Sale Here" . . **1,870.00**

Pirate Plows, paper, 20½ x 26½", 1890 . . . . **1,625.00**

Pratt's Food, tin, horse jumping fence, "Greatest Animal Regulator for Horses, Cows, Hogs, and Sheep," 6¾ x 7¼" **150.00**

Prince Albert and Camel Cigarette, enameled, 10½ x 17½", flange, two sided, one product each side **250.00**

Procter and Gamble Amber Soap, tin, 19 x 12½", emb, logo **77.00**

Putnam Horseshoe Nails, paper, 27½ x 20¾", horse–drawn carriage illus, c1888 . . . . **220.00**

Raser's Root Beer, paper, 17 x 17", diamond shape, girl sitting on floor writing on slate **660.00**

RCA Victor, canvas, "His Master's Voice," 28 x 34", frame, c1900 **575.00**

Singer Sewing Machines, paper, 14 x 24", grandmother and child at sewing machine **410.00**

Sapolin Stove Pipe Enamel, tin, 17½ x 24½", stove and furnace illus, three dimensional **360.00**

Van Houten's Cocoa, paper, boy giving younger sister boost to table, 26½ x 33", frame, 1890 . . . . . **625.00**

Walk–Over Shoe, paper, 26 x 20", factory view, product inserts **60.00**

Walter Baker & Co's Chocolate, cardboard, 27 x 23½", colonial people drinking cocoa illus **220.00**

Warner's Safe Yeast, paper, roll–down, brass bound top and bottom edges, mother, kids, and pets family scene **1,900.00**

Wrigley's Mineral Scouring Soap, tin, 19½ x 14", emb, product illus **155.00**

String Holder

Chase & Sanborn's Coffee, tin, 13¾ x 10¼" sign, 4" d wire basket string holder insert, hanging chain **825.00**

Dutch Boy Paints, tin, diecut, Dutch Boy painting door frame, hanging bucket string holder, 13¾ x 30", American Art Sign Co **2,000.00**

Es–ki–mo Rubbers, tin, cutout center holds string spool, hanging boot moves up and down on sign, 17 x 19¾" **2,500.00**

Heinz, tin, figural pickle, hanging, "57 Varieties," 17 x 14" **1,600.00**

Higgins German Laundry Soap, cast iron, black, wall mount, "Use Higgins German Laundry Soap/It is the Best," 6" h **150.00**

Lowney's Cocoa, tin, cut–out center holds string spool, cup and saucer hanger, 16 x 24" **3,000.00**

Mail Pouch Tobacco, metal sign, two piece, string held between two sections, hanging chains, hanging Mail Pouch tobacco tin, 15 x 31" h **2,000.00**

Thermometer

AC Spark Plugs, metal **175.00**

Arbuckle's Coffee, tin, yellow top, white center, red bottom, yellow coffee package, red, white, and black lettering, 19" l, 1915 . . . . **175.00**

August Flower/Boschee's German Syrup, copper, round, 9" d, 1880–1900 . . . . **210.00**

Augustus Young Hardware and Blacksmith Supplies, wood, handsaw shape, natural ground, black lettering, 24" l, 1910s **300.00**

Baity Basket Co, metal, white ground, red tobacco basket, blue letters, 15" l **25.00**

Burnett's Jamaica Ginger, round, red and black lettering, white ground, "Joseph Burnett & Co, Boston, Mass, Pat 10 Nov 1885," 9" d **160.00**

Campbell's Tomato Soup, porcelain, flat replica soup can, 12" l, 7" w, 1925 .... **1,000.00**

Clark Bar, wood, yellow ground, blue letters, orange candy bar, 19" l, 1920 .... **150.00**

Calotabs, medicinal, wood, white ground, black lettering, 15" l, 1930.................... **60.00**

Carolina Burlap Co, wood, yellow ground, black lettering, red border, 24" l, 1915 .... **100.00**

Carter White Lead Paint, porcelain, light gray ground, red "Carter," black paint bucket and lettering, 27" l, 1910s.............. **125.00**

Caterpillar Tractors, wood, yellow ground, black lettering, 40" l, 1926.................... **150.00**

Coca–Cola, tin, bottle shape, 29" l **65.00**

Doan's Pills, wood, cut–out stooping man at top, "Is Your Back Bad Today?", 5¼ x 21"............ **165.00**

Dr LeGear's Prescriptions for Livestock, Poultry, Dogs, red and yellow ground, 26" l, 1940 .... **90.00**

Dr WH Long's Vegetable Prairie Flower, wood, natural ground, black letters, 21" l, 1915. ...... **150.00**

Dry Slitz Cigars, porcelain, 8 x 38½" **170.00**

Ferris Famous Hams and Bacon, wood, white ground, red seal, black letters and numbers, 48" l, 1910s **225.00**

Hill's Bros Coffee, porcelain, red ground, white border and lettering, yellow robed magician drinking coffee illus, 21" l, 1910s **225.00**

Hire's Root Beer, bottle shape, red top and bottom, orange center, 29" l, c1950 .... **50.00**

Honest Scrap Tobacco, porcelain, 7¼ x 27¼"................. **150.00**

Humane Barn Equipment, wood, white ground, red letters, liquid barometer right side, 12" l, 1920 **80.00**

Kickapoo Indian Remedies, brass, round, "Peabody, Mass, USA, Patented May 8, 1888"........ **260.00**

King Plows & Farm Tools, wood, white ground, red and black lettering, 12" l, 1940 .... **65.00**

Mail Pouch Tobacco, dark blue ground, red, white, and black trim, 39" l, c1950............ **50.00**

Pal Orange Ade, yellow ground, red

Thermometer, Muller's Pinehurst Grade A Milk, Rockford, IL, milk carton shape, red letters, wax coated cardboard, 2½ x 6⅛", $12.00.

and white trademarks, 26" l, c1950................... **40.00**

Pepsi Cola, tan ground, blue letters, relief bottle cap, 27" l, c1950 ... **55.00**

Remington Cutlery, porcelain, 8 x 38¾" **225.00**

Royal Crown Cola, red ground, thermometer in white arrow, 26" l, c1950................... **35.00**

Sauer's Flavoring Extracts, wood, white ground, red and black lettering, 24" l, 7" w, 1915 .... **225.00**

Stafford's Ink, porcelain, dark blue, dark blue ink bottle on white area, white thermometer area, 27" l, 1910s................... **250.00**

Ward's Vitovim Bread, porcelain, yellow and dark blue ground, boy eating slice of bread illus, 21 x 9", 1910s................... **400.00**

USS American Fence and Posts, porcelain, dark blue ground, red border, lettering, and thermometer area, 19" l, 1910s........... **120.00**

CABINETS, COUNTERS, SHELVING, AND ACCESSORIES

History: When a building was built specifically as a country store building, it was customary to build–in shelving, cabinets, and counters. Much of the interior architecture was utilitarian, not ornately decorative or elaborately trimmed. A surprising number of these buildings survive. Attempting to remove and relocate these fixtures poses a major problem.

The key merchandising technique utilized by the country store was open storage. Glass cases, visible from front, top, and sides and with a back featuring a stepped shelf interior, were common. The main counter was the exception, usually containing a plank board top and solid sides with shelves or bins accessible only from the back.

The main counter usually contained several small and medium size special-purpose glass cabinets. The three most prevalent uses were candy, cheese, and notions. In addition, companies—especially thread companies—provided the country store merchant with cabinets designed to store, promote, and sell their product. Many of these featured brightly lithographed tin fronts.

In addition to the fixed pieces, the country store was home to a host of other point of purchase display units, ranging from the cracker barrel to the broom rack. Large floor bins held coffee, flour, and grains. Many of these featured stenciled advertisements.

The universal country store look is eclectic. Occasionally a merchant remodeling his store would install a matched set of counters, cabinets, and shelves. These matched sets bring a handsome premium when sold. However, carefully check the provenance of any matched set offered. The same fixtures would be used in a jewelry or small department store. Country store collectors prefer a country store provenance.

Keep your eyes open for photographs of country store interiors. They are important research sources for collectors and museums. Value ranges from $5.00 to $25.00. Add ten to twenty—five percent if the store and town are identified and the photograph dated.

Barrel
  Calumet Baking Powder, wood and
    cardboard, "The World's Great-
    est," 19¾" d, 28½" h **125.00**
  Davis Baking Powder, wood, paper
    label, 16½" d, 23½" h **165.00**

Dexter Fine Yarn, oak, four drawers, 18¾" h, 18⅛" w, 16" d, $650.00.

Cabinet
  Brainerd & Armstrong, wood frame,
    three glass panels, 16½ x 16½ x
    28", revolving spool rack **950.00**
  Clark's ONT Spool Cotton, oak, 22 x
    7½", two drawers, cased glass
    drawer inserts **250.00**
  Diamond Dyes, wood, 30" h, emb
    tin front panel, woman dyeing
    clothing illus **550.00**
  Dr Calvin Crane's Quaker Reme-
    dies, chest, mahogany, glass
    panel in slant lid, "Fully Guaran-
    teed, For Man, Woman and
    Child, In All The World No Cure
    So Sure," 10" h, 15½" w, 10"
    deep, 1880–1900 .... **1,100.00**
  Dr Lesure's
    Famous Remedies, 26" h, emb tin
      front panel, horse head, orig
      adv booklet **2,200.00**
    Veterinary Medicines, 28" h, glass
      door, three shelves, stenciled
      lettering................ **565.00**
  Dr J H McLean's Medicines, maple,
    convex glass front, four shelves,
    "Dr J H McLeans's Strengthening
    Cordial & Blood Purifier" on
    crested top, 28" h, 17½" w, 7"
    deep, 1880–1900 .... **1,975.00**
  Dr Raibert's Pine Tar Tablets, wood
    and metal frame, beveled glass
    panels, "Schmitt & Co. 209 Main
    Cin. O." on brass tag, 7" h, 4¾" w,
    9½" deep, 1890–1900........ **745.00**
  Eureka Spool Cabinet, wood, glass
    paned door, twelve shelves, 19½ x
    20 x 37" **900.00**
  Globe Dyes, wood, 28½" h, dye
    colors illus on circular paper in-
    sert, gallery top **110.00**
  Golden Fleece Gold Medal Braid
    Co, wood, 12½" h, three drawers,
    gold leafed letters........... **360.00**
  Gypsy Dye, tin, 11 x 3½ x 22", wood
    base **200.00**
  Hanford's Balsam of Myrrh, oak,
    glass door, three shelves, 24" h,
    14" w, 8½" deep, 1890–1900 ... **475.00**
  Humphrey's Homeopathic Speci-
    fics, wood, name etched on glass
    top, two drawers, 53 preparations
    in orig labeled boxes, 22" w,
    7⅞" h, c1900 .... **715.00**
  J & P Coats Spool Cotton, 22" h,
    figural spool shape, twine wrap-
    ping **440.00**
  Merrick's Spool Cotton, oak, 18" d,
    22" h, cylindrical, curved glass **715.00**
  Peerless Dyes, wood, 25½" h, tin
    front panel, woman, peacock,
    and butterflies illus.......... **715.00**

Humphrey's Veterinarian Specifics, oak, four interior shelves, composition front panel, 27½" h, 21" w, 10" d, $1,650.00.

Pratt's Food Co, veterinary remedies, wood, products illustrated
on door panel, 16½ x 6¾ x 30" h .. **625.00**
Willimantic Spool Cotton, oak,
14¼" h, four drawers, adv pulls,
side decals, Eastlake style **495.00**
Coffee Bin
  Jersey Coffee, wood, slant top lift
  lid, stenciled lettering and border
  design, 100 lbs, 31¾" h **345.00**
  Luxury Coffee, wood, stenciled lettering and border design, 32" h **375.00**
  Washburn Halligan Coffee, wood,
  stenciled lettering, 24 x 16 x 30½" **50.00**
Display Case
  Advertising, Slidewell Collars, metal
  frame, glass panels, 13 x 7 x 25½" **460.00**
  Revolving, wood frame, eight glass
  panels, octagonal, four shelves,
  32 bins, 41" h, dated 1894 . . . . . **1,500.00**
  Wood, slant top, three glass panes in
  top, four small panes across front,
  orig tobacco brown paint exterior,
  green paint interior, 42" l, 8" h,
  19th C **400.00**
Flour Sifter and Cabinet
  Cream City Flour, tin, cylindrical,
  13" d, 28" h **175.00**
  Waiten Flour Cabinet, tin cylindrical
  cabinet and lid, wood base,
  12½" d, 32" h **200.00**
Grain Bin, Wilburs Poultry Food,
wood, stenciled lettering, 17½ x 17½
x 35" **575.00**
Measure, grain, 10¾" l, oval, bent-
wood **75.00**
Rack
  Broom
    Cast Iron, round base and handle
    holder, four legs, single center

pole, holds 30 brooms, 29" h,
22" w, dated 1885 . . . . **215.00**
Wood Center Pole and round
holed base, cast iron ring
shaped handle holder, holds 18
brooms, 65" h, 24" w **125.00**
Whip Holder, bent wire, hanging,
16" d **70.00**
Wood, 18 knobbed pegs staggered
on center pole, 76" l, wire hanger **100.00**

CATALOGS

History: Catalogs played an important role in country living. First, they broadened the farmer's knowledge of what was available beyond his local community. Second, they provided a means of keeping abreast of changing technology. Finally, they decreased the sense of isolation that is part of farming.

Catalogs serve as excellent research sources. The complete manufacturing line of a given item is often described and pictured in a wide variety of styles, colors, etc. Catalogs provide an excellent method of dating objects.

Many old catalogs are reprinted for use by collectors as an aid to identification of items within their collecting interest, e.g., reprints of Heisey and Hubley catalogs. The photocopy machine also contributes to the distribution of information among friends.

Reference: Don Fredgant, *American Trade Catalogs*, Collector Books, 1984.

1855
  Arnold & Crouch, broadside price
  list, 2 pgs, joiners' bench planes,
  molding tools **125.00**
  G & D Cook & Co, first edition, 71
  tinted litho pictures, carriages . . . **475.00**
1866, Dover Stamping Co, over 200
pgs, tinners' hardware, furnishing
goods **200.00**
1870, Douglas Axe Mfg Co, cloth-
bound, 115 pgs **100.00**
1872, Greenfield Tool Co, 84 pgs,
bench planes **130.00**
1881, Wm Dent & Son Machinists'
Tools, Utica, NY, 72 pgs **160.00**
1888, Great Western Gun Works, Pittsburgh, PA, 64 pgs. **50.00**
1895, Paris Mfg Co, 16 color plates,
sleds, swings, wagons **300.00**
1897, Walworth Mfg Co, Boston, MA,
hardcover, 320 pgs, 7½ x 5¼", brass
and wrought iron hardware and architectural details **20.00**
1900, Ellwood Woven Wire Fences
and Gates, 31 pgs, 3½ x 6¼" **15.00**

Kellogg's Strawberries, R. M. Kellogg Co.,
Three Rivers, MI, 1922, 67 pages, $10.00.

1901, Gray Bros, Cleveland, OH, 176 pgs, tools	35.00
1903, Thomas, Roberts, Stevenson Co, Philadelphia, PA, 88 pgs, stoves	16.00
1908–09, Farquahar's Garden Annual Seed Catalog.	20.00
1909, Germantown Tool Works, Philadelphia, PA, 46 pgs	18.00
1910, Smith Bros Seed Co, Auburn, NY, 32 pgs, two color plates, $8\frac{1}{2}$ x $10\frac{1}{4}$"	18.00
1911, March–Brownback Stove Co, Pottstown, PA, 28 pgs	23.00
1914, Pierce Arrow, 40 pgs, 9 x 12" . .	154.00
1915, Paris Mfg Co, South Paris, ME, children's desks.	25.00
1916, Cashman's Seed	8.00

The Larkin Idea, May, 1935, orig order
blank, orange, blue, and white cover, $8\frac{1}{2}$"
h, $5\frac{1}{4}$" w, $8.00.

1917, Stover Manufacturing & Engine Co, Freeport, IL, 112 pgs, separate wholesale price list, hardware	24.00
1925, Chevrolet, loose–leaf, "A Ride in a Chevrolet" emb on cover, 65 pgs, 34 photos, 17 pen and ink spot drawings, 9 x $11\frac{3}{4}$", 16 pg booklet and two folders in cover pocket . . .	58.00
1926, William Dixon, Newark, NJ, 480 pgs, jewelers, silversmiths, die sinkers, engravers, and metalworkers tools	10.00
1927, W G Browne Mfg Co, Kingston, NY, 32 pgs, hardware, kitchen utensils, children's miniatures, separate net price list	2.00
1928, Union Fork & Hoe Co, Columbus, OH, hardcover, 120 pgs, forks, hoes, rakes, victory garden cultivator	32.00
1930, Loring Lane Co, New York City, NY, 160 pgs, household goods	3.00
1932, Sears Roebuck, Fall and Winter, 1035 pgs	40.00
1934, Montgomery Ward, seed	5.00

COUNTERTOP ITEMS

History: The country store countertop was home
to a number of items that supplemented the
counters and larger display units. Attractive lithograph tin bins housed products ranging from coffee and tea to spices and tobacco. The cast iron
decorative elements on cash registers turned
them into stylish works of art. Coffee grinders,
glass jars, paper dispensers, and string holders are
just a few of the additional items that can be
found.

The country store collector competes with the
advertising tin collector and specialized theme
collector for much of this material. Since the vast
majority was mass–produced and used in a variety of settings other than the country store, country store collectors place a premium on pieces
with a country store provenance.

References: Henry Bartsch and Larry Sanchez,
*Antique Cash Registers, 1880–1920: The Yellow
Book*, published by authors, 1987; Al Bergevin,
Tobacco Tins and Their Prices, Wallace–
Homestead, 1986; Richard Crandall and Sam
Robins, *The Incorruptible Cashier, Volume I: The
formation of an industry, 1876–1890* (1988) and
Volume II: The Brass Era, 1888–1915 (1991),
Vestal Press; Terry Friend, *Coffee Mills*, Collector
Books, 1982.

Reproduction Manufacturer: *Coffee Grinders—*
Cumberland General Store, Rte 3, Crossville, TN
38555.

Bin

Alsorbo Corn Pads, tin, feet illus on
sides, $11\frac{1}{2}$ x $6\frac{1}{4}$ x 15" **145.00**

American Sodas, tin, $10\frac{1}{4}$ x $11\frac{1}{2}$" h,
paper label, Uncle Sam holding
biscuits illus **28.00**

Baker's Baking Powder, tin, $6\frac{1}{2}$ x $4\frac{3}{4}$ x
$9\frac{1}{2}$" **60.00**

Better Service Stores Coffee, dispenses coffee beans, metal frame,
four glass panels, 14 x 14 x 28" . .   **185.00**

B F Japan Tea, tin, slant lid on lower
front, 13 x 16 x $19\frac{1}{2}$" **125.00**

Bird Brand Coffee, tin, paper label,
11 x 11 x 17" **75.00**

Dwinell–Wright Co's Royal Coffee,
tin, $19\frac{1}{4}$ x $13\frac{1}{4}$ x $21\frac{1}{2}$" **250.00**

John T Hancock & Sons Spices, tin,
ornate lettering and dec, 38" l,
$13\frac{1}{2}$" h. **1,600.00**

Honest Scrap Tobacco, tin, hinged
slant top, cat and dog illus front,
arm and hammer illus sides, 18 x
14 x 12" **750.00**

Henry Horner & Co Coffee, litho tin,
building shape, slanting roof lid,
"Happy Home Mills," 16 x $10\frac{1}{2}$ x
15" **400.00**

Imperial Tea, tin, $10\frac{1}{2}$ x $9\frac{3}{4}$ x $13\frac{3}{4}$" . . .   **80.00**

Johnson's Peacemaker Coffee, litho
tin, log cabin shape and design,
24 x 18 x 25", 1915 . . . .   **1,000.00**

Jas McClurg & Co's Unrivaled
Crackers, tin, glass insert, 10 x 10
x $11\frac{1}{2}$" **95.00**

McCormick's Tea, round, tin, glass
panel in lid and insert, $10\frac{1}{4}$" d,
$8\frac{1}{2}$" h. **80.00**

Old Glory Coffee, litho tin, curved
top, "Mocha & Java Flavored,"
$13\frac{1}{4}$ x 13 x $2\frac{1}{2}$". **650.00**

Red Cross Mocha and Java, tin,
curved hinged lid, $13\frac{1}{2}$ x $13\frac{1}{2}$ x
26" h **215.00**

Rosebud Matches, tin, floral dec, 22
x $14\frac{3}{4}$ x $10\frac{3}{4}$" h **195.00**

Royal Tiger Brand Ginger, tin, 9 x 9
x 11" h **150.00**

Schotten's Coffee, litho tin, 19 x $13\frac{3}{4}$
x $19\frac{1}{2}$" **150.00**

Sure Shot Chewing Tobacco, tin,
$15\frac{1}{4}$ x $7\frac{1}{4}$ x $10\frac{1}{4}$", Indian aiming
bow and arrow **385.00**

Sweet Cuba Tobacco, tin, 18 x 12 x
14", yellow ground, red and black
lettering, slant front **190.00**

Woolsen Spice Co, tin floral design,
$19\frac{1}{2}$ x $12\frac{1}{4}$ x $21\frac{1}{2}$" **275.00**

Canister

Blue–jay Corn Plasters, tin, 7" d,
6" h, woman applying plaster
illus, lid. **50.00**

Cash Register, National 1912 Model 442, bronze, mahogany base, small cranker, $0.00 to $9.99, 20 x $16\frac{3}{4}$ x 23", $675.00.

Fountain Tobacco, tin, $8\frac{1}{2}$" d, $8\frac{1}{2}$" h,
handled slip lid **92.00**

Cash Register

American, copper plated, 50 key . .   **1,000.00**

National

#317, 5¢ to $1.00, marble
change shelf, printer, 16" **1,200.00**

#321, brass, $17\frac{1}{4}$ x 17 x 16", ex-
tended base, 1916 . . . .   **650.00**

#452–2, oak, two drawer, crank   **850.00**

Peninsula, Muren, nickel plated,
c1912. . . . .   **250.00**

Coffee Grinder

Elma Coffee, iron, counter model,
aluminum hopper, 9 x 9 x 21" h   **550.00**

Enterprise, floor model, iron, 67" h,
$34\frac{1}{2}$" wheel diameter. **1,000.00**

Enterprize, counter model, iron, 11
x 11 x 26" **475.00**

Golden Rule Coffee, wall mount,
iron and wood, glass insert, $5\frac{1}{2}$ x 4
x 17".   **115.00**

Guinea Gold, tin body, cast iron
grinder, 15" h, Walrath & Manz   **155.00**

Cigar Cutter, The Brunhoff Mfg. Co, Cincinnati, OH, 5 x $6\frac{1}{2}$ x 3", $110.00.

Coffee Mill, Landers, Frary & Clark, New Britain, CT, No. 2, two wheels, cast iron, countertop, $500.00.

Hoffman's Coffee, wall mount, tin and wood, iron crank, old woman drinking coffee illus on front, 8 x $5\frac{1}{2}$ x 13"...............	**375.00**
Norton Bros, tin, cylindrical, 6 x $9\frac{1}{2}$", 1882...................	**400.00**
Parker, cast iron	
14" h, orig paint............	**522.00**
29" h, orig paint, #900.......	**330.00**
Collar Button Dispenser, iron, cylindrical glass case, ftd, 14" h.......	**2,200.00**
Counter Jar	
Barsam Brothers, Inc, 9 x 12", glass, octagonal, emb, lid..........	**220.00**
Bunte Candy, 6" d, 12" h, faceted, emb name, ground neck and stopper.....................	**40.00**
Dad's Cookie Co, cylindrical, emb, ''Property Of,'' 10" d, 12" h....	**70.00**
Elephant Peanuts, spherical, lid, emb elephant illus and lettering, 8" d, 9" h.................	**90.00**
Kis–Me Gum, 5 x 11" h, octagonal style, stopper..............	**55.00**
Planters Peanuts	
$12\frac{1}{2}$" h, 8" d, octagonal, emb, paper label, peanut finial lid....	**190.00**

Counter Jar, Planters Peanuts, clear, orig label, 13" h, $7\frac{1}{2}$" d top, $175.00.

13" h, $8\frac{1}{2}$" d, barrel shape, emb running peanut, peanut finial lid....................	**250.00**
14" h, 9" d, figural peanut shape, emb, peanut finial lid.......	**220.00**
Squirrel Brand Salted Nuts, 9" d, $14\frac{1}{2}$" h, emb squirrel logo, lid...	**165.00**
Walla–Walla Gum, 5 x 11" h, trademark Indian on paper label, lid..	**440.00**
Peanut Vendor, iron, glass cylinder holds peanuts, 10 x 10 x 22" h....	**3,500.00**
Peanut Warmer	
Tin, $21\frac{1}{2}$" h, curved glass front, stenciled lettering.............	**275.00**
Uncle Sam, tin, glass panel, Lutted Candy Co, 15 x $16\frac{1}{4}$ x $21\frac{3}{4}$"......	**400.00**
Pencil Vendor, metal, ''A High Grade Lead Pencil Five Cents,'' $11\frac{1}{2}$ x 17", National...................	**2,500.00**
Scale, grocery	
Computing Scale Co, light–up display.....................	**525.00**
Iron, emb shield design beneath window, $9\frac{1}{2}$ x $10\frac{1}{2}$"..........	**250.00**
Seed Box, Lake Shore Seed Co, wood, paper label, vegetables illus, 24 x 10 x 5".....................	**95.00**
String Holder, cast iron, $6\frac{1}{2}$" d, 5" h, figural ball of string on base, hinged	**100.00**
String and Paper Dispenser, cast iron, US shield design at top, holds three brown paper rolls, 18" w, 22" h...	**175.00**

PACKAGES AND TINS

History: Factory-processed food revolutionized life in the second half of the nineteenth century. Although it would be several decades before the majority of the food that constituted an American's daily diet would be ''store bought'' and not ''fresh,'' factory-processed food was eagerly embraced by most Americans.

The number of factory-processed food products was limited initially. Manufacturers quickly realized that packaging was the key to sales and the development of brand loyalty. The evolution of processed food also corresponded to the golden age of American lithography. The country store's shelves were lined with brightly colored lithographed paper and tin packages.

Unlike their historical antecedents, whose shelves contained several dozen of each item, few country store collectors have more than one example of a product on their shelves. Cost is the prohibiting factor.

Although condition and scarcity are two important value considerations, the pizzazz of the piece is the most critical value element. Many packages contain images that cross over into other collecting categories, e.g., a movie star collector is as strong or stronger a competitor than a country store collector for a Jackie Coogan Peanut Butter pail.

References: Al Bergevin, *Drugstore Tins and Their Prices*, Wallace–Homestead, 1990; —, *Food and Drink Containers and Their Prices*, Wallace–Homestead, 1978; Al Bergevin, *Tobacco Tins and Their Prices*, Wallace–Homestead, 1986; M. J. Franklin, *British Biscuit Tins 1868–1939: An Aspect of Decorative Packaging*, Schiffer Publishing, 1979; Robert and Harriet Swedberg, *Vintage Advertising Series, Tins 'N Bins*, Wallace–Homestead, 1985.

Aberdeen Creamery Co., Bossie's Best Brand Butter, one pound box, $4.50.

Boxes

Altoona Steam Bakery, wood, paper label, $22\frac{3}{4}$ x $13\frac{3}{4}$ x $13\frac{1}{2}''$ **90.00**

American Biscuit & Mfg Co, wood box, paper label, parrot illus, 18 x 12 x $10\frac{1}{2}''$. **65.00**

Bromo Seltzer, wood, stenciled, red and black ink, Emerson Drug Co, Baltimore, MD, $8\frac{1}{2}$ x $11\frac{9}{16}$ x $9\frac{1}{2}''$ . .   **175.00**

Chase's Ice Cream, cardboard, female skier illus, $\frac{1}{2}$ pint **11.00**

Coca–Cola Gum, wood, dovetailed, $12\frac{3}{4}''$ l **300.00**

Cross–Cut Cigarettes, cardboard, men sawing illus on slip cover, 8 female photo cards inside, $1\frac{1}{2}$ x 3 x $\frac{3}{4}''$ **82.00**

Dr Kilmer's Swamp–Root, wood, dovetailed, stenciled, black ink, $12\frac{1}{2}$ x 12 x 9'' **50.00**

Duryea's Stain Gloss Starch, 6 lbs, wood, dovetailed, black stencil, yellow and black paper lid label, multicolored paper end label, Glen Cove, Long Island, $10\frac{1}{4}$ x $6\frac{1}{4}$ x 6''.   **155.00**

Fellows Compound Syrup of Hypophosphites, wood, black lettering both end panels, 9'' h, 1890–1910. . . . .   **28.00**

Foley's Honey and Tar Compound, wood, dovetailed, stenciled, black ink, Foley & Co, Chicago, IL, $24\frac{3}{16}$ x $12\frac{3}{4}$ x $11\frac{1}{2}''$ **60.00**

Hood's Sarsaparilla, wood, dovetailed, stenciled, black ink, C I Hood Co, Lowell, MA, 14 x $14\frac{3}{4}$ x $10\frac{1}{4}''$ **60.00**

Hoosier Poet Brand Rolled Oats, cardboard cylinder, 4'' d, $7\frac{1}{2}''$ h . .   **55.00**

Jamestown Bakery Dairy Cream Crackers, wood, paper label, 19 x 11 x $10\frac{1}{2}''$. **85.00**

Kingsford's Silver Gloss Starch, wood, dovetailed, stenciled, green ink, multicolored paper end label, National Starch Co, Gen-

eral Offices, New York, USA, $11\frac{1}{2}$ x $6\frac{1}{2}$ x $5\frac{3}{4}''$. **105.00**

Kow–Kure, wood, dovetailed, paper label, black lettering, white ground, "For Cows Only/made only by Dairy Association/Lyndonville, VT, USA," $12\frac{1}{4}$ x $17\frac{3}{4}$ x $6\frac{1}{2}''$.   **55.00**

Log Cabin Brownies, cardboard, log cabin shape, $3\frac{1}{2}$ x $2\frac{3}{4}$ x 3'' **55.00**

Log Cabin Smoking Tobacco, wood, paper coated, interior paper label, black man smoking pipe, sitting outside cabin, $14\frac{1}{2}$ x $7\frac{3}{4}$ x $9\frac{1}{4}''$ **550.00**

Lydia E Pinkham's Vegetable Compound, one dozen, wood, dovetailed, stenciled, black ink, Lynn, MA, $9\frac{3}{4}$ x $12\frac{3}{4}$ x $9\frac{1}{4}''$ **50.00**

Medlar Co Biscuits, wood, dovetailed, paper label, $21\frac{1}{4}$ x $13\frac{3}{4}$ x 11''   **30.00**

Mother's Crushed Oats, cardboard cylinder, mother and child illus, $4\frac{1}{4}''$ d, $7\frac{1}{4}''$ h **20.00**

Perry Davis' Vegetable Pain–Killer, wood, dovetailed, paper labels, one black and white, one color, Perry Davis & Son Mfg, Providence, RI, 7 x $10\frac{3}{4}$ x $7\frac{1}{4}''$, c1871 . .   **50.00**

Fairy Soap, Gold Dust Corp, $2\frac{3}{8}$ x $3\frac{7}{8}$ x 1'', $7.50.

Nation–Wide Service Grocers, Rolled Oats, cardboard, red, white, and blue, $9\frac{1}{2}''$ h, $5\frac{1}{4}''$ d, $10.00.

Robinson Bros Bakery Crackers and Fine Cakes, wood, paper label, $23\frac{1}{2} \times 14 \times 13''$ **80.00**

Scotch Brand Oats, cardboard cylinder, Scotsman illus, Lauderbach Griest Co, Philipsburg, PA, 4" d, $7\frac{1}{4}''$ h **30.00**

Skabcura Liquid Sheep Dip, wood, stenciled, black and red ink, Skabcura Dip Co, Chicago, IL, $20\frac{1}{4} \times 8\frac{1}{4} \times 6\frac{1}{4}''$ **100.00**

Sloan's Liniment, wood, stenciled, black ink, $20\frac{3}{4} \times 14 \times 12\frac{1}{2}''$ **50.00**

Star of Empire Tobacco, wood, dovetailed, paper label, $16 \times 10 \times 7''$ **55.00**

Stickney & Poor's Extra Fine Mustard, wood, dovetailed, paper lid and side labels, multicolored, $14\frac{3}{4} \times 8 \times 4''$ **82.00**

St Jacob's Oil/The Great German Remedy, one dozen, wood, dovetailed, stenciled, black ink, old man sitting beneath tree, paper label lid, $7 \times 5\frac{1}{2} \times 7\frac{1}{8}''$ **110.00**

Warner's Safe Yeast, wood, dovetailed, Rochester, NY, $7 \times 13 \times 7''$, 1890–1900. . . . .   **38.00**

Welsh Rabbit Biscuits, tin, flower pattern, dining room scene illus, 10" l **38.00**

Winan Bros Indian Cure, wood, stenciled, black ink, Worcester, MA, $12\frac{3}{16} \times 11\frac{1}{2} \times 12\frac{9}{16}''$ **60.00**

Yankee Rolled White Oats, 2 lbs, cardboard, $4\frac{1}{4} \times 3\frac{3}{4} \times 8''$ **50.00**

Pails

Betsy Ross Peanut Butter, children playing at beach, $3\frac{3}{4}''$ d, $3\frac{1}{2}''$ h . . .   **225.00**

Bunny Coffee, 4 lbs, John W Bunn & Co, Springfield, IL, 8" d, $7\frac{1}{8}''$ h . . .   **450.00**

Choice Family Tea, black lettering, yellow ground, $4\frac{1}{4}''$ d, $4\frac{1}{4}''$ h **16.00**

Sultana Peanut Butter, tin, 4 x 4", $95.00.

Diehl's Cough Drops, 5 lbs, round, litho tin, York, PA, 6" d, $6\frac{1}{2}''$ h . . .   **35.00**

Dinner Party Brand Coffee, round, $7\frac{1}{4}''$ d, $10\frac{1}{2}''$ h **125.00**

Giant Peanuts, tin, giant watching circus parade illus, $3\frac{3}{4}''$ d, $3\frac{1}{2}''$ h . .   **138.00**

Harvard Jumbo Peanuts, 10 lb, collegiate peanut illus, $7\frac{3}{4}''$ d, $10\frac{1}{4}''$ h   **65.00**

Hoody's Famous Peanut Butter, boy and girl on peanut–based seesaw, $3\frac{1}{2}''$ d, $3\frac{3}{4}''$ h **175.00**

Jackie Coogan Peanut Butter, tin, photo portrait illustrations, $3\frac{1}{4}''$ d, $3\frac{1}{4}''$ h **330.00**

Lou–Bob Finest Grease, antique auto illus, 6" d, $5\frac{3}{4}''$ h **125.00**

Monarch Popcorn, tin, bail handle, $3\frac{1}{4}''$ d, $3\frac{3}{4}''$ h **275.00**

Penns Tobacco, $5\frac{1}{4}''$ d, 6" h. **20.00**

Pilot–Knob Coffee, tin, 5 lb, paper label, $7\frac{1}{2}''$ d, 8" h **138.00**

Plow Boy Tobacco, paper label, $5\frac{1}{4}''$ d, 6" h **40.00**

Prairie Queen Baking Powder, round, 2" d, $2\frac{3}{4}''$ h **110.00**

Sawyer Coffee, round, 9" d, 14" h   **65.00**

Schepps Cocoanut, monkey in jungle illus, $2\frac{1}{2}''$ d, $3\frac{3}{4}''$ h **150.00**

Scholl's Axle Grease, horse–drawn wagon illus, Independent Oil Co, Mansfield, OH, 6" d, $6\frac{1}{2}''$ h **75.00**

School Boy Peanut Butter, $3\frac{3}{4}''$ d, $3\frac{1}{2}''$ h **125.00**

Shamokin Packing Co Pure Lard, 8 lbs, Indian logo, $7\frac{1}{2}''$ d, $8\frac{1}{2}''$ h **66.00**

Sunny Bank Tobacco, 5" d, $5\frac{1}{2}''$ h . .   **600.00**

Sweet Cuba Tobacco, wood, $12\frac{1}{2}''$ d, 11" h **165.00**

Thresher Hard Oil, square, Standard Oil Co, $9\frac{1}{4}''$ sq, $9\frac{3}{4}''$ h **135.00**

Tins

All-American Cigars, round, Lincoln, Washington, and Franklin portraits, 5" d, $5\frac{1}{4}''$ h **230.00**

A&P Baking Powder, round, paper label, $3\frac{1}{4}''$ d, $4\frac{1}{2}''$ h **20.00**

Bokar Coffee, dark green and red can, 6" h, $4\frac{1}{4}$" d, $15.00.

Game Fine Cut Tobacco, Jno. J. Bagley & Co., Detroit, MI, litho tin, $11\frac{5}{8}$" w, 8" d, 7" h, $325.00.

Aromatic Tooth Soap, flat, rect, litho, Frederick Stearns & Co, Detroit, MI, $\frac{5}{8}$ x $3\frac{1}{4}$ x $2\frac{1}{8}$"	50.00
Auto Sliced Plug Tobacco, pocket size.	60.00
Baker Cocoa, patterned, trademark insert on two sides and cap, $3\frac{1}{4}$" sq, $5\frac{3}{4}$" h	82.00
Baker's Nursery Talcum Powder, rect, litho, stork and babies illus, 6" h	50.00
Bank Note Cigars, round, $4\frac{1}{4}$" d, $5\frac{1}{2}$" h	25.00
Black Cat Leather Preserver, flat, round, litho, cat illus, $3\frac{1}{8}$" d, $\frac{7}{8}$" h	100.00
Black Cough Drops, 5 lbs, litho, Reading, PA, $5\frac{1}{4}$" sq, $7\frac{1}{2}$" h	60.00
Borden's Meadow Brand Malted Milk, square, red and white, $9\frac{1}{2}$" h, c1910	15.00
Brunswick Dental Floss, round, litho, hole in side for floss, Johnson & Johnson, $1\frac{1}{8}$" d, $1\frac{5}{8}$" h	10.00
Bunte Marshmallows, round, $12\frac{1}{4}$" d, $9\frac{1}{4}$" h	200.00
Buttermilk and Soda Baking Powder, round, paper label, woman and cow illus, $3\frac{1}{4}$" d, $5\frac{3}{4}$" h	35.00
California Perfume, suitcase shape, Jack and Jill illus, $5\frac{3}{4}$ x $1\frac{1}{4}$ x $3\frac{3}{4}$" . . .	50.00
Carnation Corn Caps, corn removers, flat, rect, litho, $\frac{1}{2}$ x $2\frac{1}{2}$ x $1\frac{1}{8}$"	10.00
Carnation Malted Milk, square, red and white, 3 x $5\frac{3}{4}$" h	30.00
Cheney's Tooth Powder, round, litho, Cheney Chemical Co, S Manchester, CT, $2\frac{1}{8}$" d, $4\frac{1}{4}$" h	30.00
Cobb, Bates & Yerxa Nutmeg, rect, $6\frac{1}{2}$ x $4\frac{3}{4}$ x $9\frac{1}{2}$" h	45.00
Darby's Swan Tolu, medicinal candy, black on red, Somers Bros, 4 x $1\frac{1}{2}$ x $3\frac{1}{2}$".	38.00
Dill's Foot Powder, oval, litho, Norristown, PA, $4\frac{5}{8}$" h	18.00

Dr Daniel's Gall Cure, flat, round, litho, $1\frac{1}{8}$" d, $\frac{1}{2}$" h, sample	12.00
Dr J Pettit's Eye Salve, flat, round, litho, eye in lid center, $1\frac{1}{4}$" d, $\frac{1}{4}$" h	10.00
E C Harley Co Tea, square, Dayton, OH, $5\frac{1}{4}$ x $7\frac{1}{2}$" h	30.00
E C Shotgun Powder, rect, $3\frac{1}{2}$ x $1\frac{1}{2}$ x $5\frac{1}{2}$" h	50.00
Fleet's Chap Stick, round, flat, litho, 1" d, $\frac{1}{4}$" h, sample	10.00
Forest and Stream Pipe Tobacco, flying duck illus, pocket size	25.00
Friedmann & Lauterjung's Electric Razor, flat, rect, litho, $6\frac{1}{2}$" l	25.00
Frontier Boot Polish, round, flat, litho, 3" d, 1" h	40.00
Grape Nuts, 14 oz, yellow and black, Postum Cereal Co, Battle Creek, MI	18.00
Heekin's Cinnamon, rect, paper label, $6\frac{3}{4}$ x $4\frac{3}{4}$ x $9\frac{1}{2}$" h	75.00
Hoadley's Tolu Chewing Gum, chicle, Somers Bros, $2\frac{1}{4}$ x $\frac{3}{4}$ x 1".	275.00
Indian Tobacco Antidote, flat, rect, litho, Cooley & McDonald, Plymouth, IN, $\frac{5}{8}$ x $3\frac{1}{2}$ x $2\frac{1}{4}$"	20.00
Lady Hellen Coffee, round, $4\frac{1}{4}$" d, $5\frac{3}{4}$" h	45.00

Royal Gelatin Dessert, red, $3\frac{1}{2}$" d, 6" h, $7.50.

Sunbrite Cleanser, blue and orange label, tin, 5″ h, 3″ d, $7.50.

Lions Stock Remedy, livestock,
square, lion illus, $9\frac{1}{4}$ x $10\frac{1}{2}$″ h **80.00**
Little Buster Pop Corn, round, boy
popping corn, $2\frac{1}{2}$″ d, $4\frac{1}{2}$″ h **45.00**
Long Tom Smoking Tobacco,
curved corners, black man wear-
ing checkered suit, 5 x 2 x $3\frac{3}{4}$″ . . .   **165.00**
Malden Coffee, rect, 7 x 5 x $10\frac{3}{4}$″ h   **18.00**
Monarch Nut Meats, round, $6\frac{3}{4}$″ d,
$9\frac{1}{2}$″ h **30.00**
Mooney's Best Baking Powder,
round, paper label, 3″ d, $5\frac{1}{2}$″ h. . .   **22.00**
Murray's Superior Hair Dressing
Pomade, flat, round, litho tin,
3″ d, $1\frac{7}{8}$″ h **20.00**
Newton's Horse Remedy, square,
horse and surrey illus, $3\frac{1}{2}$ x $7\frac{1}{4}$″ h   **145.00**
Old Chum Smoking Tobacco, rect,
4 x $2\frac{1}{2}$ x $4\frac{3}{4}$″ h **15.00**
Old Fire Side Tea, couple by hearth,
$4\frac{1}{2}$ x $4\frac{3}{4}$ x $2\frac{3}{4}$″ **11.00**

Vision Baking Powder, E. Metzenaur Baking Powder Co., St. Louis, MO, paper label, red, blue, yellow, green, and tan, $4\frac{1}{4}$″ h, $2\frac{1}{2}$″ d, $25.00.

Old Homestead Coffee, 1 lb, $4\frac{1}{4}$″ d,
6″ h **55.00**
Par After–Shave Powder, oval, li-
tho, golfer illus, $5\frac{3}{4}$″ h **60.00**
Patterson's Seal Tobacco, square, $3\frac{1}{2}$
x $5\frac{1}{2}$″ h. **20.00**
Peacock Ink, octagonal shape, pea-
cock dec, removable ink bottle in
center, $2\frac{1}{4}$ x $2\frac{3}{4}$″ h **105.00**
Peau–Doux Styptic Powder, oval,
litho, Walgreen, Chicago, IL,
sample, $2\frac{1}{4}$″ h. **30.00**
Penetro, cold relief, round, flat, li-
tho, sample, $1\frac{5}{8}$″ d, $\frac{3}{8}$″ h **12.00**
Pickaninny Brand Salted Peanuts,
10 lbs, black girl illus, F M Hoyt &
Co, Amesbury, MA, 9″ d, $8\frac{1}{2}$″ h   **275.00**
Princine Baking Powder, handle,
used as drinking cup when empty,
pat Nov 23, 1915. . . . .   **75.00**
Red Bell Coffee, round, $5\frac{1}{4}$″ d, 4″ h   **20.00**
Robinson Crusoe Salted Peanuts,
round, $8\frac{1}{4}$″ d, $9\frac{1}{2}$″ h. **180.00**
R&R Carbolized Mutton Tallow,
flat, rect, litho, Cincinnati, OH, $\frac{7}{8}$
x 3 x $1\frac{3}{4}$″. **15.00**
Runkel's Essence of Chocolate,
square, paper label, 9 x 16″ h . . .   **90.00**
S C Smith Co Coffee, round, paper
label, Cleveland, OH, $4\frac{1}{4}$″ d, $5\frac{1}{2}$″ h   **10.00**
Shinola Shoe Polish, round, flat, li-
tho, sample, 2″ d, 1″ h **18.00**
Snowdrift Coconut, red, white, and
black paper label, wire handles,
$12\frac{1}{4}$″ d, $13\frac{3}{4}$″ h **45.00**
Squirrel Brand Fancy Salted Nuts,
round, Cambridge, MA, $6\frac{3}{4}$″ d,
$8\frac{1}{4}$″ h.   **75.00**
Star Safety Razor, blade case, flat,
rect, litho, $\frac{3}{8}$ x $2\frac{1}{4}$ x $1\frac{1}{4}$″ **15.00**
Sunray Ointment, flat, round, litho,
$1\frac{1}{2}$″ d, $\frac{1}{2}$″ h **15.00**
Tak–A–Lax, chocolate laxative,
flat, rect, litho, $\frac{1}{2}$ x $3\frac{3}{4}$ x $2\frac{3}{8}$″. **20.00**
Three Crow Cream Tartar, rect, $3\frac{1}{4}$ x
$2\frac{1}{4}$ x $4\frac{3}{4}$″ h. **20.00**
Toddy Chocolate and Malt Flavored
Food Drink, round, $3\frac{1}{4}$″ d, $3\frac{1}{4}$″ h   **50.00**
Towle's Log Cabin Syrup, 2 lbs, 1
oz, cabin shape, litho, Express Of-
fice, $4\frac{1}{2}$ x $2\frac{3}{4}$ x $4\frac{1}{2}$″ **125.00**
Tuxedo Tobacco, pocket size **12.00**
Uncle Sam Shoe Polish, round, flat,
litho, Uncle Sam illus, $2\frac{1}{4}$″ d, 1″ h   **25.00**
Victory–V Lozenges, children sled-
ding, $4\frac{1}{2}$ x 1 x 3″ **50.00**
Wabash Black Pepper, round, card-
board cylinder, lion illus, 3″ d,
5″ h **15.00**
Watkins Cocoa, paper label, square,
$3\frac{1}{2}$ x $5\frac{3}{4}$″ h. **25.00**

Wilbur's Breakfast Cocoa, paper label, $2\frac{1}{4}$ x $3\frac{1}{4}$" **150.00**

Winchester After Shave Talc, oval, litho, hunter and dog illus, $4\frac{3}{4}$" h   **50.00**

Witch Hazel Tooth Soap, flat, rect, litho, Robinson & Halstead, Cincinnati, OH, $\frac{5}{8}$ x $3\frac{1}{4}$ x $2\frac{1}{8}$" **25.00**

Zanol Baby Mine, talcum powder, pyramid shape, litho, baby with toys illus, $5\frac{3}{8}$" h. **60.00**

FOLK ART

History: Although there was a folk art consciousness among a few collectors and museum professionals prior to the 1960s, it was largely ignored by most collectors and dealers. All that changed in the late 1960s and early 1970s as museum exhibits and other events leading up to the celebration of the American Bicentennial seized upon folk art as the popular art of the American people.

The definition of what constitutes folk art is still being vigorously debated among collectors, dealers, museum curators, and scholars. Some want to confine folk art to non–academic, handmade objects. Others are willing to include manufactured material. In truth, the term is used to cover objects ranging from crude drawings by obviously untalented children to academically trained artists' paintings of "common" people and scenery.

Since this book wishes to avoid this brouhaha altogether, it has adopted the widest definition possible. If one or more groups within the field have designated a category or item as part of the folk art movement, it is listed. Since the Country community tends to emphasize the primitive, naive, and painted over the more formal, these pieces are more heavily weighted in the listings.

A major development in the folk art renaissance of the 1970s was the revival of the folk art craftsperson. Across the United States individuals and manufacturers began to copy pieces from the past, often using the same tools and techniques to produce them as was done originally. You will find more craftspersons and manufacturers listed in this section of the book than any other.

Collect pieces from individuals and manufacturers who are introducing new design and form in the vocabulary of their chosen category, rather than from those who merely copy the past. These pieces have potential long term value. While exact copies have immediate and decorative value, they will be the least sought examples in the future.

Because so many objects are being copied exactly, collectors and dealers have been fooled by them. This resulted in a slowing down of the folk art market in the late 1980s. Reproductions, copycats, and fantasy folk art pieces continue to grow in number. Until all these forms are documented with detailed information as to how to distinguish them from the originals, the folk art market will remain a perilous place.

In addition to being plagued with the problem of confusing contemporary copies, the folk art market is subject to hype and manipulation. Weathervanes, cigar store figures, and quilts are just a few of the categories that were actively hyped and manipulated in the 1970s and 1980s. Neophyte collectors are encouraged to read Edie Clark's "What Really Is Folk Art?" in the December 1986 *Yankee*. Clark's article provides a refreshingly honest look at the folk art market.

Finally, the folk art market is extremely trendy and fickle. What is hot today can become cool and passé tomorrow. Late nineteenth century quilts are cool, twentieth century quilts such as the Double Wedding Ring are hot. Whirligigs are cool, painted firemen's hats are hot.

Finally, in the 1980s, the American market began to look seriously at European material that closely resembled American folk art forms. Much was brought into the United States and sold. By the second and third transaction, many European pieces wound up with an

American attribution. Today's folk art collector needs a thorough background in both American and European folk art to collect effectively.

All in all, collecting folk art is not for the weak–of–heart or the cautious investor.

Note: After reviewing the above, the Wallace–Homestead/Warman manuscript editors insisted that "since Harry is an authority of note, he should be able to give us a definition of folk art." Since my views are widely known within the field, but have never been put into print, I have decided to take the bull by the horns and do so. The views expressed below are mine and mine alone. My personal choice would have been to remain silent, but they asked for it.

The problem with folk art is that two of the letters used to spell the word are wrong and should be replaced with two other letters. The reason is simple. Most of the individuals who buy a piece because it is folk art or pay a premium because it is folk art are being "folked." You get the drift. I think folk art is one of the biggest frauds ever perpetrated on the collecting public.

I have no problems with the objects themselves or their naivete. My collection contains many such examples. I value them for themselves, not for some artifically hyped connotation assigned to them. I wish the rest of the collecting community could as well.

References: Kenneth L. Ames, *Beyond Necessity: Art In The Folk Tradition*, W. W. Norton, 1977; Robert Bishop and Judith Rieter Weissman, *Folk Art: The Knopf Collectors' Guides To American Antiques*, Alfred A. Knopf, 1983; Jean Lipman and Alice Winchester, *The Flowering of American Folk Art 1776–1876*, Penguin Books, 1977; Henry Niemann and Helaine Fendelman, *The Official Identification and Price Guide To American Folk Art*, House of Collectibles, 1988.

Museums: Museum of American Folk Art, New York, NY; Abby Aldrich Rockefeller Folk Art Center, Williamsburg, VA.

Reproduction Manufacturers: The Calico Corner, 513 E Bowman St, South Bend, IN 46613; Conewago Junction, 805 Oxford Rd, New Oxford, PA 17350; Country Bouquet, P O Box 200, Kellogg, MN 55945; Country Loft, 1506 South Shore Park, Hingham, MA 02043; Country Wicker, 2238–D Bluemound Rd, Waukesha, WI 53186; Folk Art Emporium, 3591 Forest Haven Lane, Chesapeake, VA 23321; Good Things, P O Box 2452, Chino, CA 91708; Gray's Attic, Box 532, Manson, IA 50563; Honk 'N Quax, Ltd, P O Box 15155, 1500 Main St, Springfield, MA 01115; Mulberry Magic, P O Box 62, Ruckersville, VA 22968; The Painted Pony, 8392 West M–72, Traverse City, MI 49684; Southern Manner, Inc, 106 N Trade St, Matthews, NC 28106; Traditions, RD #4, Box 191, Hudson, NY 12534; The Vine and Cupboard, P O Box 309, George Wright Rd, Woolwich, ME 04579; Woodbee's, RR #1, Poseyville, IN 47633; Woodpenny's, 27 Hammatt St, Epswich, MA 01938.

CARVINGS

History: Carving and whittling were common pastimes in rural America. In many cases, the end product was a whimsical item or simply a pile of shavings. Skills varied tremendously.

Figures, especially those used for store displays and ship's mastheads, were professionally done. Better local carvers developed a regional reputation. Few carvers trained a successor. Nonetheless, earlier works are known to have influenced later generations, e.g., Schimmel's influence on Mountz.

Much of the "folk" carving in modern collections dates from the last half of the nineteenth through the first half of the twentieth centuries. Age is not as critical a factor in this sector as in other "folk art" categories. Identification of the carver is critical to value. Since many of the pieces are unsigned, identification is done primarily by attribution. Many attributions are loosely made and should be questioned.

Modern folklorists, such as Bishop and Hemphill, have been instrumental in the identification and promotion of contemporary carvers. Recent auction results have proven that much of the value attributed to these pieces is speculative.

References: Robert Bishop, *American Folk Sculpture*, E. P. Dutton, 1974; Jack T. Ericson, *Folk Art in America: Painting and Sculpture*, Mayflower Books, 1979; Herbert W. Hemphill, *Folk Sculpture U.S.A.*, Universe Books, 1976; Jean Lipman, *American Folk Art in Wood, Metal, and Stone*, Dover Publications, 1972; Richard and Rosemarie Machmer, *Just For Nice: Carving and Whittling Magic of Southeastern Pennsylvania*, Historical Society of Berks County (PA), 1991; John J. Stoudt, *Early Pennsylvania Arts and Crafts*, A. S. Barnes and Co., 1964.

Reproduction Craftspersons: John Jeffrey Barto, P O Box 127, Kintnersville, PA 18930; Jonathan K. Bastian, Pennsylvania German Woodcarvings, Rte 2, Box 240, Robesonia, PA 19551; Ed Boggis, Woodcarver, Old Church Rd, Box 387, Claremont, NH 03743; Connie Carlton, Shaving Horse Crafts, 1049 Rice Rd, Lawrenceburg, KY 40342; William J. Cooey, 248 Van Horn Rd, Milton, FL 32570; Sande & Steven Elkins, S. Elkins Folk Art, RR 1, Box 147A, Loudon, TN 37774; Jonathan Graves, 13708 Kenwanda Dr, Snohomish, WA 98290; Christopher Gurshin, Itinerant Painter, P O Box 616, Newburyport, MA 01950; Bill Henry, 111 N Tampa Ln, Oak Ridge, TN 37830; Sherman Hensal, The Lion & The Lamb, Box 278, Sharon Center, OH 44274; Jay V. Irwin, Wood Carver, RR 2, Box 354, Auburn Rd, Avondale, PA 19311; Paul W. Jeffries, 1158 Putnam Blvd, Wallingford, PA 19086; Alan Kohr, 144 Krause Rd, RD 2, Schwenksville, PA 19473; Christopher LaMontagne, 900 Joslin Rd, Harrisville, RI 02830; Eleanor Meadowcroft, 25 Flint St, Salem, MA 01970; Don Mounter, Rte 1, Box 54, Fayette, MO 65248; John T. Nicholas & Son, 704 N Michigan Ave, Howell, MI 48843; Donna H. Pierce, 522 Meadowpark La, Media, PA 19063; Bush Prisby, Prisby's Country, 388 Ingomar St, Pittsburgh, PA 15216; Les Ramsay, Linden Tree Gallery, 137 S Broad St, Grove City, PA 16127; Vaughn & Stephanie Rawson, The Whimsical Whittler, 1745 W Columbia Rd, Mason, MI 48854; Philip A. Sbraccia, 174 Emerald St, Maiden, MA 02148; S. Arthur Shoemaker, 2025 Plymouth Rd, Lancaster, PA 17603; Daniel G. Strawser, 2741 Buckner Rd, Thompson Station, TN 37179; Randy & Pam Tate, Knot in Vane, 805 N 11th St, DeKalb, IL 60115; Roberta Taylor, 1717 Maywood Dr, West Lafayette, IN 47906; Criss Zimmerman, RD 4, Box 2268, Lebanon, PA 17042.

Reproduction Manufacturers: Country Corner Collectibles, P O Box 422, Pitman, NJ 08071; Country House, 5939 Trails End, Three Oaks, MI 49128; Faith Mountain Country Fare, Main St, Box 199, Sperryville, VA 22740; Flying Pig Artworks, P O Box 474, Milford, MI 48042; Lace Wood 'N Tyme, 6496 Summerton, Shepherd, MI 48883; Lamb and Lanterns, 902 N Walnut St, Dover, OH 44622; Maggie MacKenzie's, P O Box 148, Beloit, KS 67420; The Magic Cottage, Inc, P O Box 438, East Meadow, NY 11554; Meadow Craft, P O Box 100, Rose Hill, NC 28458; On the Countryside, P O Box 722, Forsyth, MO 65653; Our Home, Articles of Wood, 666 Perry St, Vermilion, OH 44089; Ozark Cottage Crafts, P O Box 157, Galena, MO 65656; Pesta's Country Charm, 300 Standard Ave, Mingo Junction, OH 43938; Plantation Characters, Box 896, Painesville, OH 44077; A Special Blend of Country, RD #1, Box 56, Fabius, NY 13063; Wesson Trading Co, P O Box 669984, Marietta, GA 30066.

Reproduction Alert: Fakes, pieces deliberately meant to deceive, abound. In the early 1970s, I (Harry L. Rinker) visited a York County carver who was aging a garage full of Schimmel copies. I believe several of these have entered the market in the intervening years as Schimmel originals.

The August, 1991, issue of *Maine Antique Digest* contained David Hewitt's "Jacob Joyner: Mississippi Wood Carver or The Man Who Never Was?" An entire school of carvings, sold by some of America's most prominent folk art dealers and purchased by some of America's leading collectors, turned out to be forgeries. There are many who question whether the Joyner incident is an isolated example.

Canes
 Black Bird Handle, green, yellow, and black painted snake entwining tapering shaft, relief carved block letter initials "M.G.," 42½" l, late 19th/early 20th C **1,210.00**
 Duck's Head Handle, chased silver band at neck, relief carved canoe-shaped leaves on shaft, 37" l, late 19th C **775.00**
 Goat's Hoof Handle, relief carved scaly snake entwining shaft with incised heart and initials "A.B.," wrought iron spike, 38¼" l, late 19th C **1,550.00**
 Kitten Handle, inset eyes, smiling face, tapering bark covered shaft, 34¼" l, late 19th C **350.00**
 Man's Head Handle, looped handle, relief carved, tapering shaft, 37" l, late 19th C **275.00**
 Puzzle Cane
 Ball Handle, openwork cage contains second ball, relief carved snake entwining tapering shaft, incised leaf carving on base, 37" l, dated 1861 . . . . **325.00**
 Hunting Gun shape, butt handle, openwork carved flat shaft contains two balls, incised hunting dog, 33½" l, late 19th C **275.00**
 T-shaped Handle, tapering slat-sided shaft, puzzle slides, 35" l, late 19th C **500.00**

Snake, flat headed, incised and chip carved scales, red glass eyes, 33½″ l, late 19th C **495.00**

Stars and Stripes motif, cut and peeled bark technique, incised stars, stripes, herringbones, and diamonds, 37″ l, late 19th C **450.00**

Figures

Acrobat on Horse, whittled, blue acrobat, adjustable arms and leg, hinge and tack joints, standing on white horse, brown leather ears, blue wedge–shaped base, 10¼″ h, 8½″ l, c1880 . . . . **385.00**

Bald Eagle, raised brown incised wings, open beak, white head and tail, glass eyes, wrought strap feet, half–log base, 35″ h, 41″ l, 19th C **18,700.00**

Bluejay, relief carving, burl base, 8¼″ h, 11¼″ l, early 1900s **450.00**

Camel, standing, full bodied, leather bridle, 35″ h, 40″ l, 19th C **5,775.00**

Dandy, relief carved facial features, mustache, black top hat, bow tie, and swallowtail coat, white vest, one arm extended, white octagonal base, 29¼″ h, late 19th C **5,775.00**

Delaware Justice, two prisoners in stockade on upper platform above two hangmen and manacled black man on base, raised ladder, inscribed "Delaware Justice," 16½″ h, late 19th C **8,250.00**

Dog, seated, spotted, black and white, up–turned ears, incised orange eye ring, 7″ h, late 19th, early 20th C **225.00**

Four Soldiers, carrying black rifles, marching in formation, mounted

Eagle, carved and gilded wood, painted shield, 36″ w wing span, $3,500.00.

in pine base, 9¾″ h, 16½″ l, early 20th C **1,320.00**

Goddess of Liberty, three–quarter length, half–round, dark hair, holding sword and American flag, incised star and floral diapering on red, white, and blue costume, 29″ h, 14″ w, late 19th C **71,500.00**

Horse, dark brown, dowelled ears, white socks on rear legs, horsehair tail, 7¼″ h, 8¾″ l, c1880 . . . . **385.00**

Jonah and the Whale, black whale, moveable jaw, bearded Jonah in whale's mouth, 9″ h, 20th C **1,550.00**

Lion, Herman, standing, brush whiskers, fur mane, black felt ears, twine tail, underside inscribed "Herman was born October 26, 1901, Glen Rock, J.W. Brungart, Born Nov. 14, 1877," 10″ h, 11″ l, 1901 . . . . **875.00**

Man on Horseback, frog–bodied man wearing white cap, pearlized eyes, black and white horse, oblong white base inscribed "Made by Fred for Minnie, God Bless Him, I Miss Him So, I Love Him," 8″ h, 7¼″ l, 20th C **875.00**

Parrot, speckled white, orange, and black, cross–hatched, heart shaped wings, 5½″ h, late 19th/early 20th C **135.00**

Peacock, crested comb, turned head, blue outlined yellow body, yellow spotted tail, stick legs, relief carved feet, wood base, 5¼″ h, c1880 . . . . **275.00**

Pig, standing, cottonwood and gesso, black and white, fierce expression, bared teeth, glass marble eyes, rope tail, 17″ h, 29¼″ l, Felipe Archuleta, modern **9,350.00**

Poodle, standing, carrying swing handle basket, cross–hatched, Aaron Mountz, Cumberland Valley, PA, 4¼″ h, 5″ l, late 19th C . . **450.00**

Rabbit, hunched, black and white, red eyes, 4½″ h, 4½″ l, late 19th C **150.00**

Rooster, white, black markings, red

Architectural Element, bracket, carved face, triangular base, 12¼″ h, 7¼″ w, 8″ d, $75.00.

comb and wattle, yellow legs, green mound base, Wilhelm Schimmel, Carlisle, PA, 11" h, 9¾" w, c1875 . . . . **8,875.00**

Song Bird, relief carving, tooling, glass eyes, black, red, and orange, 5" h **200.00**

Squirrel, holding pinecone, orig polychrome paint, 5¾" h **225.00**

Steer's Head, brown, light brown stripe, white markings, leather ears, real steer horns, 21" h, 15" w, 19th C **875.00**

Strawberry/Heart, red, half round, cut sheet metal tuft, late 19th/ early 20th C **600.00**

Sulky and Driver, seated man wearing green and yellow, brown horse, leather bridle, fabric harness, plank pine base, 6½" h, 11" l, early 20th C **450.00**

Uncle Sam

On Horseback, 19" h, 16" l, painted, red, white, and blue Uncle Sam, black and white horse, brown saddle, leather tack, horsehair mane and tail, late 19th/early 20th C **4,400.00**

Standing, white top hat, white stars on blue swallowtail coat, flying tails, pink vest, striped pants, black shoes, gray stirrups, holding fabric American flag, yellow pyramid base, 17¼" h, late 19th/early 20th C. . **12,100.00**

Woman, stylized, deeply incised parted hair, broad smile, wood base, 7¼" h, 19th C **165.00**

Pilot House Figure, Columbia, half round, relief carving, golden tresses, corkscrew curls, draped robes, left hand holding gold sphere, right hand holding elongated US shield, relief carved stars and stripes on shield, pendant spray of wheat sheaves at her side, 64" h, 22½" w, mid 19th C **24,200.00**

Pipe Bowl, Uncle Sam, bead eyes, deeply carved facial features, red, white, and blue top hat and collar, 3¼" h, late 19th C **325.00**

Walking Stick, fist shaped handle, Odd Fellows insignia, knobby stick, 35" l **85.00**

Whimsey

Goblet in Cage, gold paint, dark varnish, 5½" h **95.00**

Steeple and Birds, three tapering levels covered with perched birds, swallows, crows, peacock, owl, blackbird, Canada goose, pigeon, and woodpecker, black pedestal base, 13½" h, 1800–50 **3,575.00**

DECOYS

History: Carved wooden decoys, used to lure ducks and geese to the hunter, have become widely recognized as an indigenous American folk art form in the past several years.

Many decoys are from the 1880–1930 period when commercial gunners commonly hunted using rigs of several hundred decoys. Many fine carvers also worked through the 1930s and 1940s.

The value of a decoy is based on several factors: (1) fame of the carver, (2) quality of the carving, (3) species of wild fowl (the most desirable are herons, swans, mergansers, and shorebirds), and (4) condition of the original paint.

The inexperienced collector should be aware of several facts. The age of a decoy, per se, is usually of no importance in determining value. Since very few decoys were ever signed, it will be quite difficult to attribute most decoys to known carvers. Anyone who has not examined a known carver's work will be hard pressed to determine if the paint on one of his decoys is indeed original. Repainting severely decreases a decoy's value. In addition, there are many fakes and reproductions on the market and even experienced collectors are occasionally fooled.

Decoys listed are of average wear unless otherwise noted.

References: Joel Barber, Wild Fowl Decoys, Dover Publications, 1954; Joe Engers (general editor), *The Great Book of Wildfowl Decoys*, Thunder Bay Press, 1990; Henry A. Fleckenstein, Jr., *American Factory Decoys*, Schiffer Publishing, Ltd.; Ronald J. Fritz, *Michigan's Master Carver Oscar W. Peterson, 1887–1951*, Aardvark Publications, 1988; Gene and Linda Kangas, *Decoys*, Collector Books, 1991; —, *Decoys: A North American Survey*, Hillcrest Publications, 1983; Art, Brad and Scott Kimball, *The Fish Decoy*, Aardvark Publications, Inc., 1986; Carl F. Luckey, *Collecting Antique Bird Decoys: An Identification & Value Guide*, Books Americana, 1983; William Mackey, Jr., *American Bird Decoys*, E. P. Dutton, 1965.

Periodicals: *Decoy Hunter Magazine*, 901 North 9th, Clinton, IN 47842; *Decoy Magazine*, P O Box 1900, Montego Bay Station, Ocean City, MD 21842; *The Wild Fowl Art Journal*, Ward Foundation, 655 South Salisbury Blvd, Salisbury, MD 21801.

Reproduction Manufacturers: Briere Design, 229 N Race St, Statesville, NC 28677; Lamplighter Antiques, 615 Silver Bluff Rd, Aiken, SC 29801; McClanahan Country, 217 Rockwell Rd, Wilmington, NC 28405; Tidewater Shorebirds, 2818 Lancelot Dr, Baton Rouge, LA 70816; Unfinished Business, P O Box 246, Wingate, NC 28174.

Black Duck
    Frank Schmidt, orig paint, wing carving, feather stamping, 1879–1960 . . . .   350.00
    C Ralph Wells, CT, hollow carved, orig paint 450.00
Black–Breasted Plover, Harry V Shourds, orig paint, replaced bill . .   250.00
Bluebill Drake
    Mason Factory, MI, standard grade, glass eyes, orig paint, split bottom   225.00
    Unknown Maker, Saginaw Bay area, old repaint, glass eyes, 13¼" l 40.00
Bluebill Hen
    Mason Decoy Factory, orig paint, glass eyes, 1894–1924 . . . .   275.00
    Irving Miller, MI, glass eyes, orig paint, 11½" l 150.00
Blue Wing Teal Hen, George Robert, NY, cork, bottom branded "Manning" 200.00
Brant, Miles Hancock, VA, orig paint   500.00
Bufflehead, mated pair, Paul Gibson, bottom sgd and dated 400.00
Bufflehead Drake, unknown maker, hollow, lowhead, orig paint, c1900   700.00
Canada Goose
    Madison Mitchell, Ward style head, orig paint 350.00
    Unknown Maker, Long Island area, sleeper, primitive, weathered paint, glass eyes, 20½" l 350.00
    Ward Brothers, MD, carved raised wing tips and back feathers, head turned to right 1,700.00
Canvasback Drake, Miles Hancock, orig paint 400.00
Canvasback Hen, Budgeon Sampier, Pearl Beach, MI, hollow, repaint, c1900 . . . .   200.00
Coot, unknown maker, orig paint, damaged neck joint 100.00
Curlew, unknown maker, VA, old paint, replaced bill 900.00
Eider Hen, Pete Mitchell, ME, carved, preening position, deep inlet neck 1,900.00
Goldeneye Drake, Mason Factory, MI, standard grade, tack eyes, repainted   70.00

Goldeneye Hen, glass eyes, old paint, 13" l 105.00
Golden Plover, unknown maker, carved wings, orig paint 500.00
Green–Wing Teal Drake, Mark McNair, hollow carved, bottom sgd. . .   525.00
Mallard, mated pair
    Tube Dawson, IL, hollow carved, orig paint 600.00
    Dodge Factory, MI, carved body, orig paint, restored necks 1,100.00
Mallard Drake, Hector Whittington, hollow body, turned head, glass eyes, old repaint, 16¾" l 175.00
Merganser Drake, Alec Coffin, Phippsburg, ME, orig paint, wood crest, 1920s 450.00
Merganser Hen, Doug Jester, VA, carved, unused 1,750.00
Pintail Drake, William Shaw, IL, hollow carved, repainted 200.00
Pintail Hen, Don Zeng, Chicago, carved, orig paint, glass eyes, 13½" l   375.00
Red–Breasted Merganser Drake, Samuel Squires, carved crest, orig paint, bottom branded 5,000.00
Redhead Drake, Lake St Clair, hollow, lowhead, orig paint, c1900 . . . . . .   550.00
Sandpiper, unknown maker, MA, sealing wax eyes, orig paint, replaced bill 700.00
Shorebird
    5½" h, large beak, orig paint, modern base 35.00
    6½" h, root head, whittled, shot scars, old dark finish. 150.00
    10⅞" h, primitive, cut–out silhouette, old black and white paint . .   30.00
    11" h, root head, old black and white paint, black sponged breast, shot scars 350.00

Shorebird, Blue Bellied Plover, Cape May, NJ, $350.00.

Merganser, hen and drake, Henderson Harbor, upstate NY, early 1900's, orig paint, pr, $725.00.

Snipe, unknown maker, New Gretna, NJ, metal stand, wood base, c1860 .... **875.00**

Squaw, J E Hendrickson, hollow carved, orig paint. **200.00**

Surf Scoter, Gus Wilson, ME, carved wing tips, old repaint **175.00**

Swan, unknown maker, painted, metal tack eyes, 10½" h, late 19th/early 20th C **375.00**

Widgeon Drake, Miles Pirnie, MI, orig paint **275.00**

Yellowlegs, William Mathews, VA, carved wing tips and eyes, old paint **1,500.00**

FRAKTUR

History: Fraktur, the calligraphy associated with the Pennsylvania Germans, is named for the elaborate first letter found in many of the hand-drawn examples. Throughout its history, printed, partially printed hand-drawn, and fully hand-drawn works existed side by side. Frakturs often were made by the school teachers or ministers living in rural areas of Pennsylvania, Maryland, and Virginia. Many artists are unknown.

Fraktur exists in several forms: geburts and taufschein (birth and baptismal certificates), vorschrift (writing example, often with alphabet), haus sagen (house blessing), bookplates, bookmarks, rewards of merit, illuminated religious text, valentines, and drawings. Although collected for decoration, the key element in fraktur is the text.

Fraktur prices rise and fall along with the American folk art market. The key marketplaces are Pennsylvania, the Middle Atlantic states, and Ontario, Canada.

References: Michael S. Bird, *Ontario Fraktur: A Pennsylvania–German Folk Tradition in Early Canada*, M. F. Feheley Publishers, 1977; Donald A. Shelley, *The Fraktur–Writings of Illuminated Manuscripts of the Pennsylvania Germans*, Pennsylvania German Society, 1961; Frederick S. Weiser and Howell J. Heaney (compilers), *The Pennsylvania German Fraktur of the Free Library of Philadelphia*, two volume set, Pennsylvania German Society, 1976.

Museum: The Free Library of Philadelphia, Philadelphia, PA.

Reproduction Craftspersons: Sally Greene Bunce, 4826 Mays Ave, Reading, PA 19606; Jacquelyn Trone Butera, Colonial Yard, 500 S Park Ave, Audubon, PA 19403; Ceil Cox & Kathy Hendrix, Primitives 'n' Paper, 4932 Baylor Dr, Charlotte, NC 28210; Sandra K Gilpin, 509 Baer Ave., Hanover, PA 17331; Mary Lou Harris, Aunt Sukey's Choice, 514 E Main St, Annville, PA 17003; Ruthanne Kramer Hartung, 1138 Greenwich St, Reading, PA 19604; Tom Kelly, 3 Liberty St, Mineral Point, WI 53565; Michael S Kriebel, 1756 Breneman Rd., Manheim, PA 17545; K Kerchner McConlogue, Snibbles, 701 Hunting Pl, Baltimore, MD 21229; Cheryl Ann Nash, 100 Summer St, Kennebunk, ME 04043; Sharon Schaich, 411 Woodcrest Ave, Lititz, PA 17543.

Reproduction Manufacturers: Harwell Graphics, P O Box 8, Napoleon, IN 47034; Pine Cone Primitives, P O Box 682, Troutman, NC 28166.

Adams, Rhode, 1808, vorschrift, pen and ink and watercolor on laid paper, "World interest speaks all sort languages, and acts all sorts morels, Rhode Adams, Aged 13 years, Holiston, 1808," simple floral dec, red, green, and black, 9½" h, 7¾" w. **135.00**

Baker, Aruba, 1831, book plate, "Miss Roxy Hyde, when this you see remember me, Aruba Baker, April 25, 1831," pen and ink and watercolor on woven paper, floral designs and circle, black, brown, and blue, 6⅝" h, 9¼" w. **1,150.00**

Brechall, Martin, birth certificate
1800, birth of Salome Herby, Northampton County, pen and ink and watercolor on laid paper, red, yellow, black, and bluish black, 16¼" h, 11½" w, black and red grained beveled frame **1,400.00**

1816, Schuylkill County, printed format, hand drawn pen and ink and watercolor floral dec, 11" h, 14" w, mahogany veneer frame **250.00**

Dankel, Susanna, Lancaster County, 1843, book plate, pen and ink and watercolor on laid paper, two facing pgs, birds, flowering vines, red, blue, green, and yellow, 8¾" h, 7¾" w, beveled frame **400.00**

Heydrick, Baltzer, 1837, book plate, "Hanna Heydrick 1837," pen and ink and watercolor on woven paper, red, blue, green, yellow, and black, 6⅝" h, 3¾" w. **700.00**

Krebs, Frederick, Berks County, birth certificate, "Geburts und Taufschein," printed format, hand drawn dec, pen and ink and watercolor on laid paper, two parrots and floral dec, green, red, yellow, brown, and black, records 1806 birth of Jacob Roth, 15¾" h, 19¼" w, molded frame **1,350.00**

Lappin, Susanna, 1798, book plate, pen and ink and watercolor on laid paper, bird and flowers, red, blue, green, and yellow, 8⅛" h, 5¾" w, mahogany veneer beveled frame. **500.00**

Daniel Peterman, Manheim Township, York County, PA, wove paper, watermark "P. H. & S.," multicolored decoration including women, birds, distelfinks, and floral motifs, 15¾" h, 12½" w, $1,750.00.

Leith, Maria, 1833, book plate, pen and ink and watercolor on woven paper, bird and flowers, black and red, 7" h, 4½" w 550.00

Meyer, Samuel, 1834, book plate, pen and ink and watercolor on laid paper, bird on branch, English inscription, red, yellow, green, blue, and black, 9⅜" h, 6¾" w, old frame 195.00

Moffly, Samuel, Berks County, 1805, birth certificate, pen and ink and watercolor on laid paper, hearts, large parrots, tulips, suns, crown, and stylized flowers, red, blue, green, yellow, and black, records 1789 birth of Samuel Moffly, 16⅜" h, 20½" w 1,800.00

Schmidt, Johanes, Baterland, 1806, drawing, pen and ink and watercolor on laid paper, pair of birds, red, orange, green, and black, 7" h, 9" w, framed 500.00

Sharp, Daniel, 1845, book plate, pen and ink and watercolor on woven paper, red and black, 8" h, 5⅞" w, old molded frame 75.00

Unknown Artist
  Birth Certificate
    1809, Centre County, pen and ink and watercolor on laid paper, record of birth in heart, surrounded by tulips and other flowers, orange, green, yellow, and black, 10½" h, 12½" w, grained beveled frame 1,150.00
    1815, Northumberland County, pen and ink and watercolor on laid paper, four birds, stylized flowers, red, green, yellow, blue, and black, records birth of

Ruben Poffen Miller, 15½" h, 18¾" w 2,100.00
    1850, Berks County, "Gebhurts und Taufschein," printed, hand colored, 18¾" h, 16" w, framed   25.00
  Book Plate
    1785, pen and ink and watercolor on laid paper, simple inscription, tulip, red, green, yellow, and black, 7⅜" h, 5¼" w, old frame 250.00
    1843, pen and ink on woven paper, 8⅜" h, 6¼" w, old frame . . .   150.00
  Drawing, watercolor on lined paper, two birds and tulip tree, red, blue, green, and yellow, 6" h, 8¼" w, framed 850.00
  Vorschrift, pen and ink and watercolor on laid paper, red, black, blue, and yellow, 10¾" h, 9¼" w, framed 300.00

Ziegler, Marin, Lancaster County, 1840, book plate, pen and ink and watercolor on woven paper, red, blue, yellow, and black, 8½" h, 6" w, old molded frame 500.00

LAWN ORNAMENTS AND ACCESSORIES

History: It was common to find a cast iron bench under a large tree, often a willow, or ornamental statue as part of a farmyard setting. Farmers enjoyed relaxing in the outdoors as much as working. Ornamental pieces also were used in garden and entrance settings.

Most lawn ornaments were cast from metal or concrete. Often they were painted to provide protection from the elements. Finding an example with original paint is unusual. Hitching posts are a favorite form among collectors.

The 1980s witnessed a renewed collecting interest in lawn ornaments and accessories, due in part to the Victorian decorating craze. Prices rose dramatically. Often outside ornaments became part of inside decorating schemes.

Many individuals failed to realize that excellent reproductions and copycats of nineteenth century examples were made in the 1930s and 1940s by a number of firms, e.g., Virginia Metalcrafters. Ruth Webb Lee's "Ironworks" chapter in *Antique Fakes & Reproductions: Enlarged and Revised, Seventh Edition* (Lee Publications, 1950) is well worth reading.

References: Alan Robertson, *Architectural Antiques*, Chronicle Books, 1987; J. P. Whyte's Pyghtle Works (Bedford, England), *Garden Furniture*, Apollo Books, 1987.

Reproduction Craftspersons: Michael Dutcher, 415 W Market St, West Chester, PA 19380; Joseph Hutchison, Hearthstone House, 1600 Hilltop Rd, Xenia, OH 45385; Greg Leavitt, 476 Valleybrook Rd, Wawa, PA 19063.

Reproduction Manufacturers: Cabin Fever, 5770 S Meridian, Laingsburg, MI 48848; Cape Cod Cupola Co, Inc, 78 State Rd, Rte 6, North Dartmouth, MA 02747; Country Accents, RD #2, Box 293, Stockton, NJ 08559; The Country Stippler, Rte 2, Box 1540, Pine Mountain, GA 31822; Moultrie Mfg Co, P O Drawer 1179, Moultrie, GA 31776; S. Chris Rheinschild, 2220 Carlton Way, Santa Barbara, CA 93109; Town and Country, Main St, East Conway, NH 04037.

Note: This category also includes items from around the farm that are used as lawn decorating accessories in modern suburbia. Good sense and a respect for the sublime has caused us to fail to list and price old cast iron, porcelain-lined bathtubs, used by some in an upright position (the lower third buried in the earth) as a grotto for a religious statue.

Bench
    Cast Iron, foliage design, old white
       paint, 36" l **200.00**
    Cement ends, slotted, green painted
       wooden planks, 6' l **60.00**
Birdhouse, barn form, old red finish,
    20" h **250.00**
Entry Figure, cast iron, hound, recumbent, raised head, painted white,
    18" h, 38" l **2,500.00**
Farm Bell and Yoke, cast iron, painted
    black **60.00**
Fence, one section, iron, spear finials, leafy vine and grape cluster design,
    45 x 70" **85.00**
Garden Stake, wood cutout, painted
    Black Boy, fishing, 28" h, c1950. . .   **55.00**
    Black Girl, red dress, white apron,
       holding sprinkling can, 17½" h. . .   **60.00**
Hitching Post
    Black Jockey, cement and cast iron, red hat and vest, white shirt and
       pants, holding ring, 28" h **200.00**
    Horse Head, cast iron, steel post,
       68" h, pr **90.00**
Kettle, cast iron, hog scalding, handles, 27" d, iron tripod hanger **85.00**
Planter, wood, stave construction,
    metal hoops, 32" d **35.00**
Pump, cast iron, painted white. **50.00**
Statue, cast iron
    Dalmatian, full bodied, black and white repaint, old leather collar,
       steel plate base, 48½" l, 30" h. . . .   **4,500.00**
    Deer Family, weathered repaint, 60½" h stag, 45" h doe, 31¾" h
       fawn, 3 pcs **2,900.00**

Bench, cast iron, painted white, 34" h, 44" l, $350.00.

Urn, cast iron
    19" h, 16" d, goblet shaped, anchoring rod, old white repaint, pr   **180.00**
    28½" h, removable ear handles, old white repaint, 28½" h **290.00**
Wagon Wheel, wood, painted red . . .   **45.00**
Wheelbarrow, 29" l, miniature, orig dark red paint, black and yellow
    trim **275.00**

PAINTINGS

Note: Three major types of paintings play important roles in the agrarian community—portraits, town and homestead views, and landscapes. Each provides a valuable record of the past. Their highly personal nature was both a plus and minus. The personal and local nature of the paintings meant that they would be handed down from generation to generation. However, as tastes changed or individuals moved, the importance of many of these paintings diminished. As a result there are often more paintings found in a rural homestead's attic than hanging on the walls.

The individual portrait helped preserve the sense of family continuance. The portraitist survived in rural America until the end of the nineteenth century. The talents of the artists varied widely. However, a portrait by a less skilled artist was better than no portrait at all. Today, knowing the name of the subject, date of the painting, and identity of the artist are value pluses when examining any work. By 1900 the camera replaced the portrait artist. It is worth noting that many late nineteenth and early twentieth century photographs meant to hang on the wall duplicated the size and poses of early oil and watercolor portraits.

Rural America loved landscapes, evident by the large number of oils, watercolors, and prints that survive. Many are extremely large in size, meant to occupy the major portion of a wall in a rural parlor. Most were done by academically trained artists. Alas, the location, if painted from real life, has all too often been lost. Today the frame is often more valuable than the painting or watercolor that it contains.

Farm homestead and townscapes were done in small numbers. They are valued not only as works of art, but as historical documents. Many were done by amateurs and crudely drawn. A small number were done by semi-professional and professional artists. Some of these artists have reached legendary status, e.g., the Pennsylvania Alms House painters of the mid–nineteenth century.

Many members of the rural community could not afford original works of art. Instead they relied on mass-produced etchings and prints that copied the works of popular painters of the period to decorate their walls. This is one of the most overlooked areas of collecting. Many examples sell for less than one hundred dollars.

There is no way a listing of less than several hundred paintings can accurately represent the breadth and depth of the folk painting examples sold during the last few years. The listing merely serves as an introduction to the wealth of material that is viewed as folk painting.

The art community assigns a broad definition to folk painting. The itinerant limners of the colonial period are viewed as kin to Grandma Moses. In the 1970s and 1980s ethnicity was introduced as a key element in nineteenth and twentieth century examples.

In the final analysis, what constitutes a "folk" painting is a judgment call. Since attaching a "folk" attribution to a painting usually results in a significant increase in value, learn to question the motives of individuals making such an attribution.

References: The principal purpose of this section is to assist users in identifying and valuing their paintings. The section begins with general reference books on artist identification and folk paintings in particular. Price guide listings follow. Many specialized studies, such as Barbara and Lawrence Holdridge's *Ammi Phillips: Portrait of a Painter, 1788–1865* (Crown, 1969), exist. Check with the librarian at your local art museum for help in locating them.

Artist Dictionaries: Emmanuel Benezit, *Dictionnaire Critique et Documentaire des Peintres, Sculpteurs, Dessinateurs et Graveurs*, 10 volumes, third edition, Grund, 1976; Mantle Fielding, *Dictionary of American Painters, Sculptors and Engravers*, Apollo Books, 1983; J. Johnson and A. Greutzner, *Dictionary of British Artists, 1880–1940: An Antique Collector's Club Research Project Listing 41,000 Artists*, Antique Collector's Club, 1976; Les Krantz, *American Artists*, Facts on File, 1985.

Folk Painting References: Robert Bishop, *Folk Painters of America*, E. P. Dutton, 1981; Mary

Black and Jean Lipman, *American Folk Painting*, Clarkson N. Potter, 1966; C. Kurt Dewhurst, Betty MacDowell, and Marsha MacDowell, *Artists in Aprons: Folk Art by American Women*, E. P. Dutton, 1979; John and Katherine Ebert, *American Folk Painters*, Charles Scribner's Sons, 1975; Jack T. Ericson, *Folk Art in America: Painting and Sculpture*, Mayflower Books, 1979; Herbert W. Hemphill, Jr., and Julia Weissman, *Twentieth Century American Folk Art and Artists*, E. P. Dutton, 1974; Sidney Janis, *They Taught Themselves: American Primitive Painters of the 20th Century*, Dial Press, 1942; Jean Lipman and Tom Armstrong, *American Folk Painters of Three Centuries*, Hudson Hills Press, 1980; Beatrix T. Rumford, *American Folk Portraits: Paintings and Drawings from The Abby Aldrich Rockefeller Folk Art Center*, New York Graphic Society Books, 1981.

Price Guide References, Basic: *Art At Auction in America, 1991 edition*, Krexpress, 1990; William T. Currier (compiler), *Currier's Price Guide To American Artists 1645–1945 at Auction, 1989–1990 Edition*, Currier Publications, 1989; William T. Currier (compiler), *Currier's Price Guide To European Artists 1545–1945 at Auction, 1989–1990 Edition*, Currier Publications, 1989; *Huxford's Fine Art Value Guide, Volume III*, Collector Books, 1992; Susan Theran, *The Official Price Guide To Fine Art*, House of Collectibles, 1987.

Price Guide References, Advanced: Richard Hislop (editor), *The Annual Art Sales Index*, Weybridge, Surrey, England, Art Sales Index, Ltd., since 1969; Enrique Mayer, *International Auction Record: Engravings, Drawings, Watercolors, Paintings, Sculpture*, Paris, Editions Enrique Mayer, since 1967; Susan Theran (editor), *Leonard's Price Index of Art Auctions*, Auction Index, Inc., since 1980.

Museum Directories: *American Art Directory*, R. R. Bowker Co.; American Association of Museums, *The Official Museum Directory: United States and Canada*, updated periodically.

Reproduction Craftspersons: Arlene Strader Folk Art, 100 S Montgomery St, Union, OH 45322; Cate Mandigo Editions, P O Box 221, Hadley, NY 12835; Kacey Sydnor Carneal, Rte 3, Box 988, Gloucester, VA 23061; Elizabeth F. Gilkey, 3000 Coleridge Rd, Cleveland Heights, OH 44118; Betsy Hoyt, Butternut Hill Gallery, 3751 State St W, N. Canton, OH 44720; Warren L. Kimble, RR 3, Box 3038, Brandon, VT 05773; D. Masters Kriebel, 7560 Cerro Gordo Rd, Gainesville, VA 22065; Donna Lacey–Derstine, Richardson Hollow Artworks, RR 1, Box 500, West Paris, ME 04289; Jeanne Marston, 811 S Park Ave, Audubon, PA 19407; Carol Martell, Designs Unlimited, 13401 Chestnut Oak Dr, Gaithersburg, MD 20878; Eleanor Meadowcroft, 25

Flint St, Salem, MA 01970; Diane Ulmer Pedersen, 15 Avery Rd, Holden, MA 01520.

Reproduction Manufacturer: The Battered Brush, 228 Dogwood Ave., Quitman, MS 39355.

Reproduction Alert: Unless you are thoroughly familiar with the artist, you are advised to have any folk painting that you are considering buying authenticated by an independent source. In Samuel Pennington's "The Folk Art Forger," an article about Robert Trotter's forgeries in the March 1990 *Maine Antique Digest*, he states: "No amount of money or hard time in prison, however, is likely to heal the scars his schemes inflicted on an industry that often all too readily absorbed his artistic frauds." Trotter is not the only art forger around; he just happened to get caught.

- Bird on Branch, watercolor on woven paper, red, black, and blue, 9" h, $7\frac{1}{4}$" w . . . **225.00**
- Bucket of Strawberries, sgd L Keller, oil on canvas, $14\frac{1}{2}$ x 18", late 19th C . . **875.00**
- Church, pen and pencil and watercolor on laid paper, primitive, yellow church, green, orange, and red, "No. 6," $4\frac{3}{4}$" h, $5\frac{5}{8}$" w . . . **325.00**
- Clipper Ship with American Flag, oil on tin, initialed, $6\frac{3}{4}$ x $9\frac{3}{4}$" w . . . **95.00**
- Cottage, oil on canvas, 15" h, $24\frac{1}{2}$" w **300.00**
- Family Tree, Elting Family, Hudson, NY, watercolor and paper collage on paper, $15\frac{1}{2}$ x $13\frac{1}{2}$", c1820 . . . **2,750.00**
- Farm in Summer, Henry Mohrman, oil on canvas, $23\frac{1}{2}$ x 29", signed and dated 1877 . . . **2,750.00**
- Farm of the Groves, winter, Streeter Blair, oil on canvas, 25 x $29\frac{1}{2}$", 1957 **3,575.00**
- Farm Von Herrn Adolph, Sprecher Town, Troy, WI farm scene, Paul Seifert, watercolor on paper, gilt highlights, $22\frac{1}{2}$ x 28", c1880 . . . **24,200.00**
- Four Mast Sailing Ship, pen and ink and watercolor on paper, $5\frac{3}{4}$" h, $6\frac{7}{8}$" w . . . **125.00**
- Horse, brown and black, pink cinch belt, blue grass, watercolor on paper, sgd on verso "Henry Lapp 1873," 10" h, $12\frac{1}{2}$" w . . . **1,150.00**
- House and Barn, oil on canvas, sgd "R.J. Mulloy 1893," 18" h, 24" w **70.00**
- Pennsylvania Farm Scene, house and outbuilding, farmer, horse, ducks, oil on canvas, 24 x 33", early 20th C **2,225.00**
- Portrait
  - Boy, full length, black and white check dress, holding whip, watercolor on paper, 9" h, $6\frac{3}{4}$" w, molded frame . . . **800.00**
  - Child, full length, seated, oil, signed "Thorp 1879," 36" h, 29" w . . . **900.00**
  - Child, red dress, holding green hammer, watercolor and pencil on paper, attributed to Justus Dalee, $2\frac{5}{8}$ x $2\frac{1}{4}$", c1840 . . . **495.00**
  - Girl, full length, green dress, balloon sleeves, holding book, watercolor on paper, $9\frac{3}{4}$" h, $8\frac{1}{2}$" w . . **700.00**
  - Girl with chicken and basket, pencil and watercolor on paper, bright orange, yellow, ochre, and olive green, $9\frac{1}{4}$" h, $8\frac{3}{4}$" w . . . **150.00**
  - Young Child
    - Seated, wearing plaid costume with matching hat, holding pet dog's paw, oil on canvas, $33\frac{3}{8}$ x 27", c1840 . . . **4,620.00**
    - Standing, wearing orange and black dress, eating grapes, parrot and pet dog on floor, oil on canvas, $47\frac{3}{8}$ x $36\frac{3}{8}$", New York area, c1860 . . . **7,750.00**
  - Young Girl, seated outdoors, wearing pink embroidered white dress, holding straw hat, oil on canvas, $32\frac{1}{2}$ x 27", c1840 . . . **2,310.00**
- Red Building, white picket fences, horse and surrey in foreground, oil on wood panel, $19\frac{1}{4}$ x 25", 1870 . . . **3,850.00**
- Ship Laura Ann of Boston, two smaller ships in background, oil on board, 22 x 33", c1830 . . . **7,750.00**
- Still-life
  - Cake, fruits, and wine, oil on canvas, 22 x $26\frac{1}{2}$", last quarter 19th C **1,430.00**
  - Compote of Fruit, two flower arrangements, oil on canvas, 33 x 46", c1860 . . . **12,100.00**
- Sugar Run School, Pomeroy, Meigs County, OH, oil on canvas, 14 x 20", c1860 . . . **1,875.00**
- Summer and Winter, pair of paintings, same settings in opposite seasons, barn and church in background, children and horse-drawn vehicles in foreground, oil on canvas, 14 x $17\frac{1}{2}$", inscribed and dated "Uncle Caleb, Darien, Conn, 1901 and 1902" . . . **995.00**
- Tree, flowering, two birds, watercolor on paper, blue, blue-green, yellow, and orange, stylized, 7" h, $8\frac{1}{2}$" w . . . **250.00**
- Two Girls in Landscape, birds and butterfly, watercolor and pencil on paper, Joseph H Davis, $7\frac{3}{4}$ x $10\frac{1}{8}$", c1835 . . . **16,500.00**
- Unlucky Girls, three young girls around wooden cage, escaped bird in background, watercolor, pen and ink, gouache and pin-pricking on paper, 8 x $9\frac{3}{4}$", c1820 . . . **2,200.00**
- Village, oil on academy board, 18" h, $24\frac{3}{4}$" w . . . **950.00**

View of Perkiomen Mill, Bucks County, PA, oil on canvas, Walter E. Baum, $19,250.00.

Wash Day, David Ellinger, house, tree, wash drying on line, oil on canvas, sgd, verso inscribed "Wash Day," 26 x 36", c1940 . . . . **2,640.00**

Watermelon, watercolor, cut–out paper mounted on paper, $21\frac{1}{4}$ x 28", ME, late 19th C **935.00**

Young Girl, wearing blue dress, holding rose garland, standing with white lamb, watercolor, gouache, and gold foil on paper, $11\frac{3}{4}$ x 15", Connecticut, c1820 . . . . **4,500.00**

SCHERENSCHNITTE

History: Scherenschnitte, translated as scissor–cut, is the art of decorative paper cutting. It was brought to America by German–speaking immigrants.

Scherenschnitte is found in two basic forms—complete picture and supplemental decoration. While a silhouette is technically a scissor-cutting, the term is generally reserved for full-size pictures of landscape and forest scenes. As a decorative element, scherenschnitte is found on objects such as birth certificates, marriage certificates, memorial pictures, and valentines.

The term "scherenschnitte" is generally reserved for examples cut in the late eighteenth and early nineteenth centuries. Some were cut on gilded paper. Most were mounted against a cloth or paper of contrasting background.

Scissor–cutting is a continuing tradition. Late nineteenth and early twentieth century Victorian examples do not command the same value as early examples. In Europe the tradition is especially strong in Slavic regions, especially Czechoslovakia. Many of these examples have worked their way into the American market.

Finally, some contemporary scherenschnitte

artists are experimenting with cutting techniques other than scissors, e.g., lasers. When buying a contemporary example make certain that you know how the piece was cut.

Reproduction Craftspersons: Sandra Gilpin, 509 Baer Avenue, Hanover, PA 17331; Claudia and Carroll J. Hopf, 13 Mechanic Street, Kennebunk, ME 04043.

Reproduction Manufacturers: Southern Scribe, 515 E Taylor, Griffin, GA 30223; Tree Toys, Inc, Box 492, Hinsdale, IL 60521.

Circular design, intricate cutouts, white paper mounted on black paper backing, old glue stains, $6\frac{1}{2}$" d   **475.00**

Collection of twenty–five individual designs, includes horse–drawn vehicles, trees, birds, and flowers, white paper mounted on black ground cloth, shadow box frame, $18\frac{1}{2}$" h, $22\frac{1}{4}$" w **575.00**

Landscape, pr, one with church, mill, houses, animals, and trees, other with manor house, swan pond, outbuildings, gate, animals, and trees, scissor-cut white paper on turquoise blue paper ground, $11\frac{1}{2}$ x 16", 19th C **1,100.00**

Valentine

Eight-point star center, eight hearts and birds on vines, heart border, verses inscribed on all hearts, square, watercolor, pen and ink on white paper, $14\frac{3}{4}$ x 15", c1840   **1,000.00**

Filigree birds, trees, stars, and spheres, verses inscribed on four central hearts, pale blue and yellow birds and vines painted on borders, square, white paper mounted on green silk, 19th C . .   **775.00**

Hex sign type cuttings, hearts and other borders, round, pen and ink inscription, white paper mounted on olive green ground, 13" d, dated 1842 . . . . **2,000.00**

Sixteen-point star center, verses inscribed on eight hearts surrounding center star, busts of 19th C

Modern, Claudia Hopf, hand colored, $7\frac{3}{8}$" sq handmade grained frames, image size $3\frac{3}{4}$" sq, c1979, pr, $90.00.

garbed man and woman over each heart, pairs of birds flanking small heart in each corner, square, watercolor, pen and ink on white paper, 14¾ x 15", dated 1850 .... **1,200.00**

Vignettes, pr, "Man's Abuse of Animals and the Hunted's Revenge," first grouping illustrates abuse by man of animals in hunting, farming, and playing, second grouping depicts hunted birds and deer stringing up their persecutors, scissor cut black paper on gray–green paper ground, 7¾ x 9", 19th C, pr **880.00**

THEOREM

History: Theorem describes the creation of art through the use of stencils, one for each color. As a form it was extremely popular in the early nineteenth century, especially in New England and Pennsylvania. The technique was used by furniture manufacturers as well as artists. However, when used by the antiques community, theorem means a work of art executed as a watercolor on paper or oils on velvet or cloth.

Still lifes of fruits and flowers in bowls and vases were the most popular subjects. Many of the patterns were based on examples in instruction manuals or popular prints. Although some individuals cut their own stencils and mixed their own colors, many of the young female academy students and women at home that painted theorems relied on pre–cut and ready-mixed colors.

Dating theorems can often be accomplished by noting the style of the basket or container used in the still life. Pressed glass compotes were first produced in the 1830s. Another aid is to note the stencil pattern and compare it with dated examples found in carpets, fabrics (bedspreads, curtains, pillow shams, and tablecloths), and floors. Patterns did cross over.

Two keys to value are design and originality. Add extra for the inclusion of animals, such as a bird or butterfly. Most collectors assign a fifty percent premium to a watercolor on paper theorem. However, oils on velvet theorem often acquire a mellow palette that is stunning.

Two contemporary theorem painters—David Ellinger (active between 1940 and 1980) and William Rank—deserve special mention. Ellinger's works appear on velvet, cotton, and paper and are often confused with period examples. Not all his works are signed. Rank's theorems are much more vivid in color than those of Ellinger.

Reproduction Craftspersons: Donna W Albro, Strawberry Vine, 6677 Hayhurst St, Worthington, OH 43085; Hope R Angier, Sheepscot Stenciling,

RFD 1, Box 613, Wiscasset, ME 04578; Linda Brubaker, 916 May Rd, Lititz, PA 17543; Petra & Thomas Haas, P O Box 20, Oley, PA 19547; Sharon J Mason, Olde Virginia Floorcloth & Trading Co., P O Box 438, Williamsburg, VA 23185; Nancy Rosier, Rosier Period Art, 2366 Rockingham Dr, Troy, OH 45373; Jean Smith, Stenciler, 1300 Westwood Ave, Columbus, OH 43212; Barbara Strawser, P O Box 165, Schaefferstown, PA 17088; Barbara Strickland, 728 Hawthorne, El Cajon, CA 92020; Carolyn Lloyd Swain, Folke Artstyles, Rte 3, Box 1175, Gloucester, VA 23061.

Reproduction Manufacturers: Basye–Bomberger/Fabian House, P O Box 86, W Bowie, MD 20715; Country Accents, RD #2, Box 293, Stockton, NJ 08559; Heritage Designs, 7816 Laurel Ave, Cincinnati, OH 45243.

Basket of Flowers, velvet, soft colors, 16½" h, 19½" w, early 20th C **350.00**
Basket of Fruit, velvet, red, yellow, blue, green, and brown, 10" h, 12" w **1,600.00**
Basket of Fruit, Flowers, and Foliage, watercolor on paper, 18" h, 21" w **800.00**
Bowl of Flowers, watercolor, pencil, and mica on paper, yellow and red tulips, roses, chrysanthemums, and pansies, glittering bowl, 11¼ x 8¾", c1830 .... **1,430.00**
Compote of Fruit, butterfly, velvet, 14¾" h, 17½" w **3,500.00**
Fruit, watercolor on paper, faded colors, 10" h, 12" w **450.00**
Horse, eagle, shield, and flag, watercolor and graphite was on paper, pencil mane on horse, 20½" h, 26½" w **2,850.00**
Landscape, watercolor on velvet, buildings, trees, and deer, red, yellow, green, brown, and blue, 12¼ x 13⅞" **4,800.00**
Parrot, perched on grapevine, eating strawberries from overflowing basket of fruit, velvet, soft colors, 22" h, 26" w **3,050.00**
Pot of Flowers, watercolor on velvet, sgd Jessie N. Boyer, 14 x 12¼" **500.00**
Summer's Bounty, fruits and leaves, watercolor, pen, and ink on paper, 12 x 15", 19th C **875.00**
Two Birds on Branches, watercolor on paper, blue, green, yellow, and red, 7¼" h, 9½" w **400.00**

TRAMP ART

History: Tramp art was prevalent in the United States from 1875 to the 1930s. Items were made by itinerant artists who left no record of their identity. They used old cigar boxes and fruit and vegetable crates. The edges of items were chip–carved and layered, creating the "tramp art" effect. Finished items usually were given an overall stain.

Reference: Helaine Fendelman, *Tramp Art: An Itinerant's Folk Art Guide*, E. P. Dutton & Co., 1975.

Box
  7" h, hinged, alternating yellow and orange layers form pyramids, die-cut rabbit pasted to red-paper-lined interior lid **145.00**
  $8\frac{1}{4}$" h, chip carved, sliding lid, one fitted drawer, red velvet lined interior **600.00**
  12" h, 12" w, hanging, bottom crest, old brown paint, black trim. **45.00**
  $13\frac{1}{2}$" l, gilded brass appliques **65.00**
Chest of Drawers, miniature
  6 x 12", triple arch crestrail, chip carved edge, rect top, three drawers, natural finish, green trimmed edges, ftd **160.00**
  7 x 11", rect marble top, three drawers, framed oval mirror **675.00**
  $10\frac{1}{2}$" w, 22" h, Gothic arch mirror, triptych–like back, three drawers, old varnish finish **225.00**
Clock, 27" h, chip carved, portrait medallion below clock face **500.00**
Cosmetic Box, $10\frac{1}{2}$" l, chip carved, mirror and red lined interior **85.00**
Desk, 21 x 15", miniature, pine, multi–layered chip carved stars, compasses, circles, and geometric shapes, slant front hinged lid, blue paper lined interior, six drawers, c1930 . . . .   **1,000.00**
Frame, $19\frac{1}{2}$" h, $17\frac{1}{4}$" w, rect, chip carved, diamond shape projections on corners, holds German diploma, Philadelphia, PA, dated 1915 . . . . .   **45.00**

Box, heart shaped cut–out handle, $9\frac{1}{2}$" w, $6\frac{3}{4}$" d, $7\frac{1}{2}$" h, $175.00.

Jewelry Box
  $10\frac{1}{2}$" h, brass trim and panels, red velvet insert top, lift out interior tray, hidden drawer, dated 1903   **95.00**
  $12\frac{1}{4}$" h, poplar, bird finial, floral dec, carved name "Addie," four swing out trays, center compartment, scrolled feet, old dark finish **200.00**
Magazine Rack, 15" w, hanging, brass tack dec, orig dark finish **75.00**
Mirror
  $20\frac{1}{2}$" h, $12\frac{1}{4}$" w, pine, carved, multi–layered moons, circles, hearts, and geometric designs, c1930. . .   **935.00**
  23" h, crest with confronting birds above horseshoe enclosing date "1914," center heart form frame encloses mirror, applied rosettes and wings above two birds dec . .   **220.00**
Rocker, cut–out curved sides, lyre-like splat, applied chip carved dec, two porcelain buttons in back, alligator varnish and brown paint, replaced wooden seat. **250.00**
Sewing Box, $9\frac{1}{2}$" l, pincushion frame top, drawer, orig dark finish **30.00**
Sewing Table, "Mother" on hinged lid   **850.00**
Stand, $30\frac{3}{8}$" h, diamond sides on removable planter top. **325.00**
Wall Pocket, 11 x $16\frac{1}{2}$", hanging, applied strips **125.00**

WHIRLIGIGS

History: Whirligigs are a type of whimsical wind toy. Their origins are uncertain. Some claim that they began as a "Sabbath day toy" in Pennsylvania's German regions; others see them as a weather vane variation. In 1819 Washington Irving mentions whirligigs in his famous story "The Legend of Sleepy Hollow." Whirligigs enjoyed great popularity in the rural areas of New England, the Middle Atlantic states, and the Midwest.

Whirligigs often contain more than one material in their construction; wood and wire are the most commonly found. Since most were made by amateurs, a primitive appearance dominates. Single figures usually feature rotating paddle–like arms. Multifigure examples employ a propeller that drives a series of gears and rods to make the figures move. The variety of subjects is endless.

Collectors place a premium on nineteenth century examples, many of which featured three-dimensional figures. The use of plywood and silhouette figures are signs of a twentieth century example.

Many whirligigs have been reproduced and faked. Since whirligigs were used outdoors, there should be strong evidence of weathering as well as wear where the movable parts rubbed against the body. Look for signs of rust and corrosion. Contemporary whirligig makers copy older designs. Placed outside, they can age quickly. Thus, relying solely on condition to date a whirligig is risky.

References: Robert Bishop and Patricia Coblentz, *A Gallery of American Weathervanes and Whirligigs*, E. P. Dutton, 1979; Ken Fitzgerald, *Weathervanes and Whirligigs*, Clarkson N. Potter, 1967.

Reproduction Craftsperson: Bill Muehling, 440 Yemmerdall Rd, Lititz, PA 17543.

Reproduction Manufacturer: Plantation Characters, Box 896, Painesville, OH 44077.

Amish Man and Woman, pumper, wearing leather hat and bonnet, arms attached to pumping mechanism, wind propeller, church steeple base, 60½" h, 27" l, late 19th/early 20th C **5,225.00**

Canoe, five seated Indians, wood, carved, polychrome paint, 63¼" l, 20th C **425.00**

Carousel, wood and tin, carved, painted, bicycle wheel base, horses, chariots, toy soldiers, red, white, and blue tin base and scalloped awning roof, topped by flag and brass lamp finial, four conical metal cups mounted under base catch wind and turn carousel, toy mounted on carved wood lamp stand base, 51" h, 24" d, c1900 . . . . **6,500.00**

Dandy, pine, carved, painted, stylized, sway–back figure, slicked back hair, sideburns, mustache, goatee, wearing form-fitting black narrow lapel swallowtail coat, yellow vest, brown pants, black and white tapering blades on revolving arms, black oblong base, 22" h, 1875–1900 . . . . **6,875.00**

Dirigible, pine and tin, carved, painted, silhouette of man on wood rod suspended by thin metal wires from flattened cigar–shaped balloon, green tin propellers and tail, 22½" h, 25½" l, early 20th C **4,125.00**

George Washington on Horseback, pine, carved, painted, stylized, wearing military uniform, dappled gray horse, stylized cannon, red, white, and blue propeller, green base, figures move when activated, 26¼" h, 47½" l, late 19th/early 20th C **7,150.00**

Hessian Soldier, relief carved facial features, pointed blue helmet, green swallowtail coat, black glass buttons, blue pants, yellow sword baf-

fles on angular arms, 12½" h, late 19th/early 20th C **5,500.00**

Indian, standing, dark skin, feathered headdress, white skirts, canoe oar paddles attached to arm baffles, green turned baluster and sphere base, 16½" h, late 19th/early 20th C   **950.00**

Indian, standing in canoe, real feather headdress, black and white moccasins, green canoe, green canoe paddle baffles on outstretched arms, square wood base, 12½" h, 19th C   **2,475.00**

Indian Warrior, standing, gilded, relief carved facial features, glass bead eyes, red gilt–trimmed leather headdress and costume, black metal high boots, revolving arms extend to tapering gilded paddled baffles, 16½" h, early 19th C **35,200.00**

Man, pine, carved, painted, wearing flat hat, blue coat, red vest, and tall boots, swivel feet, truncated upper arm fitted with revolving paddles, 9" h, 19th C **2,950.00**

Man and American Flag, pine and tin, carved, painted, man wearing bowler hat, jointed arms and torso, holding crank attached to red, white, blue, and yellow tin pinwheel, figure cranks when wind activates pinwheel, painted metal flag attached to red and white wood base, 7" h, 8½" l, c1900 . . . . **4,950.00**

Man Sawing Log, tin and pine, carved, painted, wooden man holding tin saw above log, standing beneath black umbrella–propeller, figure saws log as umbrella spins, 14" h, 9½" w, late 19th/early 20th C **4,500.00**

People worshipping, wood, 14" h, 18" l, $350.00.

Napoleon Soldier, pine, carved, painted, yellow hat, red swallowtail jacket, red stripe on yellow pants, high boots, relief carved and painted facial features, metal swords attached to arm paddles, 15$\frac{3}{4}$" h, c1830 . . . . **20,900.00**

Oliver Hazard Perry, pine, carved, painted, blue hat, red trimmed blue swallowtail coat, white pants, black, boots, relief carved facial features, painted black eyes, white tapering undulating baffles on revolving arms, 30" h, c1850. . . . . . . **20,900.00**

Railroad Man, wood, painted, relief carved facial features, red cap, green jacket, black pants, rotating arm baffles, 22" h, early 20th C . . . **5,225.00**

Sailor, pine, painted, carved facial features, painted hair, blue hat, metal brim, navy blue short jacket, nail head buttons, white shirt and pants, relief carved fingers and thumbs, paddle–baffles extend from hands, square black base, 14" h, early 19th C **38,500.00**

Slave and Master, pine, carved, painted, master wearing black frock coat and top hat, standing at grinding stone sharpening ax, slave wearing striped trousers and shirt sleeves turning the wheel, both figures under open shed roof between green picket fence and propeller, 19" h, 26$\frac{1}{4}$" l, late 19th/early 20th C **22,000.00**

Soldier, carved, painted, hourglass figure, red peaked cap, white metal brim, red swallowtail coat, brass nail head buttons, tapering sword paddles on shaped arm baffles, 24$\frac{1}{4}$" h, c1870 . . . . **6,500.00**

Soldier, carved, painted, rotund figure, red and black peaked cap, small goatee and mustache, red and green jacket, small copper swords on arm baffles, black wood base, 9$\frac{1}{4}$" h, late 19th C **2,500.00**

Uncle Sam, pine, carved, painted, black top hat, blue swallowtail coat and vest, red and white striped trousers, relief carved facial features, goatee, paddle arms, round black base, 11" h, 19th C **1,650.00**

Washerwoman, whirligig/weathervane combination, blue apron and tin bonnet, sheet metal washboard and yellow washtub, wood platform, red and white propeller and tail, wrought iron directional letters, figure scrubs when propeller turns, 16$\frac{1}{2}$" h, 29" l, early 20th C **4,125.00**

WINDMILL WEIGHTS

History: Windmills were an important fixture on the early prairie landscape of the Midwest. They pumped underground water for crops, household use, livestock, and steam locomotives.

Windmill weights counterbalanced the weight of the large wind wheels, which could measure as much as thirty feet in diameter. They were located at the end of the arm that ran back from the hub of the wind wheel. Although simple geometric shapes such as circles and rectangles were used, many of the weights were figural. Weight varied from ten to two hundred pounds. Windmill weights were painted to match the color of the windmill. Black was common. Blue, green, and red also were popular.

Most windmill weights were manufactured in the Midwest between 1880 and the 1920s. Leading manufacturers include the Dempster Mill Manufacturing Company (Beatrice, Nebraska), Elgin Wind Power and Pump Company (Elgin, Illinois), and Fairbury Windmill Company (Fairbury, Nebraska).

In the early 1980s windmill weights joined weather vanes as a darling of the folk art set. Although cast in molds and mass–produced, windmill weights were elevated from utilitarian objects to *objets d'art*. In 1985 the Museum of American Folk Art sponsored a traveling exhibition on windmill weights.

References: Milton Simpson, *Windmill Weights*, Johnson & Simpson, 1985; Donald E. Sites, *Windmills and Windmill Weights, published by author (P. O. Box 201, Grinnell, KS 67738).*

Reproduction Alert: Doug Clemence (Treasure Chest, 436 North Chicago, Salina, KS 67401) sells unpainted reproductions of the small chicken, Hummer #184 chicken with long shaft, Hummer #184 chicken with short shaft, "barnacle eye" chicken, short tail horse, buffalo, and squirrel. Reproductions of the BOSS bull, Fairbury flat bull (#17 in Site's book), long tail horse, and a chicken with five tail feathers (#41 in Site's book) have also been spotted.

New castings often have a finely granulated orange colored rust, which can be hidden by new paint, and rough casting edges. Modern reproductions often are done with pot metal, rather than cast iron. Finally, reproduction surfaces are rough and grainy, not weathered and smooth.

Battleship, cast iron frame, concrete–filled, Baker Mfg Co, Evansville, WI **1,000.00**

Buffalo, 16" l, painted, Dempster Mfg Co, Beatrice, NE **500.00**

Bull
   Dempster Mfg Co, Des Moines, IL, marked "BOSS" both sides, 18 lbs **700.00**

Fairbury Windmill Co, Fairbury, NE **650.00**
Hanchett, bolted halves, Simpson
Windmill and Machine Co **500.00**
Chicken, Hummer, E184, Elgin Wind-
mill Power and Pump Co, Elgin, IL **475.00**
Crescent Moon, 10" l, 27 lbs, marked
"ECLIPSE," Fairbanks Morse Co,
1900 . . . . **150.00**
Halladay Star, five points, 14½ x 14½ x
3", unpainted, US Wind Engine and
Pump Co, Batavia, IL, 1890s **400.00**
Horse, short tail, Dempster Mfg Co. . . **325.00**

Horse with Jockey, short tailed horse,
jointed sheet metal jockey on back,
painted, Dempster #4, Dempster
Mfg Co, Beatrice, NE **875.00**
Letter "W," 19½ x 9 x 2½", 22 lbs, flat
back, Althouse and Wheeler Co,
Waupaun, WI, c1900 . . . . **300.00**
Rooster, rainbow tail, painted, Elgin
Windmill Power & Pump Co, Elgin,
IL. **950.00**
Squirrel, Elgin Windmill Power and
Pump Co, Elgin, IL. **1,500.00**

FURNITURE

The Country look divides into three major categories: primitive, vernacular, and formal. A typical rural home contained all three types. Primitive work benches, shelves, and cabinets were found in the pantry, back porch, wash area, and sheds. Vernacular furniture dominated the kitchen, guest bedrooms, and living room. The parlor and master bedroom were home to more formal pieces.

Not only was the country home an eclectic mixture of furniture types, but styles were mixed as well. Pieces were passed down from generation to generation. Family heirlooms comprised much of a country home's furnishings. Further, members of the agrarian community practiced thrift. Many household furnishings and equipment were bought secondhand at country auctions.

Rural America was not isolated from the formal furniture styles of the large metropolitan areas. However, they worked their way slowly into the countryside. Further, only styles whose architecture conveyed ruggedness and a long-lasting quality were favored.

In the formal area, two major currents dominate the American furniture marketplace: furniture made in Great Britain and furniture made in the United States. American buyers continue to show a strong prejudice for objects manufactured in the United States. They will pay a premium for such pieces and accept them above technically superior and more aesthetic English examples.

Until the last half of the 19th century formal American styles were dictated by English examples and design books. Regional furniture, such as the Hudson River Valley [Dutch] and the Pennsylvania German styles, did develop. A less formal furniture, designated as vernacular, developed throughout the 19th and early 20th centuries. Vernacular furniture deviates from the accepted formal styles and has a genre charm that many collectors find irresistible.

America did contribute a number of unique decorative elements to English styles. The American Federal period is a reaction to the English Hepplewhite period. American designers created furniture which influenced, rather than reacted, to world taste in the Gothic Revival style, Arts and Craft Furniture, Art Deco, and Modern International movement.

The following chart introduces you to the formal American design styles. Note that dates are approximate.

FURNITURE STYLES [APPROX. DATES]

William and Mary **1690–1730**
Queen Anne **1720–1760**
Chippendale. **1755–1790**
Federal [Hepplewhite] **1790–1815**

Sheraton. **1790–1810**
Empire [Classical] **1805–1830**
Victorian
French Restoration **1830–1850**

Victorian (continued)

Gothic Revival	**1840–1860**	Neo-Greek	**1855–1885**
Rococo Revival	**1845–1870**	Eastlake	**1870–1890**
Elizabethan	**1850–1915**	Art Furniture	**1880–1914**
Louis XIV	**1850–1914**	Arts and Crafts	**1895–1915**
Naturalistic	**1850–1914**	Art Nouveau	**1896–1914**
Renaissance Revival	**1850–1880**	Art Deco	**1920–1945**
		International Movement	**1940–Present**

American Country pieces, with the exception of Windsor chairs, stabilized and even dropped off slightly in value. This is due to two major market developments. First, the country–designer look no longer enjoys the popularity it did during the American Bicentennial period in the late 1970s. Second, American decorators have focused more recently on the regional and European Country look.

Furniture is one of the few antiques fields where regional preferences are a factor in pricing. Victorian furniture is popular in New Orleans, and unpopular in New England. Oak is in demand in the Northwest, but not so much in the Middle Atlantic states.

References: Joseph T. Butler, *Field Guide To American Furniture*, Facts on File Publications, 1985; E & R Dubrow *Furniture, Made In America, 1875–1905*, Schiffer Publishing, Ltd., 1982; Eileen and Richard Dubrow, *American Furniture of the 19th Century, 1840–1880*, Schiffer Publishing, Ltd., 1983; Rachael Feild, *Macdonald Guide To Buying Antique Furniture*, Wallace–Homestead, 1989; Benno M. Forman, *American Seating Furniture, 1630–1730*, Winterthur Museum, W. W. Norton & Company, 1988; *Furniture Dealers' Reference Book, Zone 3, 1928–29*, reprint by Schiffer Publishing, Ltd. as *American Manufactured Furniture*, 1988; Myrna Kaye, *Fake, Fraud, Or Genuine, Identifying Authentic American Antique Furniture*, New York Graphic Society Book, 1987; William C. Ketchum, Jr., *Furniture, Volume 2: Chests, Cupboards, Desks, & Other Pieces*, Knopf Collectors' Guides To American Antiques, Alfred A. Knopf, 1982.

Kathryn McNerney, *Pine Furniture, Our American Heritage*, Collector Books, 1989; Kathryn McNerney, *Victorian Furniture*, Collector Books, 1981, values updated 1988; Milo M. Naeve, *Identifying American Furniture: A Pictorial Guide To Styles and Terms, Colonial to Contemporary, Second Edition*, American Association for State and Local History, 1989; Don & Carol Raycraft, *Collector's Guide To Country Furniture, Book II*, Collector Books, 1988; Marvin D. Schwartz, *Furniture: Volume 1: Chairs, Tables, Sofas & Beds*, Knopf Collector's Guides To American Antiques, Alfred A. Knopf, 1982; Tim Scott, *Fine Wicker Furniture, 1870–1930*, Schiffer Publishing, Ltd., 1990.

Robert W. and Harriett Swedberg, *American Oak Furniture, Style and Prices, Book III, Second Edition*, Wallace–Homestead, 1991; —, *Country Furniture and Accessories with Prices, Book I* (1983) and *Book II*, (1984), Wallace–Homestead; —, *Collector's Encyclopedia of American Furniture, Volume 1* (1990) and *Volume 2*, (1991) Collector Books; —, *Country Pine Furniture*, Wallace–Homestead, 1983; —, *Furniture of the Depression Era*, Collector Books, 1987; —, *Victorian Furniture, Book I* (1976), *Book II* (1983), and *Book III* (1985), Wallace–Homestead; —, *Wicker Furniture*, Wallace–Homestead, 1983; Gerald W. R. Ward, *American Case Furniture*, Yale University Art Gallery, 1988; Derita Coleman Williams and Nathan Harsh, *The Art and Mystery of Tennessee Furniture*, Tennessee Historical Society, 1988; Norman Vandal, *Queen Anne Furniture*, The Taunton Press, 1990; Lyndon C. Viel, *Antique Ethnic Furniture*, Wallace–Homestead, 1983.

There are hundreds of specialized books on individual furniture forms and styles. Two examples of note are: Monroe H. Fabian, *The Pennsylvania–German Decorated Chest*, Universe Books, 1978, and Charles Santore, *The Windsor Style in America, 1730–1830, Volume I* (1981) and *Volume II* (1987), Running Press.

Reproduction Craftspersons: *Beds*—Charles E. Thibeau, The Country Bed Shop, P O Box 222, Groton, MA 01450; *Clocks*—Clocks by Foster Campos, 213 Schoosett St, Pembroke, MA 02359; Edward H. Stone, C–3 Company, 13200 Forest Dr, Bowie, MD 20715; Patrick J. Terry, Terry Clocks, 2669 N. Lakeview Dr, Warsaw, IN 46580; *Frames*—William Adair, Gold Leaf Studios, P O Box 50156 NW, Washington, DC 20004; John Morgan Baker, Framer, Reed Arts and Crafts, 233 West Fifth Ave, Columbus, OH 43201; Carolyn Fankhauser, Heartwood, P O Box 458, Canfield, OH 44406; Sally Greene Bunce, 4826 Mays Ave, Reading, Pa 19606; Ted Van Valin, The Scarlet Letter, P O Box 397, Sullivan, WI 53178; *Furniture Hardware*—Charles Euston, Woodbury Blacksmith & Forge Co, P O Box 268, Woodbury, CT 06798; James W. Faust, 488 Porters Mill Rd, Pottstown, PA 19464; Steve Kayne, Kayne & Son Custom Forged Hardware, 76 Daniel Ridge Rd, Candler, NC 28715; Peter Renzetti, 301 Brinton's Bridge Rd, West Chester, PA 19382; Elmer Roush, Jr., Roush Forged Metals, Rte 2, Box 13, Cleveland, VA 24225.

General—Gary S. Adriance, Adriance Heritage Collection, 5 N. Pleasant St, South Dartmouth, MA 02748; Brian Boggs, Chairmaker, P O Box 4041, Berea, KY 40403; Joseph B. Brannen & Co, 145 West 2nd St, Maysville, KY 41056; Gordon & Christopher Bretschneider, Bretschneider & Bretschneider, Box 12, School St, Shoreham, VT, 05770; Teri M. Browning, The Wentworth Collection, P O Box 131, Wentworth, NH 03282; John W. Bunker & Son, 411 E. Lincoln Hwy, Exton, PA 19341; Michael Camp, Cabinetmaker, 636 Starkweather Rd, Plymouth, MI 48170; Steven Cherry & Peter Deen, 1214 Goshen Mill Rd, Peach Bottom, PA 17563; Gene Cosloy, Great Meadows Joinery, P O Box 392, Waylond, MA 01778; Ted Curtin & Rob Tarule, Heart of the Wood, P O Box 3031, Plymouth, MA 02361; Peter J. DiScala, Strafford House, 43 Van Sant Rd, New Hope, PA 18938; Donald A. Dunlap, Cabinetmaker, Goodell Rd, RR 2, Box 39, Antrim, NH 03440; Clint Edwards, Cabinetmaker, 5208 Brook Rd, Richmond, VA 23227; Dennis Fly, 17th & 18th Century Ltd, 1440 Pineville Rd, New Hope, PA 18938; Jim Fuller and Dolores Wood, The Craft Cove, 1516 Olive St, Coatesville, PA 19320; Jeffrey P Greene, Furnituremaker, 1 W. Main St, Wickford, RI 02852; D. T. Gutzwiller & Son, 777 Mason Morrow Rd, Lebanon, OH 45036; Chris Harter, The Country Furniture Shop, Box 125, Rte 20E, Madison, NY 13402; Jeff L. Headley & Steve Hamilton, Mack S. Headley & Sons, Rte 1, Box 1245, Senseny Rd, Berryville, VA 22611; Van Heyneker, Rte 52, Box 314, Mendenhall, PA 19357; Benjamin C. Hobbs, Rte 1, Box 517, Hertford, NC 27944; Robert Treate Hogg, 4500 Union School Rd, Oxford, PA 19363; Louis Irion III, Irion Company Furniture Makers, 44 N. Valley Rd, Paoli, PA 19301; William Kidd, Cabinetmaker, 104 Jackson Ave, Morgantown, WV 26505; R. LaMontagne & Sons, 900 Joslin Rd, Harrisville, RI 02830; James Lea, Cabinetmaker, 9 West St, Rockport, ME 04856; David LeFort & Co, 293 Winter St, Hanover, MA 02339; Terri Lipman, 437 Lombard St, Dallastown, PA 17313; Thomas Lord, P O Box 194, Canterbury, CT 06331; Michael A. McCullough, 1634 Chambersburg Rd, Gettysburg, PA 17325; Paula McDaniel, Jeff McFarlane, 1001 Election Rd, Oxford, PA 19363; Robert L. McKeown III, 227 Gallaher Rd, Elkton, MD 21921; Meredith and Chris Miller, The Copper Rooster, RD #4, Country Place, Export, PA 15632; William H. Miller, III, The Miller's, Box 562, Hatfield, PA 19440; Thomas B. Morton Cabinetmakers, The Artworks, Studio 128, 100 N. State St, Ephrata, PA 17522; Robert W. Mouland, Colonial Designs, Box 1429, Havertown, PA 19083; John T. Nicholas & Son, 704 N. Michigan Ave, Howell, MI 48843; Robert J. Nunn, P O Box 247, Unionville, PA 19375; William A. Pease, Cabinetmaker, 17 Fresh Meadow Dr, Lancaster, PA 17603; William J. Ralston, Ralston Furniture Reproductions, Box 144, Cooperstown, NY 13326; C. W. Riggs, Rte 39, Box 122A, St. Marys, WV 26170; Jack B. Robinson, American Country Reproductions, 8760 Beatty St NW, Massillon, OH 44646; William James Roth, P O Box 355, Yarmouth Port, MA 02675; Kirk Rush Reproductions, 406 Kirkwood Ln, Camden, SC 29020; Lee & Cynthia Sawyer, L. Sawyer Fine Painted Furniture, 2304 Carolina Rd, Chesapeake, VA 23322; Edward J. Schoen, Signature Gallery, Depot

Shoppes, Plank & Lancaster Aves, Paoli, PA 19301; K. Alan Styer, Cabinetmaker, P O Box 50, Greenford, OH 44422; Michael B. Timmins, P O Box 95, 140 Valleybrook Rd, Chester Heights, PA 19017; Norman Vandal, Cabinetmaker, P O Box 67, Roxbury, VT 05669; Gregory Vasileff Reproductions, 740 North St, Greenwich, CT 06831; Herman Woolfrey Furnituremakers, 1433 Whitford Rd, West Chester, PA 19380.

Grain Painting—Margorie Akin, Akin/D'Lamater Studio, Inc, 61 W. Chapel Ave, Carlisle, PA 17013; Rebecca A. Erb, 706 Brownsville Rd, Sinking Spring, PA 19608; Dorothy Fillmore Studio, 84 Pilgrim Dr, Windsor, CT 06095; David and Marie Gottshall, Gottshall's Folk Art, 210 E. High St, Womelsdorf, PA 19467; Petra & Thomas Haas, P O Box 20, Oley, PA 19547; Dorothy Wood Hamblett, P O Box 295, Millbury, MA 01527; Carol Martell, Designs Unlimited, 13401 Chestnut Oak Dr, Gaithersburg, MD 20878; Virginia Jacobs McLaughlin, Antique Cupboard, 812 W. Main St, Emmitsburg, MD 21727; Larry Plummer, 329 E. Piccadilly St, Winchester, VA 22601; Sherry A. Ringler, Ringler Design Associates, 2812 Poplar Dr, Springfield, OH 45504; Barbara Strawser, P O Box 165, Schaefferstown, PA 17088; David Bradstreet Wiggins, Itinerant Painter, Hale Rd, Box 420, Tilton, NH 03276.

Ladderback Chairs—David Barrett, Barretts Bottoms, Rte 2, Box 231, Bower Rd, Kearneysville, WV 25430; Rick & Susan Steingress, Candlertown Chairworks, P O Box 1630, Candler, NC 28715; *Miniatures*—Michael A. McCullough, 1634 Chambersburg Rd, Gettysburg, PA 17325; L. H. Peavey, 41 Wagonwheel Rd, Sudbury, MA 01776; *Pennsylvania German*—Dan Backenstose, Jr, Spring House Classics, P O Box 541, Schaefferstown, PA 17088; Jan Switzer, Painted Pony Folk Art, 8392 M–72 West, Traverse City, MI 49684; *Tin Pie Safe Panels*—Gerald Fellers, The Tin Man by Gerald Fellers, 2025 Seneca Dr, Troy, OH 45373; *Trunks*—Steven Lalloff, Traditional Leatherwork Co, 14311 Bryn Mawr Dr, Noblesville, IN 46060; *Twig Furniture*—Jane and Don Miles, The Willow Place, 374 S. Atlanta St, Roswell, GA 30075; *Upholstered Furniture*—Alexandra Pifer, 1817 Shoppe, Inc, 5606 E. State Rt 37, Delaware, OH 43015; Betty Urquhart, The Maynard House, 11 Maynard St, Westborough, MA 01581.

Windsor—Robert Barrow, 412 Thames St, Bristol, RI 02809; Curtis Buchanan, 208 E. Main St, Jonesborough, TN 37659; Jeffrey M. Fiant, 260 Golf Rd, Reinholds, PA 17569; Rolf A. Hofer, 1077 Ellis Woods Rd, Pottstown, PA 19464; Samuel J. Laity, II, RE 11, Accomac Rd, York, PA 17406; Kai Pedersen, RD 3, Box 3088A, Mohnton, PA 19540; Vince Rygelis, P O Box 231, Williams, OR 97544; David Sawyer, RD 1, Box 107, East Calais, VT 05650; Roger W. Scheffer, Straw Hill Chairs, RFD 1, Straw Hill, West Unity, NH 03743; Woody Scoville, Box 65, E. Calais, VT 05650; Mark Soukup, Rte 1, Box 27A1, Gap Mills, WV 24941; Windsors by Bill Wallick, 41 N. 7th St, Wrightsville, PA 17368; Max Wardlow, RR 1, Fillmore, MO 64449.

Reproduction Manufacturers: *Adirondack & Rustic Furniture*—Adirondack Store and Gallery, 109 Saranac Avenue, Lake Placid, NY 12946; Amish Country Collection, RD 5, Sunset Valley Rd, New Castle, PA 16105; Ptarmigan Willow, P O Box 551, Fall City, WA 98024; Wood–Lot Farms, Star Rte 1, Shady, NY 12479; *Benches*—American Country House, P O Box 317, Davison, MI 48423; *Brass Beds*—Bedlam Brass, 137 Rte 4 Westbound, Paramus, NJ 07652; *Cane and Rush Supply*—The Country Seat, RD #2, Box 24, Kempton, PA 19529; Frank's Cane and Rush Supply, 7252 Heil Ave, Huntington Beach, CA 92647; *Children's Furniture*—Nap Brothers Parlor Frame Co, Inc, 122 Naubuc Ave, Glastonbury, CT 06033; Ricyn: Country Collectables, P O Box 577, Twisp, WA 98856; Woodbee's, RR #1, Poseyville, IN 47633.

Clocks—Van Dommelen Clocks, 9–A Church St, Lambertville, NJ 08530; *Cupboards*—Ohio Painted Furniture, Rte 4, Box 200 B, Athens, OH 45701; *Cut Nails*—The Tremont Nail Co, 8 Elm St, P O Box 111, Wareham, MA 02571; *Doors*—Old 'N Ornate, P O Box 10493 H, Eugene, OR 97440; *Furniture Finishes*—Stulb's Old Village Paint, P O Box 297, 618 W.

Washington St, Norristown, PA 19404; *Furniture Hardware*—The Antique Hardware Store, 43 Bridge St, Frenchtown, NJ 08825; Old Smithy Shop, Box 336, Milford, NH 03055; Town and Country, Main St, East Conway, NH 04037; Williamsburg, Blacksmiths, Inc, Goshen Rd, Williamsburg, MA 01096.

General—Basye–Bomberger/Fabian House, P O Box 86, W. Bowie, MD 20715–0086; Bathroom Machineries, 495 Main St, P O Box 1020, Murphys, CA 95247; Carolina Leather House, Inc, P O Box 2468, Hickory, NC 28603; Chairmakers, Box 67, Melrose, WI 54642; Chinaberry General Store, 1846 Winfield Dunn Highway, Sevierville, TN 38762; Classic Furniture, Box 1544, Kansas City, MO 64141; Classics in Wood, 82 Lisbon Rd, Canterbury, CT 06331; The Colonial Keeping Room, 16 Ridge Rd, RFD #1, Box 704, Fairfield, ME 04937; Colonial Woodworks, P O Box 10612, Raleigh, NC 27605; Country Loft, 1506 South Shore Park, Hingham, MA 02043; Cumberland General Store, Rte 3, Crossville, TN 38555; Decker Antique Reproductions, P O Box 5688, Knoxville, TN 37918; Hammermark Associates, 10 Jericho Turnpike, Floral Park, NY 11001; House of Vermillion, P O Box 18642, Kearns, UT 84118; Ingrid's Handcraft Crossroads, 8 Randall Rd, Rochester, MA 02770; The Joinery Company, P O Box 518, Tarboro, NC 27886; Lace Wood 'N Tin Tyme, 6496 Summerton, Shepherd, MI 48883; Olde Mill House Shoppe, 105 Strasburg Pike, Lancaster, PA 17602; Out of the Woods, 38 Pinehurst Rd, Marshfield, MA 02050; Pine Tree Reproductions, 88160 Celery Court Rd, Decatur, MI 49045; Pure and Simple, P O Box 535, 117 W. Hempstead, Nashville, AR 71852; David T Smith & Co, 3600 Shawhan Rd, Morrow, OH 45152; Sturbridge Yankee Workshop, Blueberry Rd, Westbrook, ME 04092; The Warmth of Wood, 540 McCombs Road, Venetia, PA 15367; Yield House, North Conway, NH 03860.

Jelly Cupboards–Five Trails Antiques and Country Accents, 116 E. Water St, Circleville, OH 43113; *Miniatures*—River Bend Chair Co, Jonathan Westfield Co, P O Box 526, Westfield, IN 46074; Toncoss Miniatures, P O Box 15146, Riverside, RI 02915; *Pie Safes*— The Vine and Cupboard, P O Box 309, George Wright Rd, Woowich, ME 04579; *Porcelain Reglazing*—Guaranteed Porcelain Services, 3568 Western Branch Blvd, Portsmouth, VA 23707; *Shutters*—Historic Windows, P O Box 1172, Harrisonburg, VA 22801; *Stenciling Supplies*—Gail Grisi Stenciling, Inc, P O Box 1263, Haddonfield, NJ 08033; StenArt, Inc, P O Box 114, Pitman, NJ 08071; Stencil School, P O Box 94, Shrewsbury, MA 01545; *Tin Pie Safe Panels*—Clark Manufacturing Co, 1611 Southwind Dr, Raymore, MO 64083; Country Accents, RD #2, Box 293, Stockton, NJ 08559; *Trunks*—Lamb and Lanterns, 902 N. Walnut St, Dover, OH 44622.

Upholstered Furniture—Hunt Galleries, Inc, P O Box 2324, 2920 Highway 127 North, Hickory, NC 28603; The Seraph, P O Box 500, Sturbirdge, MA 01566; *Wicker*—Ellenburg's Wicker & Casual, I–40 & Stamey Farm Rd, P O Box 5628, Statesville, NC 28677; *Windsor*— The Guild of Gulden Cabinetmakers, Gulden Gallery Investment Replicas, P O Box 66, Aspers, PA 17304.

Reproduction Alert: Beware of the large number of reproductions. During the twenty–five years following the American Centennial of 1876, there was a great revival in copying furniture styles and manufacturing techniques of earlier eras. These centennial pieces now are over one hundred years old. They confuse many dealers and collectors.

Note: Prices vary considerably on furniture. Shop around. Furniture is plentiful unless you are after a truly rare example. Examine all pieces thoroughly. Too many furniture pieces are bought on impulse. Turn furniture upside down; take it apart. The amount of repairs and restoration to a piece has a strong influence on price. Make certain you know about all repairs and changes before buying.

The prices listed below are "average" prices. They are only a guide.

BEDS

Brass, straight top rail, curved corners, ring shaped capitals, cast iron side rails, 61" h, 55 x 94" mattress, c1900 . . . . **1,200.00**

Day

Curly maple, turned posts and rails, refinished, minor insect damage, white cotton duck cov and matching cushion, 77" l **1,600.00**

Maple, slat back, molded crest ends, nine slats, painted red, 77" l, TX, mid 19th C **1,750.00**

Four Poster

Mahogany, carved, 65" w, $86\frac{1}{2}$" l, $67\frac{1}{2}$" h, Drexel **700.00**

New England, rope bed, orig red wash finish, $80\frac{3}{4}$" h, c1800 . . . . . **700.00**

Hired Man's

Maple, folding, pine headboard, pinned sides to facilitate folding, orig first coat of red paint, $70\frac{1}{8}$" l, $45\frac{3}{4}$" w, $27\frac{3}{8}$" h **700.00**

Pine, rope, maple rails and legs, flattened ball finials, turned posts, painted red, PA, c1840 . . . . **750.00**

Poplar, rope, peaked head and footboards, turned posts

Blue–green paint **425.00**

Red paint, orig rails, minor wear and damage, $25\frac{1}{2}$" h, $39\frac{1}{2}$ x 69" mattress **500.00**

Oak

47" h headboard, 41" h footboard, 55" w, blanket roll top on head and footboards, vertical slats, scroll feet **235.00**

50" h headboard, 30" h footboard, 45" w, single size, simple winged applied dec on shaped paneled headboard, paneled footboard . . **175.00**

75" h headboard, 33" h footboard, 58" w, flower and leafy vine spoon carving, paneled, c1890 **495.00**

Bed, rope, cherry, pegs removed, $650.00.

79" h headboard, 39" h footboard, 57" w, applied medallion, feather, and fan dec on head and footboards, paneled, c1920 . . . . **525.00**

Pencil Post, walnut, scalloped head and footboard, orig rails and canopy frame, $76\frac{1}{2}$" h, $46\frac{1}{2}$ x 65" mattress . . . **4,100.00**

Rope

Curly maple, light natural refinishing, replaced side rails, $54\frac{1}{2}$" h, 47 x 74" mattress **1,500.00**

Field bed, poplar and pine, folding frame, suppressed ball finials, shaped headboard, turned legs, repinned mortised joints, old red paint, $45\frac{1}{2}$" w, 81" l, 36" h **350.00**

Low Post

Mixed woods, shaped headboard and footboard, flattened ball finials, tapered feet, orig medium green paint, VA, c1830 **585.00**

Pine, turned and painted, flattened ball finials on head and foot posts, shaped head and footboards, tapered feet, orig rope rails, orig green paint, $48\frac{1}{2}$" w, $73\frac{1}{4}$" l, PA, early 19th C **3,500.00**

Pine and poplar, peaked headboard and footboard, mushroom finials, turned posts, refinished, minor repairs, mid Atlantic, 1820–30 . . . . **750.00**

Medium Post

Pine and poplar, grain painted, scrolled headboard, blanket roll, mushroom finials, turned posts, black on red paint dec, minor repairs, PA, c1840 . . . . **4,000.00**

Poplar and curly maple, poplar headboard and rails, turned curly maple posts, trumpet shaped finials, one finial broken and reattached, 54" h headboard, 52" w, 70" l **600.00**

Poplar and yellow pine, scrolled and paneled headboard, turned blanket roll footboard, acorn finials, turned posts, refinished, minor repairs, VA, c1830 . . . . **950.00**

Painted, red, cylinder turned short headposts, compressed ball turned finials, center triangular arched headboard, tapering turned legs, conforming footposts, molded rails, $73\frac{1}{2}$" l, 48" w, 31" h, c1900 . . . . **6,600.00**

Trundle, pine and poplar, shaped headboard and footboard, ring turned posts, wooden wheels, orig red finish, 40" w, PA, c1840 **500.00**

Walnut, cylindrical turned short headposts, ball turned finials, center arched headboard, turned tapering legs, conforming footposts and footboard, later hardware added to support box spring, 73¾" l, 49⅛" w, 31" h, PA, c1900 .... **700.00**

Sleigh, mahogany and tiger maple, scrolling headboard and footboard **1,000.00**

Tall Post

Bird's eye maple, highly figured and paneled headboard, scrolling crest flanked by turned urn form posts, 80" l, 54" w, 76" h, c1830 **2,900.00**

Cherry, scrolled and paneled headboard, acorn finial posts, later molded tester, 75" l, 46" w, 87" h, mid 19th C **1,800.00**

Tester

Birch, plain turned headposts, fluted footposts, 65" h, c1800 .... **1,200.00**

Cherry, turned posts and foot rail, shaped headboard, orig canopy **1,250.00**

Cherry and maple, large scrolled paneled headboard, turned posts, refinished, missing tester, mid Atlantic, 1830–40............. **1,800.00**

Gold and red dec on orig white paint, 80¾" h, NY, early 19th C **3,000.00**

Maple, fluted posts, urn finials, restored and refinished, 73" h, c1800................... **1,500.00**

Maple and tiger maple, large paneled headboard, turned blanket roll, spiral and ring turned posts, refinished, 2" cut from legs, mid Atlantic, 1830–40........ **2,100.00**

BENCHES

Bin, pine, wide single board construction, lid seat, two part bin interior, cut out feet, scrolled ends, old dark finish, 62" l, 19" deep, 32" h...... **450.00**

Bucket

Pine

3 drawers, high back, shaped ends, double paneled doors, cut out feet, wooden pulls, refinished, 1830–40 .... **1,000.00**

3 shelves, traces of old gray paint, 45½" l, 36" h............. **550.00**

Pine and Poplar

2 shelves, overhanging top, mortised shelves, gallery back, bootjack ends, worn orig blue paint, PA, 1830–40 .... **1,900.00**

5 shelves, dovetailed top shelf, mortised shelves, Y-shaped back stretcher, old varnish, 60" l, 60" h, mid Atlantic states, 1840–60............... **1,500.00**

Cobbler, pine, top divided shelf, drawers, old nut brown patina, old repairs, 44" l **450.00**

Fireside, pine, high back, scalloped top and base, 59" h **750.00**

Mammy, decorated, worn orig red and black graining, yellow and green striping, gold stenciled floral dec, plank seat, removable baby guard, good turnings, age crack in crest, 60" l...................... **1,500.00**

Settle

60" l, 57" h, primitive, pine, dark brown repaint, cut out ends, hinged seat, horizontal board back, top board broken and repaired.................... **750.00**

64" l, 17" deep, 44" h, oak, fluted rail, shaped ends, plank seat **450.00**

87" l, plank seat, turned detail, green repaint............... **175.00**

90" l, plank seat, arrow back, simple turnings, curved arms, refinished brown................. **600.00**

Vanity, walnut, needlepoint seat, refinished, 33" l, 14" h **450.00**

Wash

Hardwood and oak, rough hewn hardwood top, square splayed oak legs wedged through top, 32" l, 15" h, WI **85.00**

Oak, rounded ends on seven separated board draining top, nut brown stain, 47" l, 18" w, 18½" h, 1890s **75.00**

Pine and Cherry, cut corner aprons, cut out feet, refinished, 52" l, 18½" h, IL................. **165.00**

Poplar, one board top

Mortised top, plain aprons, scalloped bootjack ends, orig red paint, minor repairs, PA, 1830–40............... **725.00**

Wire nail construction, weathered gray, 60" l, 18" h **195.00**

Yellow pine, scalloped apron, cut out feet, old red paint, 63½" l, 13" h **150.00**

Water

Pine

43" l, 18" w, 32¼" h, crest, cut out ends, base shelf, old blue and green paint.............. **225.00**

43½" l, 15" w, 25½" h, two drawers, one shelf, random board back, replaced knobs, IL **350.00**

48" l, two shelves, back stretchers, shaped ends, early 19th C **400.00**

61" l, 30¾" h, scalloped apron, turned legs, old blue and white repaint................. **520.00**

Pine and poplar, three dovetailed

drawers, scalloped side supports, two paneled doors, old refinishing, replaced door hinges and wooden knobs, 43¾" w, 15" deep, 50½" h **250.00**

Poplar, two shelves, square nail construction, one board bootjack ends, 36¼" l, 17⅜" w, 33½" h **350.00**

Windsor, bamboo, curved corner back with medallions, plank seat, old refinish, repaired split in crest, 79" l **75.00**

BLANKET CHESTS

Cherry, curly maple panels, turned feet and till, refinished, 38¼" w, 20" h . . **325.00**

Curly Walnut, lift top, dovetailed case, secret drawer in interior till, two drawers below, dovetailed bracket feet, fishtail hinges, crab lock, orig brass hardware, old finish, PA, 1790–1800 . . . . **7,000.00**

Decorated and Grain Painted

New England

Black diamonds on red ground, lift top, two small over two graduated large fake drawers, one large real drawer, bracket feet, 32½" w, c1810 . . . . **5,500.00**

Brown and yellow stippling, one narrow drawer, wooden pulls, bootjack ends, c1820 . . . . **5,800.00**

Burnt umber on yellow ochre, putty painted geometric design, pine, six board, 41½" l, 16" deep, 32¼" h **2,000.00**

Red and yellow mahogany graining, six board, black painted moldings and feet, interior lidded till, 36" w, 23½" h, early 19th C **375.00**

Yellow ochre and burnt umber graining, single long base drawer, covered till, replaced brass pulls, 43¾" l, 22" deep, 33" h **1,500.00**

New York

Mahogany graining, six board, central stenciled rose and yellow flowers in urn, 42" w, 29" h, Albany County, 1810–35 . . . . **1,900.00**

Ochre and burnt umber mahogany graining, painted stringing and cross banded veneer in outline, single long base drawer, old brasses, very minor blemishes on top, 45¼" l, 19⅜" deep, 34¾" h **900.00**

Vinegar painted with yellow ochre and burnt umber, pine, six board, minor imperfections, 50½" l, 21½" deep, 29½" h **1,900.00**

Ohio, poplar

Olive brown and yellow floral and heart dec on worn red ground, dovetailed, cut out heart apron, interior drawer, bracket feet, repaired, 37½" l, 17½" deep, 23½" h **850.00**

Reddish brown graining on yellow ground, brown stenciled hearts, flowers, and birds, applied base molding, lidded till, dovetailed feet, minor paint wear, Licking County, 50¼" w, 20¾" deep, 28" h **215.00**

Pennsylvania

Pine, red paint, traces of grain, three dovetailed drawers and case, orig locks, wrought iron strap hinges, brass escutcheons, stenciled initials "W H G," French feet, 50" l, 23" deep, 29¼" h **2,200.00**

Poplar, red paint, black trim, yellow striping, gold stenciled initials and date "J. B. 1878," colored floral decals, dovetailed case and bracket feet, reeded trim, two dovetailed drawers, white porcelain pulls, lidded till, 48" w, 21" deep, 26½" h, Soap Hollow, PA **3,400.00**

Unknown Origin

Pine, six board, old red repaint, one dovetailed overlapping drawer, lift lid with till, scroll cut feet, one foot chipped, replaced whittled pulls on drawer, replaced wing bat brass escutcheons, 34¾" l, 17¾" deep, 33½" h **500.00**

Pine and poplar, red graining, dovetailed case, black trim on bracket feet, interior till, wrought iron strap hinges, 50" w, 20¼" deep, 24¼" h **650.00**

Blanket Chest, dovetailed case and bracket feet, interior till, 44½" l, 19¼" deep, 26" h, $650.00.

Poplar, brown graining, flamboyant stripes, dovetailed case, turned feet, moldings, and till base and lid **1,200.00**

Maple, molded lift top, two simulated and two real thumb molded drawers in case, bracket feet, old oval brass pulls, refinished, 40½" w, 18" deep, 41½" h, New England, c1780 . . . . .   **525.00**

New England, six board, molded lid, open till, shaped sides, orig red–brown paint, 40¼" w, 25" h, early 19th C **175.00**

Oak, shaped hinged lift lid, raised front and side panels, carved dec front panel, paw feet, copper hinges, 35" w, 18" deep, 18" h **450.00**

Pine

Massachusetts, two drawer, cotter pin hinges, rose head and "T" nails, orig varnish finish, c1750   **800.00**

Mid Atlantic, six board, dovetailed case, lidded till, bracket feet, 25¼" h, 48" w, refinished, 19th C   **550.00**

New England, lift top, three graduated overlapping drawers, bracket feet, old blue repaint, 36" w, c1820 . . . .   **3,500.00**

Unknown Origin, six board, scalloped feet, 44" w, 25" h **400.00**

Pine and Maple, pine case, turned maple legs, paneled front and sides, 44" w, 24½" h, orig red washed finish, early 19th C **600.00**

Pine and Poplar, molded edge top, paneled front and ends, square corner posts, mortised and pinned frame, scalloped apron, turned feet, 44" l, 19½" deep, 25½" h, orig red paint **675.00**

Walnut

Maryland, sulfur inlay "S R 1–7–81 E.R.D.G.," crab lock, strap hinges, bracket feet, orig finish, minor repairs, c1781 . . . .   **5,750.00**

Mid Atlantic, dovetailed case, inlaid initials, two drawers, fishtail hinges, crab lock, secret drawer in till, bracket feet, c1800. . . . .   **5,500.00**

Ohio, dovetailed case, two dovetailed drawers, beaded edges, orig brasses, interior till with secret compartment and dovetailed drawer, orig lock and wrought iron strap hinge, feet and till lid replaced, old refinishing, 46¼" w, 19" deep, 26¼" h **1,200.00**

Pennsylvania

Dovetailed case, lift top, crab lock, tulip strap hinges, side handles, high French feet, refinished, c1800 . . . .   **4,600.00**

Inlaid line dec, two drawers, ogee bracket feet, 50½" w, 23¼" deep, 30¾" h, c1800. . . . .   **1,750.00**

Unknown Origin

Inlaid, dovetailed case, two overlapping dovetailed drawers, dovetailed bracket feet, interior till, repairs, refinished, 49¼" w, 18¾" deep, 25½" h **1,000.00**

Molded edge lid and till, paneled sides and ends, square corner posts, turned feet, refinished, 37½" l, 17" deep, 21½" h **400.00**

BOOKCASES

Sectional, oak

3 Sections, cornice, and base, drawer in base, ball and claw feet, 34" w, 12" deep, 49" h **525.00**

4 Sections, cornice, and base, Globe–Wernicke, Cincinnati, OH, 34" w, 10" deep, 62" h **800.00**

1 Door, oak, 6" h molded top rail, glass–paned, four shelves, applied dec on shaped apron, scrolled feet, 31" w, 14" deep, 61" h **425.00**

2 Doors, oak, pressed carving above glass–paned doors, two shelves, 43" w, 12" deep, 48" h **550.00**

CABINETS

Baker's, possum belly, cornice, two glass–paned doors, one shelf, ten drawers including four spice drawers, flour and sugar bins, cutlery, and linen drawers, pull out kneading board, turned legs, 43" w, 27" deep, 71" h **825.00**

Kitchen, 2 pc

Hawkeye, oak, cornice, two glass–paned doors, two shelves, one long and four spice drawers in top, one narrow shelf in scalloped opening, one long drawer above two graduated drawers in base, split panel door, flour bin, paneled ends, random board back, refinished, 81" h, Union Furniture Co, Burlington, IA **1,350.00**

Hoosier, oak, three paneled doors over tambour sliding doors, porcelain pull out work surface, two cutlery drawers over three graduated drawers, paneled cupboard door, square tapering legs, refinished, 41" w, 26" deep, 71" h . . .   **800.00**

McDougall, oak, three small cupboard doors with inset glass panels over pair of cupboard doors, white graniteware work surface, inset bread board, three graduated drawers, cupboard door, orig hardware and packing label, refinished, c1900 . . . .   **600.00**

Napanee Dutch Kitchenet, oak, three paneled doors, tambour pull down door, porcelain work surface, cutlery/linen drawer over paneled cupboard door, two square drawers, tapering legs, 40" w, 28" deep, 71" h, refinished, MI, patented Feb 24, 1914   **700.00**

Scheirich, oak, center glass–paned door and tambour pull down door between two tall overlapping doors over overlapping drawers in top, pull out porcelain work surface, four overlapping drawers and two doors in base, paneled ends, 40" w, 26" deep, 71" h, Louisville, KY, 1930s **625.00**

Sellers, oak frame, pine panels, one tall split panel door, two paneled doors, and tambour pull down door in top, speckled blue edge on pull out porcelain work surface, paneled cupboard door beside three graduated overlapping doors in base, paneled ends, refinished, orig door pulls marked "S," 41" w, 27" deep, 67" h, IA   **675.00**

Unknown Maker, oak

40" w, 28" deep, 70" h, frosted glass panels in three upper doors, tambour sliding doors, pull out porcelain work surface, one long drawer over paneled cupboard door, pull out cutting board over four graduated overlapping drawers, orig spice and sugar jars, patented Mar 14, 1916 . . . .   **800.00**

48" w, 26" deep, 79" h, center sugar bin above three small drawers, two glass–paned doors, and two interior shelves in top, galvanized work surface, four overlapping center drawers, one long overlapping drawer over paneled cupboard door, and flour bin in base, paneled ends, scalloped apron   **900.00**

Wilson, oak

40" w, 25" deep, 69" h, slag glass panels above wood panels in three upper doors, tambour pull down door, paneled cupboard door and three graduated overlapping drawers in base, paneled ends, tapering legs, "Wilson" inscribed on metal tag **675.00**

42" w, 27" deep, 71" h, one paneled and two glass–paned doors over triple split paneled doors, one triple split cupboard door beside three graduated overlapping drawers, scalloped apron, "Wilson Kitchen Cabinet, The Best" inscribed on metal tag, refinished **800.00**

Medicine, quarter and plain cut oak, hanging, molded cornice and base, paneled door, brass knob, 15" w, 6½" deep, 19" h **75.00**

Music, oak, square, three raised panels front and ends, five interior shelves, square wooden pull, 18" sq, 40" h   **400.00**

Pantry, oak, paneled door, interior shelves, 23¾" w, 25½" deep, 74" h   **300.00**

CANDLESTANDS

Birch

Circular dished top, turned urn form standard, cabriole legs, snake feet, 17" d, 26½" h **1,800.00**

Rect one board tilt top, cut corners, well turned column, spider legs, high feet, old varnish finish, dark varnish stain on base, 14½" w, 21¼" l, 28" h **700.00**

Birch and Maple, rect tilt top, canted corners, birdcage support, vasiform standard, cabriole legs, club feet, 24" w, 18" deep, 29" h **450.00**

Cherry

Dished top, turned column, tripod base, snake feet, worn refinishing, 15" d, 26" h **575.00**

Molded top, horizontally reeded urn design on turned shaft, tripod spider legs, spade feet, cobalt blue, CT, 1800–10 . . . .   **1,000.00**

Octagonal tilt top, turned column, tripod base, curved molded legs, refinished, 16¼ x 20", 28½" h **300.00**

Oval top, baluster and ring turned pedestal, cabriole legs, pad feet, old varnish finish, 24¾" h, NY, c1810 . . . .   **450.00**

Rect top, canted corners, spiral carved baluster standard, three arched legs, 18½" w, 29½" h, c1820 . . . .   **625.00**

Square top, chamfered corners, snake feet **600.00**

Cherry and Tiger Maple, tilt top, shaped top, curving tripod base, 27½" h, New England, c1820 . . . . .   **425.00**

Curly Maple

Round Top, two board tilt top, turned column, scrolled legs, refinished, repairs, 19" d, 26¾" h . .   **550.00**

Shaped top, turned urn column, tripod base, spider legs, refinished, PA, c1820 . . . . **1,500.00**

Mahogany

Circular dished tilt top, birdcage support, vase form standard, cabriole legs, snake feet, 23½" d, 29¼" h, Pennsylvania, c1800. . . . **4,400.00**

Oval tilt top, ring turned standard, cabriole legs, snake feet, 28½" h, New England, c1800 . . . . **1,800.00**

Rect top, carved, canted corners, turned baluster standard, paw feet, NY, c1815–25 . . . . **450.00**

Maple

Octagonal Top, applied molding on top, turned urn column, tripod base, spider legs, refinished, New England, 1820–30 . . . . **1,300.00**

Round Top, turned column, tripod base, old refinishing, 20" d, 25½" h **150.00**

Shaped Top, turned column, spider legs, spade feet, refinished **400.00**

Maple and Other Hardwood, one board rect top, beveled underside, turned column, snake feet, 26" h . . **500.00**

Poplar

Round top, orig red and black graining, gilt stenciled compote of fruit dec, turned column, turned tripod base, 17½" d, 28¼" h **250.00**

Tilting dish top, birdcage, turned urn column, cabriole legs, padded snake feet, refinished, PA, 1810–20 . . . . **2,500.00**

Tiger Maple, shaped tilt top, reeded urn column, tripod base, shaped legs, turned feet, refinished, New England, 1820–30 . . . . **990.00**

Walnut

Circular dish turned tilt top, turned column, birdcage with turned posts tripod base, snake feet, 35" d, 28½" h **900.00**

Oval top, shaped and ring turned round standard, cabriole legs, 26" w, 28¾" h, PA **275.00**

CHAIRS

Captain's, barrel shaped back, nine vase and ring turned spindles, shaped seat, apron, turned front legs and stretchers, 30" h, set of four, c1900 . . . . **500.00**

Decorated, side

Hitchcock, orig red and black graining, yellow and green striping, gilded stenciling, black painted balloon rush seat **175.00**

Red and black graining, yellow striping, rabbit ear posts, foliage and

North Carolina, hand pegged, c1790, $500.00.

fruit compote on crest, eagle on slat, three half spindles, plank seat, turned legs, 35½" h, set of six **4,200.00**

Stenciled, painted, three graduated splats, rabbit ear stiles, shaped seat, turned legs, box stretcher, labeled "Stenciled by W. Smith, Catskill, NY," set of six **800.00**

Ladder Back

36" h, arm, high seat, rabbit ear posts, two slats, replaced woven tape seat, old varnish **175.00**

36¼" h, side, simple turned finials, three slats, replaced rush seat, old red paint **75.00**

38" h, side, hardwood, turned finials, three arched slats, woven splint seat, old red repaint **125.00**

38" h, side, maple and ash, replaced rush seat, old refinish, New England, early 19th C, set of six . . . **800.00**

41¼" h, arm, hardwood, turned finials, five graduated arched slats, shaped and scrolled arms, turned arm supports, replaced rush seat, bulbous turned front stretcher, bulbous feet **210.00**

46¼" h, arm, turned finials, five graduated arched slats, shaped arms, replaced rush seat, bulbous turned front stretcher, turned feet and posts, old red repaint over orig blue and green **3,700.00**

Pressed Back, oak

Double Press, Man of the Wind and scroll design, seven turned spindles, front legs, and front stretchers, caned seat, hip rails, shaped apron, 42" h, set of ten **2,000.00**

Single Press, beaded circle surrounded by feathery vine design, five turned spindles, cane seat, hip rails, ring turned front legs and stretchers, 39" h, set of six **1,300.00**

Rush Seat, side

Banister Back, turned finials, scalloped crest, half turned slats, worn paper rush seat, turned legs and posts, old dark graining over paint, 44½" h **600.00**

Shield Back, mahogany **300.00**

Vase Splat, turned posts, yoke crest, replaced rush seat, turned legs, duck feet, turned front stretcher, old black repaint, yellow striping, 39¼" h, 19th C . . . **195.00**

Windsor

Bow Back

Arm

16" h seat, spindle back, turned arm supports, oval shaped seat, splayed base, bulbous turnings, H stretcher, old worn black and green paint **2,100.00**

16½" h seat, turned arm supports, wide flat arms, saddle seat, splayed base, bulbous turnings, H stretcher, old refinishing, repairs to seat **575.00**

17¾" h seat, hard and softwood, cherry arms, bamboo turnings, worn green paint **1,300.00**

36¼" h, spindle back, shaped arms, turned arm supports, saddle seat, H stretcher, splayed base, bulbous turnings, old refinish **1,400.00**

Side

Seven spindle back, bamboo turnings, saddle seat, H stretcher, red repaint, 18½" h seat **350.00**

Nine spindle back, "Sanborn" branded on bottom, old refinishing, early 19th C, pr . . **650.00**

Chair, Windsor, bow back, arm, maple, New England, c1800, $2,400.00.

Brace Back, side

40" h, curved ear crest, bulbous turned back posts and legs, saddle seat, H stretcher, splayed base, old alligatored brown finish over earlier paint, pr **1,400.00**

Wallace Nutting, orig natural finish, orig label **600.00**

Cage Back, side, old black paint over orig mustard yellow, early 19th C **250.00**

Comb Back, arm, Maclow, sgd and dated 1948 . . . . **700.00**

Continuous Arm, 37¾" h, spindle back, shaped arms, turned arm supports, saddle seat, H stretcher, splayed base with bulbous turnings, old black repaint **850.00**

Fan Back

Arm, shaped crest, carved ears, shaped arms, turned arm supports, oval shaped seat with plugged potty seat, bulbous turnings on splayed base, H stretcher, old worn yellow repaint over earlier green and black, repaired age cracks in seat, four replaced spindles, 16" h seat, 43¾" h overall . . . **925.00**

Side, turned posts, shaped crest, saddle seat, splayed base, bulbous turnings, H stretcher, old black paint, well executed repairs, 15¾" h seat **350.00**

Hooped Back, elm and fruitwood, wheel splat, saddle seat, flared ring turned baluster legs, H stretcher, pr **1,100.00**

Rod Back, orig dark green paint and gold dec, 19th C **120.00**

Sack Back, arm, arched top rail, spindle back, horizontal rail forms scrolled arms, canted baluster form supports, oval saddle seat, splayed baluster turned legs, H stretcher, painted dark green, PA, c1780 . . . . **1,430.00**

Step Down Crest, side, seven spindles, plank seat, splayed bamboo legs, old black repaint **100.00**

CHESTS

Apothecary

Pine and Poplar, six overlapping drawers, turned wooden knobs, old red finish, traces of green overpaint, 10½" w, 8½" deep, 10" h **175.00**

Poplar, scalloped gallery, eight overlapping drawers, orig iron pulls, simple feet, old red stain, 18" w, 6" deep, 23" h **750.00**

Carpenter's, pine and oak, dovetailed case, six drawers in fitted interior, sliding lid, old finish, 33¾" l **260.00**

Mule Chest, pine

34" w, upper half faced with false drawer fronts, hinged top, orig brown paint and hardware, New England, mid 18th C **3,300.00**

34¼" w, 35¼" h, lift lid, two dovetailed overlapping drawers, scalloped front apron, cut out feet, old brasses, old red repaint. **2,550.00**

38⅜" w, 19½" deep, 41½" h, wide single board construction, rect lift lid, blanket chest top with two fake drawers, two dovetailed overlapping drawers, scrolled feet, turned wooden pulls, orig red paint **1,800.00**

Sugar

Cherry, dovetailed case, large till, lift off lid, inlaid stars, lines, and circles, single dovetailed drawer in frame, tapered legs, cut out leg brackets, old finish and repairs, replaced moldings, 31¼" w, 15¾" deep, 36" h, attributed to NC . . . **11,000.00**

Walnut, dovetailed, divided three-section interior, single drawer in base, turned legs, sgd "Read Atlanta GA," old refinish, 29" w, 18¾" deep, 39" h **3,000.00**

CHESTS OF DRAWERS

Ash, shaped back splash, two 5" h handkerchief boxes, scribe lines on four graduated drawers, wood escutcheons, brass pulls, split paneled ends, 38" w, 19" deep, 46" h **400.00**

Birch

Bow Front, reeded columns, turned feet, refinished, 42" w **825.00**

Six graduated drawers, scalloped bracket feet, oval brass escutcheons, orig wooden pulls and finish, minor old repairs, 36¼" w, 16⅝" deep, 56¾" h, New Hampshire, early 19th C **5,000.00**

Cherry and Maple, tall chest, 58½" h, two small drawers over five graduated drawers, refinished, replaced brasses, Thetford, VT, c1800 . . . . . **4,000.00**

Cherry and Poplar, inlaid shield shaped escutcheon, turned pulls, applied edge beading on four dovetailed drawers, paneled ends, turned legs, refinished, 40½" w, 19¾" deep, 44¼" h. **500.00**

Cherry and Walnut, four dovetailed drawers, applied edge beading, turned feet, refinished, 42" w, 44½" h. **850.00**

Chiffonier, oak

28" w, 19" deep, 71" h, small oblong mirror on harp shaped swing frame, beveled mirror, five graduated drawers, six-paneled ends, square tapering legs **325.00**

33" w, 18" deep, 72" h, shaped mirror on scrolled harp shaped swing frame, beveled mirror, serpentine front, conforming top and five graduated drawers, paneled ends **525.00**

33" w, 19" deep, 45" h, applied dec on 8" h shaped rail, serpentine top, two small drawers and hat box over three long drawers, applied feather dec on hat box, shaped apron. **475.00**

34" w, 19" deep, 51" h, applied dec on shaped rail, serpentine top and two conforming top drawers above four flat drawers, scalloped apron, split panel ends, square legs, Larkin **350.00**

42" w, 21" deep, 70" h, quarter sawn oak, Empire style, rect mirror on scrolled swing frame, three shallow swell front drawers over four long drawers. **950.00**

Curly Maple, refinished, 42½" h, New England, late 18th C **1,100.00**

Dresser, oak

38" w, 20" deep, 70" h, applied dec and grotesques on oval mirror frame, serpentine front, two over two conforming drawers, shaped apron, paneled ends, ball and claw feet **500.00**

42" w, 19" deep, 64" h, adjustable triple panel mirror, two overhanging over two long drawers, wooden pulls. **425.00**

Tall Chest, cherry, PA, 1780–1790, 37" w, 23" deep, 71½" h, $4,000.00.

43" w, 19" deep, 74" h, applied dec
on rect swing mirror frame, beveled mirror, scribe lines on three
graduated drawers, paneled ends,
scalloped apron, brass hardware   **475.00**

Maple

34$\frac{3}{4}$" h, 39$\frac{3}{8}$" w, 21$\frac{1}{4}$" deep, reverse
serpentine front, rect top, con-
forming case, four graduated long
drawers, bracket feet, orig
brasses, New England, 1780–
1800. . . . .   **3,300.00**

53" h, 36" w, six graduated drawers,
molded cornice top, pad feet, refinished, replaced brasses, Salisbury, NH, area, School of Bartlett
Cabinetmaking, c1800. . . . .   **4,000.00**

84" h, two small drawers over four
graduated drawers over two small
drawers, refinished, replaced
brasses, New England, late 18th C   **2,000.00**

Oak

30" w, 19" deep, 40" h, bow front,
tiger striped veneered drawer
fronts, modified cabriole feet,
brass pulls **300.00**

41" w, 18" deep, 42" h, scribe lines
on four drawers, applied crest dec
to drawer centers, brass hard-
ware, paneled ends **350.00**

Tiger maple, projecting cornice top,
six graduated drawers, bracket feet,
42" w, 19$\frac{1}{2}$" deep, 51$\frac{3}{4}$" h **3,000.00**

CHILDREN'S

Bed

Pine, decorated, orig brown flame
graining, light colored ground,
square tapering legs, inset rockers
cut flat, mortised sides, removable round tapering posts, replaced tester frame, 54" l, 24" w,
55" h, Amish **600.00**

Tiger Maple, youth, four square tapering posts, slender ring turned
sides, old fitted mattress, Philadel-
phia, c1830. . . . .   **1,600.00**

Blanket Chest

Cherry, lift top, dovetailed case,
incised concentric rings dec front
and sides, turned feet, old finish,
15" h, PA, 1830. . . . .   **1,900.00**

Walnut, lift top, dovetailed case,
two interior drawers, bracket feet,
strap hinges, worn old finish,
24" w, PA, c1820. . . . .   **2,800.00**

Chair

Morris, oak, shaped arms, turned
spindles, adjusting rod, 19" w,
27" h **250.00**

Primitive, oak, mule ears, two hori-

Chair, child's, hickory, splint seat, $45.00.

zontal flat curved and bowed
slats, woven splint seat, 13$\frac{1}{2}$" w,
11" deep, 20" h, 1860 . . . .   **75.00**

Training, oak, shaped rail, cut out
splat, turned stiles, scrolled arms,
hinged lift lid, paneled chamber-
pot area, turned feet, 35" w, 19"
deep, 35" h **225.00**

Windsor, arm

Bow back, turned arm supports
and splayed base, shaped seat,
needlepoint seat cushion, old
varnish finish, 22$\frac{1}{4}$" h, late
19th C **525.00**

Fan Back, mixed woods, carved
ears, vase and ring turned posts,
shaped seat, splayed base,
bamboo turned legs, H
stretcher, old overpaint, PA,
c1800 . . . .   **1,400.00**

Sack Back, turned arm supports
and splayed base, shaped seat,
painted black, 25" h, New En-
gland, late 19th C **400.00**

Chest of Drawers

Cherry

20" h, two over two drawers,
reeded stiles, paneled ends,
turned feet, old finish, wooden
pulls, PA, c1830. . . . .   **2,500.00**

26" h, two drawers over three
graduated drawers, paneled
ends, shaped apron, turned
feet, refinished, replaced pulls,
PA, c1830 . . . .   **3,800.00**

Pine and hardwood, bonnet top
crest, three graduated nailed
drawers, fluted quarter columns,
dovetailed bracket feet, old worn
red finish, 18" w, 30" h **650.00**

Walnut

24" h, inlaid line and flowers, four
graduated drawers, shaped
apron, french feet, mid Atlan-
tic, c1815 . . . .   **5,000.00**

25" h, four graduated drawers, paneled ends, turned feet, old finish, glass pulls, VA, c1830 **1,800.00**

Cradle

Birch

37½" l, canted sides, scalloped headboard, turned posts and rails, refinished **300.00**

41" l, hooded, dovetailed, scalloped ends, cut out rockers . . . **500.00**

Birch and maple, scrolled hood, pinned case, shaped rockers, old finish, New England, 1820–30 **900.00**

Curly maple, fiddleback figured cherry panels, square posts, turned finials, mortised and pinned rails, cut out designs in rails, oak rockers, 38¾" l **200.00**

Hardwoods, carved, four columnar finials and tapering sides, 36" l, 27" h **175.00**

Knotty Pine, paneled sides, hoodless, 17" h, 1790–1820 . . . . **385.00**

Mahogany, dovetailed, scrolled sides and ends, old dark finish, 49½" l **500.00**

Pine

37½" l, 19¼" deep, 25½" h, tiger maple grain painting, yellow ochre and burnt umber, New England, early 19th C **375.00**

40" l, hand forged nails, old refinish, c1900 . . . . **150.00**

45" l, hooded, scalloped hood sides, plain bonnet top, orig finish, c1900 . . . . **300.00**

Poplar

39" l, dovetailed, shaped rockers, heart cut outs in scalloped ends, old worn green paint, wear and edge damage **250.00**

41" l, open, central cut out sides and ends, hand holds, trestle rockers, old dark finish **200.00**

Cradle, mixed woods, five spindle ends, patent 1869, replaced cushion, 37" l, 31½" h, $350.00.

Tiger maple, scrolled hood and footboard, dovetailed case, shaped rockers, old finish, MD, c1820. . . . . **2,200.00**

Walnut

43½" l, dovetailed, scalloped sides, hand holds, brass knobs, heart cut out in headboard, large rockers **350.00**

44" l, self-rocking, windup clockwork mechanism, flat spindles, scroll feet, patent by Aaron Dodd Crane, Feb 28, 1852 . . . **675.00**

Post and Panel, finials, scrolled head and footboards, shaped rockers, refinished, VA, c1830 **550.00**

Crib

Mixed woods, ball finials, turned posts and spindles, old red wash, PA, c1830. . . . . **300.00**

Tiger maple, acorn finials, turned posts and spindles, fold down side, refinished, PA, c1830. . . . . **1,150.00**

Desk, oak, roll top, tambour sliding door, C curve, fitted interior

1 Long Drawer, flat side and back stretchers, 24" w, 17" deep, 35" h **225.00**

4 Drawers, turned legs, paneled ends, 33" w, 21" deep, 41" h. . . . **425.00**

High Chair

Bentwood, oak, cane seat and back, pierced foot rest, flared legs, 16" w, 37" h **275.00**

Go Cart style, oak, pressed back, pressed dec on back and splats, turned spindles, foot rest supports, and stretchers, cane seat, 41" h, marked "Wait Chair Co," 1903. **425.00**

Ladder Back

Board seat, replaced seat and bottom slat, worn old brown patina, minor damage, 35½" h . . . **400.00**

Splint seat, tiger maple, finials, two slats, vase and ring turned front legs, turned front stretcher, widely splayed base, refinished, PA, c1800 . . . . **1,800.00**

Pressed Back, oak, Mother Goose design pressed in rail, five turned spindles, shaped arms, turned posts, arm supports, front legs, and front stretcher, cane seat, 42" h **250.00**

T Back, oak, turned flared legs, 18" w, 19" deep, 39" h **165.00**

Windsor

Arched Crest, volute carved terminals, six tapered spindles and shaped arms, elliptical seat, turned legs and stretchers, orig worn red and black paint, yellow highlights, c1790 . . . . **40,000.00**

Arrow Back, mixed woods, shaped arms, bamboo turned posts, legs, and stretchers, old dark green paint, PA, c1830 . . **800.00**

Bow Back, mixed woods, applied curved arms, bamboo turned spindles, legs, and H stretcher, wide oblong foot rest, old blue and red paint, Delaware Valley, c1800 . . . . **6,275.00**

Shaped Crest, medallion back, bamboo turned posts and H stretcher, old blue green paint, mid Atlantic, 1810–20 . . . . . . **1,200.00**

Rocker

Mixed woods, two arched slats, bird's eye maple dec, orig splint seat, old overpaint, PA, c1800 . . **700.00**

Oak

Mission style, three vertical arrow cut out slats, 17" w, 23" h **200.00**

Pressed back, leafy vine dec on rail, vase shaped splat, and shaped arms, turned posts, front legs, and front stretcher, leather seat, 21" w, 32" h, Stomps Burkhardt Co, Dayton, OH **250.00**

Settee, painted and dec, light green ground, green and yellow pinstriping, pink roses, 17½" h, 24¾" l **1,300.00**

Standing Cradle, tiger maple, mushroom finials, turned spindles and posts, removable side, shaped rockers, refinished, mid Atlantic, c1830 . . . . **1,500.00**

Youth Chair, oak, acorn finials, pressed back, turned spindles back and sides, rolled arms attached to seat, rect foot rest, turned legs and front stretcher, 42" h, PA **175.00**

CLOCKS

Shelf

Acorn, Forestville Mfg Co, Bristol, CT, laminated wood, lyre shaped sides, 8 day time and strike lyre fusee movements, pendulum, painted zinc dial, orig upper glass, painted green trim, 24½" h, c1847 . . . . **700.00**

Beehive

Chelsea, brass, porcelain dial, 5¼" h, c1900 . . . . **50.00**

New Haven, Guide, 1 day, strike, castle scene in glass **150.00**

Seth Thomas, inlaid mahogany case, 8 day brass time and strike

Clock, kitchen, shelf, Ingraham, Lion style, pressed oak case, 8–day movement, all orig, $350.00.

movement, quarter hour Sonora chimes, 14½" h **400.00**

Waterbury Clock Co, rosewood veneered case, 8 day time, strike, and alarm brass movement, 18¾" h, c1870 . . . . **75.00**

E N Welch, rosewood veneered case, 8 day time, strike, and alarm brass movement, 18½" h, c1875 . . . . **100.00**

Calendar, Welch Spring & Co, rosewood veneered case, 8 day time and strike, B B Lewis calendar movement, old replacement base, part of lower bezel missing, replaced glass, 19¼" h, c1870 . . . . **330.00**

Cottage

Ansonia, rosewood veneered case, 8 day time and strike brass movement, 18¼" h, c1870 . . . . **85.00**

Brewster & Ingraham, mahogany case, 30 hour time and strike movement, 13¾" h, 1845–50 **150.00**

J C Brown, rosewood veneered case, 8 day brass time and strike movement, 14¾" h, 1850–60 **400.00**

Gilbert & Co, rosewood veneered case, 8 day time and strike movement, orig glass and dial, 13½" h, c1890 . . . . **120.00**

S B Terry, mahogany case, 30 hour time and alarm ladder brass movement, 11" h, c1840 **175.00**

Seth Thomas, walnut veneered case, 30 hour time and strike movement, orig label, 9½" h . . . **225.00**

Unknown Maker

Mahogany Case, 30 hour time and alarm movement, 11½" h, c1880 . . . . **55.00**

Rosewood Veneered Case, mahogany sides, 30 hour time,

strike, and alarm movement, 12" h, c1870 . . . . **55.00**

Double Column

Sperry & Shaw, mahogany case, Union Clock Co 30 hour brass time and strike movement, minor flaking on dial, old replacement hands and glass, 26" h, c1840 . . . . **220.00**

Terry & Andrews, Empire, mahogany case, orig label and glass, 30 hour brass time and strike movement, 26½" h **200.00**

Empire, Seth Thomas, rosewood veneered case, 30 hour brass time and strike movement, orig label, minor veneer loss, refinished half columns, 25" h, c1850. . . . . . . **110.00**

Gingerbread

Ansonia, X–O.6, oak case, 8 day time, hour, and half hour strike, 22½" h **175.00**

Wm L Gilbert, Forest, oak case, tablet with bird and butterfly in marsh setting, 8 day strike, 24½" h **200.00**

F Kroeber Clock Co, Wanderer, walnut case, elaborate geometric tablet, 6" fancy dial, 8 day gong strike, 23" h **290.00**

New Haven Clock Co, pressed oak case, 8 day time, strike, and alarm movement, 24½" h, c1915 . . . . **70.00**

Seth Thomas, black walnut case, two finials flanking base, 8 day spring strike alarm, cathedral gong, 21½" h. **200.00**

Waterbury Clock Co, 8 day time, strike, and calendar brass movement, 22" h, c1880 . . . . **350.00**

Half Column

Boardman & Wells, veneered, boy fishing from boat, St Bernard sitting on pier glass illus, 30 hour wooden time and strike movement, Maine clock dealer label, 32" h, 1830–40 **110.00**

Forestville Mfg Co, mahogany veneer case, stencil dec, works stamped "W C Johnson," 8 day brass time and strike movement, 30" h, c1850. . . . . **325.00**

Silas Hoadley, foliage dec crest, 30 hour time and strike movement, ivory bushings, orig label, paint loss on lower glass door panel, 28" h, c1835 . . . . **495.00**

Eli Terry & Sons, carved columns, splat, and feet, 8 day wood time and strike movement, 37" h, c1825 . . . . **900.00**

Seth Thomas, mahogany case, dancing couple illus, 30 hour time and strike weight driven brass movement, replaced bottom table, missing part of label, 25" h, c1850 . . . . **110.00**

Half Pillar and Splat, L Byington, mahogany case, 30 hour time and strike weight driven wooden Groner movement, replaced hands and movement supports, 34¾" h, c1830 . . . . **110.00**

Kitchen, New Haven Clock Co, white painted case, 8 day time movement, 11¾" h, c1930. . . . . . **60.00**

Mantel

Birge, Mallory & Co, Bristol, CT, Empire, mahogany, enamel dial, eglomise panel with split balusters, surmounted carved eagle, c1825 . . . . **450.00**

William L Gilbert & Co, marbleized wood case, black, bell top, 8 day time and strike movement, 18½" h, c1903 . . . . **200.00**

New Haven Clock Co, tambour, mahogany case, 8 day time and strike movement, Westminster chimes, 8¾" h, c1920 . . . . . . **110.00**

Russell & Jones, marbleized wood, Tennessee marble columns, 5" dial, 8 day, 10" h . . . **125.00**

Sessions, tambour, mahogany case, 8 day time and strike movement, 10" h, c1930 . . . . **60.00**

A Stowell & Co, Boston, mahogany, rect case, arched top, engraved face, 8 day time and strike movement, Westminster chimes, key and pendulum, 18½" h, 12⅞" w **600.00**

Seth Thomas

Adamantine finish, 8 day time and strike brass movement, 9½" h, c1910. . . . . **45.00**

Rosewood Veneered Case, 8 day time, hour and half hour strike, lyre movement, refinished, replaced hands, 12½" h, c1880 . . . . **190.00**

Pillar and Scroll

Chelsea, miniature, reverse painted glass, 8 day time and strike balance wheel movement, made for Tiffany & Co, 24½" h, c1930. . . . . **715.00**

Ephraim Dohenes, Bristol, CT, Federal, carved mahogany, shaped crest, three brass urn finials above hinged glazed door, eglomise panel with houses and pond, tapering columns, bracket feet, 31 x 17½", c1830 . . . . **750.00**

Seth Thomas, miniature, scrolled crest, pillars, finials, 8 day time and strike movement, 17" h, c1920 . . . . **250.00**

Pillar and Splat

E Thayer, carved pillars and splat, 30 hour wood Groner movement, 35" h, c1830. . . . . **300.00**

Riley Whiting, carved pillars and splat, 30 hour wood time and strike movement, 34¾" h, c1830 **325.00**

Ship

Chelsea, brass, clock and Waterbury barometer with thermometer mounted on ftd rect base, 8 day time and ship's bells, door button latch missing, 7¼" h, 12¾" w, c1890 . . . . **275.00**

W A Fletcher Co, wall hanging, brass, 8 day time movement, second bit, 8½" d, 20th C **200.00**

Seth Thomas, brass, wall hanging, 8 day time and strike movement, outside bell, orig label, 6¼" d, late 19th C **575.00**

Unknown Maker, brass, wall hanging, 8 day time only balance wheel Swiss movement with second bit, repainted dial, 9¼" d, c1925 . . . . **85.00**

Waterbury Clock Co, nickel over brass, on platform, 8 day time and ship's bells, nameplate missing, 13½" h, c1890 . . . . . . **110.00**

Steeple

Birge & Fuller, 8 day time and strike wagon spring movement, 20" h, c1840 . . . . **1,000.00**

Chauncey Boardman, 30 hour fusee time and strike movement, refinished case, replaced door glass, 20" h, c1840. . . . . **100.00**

Brewster & Ingraham, Rosewood veneered case, frosted and cut door glass, 19¼" h, c1840 . . . . **350.00**

William L Gilbert, mahogany veneered case, painted glass with sailing ship, 8 day movement, restored dial, 19¾" h **250.00**

Daniel Pratt, rosewood veneered case, orig glass with St Louis Courthouse, 8 day time and strike movement, 19½" h, 1850–60 . . . . **250.00**

Tall Case

Bigelow Kennard & Co, Boston, mahogany case, carved hood, waist door, base panel, paw feet, 8 day English movement, striking Westminster, Whittington, and St Mi-

chael chimes on nest of eight bells, engraved brass dial, moon phase and seconds indicators inscribed by maker, three brass weights and pendulum, mother–of–pearl facing applied over wood, detached molding and carved feet, 101¼" h, 1920 . . . . . **3,300.00**

Philip Blazdill, Federal, cherry, inlaid, brass stop fluted columns, refinished, 91" h, dial signed "W Fitz, Portsmouth," partial paper label reads "clock case made by Philip Blazdill. . .Epping," Portsmouth, NH, c1800. . . . .**13,000.00**

A. Brown, Yorktown, PA, Chippendale case, walnut, broken arch hood ending in carved rosettes and turned finials, fluted quarter columns, raised base panel, and ogee bracket fee on lower case, painted iron dial inscribed by maker, moon phase, date indicators, 8 day time and strike movement, center sweep seconds hand, modern lead weights, period pendulum, replaced door hinges, pallet, and finial plinths, 94" h, c1790 . . . . **4,510.00**

Daniel Christ, Kutztown, PA, Chippendale, carved walnut, molded swan's neck crest hood, flowerhead carved terminals, three turned finials, arched glazed door, white painted dial with moon phases, minute and date registers, inscribed "Daniel Christ," fluted colonettes, waisted case with shaped door, fluted quarter columns, molded base with stylized leaf carved panel and fluted quarter columns, ogee bracket feet, 98¾" h, c1785 . . . . . **28,600.00**

Edward Duffield, Philadelphia, rect covered cornice and arched glazed molded door hood, brass dial with Roman and Arabic chapter rings, sweep second ring, calendar day aperture surmounted with an engraved disk marked "Edw Duffield, Philadelphia," spandrels embellished with cast eagles and urns, waisted case with arched thumb molded cupboard door, box base with bun feet, 88½" h, c1745 . . . . **9,350.00**

John Fessler, Fredericktown, MD, Federal inlaid walnut, molded swan's neck pediment hood, fan inlaid terminals, three urn finials, arched hinged door, white painted dial with moon phases, minute and date registers, inscribed "John Fessler Fredericktown," waisted case with hinged door, canted corners, paneled base with inlaid canted corners, splayed bracket feet, 99¾" h, c1810 . . . . **8,250.00**

Stephen Hassam, Charlestown, NH, Chippendale, cherry, hood with three reeded plinths, brass finials, arched molded cornice, glazed door, engraved brass dial inscribed "Stephen Hassam," 8 day brass weight driven movement, brass mounted reeded columns, tombstone molded door flanked by brass mounted reeded quarter columns, base with scrolled ogee bracket feet, old finish, c1780 . . . **5,000.00**

Silas Hoadley, Plymouth, CT, pine case, scrolled fret, three brass finials, glazed door, enameled wood dial inscribed by maker, seconds indicator, primitive scene in arch, turned hood columns, rect waist door, cut out bracket feet, 30 hour time and strike wood works movement, period tin can weights and pendulum bob, refinished, replaced finials, 90" h, 1830 . . . . . **1,750.00**

Wallace Nutting, case copied from John Goddard, Chippendale, mahogany, 8 day brass time and strike movement with moon phases, two block and shells, broken arch hood with three flame finials, carved rosettes, fluted hood column, fluted quarter column, blocks and shells on waist, door, and base panel **7,250.00**

Robert Peaslee, Boston, MA, Queen Anne, inlaid walnut, coffered bonnet hood over coved molding above paneled pediment, arched glazed door with cylindrical colonettes, molded capitals and bases, brass dial with Roman and Arabic chapter rings, sweep seconds ring and calendar day aperture, circular engraved convex disk inscribed "Rob. Peaslee, Boston," waisted line inlaid case with arched line inlaid box, line inlaid applied base molding, some repairs to case molding, 91½" h, 18" w, 9¾" deep, c1730–40 . . . . **9,900.00**

Rogers & Son, Berwick, MN, cherry, 8 day weight driven iron and brass movement, old refinish, 88½" h, late 18th C **2,000.00**

David Seip, Bucks County, PA, Chippendale style, birch, arched

hood with swan's neck and dentilated cornice, waisted case, fluted corner columns, French bracket feet, enamel dial with second hand, lunette dial, 96" h, 19th C **13,500.00**

S. Taber, New England, country Federal, grain painted, arched glazed door flanked by freestanding columns, flat top hood, waisted case with thumb molded door, molded base, short bracket feet, painted dial, 83" h, early 19th C **1,600.00**

Unknown Maker

Grain Painted, pine, tall case clock, 30 hour pull chain weight driven brass and wood movement, painted to resemble rosewood, painted wood dial, 85½" h **1,210.00**

Hepplewhite, pine, freestanding columns and high arched gooseneck hood, wood works and painted wood face, pewter hands, orig brown graining weights and pendulum, cut out feet, 82" h **1,550.00**

Pennsylvania, inlaid stars and initials "B–R," four turned columns and tapering moldings ending in carved rosettes on fully developed hood, shell carved door and turned quarter columns on lower case, ogee bracket feet and raised panel set into base, 8 day time and strike movement, center sweep seconds hand, moon phase indicator, orig lead weights and pendulum, center finial missing, replaced feet and attached molding, 90½" h, c1780 . . . . . **6,050.00**

New England, Federal, mahogany, Roxbury type hood with brass stop fluted colonettes, enamel dial with date ring, waisted case with arched door, brass stop fluted quarter columns, ogee bracket feet, 96" h, early 19th C **3,750.00**

Quarter Grained Oak, three finials, scrolled crest, two columns, 8 day weight driven time and strike movement, second bit, moon phase, replaced pendulum and weights, restoration on face of broken arch pediment, 97¾" h, c1900 . . . . **1,400.00**

Waltham Clock Co, Waltham, MA, mahogany case with cross banded veneers, three brass finials, glazed door, maker's name engraved on silver and gilt dial, seconds indicator, strike/silent lever, chime/silent lever, and chime selection lever, 8 day movement, hour strike, chimes on nine nickel plated tubes, pendulum, key, and three brass weights, cloth fabric replaced on pierced openings in sides of hood, case refinished, 103" h, 1920 . . . . **2,200.00**

Riley Whiting, grain painted, painted eagle with trophy in crest of wooden dial, signed, 84" h, 1820–30. . . . . **3,500.00**

Aaron Willard, Jr., Boston, Federal, inlaid mahogany, pierced fretwork crest on hood, three brass ball and steeple finials, arched glazed door, white painted dial, polychrome basket of fruit above inscription "Aaron Willard, Jun'r, Boston," minute and calendar date registers, waisted case with hinged molded door, fluted quarter columns with brass capitals, splayed bracket feet, 99½" h, c1810 . . . . **19,800.00**

Wall
Banjo
William Cummens, Boston, MA, cross banded mahogany frames, painted tablets, sea creatures pulling shell boat with driver, 8 day T bridge movement, old finish, orig brass finial, 34" h, c1810 . . . . **2,000.00**

Howard & Davis
#2 Size, fine grained case, 8 day weight driven time only movement, "Made for Riggs Philadelphia" marked on works, dial repainted, bottom board replaced, 43¾" h, c1860 . . . . **2,310.00**

#4 Size, fine grained case, 8 day time only weight driven brass movement, two replaced glue blocks, bottom board removed, 32" h, c1860   **440.00**

Levi Hutchins, Concord, NH, gold front, painted iron dial, 8 day time movement with T–bridge and step train, pendulum, 42" h, 1820 . . . . **800.00**

New Haven Clock Co
17¼" h, miniature, 8 day movement, cast eagle finial, replaced door glass, 1920s . . .   **65.00**

39" h, mahogany case, 8 day time and strike movement, replaced eagle finial, c1920   **165.00**

Plymouth Clock Co, Thomaston,

CT, mahogany, eagle finial, two glasses with Washington and Mount Vernon dec, painted dial, 8 day time and strike movement, chime rod, 29" h, 1930 . . . .   **120.00**

Tifft, mahogany case, 8 day time only movement, replaced glasses, 34" h, 1830–40 . . . . .   **770.00**

Unknown Maker
Baltimore, mahogany case, 8 day weight driven time only movement, Howard glasses, "W.H.C. Riggs/Philada" marked on dial, throat glass cracked, minor flaking on dial, 33½" h, c1870. . . . .   **2,640.00**

Boston, MA, gold stenciled frames, brass eagle finial, two painted tablets, painted iron dial, 8 day time movement with iron weight and pendulum, inscribed "Cleaned by E. Taber, Oct 4, 1836," J. J. Beals paper label, 35" h, c1820 . . . .   **2,700.00**

Howard type, #4 size, 8 day time only brass driven movement, sgd "J. Pousey," dial touched up, 32" h, c1860 . .   **990.00**

Calendar
Ansonia, drop octagon, rosewood veneer, gilt molding, 8 day strike, 24" h **300.00**

Seth Thomas, office, rosewood veneered case, 8 day time movement, calendar on bottom, 32½" h, c1875 . . . .   **1,600.00**

Figure 8
Howard, #8 size, black walnut case, 8 day weight driven brass time only movement, 44½" h . .   **4,400.00**

Ingraham Clock Co, rosewood case, 8 day time and strike movement, B B Lewis calendar, two labels, 30" h, 1870–80. . . .   **650.00**

Seth Thomas, regulator, cherry case, 8 day time only movement, refinished, orig dial, tablet, and label, 28¾" h, c1880 . .   **825.00**

Gallery
Brewster & Ingraham, round, 8 day east/west time movement, sgd orig wood dial, 13" d, c1840 . . . .   **400.00**

E Howard, electric, 21" d, c1925   **85.00**

Seth Thomas, round, mahogany finish case, 30 day time only movement, missing down fore pin, 27½" d, c1890 . . . .   **990.00**

Marine Lever, octagonal
D Pratt & Son, 30 hour time only movement with second bit, mi-

nor veneer damage, 8" d,
c1880 . . . .   **100.00**
Seth Thomas
    Mahogany case, 8 day double
    wind brass movement, 8¼" d,
    c1910 . . . .   **100.00**
    Oak veneered case, 15 day
    time only movement, two
    barrels, new paper dial, sec-
    ond hand missing, 8½" d,
    c1890 . . . .   **75.00**
    Waterbury, mahogany case, 8
    day time only movement with
    second bit, repaired bezel, bro-
    ken spring, 10¾" d, c1870 . . . .   **55.00**
Octagon, E N Welch, mahogany ve-
    neered case, 8 day time, strike
    balance wheel movement, orig la-
    bel, 12½" d, c1860 . . . .   **300.00**
Regulator
    Atkins Clock Co, short drop, ma-
    hogany veneered case, applied
    carving, 8 day time movement,
    25½" h, c1850. . . . .   **350.00**
    Boston Clock Co, painted cherry
    case, 8 day time movement,
    34" h, 1880–90 . . . .   **800.00**
    Gilbert, store box, birch case, 8
    day time and calendar spring
    driven movement, refinished,
    new paper dial, small piece
    broken from bottom, 34" h,
    c1920 . . . .   **275.00**
    E Howard & Co
    Model #13, 8 day weight
    driven time only movement,
    42" h, c1880 . . . .   **2,640.00**
    Model #58, store box, cherry
    case, 8 day time only weight
    driven movement, 39" h,
    c1880 . . . .   **1,925.00**
    Model #70, solid Circassian
    walnut facings, cherry side, 8
    day time only movement,

**Regulator, Seth Thomas, oak case, re-
stored and refinished, $750.00.**

script signature on face, re-
placed hands, 41½" h, c1880   **1,870.00**
Ingraham
    Dew Drop, walnut case, time
    and calendar movement,
    24" h, c1890 . . . .   **275.00**
    Ingot, miniature, oak case, time
    only movement, 19½" h,
    c1910 . . . .   **190.00**
Little & Eastman Co, Boston, MA,
    quarter grain oak case, sgd 8
    day time movement, 35¼" h,
    c1890 . . . .   **650.00**
Daniel Pratt & Sons, short drop,
    rosewood veneered case, 8 day
    time only movement, over label
    for Waterbury Clock Co, minor
    veneer damage, 21½" h, c1870   **220.00**
Sessions, store box, pressed oak
    case, 8 day time and calendar
    spring driven brass movement,
    top missing, replaced hands
    and pendulum rod, 35" h,
    c1915 . . . .   **275.00**
Seth Thomas
    Bank Model, long case, solid
    quarter grain oak case, 30
    day time only movement
    with second bit, small chip
    from side top molding, 68" h,
    c1900 . . . .   **1,100.00**
    Model #1, Extra, rosewood ve-
    neered case, 8 day double
    wind time and strike move-
    ment with second bit, sgd
    pendulum, tulip hands, orig
    label, minor veneer loss,
    black missing from door
    glass, 44" h, c1860 . . . .   **2,035.00**
    Model #2, quarter grain oak
    veneered case, 8 day weight
    driven time only movement
    with second bit, bottom
    molding missing, 36" h,
    c1890 . . . .   **825.00**
    Model #13, pressed oak case,
    calendar, 8 day weight
    driven time only movement
    with second bit, door refin-
    ished, crest missing, 48" h,
    c1875 . . . .   **875.00**
    Model #18, long drop, quarter
    grain oak veneered case, 8
    day weight driven time only
    movement with second bit,
    slight loss of veneer on bezel,
    54" h, c1875 . . . .   **1,320.00**
    Short Drop, solid walnut case,
    8 day time and strike move-
    ment, latch tab missing,
    17½" h, c1910 . . . .   **275.00**
Waltham Clock Co, Waterbury,
    CT, oak case, Regulator tablet,

painted zinc dial, 8 day time
and strike movement and half
hour strike, pendulum, 32" h,
1910 . . . .   375.00
Waterbury Clock Co, Regent long
drop, 8 day time only brass
movement, orig finish, full labels on back, professionally refinished dial, 31" h, c1905 . . .   385.00
E N Welch, ripple, rosewood
case, 8 day time only movement, J C Brown label, 25¼" h,
c1865 . . . .   650.00
Schoolhouse
Ingraham, pressed oak case, 8 day
time, strike, and calendar
movement, 18¾" h, c1900 . . . .   325.00
Jerome, mahogany and rosewood
case, octagon, 8 day, 12" dial,
c1850 . . . .   300.00
New Haven Clock Co, mahogany
veneered case, 8 day time only
movement, pendulum missing,
paint flaking on door, minor veneer damage, 24" h, c1870 . . .   225.00
Russell & Jones, walnut and oak
case, gilt glass, 8 day spring
movement, 12" d, 26" h, c1889   350.00
Sessions
Century model, short drop,
pressed oak case, 8 day time,
strike, and calendar movement, orig label, replaced
calendar hand, 26½" h,
c1900 . . . .   415.00
Regulator, pressed oak case, 8
day time only brass move-
ment, orig finish, professionally refinished dial and tab-
let, 27¼" h, c1910 . . . .   300.00
Seth Thomas
Long Drop, Globe model,
rosewood veneered case, 8
day time only movement,
orig label, 31½" h, c1875 . . .   715.00
Short Drop, rosewood case, 8
day time and strike move-
ment, minor veneer damage
and flaking of dial, 22" h,
c1875 . . . .   325.00
Waterbury, short dew drop, ma-
hogany veneered case, 8 day
time and calendar movement,
calendar gears missing, 24" h,
c1890 . . . .   220.00
E N Welch, #1 Drop Octagon
Calendar, short drop, rosewood
veneered case, 8 day time and
calendar spring driven movement, minor veneer loss,
24½" h, c1880. . . . .   275.00
Wag–On–The–Wall, sgd "Gabrie

Constant/A Orleans," brass and
iron case, 8 day time and strike
brass weight driven movement,
small repair on crest, 58" h,
c1860 . . . .   440.00
Wall Master, Standard Electric Time
Co, electric
Mercury Pendulum, pressed quarter grained oak case, 73" h,
c1915 . . . .   1,210.00
Nickel Pendulum, pressed quarter
grained oak case, 74" h, c1915   715.00
Simulated Mercury Pendulum,
mahogany case, 65" h, c1920   495.00
Watchman's, Howard Co, 8 day
weight driven time only movement, refinished case, traces of
old finish, 54" h, c1880 . . . .   880.00

CUPBOARDS

Chimney, pine
12" w, 10½" deep, 91" h, full length
overlapping door, seven mortised
shelves, wrought iron hinges and
slide bolt latch 2,250.00
14" w, 25½" deep, 64¾" h, dovetailed
case, cornice, paneled door,
open shelf, green wash repaint,
base recut 350.00
Corner
Butternut, beaded edge, paneled
doors, applied molding waist and
cornice, carved inscription "May
the 31, 1856, Made by Jo
Younker," 41" w, 79" h 1,200.00
Cherry
45" w, 25" deep, 86" h, dentil

**Cupboard, corner, pine, nine pane glass
door over single door base, 25" d, 38" l,
61" h, $1,850.00.**

molding, glazed upper section, pair of paneled cupboard doors, scalloped apron, refinished with strong traces of orig red paint, some orig glass, c1800 . . . . **4,200.00**

47" w, 86½" h, glazed, inlaid, molded cornice, two eight-paned doors, two paneled doors with inlaid star centers, refinished, early 19th C. **3,250.00**

50" w, 20" deep, 79" h, molded cornice above conforming case, pair of glazed doors, short drawer, two paneled cupboard doors, block feet. **1,300.00**

86½" h, one piece, cove molded cornice, one twelve-paned door, serpentine interior shelves, two paneled doors with molded stiles and rails, scalloped apron, bracket feet, old refinish. **4,000.00**

Cherry and mahogany, 2 pc, stepback, molded cornice, double eight-pane doors, three convex front doors, two paneled cupboard doors, turned feet, refinished, interior painted white, PA, c1830. . . . . **2,500.00**

Grain Painted
96" h, 53" w, pine, red and black graining, thumb molded cornice above stylized flowerhead carved dentil frieze, two arched paneled doors, red painted interior top, two doors on bottom with shelf interior, fluted columnar stiles, PA, 18th C. **6,600.00**

98½" h, 58½" w, molded cornice above arched double glazed cupboard doors, three shaped interior shelves, arched chip carved molding with center cartouche, doors flanked by molded pilasters, two molded edge panel doors, molded base, losses to glass, minor restoration **3,775.00**

Hanging
Cherry, carved potted tulip on molded flat panel door, molded cornice, carved ferns on case, spiral inset corner columns, reeding, scalloped apron, cut out feet, refinished, PA, c1815 . . . . **10,000.00**

Painted, orig tobacco brown and red-brown paint, wrought and "T" nails, cotter pin hinges, 41" h, Hudson Valley, NY, c18th C **350.00**

Tiger maple, recessed flat panel door, cornice and base molding, old finish, OH, c1820 . . . **3,750.00**

Walnut, raised panel door, molded cornice, old finish, restored H hinges, VA, c1780. . . **6,000.00**

Oak
29½" w, 17" deep, 37" h, carved, raised paneled door, shelf interior, shaped apron and feet . . . **900.00**

51" w, 18" deep, 85" h, cornice, two glass-paned doors, three interior shelves, one drawer over two split panel doors **1,300.00**

Pine and poplar
Blind door, 2 pc, stepback, molded cornice, two double paneled doors over two paneled doors, applied bracket feet, 25" w, orig paint, NJ, c1820 . . . . **5,000.00**

Cherry finish, 2 pc, top with single door of twelve panes of old glass, molded cornice, pr paneled cupboard doors, scalloped apron, bracket feet, traces of old paint, refinished, replaced hinges and door latches, minor edge damage, 42" w, 84½" h **4,500.00**

Decorated, dark green trim, red ground, light green interior, cove molded cornice with reeded frieze, twelve pane glass top door, picture frame molding, raised paneled bottom doors, bracket feet, 44" w, 88½" h **8,250.00**

Poplar, red paint, double cove molded cornice, one nine-paned door, dovetailed drawer, two paneled doors, cast iron latches, brass knobs, 75½" h **4,600.00**

Tiger maple, 2 pc, molded cornice, twelve-paned arcade door, spoon slotted shelves, two drawers, two reeded paneled doors, black turned feet, orig finish, PA, c1825 . . . . **21,000.00**

Walnut, dentil molding on well developed cornice, raised panel doors, beaded frames, applied corner molding, replaced bracket feet, old varnish finish, replaced hinges and hardware, 49" w, 90¼" h **4,000.00**

Yellow pine, dentil molding below 1 pc cornice, six-paned arcade double doors, paneled cupboard doors, applied bracket feet, traces of orig blue and cream paint, MD, c1810 . . . . **4,500.00**

Dutch Cupboard, pine, painted, dry sink base, 48″ w, 21½″ deep, 90″ h, $4,800.00.

Dutch
Butternut and cherry, 2 pc, wide molded cornice, six–paned double doors, two drawers in waist, turned quarter columns, raised panels in lower doors, applied bracket feet, refinished, Soap Hollow, PA, c1850 . . . . **3,800.00**
Cherry, 2 pc, molded cornice, six–paned double doors, scalloped opening, three overlapping drawers in waist, chamfered corners, split panel doors below, split paneled ends, turned feet, refinished, PA, c1830 . . . . **7,800.00**
Curly walnut, 2 pc, blind door, cornice, quarter paneled doors upper case, three overlapping drawers in waist, two paneled doors lower case, ogee feet, refinished, c1800 . . . . **11,000.00**
Maple and cherry, 2 pc, molded cornice, six–paned double doors, two beveled candle drawers, three beveled drawers in waist, split panel doors below, turned feet, refinished, PA, c1840 . . . . . **4,400.00**
Pine and poplar
Four spice drawers in upper case, 2 pc, molded cornice, six–paned double doors, three drawers in waist, raised panel doors, turned feet, refinished, PA, c1830 . . . . **4,500.00**
Six–paned double doors, 2 pc, wide molded cornice, three drawers in waist, two paneled doors, turned feet, old red var-

nish, left rear foot missing, PA, c1830 . . . . **4,200.00**
Nine–paned single door, 2 pc, molded cornice, two drawers in waist, paneled lower doors, turned feet, 42″ w, old red finish, interior painted white, PA, c1835 . . . . **4,200.00**
Poplar
Blind door, 2 pc, molded cornice, double raised panel upper doors, one small drawer flanked by two drawers in waist, raised panel lower doors, missing feet, late grain paint, PA, c1800 . . . . **7,500.00**
Three–paned double doors, 2 pc, cornice, two drawers in waist, two paneled doors below, wooden pulls, cut out feet, overpainted, PA, c1840 . . . . . **2,000.00**
Tiger maple and walnut, 2 pc, molded cornice, eight–paned double doors with one column of four narrow panes beside one column of four wider panes, three overlapping drawers in waist, two paneled doors below, bracket feet, refinished, PA, c1830 . . . . . **8,000.00**
Walnut
Single blind door, 2 pc, molded cornice, tall pie shelf, three overlapping drawers in waist, diamond facet paneled doors below, turned feet, overpainted white, feet removed, OH, c1820 . . . . **8,000.00**
Two double raised panel doors upper case, 2 pc, cornice, three overlapping drawers in waist, raised panel doors lower case, shaped apron, cut out feet, VA, c1815 . . . . **12,000.00**
Hanging
Cherry
1 Door, raised panel, cornice, four spice drawers inside, H hinges, refinished, c1820 . . . . **4,000.00**
2 doors, paneled, painted shelves, 25″ w, 11″ deep, 26″ h, mid 19th C **450.00**
Pine, worn orig blue paint, raised panel door, bat wing brass, beaded frame, perimeter molding, interior shelf dated "1835," 23″ w, 8¼″ deep, 25″ h **600.00**
Pine and poplar, orig rosewood graining, paneled doors, step back shelves, 34½″ w, 33″ h **200.00**
Poplar, one door over one drawer, scalloped lower shelf, orig red

paint, forged hinges, 20" w, PA, c1790 . . . . **7,150.00**

Walnut

Flush panel door, base and cornice molding, reeded stiles, relief carved star flower designs, stamped sunbursts, relief carved design on door, shelf and two dovetailed drawers interior, worn finish, 25" w, 34¾" h **525.00**

Four-pane door, dentil section on large cornice, molded pilasters and base, old finish, rat tail hinges, 28" w, PA, c1780 . . . . **8,500.00**

Jelly

Cherry and poplar, paneled ends and doors, applied molding, one dovetailed drawer, square tapered feet, refinished, 37¾" w, 50½" h . . **875.00**

Pine, gallery top, two doors, four shelves, orig red paint, 15" w, 33" deep, 57½" h, c1850 . . . . **750.00**

Pine and poplar

Grain painted, red flame graining, dovetailed drawer, two paneled doors, cut out feet, 36¼" w, 45" h **1,000.00**

Open bucket bench bottom, molded cornice, dovetailed case, two double paneled doors, cut out tapered legs, orig red paint, PA, c1830 . . . . **5,000.00**

Painted, two shallow raised panel doors, cut out feet, old green paint, PA, c1820 . . . . **1,100.00**

Single door

34" w, dovetailed case, paneled door, applied bracket feet, old reddish brown finish, PA, c1820 . . . **1,800.00**

38" w, dovetailed case, raised panel door, cornice and base molding, applied bracket feet, refinished, PA, c1830 **1,500.00**

Two drawers over two paneled doors, scalloped dovetailed gallery, paneled ends, tapered cut out feet, old varnish, wooden pulls, VA, c1840 . . . . **550.00**

Poplar, two overhanging drawers, two paneled doors, shaped skirt, red and black graining, orig hardware, 41½" w, 21½" deep, 46" h **650.00**

Walnut, dovetailed gallery, two beveled drawers, two paneled doors, paneled ends, cut out feet, refinished, wooden pulls, mid Atlantic, c1830 . . . . **1,200.00**

Yellow pine

1 Door, flat panel door, scalloped apron, cut out feet, old finish,

Jelly Cupboard, shaped gallery, two drawers over two doors, orig hardware, $850.00.

worm damage inside, VA, c1820 . . . . **850.00**

2 Doors, double flat paneled doors, paneled ends, tapered legs, overpainted, VA, c1840 **1,000.00**

Linen Press

Cherry

Bull's eye molding front and sides, 2 pc, stepback, reeded pilasters top and bottom, two paneled doors, three graduated drawers, overhanging top drawer, paneled ends, turned feet, 38" w, refinished, mid Atlantic, c1840 . . . . **4,000.00**

Dentil detail below wide cornice, 2 pc, stepback, line and fan inlay on two paneled doors, molded waist, line inlay on four graduated drawers in base, chamfered fluted corners top and bottom, ogee feet, refinished, New England, c1790 . . . **24,000.00**

Inlaid band below cornice, 2 pc, two paneled doors, four graduated drawers, beaded shaped apron, French feet, refinished, orig brass eagle pulls, mid Atlantic, c1800 . . . . **5,000.00**

Pine

34¾" w, 20" deep, 77" h, projecting fret carved and dentil molded cornice, arcaded raised panel doors, shelf interior, three short and one long drawer, bracket feet, stained, orig brasses **1,800.00**

46½" w, 20½" deep, 78½" h, projecting molded cornice, raised paneled doors, shelf interior, three graduated drawers, scrolled bracket feet, stained, PA **2,600.00**

Pine and Walnut, dovetailed case, paneled doors, base and cornice molding, two dovetailed drawers in bottom interior, turned feet, orig paint with red wash, 42" w, 75" h **900.00**

Tiger maple, 2 pc, stepback, large fretwork cornice, tombstone flat panels in doors, chamfered reeded corners, H hinges, six drawers, three over two over one long drawer, applied bracket feet, old finish, mid Atlantic, c1800 .. **24,000.00**

Walnut

2 paneled doors, 2 pc, molded and dentil cornice, lower section with three graduated thumb molded long drawers, molded base, bracket feet, 50" w, 20" deep, 78" h, late 18th C **3,200.00**

4 paneled doors, 2 pc, stepback, two drawers in base, shaped apron, tall French feet, old finish, VA, c1810 .... **8,500.00**

4 quarter paneled raised panel doors, dentil section on large cornice and waist molding, raised panel ends upper case, split raised panel ends lower case, turned feet, old finish, mid Atlantic, c1825 .... **10,000.00**

Pewter Cupboard, pine, open, one piece

Painted, board and batten door, wrought iron H hinges, blue repaint over traces of earlier red, feet worn down, old replaced hinges, 37$\frac{3}{4}$" w, 14$\frac{1}{4}$" deep, 59$\frac{1}{2}$" h **1,700.00**

Refinished, bent back, scalloped opening, two doors in base, 48$\frac{3}{4}$" w, 82$\frac{1}{2}$" h, c1900 .. **700.00**

Traces of old reddish brown finish, simple cornice, board and batten door, wide one board ends, slightly truncated top with three shelves, minor edge wear, feet shortened, 37$\frac{1}{2}$" w, 22$\frac{1}{2}$" deep, 81" h **1,200.00**

Schrank, walnut

Large blocked cornice with dentil section, fluted pilasters, tombstone raised panels in doors and ends, two overlapping and three hidden drawers in base, hidden drawers disguised as pilasters, ogee feet, H hinges, refinished, MD, c1780 .... **40,000.00**

Large stepped cornice, two double raised panel doors between double side panels, molded stiles, two overlapping drawers between dia-

mond moldings below, applied bracket feet, refinished, repairs to drawers and base, mid Atlantic, c1800 .... **14,000.00**

Stepback

Oak, 2 pc

39" w, 20" deep, 82" h, molded cornice, two single–paned doors, two over one drawers, two paneled cupboard doors, scalloped apron, brass pulls .. **800.00**

40" w, 19" deep, 74" h, molded cornice, two single–paned doors, scribe lines on stiles and cupboard doors, two overlapping drawers in top, two drawers in base, two paneled cupboard doors, split panel ends **750.00**

47" w, 24" deep, 85" h, applied dec and roll on cornice, two single–paned doors, two interior shelves, and two drawers in top, scribe lines on stiles and long overhanging drawer and two split panel doors in base, shaped apron, paneled ends .. **950.00**

Pine, molded cornice, paneled doors, beaded edges on two dovetailed drawers, bracket feet, brass thumb latches, mellow refinishing **1,600.00**

Pine and poplar, six–paned double doors upper case, 2 pc, molded cornice, two overhanging drawers in waist, paneled doors lower case, reeding in stiles, drawers, and doors, applied half columns in lower case, turned feet, refinished, NJ, c1830 .... **8,500.00**

Poplar, blind door, 2 pc, molded cornice, double raised panel upper doors, molded waist, one small between two longer overlapping drawers in waist, two raised panel doors below, late grain paint, missing feet and part of cornice, PA, c1800 .... **7,500.00**

Walnut

2–Pane center panel flanked by 4–pane double doors above two paneled door blind mid–section, molded waist, two paneled doors in base, cut out feet, refinished, c1850 ...... **3,200.00**

6–Pane double doors, 2 pc, beaded molding on two drawers in waist, two paneled doors in base, turned legs, old finish, VA, c1835 .... **2,500.00**

8–Pane double doors, 2 pc, wide cornice, two overhanging drawers in waist, applied turned half columns and split paneled doors on base, paneled ends, turned feet, 96" h, CA, c1835 . . . . **2,600.00**

12–Pane old glass double doors, 2 pc, wide molded cornice, dovetailed cases, spoon cut outs, pie shelf with curved molding, corner columns, three dovetailed overlapping drawers in waist, four small center dovetailed overlapping drawers in base, two double paneled doors, walnut and poplar secondary wood, dovetailed bracket feet, H hinges, old finish, replaced brass hardware, renailed back boards, 66¾" w at cornice, 95" h **4,100.00**

Blind door, 2 pc, dentil section below cornice and waist molding, four paneled doors, cut out feet, refinished, 38" w, MD, c1835 . . . . **2,800.00**

Wall
Cherry, poplar secondary wood, molded cornice, two eight–paned top doors, two dovetailed drawers, raised panel doors, simple cut out feet, orig finish, later brass pulls, minor repairs, 48" w, 13¼" deep, 84" h **3,500.00**

Oak
37" w, 15" deep, 83" h, applied dec on cornice, two single–paned doors, two interior shelves, two overlapping drawers over two paneled cupboard doors, split panel ends, shaped apron **900.00**

38" w, 16" deep, 72" h, two single–paned doors, two overlapping drawers, two split panel cupboard doors, split panel ends, shaped apron **700.00**

Pine
36½" h, beaded frame, board and batten door, reset H hinges, old red finish **550.00**

54" h, two double vertical paneled doors, orig hardware and red paint, NY, early 19th C **1,000.00**

66" h, breadboard end doors, picture frame molding, bootjack ends, five shelves, wooden knobs, brass locks, orig graining, NY, c19th C **850.00**

Poplar
52" w, 18" deep, 82¼" h, 2 pc, molded cornice, glass panes in double doors, two dovetailed drawers, paneled doors, simple

cut out feet, beaded trim, old red paint, originally a 1 pc cupboard **1,250.00**

53" w, 18½" deep, 85½" h, closed face, pair of cupboard doors with arched panels, four small drawers over two drawers, paneled lower cupboard doors flanked by turned columns, refinished with traces of orig paint, two drawer pulls missing, replaced hinges and glass, PA, 19th C **2,300.00**

55¼" w, 85" h, 2 pc, cove molded cornice, pie shelf, dovetailed drawers, paneled doors, scrolled base, cast iron latches, refinished **2,600.00**

90" h, 2 pc, wide molded cornice, six–pane wavy glass double doors over three dovetailed overlapping drawers and two paneled doors, pie shelf, chamfered corners, dovetailed bracket feet, turned knobs, old red finish **4,500.00**

Walnut
1 Pc, cornice, eight–paned double doors, two paneled doors, applied scalloped bracket feet, orig finish, part of cornice and one foot missing, VA, c1820 **3,500.00**

2 Pc, molded cornice, eight–paned double doors over two dovetailed drawers and paneled doors, old red repaint, 49¾" w, 22¼" deep, 88" h **1,100.00**

DESKS

Bookcase Combination
Cherry, two paneled bookcase doors, four graduated drawers, refinished, replaced brasses, 36¼" w, 73¼" h, CT, late 18th C **2,500.00**

Cherry and tiger maple, cornice, two eight–paned double doors on bookcase, four small drawers in top, two drawers in base, turned legs, matching stripe in drawer fronts, refinished, PA, c1830. . . . **2,800.00**

Curly and bird's eye maple, large cornice, fold down writing board, two drawers in upper case, one large flanked by two small drawers in bottom, turned legs, refinished, wooden pulls, mid Atlantic, c1830 . . . . **2,200.00**

Oak
38" w, 12" deep, 69" h, quarter sawn, applied dec on crest, single glass–paned door and four

Bookcase Desk, pine, two doors with replaced glass, four int. shelves, single center drawer, eight small drawers, brass hardware, c1860, 24¼" d, 45¼" l, 87" h, $1,875.00.

interior shelves in bookcase, shaped beveled glass mirror above drop lid, one swell drawer over two flat drawers, paw feet. **1,000.00**

39" w, 12" deep, 71" h, applied dec on shaped gallery and drop lid, leaded glass panel in bookcase door, fretwork design above desk, scalloped aprons, cut out feet. **725.00**

54" w, 13" deep, 74" h, quarter sawn, double bookcase, convex glass doors, applied dec on crest and drop lid, shaped beveled mirror, one swell drawer over two flat drawers. **875.00**

Walnut, molded cornice, twelve–paned door, one drawer in base, turned legs, refinished, wooden pulls, MD, c1835. . . . .   **1,800.00**

Box

Grain painted, pine, hinged slope lid, three compartments above three drawers, imperfections, 15½" l, 11" deep, 7¾" h, New England, early 19th C **750.00**

Pine

20" h, 28" w, mortise and tenon and dovetailed construction, handwrought nails, pigeonhole interior, orig tobacco brown finish, Hudson Valley, NY, c18th C. **500.00**

20¾" h, 28" w, 17" deep, slant top lift lid, applied edge molding, three drawers, turned bulbous

feet, replaced lid and feet, restored molding. **200.00**

Poplar, dovetailed case, slant top lid, scrolled gallery, old dark finish over earlier red, edge damage, holes and deterioration in bottom board, 24¾" w, 15¼" deep, 10½" h   **90.00**

Butler's, walnut, inlay, fitted interior, three dovetailed drawers, scalloped apron, straight feet, repairs, 43" w, 42" h **1,500.00**

Clerk's, pine, slant top lift lid, eleven pigeonholes in fitted interior, dovetailed drawer, tall square tapered legs, layers of old blue and gray paint, damage to top and edge molding, added interior iron brace, 30½" w, 24½" deep, 55" h **450.00**

Cylinder, incised dec on shaped gallery, drawer, and door, fitted interior, leather covering on pull out writing surface, long overhanging drawer over two drawers and lower door, fluted stiles and apron, brass hardware, 32" w, 22" deep, 49" h   **1,500.00**

Decorated, thin washed red and brown finish, cobalt blue dec, stylized flowers and date "1817" on upper crest, "My Country and My Glory" on face, initials "J" and "G" on uprights, stars, pinwheels, swags, and pendants of flowers, three drawers inside and outside, 34½" w, 48" h, PA **3,500.00**

Fall Front, oak

29" w, 18" deep, 44" h, two concave top drawers, applied dec to front legs, shaped lower drawer   **425.00**

38" w, 23" deep, 52" h, scribed lines on lid and drawer front, paneled ends, table base, turned legs **700.00**

Cylinder Desk, Eastlake, lady's type, cylinder top, fitted interior, $800.00.

Lady's

Oak, open baluster gallery flanking shaped crest, applied dec, fall front, single drawer, shaped mid shelf, French legs, 26" w, 14" deep, 50" h **350.00**

Pine, lift top lid, plain back rail, dovetailed body, interior compartments, ¾" molding around lid, molding on apron, square tapered legs, orig red paint, 33" h, c1790 **1,500.00**

Parlor, quarter sawn oak, fall front

29" w, 15" deep, 57" h, straight crest, two small glass–paned doors over fall front desk, one long drawer over two paneled lower doors, scrolled feet **650.00**

32" w, 16" deep, 47" h, one long drawer over two drawers and small door, bootjack ends **525.00**

Plantation, oak and bird's eye maple, cornice, bird's eye maple panels on 2 blind bookcase doors, slanted hinged lift lid writing surface, drawer, turned legs, 36" w, 27" deep, 72" h, KY **750.00**

Roll Top, kneehole, S curve tambour sliding door, fitted interior, two sets of four graduated drawers, single center drawer, paneled ends, "Rowlett Desk Manufacturing Co., Richmond, Ind." inscribed on metal tag, 54" w, 30" deep, 48" h **1,725.00**

School Master's

Oak, slanting lift lid, overhanging top, paneled door storage space in front, shaped top and foot braces, 38" w, 20" deep, 41" h **425.00**

Pine, lift top, tapered legs, refinished, replaced hinges, 19th C . . **250.00**

Walnut, two pc, dovetailed removable desk has slant top lid and two interior dovetailed drawers, base has square tapered legs and one dovetailed drawer, refinished, 44½" h **400.00**

Slant Front

Birch, wavy, divided pigeonholes and two tiers of four drawers in fitted interior, four long drawers, orig brasses, old refinish, interior blocks and casters added, 29" w, 18⅜" deep, 44¼" h **3,000.00**

Cherry, 38" w, 19" deep, 42½" h, slant front, dovetailed case and four drawers, beaded frame, fitted interior, bracket feet **3,400.00**

Curly maple, rect top, four overlapping graduated drawers, molded edge lid, stepped arrangement fitted interior with seven dovetailed drawers, pigeonholes,

and center door, ogee feet, old finish, replaced brasses, minor damage, 36" w, 18" deep, 41⅜" h **10,000.00**

Mahogany, slant front, nine interior drawers, four pigeonholes, two small drawers over three graduated drawers, refinished, orig brasses, 41¾" w, 44¼" h, MA, 18th C **4,750.00**

Standing

Cherry, dovetailed gallery, hinged lift lid, slide out writing board, four nailed interior drawers, old finish, porcelain pulls on slide, PA, c1830 . . . . **750.00**

Decorated, poplar and pine, salmon dec, hinged lift lid, one drawer below case, block and turned legs, H stretcher, PA, c1810 . . . . **2,400.00**

Pine and poplar

Fold down top, pull out supports, six inside drawers, turned legs, overpainted, mid Atlantic, c1830 . . . . **500.00**

Hinged lift lid, square tapering legs, old varnish, PA, c1840 . . **350.00**

Poplar, plain gallery, hinged lift lid, turned legs, orig brown and gold dec, CT, c1830 . . . . **450.00**

Tiger maple, hinged lift lid, two overlapping drawers below case, three interior drawers, turned legs, old finish, PA, c1830 . . . . . **2,100.00**

Walnut, straight gallery, hinged lift lid, two interior drawers, turned legs, refinished, MD, c1830 . . . . **650.00**

Yellow Pine, hinged lift lid, one interior drawer

Block and turned legs, H stretcher, one overlapping drawer below case, wooden pulls, old varnish, Delaware Valley, c1780 . . . . **1,100.00**

Square tapering legs, overpainted, VA, c1840 . . . . **600.00**

DOUGH BOXES

Pine

23" l, 8½" h, slanting sides, inchworm carved handles, 19th C . . . **350.00**

41⅝" l, 22½" w, 26½" h, slanted sides, turned legs, orig dark brown paint under white overpaint, c1875 . . . **375.00**

Poplar, overhanging lid, dovetailed case, turned legs on base, refinished, PA, 1830–40 . . . . **450.00**

Yellow Pine, dovetailed case, strap handles, sawbuck base, mortised stretcher, traces of orig blue paint through overpaint, top handle missing, VA, 1830–40 . . . . **850.00**

DRY SINKS

Butternut, two doors, one interior shelf, orig stippling and finish, 42" w, 20" deep, 35" h **500.00**

Cherry, 2 pc, two paneled doors on top, rect sink over two paneled base doors, 46" w, 23½" deep, 77" h **1,000.00**

Curly Maple, rect well, work surface to right with short drawer, two poplar wood cupboard doors, short bracket feet, hardwood edge strips, refinished, minor repairs, 55" w, 34½" h   **2,200.00**

Decorated, salmon paint dec, pine and poplar, two small drawers flanking shelf in high back, two paneled doors in base, cut out feet, orig paint, PA, c1850 . . . .   **4,000.00**

Grain Painted

Brown graining, pine and poplar, cornice, two raised panel doors in cupboard top, paneled back board, shaped ends, three graduated overlapping drawers beside two raised panel doors in base, cut out feet, orig paint, PA, c1850   **2,800.00**

Oak graining, cupboard top with two paneled doors, hood opening over dry sink, base with four graduated drawers and two cupboard doors, cast iron hardware, 54" w, 21¼" d, 78" h, mid 19th C **1,400.00**

Yellow graining, pine and poplar, scalloped splash back, overhanging top, and three drawers in high back, raised panel doors in base, cut out feet, orig paint, PA, c1860 . . . .   **1,800.00**

Pine

45" w, 22" deep, 29" h, shallow well top over recessed pair of paneled cupboard doors, bracket feet, 19th C **950.00**

51" w, 20" deep, 46" h, shelf top, zinc lined well, double paneled doors flanked by two small drawers, IL **525.00**

54" w, 17½" deep, 30" h, crest, paneled doors, one drawer **450.00**

Pine and Poplar

34" w, oak graining, hinged lift top, one side drawer, two paneled doors, cut out feet, PA, c1850 . . .   **750.00**

49" w, 21½" deep, 33" h, vertical seam in backboard crest, lift lid cover on well, one dovetailed drawer, paneled doors, old mustard yellow graining, orig cast iron latches **1,150.00**

52" w, 22½" deep, 50⅜" h, shelf back with two small drawers, pair of base cupboard doors, refinished,

minor restoration, attributed to PA, c1825 . . . .   **850.00**

62½" w, 19¾" deep, 34" h, crest, paneled doors, one small nailed drawer, refinished **900.00**

Double lift top, two paneled doors, cut out feet, old brown paint, PA, c1850 . . . .   **1,100.00**

Poplar

33" w, 18½" deep, 26" h, crest, swing–out shelf attached to off center door, simple cut out feet, stripped finish, orig cast iron thumb latch **350.00**

42" w, 19¾" deep, 34" h, paneled doors, one small drawer, simple cut out feet, worn layers of old green paint, porcelain pull, plugged hole in side **550.00**

48" w, 19¾" deep, 48¾" h, shelf top, paneled doors, dovetailed drawer, cut out sides, simple cut out feet, old worn refinishing . . .   **1,125.00**

Wainscot Sides, peaked splash back, single center door, orig hardware, 45" w, 18" deep, 32" h, IN **325.00**

Walnut and Poplar, two paneled doors, one drawer, old finish, dark green paint on interior of hutch top, orig cast iron latches with brass knobs, bottom end damage on feet, 52" w, 18½" deep, 49" h **800.00**

HUNTBOARDS

Walnut, three drawers, square tapering legs, refinished, 48" l, VA, 1810–20 . . . .   **14,000.00**

Yellow Pine

2 Drawers, recessed panel on small center drawer, square tapering legs, refinished, Southern, 1820–30 . . . .   **3,500.00**

6 Drawers, scalloped backboard, two rows of three drawers, square tapering legs, refinished, wooden pulls, warped and broken rear leg, Southern, c1820 . . . .   **3,750.00**

ICE BOXES

1 Door, oak, split raised panel, paneled ends, "Victor, Challenge Refrigerator Co., Grand Haven, Mich. U.S.A." inscribed on metal tag, zinc lined, orig hardware, 22" w, 15" deep, 40" h **500.00**

2 Doors, oak, applied dec on paneled doors, paneled ends, bracket feet, "North Pole" inscribed on metal tag, zinc lined, orig hardware, 25" w, 19" deep, 55" h **475.00**

3 Doors, paneled doors and ends, zinc lined, orig hardware, 35" w, 18" deep, 39" h **425.00**

MINIATURES

Blanket Chest

$8\frac{1}{4}$" l, poplar, six board, cut out feet, wire staple hinges and till, orig white paint, smoked graining . . . **2,175.00**

$9\frac{1}{2}$" l, Lehneware, pine, turned feet, old red paint, green and white striping, painted floral vines, floral transfer designs, woman's portrait, alligatored surface **1,100.00**

10" l, pine, six board, till, wire hinges, old red paint. **475.00**

$15\frac{1}{4}$" l, poplar, applied lid edge molding, bracket feet, old red stain **375.00**

$18\frac{1}{4}$" l, pine, applied lid and base molding, old leather hinges, orig reddish brown vinegar graining **3,350.00**

$18\frac{3}{4}$" l, pine, dovetailed, lid and base edge moldings, turned feet, wrought iron strap hinges, bear trap lock with key. **650.00**

$24\frac{1}{2}$" l, $11\frac{1}{2}$" deep, 13" h, poplar, orange graining, molded edge lid, brass escutcheon, dovetailed, bracket feet **900.00**

25" l, 13" deep, $17\frac{1}{4}$" h, pine, dovetailed, lid and base edge molding, turned feet, orig polychrome painted stylized tulips, floral designs, and initials and date "1844" on front panel, orig red finish, Somerset County, PA **5,200.00**

Chest of Drawers, $13\frac{1}{2}$" h, $10\frac{1}{2}$" w, $5\frac{3}{4}$" deep, pine, one small drawer over two bottom drawers, turned feet, orig red and black graining. **600.00**

Table

Parlor, quarter and plain cut oak, salesman's sample

Miniature, Windsor chair, yellow ground, black lines, red flowers, green leaves, $9\frac{1}{2}$" h, $95.00.

Round Top, chamfered top edge, turned legs, mid shelf, golden finish, $14\frac{3}{4}$" d, $18\frac{1}{2}$" h, 19th C **175.00**

Square Top, molded apron, splayed base, ball and vase turned legs, mid shelf, ball feet, 16" sq top, 18" h **250.00**

Tilt Top, poplar, 8" d, $8\frac{1}{2}$" h, tripod base, spider legs, turned column, round top, old red paint **875.00**

PIE SAFES

Butternut and Poplar, six tin panels, two doors, three panels each door, star and circle design, two overlapping drawers below, scalloped apron, cut out feet, overpainted, wooden drawer pulls, OH, c1850 **1,800.00**

Oak, four tin panels on door fronts, circle and diamond design, two doors over long dovetailed drawer, two interior shelves, 33" w, 15" deep, 49" h **625.00**

Painted, three tin panels, pierced rooster design in front hinged door, pierced hex signs in side panels, corners form feet, painted white, 30" w, $19\frac{3}{4}$" deep, $33\frac{1}{4}$" h **2,310.00**

Pine and Poplar

2 large tin panels, 2 small tin panels, two drawers over two doors, large tins in doors, small tins in ends, potted flower design, turned feet, late red wash, VA, c1835 . . . . . . **1,750.00**

4 tin panels, punched star in circle design, one drawer above two doors, panels in doors, paneled ends, square tapering legs, old brown finish, VA, c1840 . . . . . . **900.00**

6 tin panels, gallery, two doors, three panels each door, paneled ends, two paneled cupboard doors below, cut out feet, old finish, VA, c1840. . . . . **1,700.00**

8 tin panels, dovetailed gallery, two doors, punched arc designs, tall square tapering legs, overpainted, mid Atlantic, c1850 . . . . **1,000.00**

12 tin panels, two overhanging drawers over two doors, punched tulips in flower pot designs, initials "RK" on pots, paneled ends, turned feet, overpainted, front foot repaired, VA, c1840 . . . . . . **1,200.00**

13 tin panels, single door, row of three panels in door flanked by two rows of three panels, two panels each end, star design, square legs, brown finish, PA, c1835 . . . . **5,500.00**

Hanging, four tin panel sides, punched diamond and floral design, single door, refinished, PA, c1835 . . . .   **1,400.00**

Tin, three tin panels, rect molded top, hinged door pierced with animals and figures designs, sides pierced with animals and hearts designs, side inscribed "Centennial Safe G H Read 1876," old restoration to back of top, 31" w, 25½" deep, 35" h **1,650.00**

Walnut

3 tin panels, double doors punched star, circle, and heart designs, two dovetailed drawers, cut out feet, refinished, 42¾" w, 48½" h **850.00**

12 tin panels, dovetailed gallery, two doors, turned legs, refinished, VA, c1850 . . . .   **1,000.00**

24 tin panels, two doors, six panels each door and end, large pinwheel and floral design, tall turned feet, overpainted, VA, c1835 . . . .   **2,000.00**

Walnut and Cherry, twelve tin panels, dovetailed gallery, two drawers above two doors, six panels each door, three panels each side, star in circle design, square tapering legs, refinished, VA, c1850 . . . .   **1,800.00**

ROCKERS

Arrow Back

Ink graining, scrolled arms, widely splayed back **200.00**

Painted and decorated, old black paint, gold stenciled dec, unpainted arms, 33¾" h, New England, c1830 . . . .   **200.00**

Boston, grain painted, gilt stencil dec, scenic dec crest, rosewood grained seat, mid 19th C **500.00**

Decorated

Plank seat, red flowers on crest rail, arrow form uprights, shaped arms, turned legs, light green ground, attributed to NY state, c1825 . . . .   **2,100.00**

Writing arm, worn orig red and black paint, white striping, black stenciled detail, damaged woven splint seat, wear and minor age cracks in writing arm **200.00**

Grain Painted, rosewood grained, olive green stenciled crest, thumb back, yellow striping, 15¼" h seat, 32¼" h, New England, c1830 . . . . .   **350.00**

Ladder Back

Arm

Primitive, oak, four shaped slats, crossrails flanking bottom slat,

Rocker, slat back, mixed woods, replaced basketweave seat, $175.00.

rod rails connecting back stiles to front posts, wide arm rest supported by projecting turned spindles, woven splint seat, cheese cutter rockers, black stain, 19½" w, 20" deep, 42" h   **300.00**

Rabbit ear back posts, turned arms and posts, four slats, paper rush seat, refinished **85.00**

Turned finials, turned and chip carved bulbous back and arm supports, four wide step down slats, scrolled arms, turned upper stretcher, worn black repaint over orig blue, replaced woven splint seat, Belmont County, 47" h overall **350.00**

Side, turned finials, four slats, turned front stretchers, cheese cutter rockers, old green repaint over earlier red, replaced paper rush seat, 39" h **35.00**

Nursing, oak, buttons on pressed back, turned groove and ball finials, nine rods, hip rails, cane seat, turned legs, 20" w, 28½" deep, 42" h **275.00**

Pressed Back, oak

Double pressed back, six turned spindles, cane seat, hip rails, turned front legs and stretchers, 40" h **185.00**

Single pressed back, shaped headpiece, seven arrow splats, four turned spindle arm supports each side, rolled under arms fastened to plank seat, turned legs and front stretchers, 21½" w, 19½" deep, 40" h, PA **400.00**

Triple pressed back, shaped rails, seven turned spindles, turned spindles below sloping arms, cane seat, turned arm supports

Rocker, Windsor, fan back, bamboo style, old black repaint, 29½" h, 22½" w, $425.00.

and front legs and stretchers, shaped apron, 43" h **500.00**

Pressed and Carved Back, oak, leafy design, turned finials, fluted posts, upholstered seat, turned and fluted front legs and H stretcher, 37" h . . . **225.00**

Spindle Back, oak and walnut, acorn finials, four flat shaped spindles, walnut arms, woven splint seat, band turning on legs, 28" w, 17" deep, 42" h, c1905 . . . . **250.00**

Windsor
Arrow Back, decorated, orig cornucopia, flower, and leaf designs in black, yellow, and persimmon, c1830. . . . . **300.00**
Bow Back, seven spindle back, saddle seat, old finish, repairs **125.00**
Comb Back
Maple and ash, refinished, 42½" h, New England, c1820 . . . . **425.00**
Painted holly crest, arrow slats, black repaint **150.00**

SHELVES

Hanging
Bird's eye maple graining, 39" h, 23¾" w, 5½" deep, four shelves . . . **850.00**
Hardwood, 23¼" h, 25" w, 8" deep, three shelves, red stain **200.00**
Pine, 23¾" h, 20" w, two shelves, scalloped ends. **225.00**
Poplar, 26" h, 26" w, 7½" deep, three shelves, truncated sides, molded front edges, old red paint **1,050.00**
Poplar, 30" h, 24½" w, 8½" deep, four shelves, scalloped ends and crest **400.00**
Soft wood, 27¾" h, 30¾" w, curved tapering ends, molded edges, old red **800.00**
Walnut, 18" h, 14" w, one shelf, applied pine cut outs, scalloped

brackets and shelf, chip carved detail, two candle sockets, old varnish **325.00**

SETTEES

Oak, shaped crest, fretwork back and arm supports, shaped arms, oblong cane seat, bentwood oblong one pc stretcher, ring turned legs, curved tapering legs, 47" w, 18" deep, 38" h **500.00**
Plank Bottom
Mixed woods
Scrolled crest, dec crest and upper rail, multicolored dec on dark ground, turned half spindle back, scrolled arms, spindle arm supports, turned legs, tapering stretchers, orig paint, PA, c1850 . . . . **925.00**
Tablet Crest
Arrow back, floral dec crest, multicolored dec on dark ground, scrolled arms, turned spindle arm supports, turned legs and stretchers, orig paint, mid Atlantic, c1850 . . . . **675.00**
Spindle back, floral dec crest, multicolored on black ground, floral dec crest, scrolled arms, turned legs, long flat stretchers front and back, turned stretchers front to back, orig paint, PA, c1850 . . . . **1,500.00**
Windsor, mixed woods
Birdcage, rod back, plank seat, bamboo turned legs and stretchers, dark brown graining, old paint, PA, c1800 . . . . **9,500.00**
Low Back, curved, rod back, knuckle arm, vase and ring turned arm supports, plank seat, bamboo turned legs, bulbous stretchers, stamped "T. Mason" on bottom, late overpaint, Philadelphia, c1780. . . . . **3,850.00**
Rail Back, rod back, scrolled arms, vase and ring turnings, H stretcher, old finish, 35¾" l, mid Atlantic, c1800 . . . . **4,200.00**
Scrolled Crest, dec crest and upper rail, multicolored floral dec on dark green ground, turned half spindle back, scrolled arms, turned arm supports, plank seat, turned legs, straight stretchers, orig paint, mid Atlantic, c1820 **1,750.00**
Shaped Crest, carved ears, rod back, knuckle arms, plank seat, bamboo turned legs and stretchers, overpainted, mid Atlantic, c1830 **5,200.00**

Step–down, cut out crest rail, arched rod back, outswept arms, plank seat, bamboo turned legs, old brown paint, New England, c1800................... **4,950.00**

Straight Crest, rod back, bamboo turnings, plank seat, refinished, 38" l, mid Atlantic, 1810–20 ... **2,700.00**

Tablet Top, bamboo turned spindle back, arms, arm supports, and stretchers, plank seat, turned legs, refinished, mid Atlantic, c1820 **1,650.00**

SOFAS

Carved, 30" h, 73½" w, orig olive green paint, PA, 19th C............. **1,700.00**

Sheraton Style, 72" l, mahogany frame, turned legs, turned freestanding arm posts, short arms, reupholstered.................... **2,400.00**

STANDS

Bakery Cooling Rack, softwood, beveled edge cornice, removable shelves, chamfered edges on shoe feet, old red paint over black, 63½" h **525.00**

Commode Washstand

Oak

29½" w, 15" deep, 28" h, horizontal reeding on back splash, two long drawers over two raised panel doors, split panel ends **275.00**

31" w, 17" deep, 51" h, harp shaped towel bar, serpentine front long drawer over two flat drawers and paneled door, shaped apron, paneled ends .. **295.00**

32" w, 18" deep, 29" h, carved ears, horizontal fluting, open baluster gallery, and scribed design on 13" h back splash, one long overhanging drawer over two flat drawers and paneled door, fluted stiles, split paneled ends, metal towel bar on side **350.00**

Stand, one drawer, decorated top, orig paint, c1800, 18 x 22½ x 28", $575.00.

Pine and poplar, shaped dovetailed gallery, single drawer over two paneled doors, paneled ends, turned feet, rosewood graining, sponge and pinstripe dec, orig paint, wooden pulls, c1830 .... **1,000.00**

Tiger maple, shaped gallery, single drawer over two paneled doors, paneled ends, turned feet, striped figuring throughout, refinished, wooden pulls, PA, c1830 ...... **825.00**

Crock, primitive, five stepped shelves, old green repaint, late wire nail construction, 38" w, 30" deep, 31" h .. **125.00**

Night

Birch and cherry, 26¾" h, two dovetailed drawers, turned legs **375.00**

Bird's eye maple, shaped serpentine top and front, one drawer, block and turned legs, figured wood throughout, refinished, New England, c1830.............. **2,100.00**

Cherry

17¼" w, 16⅜" deep, 27" h, molded edge one board top, boldly scalloped aprons all sides, curly maple drawer, square tapering legs, poplar secondary wood, minor edge repair to scalloped apron one side, replaced drawer support........... **65.00**

21⅛" w, 25¾" deep, 28¼" h, molded edge on top and skirt, old finish, orig brass, RI, 1780–1800.................. **1,800.00**

22½" w, 17½" deep, 28½" h, curly and bird's eye maple veneer, turned legs, two dovetailed drawers, one with ogee, other with curved front, refinished .. **300.00**

24" w, 18¾" deep, 29" h, two board scalloped top, applied beading on dovetailed drawer, walnut inlay on posts, turned legs, refinished........... **275.00**

24⅜" w, 24¾" deep, 28¼" h, applied gallery, bevel–edged one board top, underside finger hold lip on dovetailed drawer, square tapered legs, old finish **1,400.00**

Square top, bead molding on single deep drawer, square tapering legs, old finish, PA, c1825 .... **700.00**

Cherry and tiger maple, three drawers, paneled ends, turned legs, refinished, wooden pulls, mid Atlantic, c1830.............. **700.00**

Chestnut, overhanging top, drawer, block and turned legs, tapering feet, wooden pulls, 22" w, 19½" deep, 29½" h **125.00**

Curly maple and cherry, two board

molded edge top, dentil molding at top edge of apron, beaded edge on dovetailed drawer, square tapering legs, damaged dentil molding, replaced drawer support, 25¼" w, 21½" deep, 29" h **115.00**

Drop Leaf

Birch, drop leaf, cut out ovolo corners on two 7½" leaves, two dovetailed drawers, turned legs, refinished, 21¾" w, 17" deep, 28¾" h **375.00**

Cherry and other hardwood, two dovetailed drawers, turned legs, brass pulls, old red paint, 29" h **1,000.00**

Pine and poplar, two shaped drawers, turned legs, rosewood graining, gold pinstriping, PA, c1830 . . . .   **875.00**

Walnut, two dovetailed drawers, applied pressed edge molding, turned legs, 16" w, 20" deep, 29" h **225.00**

Folk Art, cherry, cut out ovolo corners on two board top, two dovetailed drawers, turned legs, relief flower carving on facade, sides of apron, and front legs, punched designs, old worn finish, 21" w, 21¼" deep, 29" h **600.00**

Mahogany

Oval top, inlaid, single drawer, square tapering legs, H stretcher, refinished, VA, c1810 . . . .   **1,870.00**

Rect top, thumb molded, incised beaded drawer, plain apron, thin turned tapering legs, bulbous cuffs, 15" w, 21½" deep, 27" h, NY, 1790–1810 . . . . . .   **1,760.00**

Maple

18" w, 15½" deep, 28½" h, one board top, dovetailed drawer, turned legs, old natural refinish   **275.00**

18¼ x 19" top, shaped corners, one drawer, square tapered legs, refinished, replaced drawer pull, New England, c1800 . . . .   **650.00**

Oak, serpentine front, drawer over door, shaped apron, cabriole legs, 22" w, 16" deep, 30" h **250.00**

Pine and poplar

Square top, wide molded apron, splayed ring turned legs, button feet, refinished, PA, c1830 . . .   **600.00**

Three drawers, shaped splash back and apron, applied columns, paneled ends, turned legs, old grain painting, PA, c1830 . . . .   **680.00**

Tiger and bird's eye maple, two

graduated drawers, turned legs, highly figured wood, refinished, mid Atlantic, c1830 . . . .   **900.00**

Tiger maple

1 drawer, overhanging top, ring turned legs, refinished, 17¼" h, New England, 1820s **450.00**

2 drawers, paneled ends, turned legs, figured wood throughout, refinished, PA, c1830 . . . .   **1,000.00**

Notched corner top, shaped apron, splayed square tapering legs, refinished, PA, c1800 . . .   **2,200.00**

Walnut, one dovetailed drawer, square tapering legs, refinished, wooden pull, VA, c1830 . . . . . .   **400.00**

Parlor, oak

Round top, quarter and plain cut, splayed base, spool turned legs, shaped mid shelf, button feet, golden oak finish, 23" d top, 29" h   **275.00**

Square top, scalloped edge top, molded apron, splayed base, flat button turned legs and feet, scalloped edge mid shelf, 28¾" sq top, c1880 . . . .   **245.00**

Plant, burled ash top, ash column, three cast iron branch legs, 10½" d, 33¼" h **150.00**

Sewing, mahogany, Martha Washington type, shaped lift top, two drawers, sliding tops on side compartments, flaring tapered legs, refinished, Baltimore, MD, c1800   **3,200.00**

Telephone Stand, cherry and poplar, dovetailed drawer, old finish, 23" w, 14¾" deep, 36" h **245.00**

Wash

Cherry

28" h, 19½" w, 16½" deep, dovetailed drawer and gallery, turned feet and posts, refinished   **300.00**

32¾" h, four board top, dovetailed drawer and gallery, turned legs, base shelf, refinished **325.00**

Corner, scalloped dovetailed gallery, bow front, two holes in top shelf, drawer under bottom

Quilt Stand, pine, shoe foot, $275.00.

shelf, turned legs, refinished,
PA, c1830 . . . .   **900.00**

Pine

20¾" w, 16¼" deep, 32¾" h, decorated, corner shelves on crest,
dovetailed drawer, turned legs
and posts, orig red and green
striping on white ground, hole
for bowl, white porcelain knobs   **225.00**

29¼" w, 16½" deep, 31¼" h, lift lid
top, one dovetailed drawer,
paneled door, simple turned
feet and pilasters. **210.00**

33¼" h, dovetailed gallery and
drawer, turned feet and posts,
orig red and black graining, yellow striping, and stenciled gold
dec **200.00**

Pine and poplar, scrolled back
splash, two towel bars, shaped
overlapping drawer, hexagonal
tapering legs, orig yellow finish,
PA, c1830 . . . .   **1,500.00**

Poplar, red paint, stenciled black tulip and heart design on top,
splayed base, square tapered legs,
one dovetailed drawer with overlapping edge dec, chip carving
and molded edge, 17½ x 17½",
26½" h **425.00**

Tiger maple

Back splash, single drawer,
turned legs, ball feet, replaced
shelf cracked, early 19th C . . .   **500.00**

Dovetailed gallery, single drawer,
lower shelf, block and turned
legs, old finish, wooden pull,
PA, c1830 . . . .   **800.00**

Yellow pine, gallery, single drawer,
square tapering legs, overpainted,
part of gallery missing, VA, c1825   **600.00**

STOOLS

Broom Maker's, splayed turned legs,
mid shelf, wood and wrought iron
clamps, worn gray paint, 36" h **225.00**

**Foot Stool, pine, five board, 17 x 6¾ x 9",
$45.00.**

Foot

Decorated

7½ x 13½" h, rect top, splayed
turned legs, old dark green
paint, yellow and green "F"
and flower **65.00**

14¼" x 8" h, pine, cut out legs, orig
green paint, two dogs, loving
couple and lovebirds scenes . .   **180.00**

15 x 9" h, pine, square nail construction, half moon cut outs on
ends, yellow pine trees, green
leaves, yellow and green dots,
mid 19th C **100.00**

Hardwood, splayed legs, old brown
finish, 9⅝ x 12⅜" h **45.00**

Oak, oval, turned splayed legs, dark
finish, 13" l **55.00**

Pine, cut out feet, old red finish,
12½" l **125.00**

Piano, adjustable, mahogany, round
seat, turned legs, worn leather up-
holstery, 21" h **75.00**

TABLES

Baker's, oak, overhanging top, two
chamfered drawers over two possum bellied grain painted bins,
golden oak finish, 46" l, 25" w,
30" h **575.00**

Breakfast, drop leaf, one drawer,
square tapering legs, refinished, replaced pull, 32½" l, 19½" w, 29" h,
New England, c1810 . . . .   **800.00**

Dining, oak

Round top, pedestal, feathered legs,
carved lion's feet, 54" d, 31" h,
c1880 . . . .   **800.00**

Square top, two leaves stored in
well, corner applied carved
shields, onion turned tops and feet
on five chubby legs, 48" sq top,
29" h **850.00**

Drop Leaf

Bird's eye and tiger maple, shaped
rect top and leaves, turned reeded
legs, scrolled cross stretchers, refinished, New England, c1820 . .   **3,000.00**

Cherry

39" l, 17½" w, 27½" h, rect top, two
12¼" drop leaves, turned legs,
refinished, replaced hinges . . .   **315.00**

42" l, 19" w, 28" h, rect top, deep
drop leaves, conforming frieze,
straight tapered legs, early
19th C **850.00**

42½" l, 41¾" w, 27¾" h, rect top,
two drop leaves, plain apron,
square tapering legs, New En-
gland, 1790–1810 . . . .   **2,860.00**

48" l, 47½" w, 28" h, rect top, two

drop leaves, plain apron, turned reeded tapering legs, MA, 1800–15 . . . . **2,750.00**
Cherry and maple, rect top, two drop leaves, swing legs, pad feet, refinished, 47" l, 27½" h **3,500.00**
Cherry and tiger maple, rect top, six legs, refinished, 42" l, 29¼" h. . . . **350.00**

Maple
Rect top, square tapering legs, refinished, 35¾" l, 18½" w, 28" h   **425.00**
Round top, cabriole legs, pad feet, refinished, New England, c1790 . . . . **2,700.00**
Tiger maple, rect top, deep drop leaves, turned legs, figured wood throughout, old finish, mid Atlantic, c1830 . . . . **1,500.00**
Walnut, rect top, two drop leaves, cabriole legs, refinished, repairs to top, 48½" l, 19" w, 28" h, PA, late 18th C **1,500.00**

Farm
Maple, rect overhanging top, square tapering legs, old finish, mid Atlantic, c1830. . . . . **1,500.00**

Walnut
60" l, rect overhanging top, one small between two longer drawers, turned legs, old finish, wooden pulls, VA, c1830 . . . . **2,600.00**
Rect two board overhanging top, dovetailed cleats, turned legs, old finish, VA, c1820 . . . . **900.00**

Harvest
Birch, oblong top, oblong drop leaves, turned legs, 85" l. **3,000.00**
Pine and birch, square chamfered legs, mortised and pinned apron and stretchers, worn finish, 84" l, 27¾" h **1,000.00**

Hutch
Hardwood and pine, round two board pine top, square legs, mortised and pinned apron and stretchers, pine seat, old red paint, 47" d, 29" h **3,000.00**

Pine
Circular tilt top
41" d, 28" h, square seat, turned legs, c1820 . . . . **850.00**
44" d, 26" h, red paint, square seat, square molded legs, box stretcher, late 18th C. . . **1,300.00**
47⅝" d, 27¾" h, orig red paint, mid Atlantic, 19th C **4,500.00**
Rect top, three board top, cut out feet, lift lid seat, old worn dark patina, age cracks and scorching, 60" l, 30" w, 29" h **850.00**
Pine and maple, painted and grained, all–over mustard paint,

Hutch Table, New England, oval, pine, oak shoe feet and cleats, 46 x 66½ x 26½", 18th C, $4,500.00.

underside of top comb grained and outlined, 17½" h hinged seat, 54" l, 35¾" w, 51¼" h, PA, 1825–50 . . . . **1,300.00**
Pine and poplar
Rect cleated pin top, hinged lift lid seat, paneled bootjack ends, worn orig graining, PA, c1850 **1,300.00**
Two board rounded corner top, hinged seat, cut out ends, old refinish, 61½" l, 40" w, 28½" h **1,100.00**
Kitchen, chestnut, rect rounded corner top, five turned and fluted legs, 42" l, 27" w, 30" h. **350.00**
Sawbuck, pine
35¾" l, 23¼" w, 27½" h, two board top, square nail construction, old nut brown finish. **250.00**
71¾" l, 34¾" w, 28¾" h, two board top, old nut brown finish, minor age cracks **85.00**
Tavern
Cherry, shaped sides, triangular pad feet, old refinishing, replaced glue blocks, 28¾" l, 27" h. **2,500.00**
Cherry, maple, and pine, pine one board top with breadboard ends, mortised and pinned apron, one dovetailed drawer, square tapering legs, reattached top, drawer pull missing, 43" l, 28½" w, 27½" h **500.00**

Tavern Table, New England, single center drawer, spade feet, 44" l, 27¼" d, 28½" h, $900.00.

Cherry and walnut, turned legs, plain stretchers, old finish, 53½" l, 33¾" w, 25" h, NY, 18th C **2,300.00**

Hardwood and pine

38½" l, 24" w, 26¼" h, one board breadboard top, splayed base, square tapering legs, old red repaint **450.00**

38¾" l, 28" h, scrubbed finish, turned legs, mortised and pinned apron and stretcher, repaired **250.00**

Maple and pine

24" round top, shaped apron, vase and ring turned legs, molded box stretcher, traces of orig paint, one leg repaired, PA, c1780 . . . . **6,500.00**

32" l, 27" h, oval pine top, plain apron, block and turned cylindrical legs with cylindrical feet, 32" l, 27" h, 18th C **1,980.00**

34⅞" l, 26½" h, pine top, single large drawer, turned legs, molded stretchers, old refinishing, Rhode Island, early to mid 18th C. **2,700.00**

37½" l, 26½" h, pine breadboard scrubbed top, mortised and pinned pine apron, square tapering maple legs, red traces on base **750.00**

37½" l, 26¾" w, 26" h, mortised and pinned apron, molded edge, one dovetailed drawer, turned tapering legs, duck feet, old dark red repaint, worm holes in base, age cracks, replaced warped top **600.00**

Pine and poplar

24" l, 15½" w, 22¾" h, pine and poplar, turned legs and stretchers, old finish **1,050.00**

29¼" l, 20½" w, 29½" h, one board removable top, applied edge molding on apron, square tapering legs, orig red and black flame graining **2,800.00**

Pine and walnut, two board pine top, mortised and pinned apron, walnut base, widely splayed square tapering legs, dark blue repaint, 26" l, 22¾" w, 28¼" h **250.00**

Walnut, overhanging molded pin top, dovetailed cleats, single overlapping drawer, scalloped apron, vase and ring turned legs, molded box stretcher, refinished, PA, c1780 . . . . **7,800.00**

Tea

Maple, oval overhanging top, shaped apron, four turned off cen-

ter legs, pad feet, old brown paint, New England, c1780 . . . . **18,000.00**

Pine, oblong scrubbed overhanging one board top, molded apron, molded splayed square tapering legs, traces of old paint, New England, 1810–20. . . . . **1,750.00**

Pine and maple, oval top, cleat, splayed turned legs, button feet, refinished, 33¾" l, New England, c1800. . . . . **3,000.00**

Walnut, circular tilting dish top, birdcage, suppressed ball column, tripod base, cabriole legs, padded snake feet, refinished, Delaware Valley, c1780. . . . . . . **3,750.00**

Walnut and maple, rect overhanging top, single drawer, turned off center legs, pad feet, old red paint, wooden pull, PA, c1780. . . . . **7,500.00**

Work

Cherry

19¾" l, 28¾" h, rect top, rounded corners, two drawers, ring turned stiles form tapering cylindrical legs, MA, c1815 . . . . **610.00**

27¾" l, 23½" w, 29¾" h, turned legs, one dovetailed drawer, refinished **625.00**

34" l, 18¼" w, 28¾" h, drop leaf, rect scrubbed top, one drawer, square tapering legs, red painted base, replaced brass pull, New England, 1810–20 **350.00**

Cherry and pine, single drawer, turned legs, orig red finish, wooden pull, 29" h, early 19th C **150.00**

Maple and pine, one dovetailed drawer, turned posts and feet, refinished, 42½" l, 29" h **500.00**

Pine

24¾" l, 17¾" w, 29" h, octagonal top, decorated, red, green, yellow, and blue floral dec and

Mirror, bureau type, mixed woods, orig finish, movable mirror, 7" d, 13½" w, 21" h, $350.00.

striping on orig light blue paint, gilded cluster of musical instruments in center top, dovetailed drawer over pull out bag frame, two smaller drawers in ends, square tapering legs, orig brass pull, worn paint, repaired split in one leg **175.00**

36" l, 19¾" w, 29¼" h, dovetailed drawer, turned legs, orig red flame graining **450.00**

48" l, 26½" w, 28¾" h, two board scrubbed top, base with old dark paint, square tapering legs **300.00**

Pine and poplar, removable three board top, two dovetailed overlapping drawers, turned legs, professional red and black repaint base, 54½" l, 29½" w, 29½" h, PA **950.00**

Poplar, rect overhanging top, pin top with dovetailed cleats, two deep drawers, turned drawers, orig red paint, PA, c1830 . . . . . . **6,000.00**

Tiger maple, one drawer, refinished **850.00**

Walnut, drop leaves, one drawer . . **250.00**

TRUNKS

27" w, 18" deep, 13" h, oak, dovetailed case, molded lid and base, iron bail handles **250.00**

46¼" w, 17½" deep, 19" h, oak, hand made, chamfered panel each side, recessed brass combination lock, NY, late 19th C **400.00**

WARDROBES

Oak

43" w, 16" deep, 72" h, breakdown, molded cornice, applied lily top front corners, two paneled doors, long base drawer, paneled sides, horizontal reeding, shaped apron **500.00**

48" w, 17" deep, 94" h, ornate applied dec on shaped and molded

cornice, two paneled doors, scribe lines on two base drawers, paneled ends, cut out feet **1,250.00**

Pine, simple detail, molded cornice, raised panel door, beaded edge stiles, shelves and wood hooks interior, worn dark brown finish, 75¾" h **510.00**

WICKER

Bench, window, scrolling arms, cane seat, scrolling on skirt, 34 x 18 x 29" **300.00**

Bookcase, four oak shelves, turned wood frame, reed and wood fancy sunburst back, natural finish, c1890 **500.00**

Chair

Arm

Geometric diamond shape design on back panel, rattan wrapped, tight weave, upholstered seat **350.00**

Inverted triangle design woven in back, Heywood Brothers, painted, c1890. . . . . **400.00**

Side, shaped woven crest, vase shaped ornate splat, pressed seat, 17½" w, 39" h **175.00**

Chaise Lounge, rolled arms with scrollwork, continuous and star caned back, wrapped legs, rolled footrest, yellow floral cushion, Wakefield Rattan Co, c1890 . . . . **800.00**

Chest of Drawers, rattan wrapped, tightly woven, three drawers, 27" w, 18" deep, 32" h, c1900 . . . . **325.00**

Desk, natural, wood gallery, basketweave and openweave design, one drawer, shelf on top with arched front, ball feet, c1900 . . . . **325.00**

Etagere, rattan wrapped, fancy scrollwork, 6 tiers, arched crest insert with oval mirror, X stretchers, cabriole legs, 69" h **1,000.00**

Ferner, cane and wicker, wrapped legs, 31" h **240.00**

Foot Stool, upholstered seat, painted **150.00**

High Chair, shell design back, machine woven cane seat, wooden

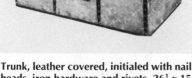

Trunk, leather covered, initialed with nail heads, iron hardware and rivets, 26½ x 15 x 12½", $175.00.

Stool, wicker, painted white, 13½" h, $165.00.

footrest, turned wooden legs, natural finish, c1880 . . . .   **275.00**
Rocker
  Braidwork design, serpentine edges, wooden rockers, painted white, Wakefield Rattan Co **225.00**
  Platform, rolled edge, high back, patent, 25" w, 47" h **450.00**
Settee, rect back, upholstered section on back and seat, woven arms, scalloped skirt. **425.00**
Smoking Stand, brass tray, 28" h **60.00**
Sofa, scrolled back, diamond design, upholstered seat, 65" l, 37" h **275.00**
Stand
  Lamp, circular wooden top and mid shelf, scrolled supports, 16" d, 30½" h **200.00**
  Music, three oak shelves, Wakefield Rattan Co paper label, c1883 . . .   **250.00**
  Sewing, hinged circular cov, spiderweb caned top basket, lower shelf open basket, three legs, natural finish, c1870 . . . .   **300.00**
Steamer Chair, tightly woven back and seat, diamond design, wide arm rests, magazine holder, old dark green paint, 56" l **350.00**
Table
  End, looped edge on sq top, stick, ball, and curlicue detail, small woven tier middle, wrapped legs with stretcher, c1890 . . . .   **375.00**
  Library, oval, Karpen Guaranteed Construction Furniture paper label **300.00**
  Oval, braided edge on wooden inset top, wrapped legs and X stretcher, woven mid shelf, bowed legs, 36½" w, 20½" deep, 30" h **325.00**
  Tea, natural, oak top and serving shelves, rounded corners on top, stick, ball, and scroll detail, flared wrapped legs and balls, c1890 . .   **575.00**
Towel bar, hanging, oval beveled mirror, 24" l **80.00**

ADIRONDACK AND OTHER RUSTIC FURNITURE

History: The use of natural materials in furniture construction, ranging from tree branches to rattan, enjoyed great popularity in the latter half of the nineteenth century and first quarter of the twentieth century. The rustic look was found in cottage, porch, and some garden furniture.

It is extremely important to differentiate between rustic and primitive furniture. Although much rustic furniture appears primitive in form and construction, factory and craftsperson exam-

ples dominate. Among the catalogs in the collection at Rinker Enterprises is *Rustic Furniture—Rustic Bird Houses* of the Ye Olde Rustic Furniture Company of Philadelphia, who advertise their products for "porches, lawns, summer homes, parks, country clubs, gardens, pavilions, theaters, hotels, dens, sanatoriums, etc."

One of the best known manufacturers of rustic furniture is the Old Hickory Furniture Company of Martinsville, Indiana, which celebrated its fortieth anniversary in 1931. Their "Pioneer" suite of porch furniture featured a chair, rocker, rocker settee, settee, stool, swing and chains, and table. Note the use of the term "Pioneer." Rustic furniture is sold as part of the Western as well as the Country look.

Adirondack furniture is a type of rustic furniture. It features a number of unusual designs and painted decoration. As a result, it became a darling of the folk art set in the 1980s. The collecting ardor for Adirondack furniture quickly cooled in the late 1980s when a large number of reproductions, copycats, and fakes arrived upon the scene. Beware of small end tables featuring a birdhouse motif.

Reference: *Rustic Hickory Furniture Co., Porch Lawn, and Cottage Furniture: Two Complete Catalogs, ca. 1904 and 1926*, Dover Publications, 1991.

Breakfront, pine, stripped bark, four doors, oak and walnut geometric wood facings, one initial "J," "O," "H," and "N" over each door, 87" w, 94½" h, 1875–1900 . . . . . .   **250.00**
Chair
  Log
    Bark Covered, straight upper rail Cedar, three spindles, V-shaped arm supports, six board seat, inverted V-shaped braces between upper and lower stretchers, c1910 . . . .   **150.00**
    Hickory, seven spindles, woven splint seat, 20" w, 18" deep, 21" h, Old Hickory Furniture Co, IN, 1930s **185.00**
    Stripped bark, painted, straight crest, sloping arms, dark green, 30¼" h, NY, 19th C **175.00**
  Log and Twig
    Andrew Jackson style, hickory, bark covered, woven splint back and seat, continuous arms, 20" w, 18" deep, 21" h, Old Hickory Furniture Co, IN, 1930s **225.00**
    Continuous arm woven splint back and seat, hickory, orange and black wiped enamel finish,

20" w seat, 19" deep, 20" h, Old Hickory Furniture Co, IN, 1930s **350.00**

Dining, hickory, woven seat, Indiana Hickory Furniture Co branded mfg mark, Paine Furniture Boston metal retailers tag, set of four. **800.00**

Clothes Tree, hickory, six peg hooks, tripod base, arched legs, 68" h, Old Hickory Furniture Co, IN, c1935 . . **125.00**

Corner Bench, log, cedar, straight upper rails, three posts, smooth planed 35 board seat, diamond shaped braces between upper and lower rails, c1915 . . . . **235.00**

Corner Cupboard, oak and hickory, spindled gallery, two glass–paned doors, interior shelf, two paneled cupboard doors, ftd, dark oak finish, wooden pulls, 66" h, 20" w, Old Hickory Furniture Co, IN, 1930s. . . **775.00**

Desk, hickory and oak, arched spindled rail, oak top and two mid shelves each side, spindles on curved shelf supports, drawer, dark oak finish, 36" l, 24" w, 30¼" h, Old Hickory Furniture Co, IN, 1930s. . . **475.00**

Divan, hickory, spindled back, arms, and base, wrapped woven splint rail, arms, and seat, checkered diamond design on cushions, 64" l, 22" deep, 18" h back, Old Hickory Furniture Co, IN, 1930s **500.00**

Fainting Couch, hickory, raised curved backrest, continuous woven splint top reinforced with coil springs under weaving, 29" w, 82" l, Old Hickory Furniture Co, IN, 1930s. . . **450.00**

Fern Stand, twig, stripped bark, painted, black and silver, 14" square top, NY **65.00**

Flower Box, log, cedar, bark covered, two rows of eight upright logs, joined together, cut out rect planting area, 33" l, 12" w, 8" deep, 1910s **45.00**

Flower Vase, log, cedar, bark covered, twelve upright pickets form circular planter, tripod column, random logs form base, c1915 . . . . **50.00**

Footstool

9" h, 10½ x 13", worn blue and white cloth upholstery, NY **100.00**

12" h, 10" sq woven splint top, splayed base **65.00**

High Chair, hickory, spindle back, railed tray, woven splint seat, splayed base, 19" w, 39" h, Old Hickory Furniture Co, IN, 1930s. . . **250.00**

Lawn Seat, log, cedar, bark covered, straight rails, geometric and random twig designed back, twig braces,

wide spindled arm rests, 14 board seat, c1910. . . . . **275.00**

Magazine Stand, square oak top and three shelves, four hickory legs, woven splint panels sides and back, dark oak finish, Old Hickory Furniture Co, IN, 1930s. **100.00**

Planter, ftd, painted

24" l, log, cedar, bark covered, upright pickets surrounding square box. **35.00**

36" l, stripped bark, black and silver dec, NY **50.00**

51" l, stripped bark, orange and lime green, ornately decorated, NY . . **450.00**

Rocker

19½" h, child size, hickory, stripped bark, rect back, straight stiles and rails, two mortised spindles, splint seat, straight legs, four stretchers, NY, c1910 . . . . **125.00**

21" h, 20" w seat, 18" deep, Andrew Jackson style, hickory, bark covered, continuous arms, woven splint back and seat, Old Hickory Furniture Co, IN, c1930 . . . . **275.00**

22" h, child size, bark covered, oak splint seat, NY, c1900 . . . . **115.00**

30" h, child size, stripped bark, arms, painted, black, red, and silver, NY. **120.00**

40" h, log, cedar, bark covered, straight upper and lower rails, five straight spindles, six board seat, double stretchers, 1910s. **200.00**

49" h, hickory, stripped bark, painted, brown, NY **275.00**

Settee, bark covered

Arched Rail, hickory, woven splint back and seat, 43" l seat, 19" deep, 25" h, Old Hickory Furniture Co, IN, 1930s **350.00**

Curved Back, hickory, center post, continuous arm, woven splint back and seat, 45" l seat, 20" deep, 21" h, Old Hickory Furniture Co, IN, 1930s **325.00**

Spindle Back, straight rails, woven splint seat, 43" l, 19" deep, 21" h, Old Hickory Furniture Co, IN, c1930. . . . . **375.00**

Steamer Chair, hickory, woven splint back and seat, 12 x 24" writing table arm, spindled base, 22" w, 48" deep, 30" h, Old Hickory Furniture Co, IN, 1930s **425.00**

Stool, hickory, woven splint saddle seat, 15 x 18" seat, 15" h, Old Hickory Furniture Co, IN, 1930s **75.00**

Table

End, log, cedar, bark covered frame, smooth planed square top and lower shelf, X–shaped braces between table top and stretchers, 1910–20. . . . .   **75.00**

Gate–leg, oak and hickory, stripped bark, rect top, rounded corners, rounded edges on two triangular leaves, thick legs, 22 spindles supported by stretchers and rails, two swing–out legs, cast iron hinges, $33\frac{1}{2}''$ h, $43\frac{1}{2}''$ l, 40" deep, NY, c1915 . . . .   **350.00**

Lamp, log and twig, hickory, bark covered

Octagonal oak top, splayed hickory legs, double stretchers, dark oak finish, 24" d, 30" h, Old Hickory Furniture Co, IN, c1932 . . . .   **225.00**

Round oak top and mid shelf, arched shelf supports, three straight hickory legs, stretchers radiating from center hub, dark oak finish, 30" d top, 18" d shelf, 30" h, Old Hickory Furniture Co, IN, 1930s **275.00**

Pedestal, log, cedar, bark covered, hexagonal top, tripod table top support and base, stretchers, 1910–20. . . . .   **125.00**

Trestle, oak top, pinned trestle, hickory base, dark oak finish, 42" l, 24" w, 30" h, Old Hickory Furniture Co, IN, 1930–35. . . . .   **475.00**

Tabourette, hickory, 16" sq oak top, shaped corners, splayed base, double stretchers, dark oak finish, 17" h, Old Hickory Furniture Co, IN **85.00**

Tennis Seat, log, cedar, bark covered, no back, X–shaped braces between front and back arm posts, nine board seat **225.00**

Tete–a–tete, log, cedar, bark covered, two seats opening to opposite sides, straight rails, four spindles on backs

Wash Stand, painted, faked grains, mixed woods, double mirrored doors, $19\frac{3}{4}''$ d, $16\frac{1}{2}''$ w, 31" h, $325.00.

and arms, six board seats, double stretchers front and back, 1910s . . .   **300.00**

Whatnot Stand, corner, oak and thornwood, stripped bark, six tiered, $55\frac{1}{2}''$ h, NY, late 19th C **325.00**

ENGLISH COUNTRY FURNITURE

History: The role of the English gentry is glorified in fact and fiction. The concept of the "gentleman farmer" enjoys great popularity in America. Although American views about life in the English countryside are mythic and idealistically oriented, their influence on American Country collecting is very strong.

Among early "antiques" collectors, there was a strong prejudice for things English. The concepts of England as the source for American design and that somehow English goods were simply superior resulted in English pieces occupying positions of prominence in many American collections.

English Country is found in both formal and vernacular styles. Formal was reserved for the manor house; vernacular suited the common folk and local tavern crowd. In the 1930s and 1940s English vernacular furniture from Welsh dressers to Windsor chairs was eagerly sought by American collectors. In the 1960s and 1970s emphasis was placed on things American. English Country vernacular lost favor.

The return to the formal look in the 1980s and the desire to replace the American Country look that evolved during the Bicentennial era resulted in the rediscovery of English Country by collectors and decorators. In essence, the market has come full cycle. Pieces that were popular in the 1930s and 1940s are popular again in the 1990s.

The lack of adequate reference and decorating texts makes collecting English Country a hodgepodge operation. It is highly recommended that anyone wishing to focus on English Country travel to Great Britain and visit regional and local museums and historic sites.

References: Bernard D. Cotton, *The English Regional Chair*, Antique Collector's Club, 1990; Howard Pain, *The Heritage of Country Furniture: A Study in the Survival of Formal and Vernacular Styles from the United States, Britain, and Europe Found in Upper Canada, 1780–1900*, Van Nostrand Reinhold, 1978.

Reproduction Alert: A fair amount of English Country enters the American market via preassembled containers. Buyers should be aware that great liberties are taken in respect to rebuilding and reconstructing this furniture. Have any "period" piece authenticated by an expert.

Settle Bench, pine and oak, paneled front, sides, and back, lift top seat, worn finish, late 17th C, 30" l, 19" d, 27" h, $600.00.

Bed, four post, mahogany, reeded and vase turned posts, 62" w, 81" l, 90" h, late 18th C **7,200.00**

Bureau, cylinder, mahogany
  30" w, inlaid, urn dec on cylinder front, one drawer, long square tapering legs, 1901–10 . . . . **850.00**
  42" w, tambour shutter door, fitted interior, three drawers, c1820 . . . **1,750.00**

Chair
  Elbow, ash and elm, rod back, straight rail, wide shaped plank seat, splayed base, turned legs, c1800 . . . . **1,100.00**
  Windsor, side, yew and beech, wheelback, braced, shaped plank seat, turned legs, crinoline stretcher, 19th C, pr **1,275.00**

Chest of Drawers
  Mahogany, two over four graduated drawers, bracket feet, replaced bail handles, 46¼" w, c1770 . . . . **750.00**

Chair, Windsor, elm and ash, broad arm, Christmas tree splat, $950.00.

Oak, molded cross banded top, two over three graduated drawers, bracket feet, 37" w, c1800 . . . . . **2,500.00**

Clothes Press, oak
  Paneled Doors, cornice, three arched panel doors, three waist drawers with drop pulls, two four–paneled cupboard doors, square feet, mid 18th C **3,500.00**
  Welsh, cornice, three raised panel doors in top, three waist drawers over two raised panel cupboard doors, paneled ends, 53" w, c1790 . . . . **3,200.00**

Corn Chest, oak, narrow shelf on shaped gallery, hinged cov, four fielded panels, four apron drawers, bracket feet, 63" w, c1760 . . . . . . **1,450.00**

Cradle
  Cane–filled frame, ogee–arched hood, shaped supports and legs, 41" l **1,600.00**
  Oak, peaked hood, turned finials, raised panels, shaped rockers, 36" l, 18th C **1,450.00**

Cupboard
  Corner, oak, dentil design below wide molded cornice, single paneled door, molded base, c1780 . . . . **1,800.00**
  Hanging, oak, cornice, molded panels, two doors, square legs, 60" w, 18th C **1,750.00**
  Livery, oak, molded cornice, arched raised panel doors in top, two over one drawers in base, paneled ends, square feet, orig pegs inside, iron H hinges, mid 18th C **5,200.00**
  Welsh, chestnut, wide cornice, two paneled doors, two drawers in waist, two paneled cupboard doors, bracket feet, c1820 . . . . . **3,500.00**

Desk, slant front, mahogany, four graduated drawers, bracket feet, 36¼" w, mid 18th C **5,200.00**

Dresser
  Canopy, oak, molded cornice, shaped sides, two open shelves, two arched cupboard doors, paneled ends, square feet, 50" w, c1740 . . . . **12,000.00**
  Oak, closed, molded cornice, pierced scrolling frieze, three shelves, and two raised arch panel doors in rack, two columns graduated drawers flanking one center drawer over two raised arch panel doors in base, bracket feet, crossbanded in mahogany, 87" w, Lancashire, mid 18th C **7,500.00**
  Oak and Fruitwood, molded cornice, three open shelves, three

drawers at waist, base shelf, turned center support, 55½" w, c1750 . . . .   **6,000.00**
Oak and Pine, five drawers above arched apron, baluster turned supports, pine platform base, 60½" l, c1750 . . . .   **4,000.00**
Welsh, oak
  Denbighshire, molded cornice, scalloped and shaped rack, two shelves, three bevel edged drawers in waist, split arch raised panels on two lower cupboard doors, paneled ends, square feet, 60" w, early 18th C **14,000.00**
  North Wales
    50" w, cornice, shaped sides, two open shelves and overhanging shaped rack, two beveled drawers in waist, two raised panel cupboard doors, paneled ends, square feet, early 18th C **15,000.00**
    60" w, cornice, scalloped rack, three shelves, three drawers in waist over three center drawers, two molded paneled cupboard doors, square legs, drop pulls, 18th C **6,500.00**
    73" w, cornice, shaped sides, three open shelves, and seven spice drawers in rack, four parallel drawers over three center drawers, two paneled cupboard doors, and paneled ends in base, early 18th C **18,000.00**
  Walnut, Queen Anne, oak, cornice, open back rack with twelve peg hooks, three plate shelves, cup hooks, and spoon slots in top, shaped crest, three drawers in waist, elaborately shaped triple apron, four turned front legs with block feet, lower shelf, 62" w, early 18th C **13,000.00**
Kettle Stand, mahogany, carved, round top, open baluster gallery, turned column, tripod base, 11¾" d, 29" h **2,500.00**
Settee, double chair back, elm, rect back, pierced strapwork splats, brown repp cov on padded drop–in seat, 45" w **2,000.00**
Table
  Gateleg
    57½" l, mahogany, oval top, tapering legs, flared feet, c1750   **1,800.00**
    60¼" l, oval top, block and ring turned legs, late 17th C **1,200.00**

Library, drum, mahogany, tooled leather inset, drawers stamped "A. Blain, Liverpool," turned column, tripod base, 47" d **2,500.00**
Refectory, trestle ends joined by flying stretcher on plinth bases, shoe feet, 113" l, early 18th C. **1,250.00**
Tea, mahogany, open baluster gallery, birdcage, turned column, tripod base, carved ogee legs, 27½" w **1,200.00**
Wardrobe, oak, stepback, cornice, two arched raised panel doors over two raised panel drawers, paneled ends, tapering feet, c1740 . . . .   **6,500.00**

FRENCH COUNTRY FURNITURE

History: Like its English counterpart, French Country furniture is found in formal and vernacular styles. Formal French Country tends toward the high style. Its American popularity is confined to collectors and decorators living in metropolitan areas.

French vernacular pieces, especially the bleached examples from Southern France, were discovered by collectors and decorators in the mid–1980s. As the 1990s progress, their popularity appears to be waning. This is due in part to the large number of reproductions, copycats, and fakes that flooded the American market.

French Canadian furniture is attracting the strong attention of American Country collectors and decorators. It recently was revealed that a large amount of furniture that sold in the market from the 1960s through the 1980s as painted rural New England Country furniture was actually from the rural regions of French Canada.

References: Warren Johansson, *Country Furniture and Accessories from Quebec*, Schiffer Publishing, 1991; Howard Pain, *The Heritage of Country Furniture: A Study in the Survival of Formal and Vernacular Styles from the United States, Britain, and Europe Found in Upper Canada, 1789–1900*, Van Nostrand Reinhold, 1978.

Armoire
  Cherrywood, stepback, molded chamfered cornice, two upper doors, long drawer over two lower doors, shaped paneled doors, paneled ends, squat cabriole legs, 56" w **6,500.00**
  Fruitwood, molded cornice, two shaped paneled doors, paneled ends, shaped aprons, squat cabriole legs, 61" w, late 18th C **3,000.00**
  Oak, cornice, two paneled doors, paneled ends, shaped apron,

squat cabriole legs, 59¾″ w, late
18th C **4,250.00**
Banquette, painted white, rect back,
bowed seat and squab, blue floral
chintz upholstery, 53″ w **1,750.00**
Bed, sleigh, butternut, rollover carved
molding at top of paneled head and
foot boards, shaped side rails have
hand wrought flat metal hook fitt-
ings, Alsatian leg, twin size **1,100.00**
Chair
Bergere, stained beechwood frame,
plum colored velvet upholstery on
back, seat, and squab, tapering
legs, Louis XVI **1,875.00**
Chaise, elm, oval back, serpentine
seat, tufted upholstery, Louis XVI,
pr **2,500.00**
Fauteuil, walnut, close–nailed floral
needlework upholstery, Louis
XVI, pr **2,500.00**
Side, carved, cream decorated,
cane back, bowed seat, molded
cabriole legs, Louis XV, set of four   **4,000.00**
Chest of Drawers, mahogany
44½″ w, marble top, one shallow
over three deep drawers, Louis
Philippe, c1840 . . . .   **650.00**
51½″ w, Napoleon III style, carved,
urn finials, two over six drawers,
raised oblong panel fronts, rope
turned columns, mid 19th C **550.00**
Commode Cabinet
26½″ w, three drawers, shaped
apron, cabriole legs, parquetry in-
lay on door fronts, 19th C **600.00**
40″ w, demi–lune, walnut, cross-
banded and parquetry, two drawers, tapering reeded legs, late
18th C **6,500.00**
Cupboard, stepback, cherry, carved
and applied yellow maple borders
on cornice and door panels, two
molded frame upper doors, mitered
edges on two drawers at waist, two
lower molded frame cupboard
doors, carved block feet, 60″ w,
84″ h, Peter Detuncq, second half
19th C **5,000.00**
Fire Screen, painted gray, floral dec on
rect silk panel, 17¼″ w **1,800.00**
High Chair, sloping arms, paneled
storage area below seat, door in
back, high knees, tapering feet **900.00**
Secretary Chest, shaped crest, small
arched center door flanked by four
drawers in top, ogee door front, false
top drawer is pull down writing surface with deeply carved sliding
block braces, fitted interior, two
lower drawers, wooden pulls,
66″ w, 60″ h, second half 19th C . .   **3,500.00**

Side Cabinet, chestnut, two drawers
over two shaped paneled doors, applied turned half columns, cabriole
legs, 49″ w, mid 18th C **2,500.00**
Table
Card, Louis XVI style, demi-lune,
brass bound mahogany, round
top, five square tapering legs,
42½″ d, late 18th C **700.00**
Dining, Louis XVI style, drop leaf,
walnut, oval top, six turned ta-
pering legs, 42¾″ w **2,750.00**
Tric–Trac, Louis XVI style, mahog-
any, leather lined reversible tray
top, two drawers, ebony and fruit-
wood chess players, 44½″ w **3,000.00**

PENNSYLVANIA GERMAN FURNITURE

History: The first German settlers arrived in
Pennsylvania in 1683. With Philadelphia as a
hub, they spread north, west (to Harrisburg,
Pennsylvania), then south, and east. The initial
period of immigration ended in the 1740s at
which time Pennsylvania German communities
dotted southeast Pennsylvania, the Shenandoah
Valley from Hagerstown, Maryland, to the Southern back country, and portions of Ontario in Canada.

The Germans brought with them a strong craft
tradition. Next to Shaker, Pennsylvania German
is the most widely collected form of American
regional furniture. Although Pennsylvania German painted furniture has received the most attention in exhibits and print, there was also a
strong tradition of unpainted formal pieces as
well.

Pennsylvania German vernacular forms survived for centuries. One of the most valuable
reference sources is Henry Lapp's handbook. This
book illustrates vernacular forms made by Lapp
well into the twentieth century.

Pennsylvania German furniture was meant to
be used and survive. Its sturdy construction and
vertical lines make it easy to distinguish from
other regional forms. Most examples were made
by furniture craftsmen. The Pennsylvania German
farmer as maker of his own furniture is largely a
myth.

References: Bernard Deneke, *Bauernmobel: Ein
Handbuck Fur Sammler and Liebhaber*, Deutsche
Taschenbuck Verlag, 1983; Monroe Fabian, *The
Pennsylvania–German Decorated Blanket Chest*,
Universe Books, 1978; Beatrice Garvan, *The
Pennsylvania German Collection*, Philadelphia
Museum of Art, 1982; Alan Keyser, Larry Neff,
and Frederick S. Weiser (trans. and eds.), *The
Accounts of Two Pennsylvania German Furniture*

Makers—Abraham Overholt, Bucks County, 1790–1833, and Peter Ranck, Lebanon County, 1794–1817, Sources and Documents of the Pennsylvania Germans III, Pennsylvania German Society, 1978; Henry Lapp, *A Craftsman's Handbook,* Good Books, 1975.

Blanket Chest
  Pine
    Red Ground, miniature, dovetailed, lid and base edge molding, turned feet, orig polychrome painted stylized tulips, floral designs, and initials and date "1844" on front panel, orig red finish, Somerset County, 25" l, 13" deep, 17¼" h **5,200.00**
    Dark Blue, two painted arched panels with pots of stylized flowers in red, blue, green, black, and brown on white ground, two white and brown stars on lid, dovetailed case, till, and bracket feet, wrought iron strap hinges and bear trap lock with escutcheon and key, professional molding replacement, 50" w, 21¾" deep, 21" h **2,800.00**
  Poplar
    Black and orange, white trim, twelve pointed stars, hearts, and meandering vine and dots dec, sgd "CS 1820," two drawers, bracket feet, c1820. **7,000.00**
    Brown Ground, sponged blue arched panel designs, red and black diamond border, orange and blue base, lift top, three drawers, bracket feet, c1790 **15,000.00**
    Green ground, large yellow hearts inscribed "Phillip Dutrer 1775," lift top, two overlapping drawers, dovetailed bracket feet, worn orig paint, minor repairs, c1795. **5,000.00**

Miniature, blanket chest, pine, decorated, lift top, orig hardware, 13" l, 7¼" w, 6" h, $400.00.

Corner Cupboard
  Pine
    Decorated, 2 pc, upper section with molded cornice, arched glazed door, and plate rails and spoon slots on shelf interior, projecting lower section with two drawers over pair of cupboard doors, turnip feet, painted red, stippled yellow highlights, door painted white, 28" w, 90" h, first quarter 19th C. **21,000.00**
    Grain Painted, 1 pc, blind door, molded cornice, double paneled doors top and bottom, cut out feet, orig red and yellow graining, c1840 **7,000.00**
    Pine and Poplar, decorated, orange and red geometric stripe design, pine and poplar, 2 pc, three–paned double doors, single drawer, two paneled doors, cut out bracket feet, c1840. **6,500.00**
    Poplar, grain painted, 2 pc, simulated tiger maple and rosewood graining, yellow, red, and black dec, double molded cornice, twelve–paned door, three nailed drawers in waist, shaped apron, cut out feet, orig finish, c1840. **17,000.00**
Chair, side, dec, brown ground, white striping, polychrome floral dec on crest, set of four. **300.00**
Cradle
    Pine and Poplar, dec, post and panel construction, mushroom finials, heart cut outs on scrolled headboard and shaped footboard, shaped rockers, black panels on orange–red frame, c1825. **6,000.00**
    Walnut, heart cut out in head and footboards, scrolled headboard, arched footboard, dovetailed case, shaped rockers, old finish, c1830. **650.00**
Dry Sink, pine and poplar, decorated, dovetailed gallery, two drawers, two flat paneled doors, paneled ends, turned feet, yellow and brown stippled panels, c1820 **4,200.00**
Dutch Cupboard, pine and poplar, blind door, mustard grained, 2 pc, molded cornice, two paneled doors in top, two drawers in waist, two paneled doors below, cut out feet, old paint, wooden pulls, c1850 **1,800.00**
Jelly Cupboard, pine, brown graining, cornice, two double raised panel doors, chamfered corners, turned feet, c1830. **2,400.00**

Schrank
Pine and Poplar
Large blocked cornice, two split raised panel doors, fluted pilasters, two overlapping drawers in base, overpainted, missing ball feet, c1780 . . . . **2,000.00**
Stepped cornice, raised panel doors, front, and end panels, waist molding, three overlapping drawers, applied bracket feet, red case, black feet, orig paint, c1790 . . . . . . **37,000.00**
Walnut
Inlaid pilasters below cornice, two shaped recessed paneled doors between shaped recessed side panels, fluted quarter columns top and bottom, three over two overlapping drawers in base, applied French bracket feet, refinished, orig H hinges, c1795 . . . . **11,000.00**
Holed Dentil section and fluting below molded cornice, two double molded raised panel doors and fluted quarter columns above, three over two overlapping drawers and chamfered corners in base, ogee feet, refinished, orig H hinges, c1795 . . . . **18,000.00**

Stepback Cupboard
Glazed Pine, molded cornice, two six-pane doors, spoon holder shelf, three drawers over two paneled doors in base, refinished, replaced pulls, 44¼" w, 78½" h, c1830 . . . . . . **1,500.00**
Pine, 2 pc, open top, large stepped cornice, molded waist, raised panel doors lower case, tall scalloped bracket base, orig red paint, c1810 . . . . **11,000.00**
Poplar, 2 pc, 16-paned double doors, cornice, five overlapping drawers in waist, four paneled doors in base, scalloped apron, cut out feet, old graining, 84" w, 84" h, c1830 **4,200.00**
Trunk, miniature, dome lid, decorated, multicolored finger graining and flowers, 9½" h, late 18th C **575.00**
Wall cupboard, closed face, paneled doors and sides, molded flaring cornice, pair of paneled top drawers, shelved interior, three small midsection drawers, molded waist, pair of paneled cupboard base doors, old refinishing, traces of old red paint, molding loss, 83" h, early 19th C . . **3,000.00**

GLASS

Glass serves two key functions in Country: utilitarian and decorative. Glass used in rural America was manufactured to last. Most pieces were thickly made and would last a long time when handled carefully. Glass had a permanence attached to it that was easily understood by the agrarian housewife.

Glass was recyclable. It could serve the same purpose over and over again. Every agrarian home had a place in the pantry or basement where jars and other glassware were stored awaiting reuse. Further, manufacturers of food products quickly realized the value placed upon glass by the agrarian housewife. Sales increased when prepackaged foods were placed in reusable glass.

The arrival of inexpensive glassware revolutionized country life. Storage possibilities increased considerably. Home canning became a seasonal activity. Inexpensive pattern glass added a touch of elegance to everyday life. The level of sanitation increased.

The country housewife classified her glassware in three categories: storage vessels, everyday glassware, and special occasion glass. Glass storage vessels were limited until the arrival of the refrigerator. The most common glass storage vessel was the fruit jar. The fruit jar, along with the cold cellar, were the principal means of food storage in rural America until the arrival of electricity. You cannot run a refrigerator without it. Although some farmsteads had icehouses, most did not. Individuals living in towns fared better, albeit ceramic and tin storage dominated in an icebox.

Everyday glassware consisted primarily of drinking glasses and table accessories such as spoon holders and salt and pepper shakers. The kitchen and Depression era glasswares of the 1920 to 1950 period found favor with the rural housewife. It was colorful and affordable. Although more glass forms appeared throughout the house, the most heavily used items, e.g., dinner plates, still tended to be ceramic.

Cut glass was the most highly prized glassware in rural America. It graced the dining room buffet and was used only for special occasions. It was passed down from generation to generation more than any other glass type. Those who were unable to afford cut glass turned to pattern glass that imitated cut glass patterns.

Glass played a major role in lighting. See the "Lighting" section for more detailed information.

Practicality aside, the agrarian housewife loved the decorative nature of glass. Leaded cut glass sparkled with brilliance on a dining room buffet. Shelves were installed in a kitchen window so light could reflect through a host of colored glasswares. A surprising amount of early American glass and flasks survived because they fulfilled this latter role.

One final glass form—souvenir glass—deserves mention. Since farming is primarily a seven-day-a-week occupation, individuals who traveled loved to bring home souvenirs from the places that they visited. Glass souvenirs were especially popular. Whether a ruby stained mug acid–etched with the name of the place and date or a milk glass canoe with a decal of the site, these glass souvenirs enjoyed a place of honor in the country home.

References: Corning Museum of Glass and The American Committee of the International Association for the History of Glass, *Glass Collections in Museums in the United States and Canada*, The Corning Museum of Glass, 1982; Harold Newman, *An Illustrated Dictionary of Glass*, Thames and Hudson, 1977; Jane Spillman, *Glass*, The Knopf Collectors' Guides to American Antiques, *Volume 1: Tableware, Bowls & Vases* (1982) and *Volume 2: Bottles, Lamps & Other Objects* (1983), Alfred A. Knopf.

Periodicals: *Antique Bottle & Glass Collector*, PO Box 187, East Greenville, PA 18041; *Antique Glass Quarterly*, PO Box 1364, Iowa City, IA 52244; *Glass Collector's Digest*, PO Box 553, Marietta, OH 45750; *The Daze*, PO Box 57, Otisville, MI 48463.

Museums: Historical Glass Museum, Redlands, CA; Corning Museum of Glass, Corning, NY; Toledo Museum of Art, Toledo, OH; Chrysler Museum, Norfolk, VA; Bennington Museum, Bennington, VT.

EARLY AMERICAN

History: Early American glass covers glass made in America from the colonial period through the mid–19th century. As such, it includes the early pressed glass and lacy glass made between 1827 and 1840.

Major glass producing centers prior to 1850 were: Massachusetts with the New England Glass Company and the Boston and Sandwich Glass Company; South Jersey; Pennsylvania with Stiegel's Manheim factory and Pittsburgh; and Ohio with Kent, Mantua, and Zanesville.

Early American glass was collected heavily during the 1920 to 1950 period, regaining some of its earlier popularity in the mid–1980s. In the Country movement, its role is largely as a decorative accessory.

Leading sources for the sale of early American glass are the mail auctions of Collectors Sales and Services and Glass Works Auctions and the auctions of Richard A. Bourne, Early Auction Company, Garth's, Norman C. Heckler & Company, and Skinners.

References: William E. Covill, *Ink Bottles and Inkwells*, 1971; Lowell Inness, *Pittsburgh Glass: 1797–1891*, Houghton Mifflin Company, 1976; George and Helen McKearin, *American Glass*, Crown, 1975; George and Helen McKearin, *Two Hundred Years of American Blown Glass*, Doubleday and Company, 1950; Helen McKearin and Kenneth Wilson, *American Bottles And Flasks*, Crown, 1978; Adeline Pepper, *Glass Gaffers of New Jersey*, Scribners, 1971; Jane S. Spillman, *American and European Pressed Glass*, Corning Museum of Glass, 1981; Kenneth Wilson, *New England Glass And Glassmaking*, Crowell, 1972.

Collectors' Club: The National Early American Glass Club, 7417 Allison Street, Hyattsville, MD 20784.

Museum: Sandwich Glass Museum, Sandwich, MA.

Reproduction Manufacturer: The Ebenezer Averill Co., PO Box 156, Milford, NH 03055.

Cologne Bottle, 9⅜" h, clear, pontiled, flared lip, 1840–1850 . . . . **90.00**
Carafe, 5⅜" h, purple blue, blown three mold, barrel shaped, geometric pattern, open pontil, tooled and flared lip, orig blown stopper, 1820–1830 **800.00**
Castor Bottle, 4⅛" h, clear, blown, three 3-piece molds, cylindrical, concave sloping shoulders, open pontil, sheared and tooled lip, 1820–1830 . . . . **50.00**
Decanter, 8¼" h, clear, blown three mold, semi-barrel shaped, sloping shoulders, applied neck bands, pontil mark, tooled and flared lip, matching blown stopper, 1820–1830 . . . . **120.00**
Flask, 6½" h, light olive green, free-blown, chestnut shaped, open pontil, rolled lip, 1800–1820. . . . . **85.00**
Ink Bottle
Cylindrical, emb "E Waters, Troy, NY", 2⅜" h, 1½" d, aquamarine, open pontil, applied mouth, 1830–1850. . . . . **235.00**
Pitkin, 1¾" h, 2" d, medium olive yellow, 36 ribs swirled to left, open pontil, disc mouth, 1800–1820. **300.00**
Twelve-Sided, emb "Harrison's Columbian Ink/Patent," 4⅞" h, 2½" d, aquamarine, open pontil, applied mouth, 1840–1850 . . . . **150.00**
Umbrella, octagonal base, 2½" h, 2½" d, deep cobalt blue, smooth base, rolled lip. **825.00**
Medicine Bottle
Dr Mann's Celebrated Ague Balsam, deep aquamarine, open pontil, applied mouth, Galion, OH **230.00**
Swaim's Panacea, 8" h, medium olive green, pontil scarred base, applied mouth, 1830–1850 . . . . **275.00**
Pill Jar, 2½" h, medium yellow amber, blown, 12=sided, open pontil, sheared and tooled lip, 1820–1830 **525.00**
Salt, 2⅝" h, clear, 20 vertical ribs, pontil scar, applied foot, tooled rim, 1830–1840 . . . . **70.00**
Snuff Jar
Rectangular, 4⅝" h, medium yellow olive, blown, open pontil, flared and tooled lip, partial label for "Mahcoby Snuff," 1810–1830 **55.00**
Square, 4⅝" h, deep root beer amber, blown, open pontil, flared and tooled lip, 1790–1820. . . . . **575.00**
Storage Jar, 12⅞" h, deep olive amber, blown, pontiled, flared and tooled lip, 1800–1820. . . . . **230.00**
Toilet Water Bottle
Clear, blown three mold, 5¼" h, cylindrical, sloping shoulder, rayed, blown, open pontil, tooled and flared lip, molded rib at base of neck, 1820–1830 . . . . **35.00**
Purple Blue, blown, two 3-piece molds, 5½" h, tapering ovoid shape, ringed, open pontil, tooled and flared lip, 1820–1830 . . . . . **80.00**
Utility Bottle
Bladder shape, 8⅛" h, deep root beer amber, free-blown, open pontil, rolled lip, 1790–1810 . . . . **185.00**
Cylinder shape, 8⅛" h, light apple green, blown, open pontil, heavy

Ink Bottle, square, emb "Caw's Ink New York," 2¼ x 1⅞", $275.00.

Medicine Bottle, Warners Safe Kidney & Liver Cure, Rochester, NY, amber, 9½" h, $300.00.

rolled lip, Pittsburgh district,
1820–1830. . . . .   **65.00**
Squat, 4" h, medium olive amber,
freeblown, open pontil, applied
string lip, 1790–1810 . . . .   **250.00**
Utility Jar, 4½" h, 2" base diameter, medium yellow olive, blown, open
pontil, slightly flared and tooled lip,
1800–1820 . . . .   **350.00**

HISTORICAL FLASKS

History: A flask is a container for liquids. Early
American glass companies frequently formed
them in molds which left a relief design on the
front and/or back. Historical flasks with a portrait,
building, scene, or name are the most desired.

Most flasks have a narrow neck. A chestnut is
hand blown, small, and has a flattened bulbous
body. The pitkin has a blown globular body with
vertical ribs with a spiral rib overlay. Teardrop
flasks are generally fiddle shaped and have a
scroll or geometric design.

Dimensions can differ for the same flask because of variations in the molding process. Color
is important, with scarcer colors demanding more
money. Aqua and amber are the most common
colors. Bottles with "sickness," an opalescent
scaling which eliminates clarity, are worth much
less.

Relief decorated flasks, especially those featuring patriotic or historical themes, are the most
popular among Country collectors. Although
aqua is the most common color, it is favored
because of its ability to blend well into any Country decorating scheme.

Reference: George L. and Helen McKearin,
American Glass, Crown Publishers, 1941 and
1948.

Collectors' Club: The National Early American
Glass Club, 7417 Allison Street, Hyattsville, MD
20784.

Reproduction Manufacturer: The Ebenezer Averill Co., PO Box 156, Milford, NH 03055.

Columbia–Eagle, McKearin GI–121,
pint, aquamarine, three vertical ribs,
sheared lip, pontil mark, American,
1820–1840 . . . .   **215.00**
Cornucopia–Urn
McKearin GIII–7, half pint, olive
amber, three vertical ribs, sheared
lip, pontil mark, American,
1830–1840. . . . .   **120.00**
McKearin GIII–14, half pint, emer-
ald green, three vertical ribs,
sheared lip, pontil mark, Lancas-
ter, NY Glass Works, 1830–1840   **385.00**

George Washington, Father Of His Country, Gen. Taylor Never Surrenders, Dyott-
ville Glassworks, Philadelphia, 6¾" h,
$450.00.

Eagle–Cornucopia, McKearin GII–11,
half pint, aquamarine, horizontal
beading, vertical medial rib,
sheared lip, pontil mark, Monon-
gahela and early Pittsburgh district,
1830–1840 . . . .   **175.00**
Eagle–Eagle, McKearin GII–24, pint,
sapphire blue, corrugated horizontally, vertical medial rib, sheared
lip, pontil mark, American, 1840–
1850 . . . .   **2,200.00**
Eagle–Oak Tree, McKearin GII–60,
half pint, amber, heavy vertical medial rib, circular beading, sheared
lip, pontil mark, American, 1830–
1840 . . . .   **950.00**
Franklin–Dyott, McKearin GI–96,
quart, aquamarine, vertically
ribbed, sheared and tooled lip, pontil mark, Kensington Glass Works,
Philadelphia, PA, 1830–1840 . . . .   **230.00**
Jenny Lind
McKearin GI–99, quart, calabash,
deep emerald, broad sloping
collar, pontil mark, S Huffsey
Glass Works, 1850–1860. . . . . .   **685.00**
McKearin GI–101, quart, calabash,
aquamarine, broad sloping collar,
pontil mark, Millfora Glass
Works, 1850–1860 . . . .   **145.00**
Kossuth, McKearin GI–112, quart,
calabash, aquamarine, fluted edges,
sloping collar, pontil mark, S Huff-
sey Glass Works, 1850–1860. . . . .   **240.00**
Lafayette, McKearin GI–86, half pint,
five vertical ribs, olive amber,
sheared lip, pontil mark, Coventry,
CT, 1825–1835 . . . .   **325.00**
Masonic–Eagle
McKearin GIV–32, pint, golden amber, vertically ribbed, flared and

rolled lip, pontil mark, J Shepard & Co, White Glass Works, Zanesville, OH, 1830–1840 . . . . **1,200.00**

Success to the Railroad, McKearin GV–1, pint, aquamarine, three vertical ribs, sheared lip, pontil mark, two reversed numeral "5"s on base, Lancaster, NY Glass Works, 1830–1840 . . . . **415.00**

KITCHEN GLASSWARE

History: The first quarter of the twentieth century brought inexpensive kitchen and table products to center stage. Hocking, Hazel Atlas, McKee, U. S. Glass, and Westmoreland were companies which led in the production of these items.

Utilitarian kitchen glassware complements Depression Glass tablewares. Many items were produced in the same color and style. Because the glass was molded, added decorative elements included ribs, fluting, arches and thumbprint patterns. Kitchen Glassware was thick to achieve durability, which resulted in forms which were difficult to handle at times and often awkward aesthetically. After World War II, aluminum products began to replace Kitchen Glassware.

Kitchen Glassware was made in large numbers. Although collectors do tolerate signs of use, they will not accept pieces with heavy damage. Many of the products contain applied decals; these should be in good condition. A collection can be built inexpensively by concentrating on one form such as canister sets, measuring cups, reamers, etc.

References: Gene Florence, *Kitchen Glassware of the Depression Years, Fourth Edition*, Collector Books, 1990; Shirley Glyndon, *The Miracle In Grandmother's Kitchen*, privately printed, 1983; Mary Walker, *Reamers–200 Years* (1980, separate price guide) and *The Second Book, More Reamers—200 Years* (1983), Muski Publishers.

Collectors' Club: National Reamer Collectors Association, Rt 3, Box 67, Frederic, WI 54837.

Ash Tray
Green Transparent, flared lip **8.00**
Jadite, light, six–sided, Jeannette . . **6.00**
Baker, jadite, dark, oval, 5 x 3½", McKee **10.00**
Batter Bowl, Anchor Hocking
Green Transparent, spiraled **18.00**
Jadite, dark **10.00**
Mayfair Blue, vert rib **115.00**
Opaque Yellow, vert rib **70.00**
Turquoise Blue **32.00**
White, peach and grape design, Fire–King **12.00**
Batter Jug
Amber, dark, lid, Paden City **45.00**

Black, glass insert, metal frame, handle, and attached lid, McKee **65.00**
Clear, emb floral design, cobalt cov, Paden City **40.00**
Forest Green, cov, New Martinsville **50.00**
Jadite, light, rect, glass lid, Jeannette **175.00**
Green Transparent, glass lid, melon rib, Jenkins **275.00**
Pink, knobbed cov, round, Cambridge **65.00**
Red, metal frame, lid, and handle, McKee **80.00**
Batter Set
Amber, square pitchers, vert rib corners, inset handle covers, rect tray, New Martinsville **110.00**
Black, square pitchers, knobbed covers, tab handle rect tray, Paden City **185.00**
Cobalt, square pitchers, vert rib corners, inset handle covers, tab handle rect tray, New Martinsville . . **275.00**
Pink Pitchers, knobbed covers, black rect tab handle tray, Paden City **125.00**
Bowl
Cobalt, 11⅝" d, rolled lip, Hazel Atlas **60.00**
Custard, 8" **15.00**
Delphite, 7½", horiz rib, Jeannette **35.00**
Green Transparent, cov, 9" d, Jeannette **35.00**
Jadite, light, black "Tom & Jerry" lettering, McKee **70.00**
Pink, 9¾" d, marked Cambridge . . . **20.00**
Butter Dish, rect, cov
¼ lb
Amber, vert rib, Federal **22.00**
Cobalt, Crisscross pattern **75.00**
Crystal, frosted, vert rib, Federal **12.00**
1 lb
Amber, light, rect, vert rib, Federal **25.00**
Chalaine Blue, vert rib, tab handles **250.00**
Cobalt, emb "Butter Cover" on lid, tab handles, Hazel Atlas . . **160.00**
Delphite, emb "Butter," tab handles, Jeannette **150.00**
Jadite, dark, emb "Butter," Jeannette **35.00**
Pink, emb Scotty top **35.00**
Seville Yellow, tab handles, McKee **60.00**
Ultra–marine, ribbed, "Jennyware" **85.00**
White, red ships, McKee **22.00**
2 lb
Green Transparent **120.00**
Pink, emb "B" lid **100.00**
Butter Tub, round, cov, amber, light, vert ribs, Federal **22.50**

Cake Plate
  Cobalt, 3 ftd, Fry 80.00
  Pink, snowflake pattern 18.00
Canister, cov
  Caramel, 40 oz, round, caramel
    glass cov 70.00
  Chalaine Blue, "COFFEE," press–
    on lid 180.00
  Clambroth, large, snap–on lid 25.00
  Clear, large
    Dutch Boy design, pink lid 18.00
    Green "Taverne" scene and lid   20.00
  Clear Frosted, 40 oz, swirl pattern,
    labeled "Coffee," screw–on lid,
    Owens–Illinois 12.50
  Cobalt, vert lettering 275.00
  Crystal, 128 oz, melon rib, emb
    "FLOUR," snap–on lid 35.00
  Custard, square, black lettering,
    screw–on lid 45.00
  Delphite, round, 20 oz, "TEA," ho-
    riz rib, Jeannette 90.00
  Forest Green, 20 oz, rice, diagonal
    ridged, Owens–Illinois 14.00
  Jadite
    47 oz, vert rib, diagonal label,
      glass lid, Hocking 38.00
    48 oz, 5½" h, square, glass cov,
      black lettering, Jeannette 30.00
  Peacock Blue, 5 lb, sugar, melon
    rib, snap–on lid 185.00
Casserole, cov, clambroth, oval, Pyrex   85.00
Cheese Dish, cov, clear, emb "Sani-
  tary Preserver" 30.00
Coaster
  Cobalt, round, four raised lines in
    center 6.00
  Jadite, round, McKee 40.00
Cocktail Shaker, cobalt, barbell shape,
  chrome cov 80.00
Coffee Dispenser, green transparent
  jar, vert rib, metal screw–on lid and
  dispenser, wall mount 300.00
Coffee Dripolator, crystal 10.00
Coffee Pot, clear, glass cov, red finial,

red, yellow, and blue ring dec, Glas-
  bake 25.00
Cookie Jar
  Black, cov, horiz rib, LE Smith 55.00
  Green Transparent, barrel shaped,
    glass cov 45.00
  Peacock Blue, cov, barrel shaped,
    three horiz ribs at top and bottom,
    LE Smith 70.00
Crock, 40 oz, glass cov, jadite, light,
  round, knob on top, Jeannette 38.00
Cruet
  Clear Frosted, rooster decal, clear
    stopper 10.00
  Forest Green, paneled, clear faceted
    stopper 32.00
  Green Transparent, pyramid shape,
    stopper, Jeannette 80.00
  Jadite, light, square, black "Vine-
    gar" lettering, stopper 115.00
  Pink, set, two cruets and tray, Impe-
    rial 70.00
Cup, jadite, light, black "Tom & Jerry"
  lettering, McKee 8.00
Curtain Ring, forest green 9.00
Curtain Tie Back
  Amber, feathered, pr 20.00
  Cobalt, Sandwich, round, large . . .   15.00
  Peacock Blue, plumed, pr 28.00
Custard Cup, jadite, light, McKee 4.00
Decanter, Peacock blue, long neck,
  horiz ribs at shoulder, orig stopper,
  Imperial 25.00
Door Knob Set
  Green Transparent, faceted knobs   90.00
  Jadite, faceted knobs 40.00
Drawer Pull
  Double
    Chalaine Blue 15.00
    Green Transparent 18.00
  Single
    Black, six–sided 8.00
    Cobalt, small 10.00

Casserole, Fire King, cov, blue, 5" w, $6.00.

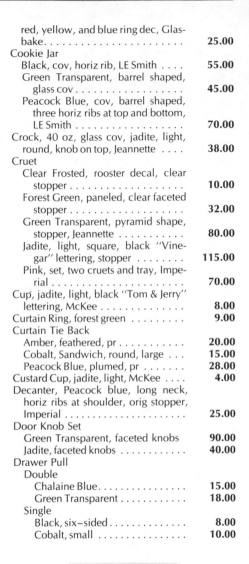

Cruet, Cathedral pattern, amber, Bryce Bros., $120.00.

Drippings Jar
  Delphite, black lettering, horiz rib,
    Jeannette 55.00
  Jadite, light, horiz rib, black let-
    tering, Jeannette 32.00
Egg Beater Bowl, spout
  Chalaine Blue, 4½″ h 32.50
  Jadite, light, McKee 10.00
Egg Cup, Chalaine blue 12.00
Funnel
  Crystal, 9″, vert rib, conical 12.00
  Green Transparent, 4½″, vert rib,
    conical 32.00
  Yellow, canning 40.00
Gravy
  Green Transparent, underliner,
    Cambridge 48.00
  Pink, double spout, Cambridge . . .   20.00
  Red, platter, Imperial 150.00
Horseradish Jar, cov, crystal, emb let-
  tering 10.00
Ice Bucket
  Black, cov, wrapped bale handle . .   65.00
  Clear, tab handles, black, yellow,
    and red rings, Hocking 15.00
  Jadite, cov, bale handle 80.00
Ice Tub, Peacock blue, straight sides,
  tab handles 25.00
Instant Coffee, crystal, emb lettering,
  sterling top and base 28.00
Knife
  Amber, ribbed handle, 8¼″ l, Stonex   95.00
  Blue, light, Three Star, 8½″ l, Vitex–
    Glas 18.00
  Crystal, Three Leaf, 8½″ l, Dur–X . . .   8.00
  Green, plain handle, 9¼″ l 32.00
  Pink, Steel–ite 65.00
Knife Rest, amber 18.00
Ladle
  Black 55.00
  Cobalt, Fostoria 32.00
  Forest Green, Cambridge 20.00
  White, Imperial 40.00
Marmalade Jar, green transparent,
  metal lid and spoon 20.00
Match Holder
  Delphite, black lettering, Jeannette   42.00
  Jadite, light, no lettering, Jeannette   10.00
Measuring Cup, 1 Cup
  Amber, light, three spouts, Fed-
    eral 35.00
  Caramel, 2 spout 450.00
  Chalaine Blue, 2 spout 525.00
  Cobalt, 3 spout, Hazel Atlas 275.00
  Jadite, Hocking 140.00
  Red, fired–on, McKee Glasbake . . .   25.00
  Seville Yellow, 2 spout 165.00
  White, red rim, Glasbake 48.00
Measuring Cup Set, dry, 4 pcs, ¼, ⅓, ½,
  and 1 cup, tab handles, Jeannette
  Delphite 125.00
  Jadite 40.00

Pink 115.00
Measuring Pitcher
  2 Cup
    Custard, orange dots, McKee . . .   32.00
    Delphite, McKee 65.00
    Green Transparent, Sunflower
      bottom, Jeannette 85.00
    Jadite, dark, Sunflower bottom,
      Jeannette 45.00
    Vitrock White, cov 35.00
    White, red bows, McKee 25.00
    Yellow 210.00
  4 cup
    Caramel, handle, McKee 475.00
    Chalaine Blue, no handle 550.00
    Crystal, no handle 35.00
    Custard, handle 28.00
    Delphite, handle 425.00
    Jadite, light, handle, McKee 28.00
    Seville Yellow, no handle 275.00
Measuring Spoon, crystal, marked ta-
  ble, dessert, and tea, curled handle   4.50
Meat Platter, amber, oval, ftd, Fry . . .   40.00
Milk Pitcher
  Clear base, cobalt cov, Paden City   40.00
  Cobalt, paneled, Hazel Atlas 55.00
Mixing Bowl
  Black, 7⅜″ d, McKee 30.00
  Jadite, 8¾″ d 18.00
  Pink, 9″ d, slick handle, 2 spout, lid   40.00
Mug
  Cobalt, paneled, Cambridge 45.00
  Custard, black lettering "Tom &
    Jerry" 12.00
  Green Transparent, paneled, ftd,
    Jeannette 25.00
  Jadite, light, bottoms down, McKee   130.00
  Peacock Blue, flared base 25.00
  Pink Frosted, root beer 25.00
Mustard Pot, cobalt, clear finial on
  cov, spoon 25.00
Napkin Holder
  Black, marked "Naro–O–Fold
    Napkin Company Chicago, USA"   125.00
  Jadite, emb "Serv–All" 125.00
  White
    Fan Fold, Diana Mfg, Green Bay   65.00
    Handi–Nap, Ft Howard 45.00
    Party Line, Paden City 40.00
Pickle Jar, green transparent, barrel
  shaped, metal screw–on lid and
  bale handle 90.00
Pitcher and Reamer Set
  2 cup
    Blue, Fenton 1,375.00
    Cobalt, Hazel Atlas 225.00
    Crystal, ftd, orange dec, US Glass   25.00
    Green Transparent, Jeannette . . .   95.00
    Red, Fenton 900.00
    White, 5 blue dots, Hazel Atlas   32.00
  4 Cup
    Crystal, Hocking 22.50

Green Transparent, ftd, Hocking	**35.00**
Pink, Party Line, Paden City	**135.00**
Pot Watcher, clear, round	**8.00**

Reamer

Amber

Baby, 2 pc, Westmoreland	**175.00**
Large, dark, Cambridge	**650.00**
Small, light, tab handle, Federal	**10.00**

Black

Large, Saunders, emb lettering, high pointed cone.	**800.00**
Small, fired-on, tab handle, Hocking	**12.00**

Blue, 2 pc

Baby, double handle	**425.00**
RE–GO.	**1,000.00**
Caramel, grapefruit size.	**700.00**
Chocolate, large, emb "Sunkist" . .	**400.00**

Clambroth, large

Boat shaped	**175.00**
MacBeth–Evans	**325.00**

Cobalt

Large, Crisscross, Hazel Atlas . . .	**215.00**
Lemon, tab handle, Hazel Atlas	**275.00**

Crystal

Baby, double handle, elephant dec base, 2 pc, Fenton	**70.00**
Large, tab handle, Hazel Atlas. . .	**5.00**
Small, chisel cone, Easley's	**70.00**
Crystal Frosted, baby, double handle, flower dec, 2 pc	**90.00**
Custard, 6", red trim, emb "McK," McKee	**38.00**

Delphite

Large, Jeannette.	**950.00**
Small, emb "McK," McKee	**250.00**

Green Transparent

Large, slick handle, US Glass Co	**60.00**
Small, ftd, Cambridge	**350.00**
Jadite, dark, large, Jeannette.	**22.00**
Jadite, light, Saunders, emb lettering, high pointed cone, McKee	**750.00**
Opalescent White, small, square, Easley's.	**165.00**

Pink

Baby, tab handle, 2 pc, L E Smith	**235.00**

Large, emb "Lindsay"	**400.00**
Pink Frosted, 2 pc, Westmoreland	**115.00**
Sun–Colored Amethyst, baby, 2 pc, Westmoreland.	**65.00**
Turquoise Blue Milk Glass, emb "Sunkist"	**275.00**
Reamer Bucket, green transparent, Hex Optic, Jeannette	**35.00**

Refrigerator Dish, cov, stacking

Chalaine Blue, 4 x 5"	**40.00**
Clear, jade cov, wedge shape.	**8.00**
Cobalt, round, 5¾" d, Hazel Atlas . .	**55.00**
Delphite, 4 x 5", McKee	**25.00**
Green Transparent, dark, 4½ x 5", tab handles, Jeannette	**20.00**

Jadite

Light, oval, 7", vert rib, Hocking	**24.00**
Dark, 10 x 5", floral lid	**28.00**
Pink, 8 x 8", vert rib, Federal.	**30.00**
Ultra–marine, 4 x 8", Jeannette . . .	**25.00**
White, blue wheat and rooster dec, clear lid, 4¼ x 6¾", Pyrex	**4.50**
Yellow, 4½ x 5", Hazel Atlas Co. . . .	**32.00**

Rolling Pin

Amethyst, blown type	**90.00**
Black, blown type	**275.00**
Chalaine Blue, shaker cap	**375.00**
Clambroth, wooden handles	**80.00**
Cobalt, wooden handles attached to metal rod inside pin	**325.00**
Crystal, screw–on cobalt handles	**175.00**
Custard, circular band opposite shaker top, McKee	**160.00**
Forest Green, blown type	**135.00**
Jadite, light, smooth end opposite shaker top, McKee	**265.00**
Peacock Blue, wooden handles attached to metal rod inside pin . . .	**175.00**
Pink, screw–on wooden handles . .	**300.00**
Robin Egg Blue, blown type	**325.00**

Salad Set

Amber, flattened handles, edge down sides	**32.00**
Black, Cambridge	**90.00**
Blue, light, Imperial.	**70.00**
Cobalt, rounded ribbed handles . . .	**40.00**
Peacock Blue, large pointed handles, clear bowl and tines	**65.00**
Pink, flattened handle	**42.00**
Red, Cambridge	**135.00**

Salt Box, cov

Amber, dark, vert rib, emb "SALT," Sneath	**135.00**
Chalaine Blue, metal hinged cov . .	**165.00**
Crystal, emb lettering.	**15.00**
Green Transparent, 6" d, emb "SALT," Jeannette	**155.00**
Jadite, light, black lettering, wooden lid, wall mount, Jeannette.	**185.00**
White, rect, scalloped crest, emb "SALT," wall mount.	**110.00**
Serving Dish, clambroth, 7⅜" d, round	**10.00**

Reamer, US Glass Co., No. 119, clear, green, two cup measuring pitcher base, 4¾" d, 5¼" h, $30.00.

Shaker
  Amber, dark, sugar, hourglass
    shape, Paden City **130.00**
  Black, cylindrical, hobnail, Fenton   **25.00**
  Chalaine Blue, "NUTMEG" **45.00**
  Clambroth, sugar, one hole lid **35.00**
  Clear, ovoid shape, vert rib, red la-
    bel and lid, Owens–Illinois **6.00**
  Crystal, John Alden salt and Priscilla
    pepper, blue illus, red lettering
    and lid, pr **18.00**
  Custard, roman arch side panel,
    black lettering **12.00**
  Delphite, round, black lettering, ho-
    riz rib, Jeannette **18.00**
  Green Transparent, sugar, Hex Op-
    tic, Jeannette **135.00**
  Jadite
    Dark, flour, black lettering **15.00**
    Light, roman arch side panel,
      black lettering, McKee **32.00**
    Orange, fired–on, roman arch sides,
      black lettering, McKee **9.00**
    Seville Yellow, square, flour, black
      lettering, McKee **13.00**
    White, tulip dec, red and blue stripe
      on white lid, Hocking. **4.50**
    Yellow, fired–on, black lettering,
      Hocking **5.00**
  Sherbet, green clambroth, paneled . . .   **6.00**
  Skillet, clear, Range Tec, McKee **8.00**
  Spoon, peacock blue bowl, clear stem   **20.00**
  Spoon Holder, crystal, scalloped top,
    "Pat Feb 11, 1913" **18.00**
  Spoon Rest, green, double **165.00**
  Sprinkler, crystal, red stopper, emb let-
    tering and design, cardboard in-
    structions **18.00**
  Stack Set, green transparent, creamer,
    sugar, plate, and salt and pepper
    shakers, Westmoreland **55.00**
  Straw, black **4.00**
  Straw Holder, peacock blue, cov, cy-
    lindrical, 1950s. **175.00**
  Sugar Canister and Salt and Pepper
    Shaker Set, black, round, wire ftd
    base, Sellers **100.00**
  Syrup
    Amber, dark, chrome cov, bulbous,
      ringed bottom, Cambridge **45.00**
    Black, cov, Fenton **45.00**
    Clear, 1 qt, horiz rib, paper label
      "No Drip Server," blue top, Fed-
      eral Tool Corp **6.00**
    Green, swirl, metal cov, Hocking   **35.00**
    Pink, square, vert rib corners, glass
      cover, New Martinsville **42.00**
  Tea Kettle, clear, horiz rib, glass han-
    dle, Glasbake **18.00**
  Toast Holder, crystal, holds six slices   **48.00**
  Tray
    Black, rect **25.00**

Sugar Shaker, Optic pattern, cranberry, ring neck, Hobbs, Bruckunier & Co., $125.00.

  Clambroth, 10⅝" square **17.50**
  Tumbler
    Cobalt, straight sided, marked
      "HA," Hazel Atlas. **12.50**
    Jadite, light, 12 oz, horiz rib, Jean-
      nette **10.00**
  Tumble–Up Night Set, cobalt **35.00**
  Vase, jadite, light, horiz rib, Jeannette   **10.00**
  Water Bottle
    Cobalt, metal cap, 64 oz, 10" h, Ha-
      zel Atlas **60.00**
    Forest Green, sloping shoulders,
      metal cap, Duraglas **20.00**
  Water Dispenser
    Cobalt, rect, swirled, rect cov, metal
      spigot, L E Smith **325.00**
    Crystal, cylindrical, horiz rib, metal
      spigot, separate ice holder insert,
      McKee **70.00**
    Custard, rect, rect cov, metal swivel
      spout, McKee **120.00**
    Jadite, light, round crystal cov,
      metal swivel spout, Sneath **50.00**
  Whipped Cream Pail, green clam-
    broth, metal bale handle, Fenton . .   **30.00**

VICTORIAN GLASSWARE

History: Glassware was popular during the Victorian era for a variety of reasons. First, a wealth of new utilitarian forms ranging from cruets to spooners were introduced. They were adopted universally.

Second, the glass industry adopted mass–production. Glass items were no longer a prerogative of the upper class. They were affordable by everyone.

Third, glass manufacturers produced glass in a wide range of patterns and colors. You did not have to have the same type of glass as your neighbors. Glassware allowed the Victorians to introduce individuality into their home.

Finally, combining glass with inexpensive silver plated frames allowed the creation of a wide variety of elegant appearing pieces, such as pickle castors, that were modest in cost. As a result, a touch of class could be introduced to even the poorest household.

During the Victorian era, the glass industry also produced some of the finest art glass ever made in America. Mount Washington Glass Company (New Bedford, Massachusetts) introduced Burmese, Crown Milano, and Royal Flemish. The New England Glass Works (Boston, Massachusetts) and Hobbs, Brochunier & Co. (Wheeling, West Virginia) manufactured Peachblow. Amberina, cosmos, cranberry, Mary Gregory type, pomona, and satin glass are just a few of the other highly collectible areas of Victorian glassware.

References: William Heacock, Encyclopedia of Victorian Colored Pattern Glass, Antique Publications—*Toothpick Holders from A to Z, Book 1* (1981); *Opalescent Glass from A to Z, Book 2* (1981); *Syrups, Sugar Shakers & Cruets, Book 3* (1981); *Custard Glass from A to Z, Book 4* (1980); *U. S. Glass from A to Z, Book 5* (1980); *Oil Cruets from A to Z, Book 6* (1981); *Ruby Stained Glass from A to Z, Book 7* (1986); and, *More Ruby Stained Glass, Book 8* (1987); William Heacock and William Gamble, *Cranberry Opalescent from A to Z, Book 9*, Encyclopedia of Victorian Colored Pattern Glass, Antique Publications, 1981.

Bill Jenks and Jerry Luna, *Early American Pattern Glass, 1850–1910: Major Collectible Table Settings with Prices*, Wallace–Homestead, 1990; Dori Miles and Robert W. Miller, *Wallace–Homestead Price Guide to Pattern Glass, 11th Edition*, Wallace–Homestead, 1986; John A. Shuman III, *The Collector's Encyclopedia of American Art Glass*, Collector Books, 1988.

Periodical: *Glass Collector's Digest*, PO Box 663, Marietta, OH 45750.

Biscuit Jar, cov
    Pigeon Blood, Beaded Drapery pattern, ornate silverplate rim, handle **200.00**
    Wavecrest, pink and blue ground, robins and violets dec. **300.00**
Bread Plate, pattern glass, Dahlia, amber. **55.00**
Butter Dish, cov
    Button Arches, ruby stained, Lancaster Fair, 1916 . . . .   **150.00**
    Cosmos Glass, pink band, c1900 . .   **195.00**
    Wildflower, vaseline, pattern glass, collared base. **45.00**
Cake Stand, 10", Bleeding Heart pattern, clear. **85.00**
Castor Set
    Cranberry glass, three–bottle, open salt, pepper shaker, and mustard jar, heavy paneled sides, silverplate frame, mother–of–pearl handle **250.00**

Biscuit Jar, pigeon blood, ribbed, silver plated fittings, 8½″ to top of finial, $250.00.

Cut Glass, six–bottle, ribbed trim on pedestal base, deep skirt, bale handle holds bell and plunger, marked "Meriden B Co," 7″ h . . .   **225.00**
Satin Glass, three–bottle, white, ribbed, silverplate holder marked "Pairpoint" **225.00**
Celery
    Diamond Quilted, cut velvet, deep blue, box pleated top, 6½″ h **725.00**
    Burred Hobnail, milk glass **35.00**
    Wildflower, apple green **60.00**
    Inverted Thumbprint, rubena, ruffled rim **85.00**
Creamer, ruby stained, Star of David, St Louis World's Fair, 1904. . . . . . .   **125.00**
Cruet
    Daisy and Fern, swirl mold, opalescent, blue ground, applied blue handle, clear faceted stopper, 6¼″ h **165.00**
    Inverted Thumbprint, pigeon blood, orig stopper **225.00**

Muffineer, Reverse Swirl pattern, opalescent cranberry and white, Buckeye Glass, $200.00.

Pickle Castor, clear, swirl pattern insert, begging dog finial, Hartford Quadplate, 10" h, $175.00.

Egg Cup, double, Dahlia pattern, clear	**50.00**
Fish Set, milk glass, fish platter, four serving dishes, patent date, Atterbury	**200.00**
Lemonade Set, Thumbprint pattern, cranberry, pitcher and six tumblers	**150.00**
Muffineer	
Cranberry, cylindrical, bulbous base, sterling silver top, 6½" h . . .	**75.00**
Maize, custard, 6" h, Libbey.	**200.00**
Pineapple and Fan pattern	**35.00**
Pickle Castor	
Cranberry, barrel insert, multi-colored enamel floral dec, figural frame with acorns and dog's feet	**400.00**
Green Glass, enameled florals, ornate silverplate frame	**225.00**
Daisy and Fern, apple blossom mold, opalescent blue, ornate ftd silverplate frame, orig tongs	**265.00**
Diamond Quilted, rubena, decorated insert, ftd, fancy frame, orig tongs	**275.00**
Spooner	
Cosmos Glass, pink flowers, c1900	**130.00**
Bleeding Heart pattern, clear	**25.00**
Syrup	
Cranberry, inverted cut design, sterling silver holder	**500.00**
Wildflower pattern, clear	**65.00**
Scroll and Net, pigeon blood, satin finish, applied frosted handle, orig top	**575.00**

WHIMSIES

History: Glass workers occasionally spent time during lunch or after completing their regular work schedule creating unusual glass objects, known as whimsies, e.g. candy striped canes, darners, hats, paperweights, pipes, witch balls, etc. Whimsies were taken home and given as gifts to family and friends.

Because of their uniqueness and infinite variety, whimsies can rarely be attributed to a specific glass house or glass worker. Whimsies appeared wherever glass was made, from New Jersey to Ohio and westward. Some have suggested that style and color can be used to pinpoint a region or factory, but no one has yet developed an identification key that is adequate.

Glass canes are one of the most collectible types of whimsies. Glass canes range from very short, under one foot, to lengths of ten feet and beyond. They come in both hollow and solid forms. Hollow canes can have a bulb type handle or the rarer "C" or "L" shaped handle. Canes are found in many fascinating colors, with the candy striped being a regular favorite with collectors. Many canes are also filled with varied colored powders, gold and white being the most common, silver being harder to find. Many canes were made to be carried in regional parades organized to display craftsmen's wares. Others were used as candy containers.

References: Joyce E. Blake, *Glasshouse Whimsies,* printed by author, 1984; Joyce E. Blake and Dale Murschell, *Glasshouse Whimsies: An Enhanced Reference,* printed by author, 1989.

Collectors' Club: The Whimsey Club, 4544 Cairo Drive, Whitehall, PA 18052.

Barber Bottle, opalescent white stars and stripes on cranberry, 8" h, white porcelain corked stopper	**275.00**
Bracelet, clear, multicolored spirals entwining gold spiral, Sandwich, 1840–70	**200.00**
Chain, thirteen feet long, plain cobalt blue, amber, and aqua links	**250.00**
Darner	
Peachblow, glossy finish, 6" l, c1900.	**225.00**
White Milk Glass, blue loopings, straight sheared open end	**175.00**
Egg, 2⅜" h, milk glass, cobalt blue and pink spattering	**75.00**
Fairy Lamp, 3 pc, peach–pink shading to yellow, sgd "Queen's Burmese Ware Thomas Webb & Sons Patented" on base and "S. Clarke Patent Trade Mark Fairy," c1880	**850.00**
Hatchet	
7" l, vaseline, raised molded letters "World's Fair 1893" and "George Washington Father of this Country," George Washington relief bust, sgd "Libbey Glass Co Toledo Ohio"	**485.00**
8⅜" l handle, 5⅛" l blade, clear, twisted handle	**120.00**

Witch Ball, pale blue, white looping, Nailsea type, 4¾″ d, $120.00.

Hat Stand, 14¾″ h, blown, blueish–
white base, pink top, pontiled, En-
gland, c1850 . . . .   **215.00**
Muddler, 4½″ l, crystal rod, duck crest,
New York World's Fair, 1939 . . . . .   **20.00**
Pear, 5½″ h, amber **85.00**
Pipe
9″ l, twisted stem, white dashes on
scalloped pink–edged bowl,
c1800. . . . .   **225.00**
15″ l, cranberry, one large band
flanked by two smaller bands on
deep bended stem, white bor-
dered bowl, c1800. . . . .   **250.00**

40″ l, aqua, white spirals entire
length, Philadelphia Exposition,
1876. . . . .   **165.00**
Powder Flask, 13″ l, clear, milk glass
loopings **225.00**
Rolling Pin, 15″ l, freeblown, knobbed
ends, medium sapphire blue,
painted red floral dec and gold inscription "A Present from New-
castle," c1850 . . . .   **175.00**
Walking Stick, blown
36″ l, grape colored, hollow, simulated branch body, raised spirals,
right angle bulbous handle **135.00**
39″ l, aqua, applied swirled ribs . . .   **50.00**
50″ l, clear, alternating close red,
white, and blue spirals **175.00**
58¾″ l, clear, mahogany spiral, inte-
rior gilding **85.00**
59″ l, clear, white, yellow, and ma-
hogany looping **150.00**
Witch Ball
4″ d, clear, milk glass loopings **185.00**
9½″ d, freeblown, aqua, contains pa-
per flower, leaf, butterfly, and
people cut outs, red, blue, green,
and white interior powder, New
England, 1850–80. . . . .   **450.00**

KITCHEN COLLECTIBLES

Family life in rural America focuses around the kitchen. A substantial breakfast at the break of dawn and a robust satisfying meal at the end of a day's hard work are standard fare. At the conclusion of the evening meal, it was not uncommon to sit around the table and converse, often for hours. In an agrarian environment, the kitchen table is as important a social center as the living room or parlor.

The kitchen remained a central focal point in the family environment until frozen foods, TV dinners, and microwave ovens freed the family to congregate in other areas of the house during meal time. Initially, food preparation involved both the long and short term. Home canning remained popular through the early 1950s.

Many early kitchen utensils were handmade and prized by their owners. Next came a period of utilitarian products manufactured of tin and other metals. Design began to serve both an aesthetic and functional purpose. Brightly enameled handles and knobs were made to appeal to the busy housewife. With the advent of bakelite and plastic even more color found its way into the kitchen.

Multicolored enameled matchsafes, pot scrubbers, and string holders were not only functional, but advertised a product or service. These early advertising giveaways are prized by country collectors.

The new fangled gadgets and early electrical appliances changed the type and style of kitchen products. Many products became faddish. Electric waffle makers were popular in the 1930s and breakfast was served on special waffle dinnerware sets, complete with serving platters and syrup pitchers. Old hand operated egg beaters were replaced by aerators and mixers.

References: Jane H. Celehar, *Kitchens and Gadgets, 1920 To 1950,* Wallace–Homestead, 1982; Linda Campbell Franklin, *300 Years Of Kitchen Collectibles: An Identification and Value Guide, 3rd Edition,* Books Americana, 1991; Bill and Denise Harned, *Griswold Cast Collectibles: History & Values,* privately printed, 1988; Mary Lou Mathews, *American Kitchen And Country Collectibles,* L–W Promotions, 1984; Gary Miller and K. M. Scotty Mitchell, *Price Guide To Collectible Kitchen Appliances: From Aerators to Waffle Irons, 1900–1950,* Wallace–Homestead, 1991; Ellen M. Plante, *Kitchen Collectibles: An Illustrated Price Guide,* Wallace–Homestead, 1991; Frances Thompson, *Antiqu From The Country Kitchen,* Wallace–Homestead, 1985.

Reproduction Manufacturers: American Country House, PO Box 317, Davison, MI 48423; Conewago Junction, 805 Oxford Rd, New Oxford, PA 17350; Cumberland General Store, Rte 3, Crossville, TN 38555; Lemee's Fireplace Equipment, 815 Bedford St, Bridgewater, MA 02324; Matthew's Wire & Wood, 654 W Morrison, Frankfort, IN 46041; Matthews Emporium, PO Box 1038, Matthews, NC 28106; McClanahan Country, 217 Rockwell Rd, Wilmington, NC 28405; Old Smithy Shop, Box 336, Milford, NH 03055; Our Home, Articles of Wood, 666 Perry St, Vermillion, OH 44089; Town and Country, Main St, East Conway, NH 04037.

BAKING ITEMS

History: The country kitchen is readily acknowledged as the source of nourishing, hearty meals. A country kitchen isn't complete without a freshly baked pie cooling on the window sill. The smell of freshly baked goods lingers in the minds of many individuals. Homemade bread is a must. Dessert is an integral part of dinner. In fact, dessert products have a habit of showing up at breakfast as well as in the lunch box.

All items associated with baking are collectible, from ingredient packaging to utensils used to serve the end product. Collectors concentrate on three distinct periods: 1850 to 1915, 1915 to 1940, and 1940 to the present. The presence of the original box is extremely important for items made after 1915.

Pieces containing a manufacturer's or patent date marking and highly decorated pieces, either painted or lithographed, are more highly valued than unmarked or plain examples. Many collectors like to use these old implements (hence the desirability of pieces that are in working condition). Finally, the category is subject to crazes. Pie birds are the "hot" collectible of the moment.

Collectors' Club: International Society of Apple Parer Enthusiasts, 3911 Morgan Center Road, Utica, OH 43080.

Reproduction Craftsperson: *Cookie Cutters—* Robert and Sylvia Gerlack, PO Box 213, Emmaus, PA 18049.

Reproduction Manufacturer: *Cookie Cutters—* Gooseberry Patch, PO Box 634, Delaware, OH 43015.

Apple Corer, tin, wood handle, Boye Needle Co, 1916	**12.00**
Apple Parer	
Cast Iron, heart design gear wheel, eight gears, Sinclair Scott Co, Baltimore, MD, c1880	**60.00**
Wood, bird's eye maple, forged iron fork and handle, table clamp, 19th C	**215.00**
Apple Slicer, wood and iron, six blades, 42" l, 19th C	**150.00**
Beaten Biscuit Machine, wood, table model, c1860s	**185.00**
Biscuit Cutter, tin, fluted edge, strap handle	**8.00**
Bread Board, carved motto "Give Us This Day Our Daily Bread" around border, 9½" d, early 20th C	**50.00**
Bread Fork, wooden handle, carved "Bread," three prong, silver plated	**95.00**
Bread Grater, tin, cylindrical, punched, handle, 10" l	**20.00**

Apple Corer, wooden, 22 x 13½", PA, $175.00.

Bread Knife, "Bread" carved on wooden handle, carbon steel blade, 12½" l, 19th C **30.00**

Bread Maker, tin, cast iron gears, table mount, White House Bread Maker, 1902 . . . .   **115.00**

Bread Pan, tin, double loaf, side by side tubes, Ideal **28.00**

Bread Raiser, tin, stamped, ventilated dome lid, 8 quart. **40.00**

Bread Rising Tray, wood, six loaf, 39 x 7", late 19th C. **200.00**

Bread Slicing Box, wood, 13½" l, 5¾" h, varnished, 19th C **65.00**

Cake Decorator, tin, eight different design heads. **25.00**

Cake Filler, tin, table mount, Jaburg Bros, 1908 . . . .   **30.00**

Cake Mixer, tin and cast iron, table mount, Universal, Landers, Frary & Clark, c1900. . . . .   **50.00**

Cake Mold
  Lamb, cast iron **55.00**
  Turk's Head, redware, 7¾" d **90.00**

Cake Pan, angel cake, tin, tube and handles, Vanity Co **18.00**

Cake Turner, tin, wooden handle, Androck. **3.00**

Cherry Pitter
  Duke, cast iron, long hopper, swiveling hinge above fastening clamp, table mount, 11" l, Duke, Reading Hardware Co, Reading, PA, 19th C **75.00**
  Enterprise #2, cast iron, tinned finish, Enterprise Mfg Co, patented 1903.   **70.00**

Chocolate Mold, running rabbit, marked "Brandt's" **20.00**

Coconut Grater, turned iron shaft, serrated blades, brass and wood handle, 7" h, mid 19th C **95.00**

Cookie Board, rect
  Beech, relief carved rooster one side, folk art couple reverse, worm holes, 7 x 11". **375.00**
  Walnut, carved, flowers, fruit, and compote in toothed almond shaped border, 6¼ x 16" **260.00**

Cookie Cutter
  Roller, tin, wire handle, diamonds, waffling, or swirl patterns, interchangeable rolls, Guirier, orig box, c1930 . . . .   **40.00**
  Scottie Dog, running, tin, flatback, strap handle, 4½" l, 3" w **25.00**

Cookie Mold
  Cast Iron, oval, bird on branch, 5" l   **75.00**
  Pine, primitive, carved bird design both sides, 4½ x 6¼". **225.00**

Cookie Press, tin, wooden plunger, star shaped opening, 10½" l. **35.00**

Cookie Cutter, tin, walking horse, two finger holes, patina, 7½" w, 5½" h, $35.00.

Corn Stick Mold, cast iron, wire handles, four stick, Wagner Ware, c1880 . . . .   **25.00**

Cream Whip, glass jar, tin whip, cast metal gear, 10" h, Whippo Super–Whip, early 20th C **45.00**

Crimper, aluminum, 5½" l, Juice Tite Pie Sealer **15.00**

Dough Mixer, two loaf, tin pail, side handles and crank, "U"-shaped wire blade, crimped dome lid, wooden knob, screw clamp, Chauvauquat Bread Mixer, S & H Co, NY, c1909 . . . .   **30.00**

Doughnut Cutter, tin, "Rumford Baking Powder" **12.00**

Egg Beater
  Big Bingo #7, metal, heavy gauge wire handle, sheet metal gear wheel, coiled wire knob, A&J, Binghamton, NY, patented 1923   **25.00**
  Clipper, Archimedean drill action, nine twist shaft, wooden spool, two small ballooned blades, 13" h, patented Aug 1930 . . . . . .   **65.00**
  Jewel Beater Mixer Whipper Freezer, cast iron gear and crank, wooden knob, black, screw–on lid, wire beaters, straight sided emb glass jar, 7" h, Juergens Brothers, Minneapolis, MN, c1900. . . . .   **60.00**

Dough Scraper, wrought iron, triangular, 4¾" base, 4½" handle, $25.00.

Egg Beater and Measuring Cup Set, 2 cup, emb glass jar, cast iron gears and lid, scalloped edge, wire blades, New Keystone Beater **45.00**

Egg Whip, sheet metal, wire frame, four large cutouts on large flat spoon, 11" l, Vandeusen Egg Whip, C A Chapman, Geneva, NY, patented Mar 13, 1894 . . . . **25.00**

Flour Dredger, tin, ftd, domed pierced lid, strap handle, 6" h, c1825 . . . . . **20.00**

Flour Grinder, cast iron, graniteware hopper, wooden pusher, late 19th C **65.00**

Flour Scoop, metal bowl, wire handles stamped "Airy Fairy Kwik Bis–kit Flour" and "Airy Fairy Cake Flour," $7\frac{1}{2}$" l **10.00**

Flour Sifter

Gem Flour and Saucer Sifter, tin bucket, crank, three iron paddles, screen bottom, three cast iron legs, painted black, 11" h, patented Dec 26, 1865 . . . . **80.00**

Kwik, tin, double ended, yellow wooden handle, 5 cup, 20th C . . **18.00**

Sift–Chine, tin, wire mesh bottom, side handle, squeeze action, Meets a Need Mfg Co, Seattle, WA, c1931 . . . . **12.00**

Fruit Baller, red turned wooden handle, hinged perforated cutting ring, $5\frac{1}{4}$" l, 1920s **6.00**

Fruit Press, plated cast iron, bowl shaped hopper, table model, 12" h, 11" l, Enterprise Mfg Co, Philadelphia, patented Sept 30, 1879 . . . . . **60.00**

Funnel, tin, attached hinged wire mesh strainer, 9" l, $3\frac{3}{8}$" d, patented Aug 24, 1875 . . . . **18.00**

Herb Mill, 2 pc, cast iron, 17" l boat shaped ftd base, 7" d wooden handled wheel, 19th C **185.00**

Kettle Strainer, tin and wire, pierced, 16" l, 10" w, patented 1898 . . . . . . **15.00**

Lard Press, varnished wood, nickeled iron hinge, long paddle handles, corrugated interior, 12" l, late 19th C **45.00**

Lemon Squeezer, japanned cast iron, "American Queen," c1906 . . . . . . **25.00**

Measure, tin, wraparound pouring lip, strap handle, 1 pint, c1875 . . . . . . **24.00**

Measuring Cup, spun aluminum, emb "Swans Down Cake Flour Makes Better Cakes" on side, 1 cup **15.00**

Measuring Pitcher, tin, 1 quart, Dover **6.00**

Measuring Spoons, tin, marked $\frac{1}{4}$, $\frac{1}{2}$, and 1 tsp and 15, 30, and 60 drops, marked "Original," patented 1900 **15.00**

Mixer

Kwikmix, nickeled metal, vertical cranked wheel, metal band holds

container, mounted on board, 8" h, Schenker Mfg Co, NY, patented 1922 . . . . **55.00**

Maynard Mixer, plastic, red, chromed white metal gears, $11\frac{1}{8}$" l, Los Angeles, CA, patented 1933 . . . . **15.00**

Mixing Spoon, nickeled metal, stamped and slotted bowl, green wooden handle, marked "Rumford Baking Powder," $10\frac{3}{4}$" l, 20th C . . . **18.00**

Muffin Pan, cast iron, 11 muffins, Griswold **20.00**

Nut Cracker

Alligator shape, cast iron, late 19th C **100.00**

Pliers type, hand held, cast iron, knobbed ends, cracks two sizes, $5\frac{1}{8}$" l, 19th C **15.00**

Nut Grinder, cast iron and tin, glass jar, screw–on tin hopper, Climax, 1940s **12.50**

Nutmeg Grater

Cast Iron crank, wire handle, 7" l, 19th C **115.00**

Tin cylinder and barrel, wooden handled wire crank, spring loaded plunger, $3\frac{1}{2}$" l, 19th C **85.00**

Pastry Blender, six hooped wires, sheet metal handle, Lambert, Clara Burchard Lambert, Pasadena, CA, $4\frac{1}{4}$" w, patented Mar 11, 1924 . . . . . **14.00**

Pastry Brush, turned wood handle, $8\frac{1}{4}$" l, Shaker **120.00**

Pastry Knife, steel, cylindrical handle at top rolled edge, no finger cutout, $4\frac{1}{2}$" h, 5" w, c1900 . . . . **15.00**

Peach Parer, cast iron, wooden board base, two opposing forks, David H Whittemore, MA, 1860s **95.00**

Pie Bird, china, glazed

Chicken **48.00**

Duck, blue **23.00**

Pie Bird, ceramic, yellow, green, red, and white, $18.00.

Rolling Pins, top with incised design, 18" l, $24.00; bottom with turned handle, 18½" l, $28.00.

Man, black suit and hat, white face, black features	**52.00**
Pie Crimper, bone, carved, cross hatching, 6¼" d	**120.00**
Pie Filler, tin, braced tubular handle, 1 quart, Jaburg Bros, 1908	**45.00**
Pie Lifter, wire, wooden handle, two prongs, 17½" l	**20.00**
Pie Pan, tin, "Mrs Smith's"	**5.00**
Popover Pan, cast iron, slanted cups, 11 popovers, 11" l, Wagner Ware	**24.00**
Poppyseed Mill, cast iron, painted turquoise green, spun brass hopper, table clamp, Standard, 9¼" h, 1890s	**35.00**
Pudding Mold, tin, melon shape, flat lid, c1890.	**40.00**
Raisin Seeder, cast iron, four legs, 8–wire levered press, 6" l, patented May 7, 1895	**50.00**
Roll Cutter, tin, cuts fourteen 5" l rolls each revolution, 11" l, Mennonite	**25.00**
Rolling Pin	
Hardwood, turned bone handles, 15" l, 19th C	**200.00**
Maple, one piece, turned, 14" l, 3½" d	**25.00**
Strawberry Huller, tweezer shape, folded spring steel, concave round disc ends, cutout centers, A S Bunker, Lawrence, MA, c1877.	**4.00**
Sugar Shaker, tin, domed perforated lid, strap handle, 4" h, 2½" d, Fries, c1900	**20.00**
Tart Sealer, tin and cast aluminum, wooden knob handle, spring loaded, Tart Master, patented 1938	**18.00**
Wafer Iron, cast and forged iron, heart shaped wafer, 29½" l	**250.00**
Waffle Iron	
Abbot & Lawrence, cast iron, stand, hearts and diamonds, 8½" l	**60.00**
Wagner, cast iron, two piece, bale handle, 1920.	**20.00**
Whisk, wire, marked "Omar Wonder Flour," 20th C	**8.00**

CANNING ITEMS

History: The bountiful harvest is a common theme in Country collecting. However, a bountiful harvest meant plenty of hard work, especially for the country housewife. The products of one harvest had to last until the next harvest was gathered. Further, one had to plan ahead, laying away extra in case the next year's returns were insufficient.

Canning, also known as jarring, is labor intensive. Time passed quicker and more was accomplished when extra hands were available. Canning bees, similar to quilting bees, were common occurrences. Most canning parties consisted of the women from one's extended family. Often the group moved from one home to another during a harvest season.

An innovative Philadelphia glass maker, Thomas W. Dyott, began promoting glass canning jars in 1829. John Landis Mason patented the screw type canning jar on November 30, 1858. The progress of the American glass industry and manufacturing processes can be studied through fruit jars. Early handmade jars show bits of local history.

Many ways were devised to close the jars securely. Lids of fruit jars can be a separate collectible, but most collectors feel it is more desirous to have a complete fruit jar. Closures can be as simple as a cork or wax seal. Other closures include zinc or glass lids, wire bails, metal screw bands, and today's rubber sealed metal lids.

Many fruit jar collectors base their collections on a specific geographical area, others on one manufacturer or one color. Another way to collect fruit jars is by patent date. Over 50 different types bear a patent date of 1858. Note: The patent date does not mean the jar was made in that year.

Most canning collectors do not limit their focus to fruit jars. Canners, funnels, sealing equipment, and cooking thermometers also are sought.

References: Alice M. Creswick, *The Fruit Jar Works, Volume I* and *Volume 2,* published by author; Alice M. Creswick, *Red Book No. 6: The Collector's Guide To Old Fruit Jars,* published by author, 1990; Dick Roller, *Standard Fruit Jar Reference,* published by author, 1987; Dick Roller, *Supplementary Price Guide to Standard Fruit Jar Reference,* published by author,1987; Bill Schroeder, *1000 Fruit Jars: Priced And Illustrated,* 5th Edition, Collector Books, 1987.

Periodical: *Fruit Jar Newsletter,* 364 Gregory Avenue, West Orange, NJ 07052.

Note: Fruit jars listed below are machine made unless otherwise noted.

Canner	
Iron Horse Cold Pack, blackened tin, double seamed bottom, wood handles, seven quart jar rack, wire jar lifter, 13¾" d, 9" h, Rochester Can Co, c1930	**65.00**
Mudge's Patent Canner, tin and copper, Biddle–Gaumer Co, late 1880s	**225.00**

Canning Rack, wire, rect, used in two–hole boiler **12.00**

Corn Dryer, twisted wire, hanging ring at top, c1910 . . . . **12.00**

Fruit Dryer, tin frame, wire screen, three shelves, removeable trays, Arlington Oven Dryer, 9″ h **135.00**

Fruit Jar

American Fruit Jar, light green, handmade, glass lid, wire bail, 1 quart. **100.00**

Atlas Mason, aqua, handmade, zinc lid, 1 quart **25.00**

Ball, Sure Seal, blue, smooth lip, lightning beaded neck seal **4.00**

Blue Ribbon, clear, glass lid, wire clip, 1 quart. **7.50**

Clark Fruit Jar Co, blue, handmade, glass lid emb "Clark Fruit Jar Cleveland," 1 quart **7.50**

Dexter, aqua, ground lip glass insert and screw band, patented Aug 8, 1865. **35.00**

Economy, amber, metal lid, spring clip, 1 pint. **5.00**

Empire, aqua, handmade, stopper neck, name emb in arch, 1 quart **215.00**

Forster Jar, clear, smooth lip, glass insert and screw band. **8.00**

Good House Keepers, clear, machine made, zinc lid, 2 quart. . . . **2.00**

Hazel Atlas E Z Seal, clear, smooth lip **10.00**

Hoosier, aqua, handmade, threaded glass lid, emb "Hoosier Jar," 1 quart. **315.00**

Independent, aqua, handmade, glass screw lid, 1 quart **40.00**

Kerr, sky blue, smooth lip, two pc lid, 1 pint **25.00**

Lightning Putnam #31, aqua, bail handle **10.00**

Lyon Jar, clear, patented Apr 10, 1900. **2.00**

Mason

Aqua, Midget, 1858 . . . . **25.00**

Green, handmade, zinc lid, emb "S Mason's Patent 1858," 1 quart **4.50**

Millville Atmospheric, aqua, 1 quart, 1861 . . . . **40.00**

Ohio, clear, handmade, zinc lid, emb "Ohio Quality Mason," 2 quart. **12.00**

Putnam, amber, 1 quart **15.00**

Regal, clear, handmade, glass lid, emb "Regal" in oval, 1 quart. . . . **3.00**

Smalley & Co, amber, rect, arched shoulders, tin lid, 2 quart, patented Apr 7, 1896 . . . . **38.00**

Swayzee's Improved, green **12.00**

Tropical, clear, machine made, zinc lid, name emb in script, 1 quart **2.75**

Yeoman's Fruit Bottle, aqua, wax cork closure **45.00**

Fruit Jar Holder, wire, 6″ h **6.00**

Fruit Jar Lifter

E–Z Lift, iron. **4.00**

Mason Jar Sealer and Opener, cast iron frame, steel blade, adjustable leather strap, c1912 . . . . **18.00**

Simplex, metal, Gorman Mfg Co, late 19th C **15.00**

Fruit Jar Wrench

Presto, iron, Cupples Co, orig box, 20th C **7.50**

Speedo, cast metal, geared mechanical, c1900 . . . . **10.00**

Wilson's, cast iron, Wilson Mfg Co, early 20th C **12.00**

Funnel

Enamelware, wide untapered neck, 5″ l, c1900 . . . . **12.00**

Tin, ring handle, large mouth, c1900. . . . . **8.00**

Herb Drying Rack, wood, orig blue paint, 28″ l, 19th C **425.00**

Jelly Glass, pressed glass, clear **3.00**

Scale, spring, cast iron and stamped sheet iron, Simmons Hardware Co, 20th C **28.00**

Soldering Iron, copper, bullet shaped

Atlas E–Z Seal, quart, clear, blue glass, glass lid, clamp top, $10.00.

Bull Dog Jar Rubbers, $3\frac{3}{8}$ x $3\frac{1}{4}$ x $1\frac{3}{8}$″ orig box, $4.00.

head, iron wire shaft, wooden handle, 8" l, late 19th C **8.00**
Thermometer, jelly, knife shaped, calibrated metal plate, glass tube, tapered turned wooden handle, hanging loop, Taylor Instrument Co, NY, mid 1930s **7.50**

CLEANING AND WASHDAY

History: Living and working in a rural environment was dirty business. Field work and feeding the animals generated large amounts of dust. Wet weather meant mud and plenty of it.

The housewife faced a never-ending battle to keep things clean. Dusting was a daily chore. Washday was not limited to Mondays on most farms. Rural society always has judged wives on how they kept house and family. Women's liberation may have changed some things, but not this.

Many individuals who decorate in Country favor the weathered look. Cleaning and washday material fills the bill. These implements were meant to be used, used hard, and to last. Try beating a rug with a carpet beater.

Because electricity came late to many rural areas, most pre–1940 implements are hand powered. The number of variants within each product is overwhelming. Mail order catalogs are a great research source to determine what was available during a given time period.

Reproduction Craftsperson: *Brooms*—Kenelm Winslow III, 252 Clover Hill Rd, Newburg, PA 17240.

Broom, wood splinters and handle, c1825 . . . . **50.00**
Broom Holder, cast iron, emb "Gem Broom Holder" **12.50**
Carpet Beater
  Oak, Silver Streak, Bissell, early 1900s **30.00**
  Wicker, knot design, 35" l **28.00**
  Wire
    Braided, wooden handle, 30" l, c1905 . . . . **25.00**
    Twisted, bulbous onion shape, turned wooden handle, 31" l **30.00**
Clothes Dasher
  Tin, star stamped on cone, wooden broomstick handle **12.00**
  Wood, X frame, vertical handle, 18" l **45.00**
Clothes Dryer, folding, wood **18.00**
Clothespin Bag, cotton, embroidered **10.00**
Clothes Sprinkler, ceramic, figural Mammy, white dress, red trim, 1935–45 . . . . **80.00**
Dusting Brush, horsehair, wooden handle, 9" l **18.00**

Pot Scraper, advertising, Sharples Tubular Cream Separator, The 1909 Tubulars Are Better Than Ever, red cream separator, sepia and blue highlights, advertising and list of company locations on back, 3½" h, 2¼" w, $250.00.

Dustpan, tin, tubular handle, 8" w . . . **40.00**
Iron
  Box, iron slug, lift gate at back, wrought iron handle, 1850 . . . . . **150.00**
  Charcoal, tall chimney, 7" h, W D Cummings & E Bless, patented 1852 . . . . **75.00**
  Fluter, nickeled cast iron, wooden handle, hinged base plate, two heating plates, 2½" d roller, 6¾" l base, Empire Fluter, Heinz & Munschauer, Buffalo, NY **110.00**
  Gasoline, nickel plated, blue enamel handle, Coleman #3 . . . **60.00**
  Sad Iron, raised star center, wooden handle, 2½" **95.00**
  Sleeve, cross–hatched iron handle, 7" l, Hub **45.00**
Ironing Board, poplar, folding, one board top, four turned legs, old green paint on base, 30 x 14¾ x 59½" **150.00**
Soap Saver, tin frame, twisted wire handle, hanging loop, wire mesh container, 3½ x 2½", 7" l handle **20.00**
Sprinkler Bottle, glass
  Bulbous, mold blown **18.00**
  Cat, blue and white **20.00**
Washboard
  Atlantic No. 14, wood frame, glass scrubber **20.00**
  Columbus, wood **24.00**
  Midget–Washer, glass, orig label, 8½ x 6" **12.00**
  National, wood frame, stenciled pilgrim scene, brass scrubber, 24" h, 12½" w **30.00**
  The Zinc King, wood frame, zinc scrubber **15.00**
Washer, copper–bottom tub, wringer **180.00**

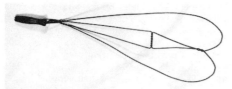

Rug Beater, wire, wooden handle, 31" l, $20.00.

Washing Machine, tin tub, wood
dasher, iron crank, 1883 . . . .   **175.00**
Wash Stick, 36" l **12.00**
Whisk Broom, Mammy, 4½" l **18.00**

COOKBOOKS

History: Among the earliest Americana cookbooks are *The Frugal Housewife; or, Complete
Woman Cook* by Susanna Carter, published in
Philadelphia in 1796 and *American Cookery* by
Amelia Simmons, published in Hartford, Connecticut in 1796. Cookbooks of this era are
crudely written, for most cooks could not read
well and measuring devices were not yet refined.

Other types of collectible cookbooks include
those used as premiums or advertisements. This
type is much less expensive than the rare 18th
century books.

References: Bob Allen, *A Guide to Collecting
Cookbooks and Advertising Cookbooks: A His-
tory of People, Companies, and Cooking*, Collec-
tor Books, 1990; Mary–Margaret Barile, *Just
Cookbooks!—The only directory for cookbook
collectors*, Heritage Publications (PO Box 335,
Arkville, NY 12406); Linda J. Dickinson, *Price
Guide to Cookbooks and Recipe Leaflets*, Collec-
tor Books, 1990; Linda Campbell Franklin, *300
Years of Kitchen Collectibles, 3rd Edition*, Books
Americana, 1991.

Periodical: *Cookbook Collectors' Exchange*, PO
Box 32369, San Jose, CA 95152.

Collectors' Club: Cook Book Collectors Club of
America, PO Box 56, St James, MO 65559.

All About Home Baking, General
Foods, hard cov, 144 pgs, 1933 . . .   **6.00**
America's Cook Book, Home Institute,
NY, hard cov, 1,006 pgs, 1937. . . .   **18.00**
American Family Cookbook, L Wal-
lace, hard cov, 831 pgs, 1949 . . . .   **16.00**
American Housewife Cookbook, H
Anners, 95 pgs, 1850. . . . .   **55.00**
American Regional Cookery, S Hib-
bon, hard cov, 354 pgs, 1946. . . . .   **18.00**
American Way of Progress, Kraft, NY
World's Fair, leaflet, 20 pgs, 1939   **4.00**

Anyone Can Bake, Royal Baking, hard
cov, 100 pgs, 1928 . . . .   **15.00**
Apple–Dore Cook Book, A Graves,
soft cov, 234 pgs, 1872 . . . .   **35.00**
Arm & Hammer Soda Valuable Reci-
pes, leaflet, 32 pgs, 1900 . . . .   **6.00**
Art of Cooking and Serving, Crisco,
soft cov, 252 pgs, 1934 . . . .   **10.00**
Art of German Cooking and Baking, L
Meir, 394 pgs, 1944 . . . .   **10.00**
Art of Making Bread at Home, North
Western Yeast Co, IL, black and
white cov, 28 pgs, c1930. . . . .   **6.00**
Atlas Book of Recipes & Helpful Infor-
mation on Canning, Hazel Atlas
Glass Co, c1930 . . . .   **13.00**
Aunt Jenny's Favorite Recipes, Spry,
soft cov, 48 pgs, 1940 . . . .   **18.00**
Ball Blue Book, Russel, soft cov, 56
pgs, 1930 . . . .   **15.00**
Berk's County Cookbook, Pennsylva-
nia Dutch Recipes, soft cov, 48 pgs,
c1945 . . . .   **7.00**
Best Chocolate Recipes, Baker's Choc-
olate, 60 pgs, 1932 . . . .   **2.00**
Betty Crocker All Purpose Baking, soft
cov, 100 pgs, 1942 . . . .   **4.00**
Biscuit & Cakes, Reliable Flour, leaflet,
62 pgs, 1922. . . . .   **7.50**
Biscuits for Salads, National Biscuit,
leaflet, 8 pgs, 1926 . . . .   **2.00**
Bond Bread Cookbook, soft cov, 30
pgs, 1932. . . . .   **8.00**
Book of Cookies, Good Housekeep-
ing, soft cov, 68 pgs, 1958 . . . .   **4.00**
Borden's Cooking New York World's
Fair, soft cov, 1939 . . . .   **4.00**
Boston Cooking School Cookbook,
Fannie Farmer, hard cov, 648 pgs,
1912 . . . .   **20.00**

**Aunt Jenny's Favorite Recipes, Spry,
$10.00; Betty Crocker's 101 Famous Bis-
quick Recipes, $12.00; Crisco, The Art of
Cooking And Serving, $10.00; The Ball
Blue Book, $15.00; Be An Artist At The
Gas Range, $9.00.**

Bride's Favorite Receipts, Indianapolis, hard cov, 1909.	**18.00**
Calumet Baking Powder Recipe Book, 80 pgs, 1922.	**12.00**
Candy Making at Home, M Wright, 188 pgs, 1920.	**20.00**
Chicken of the Sea Tuna Hoppy Bar—20 Ranch Recipes, 1951	**5.00**
Clabber Girl Baking Book, 15 pgs, 1934	**4.00**
Come Into the Kitchen, D Jerdon, L Pinkham, 32 pgs, c1920	**10.00**
Common Sense Papers on Cookery, Payne, c1920	**30.00**
Congress Cookbook, Congress Yeast Powder, soft cov, 80 pgs, 1899.	**5.00**
Cookery Calendar 1925, Women World Magazine, hard cov, 56 pgs	**17.50**
Cottolene Shortening—52 Sunday Dinners, 192 pgs, 1915	**4.00**
Cow Brand Cookbook, leaflet, 32 pgs, 1900	**3.00**
Daniel Webster Flour Cook Book, soft cov, 120 pgs, 1907	**16.00**
Durkee Famous Food Cookbook, Century of Progress, 1933	**5.00**
Edna Eby Heller's Dutch Cookbook, soft cov, 65 pgs, 1953	**5.00**
Eggs At Any Meal, US Dept of Agriculture, leaflet #39, 8 pgs, 1931	**12.00**
Enterprising Housekeeper, Johnson, soft cov, 79 pgs, 1898	**20.00**
Famous Dishes from Every State, Frigidaire, soft cov, 1936	**2.00**
Farm Journal's Country Cookbook—More Than 1,000 Tested Recipes, Nell B Nichols, Farm Journal, soft cov, special edition, 420 pgs, 1959	**7.50**
Feeding the Child from Crib to College, Wheatena, 44 pgs, 1928	**12.50**
Foodarama Party Book, Kelvinator, 128 pgs, 1959.	**3.00**
Gem Chopper Cook Book, Sargent & Co, NY, cloth cov, 1890s.	**20.00**
Given's Modern Encyclopedia of Cooking, hard cov, 1,724 pgs, 1947	**15.00**
Gold Medal Flour Cook Book, Washburn Crosby Co, soft cov, 74 pgs, 1917	**17.50**
Gone with the Wind Famous Southern Recipes Cookbook, Pebeco Toothpaste	**35.00**
Good Housekeeping Book of Menu Recipes, hard cov, 253 pgs, 1922	**8.50**
Grandma's Old Fashioned Molasses, soft cov, 34 pgs, 1931	**8.00**
Heinz Book of Meat Cookery, Heinz, soft cov, 54 pgs, 1930	**5.00**
Hood's Cookbook # 1, Hood's Sarsaparilla, soft cov, 32 pgs, 1879.	**7.00**
Housekeeping in Old Virginia, J Morton, 1879	**98.00**
How to Bake Ration Book, Swans Down, soft cov, 23 pgs, 1923	**3.00**
How to Make Jams, Jellies, & Marmalade, Certo, soft cov, 1927	**5.00**
Institute Cookbook, H Cramp, hard cov, 507 pgs, 1913	**10.00**
Jell-o Secrets for Automatic Refrigerators, leaflet, 1929	**6.00**
Karo Cook Book, Hewitt, 47 pgs, 1909	**10.00**
Kerr Home Canning, Kerr, 56 pgs, 1943	**15.00**
Kickapoo Indian Medicine Co Cookbook, 1891	**9.00**
Kitchen Tested Recipes, Sunbeam, 40 pgs, 1933	**3.50**
Knox Gelatin Desserts, Salads, Candies, & Frozen Dishes, leaflet, 75 pgs, 1933	**7.50**
Lippincott's Housewifery, L Balderston, 1919	**35.00**
Martha Washington Cookbook, M Kimball, 1940.	**8.00**
Metropolitan Cookbook, Metropolitan Life, soft cov, 65 pgs, 1914.	**6.00**
Milk, the Way to Health and Beauty, Milk Association, NY, 55 pgs, 1939	**3.50**
Mrs Curtis's Cookbook, hard cov, 1,173 pgs, 1913	**25.00**
Mrs Winslow's Domestic Receipt Book For 1873, Jeremiah Curtis & Sons, John I Brown & Sons, soft cov, 32 pgs, 1873	**28.00**
Naturopathic–Vegetarian Cookbook, 72 pgs, 1907.	**25.00**
New England Yankee Cookbook, I Wolcott, hard cov, 398 pgs, 1939	**8.00**
New Art of Buying, Preserving and Preparing Foods, General Electric Kitchen Institute, soft cov, 1934	**10.00**
New Orleans Creole Recipes, M Brenner, 76 pgs, 1955	**8.00**
New Process Cookbook, Stove Co, soft cov, 65 pgs, c1890	**4.50**
Old Fashion Molasses Goodies, Brer Rabbit, soft cov, 48 pgs, 1932	**2.50**
Pennsylvania Dutch, soft cov, Sunbonnet girl cov, 1936	**15.00**
Pillsbury Cook Book, soft cov, 125 pgs, 1911	**18.00**
Proven Recipes—Three Great Products from Corn, Corn Products Refining Co, NY, Indian cov, leaflet, 66 pgs	**5.50**
Quaker Recipes, Woman's Auxiliary, NC, soft cov, 198 pgs, 1954	**8.00**
Ralston Mother Goose Recipe Book, soft cov, 15 pgs, 1919	**12.00**
Rawleigh's Almanac Cook Book & Medical Guide, soft cov, 99 pgs, 1916	**16.50**
Reliable Recipes, Reliable Flour, soft cov, 32 pgs, 1904	**8.00**

Dr. King's Guide To Health, 34 pages, red building, green and blue highlights, yellow background, recipes and health tips, 9⅜" h, 6¾" w, $8.00.

Royal Baker and Pastry Cookbook, Royal Baking Powder, leaflet, 1906	4.00
Savory Dishes, Kitchen Bouquet, leaflet, 1916	2.50
Science of Food & Cookery, Anderson, 297 pgs, 1938	12.00
Selected Recipes That Keep Families Happy, McCormick Spice, soft cov, 31 pgs, 1928	5.00
Settlement Cookbook, S Kander, hard cov, 22nd edition, 623 pgs, 1938	20.00
Sloan's Y Hints and Up To Date Cookbook, soft cov, 47 pgs, 1901	6.00
South Carolina Cookbook, Farm Women, 426 pgs, 1954	9.50
Standard Family Cookbook, G Wilkinson, hard cov, 640 pgs, 1959	5.00
Successful Preserving with Kold-pak Rubber Jars, 16 pgs, 1917	6.00
Tested and Proven Recipes, Mueller's, soft cov, 40 pgs, 1930	6.50
Union Gas & Electric Company Cookbook, Cincinnati, soft cov, 168 pgs, 1907	10.00
Vaughn Feed Store—Vegetable Cookbook, 1919	7.50
Vitality Demands Energy, General Mills, soft cov, 50 pgs, 1934	64.00
Watkin's Almanac Home Doctor and Cookbook, Watkins, soft cov, 92 pgs, 1932	4.50
White House Cookbook, hard cov, 490 pgs, 1899	25.00
Women's Temperance Kitchen Wall Cookbook, 27 pgs, 1888	45.00
Young Housekeeper or Thoughts on Food & Cookery, Alcott, 424 pgs, 1838	50.00

COOKIE JARS

History: Cookie jars, colorful and often whimsical, are one of the fastest growing categories in the collectibles field. Many cookie jars have been made by more than one company and as a result can be found with different marks. This resulted from mergers or splits of manufacturers, e.g., Brush–McCoy which is now Nelson McCoy. Molds were also traded and sold among companies.

Cookie jars often were redesigned to reflect newer tastes. Hence, the same jar may be found in several different style variations.

Cookie jars are subject to chips and paint flaking. Collectors should concentrate on jars which have their original lid and are in very good or better condition. Learn to identify makers' marks and codes. Do not fail to include some of the contemporary manufacturers in your collection.

Above all, ignore the prices and hype associated with the cookie jars sold at the Andy Warhol sale in 1988. Neither are realistic.

References: Harold Nichols, *McCoy Cookie Jars: From The First To The Latest,* Nichols Publishing, 1987; Fred and Joyce Roerig, *Collector's Encyclopedia of Cookie Jars,* Collector Books, 1990; Mike Schneider, *The Complete Cookie Jar Book,* Schiffer Publishing, 1991; Ermagene Westfall, *An Illustrated Value Guide To Cookie Jars,* Collector Books, 1983.

Periodical: *Crazed Over Cookie Jars,* PO Box 130, German Valley, IL 61039.

Museum: The Cookie Jar Museum, Lemont, IL.

Abingdon Pottery Company	
Baby, blue, marked "Abingdon USA 561"	115.00
Hippo, sitting up, red, green, black, and yellow floral trim on white, marked "Abingdon USA, 549," c1942	190.00
Humpty Dumpty, yellow brick wall, brown and white striped suit, marked "Abingdon USA 663," c1949	175.00
Jack–in–the–Box, multicolored trim and "COOKIES" on white, marked "Abingdon USA 611," c1947	130.00
Little Old Lady, wearing apron, green, marked "Abingdon USA 471," 1939	70.00
Miss Muffet, sitting on tuffet, white ground, yellow hair, blue bow, red flowers on dress, black spider on base, marked "Abingdon USA, 622," c1949	115.00
Money Bag, white, pink trim, marked "Abingdon USA 588," c1947	50.00

Windmill, white, blue trim, red and
green tulips, marked "Abingdon
USA 678," c1949 . . . .   **95.00**

American Bisque Company

Baby Elephant, white, blue cap and
bib, yellow and pink trim, un-
marked **50.00**

Cat in Basket, blue trim on white,
marked "Patent Pending" **35.00**

Clown, raised arms, yellow shirt,
blue pants, pink shoes, marked
"USA" **40.00**

Coffee Pot, brown, red flowers, bail
handle **20.00**

Cookie Barrel, brown, marked
"USA" **15.00**

Davy Crockett, brown outfit, green
foliage background, marked
"USA" **180.00**

Gift Box, white, blue ribbon and
bow, marked "USA," c1958. . . .   **50.00**

Kitten and Beehive, white kitten,
flowers and bees on yellow bee-
hive, marked "USA," c1958. . . .   **35.00**

Milk Can, bell in lid, "After School
Snacks" in black, marked "USA"   **35.00**

Olive Oyl, green hat and collar,
black hair, marked "USA" **425.00**

Pedestal Jar, yellow, marked "USA"   **15.00**

Pennsylvania Dutch Girl, red dress,
yellow bonnet and hair, red tulip
on yellow apron, marked "USA"   **125.00**

Pig with Straw Hat, white, yellow–
brown hat, blue neckerchief,
black hooves, marked "USA" . . .   **45.00**

Pot Belly Stove, black, red trim,
marked "USA" **20.00**

Tugboat, brown and yellow, bell in
lid, marked "USA" **90.00**

American Pottery Co

Clown, stripes on collar, marked
"USA, APCO". **20.00**

Cow in Overalls, red and black trim
on white, marked "USA, APCO"   **20.00**

Dutch Boy, red, yellow, and black
trim on white, marked "USA
APCO". **30.00**

Brayton Laguna

Dog, red, white, and blue gingham,
unmarked **80.00**

Goose Woman, holding goose and
pumpkin, marked "Brayton La-
guna Pottery" **140.00**

Lady, red and blue striped dress,
marked "Brayton Laguna" **120.00**

Mammy, striped blouse, green skirt,
white apron, marked "Brayton La-
guna Pottery, copyright" **225.00**

Brush

Circus Horse, black dog finial,
brown and green trim on white,
unmarked, early 1950s. **185.00**

Cookie House, green and white, red
chimney, "W/31," c1962. . . . . .   **45.00**

Cow, cat finial, brown, "W 10
Brush USA," early 1950s **65.00**

Crock, duck finial, pink, "K/26,
USA," c1956. . . . .   **30.00**

Davy Crockett, brown, gold trim,
"USA," c1956. . . . .   **160.00**

Hen on Basket, red and yellow trim
on white, unmarked, c1969 . . . .   **70.00**

Humpty Dumpty, white ground,
brown peaked hat, gloves, and
shoes, "W 29 Brush USA," c1962   **70.00**

Lantern, brown and cream, "K 1
Brush USA". **45.00**

Old Shoe, yellow, green and brown
trim, "W/Brush USA," c1959 . . .   **55.00**

Teddy Bear, feet together, brown,
"014 USA," c1947 . . . .   **85.00**

California Originals

Pelican, brown, baby pelican finial,
unmarked **35.00**

Santa Claus, leaning on sack, reverse
"871" impressed on back **55.00**

Squirrel on Stump, small, brown,
"2620, C". **20.00**

W C Fields, black band on white
straw hat, pink nose, gray tie,
black suit, Cumberland Ware . . .   **80.00**

Yellow Cab, black "TAXI" and
checkerboard design, unmarked   **50.00**

Cardinal China Company

Pig Head, black and pink trim on
white, #301 . . . .   **50.00**

Telephone, pink and black trim on
white, #311 . . . .   **35.00**

Doranne of California

Cow on Moon, yellow, black trim,
"J 2, USA," late 1950s **80.00**

Mother Goose, olive green, "C J 16
USA," late 1960s. **65.00**

Fredericksburg Art Pottery Co

Hen, brown, marked "F.A.P.Co
USA" **25.00**

Windmill, white, blue trim, marked
"F.A.P.Co". **25.00**

Gilner

Mother Goose, white, blue bonnet,
blue polka dots on yellow apron,
marked "Gilner USA G–720" . . .   **70.00**

Rooster, gray feathers, red and yellow trim, marked "Gilner, G–22"   **30.00**

Hull Pottery Company

Big Apple, red and yellow, green
leaves, unmarked **25.00**

Cookie Crock, brown, white lettering and flowers, marked "Hull
Oven Proof, USA". **20.00**

Duck, orange, red, and black trim
on white, marked "Hull 966,
USA" **30.00**

Gingerbread Boy, brown, marked

"Hull, copyright, Crooksville, Ohio, USA, Ovenproof" **35.00**

Little Red Riding Hood, marked "967 Hull Ware, Little Red Riding Hood Pat, applied for USA" **185.00**

Maddux of California

Beatrix Potter Rabbit, carrying umbrella and basket, marked "copyright, Maddux of Calif." **65.00**

Raggedy Ann, blue and red outfit, sitting on base, marked "copyright, Maddux of Calif. USA 2108"   **40.00**

McCoy Pottery

Apple, red on green, one leaf, marked "McCoy USA," 1950s. . .   **20.00**

Bananas, bunch, yellow and brown, marked "McCoy," c1950 . . . . . .   **55.00**

Bean Pot, floral dec on black, marked "USA," 1939. . . . .   **15.00**

Christmas Tree, marked "McCoy USA, 1959" **325.00**

Corn, single cob, marked "McCoy USA," 1958–59 . . . .   **95.00**

Fruit Cylinder, multicolored fruit on white jar, marked "McCoy USA," 1946–54. . . . .   **15.00**

Hen on Basket, red and yellow trim on white, marked "USA," c1958   **40.00**

Hen on Nest, brown hen and straw nest on yellow base, red lettering, marked "USA," 1958–59. . . . . .   **40.00**

Hobby Horse, red, brown, blue, and black trim on white, marked "McCoy USA," c1950 . . . .   **60.00**

Mother Goose, wearing scarf, carrying basket, marked "McCoy USA," 1948–52 . . . .   **65.00**

Pears on Basketweave, marked "McCoy USA," c1957 . . . .   **30.00**

Strawberry, red, green hull, marked "McCoy USA," 1955–57 . . . . . .   **25.00**

Two Kittens in Basket, black and white kittens, yellow basket, red yarn, marked "McCoy USA" . . .   **200.00**

Tulip, red tulip and band on white pot base, red tulip finial, marked "McCoy USA," 1958–59. . . . . .   **60.00**

Metlox Pottery Company

Barn, rooster finial, animals at windows, brown, marked "Metlox Calif. USA". **55.00**

Polka Dot Topsy, black child, blue polka dots on white dress, marked "Metlox, Calif. USA". **90.00**

Cat, white, blue eyes, pink nose, marked "Metlox Calif. USA" . . .   **55.00**

Drum, bisque, brown drum, children and animals dec, marked "Made in Poppytrail, Calif.". . . .   **30.00**

Mrs Rabbit, holding carrot, blue trim on white, marked "Metlox, Calif. USA" **60.00**

Piggy, bisque, brown, marked "Made in Poppytrail, Calif. USA"   **50.00**

Rabbit on Cabbage, brown rabbit finial, green cabbage head, unmarked **35.00**

Sir Francis Drake, white, yellow beak and feet, green grass, unmarked **40.00**

Morton Pottery Company

Coffee Pot, multicolored cookies and lettering on white pot, marked "USA 3621". **20.00**

Fruit Basket, multicolored fruit, green basket, marked "USA 3720". **30.00**

Hen, chick finial, black and white feathers, red and yellow trim, unmarked **35.00**

Milk Can, multicolored "COOKIES" on white can, marked "USA 3539".   **25.00**

Pottery Guild

Balloon Lady, unmarked **70.00**

Elsie, standing upright in barrel, brown and white, unmarked. . . .   **90.00**

Rooster, red, green and yellow accents on white, marked "Hand Painted Pottery Guild of America"   **40.00**

McCoy Pottery, Mammy, $85.00.

Morton Pottery, Clown, $25.00.

Red Wing Pottery
  Chef, red and black, marked "Red
    Wing USA" **70.00**
  Jack Frost on Pumpkin, unmarked   **135.00**
  King of Tarts, wearing crown, hold-
    ing heart scepter and bag marked
    "TARTS," marked "Red Wing
    USA" **150.00**
  White Crock, illegible mark **25.00**
Regal China
  Alice in Wonderland, marked "Walt
    Disney Productions, copyright,
    Alice in Wonderland," 1950s . . .   **575.00**
  Barn, red roof, brown walls, animals
    at windows, bird finial, marked
    "Pat. Pending 381" **100.00**
  Davy Crockett, bust, marked "Trans-
    lucent Vitrified China, copyright,
    C. Miller 55–140 B" **145.00**
  Quaker Oats, replica canister,
    marked "Regal" under recipe . . .   **110.00**
Robinson–Ransbottom
  Hi Diddle Diddle, full yellow moon,
    cow finial, cat playing fiddle,
    dish, and spoon, gold trimmed,
    marked "RRP Co. Roseville, Ohio
    317" **75.00**
  Peter, Peter, Pumpkin Eater, Peter
    and wife on yellow pumpkin,
    marked "RRP Co. Roseville, Ohio
    1502" **65.00**
Shawnee Pottery Company
  Clover Bloom Winnie, white cow,
    wearing clover dec hat and dress,
    marked "Winnie USA" **115.00**
  Corn, single ear, yellow and green,
    marked "Shawnee 66" **70.00**
  Cottage, brown roof, red door, blue
    windows, marked "USA 6" **110.00**
  Fruit Basket, multicolored fruit, yel-
    low basket, marked "Shawnee
    84" **40.00**
  Jug, ovoid, blue, marked "USA". . .   **50.00**
  Puss 'n Boots, gold trim and decals,
    marked "Patented Puss 'n Boots
    USA" **165.00**
  Tulip Smiley, white pig, wearing red
    neckerchief, tulip dec, gold trim,
    marked "USA" **145.00**

EGG AND DAIRY

History: Most farms were self–sufficient. Even grain farmers kept a cow and flock of chickens to meet their need for dairy products. What was not used on the farm was sold for extra income. Many a farming wife bought Christmas presents with the egg money.

Egg and dairy products were both primary and secondary food stuffs. They were an important ingredient in baking. It was necessary to process many products before use. Churning butter was an after–dinner task that often fell to young children. Of course, there was a pleasurable side, especially when the ice cream freezer was brought out.

Butter prints are divided into two categories: butter molds and butter stamps. Butter molds are generally of three–piece construction—the design, the screw–in handle, and the case. Molds both mold and stamp the butter at the same time. Butter stamps are of one–piece construction, sometimes two pieces if the handle is from a separate piece of wood. Stamps are used to decorate the top of butter after it is molded.

References: Paul Dickson, *The Great American Ice Cream Book*, Galahad Books, 1972; Paul Kindig, *Butter Prints and Molds*, Schiffer Publishing, 1986; Ralph Pomery, *The Ice Cream Connection*, Paddington Press, Ltd., 1975; Wayne Smith, *Ice Cream Dippers: An Illustrated History and Collector's Guide to Early Ice Cream Dippers*, published by author, 1986.

Periodicals: *Cream Separator News*, Rte 3, Box 189, Arcadia, WI 54612; *Eggcup Collectors' Corner*, 67 Stevens Ave., Old Bridge, NJ 08857; *The Udder Collectibles*, HC 73, Box 1, Smithville Falls, NY 13841.

Collectors' Club: The Ice Screamers, 1042 Olde Hickory Road, Lancaster, PA 17601.

Reproduction Manufacturers: *General*— Chinaberry General Store, 1846 Winfield Dunn Highway, Sevierville, TN 38762; *Molds*— Holcraft, PO Box 792, Davis, CA 95616; Olde Mill House Shoppe, Box H, Lancaster, PA 17602.

Butter
  Box, bentwood, tin bands at top and
    bottom, 2 quart, late 19th C **25.00**
  Carrier, cov, wood, painted, red,
    wire bail handle, 12" d, 19th C   **110.00**
  Churn
    Cylinder type, Fairy Churn,
      wooden barrel and frame, side
      crank, lock–on lid, Palmer Co,
      Rockford, IL, c1900 . . . .   **90.00**
    Dasher type
      Stoneware, salt glazed, ear
        handles, wooden lid and
        dasher, 4 gallon, 19th C . . .   **125.00**
      Tin, flared lip, tapering cylin-
        drical body, two handles,
        orig mustard paint, 25" h,
        c1875 . . . .   **275.00**
      Wood, barrel construction, ta-
        pered sides, elongated stave
        handle, orig old red paint,
        New England, 18½" h, c1825   **400.00**
    Electric, Gem Dandy, emb cow
      on glass barrel, aluminum

Butter Churn, 4 quart size, Dazey Churn & Mfg. Co, St. Louis, square glass base, wooden beaters and handle, cast metal and tin top, silver paint coating, 4⅝″ sq, 12¼″ h, $85.00.

shaft, adjustable triangular cutout dasher blade, screw-on lid, bail handle, emb cow, "Duraglas," and "Use with Gem Dandy Electric Churn" on barrel, Alabama Mfg Co, 2 gal, c1950 . . . . 65.00
Rocker type, wooden churn and cradle, red milk paint 250.00
Tabletop
Elgin, glass jar, wooden paddles, 2 quart, 20th C 80.00
Perfection MixMaster, glass jar, iron gears, wooden paddles, 1 gallon 50.00
Cutter, cast iron, nickel plated, painted, table mount, wire cutter, early 20th C 50.00
Fork, wood, painted, five tines, "Mrs Bragg's Butter Fork," 6″ l, late 19th C 15.00
Merger, Mak-Mor Butter Machine, tabletop glass jar, cast iron frame and gears, metal blades, NY, patented May 30, 1911 . . . . 60.00

Butter Stamp, sheaf of wheat, crimped border, 4⅜″ d, 3″ h, $150.00.

Mold
Cow, round, 4¾″ d 75.00
Flowers and Stars, box type, wood, marked "Porter Blanchards Son's Co," 19th C 125.00
Goose, plunger type, wood, ½ lb, 3¾″ d, late 19th C 145.00
No Pattern, wood box, iron frame and handle, 1 lb, 5¾″ l, 3⅝″ w, 19th C. 70.00
Star, cast aluminum, ½ lb, 3½″ d, R Hall, Burlington, NC, c1940 20.00
Paddle, maple handle, wire blade, 8¾″ l, c1900. . . . . 18.00
Slicer, iron, nickel plated, 11 cutting wires, enameled base, Elgin #48, 8½″ h, 8½″ l, c1911 . . . . 50.00
Stamp, wood, carved, 19th C
Bird, standing in grass, corrugated border, 3″ d 250.00
Cow, fence in background, pointed udders, 3⅝″ d 275.00
Double Pineapple, rect, 2¾ x 4⅞″ 110.00
Eagle, eight point star, 2¾″ d 200.00
Five Fish, piecrust border, handle, 3½″ w. 350.00
Flower, six petals, serrated border, lollipop type, elongated shield shaped handle ends in heart, 10″ l. 600.00
Rooster, lathe-turned blank, 3½″ d 70.00
Rose, rosebud, and leaves, lathe-turned blank, 2″ d. 60.00
Tulip, rect, 3⅜ x 5″ 250.00
Two Sided, dove one side, vase of flowers other side, 3¼″ d 175.00
Worker, tabletop, wooden frame and gears, bentwood holder, iron crank handle, 13½″ h, 19th C. . . . 300.00
Cheese
Curd Whipper, spring steel blades, wooden handle, 24½″ l, c1880 . . 75.00
Drainer, basket, round top, tightly woven sides, square bottom, two handles, 6″ h, 12½″ d, 19th C . . . 250.00
Mold, round, wood, carved, pig, 12″ d, 19th C. 75.00
Press, round, tin cylinder, three legs, pierced bottom and lower sides, ring handle, handmade, 7⅛″ h, 6⅜″ d, 19th C 130.00
Sieve
Round, tin cylinder, alternating rows of vertical slits and round pierced holes, three peg feet, 4″ h, 4¼″ d, mid 19th C 135.00
Slicer, aluminum, Cut-Rite, No 300, Wagner Ware, OH, 7″ l, 3⅛″ w, 20th C. 35.00
Cream Separator, tabletop, Royal Blue Junior, c1900 . . . . 60.00

Cheese Sieve, heart shaped, punched tin, footed, 5¾ x 5⅝ x 3⅝", late 19th C, $200.00.

Egg
  Basket, iron wire, 8" d, c1905 . . . . **25.00**
  Candler, tin cylinder, pierced, strap handle, The Family Egg–Tester, 3" h, patented Mar 13, 1876 . . . . **30.00**
  Grading Scale
    Oakes Mfg Co, tin, painted, 7" h, 20th C **25.00**
    Zenith Egg Grader, red cast iron, weight and balance, blue cast iron base, aluminum egg pan and scale, brass pointer, #1002, early 20th C **28.00**
  Timer
    Alarm Whistle, aluminum insert, orig box and instructions, 20th C **15.00**
    Wall Mounted, enameled tin, milk bottle shaped backplate, small glass–bulbed flip timer attached, 6" h, c1900 . . . . **50.00**
    Wood Frame, turned, holds glass bulbs, painted red, 4" h, 19th C **30.00**
Ice Cream
  Carrier, oak box, zinc lined, side door for ice cream storage, lift–off top for ice, Bradley Ice Cream Cabinet, 8½" h, late 19th C **250.00**
  Freezer
    Arctic, wood bucket, cast iron works, White Mountain Freezer Co, NH, patented 1889 . . . . . . **40.00**
    Kwik Freeze, galvanized tin, blue, paper label, 20th C **50.00**
  Mold
    Battleship, pewter, E & Co #1069, 20th C **100.00**
    Bride and Groom, pewter, Krauss, #627–K, 20th C **45.00**
    Daisy, pewter, two part, hinged, 2½" d, late 19th C **45.00**
    George Washington, profile bust, hatchet shaped mold, pewter, two part, hinged, S & Co #336, 4" h, early 20th C **60.00**

Straw Basket, pewter, three part, #598, early 20th C **35.00**
Turkey, dressed, pewter, 5" l. . . . **20.00**
Scoop
  Dover #20, nickeled brass, round bowl, turned wooden handle, lever–activated scraper, 10½" l, 1930s **40.00**
  Gilchrist, nickeled brass, cone type, key mechanism, loop handles, 7½" l, 1920–31 . . . . . **35.00**
  Indestructo #30, bowl shape cup, nickeled brass, wooden handle, Benedict Mfg Co, 10½" l, 1920s **50.00**
  Nuroll, cast aluminum, non–mechanical, 1940s **10.00**
  Quick and Easy #486, nickeled brass, cone shaped, thumb lever, turned wood handle, Erie Specialty Co, c1910 . . . . **75.00**
  Rainbow Ice Cream Dispenser Cake Cone Co, Inc, sandwich scoop, stainless steel, cast aluminum handle, 10" l, 20th C **85.00**
  Trojan #16, nickeled brass, wooden handle, lever action, Gem Spoon Co, early 20th C **30.00**

FOOD PREPARATION

History: A country housewife cooked, and cooked, and cooked. Just as farming was a seven-day-a-week occupation, so too was cooking. The country cook was willing to try any labor saving device at least once. This explains why so many mint examples remain with their original box. Not every device worked well.

Many of these implements were mechanical. Collectors prefer examples in working order. Value decreases rapidly if an object is rusted or pitted.

Look for unusual shapes, highly decorated pieces, and examples that obviously have been used but carefully cared for. A marked piece is a plus. Most collections focus on one form and its many variations.

Reproduction Craftspersons: *Utensils—* Horwood's Country House, 4307 Gotfredson Rd, Plymouth, MI 48170; Jonathan Marshall, Blacksmithing, 1310 Westview, East Lansing, MI 48823; Virginia Petty, Whistlin' Whittler, 1684 Three Forks–Flatrock Rd, Oakland, KY 42159; Ronald Potts, Blacksmith, Chriswill Forge, 2255 Manchester Rd, North Lawrence, OH 44666; Roush Forged Metals, Rte 2, Box 13, Cleveland, VA 24255.

Reproduction Manufacturer: *Utensils—* Applecore Creations, PO Box 29696, Columbus, OH 43229.

Bean Slicer, cast iron, painted, blue, emb leaf design, tin cover, screw clamp, 9" h, c1900 . . . . **65.00**

Bean Stringer, Bean–X, blued steel blade, springs, 6½" l, Orange, NJ, c1900 . . . . **12.00**

Cabbage Cutter

Handmade, wood, box style, peg construction, carbon steel blade, 30" l, 19th C **45.00**

Indianapolis Kraut Kutter, wood, two steel blades, Tucker & Dorsey Mfg Co, Indianapolis, IN, patented 1905 . . . . **50.00**

Pine, 14½" h, 5¾" w, scalloped edge, twin blades, old finish **85.00**

Chopping Knife

A & J, wooden handle, painted green, four stainless steel blades form bell shape, Binghamton, NY, 6" h, 3" w, c1925 . . . . **12.00**

B Denton, wooden handle, wrought iron blade, crescent shape, two wide tangs, riveted, 6" w, Auburn, NY, c1860 . . . . **65.00**

Double Action, cast iron handle, cast steel blade, patented Oct 20, 1892. . . . . **15.00**

Perk, wooden handle, half–ovoid blade, one tang, 5" w, c1875 . . . **55.00**

Cleaver, wooden handle, tool steel blade, 4" w, 13" l, marked "Samuel Lee, L.F. & C.," patented May 1886 **25.00**

Corn Grater, arched steel blade, oval hole in wooden board, 12" l, c1875 **12.00**

Cutting Board, fish shape, wood, burn rings, 12" l, 7¼" w, early 20th C. . . . **45.00**

Fish Scaler, Champion, cast iron, 20th C **12.00**

Food Chopper, Kitchmaster, plated metal, table mount, crank, three

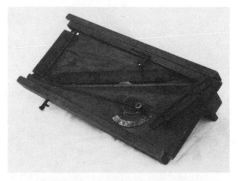

Cabbage Cutter, marked "Arcadia Manufacturing Co., Newark, New York, Pat'd 1885–1891," adjustable blade, iron handle, fold–down locking legs, 9¾ x 21¾", $85.00.

Colander, wire frame and mesh, painted wooden handles, white lines on green, 8⅛" d, 5¼" h, $15.00.

discs, Chicago Flexible Shaft Co, c1934 . . . . **25.00**

Food Grinder

Classic #1, cast metal, 20th C **18.00**

Keen Kutter #K110, tinned cast iron, Simmons Hardware, 20th C **25.00**

Vitantonio Co, No 1 Fruit Strainer, cast iron, brass plated, sheet iron chute, table mount, large hopper, side crank, metal cutter insert, 9¼" h, Cleveland, OH, patented Feb 15, 1888 . . . . **80.00**

Food Mill

Dana Mfg Co, cast iron, Cincinnati, OH, c1900 . . . . **18.00**

Universal, cast iron, two cutters, Landers, Frary & Clark, patented 1897 and 1899 . . . . **30.00**

Food Press, Starrett's Patent Food Press #1, cast iron frame, iron presser foot, rect sheet iron press box, painted and japanned, dark red and gold, vertical screw press action, perforated bottom insert, 9½" l, 6¼" w, Athol Machine Athol, MA, patented Apr 15, 1873 . . . . **80.00**

Fork

10⅜" l, wrought iron, tooled handle **50.00**

15⅝" l, wrought iron, down–hearth, applied scrollwork dec on sides of handle, three tines, delicate hanger, 18th C **100.00**

30½" l, wrought iron, heart ornament in tines **185.00**

French Fry Cutter

Maid of Honor, tin, stamped, table top model, 1930s. **6.00**

Silver's Sure Cut, tin cross–hatched blades in ring, 4" d, c1900 . . . . . **25.00**

Garlic Press, wood, two piece, hinged, 19th C **80.00**

Grater

Brass, punched, curved grating surface, wrought steel frame, 15" l, stamped "D.R.G.M. & D.R.R." **95.00**

Cast Iron, revolving, painted green, wooden handle, screw clamps, $8\frac{1}{2}$" h, Lorraine Metal Mfg, 20th C   **20.00**

Tin, punched, half cylinder, wooden paddle back, 10" h, $3\frac{1}{2}$" w, late 19th C. **35.00**

Tin and Cast Iron, revolving, table mount, c1880 . . . .   **20.00**

Tin and Wire, two grating surfaces, slicer, and french fry slicer, $10\frac{1}{2}$" l, Ekco, 20th C **10.00**

White Enamel, tabletop style, 19th C **38.00**

Grist Mill, Arcade, cast iron, table mount, c1900 . . . .   **40.00**

Herb Mill, japanned tin, sheet iron hopper, wooden drawer and crank handle, 7" h, 19th C **85.00**

Kitchen Saw, Keen Kutter, carbon steel blade, turned wooden handle, $13\frac{1}{2}$" l, Simmons Hardware, 20th C   **12.00**

Ladle

Brass Bowl, copper rivets, flat ended iron handle, $21\frac{1}{2}$" l, late 18th/early 19th C **75.00**

Iron, hand forged, impressed dec on flat handle, $20\frac{1}{2}$" l, Hudson Valley, NY, late 18th/early 19th C . .   **50.00**

Lemon Squeezer

Union Porcelain Works, wood, white porcelain insert. **135.00**

Walker's Quick & Easy No 42, table mount, sheet metal frame, iron lever, cast aluminum perforated cup, concave glass receiving tumbler, Erie Specialty Co, Erie, PA, c1906. . . . .   **55.00**

Meat Grinder

Family No 1, plated cast iron, long barrel, flared hopper, two leg screw clamp, worm screw cutter, crank, two interchangeable plates, Ellrich Hardware Mfg Co,

Meat Grinder, Harras, No. 52, cast metal side, painted white, white enamel body, orig wood plunger and handle, $50.00.

Plantsville, CT, patented May 15, 1888. . . . .   **35.00**

Perry's Patent No 1, cast iron, japanned, table mount, 2 piece horiz cylinder, cutter drum in hinged top half, crank handle, Peck, Stow & Wilcox Co, 1890s. **120.00**

Meat Press

Columbia #2, cast iron, three piece, screw action press, Landers, Frary & Clark, 19th C **100.00**

Quick & Easy, table mount, cast iron frame, T bar screw attached to press plate, removable cup, Erie Specialty Co, Erie, PA, c1905 . . .   **75.00**

Meat Slicer, Dandy, tin, wooden handle, 20th C **12.00**

Meat Tenderizer

Cast iron head, pattern of four concentric rings, turned wooden handle, $8\frac{1}{2}$" l, Philadelphia, PA, 19th C **35.00**

Rolling type, steel blades set in small roller, turned wooden handle, 9" l, 19th C **30.00**

Mortar and Pestle

Cast Iron, polished, ftd, flared sides, swag design around side, $\frac{1}{2}$ lb, long handled pestle, Thomas Burkhard, 1870s **40.00**

Tiger Maple, turned, pestle ends interchangeable, 7" h, 6" d mortar, 9" l pestle, c1925 . . . .   **175.00**

Noodle Cutter, The Ideal, rolling type, wire handle and frame, 14 blades, Toledo Cooker Co, Toledo, OH, c1910 . . . .   **15.00**

Pea Sheller, Holmes Pea–Sheller, sheet metal, painted green, yellow wooden knob on crank, hard rubber rollers and feet, $5\frac{1}{4}$" l, Holmes Mfg Co, Los Angeles, CA, c1920. . . . . .   **45.00**

Potato Masher, nickeled iron wire mashing head, openwork snowflake design, turned wooden handle, 9" l, late 19th C **15.00**

Potato Ricer, tinned metal presser and perforated cup, iron lever handles painted red, 12" l, Handy Things, Ludington, MI, c1940 . . . .   **10.00**

Potato Slicer, cast iron, table mount, crank, 1870s. **110.00**

Sausage Stuffer

Angers Perfect No 1 Filler, tin and cast iron, spring loaded lever action, table mount, Sargent & Co, late 19th C **55.00**

Wagner Stuffer No 3, cast iron, mounted on plank, crank, Salem Tool Co, Salem, OH, c1900 . . . .   **40.00**

Sieve

Bentwood frame, two finger con-

struction, woven horsehair mesh,
4½" d, 19th C **150.00**
Tin frame, brass screen, adjustable,
2½ to 9½" d, c1900 . . . .   **10.00**
Skimmer
Brass, pierced, copper rivets hold
oval bowl to handle, 20" l **65.00**
Enamelware, yellow spatter, brown
handle, 20th C **30.00**
Iron, wrought, looped handle, 9½" l,
c1900 . . . .   **70.00**
Spatula
Wrought iron, rope twist handle,
delicate hanging hook, pitted,
18¾" l, 18th C **200.00**
Wrought steel, 16" l, pitted **35.00**
Spoon, handwrought iron, down—
hearth, incised dec on upper face of
handle, delicate scrolled hanger,
15¾" l, 18th C **50.00**
Strainer, pierced tin, conical bowl,
hanging ring on tubular handle,
17" l, 8½" d, late 19th C **30.00**
Vegetable Slicer
A & J, turned wooden handle,
twisted wire blade, 16" l, Bing-
hamton, NY, c1930 . . . .   **18.00**
Universal Vegetable Slicer, table
mount, zinc plated iron, wooden
handle, 12" l, Landers, Frary &
Clark, New Britain, CT, c1900 . .   **45.00**

GRANITEWARE

History: Graniteware is the name commonly
given to iron or steel kitchenware covered with an
enamel coating.

The first graniteware was made in Germany in
the 1830s. It was not produced in the United
States until the 1860s. At the start of World War I,
when European manufacturers turned to the making of war weapons, American producers took
over the market.

Colors commonly marketed were white and
gray. Each company made their own special
colors, including shades of blue, green, brown,
violet, cream, and red. Graniteware still is manufactured with the earliest pieces in greatest demand among collectors.

Old graniteware is heavier than new graniteware. Pieces with cast iron handles date from
1870 to 1890; wood handles date from 1900 to
1910. Other dating clues are seams, wood knobs,
and tin lids.

References: Helen Greguire, *The Collector's En-
cyclopedia of Graniteware: Colors, Shapes &
Values*, Collector Books, 1990; Vernagene
Vogelzang and Evelyn Welch, *Graniteware, Col-
lectors' Guide With Prices, Volume 1* (1981) and
Volume 2 (1986) Wallace–Homestead.

Collectors' Club: National Graniteware Society,
4818 Reamer Road, Center Point, IA 52213.

Reproduction Manufacturer: Faith Mountain
Country Fare, Box 199, Sperryville, VA 22740.

Angel Food Pan, 11" d, fluted, gray
mottled **25.00**
Baking Pan
Blue and white swirl, black trim, ob-
long, applied handles **145.00**
Cobalt blue and white swirl **100.00**
Batter Jug, dark blue and white relish
pattern, tin lid, bail handle **275.00**
Bedpan, cov, gray and white speckled   **30.00**
Berry Pail, lid
Dark green and white swirl. **135.00**
Gray and black mottled, 7" d, 4¾" h   **45.00**
Bowl
Blue and white mottled, 7" d **25.00**
Blue and white speckled, 11" d. . . .   **10.00**
Creamware, green trim **12.50**
Dark brown and white mottled,
7½" d, 3¼" h, Onyxware. **20.00**
Bread Box, round, white, black letters
and trim, vented top **125.00**
Bread Pan, gray mottled **15.00**
Bread Riser, cov
Blue and white swirl, tin lid, large   **175.00**
Cobalt blue and white medium mot-
tled, black trim, ftd, small **475.00**
Bucket, 2 quart, aqua swirl, bail han-
dle **20.00**
Butter Carrier, oval, aqua and white
swirl, cobalt blue trim **300.00**
Cake Pan
Blue and white swirl, 10" d **25.00**
Gray, 10 x 14". **10.00**
Robin's egg blue and white marble-
ized, 7½" d **45.00**
Chamber Pot
Cobalt blue and white swirl **180.00**
Gray mottled, 8" h, 9½" d **75.00**
Cocoa Dipper, gray, hollow handle   **225.00**
Coffee Biggen, red and white medium
mottled, 4 pc **575.00**

**Berry Pail, gray and black, 7" d, 4¾" h,
$45.00.**

Coffee Boiler
    Brown, white interior. **25.00**
    Gray mottled, 2½ gallon, hinged lid   **60.00**
Coffeepot
    Black and white speckled, large . . .   **30.00**
    Blue and white marbleized, 8 cup   **80.00**
    Blue spatter, six cup. **55.00**
    Brown swirl, large **250.00**
    Dark green and White Swirl **225.00**
    Gray, V neck, wooden handle **75.00**
    White **20.00**
Coffee Roaster, black and white me-
    dium mottled, screen drum **425.00**
Colander
    Blue and white marbleized. **75.00**
    Blue and white swirl **35.00**
    Gray, pedestal base, 12" d **20.00**
Creamer, turquoise swirl, 5" h **12.00**
Cup
    Blue and white swirl **30.00**
    Gray mottled. **12.00**
Cup and Saucer, creamware, green
    trim **6.50**
Cuspidor, blue and white swirl. **325.00**
Custard Cup
    Blue and white marbleized. **75.00**
    Gray mottled. **8.00**
Dipper
    Cobalt blue swirl **25.00**
    Dark brown and white mottled,
      Onyxware. **40.00**
Dishpan, gray, 5" h, 16" d **10.00**
Double Boiler
    Blue swirl, 3 pc **60.00**
    White, red trim **20.00**
Egg Cup, blue. **35.00**
Funnel
    Cobalt blue and white marbleized,
      large.   **45.00**
    Gray mottled, wide mouth **45.00**
Grater, medium blue. **115.00**
Jelly Roll Pan, round, medium blue
    swirl. **65.00**
Kettle, cov, gray mottled, 9" h, 11½" d   **45.00**
Ladle
    Blue and white marbleized. **55.00**

Coffeepot, gray, 8½" h, $65.00.

Lavender and white swirl, white in-
    terior **45.00**
Loaf Pan, gray. **25.00**
Lunch Pail, gray mottled, tin lid **40.00**
Measure, gray, 1 cup. **48.00**
Milk Can
    Black and white speckled, lock top,
      wire handle, 8" h **35.00**
    Green and white swirl, blue trim,
      handle, Emerald Ware **350.00**
Milk Pail, blue and white marbleized   **75.00**
Milk Pan
    Blue and white **35.00**
    Gray, 1 quart **30.00**
Mixing Bowl, brown swirl **85.00**
Mold
    Brown to tan shaded, shell shape,
      white interior, hanging ring. **135.00**
    Turquoise and white swirl, Turk's
      head.   **200.00**
    White, fluted. **40.00**
Muffin Pan
    Blue and white mottled, eight cup   **250.00**
    Gray mottled, nine cup **40.00**
Mug
    Cobalt blue and white marbleized   **20.00**
    Cream, green trim **6.50**
Mush Mug
    Blue and white swirl, black trim . . .   **185.00**
    Green and white swirl, black trim,
      Emerald Ware, large. **115.00**
Mustard Pot, cov, white, handle, 3½" h   **45.00**
Pie Pan, cobalt blue, white veins, 6" d   **25.00**
Pitcher
    Blue and white mottled, blue trim   **140.00**
    Gray, ice lip, 11" h **110.00**
    Green shaded, 6" h **20.00**
Pitcher and Bowl Set
    Blue. **365.00**
    Gray **115.00**
    Red, black handle and trim, squatty   **100.00**
Plate
    Gray, 8" d. **8.00**
    Gray mottled. **40.00**
    Red and white mottled, white inte-
      rior, 12 sided **45.00**
    Turquoise, divided **45.00**
Platter, white, blue trim. **25.00**
Preserving Kettle
    Blue and white mottled, seamless,
      bail handle **140.00**
    Light Gray, side handles. **30.00**
Pudding Pan, cobalt blue and white
    swirl, 8" d **40.00**
Roaster
    Cobalt blue and white mottled **20.00**
    Emerald green swirl, large **250.00**
    White, black trim, oval, 18" l, Voll-
      rath. **35.00**
Salt Box, light blue, hanging **125.00**
Sauce Pan, green and white swirl,
    white interior **195.00**

Soap Dish, gray, wall hanging, $30.00.

Scoop, grocer's, gray mottled, tubular handle riveted to bowl	**135.00**
Sink Strainer, cobalt blue and white mottled, triangular, wire feet	**130.00**
Skimmer	
Gray mottled, 10" l	**25.00**
White, pierced diamond pattern bowl	**120.00**
Soap Dish, blue and white swirl, hanging	**110.00**
Soup Tureen, cov, gray, flat bottom . .	**300.00**
Spatula	
Gray	**24.00**
Gray mottled, large	**85.00**
Strainer	
Light blue and white mottled, black handles and trim, squatty	**275.00**
Light blue and white speckled, pierced bottom	**35.00**
Sugar, cov, white	**45.00**
Tea Kettle	
Green and white mottled, green trim	**225.00**
Red, 1960s	**50.00**
Teapot	
Gray, gooseneck	**90.00**
Red swirl, gooseneck	**300.00**
Tray	
Blue and white spatter, 18" d	**100.00**
Red and white mottled, dark blue trim, 1960s	**85.00**
Tube Pan, gray mottled, octagonal . . .	**40.00**
Tumbler, azure blue, orig label	**35.00**
Vegetable Bowl, oblong, red and white large swirl, black trim, 1950s	**135.00**
Wash Basin	
Blue and white marbleized, 13½" d	**35.00**
Green swirl	**25.00**
Wash Bowl	
Red and white large swirl, black trim	**295.00**
White, red trim, oval	**18.00**

STRING HOLDERS

History: The string holder developed as a utilitarian tool to assist the merchant or manufacturer who needed tangle–free string or twine to tie packages. Early holders were made of cast iron, some patents dating to the 1860s.

When the string holder moved to the household, lighter and more attractive forms developed, many made of chalkware. The string holder remained a key kitchen element until the early 1950s.

Reproduction Manufacturer: Bullfrog Hollow, Keeny Rd, Lyme, CT 06371.

Brass, ball, nickeled, pedestal stand, c1910	**115.00**
Cardboard, 3½" d, 2¼" h, round, pink ground, olive green dots, impressed label "Sealright"	**50.00**
Cast Iron	
Ball, 6" d, wire hanger	**5.00**
Beehive, 6" h, dated Apr 1865	**55.00**
Dutch Girl, hanging type	**20.00**
Fish	**60.00**
Gypsy Kettle	**145.00**
Ceramic	
Apple, red	**20.00**
Cat	**15.00**
Jack–O–Lantern	**50.00**
Mammy, blue turban, blue and white dress and apron, holding flowers, marked "Japan, Fred Hirode," 6¾" h, 1940s	**65.00**
Chalkware	
Girl, wearing blue bonnet	**45.00**
Mammy Head, red polka dots on white turban, 5" h, 1910–20. . . .	**135.00**
Old Lady, sitting in rocking chair . .	**25.00**
Peach	**30.00**
Pear, yellow	**20.00**
Pottery, Mammy, wearing red turban and checkered dress, 6¾ x 6"	**110.00**
Redware, bust of lady, curly hair	**95.00**
Stoneware, cobalt blue bird dec	**60.00**
Tin	
Apple, marked "Shenandoah Valley Apple Candy, Winchester, VA," 4 x 4"	**150.00**
Woman, knitting, cat playing with yarn	**18.00**
Wood, teapot, chef decal	**25.00**

Kitten, cream colored, red yarn, plaster, $45.00.

LEISURE AND PLAY

Life in rural America is hard and repetitive. Members of the agrarian community work hard and play hard. They are believers in the adage that "all work and no play makes Jack a dull boy."

It is difficult to escape from farming for an extended vacation. As a result, leisure activity often centered around day long or half day events. Extended leisure time was possible only when someone stayed behind to do the chores.

Leisure activities and social interaction are closely linked. Rural America is held together by its strong sense of community. It is only natural to spend time with family and friends during holidays, outings, and religious events.

A day away from the daily routine is a day in which memories are created. Souvenirs, mementos, and photographs document and rekindle the event. These treasured keepsakes grace the parlor or a favored corner of the bedroom chest of drawers.

Not all leisure and play is socially interactive. Some allows individuals a little time to themselves. Until the post–World War II era, rural families were large and often nuclear. Finding one's own space (to use a modern phrase) was difficult. The means to achieve that space, whether a toy or hunting rifle, is among the most cherished of possessions.

The Country decorator too often misses the leisure and play side of country life. The tendency is to stress decorative elements that convey hard work and products derived from that work. A true Country decorating scheme never fails to illustrate the agrarians' ability to celebrate life itself.

AMUSEMENT PARK, CARNIVAL, CIRCUS, AND COUNTRY FAIR ITEMS

History: The biggest social events in the lives of most agrarians were the county and state fairs. Participation often occurred on two levels— through membership in a local agrarian organization, usually The Grange, and individually. One planned for the fair for a year. For many, it was their one trip away from home.

A trip to the fair usually netted many keepsakes. First, there were the prizes ranging from trophies and ribbons that were won. Second, manufacturers often handed out premiums such as bookmarks, calendars, and sewing implements to help remind individuals of their products. Finally, there were the souvenirs, from a pinback button to a pennant.

Although most county and state fairs contained a midway, the primary reason for going was business and education. Pleasure came only after the business at hand was concluded. Rest assured that entering a pie in the pie contest was serious business. Local reputation stood or fell on the results of the judging.

When the agrarian family simply wanted to get away from it all, they went to an amusement park, carnival, or circus. These were purely social events.

Carnivals normally were sponsored by a local group, ranging from the church to a fire company. Often they contracted with professional groups to provide rides and booths featuring games of chance. Food was provided locally. The most commonly found memento is a piece of carnival chalkware.

Carnival chalkware, cheerfully painted plaster of paris figures, was manufactured as a cheap, decorative, art form. Doll and novelty companies mass produced and sold chalkware pieces for as little as a dollar a dozen. Many independents, mostly immigrants, molded chalkware figures in their garages. They sold directly to carnival booth owners.

Carnival chalkware was marketed for a nominal price at dime stores. However, its prime popularity was as a prize at games of chance located along carnival midways. Some pieces are marked and dated; most are not. The soft nature of chalkware means it is easily chipped or broken.

By the mid–19th century the tent circus with accompanying side shows and menagerie became popular throughout America. There were hundreds of circus companies, varying in size from one to three rings. The golden age of the tent circus was the 1920s to the 1940s when a large circus would consist of over 100 railroad cars.

Almost every rural town of any size was visited by a circus. It was a day eagerly anticipated by the local youth, who would gather at the rail siding to watch the circus unload, follow it to the field where it set up, and hang around until performance time.

The most commonly found circus souvenir is the program. A few individuals saved the large promotional broadsides. Country collectors often incorporate the circus theme into their settings through games, puzzles, and toys. Although not obtained at a circus, they capture the excitement that the circus creates.

A trip to the amusement park meant a trip to the big city. It was quite common for a town or township to have "community" or "church" day at an amusement park. Mothers and their children arrived in the morning. Fathers joined the festivities when work was done. Of all the features, it is the amusement park carousel which is best remembered.

By the late 17th century carousels were found in most capital cities of Europe. In 1867 Gustav Dentzel carved America's first carousel. Other leading American manufacturers include Charles I. D. Looff, Allan Herschell, Charles Parker, and William F. Mangels. The price of carousel figures skyrocketed in the 1980s when folk art collectors took the market for themselves. Today most Country collectors who want a carousel figure as an accent piece utilize a modern reproduction.

References: Charlotte Dinger, *Art Of The Carousel*, Carousel Art, Inc., 1983; Tobin Fraley, *The Carousel Animal*, Tobin Fraley Studios, 1983; Frederick Fried, *The Pictorial History Of The Carousel*, Vestal Press, 1964; William Manns, Peggy Shank, and Marianne Stevens, *Painted Ponies: American Carousel Art*, Zon International Publishing, 1986; Thomas G. Morris, *The Carnival Chalk Prize*, Prize Publishers, 1985; Ted Sroufe, *Midway Mania*, L–W, Inc., 1985.

Periodicals: *Carousel Art*, PO Box 992, Garden Grove, CA 92642; *The Carousel News & Trader*, 87 Park Avenue West, Suite 206, Mansfield, OH 44902.

Collectors' Clubs: The American Carousel Society, 60 East 8th Street, #12K, New York, NY 10003; Circus Fans of America, Four Center Drive, Camp Hill, PA 17011; The Circus Historical Society, 743 Beverly Park Place, Jackson, MI 49203; National Amusement Park Historical Association, PO Box 83, Mount Prospect, IL 60056; National Carousel Association, PO Box 8115, Zanesville, OH 43702.

Museums: The Barnum Museum, Bridgeport, CT; Circus World Museum, Baraboo, WI; Ringling Circus Museum, Sarasota, FL.

Reproduction Craftsperson: *Carousel Horses*— J T Nicholas & Son, 704 N Michigan Ave, Howell, MI 48843.

Reproduction Manufacturer: *Carousel Horses*— Ed Boggis, Box 287, Claremont, NH 03743.

Admission Pass	
Luna Park, Washington, DC, cardboard, complimentary, yellow crescent moon and black lettering on blue ground, $2\frac{1}{2}$ x $4\frac{1}{4}$", c1900	**20.00**
P T Barnum, Bridgeport, CT, white card, blue seal, "Two to See Bailey Elephant From 2 to $3\frac{1}{2}$ P.M./ P.T. Barnum" signed in black, Feb 8, 1882	**150.00**
Advertising Trade Card, Jumbo the elephant, arrival at Castle Garden, Clark's ONT Spool Cotton, copyright 1889	**8.00**
Banner, circus freak, "Eeka the Cannibal"	**1,000.00**
Carnival Chalkware	
Cat, 10", bank, c1940	**10.00**
Dog	
Collie, 18", c1940	**15.00**
Terrier, 8", black and white, rhinestone eyes, c1940	**10.00**
Fan Dancer, 16", marked "Portland Statuary Co," c1935	**50.00**
Kewpie, $12\frac{1}{2}$", bank, 1935–45	**20.00**
Lady and Dog, $11\frac{1}{4}$", full ruffled skirt, floral trim, c1935	**12.00**
Lamp Doll, 15", movable arms, long marcelled hair, c1920	**125.00**
Little Red Riding Hood, 14", marked "Connie Mamat," 1930s	**30.00**
Pig, 10", standing, carrying tray, wearing jacket and hat, marked "J Y Jenkins," 1937	**20.00**
Windmill, $6\frac{1}{4}$", 1935–40	**4.00**
Carousel Band Organ, Wurlitzer, style 146A, approx 40 keys, cymbals, pair of drums, elaborately carved painted facade with foliage motifs and painted panels, 3' d, 6' h, 8' l, c1922	**17,600.00**
Carousel Figures, carved wood	
Charles Carmel	
Lead Stander, outside row, wildly flowing mane, draped forelock, elaborately jeweled trappings, full sword and scabbard, fish–scale armor, fringed fabric, layered straps, 64" l, Sherman's Park, Caroga Lake, NY, c1915	**29,700.00**
Stander, alert expression, long windswept mane, jeweled scalloped trappings, 43" l, c1905	**8,800.00**
Dentzel	
Cat, finely carved fur detail, fish clamped in jaws, 54" l, President's Park, Carlsbad, NM, c1903	**27,500.00**

Carousel Horse, jumper, 38" l, $2,100.00.

Giraffe, outside row, whimsical expression, elaborately deeply carved trappings include large leaves and draped blanket, 70" h, Fun City Park, Johnstown, PA **42,900.00**

Mare Prancer, inner row, expressive face, long flowing mane, parted forelock, scalloped straps, draped blanket, period body paint, 54" l, c1900 . . . . . . **16,500.00**

Prancer, alert expression, full entricately carved mane, layered straps, rippled blanket, western saddle, 64" l, c1900 . . . . **13,200.00**

Armitage Herschell, track horse, jumper, pleasing expression, parallel leg position, suggestion of bird at saddle cantle, orig paint, mounted on rocking mechanism, 54" l, c1895 . . . . **6,600.00**

Herschell–Spillman

Deer, outside row, standing pose, elaborately decorated trappings, dog's head at cantle, deeply carved fur, real antlers, 58" l, Newtown Lake Park, Carbondale, PA, c1910 . . . . **23,100.00**

Dog, jumping, sweet expressive face, 54" l, portable carousel, c1905 . . . . **6,875.00**

Mule, jumping, animated pose, pleasant expression, folded blanket, 52" l, Rocky Point Park, RI, c1914 . . . . **6,600.00**

Pig, jumping, elaborate trappings, deeply rippled blanket, huge ribbon and bow at neck, curly metal tail, 44" l, c1914 . . . . **16,500.00**

Illions

Jumper, slim tapered head, spirited expression, full reverse swept mane, 52" l, c1910 . . . . . **5,500.00**

Stander, outside row, gentle expression, protruding peek–a–boo mane, ornately carved jeweled trappings and blanket, buckle on girth strap, 62" l, Supreme Carousel, c1921 . . . . . . **45,100.00**

Looff

Giraffe, expressive face, criss–cross blanket, twin eagles' heads at saddle cantle, 48" l, c1895 . . . . **13,200.00**

Prancer, gentle expression, full mane, checkered blanket, two eagles' heads with glass eyes at saddle cantle, 66" l, c1895 . . . . **7,700.00**

Sea Dragon, fierce expression, bared teeth, shell–like saddle, jeweled straps and blanket, fish scale tail, 66" l, c1900 . . . . . . **20,900.00**

E Joy Morris, rounding board, ornately carved, scrolls and foliage motif, central mirror, 90" l, Lake Quassy, Middletown, CT . . . **2,200.00**

Daniel Muller, panel, jester head wearing garland of bells, 50" h, c1912 . . . . **1,540.00**

Parker

Jumper, armored, upright pose, lattice work on blanket, jeweled trappings, large medallion on breastplate, 50" l, c1905 . . . **6,600.00**

Wild Boar, aggressive expression, bared tusks, scalloped layered blankets, 52" l, c1895 . . . . **2,200.00**

PTC

Goat, jumping, animated pose, heavily carved fur detail, layered trappings, 45" l, c1906 . . . **5,500.00**

Jumper, Muller period, sensitive expressive face, parted and curled mane, fancy forelock, jeweled straps and blanket, c1905 . . . . **9,625.00**

Stander, outside row, reverse flowing windswept mane, raised forelock, layered jeweled trappings, large detailed rifle from saddle cantle to front leg, 60" l, c1914 . . . . **22,000.00**

Stander, outside row, Zalar style, gentle expression, full flowing mane, long draped forelock, tucked head, multi–layered strap decoration with star motif and large jewel at bridle rosette, 65" l, PTC Carousel #49, Clementon Park, NJ, c1919 . . . . **22,000.00**

PTC/E Joy Morris, zebra, outside row, proud stance, layered blanket, elaborately fringed straps, 56" l, Lakemont Park, Altoona, PA, c1903 . . . . **22,000.00**

Spillman, jumper, jeweled layered trappings, fringed blanket, large single rose on breast strap, 58" l, c1924 . . . . **5,500.00**

Stein and Goldstein, jumper, roached mane, criss–cross bridle,

wide decorated breast strap, 44" l,
c1905 . . . . **3,300.00**
Unknown Artist, elephant, realistic
proportions, expressive face, scal-
loped blanket, 52" l, c1880 . . . . . **11,550.00**
Carousel Platform Panel, Coney
Island, NY, mirrored, Illions signa-
ture **600.00**
Pinback Button
Annual Fair, lettering on banner
above farm animal heads, horse
race below, multicolored, 1¼" d,
c1900 . . . . **4.00**
Clyde Beatty Circus, photo illus, lion
tamer Beatty and lion, black and
white on blue ground, 1¾" d,
1940s **10.00**
Coney Island, NY, "The Great Coal
Mine/Coney Island," mule pulling
cart and miner swinging axe at
mine shaft, multicolored, 1¼" d,
c1905 . . . . **18.00**
Dreamland Park, NY, "Meet Me at
Dreamland Park," white lettering,
red ground, 1" l oval, 1900s **5.00**
Elks Carnival & Midway, small girl
sitting in bird cage inscribed "A
Bird in a Gilded Cage" and "Baby
Vera," gold colored, 1¾" d, c1905 **15.00**
Hershey Park, PA, "Hershey Park,"
child holding candy bar, sitting in
cocoa bean, multicolored, 1¼" d,
c1908 . . . . **35.00**
Long Beach, CA, "Aviator/I Flew on
the Air Ship/Spiralway/Long
Beach, Cal," red and blue lettering and ride illus, white
ground, 1¼" d, 1910s **20.00**
Luna Park, Washington, DC, "New
Virginia Reel/Luna Park," six
adults on amusement park ride,
multicolored, 1¼" d, 1910s **35.00**
Midway Amusement Park, FL,
"7115/$2,000,000 Playground,"
red and blue lettering, white
ground, ⅞" d, 1930s **3.00**
Moxahala Park, "I Rode the
Swooper/Gee It's Great/Moxahala
Park," black lettering, white
ground, ⅞" d, 1930s **5.00**
Ringling Bros, "Souvenir Ringling
Bros./World's Greatest Shows,"
black lettering, black and white
Ringling Bros photo, white
ground, 1½" d, 1910s **35.00**
Royal–Adams Circus, "Broadway
Arsenal Dec. 12–17th," caricature clown illus, red, white, and
black, 1¾" d, 1900s **20.00**
Steeplechase Park, NY, "Steeple-
chase Funny Place," smiling man
illus, multicolored, ⅞" d, 1910s **20.00**

Texas State Fair, state flag illus,
multicolored, ⅞" d, c1905 . . . . . . **2.50**
Plate, Ocean Pier & Fun Chase, Wild-
wood, NJ, pierced border, 4" d **8.00**
Post Card
Atlantic City, NJ, "Famous Old
Landmark/The Elephant at South
Atlantic City," photograph, #9,
Chilton Publishing Co **4.00**
Circus Performer, photo, snake han-
dler Millie Leatrice, copyright
Campboll's Photo Art Shop, Rich-
mond, IN **30.00**
The Great Allentown Fair, Allen-
town, PA, Dan Patch race horse
illus, undivided back, 1906 . . . . . **75.00**
Poster
Christy Bros Big 5 Ring Wild Animal
Shows, "The Wonder Show," li-
tho, camels in foreground with
trained bison, oxen, and deer,
Christy Bros in vignette at upper
left, 27 x 41", c1925 . . . . **150.00**
Downey Bros Big 3 Ring Circus
"Leaps—Revival of that Astound-
ing and Sensational Exhibition,"
group of elephants, camels, and
horses in line, aerial artist leaping
overhead, audience background,
41 x 27", c1925 . . . . **125.00**
Ringling Bros Barnum & Bailey,
"Rudy Rudynoff, Peerless Eques-
trian," Rudynoff in Cossack–like
costume flanked by steed and
Great Dane, 28 x 41" **200.00**
Sells Bros Circus, 1893 . . . . **775.00**
Program, Sells–Floto Circus, 20 pgs,
sepia photos, 5¼ x 8½", 1932 . . . . . . **15.00**
Ruby–Stained Glass
Bell, Elkhorn Fair, Button Arches
pattern, clear paneled handle,
6½" h, 1913 . . . . **65.00**
Butter Dish, cov, Lancaster Fair,
Button Arches pattern, 1916 . . . . **150.00**
Syracuse Fair, cordial, 1905 . . . . . . **45.00**

**Fan, Moolah Shrine Circus, advertising on
back for Wabash Railroad, $15.00.**

Trade Card, Come to the Audubon County Fair, flirting cats, $7.50.

Tumbler, etched "Carnival, July 29, 1904," and "J. M. Craig," Button Arches pattern, $3\frac{7}{8}$" h, $2\frac{7}{8}$" d	30.00
Shooting Gallery Target	
Duck, cast iron, worn repaint, $5\frac{3}{4}$" h	35.00
Muskrat, cast iron, worn repaint, 9" h	25.00
Spoon, "Goin' to the Fair," Chicago Children's Home, young girl, 1892	40.00
Stereograph	
Asbury Park, NJ, buildings, G W Pach, 1870s	10.00
Bostock Wild Animal Show, tamer and lions, #74, whiting	25.00
Coney Island, NY, #501, trained bears riding carousel pulled by pony, H C White	18.00
Costello's Circus, Sacramento, CA, #1119, The Educated Elephant, Soule, 1870.	65.00
Wheel, circus wagon, sunburst	525.00
Wheel of Fortune	
24", wood, painted, horses and jockeys, mounting hardware. . . .	175.00
30", wood, thirty numbers, mounting hardware, marked "Will & Finck, San Francisco"	400.00

BIRD CAGES

History: During the Victorian era, the keeping of exotic pets, such as parrots and other types of birds, was common among the middle and upper classes. A standing bird cage often graced a solarium or living room. Well–to–do farmers and small town merchants imitated their big city counterparts.

Bird cages were constructed from a variety of materials ranging from wire and wood to wicker. Few period cages survive in good condition.

Bird cages became a "hot" decorator item in the late 1980s. Although primarily associated with the Victorian revival, they quickly found a place in the Country community. The most decorative examples made from natural materials also attracted the attention of the folk art collector.

Reproduction Alert: The vast majority of the bird cages being offered for sale today are reproductions. Before buying any bird cage become familiar with the Victorian Fantasies catalog from J. K. Reed, 1805 SE Union Ave, Portland, OR 97214.

24" h, brass plated, dome shape, 66" h gooseneck floor stand, replated . . .	**525.00**
26" h, tramp art, painted, wooden frame and wire, carved, gold and silver	**600.00**
$26\frac{1}{2}$" h, $28\frac{1}{2}$" l, paddle–wheeler boat design, painted, red, white, and blue, three–tiered, flying two American flags, two smoke stacks, anchor, two paddle wheels, American eagles stenciled on wheel houses, filigree doors and panels, figural Captain standing at wheel on foredeck, two frolicking dolphins painted on base floor	**6,875.00**
30" h, 17" d, wrought iron, dome shape, $\frac{1}{8}$" w vertical strips, four horizontal braces, hanging ring	**225.00**
31" h, wood base and finial, wire and tin construction, old red and black paint	**275.00**
34" h, wood base, wire construction, peaked roof, straight sides, painted black	**400.00**
38" h, $34\frac{1}{4}$" w, tin and glass, painted, three story house, seven compartments, painted floral and leaf dec on paneled swinging glass doors, ring perches in third story, late 19th/early 20th C	**2,225.00**

Victorian, wirework center dome with pair of arched cages on each side, painted wooden base, orig feeders and swings, $2,250.00.

CHILDREN'S RIDE-ON TOYS

History: Many toys found in agrarian homesteads were handmade. Among the most common were children's ride–on toys, especially rocking horses. Since rural families were large, especially during the nineteenth and first half of the twentieth centuries, ride-on toys were made to survive. Repainted and repaired examples are typical.

During the late nineteenth century, mass produced riding vehicles and wagons arrived upon the scene. Many were made by the same companies that manufactured larger vehicles. Wood was the most commonly found construction element.

By the 1920s pressed metal riding vehicles appeared. Many of these automobiles, fire trucks, and planes mimicked their real–life counterparts. Pedal cars from the 1920s through the 1950s are one of the "hot" collectibles in today's market.

References: Neil S. Wood (ed.), *Evolution of The Pedal Car and Other Riding Toys, 1884–1970's*, L–W Book Sales, 1989; —, *Evolution of the Pedal Car, Vol. 2*, L–W Book Sales, 1990; —, *Evolution of the Pedal Car, Vol. 3*, L–W Book Sales, 1992.

Reproduction Craftsperson: John T Nicholas & Son, 704 N Michigan Ave, Howell, MI 48843.

Reproduction Manufacturers: The Colonial Keeping Room, RFD 1, Box 704, Fairfield, ME 04937; Woodshed Originals, Box 3, Itasca, IL 60143.

Airplane
    44" l, Scout Master, wood and sheet metal, painted **750.00**
    48" l, sheet metal, painted, gray, short wings, rubber rims on three wide metal wheels, repainted, rust and pitting **500.00**
Baby Carriage, 42½" h, 56" w, wood carriage and wheels, fringed top supported by iron framework, painted and decorated, white ground, blue and yellow pinstriping, polychrome swans, late 19th C . . .   **550.00**
Bear, 30¾" h, 38" l, brown mohair, tan muzzle, glass eyes, steel frame, wheels, Steiff, c1940 . . . . **2,800.00**
Carriage, 54" l, horse–drawn, painted wicker seat, three wheels **2,500.00**
Hobby Horse, on frame
    24½" h, 51" l, dapple gray, green saddle, heart shaped supports, New England, early 19th C **1,200.00**
    26½" h, 48½" l, solid head mounted on bentwood frame, yellow pinstriping, red ground, 19th C **10,500.00**
    34½" h, 56¾" l, bouncing, brown and white calfskin, glass eyes, horse-

Carriage, wicker, toddler type, painted beige, c1930, $210.00.

    hair mane and tail, fringed cut velvet and leather saddle, leather tack, wooden frame, red, pinstriping, late 19th C **1,550.00**
    36" h, bouncing, wood, carved, painted, white, galloping, glass eyes, horsehair mane and tail, leather ears and tack, painted wooden arched base, cast iron fittings, black, gold, and white pinstriping and dec on red painted platform, c1900 . . . .   **725.00**
Horse
    27", wooden platform, lever action stirrups **1,500.00**
    36" h, 45" l, wood, hide cover, glass eyes, horsehair mane and tail . . . **1,300.00**
Pedal Car
    Cannonball Express, 27" l, red **300.00**
    Car, wooden spoke wheels, chain drive, c1905 . . . .   **225.00**

Rocking Horse, wood head, red burlap covering, straw filled, wood legs, red paint, red felt and leather saddle, hair mane, marked "Cebasco, Made in Germany," 34" l body, 58" l rockers, 40" h, $1,200.00.

Pedal Car, Packard, orig paint, minor rusting, c1920, 28" l, 15" h, $7,500.00.

City Fire Dept, 35" l, metal, red and
   white, ball bearing drive **150.00**
Coupe, 36" l, 1920s **400.00**
Dump Truck, 46" l, sheet metal,
   painted, yellow and black, Mur-
   ray Ohio Mfg Co, 1950s **475.00**
Hook & Ladder Pumper, 45" l, sheet
   metal, worn metallic red paint. . .   **85.00**
Hudson, wood and steel, folding
   windshield **150.00**
Packard Dual Cowl Phaeton, 72" l,
   American National **3,300.00**
Race Car, 51" l, metal, painted,
   hinged hood, Eureka, c1940 . . . .   **600.00**
Roadster, 34" l, yellow and black
   trim, green ground **600.00**
Station Wagon, 44" l, pressed steel,
   painted **150.00**
Rocking Horse, wood
   21" h, primitive, painted, carved
   body, straight legs, dapple gray,
   painted mane, horsehair tail, leather type harness and saddle,
   polychrome floral dec and brown
   pinstriping on cream colored
   rockers and center base platform   **950.00**
   23" h, 45" l, wood, painted, gray,
   black mane and horsehair tail,
   leatherette saddle, brown stained
   rockers, 19th C **650.00**
   23½" h, 41¼" l, stylized, pine,
   carved, painted, incised eyes,
   sides form rockers, yellow, red,
   and black outline and feather
   painting, black leather bridle,
   black and white printed oil cloth
   cushioned saddle seat, c1840 . . .   **1,325.00**
   30½" h, 51" l, full figured, pine,
   carved, painted, white horse, leather star and shield stitched saddle
   and bridle, cast iron stirrups, brass
   button eyes, real horsehair tail,
   yellow pinstriping on red rockers,
   sailboat motif on platform, 1875–
   1900 . . . .   **17,600.00**

   32" l, painted, two horse cut–outs
   on rockers, center seat **250.00**
   33" l, black plush velvet seat, c1880   **650.00**
   42" l, painted, dapple gray, leather
   saddle **1,100.00**
   50" l, painted, turned legs, pinstrip-
   ing **550.00**
   54" l, carved wooden body, beige
   repaint, leather saddle and harness, replaced mane and tail,
   arched wooden rockers painted
   red, rockers repaired **375.00**
Sled
   36" l, pansies and geometric designs, yellow on red painted
   panel, orig finish, "RH White/
   Boston/Kitchen DP" stenciled sig-
   nature on bottom **150.00**
   37½" l, wood, painted, oblong plat-
   form, red and black, "Grant,"
   pinstriping and floral dec, iron
   tipped looped fronts on wooden
   runners, missing one brace **450.00**
   39" l, wood, steel runners, stenciled
   "King of the Hill," striping, orig
   red paint and varnish **275.00**
   40" l, iron tips on wood runners, old
   yellow repaint **100.00**
   45" l, horse head, scrolls, and pin-
   stripes on red ground **650.00**
   49" l, running horse dec, brown and
   beige "Chester" inscription, black
   and yellow pinstriping, red
   painted deck, late 19th C **325.00**
   72" l, oak and walnut, no dec, iron
   runners **115.00**
   Landscape surrounded by stenciled
   dec, orig label reads "THE
   CHAMPION/No. 4/The Deposit
   Mfg. Co.," late 19th C **800.00**
Sleigh, 43" l, wood, painted, tufted upholstered seat **650.00**
Tricycle
   Thunderbolt, 34" l, pulley type,
   wooden seat **200.00**
   Wood, spoke wheels, wooden
   pedals, cast iron fittings **400.00**
Velocipede, 32" h, 40" l, wood,
   carved, painted, dapple gray, glass
   eyes, horsehair mane and tail, tricycle base, black striping on red
   wheels, wrought iron pedals, fili-
   greed cast iron hardware, late
   19th C **6,875.00**
Wagon
   28" l, wood bed, painted, red and
   green, cast iron wheels **250.00**
   31" l, wood, Hibbard Playmate . . .   **175.00**
   42" l, Lightning Wheel Coaster,
   wood, wooden spoke wheels . . .   **385.00**
   43" l, Pioneer Coaster, wood artil-
   lery wheels, 1900 . . . .   **450.00**

FIREPLACE EQUIPMENT

History: The fireplace was a gathering point in the colonial home for heat, meals, and social interaction. In the urban environment, it maintained its dominant position until the introduction of central heating in the mid–19th century. In the countryside, the fireplace as a heat source remained dominant well into the 20th century.

Even after central heating was introduced, the rural farmhouse retained working fireplaces. There was something nostalgic and comfortable about a roaring fire.

The open fireplace was one of the most popular decorating motifs of the early American decorating revival of the 1920s and 1930s. When Country became popular in the 1970s and 1980s, the living room and parlor fireplace became a major decorative focus.

Because of the continued popularity of the fireplace, accessories still are manufactured, usually in an early American motif. In the 1970s the folk art community developed a strong interest in fireboards, a device put in front of the fireplace to hide the opening when it was not in use during the late spring, summer, and early fall. It was not long before several reproduction craftspersons began providing contemporary copies of old fireboards.

Reproduction Alert: Modern blacksmiths are reproducing many old iron implements.

Reproduction Craftspersons: *Firebacks—* Patricia Euston, New England Firebacks, PO Box 268, Woodbury, CT 06798; Kurt P Strehl, Orpheus Coppersmith, 52 Clematis Rd, Agawam, MA 01001; *Fireboards—*Hope R Angier, Sheepscot Stenciling, RFD 1, Box 613, Wiscasset, ME 04578; Dorothy Fillmore Studio, 84 Pilgrim Dr, Windsor, CT 06095; Betsy Hoyt, Butternut Hill Gallery, 3751 State St W, N Canton, OH 44720; Sharon J Mason, Olde Virginea Floorcloth & Trading Co, PO Box 438, Williamsburg, VA 23185; *Fireplace—*James W Faust, 488 Porters Mill Rd, Pottstown, PA 19464; Jonathan Marshall, Blacksmith, 1310 Westview, E Lansing, MI 48823; Charles R Messner, Colonial Lighting and Tinware Reproductions, 316 Franklin St, Denver, PA 17517; Ronald Potts, Blacksmith, Chriswill Forge, 2255 Manchester Rd, N Lawrence, OH 44666.

Reproduction Manufacturers: *Firebacks—*The Country Iron Foundry, PO Box 600, Paoli, PA 19301; *Fireboards—*The Country Hand, PO Box 212, West Terre Haute, IN 47885; Heritage Designs, 7816 Laurel Ave, Cincinnati, OH 45243; The Prairie Stenciler, 7215 Nobel Court, Shawnee, KS 66218; *Fireplace—*Lemee's Fireplace Equipment, 815 Bedford St, Bridgewater, MA 02324; The Reggio Register Co, PO Box 511, Ayer, MA 01432; *Mantels—*Maurer & Shepherd

Joyners, Inc, 122 Naubuc Ave, Glastonbury, CT 06033.

Andirons, pr
  Brass
    9¾" h, faceted finial, shaped stem, double spurred arch supports, ball feet, miniature, Boston area, c1830 . . . . **1,425.00**
    15" h, Queen Anne, banded ball standard, spurred arched supports, snake feet, late 18th C   **450.00**
    16" h, Federal, urn form standard, square plinth, cabriole legs, club feet, early 19th C **400.00**
    18½" h, ball and steeple finial engraved with floral and leaf festoons, engraved plinth base, house and tree by water on front, flowers on sides, spurred arched supports, snake feet, attributed to R Wittingham, NY, 1800–25. . . . .   **2,425.00**
    19" h, turned finial and shaft, spurred arched legs, ball feet   **200.00**
  Brass and Wrought
    20¼" h, brass urn finials, knife blade shape, penny feet **450.00**
    22" h, brass finials, penny feet, 18th C **400.00**
    22½" h, brass swirled flame finial above faceted ball, wrought iron open twisted standard with arched supports and penny feet, twisted log guard, matching fireplace poker, c1785 . . . .   **3,000.00**
    26" h, brass lantern form finials, faceted spurred arch supports, ball and claw feet, c1810 . . . . .   **5,775.00**
  Cast Iron
    Bulldogs, front views, heads turned opposite directions, c1870 . . . .   **200.00**
    Cat, 17" h, sitting, yellow glass eyes **120.00**

Andirons, pr, brass, Connecticut, acorn finials, late 18th C, 17½" h, $375.00.

George Washington, 20" h, figural.................... **250.00**

Heart finials, 12½" h.......... **400.00**

Hessian, 20" h, figural, hand on hip, walking to left........ **225.00**

Owls, 16" h, glass eyes, dated 1887.................. **375.00**

Snakes, 16" h, intertwined, late 19th C................. **135.00**

Wrought Iron, 17½" h, knob finials, open cage style scrolled design, knob feet................. **200.00**

Apple Roaster, wrought iron, hinged apple support, heart–pierced end on slightly twisted projecting handle, 34¼" l, late 18th C......... **1,650.00**

Ash Shovel, wrought iron

14½" l, broom shape, partially twisted handle, late dec....... **110.00**

28" l, scrolled detail, pitted blade **25.00**

Bellows

16½" l, wood and brass, painted fruit and foliate dec............. **110.00**

16¾" l, red and black graining, stenciled and freehand fruit and foliage, brass nozzle.......... **230.00**

17¾" l, turtle back, white paint, smoked graining, stenciled and freehand fruit and foliage, brass nozzle **225.00**

18¼" l, leather, polychrome cornucopia, smoke grained back, brass nozzle, mid 19th C.......... **75.00**

20" l, walnut, carved roses, basket of flowers, fruit, and tassels, punchwork ground, brass nozzle, c1800.................... **19,800.00**

Bird Roaster, tin reflector, four hooks, 1870s..................... **175.00**

Bird Spit, wrought iron, hanging, three elongated hooks suspended from ring, one suspended from chain in center, 19" h, c1900.......... **300.00**

Bellows, orig red and gold paint, worn leather, 14¾" l, 7½" w, $45.00.

Broiler, wrought iron

20" h, narrow rods, four feet, handle **85.00**

26½" h, adjustable lyre shape rack with tines, tripod base, penny feet, cast finial.............. **400.00**

Chestnut Roaster, pierced iron, heart shape, long twisted handle, 28½" l, 18th C **900.00**

Coal Box, copper, emb laurel wreath dec, 12" w, 12" d, 13" h........ **150.00**

Coals Carrier, wrought iron, sliding lid, 31" l..................... **235.00**

Coal Grate, bell metal, rect basket, cast iron back plate, dancing maidens ornament, pierced front skirt, surmounted by urns, straight tapered legs, spade feet, 32" w, 17" d, 38½" h, late 18th C........ **300.00**

Crane, wrought iron

35½" l, 18th C **150.00**

52" l, Y–shaped, folds in center ... **85.00**

Down–Hearth Gridiron, wrought iron, rotary, four decorated spear points, three legs, long hook end handle, 24½" l, 18th C **600.00**

Dutch Oven, tin, iron spit, 19" l..... **200.00**

Ember Carrier, tin and iron, long wooden handle.............. **400.00**

Ember Tongs, wrought iron

9¼" l, primitive **50.00**

14½" l, scissor extension **125.00**

Fender

20¾" l, iron, wire grill, brass top rail **275.00**

43¼" l, brass, three engraved eagles, geometrically pierced, early 19th C **8,250.00**

47" l, cast iron, shell and ribbon design, paw feet **175.00**

51½" l, brass, D–form, pierced **225.00**

67" l, 6¾" h, brass, double rail, six posts..................... **55.00**

Fire Back, cast iron

Classical Bust in laurel wreath, relief design, marked "H W Stiegel, Elizabeth Furnace, 1769," 23" h, 27" w **6,200.00**

Floral dec, rose and portcullis, arched, 22" h, 16" w **1,550.00**

General Wolfe, portrait in medallion surrounded by flags, early 19th C **1,200.00**

Man and Horse, inscription at top, foliage, 17 x 23"............. **200.00**

Tree of Life pattern, 24" w, 21" h, Lancaster, PA, 18th C........ **300.00**

Fire Board

Bird's Eye Maple wood graining, line borders, three–section..... **900.00**

Geometric Pattern, painted, blue, yellow, green, sienna, black, and white, 22¾ x 36¼", 19th C **2,000.00**

Fire Cover, wrought iron, gooseneck, penny feet, 9½" h, 18th C **140.00**

Fire Lighter, brass, mug shape, round finial on hinged lid, strap handle, round tray, brass and composition lighter wand, Todhunter, NYC, NY, 1930s.................... **24.00**

Fire Mark

Cast Iron

3$\frac{1}{16}$" h, oval, eagle, "1792," traces of old paint.......... **45.00**

7$\frac{1}{4}$ x 10$\frac{1}{2}$", relief design, four clasped hands, marked "No 906" **300.00**

7$\frac{3}{8}$ x 11$\frac{1}{2}$", hydrant and hose, marked "F A," polychrome paint, pitted............. **210.00**

9 x 11$\frac{1}{4}$", oval, pumper, marked "U. F.," painted black, pitted **135.00**

Copper, fireman holding hose, burning building, marked "Protector, 1825".............. **190.00**

Flue Cover

Brass frame, reverse painted floral illus on glass center, hanging chain, late 19th C **30.00**

Cast Iron, plain **20.00**

Tin, emb, painted, paper litho farm scene, c1900.............. **15.00**

Grate, cast iron, basket type, short legs, 18" w, late 19th C **35.00**

Grill, wrought iron twisted rattail handle...................... **85.00**

Hake, forged iron, S–shaped, 6" l, early 19th C **15.00**

Hearth Bar, wrought iron, free standing, 54" l, 26" h.............. **455.00**

Hearth Broom, 50" l, birch splint, 1700–1820 .... **135.00**

Hearth Brush

15" l, turned wooden handle, red and black highlights on gilt leaf design, green ground **700.00**

22" l, turned wooden handle, traces of old black paint........... **70.00**

23" l, gild dec on old green painted wooden handle, horsehair bristles **40.00**

27" l, baluster turned wooden handle, grain painted, smoke decorated, leaves and flowers, gray on yellow ground, c1830 .... **450.00**

Heat Reflector, tin, semi–circular form, pierced heart, diamonds, dots, and stars design, loop handle **500.00**

Kettle Pusher, down–hearth implement, fitted with lid lifter, hand-wrought iron, 6" w, 4$\frac{3}{8}$" h, c18th C **90.00**

Kettle Shelf, cast iron, pierced design on 11 x 16$\frac{1}{2}$" shelf, 10" h........ **70.00**

Kettle Stand, wrought iron, reticulated brass top, turned wooden handle, 11" h **225.00**

Kettle Tilter, wrought iron, acorn finial on swivel ring, 14" w, c1810 ..... **375.00**

Kindler, bulbous head, asbestos–filled, wire handle, Yankee, late 19th C **6.00**

Kindling Tub, coppered oak, brass bound, oval, 24" w, 17" d, 16" h .. **1,500.00**

Log Basket, brass, turned rod spindles, stationary handle, 17 x 16 x 12" ... **150.00**

Mantel

Pine, carved by Adam Deal, 53 x 72", late 18th C **300.00**

Poplar, brown stain finish, 28 x 30$\frac{3}{4}$" opening, 51 x 46$\frac{1}{2}$" overall **160.00**

Match Safe

Advertising, tin, hanging

American Steel Farm Fences, fence illus, "Made In All Heights," 3$\frac{1}{2}$ x 5" h **70.00**

Billings–Chapin Paints, paint can and brush illus, 3$\frac{1}{2}$ x 5" h **70.00**

Bullock, Ward & Co, factory illus, "Compliments Of," 3$\frac{1}{2}$ x 5" h **125.00**

De Laval Cream Separators, die-cut, emb, figural separator, 4 x 6$\frac{1}{4}$" h, orig box **310.00**

Dutch Boy Paints, emb, trademark Dutch Boy holding three–dimensional paint bucket, 3 x 6$\frac{1}{2}$" h **180.00**

Juicy Fruit Gum, portrait illus, "The Man Juicy Fruit Made Famous," 3$\frac{1}{2}$ x 5" h.......... **220.00**

Moxie, diecut bottle shape, "Learn to Drink Moxie/Very Healthful," 2$\frac{1}{2}$ x 7" h **525.00**

Old Judson, child handing glass to father, mother watching, 3$\frac{1}{2}$ x 5" h **140.00**

Sharples Cream Separator, diecut, mother and child using machine, "The Pet of the Dairy," 2 x 7" h **115.00**

Matchsafe, tin, enameled, Ceresota Flour, marked "Nell Sign & Poster Co. NY," 2$\frac{1}{4}$ x 5$\frac{1}{2}$" h, $385.00.

Brass
    Fire Department, copper colored, hinged lid, Reading, PA, Fire Hall cello insert in lid, 2 x 2½", early 1900s **40.00**
    Milk Pail, figural **185.00**
    Punched Tooling, polished, hanging, 5½" l **70.00**
Cast Iron
    Horseshoe Shape, antlered stag crest, knob finial on cov box base, hanging **35.00**
    Lady's Shoe, figural, red, mounted on gild leaf, 4½ x 5" . .   **100.00**
    Open Scrollwork, dated 1867 . . .   **55.00**
    Tin, top hat shape, hinged lid, black band on green ground, 2⅜" h **60.00**
    Wood, heart shape, angled pocket, chip carved edges, white sanded paint, gold trim, 5¼" h, hanging   **60.00**
Peel, wrought iron, ram's horn handle, 42¾" l **100.00**
Pot Chain, forged iron, hook at both ends, 40" l, 18th C **75.00**
Reflector Oven, sheet iron, crank spit, ftd, 11" w, 19th C **275.00**
Roasting Rack, wrought iron, tripod base, penny feet, 30¼" h **550.00**
Screen
    30" h, 19" w, brass and mesh, spindle gallery, arched feet **75.00**
    34¼" h, brass, three panels, folding, c1930. . . . .   **70.00**
    51" h, mahogany, circular frame, young boy illus on needlework panel, tripod base, New England, 19th C **3,300.00**
    52" h, rosewood, circular needlework panel, brass and rosewood standard, incurvate triangular base, melon reeded parcel gilt feet, early 19th C **450.00**
Skewer, wrought iron, twisted handle, delicate hanger, 10½" l **75.00**
Skewer Rack, iron
    4" l, 4" h, tulip pattern, two twisted and two straight skewers, early 19th C **450.00**
    6½" l, wrought, stamped "R.E.," handmade, three skewers **110.00**

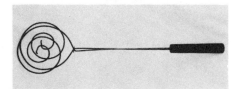

Toaster, wire toast holder, sliding ring, wooden handle, 19¾" l, $24.00.

7" l, wrought, three skewers, 9¼" l largest skewer, 18th C **400.00**
16" l, four skewers, pitted. **300.00**
Spider, cast iron, straight sides, flat bottom, long handle, three feet, 5" h, 20" l, 18th C **65.00**
Toasting Fork, wrought iron, rattail handle, 28" l **95.00**
Tool Set
    Brass, tongs, hearth brush, ash shovel, and poker, matching stand **120.00**
    Wrought Iron, hammered finish, sailing ship on tripod stand, knobs hold tongs, hearth brush, ash shovel, and poker, Heather, NYC, NY, c1925 . . . .   **60.00**
Tongs
    Brass steeple tops, 1775–1800 . . . .   **130.00**
    Iron, 28" l **18.00**
Trammel
    Adjustable, wrought iron, hanging, turned hook standard, single candlecup and bobeche, New England, 18th C **2,530.00**
    Chain
        50" l, wrought iron, early 19th C   **55.00**
        65" l, hand forged iron, twisted shafts and ram's horn terminations on ends of rod and hooks, two sets of four interlocking flat wrought iron rings, one large hook, one rounded flat hook, Hudson Valley, NY, late 18th C   **150.00**
    Ratchet, wrought iron, crane ring, 45 to 60" l, early 19th C **200.00**
    Sawtooth, wrought iron, ram's horn finial, scrolled ratchet. **225.00**
Trivet
    11" d, wrought iron, revolving, high legs, early 18th C **210.00**
    21½" h, wrought iron, adjustable roasting fork, wooden handle . . .   **200.00**

FISHING COLLECTIBLES

History: Water is a precious commodity in rural America. The location of a stream often dictated the site of a town or farmstead. The farm pond, usually stocked with a variety of fish, provides a hedge against drought.

Fishing was more a means of relaxation than sport for the farmer. Many a cartoon of "the lazy farmer" pictured him asleep with his back against a tree while fishing along the bank of a stream that ran through his farm.

Early man caught fish with crude spears and hooks made of bone, horn, and flint. By the middle 1800s metal lures with hooks attached were produced in New York State. Later, the metal was curved and glass beads added for greater attraction. Spinners with wood–painted bodies and glass eyes appeared around 1890. Soon after, wood plugs with glass eyes were being produced by many different makers. A large number of patents were issued in this time period covering developments of hook hangers, body styles, and devices to add movement to the plug as it was drawn through the water. The wood plug era lasted up to the mid–1930s when plugs constructed of plastic were introduced.

With the development of casting plugs, it became necessary to produce fishing reels capable of accomplishing that task with ease. Reels first appeared as a simple device to hold a fishing line. Improvements included multiplying gears, retrieving line levelers, drags, clicks, and a variety of construction materials. The range of quality in reel manufacture varied considerably. Collectors are mainly interested in reels made with quality materials and workmanship, or those exhibiting unusual features.

Early fishing rods were made of solid wood which were heavy and prone to break easily. By gluing together strips of tapered pieces of split bamboo a rod was fashioned which was lighter in weight and had greatly improved strength. The early split bamboo rods were round with silk wrappings to hold the bamboo strips together. With improvements in glue, fewer wrappings were needed, and rods became slim and lightweight. Rods were built in various lengths and thicknesses, depending upon the type of fishing and bait used. Rod makers' names and models can usually be found on the metal parts of the handle or on the rod near the handle.

The fishing collectibles category has broadened significantly beyond rod, reel, and lure to include landing nets, minnow traps, bait boxes, advertising signs, catalogs, and fish decoys used in ice spearing. Items in original containers and in mint condition command top prices. Lures that have been painted over the original decoration or rods that have been refinished or broken have little collector value.

References: Jim Brown, *Fishing Reel Patents of The US, 1838–1940*, published by author; Clyde A. Harbin, *James Heddon's Sons Catalogues*, CAH Enterprises, 1977; Art and Scott Kimball, *Collecting Old Fishing Tackle*, Aardvark Publications, Inc., 1980; Art and Scott Kimball, *Early Fishing Plugs of the U. S. A.*, Aardvark Publications, Inc., 1985; Art and Scott Kimball, *The Fish Decoy*, Aardvark Publications, Inc.; Carl F. Luckey, *Old Fishing Lures and Tackle: Identification and Value Guide, Volume I and II*, Books Americana; Albert J. Munger, *Those Old Fishing Reels*, privately printed, 1982; J. L. Smith, *Antique Rods and Reels*, Gowe Printing, 1986; Richard L. Streater, *Streater's Reference Catalog of Old Fishing Lures, Volume I and II*; Steven K.

Vernon, *Antique Fishing Reels*, Stackpole Books, 1984.

Periodicals: *Antique Angler*, PO Box K, Stockton, NJ 08559; *Sporting Classics*, PO Box 1017, Camden, SC 29020.

Collectors' Club: National Fishing Lure Collectors Club, PO Box 1791, Dearborn, MI 48121.

Museums: American Fishing Tackle Mfg. Assn. Museum, Arlington Heights, IL; American Museum of Fly Fishing, Manchester, VT; National Fishing Tackle Museum, Arcadia, OK; National Fresh Water Fishing Hall of Fame, Hayward, WI; Sayner Museum, Sayner, WI.

Reproduction Alert: Lures and fish decoys.

Bait Box, circular, label on white interior, black exterior, W J Cumming	**10.00**
Bait Bucket	
Rectangular, stenciled "T J Conroys special rectangular floating minnow bucket No. 28," and rod, reel, and fly dec, orig green paint, lift–out bait compartment, 11 x 5 x 10½"	**550.00**
Round	
Punched hole fish design, homemade, orig wooden latch	**28.00**
Stenciled "St Lawrence Bucket," gold lettering, green ground, lift–out bait compartment, 8 x 9"	**120.00**
Bobber	
Panfish float, hp, black, red, and white stripes, 5" l	**10.00**
Pike float, hp, yellow, green, and red stripes, 12" l	**24.00**
Box, fishing tackle salesman's, lettered, 5' l, 2' w, from buggy of Thomas Kenyon, Gladding Co, New England, late 19th C	**550.00**
Canoe	
17' l, 34" w, dark green canvas covered, cane seats, four paddles, B N Morris Canoes, Veizne, ME	**500.00**
17½' l, 35" w, light blue canvas covered, yellow trim, two cane seats	**150.00**
Canoe Seat, rattan, folding	**360.00**
Creel	
Canvas, netting front, leather trim, J Venables & Son, St Aldates St, Oxford, 16"	**205.00**
Crushed Willow, leather bound, form fit, 14 x 9 x 7"	**24.00**
Mahogany, half–round, brass fixtures, round center hole in hinged lid, 13"	**990.00**
Split Willow, orig rattan hinges and lid latches	**100.00**
Tin, oval cylinder, painted, silver ferns dec on green ground, chil-	

Creel, Form–Fit, crushed willow, leather bound, curved back, carrying straps, printed ruler on back, 14″ l, 7″ w, 9″ h, $25.00.

dren hunting and fishing illus on hinged door, web strap, some rust inside, 14¾″ l **300.00**

Toleware, lady's, matching padlock–style worm box, stenciled red roses and gold border on green ground, center hole on hinged lid **880.00**

Whole Willow, woven rim, center hole, orig latch, strap and loop, leather harness, wire hinges **330.00**

Wicker, center lid hole, early 1900   **55.00**

Decoy

Bass

Lake Chautauqua, NY, 7″ l **2,475.00**

Nathan Meyer, NY, glass eyes, orig polychrome paint, 22″ l . .   **150.00**

Oscar Peterson, Cadillac, MI, 7½″ l **1,760.00**

Brook Trout, full bodied, 17″ l, orig paint **210.00**

Brown Trout, painted scales, Oscar Peterson, 9″ l, minor spearpoint marks, tip of tail re–glued, 1907–19 . . . .   **6,050.00**

Fish, multicolored, spinner in body opening, carpet tack eyes, 8″ l. . .   **230.00**

Perch

Ice King, painted, Bear Creek Co, 7″ l **65.00**

Isaac Goulette, 9″ l, age chipping, paint off belly weight **660.00**

Lake Chautauqua, NY, 9″ l, late 19th C. **4,125.00**

Decoy, perch, Michigan, c1940, 5½″ l, $50.00.

Pike, tin fins, carved tail, mouth, and gills, green, white spots, 12″ l   **85.00**

Rainbow Trout, Oscar Peterson . . .   **2,750.00**

Sucker

Oscar Peterson, Cadillac, MI, 8″ l   **1,540.00**

Randall, cast aluminum, painted gold scales, 6″ l **40.00**

Sunfish, tin fins and tail, bead eyes, painted gills and scales, carved and painted body, green and yellow spots, 6″ l **45.00**

White Mackerel, pearlescent bronze and silver back, white belly, Kenneth Bruning, 14″ l, some chipping **1,265.00**

Fly Chest, 21 slide–out trays, 600 salmon flies **3,960.00**

Guide Boat, mahogany and cedar, laminated decks, painted black sides, caned seats and back rest, oars, brass oarlocks, 14′ 7″ l, 38½″ w   **3,800.00**

Line Drier, wooden handle, 15″ spool   **10.00**

Lure

Arbogast, Weedless Sunfish, glass eyes, 1¾″ l body **200.00**

Edkins, minnow, silver tinsel inside clear hollow glass body, painted brass head, painted eyes, German silver tail stamped "C. Edkins–Patent," five clear glass beads between treble hook and tail, spinner, 3½″ l **400.00**

Riley Haskell, minnow, handmade, silver plated copper body, brass tail and fins, wire wrapped double hook, marked "R. Haskell, Painesville, O. Pat'd Sep. 20, 1859," 4½″ l **8,500.00**

Heddon

200 Special, red head, radiant paint, three hooks **70.00**

Coast Minnow #630, green crackle back, hp gills, rubber tail, damaged tail, missing hook . . .   **200.00**

Dowagiac Killer #450, 2⅝″ l **1,705.00**

Dowagiac Minnow #100, yellow

Lure, Kingfisher, Wood Minnow, Series 101, glass eyes, green, orange, and red body, orig box, 3″ l, $30.00.

sides, black and red stripes, L–rig ... **85.00**

Expert, slope nose, white body, blue nose, red paint collar, 1906 ... **190.00**

Spin–Diver, orig box ... **605.00**

K & K, Minnowette, jointed body, plug in silver shiner finish, green top, silver bottom with scales, metal tail, $3\frac{1}{2}''$ l ... **325.00**

Miller's Reversible Minnow, $4\frac{1}{4}''$ l, c1916 ... **1,650.00**

Moonlight, Musky Pikaroon, yellow body, black and red on back, glass eyes, 1922 ... **80.00**

Pflueger

May Bug, spoon ... **990.00**

Monarch Minnow, through wire, glass eyes, gold finish painted gills, unmarked prop, three hooks, $3\frac{1}{2}''$ l ... **35.00**

Shakespeare

Evolution, prop type, stamped "Pat. Appl'd For," 3" l body, hooks removed, c1902 ... – **100.00**

Frog Skin Bait, glass eyes, $3\frac{3}{4}''$ l ... **65.00**

Revolution, smooth spade props, acorn style aluminum body, $3\frac{1}{4}''$ l, no tail hook, c1906 ... **100.00**

M A Shipley, metal fish–shape spoon, large fixed hook, $4\frac{3}{4}''$ l, Philadelphia, PA ... **45.00**

Van DeCar, Bonafide Aluminum Minnow, 1907 patent ... **4,125.00**

Minnow Trap

Camp, aqua colored glass, plated steel cap, three off–center entry holes, 11" l, Checotah, OK ... **100.00**

Handmade, metal and mesh, hinged door, 12 x 10 x 10" ... **32.00**

Shakespeare, glass, pale green, metal lid, emb name, 1 gallon ... **85.00**

Reel

Abbey & Imbrie, Imbrie Surf Reel, $3\frac{3}{8}$, hard rubber and German silver, jeweled bearings, "No–Off" free spool and lock button, two click buttons, "Feb 6, 1912 Pat. Date" on thumb drag, NY ... **175.00**

Appleton & Litchfield, fly reel, German silver and black hard rubber, $2\frac{3}{8}''$ d pillar to pillar, built–in click, Boston, MA ... **500.00**

Bond, bait casting, cardboard tube, Detroit ... **40.00**

Fin–Nor #4, spinning ... **250.00**

Hardy Bros

The Perfect, salmon reel, hard rubber handle, no ring guide, brass foot, adjustable drag, $4\frac{1}{4}''$ ... **225.00**

The Silex, salmon reel, quick change spool, rim click lever,

ridge foot, two knob handles, orig fitted case, 4" ... **110.00**

The Uniqua, black handle, enforced crescent latch, ridged brass foot, $3\frac{1}{8}''$ ... **55.00**

James Heddon's Sons, Bait Casting Level Wind, #3–36, German silver S handle, click button ... **70.00**

L A Kiefer, baitcasting, slide and pull drag, pat Aug 23, 1881/Feb 21, 1882, missing rear bearing cap ... **500.00**

B F Meek & Sons

#2, narrow spool, Louisville, KY, c1880 ... **650.00**

#44, flat back design ... **5,500.00**

Meek & Milam, #1 ... **2,200.00**

Meyer Co, Flo–Line, spinning reel and bait caster, orig box and instructions, Kenosha, WI ... **25.00**

B C Milam & Son, #5 ... **3,300.00**

Mills, Fairy, aluminum, trout, $2\frac{1}{4}''$ d, c1919 ... **3,300.00**

Orvis, Green Mountain II, adjustable sliding foot, quick change spool, exposed spool rim on/off click, center plate screw drag, cloth bag, $3\frac{1}{2}''$ ... **60.00**

Pflueger

Golden West, large size, orig box, OH, 1923 ... **45.00**

Medalist, USA Model #1496½, Diamolite line guard, rim drag, leather–type pouch ... **35.00**

Shakespeare

President, leather case, 1941 ... **30.00**

Special Tournament, #1740, free spool, 1920s ... **90.00**

Sterling #230, multiplying, hard rubber and nickel plated, click and drag, 100 yds, orig box ... **70.00**

Talbot, Ben Hur, trout, 1901 patent **6,600.00**

Uslan 500, model 1, line grab and under spool tension adjustment ... **50.00**

Edward Vom Hofe

6/0 #521, two rim levers, German silver and hard rubber, anti–reverse stud, click button, 1902 and 1896 patent dates ... **110.00**

Perfection model 360, handmade, size 2, trout ... **6,050.00**

Julius Vom Hofe, raised pillars, German silver and hard rubber S handle, 2 to 1 multiplier, off center turn click button ... **100.00**

Winchester, fly, black finish over brass, $2\frac{5}{8}''$ ... **50.00**

Rod

Abercrombie & Fitch Co, Triton, trout, $8\frac{1}{2}'$, 3–pc, 2 tips, brown wraps, wood reel seat, orig bag and aluminum tube ... **170.00**

Andrus, 8', 3–pc, 2 tips, red and

black intermediates, wood reel seat, "Made by H. Andrus–1918–Hartford, CT." engraved on nickel–silver butt cap **150.00**
Barney & Berry, trout fly, 8½', 3–pc, 2 tips, honey wraps, black intermediate winds, German silver and screw–down reel seat, orig cane case and bag **160.00**
Forest, Maker & Kelso, salmon, wood, 10', 2–pc, 1 tip, dark brown finish, brass sliding reel bands, cork butt, rubber butt cap   **10.00**
Garrison, 8', 2–pc, 2 tips **3,520.00**
Gilam, trout, 8', 3–pc, 2 tips, light line **4,400.00**
Halstead, 8', 2–pc, 2 tips **3,575.00**
Hardy
  Palakona—The De Luxe, 502 3 DMS, 9', maroon wraps, honey intermediates, aluminum screw–type reel band, wooden ferrule plugs, orig bag, tag, and tube **90.00**
  Salmon, 16', 3–pc, 2 tips, cane, dark maroon wrap and intermediates, patent steel center, cork grip butt, ferrule plugs, old rod bag and 65" wooden rod box   **150.00**
R H Kiffe Co, NY, salmon and boat rod, fine grain wood, 10½' and 7' lengths, 4–pc, 2 tips for 10½', 1 tip for 7', and 2 mid–sections, white and black wraps fore and aft of reel seat, sliding reel band, tube guides with red and black wraps and intermediates **60.00**
H L Leonard
  The Leonard Rod, Tournament, 8', 3⅞ oz, 3–pc, 2 tips, light brown wraps, wooden foot, sliding reel band, orig bag, tag, and tube **400.00**
  Special Tournament, salmon dry fly, 9', 3–pc, 2 tips, honey wraps, red tip, German silver reel seat, orig bag, tag, and tube   **175.00**
  Tournament, 9½', 6⅝ oz, 3–pc, 2 tips, dark maroon wraps and intermediates, sliding reel band, German silver reel seat, orig bag, tag, and tube **200.00**
  Trout, 8', 3–pc, 2 tips, engraved   **5,500.00**
Montague, trout, 9', 3–pc, 2 tips, black and maroon wraps and intermediates, silver screw–down reel band, fitted case **35.00**
Orvis, 8½', 3–pc, 2 tips, red wraps, screw–down reel band, cedar foot, orig bag and tube **225.00**
Payne
  Bait Caster, 5' **935.00**

Canadian Canoe, 8½', 5½ oz **4,125.00**
F E Thomas, salmon, 13½', 3–pc, 2 tips, gold wrap and intermediates, extension butt, locking reel band, German silver hardware, orig bag and tube **75.00**
Rod and Reel, Hurd Supercaster, wooden handle, built–on reel **70.00**
Rowboat, 12' l, 45" w, brown canvas, canoe–type construction, three seats, some cracked ribs **150.00**
Salmon Fly
  Col Esmond Drury, double hook, General Practitioner **275.00**
  Dr T E Pryce–Tannat **550.00**
  Jimmy Younger, Wilkinson **132.00**
Spring Gaff, wooden handle, 37½" l, MSA Co, Gladstone, MI, pat June 1900 . . . .   **275.00**
Tackle Box
  Leather, fitted metal interior, contains assorted weights, small vise, one reel, hooks, hardware, and old floats **60.00**
  Wooden, canvas covered, contents include one each small S handle Multiplier, unmarked reel, 2⅝ Multiplier Trout reel, Pepper–type spinner–fly lure, and hooks, leather fly keeper, two Phantoms, and assortment of flies **90.00**
Trophy, swordfish, head section, no back plaque **100.00**
Trout Basket
  Birch Bark, center hole in tin lid . . .   **525.00**
  Splint, high neck, web strap **495.00**
  Whole Willow, loops on sides, small lid opening, replaced hinge and latch loop **120.00**

HOLIDAY COLLECTIBLES

History: Holidays provided a welcome break from the tedious daily chores that were a constant in country living. Work could not be totally ignored. The cows had to be milked and the animals fed, holiday or not. The rural community followed a Sunday, rather than a weekday schedule.

Religious holidays tended to be family oriented and personal. Coming together was achieved at the traditional church service. Patriotic holidays were community celebrations, a time when frivolity prevailed.

Many holidays have both religious and secular overtones, such as Christmas, St. Patrick's Day, Easter, and Halloween. National holidays such as the Fourth of July and Thanksgiving are part of one's yearly planning. There are regional holidays. Fastnacht Day in Pennsylvania–German country is just one example.

Some holidays are the creation of the merchandising industry, e.g., Valentine's Day, Mother's Day, Father's Day, etc. The two leading forces in the perpetuation of holiday gift giving are the card industry and the floral industry. Through slick promotional campaigns they constantly create new occasions to give their products. Other marketing aspects follow quickly. Holiday items change annually. Manufacturers constantly must appeal to the same buyer.

Collectors tend to specialize in one holiday. Christmas, Halloween, and Easter are the most popular. Christmas collectors split into two groups—those who collect material associated with the Christmas tree and those who collect Santa Claus-related material. Halloween and Easter collectors tend to be generalists, albeit some Easter collectors limited their collection to Easter bunnies. New collectors still can find bargains, especially in the Thanksgiving and Valentine's Day collectibles.

Many holiday collectibles were manufactured abroad. Germany and Japan are two of the leading exporters of holiday items to the United States. German items from the turn of the century are highly prized.

It is possible to build a holiday collection around a single object. Two possibilities are post cards and papier mache candy containers. Among contemporary material, it is possible to find one or more limited edition collectors' plates issued for most holidays.

One of the most overlooked holiday collectibles is the greeting card. A greeting card's message and artwork is an important reflection of the values of the time the card was printed. With the exception of Valentines, most examples, even those from the early decades of the twentieth century, are priced under two dollars.

References: Helaine Fendelman & Jeri Schwartz, *The Official Price Guide to Holiday Collectibles*, House of Collectibles, L–W Book Sales (pub.), *Favors & Novelties: Wholesale Trade List No. 26, 1924–1925*, price list available; Margaret Schiffer, *Holiday Toys and Decorations*, Schiffer Publishing Ltd., 1985.

Newsletters: *Hearts to Holly: The Holiday Collectors Newsletter*, PO Box 105, Amherst, NH 03031; *Trick or Treat Trader*, PO Box 1058, Derry, NH 03038.

Reproduction Craftspersons: *Easter Eggs*—John J Hejna, 4529–289th St, Toledo, OH 43611; Valerie M Martz, Eggstrordinaire!, PO Box 118, Doylestown, PA 18901; Elizabeth Mayer, RR 3, Box 290, Langhorne, PA 19047; *General*—Johnathan K. Bastian, Pennsylvania German Woodcarvings, Rte 2, Box 240, Robesonia, PA

19551; Will Carlton, Carlton Studio, 2925 McMillan Rd, San Luis Obispo, CA 92401; Bruce Catt, C & V Emporium, PO Box 985 Planetarium Sta, New York, NY 10024; Lois Clarkson, Snowdin Studios, Box 28, Buckingham, PA 18912; Ruth Clotfelter Camenisch, Clotfelter Creations, Rte 2, Box 207–A, Monett, MO 65708; Sandra Coker, A Visit From St Nicholas, 1213 W Mulberry St, Salem, IN 47167; Glenn F Hale, Star Route, Harmonyville Rd, Pottstown, PA 19464; Joretta & Ron Headlee, 22 Downing Circle, Downingtown, PA 19335; Gerard Lavoie, Glassblower, Gerard Originals, PO Box 531, Methuen, MA 01844; Lydia Withington Holmes, Pewterer, Barton Hill, Stow, MA 01775; David & Sharon Jones, Three Feathers Pewter, Box 232, Shreve, OH 44676; Ed & Amy Pennebaker, Red Fern Handblown Glass, HCR 68, Box 19A, Salem, AR 72576; Pamela F Pizzichil, RD 2, Pottstown, PA 19464; Randy & Pam Tate, Knot in Vane, 805 N 11th St, DeKalb, IL 60115; Roberta Taylor, PO Box 336, Jeromesville, OH 44840.

Reproduction Manufacturers: Amazon Vinegar & Pickling Works Drygoods, 2218 E 11th St, Davenport, IA 52803; Applecore Creations, PO Box 29696, Columbus, OH 43229; Briere Design, 229 North Race St, Statesville, NC 28677; Checkerberry Hill, 253 Westridge Ave, Daly City, CA 94015; Country at Heart Creations, PO Box 67–B, Forest City, PA 18421; Country Bouquet, PO Box 200, Kellogg, MN 55945; Country House, 5939 Trails End, Three Oaks, MI 49128; Country Lady, PO Box 68, 201 E. Main St, Larwill, IN 46764; Designs in Copper, 7541 Emery Rd, Portland, MI 48875; The Evergreen Press, Inc, 3380 Vincent Rd, Pleasant Hill, CA 94523; Faith Mountain Country Fare, Main St, Box 199, Sperryville, VA 22740; Fernswood Strawwork, Box 26, R.D. 2, New London, OH 44851; Five Trails Antiques and Country Accents, 116 E Water St, Circleville, OH 43113; Gooseberry Patch, PO Box 634, Delaware, OH 43015; Gray's Attic, Box 532, Manson, IA 50453; Lamplighter Antiques, 615 Silver Bluff Rd, Aiken, SC 29801; Lancaster Collection, PO Box 6074, Lancaster, PA 17603; Mathew's Wire & Wood, 654 W Morrison, Frankfort, IN 46041; Matthews Emporium, 157 N Trade St, PO Box 1038, Matthews, NC 28106; McLeach, Box 575, Fitchburg, MA 01420; Mulberry Magic, PO Box 62, Ruckersville, VA 22968; The Painted Pony, 8392 West M–72, Traverse City, MI 49684; Pure and Simple, PO Box 535, 117 W Hempstead, Nashville, AR 71852; The Roos Collection, PO Box 20668, New York, NY 10025; Rustique Designs, Rte 4, Box 295, Parsons, KS 67357; The Tinhorn, 9610 W 190th, Lowwell, IN 46356; Unfinished Business, PO Box 246X, Wingate, NC 28174; Vaillancourt Folk Art, PO Box 582, Millbury, MA 01527; Woodpenny's, 27 Hammatt St, Ipswich, MA 01938.

Christmas
Angel, hard plastic, 10" l, tree top-
per, white and gold robe, clear
wings, 1950s **18.00**
Building
Bank, chalk, 3" h, corner build-
ing, white, marked "Made In
Japan" **10.00**
House, cardboard, 4" h, white
mica, cellophane windows . . .   **5.00**
Village, litho paper, 5" h, five
buildings, USA **25.00**
Candy Cane, chenille, 5" l, red and
white, Japan **6.00**
Candy Container
Father Christmas
Green Glass, 4" h, metal lid on
bottom **225.00**
Papier Mache, 7" h, belsnickle,
holding feather tree, white
coat, black boots, Germany,
c1900 . . . .   **350.00**
Santa
Net Body, 7" l, white, celluloid
head, hands, and boots,
three pom–pom buttons, Ja-
pan **75.00**
Composition and Felt, 8" h, red
felt suit, pink composition
face, cotton beard, remov-
able feet **90.00**
Molded Cardboard, 10" h,
holding sack on chimney,
candy cane holder, red and
white, USA, late 1940s **50.00**
Deer
Celluloid, 3" h, white, antlers . . .   **7.00**
Composition, $4\frac{1}{2}$" h, wooden legs,
metal antlers, brown, Germany   **45.00**

**Father Christmas belsnickle, papier ma-
che, red coat, black boots, holding
feather tree, Germany, $265.00**

Metal, 5" h, brown, marked "Ger-
many" **35.00**
Light Bulb
Bear, clear glass, early, marked
"Germany" **100.00**
Clown, clear glass, red and green
trim, marked "Germany" **55.00**
House, $2\frac{1}{2}$" h, milk glass, pink and
blue, Japan **10.00**
Santa, 3" h, milk glass, one leg in
chimney, Japan **25.00**
Street Lamp, 2" h, milk glass, Ja-
pan **12.00**
Light Strings
Bubble, Noma, orig box, 1940s   **35.00**
Celluloid, assortment of figures on
large string **150.00**
Nativity Figures
Angel, $4\frac{1}{2}$" l, composition, wax
covering, spun glass wings, hu-
man hair, net and lace robe,
Germany **40.00**
Camel, 5" l, composition body,
hide covering, wooden legs,
Germany **38.00**
Chicken, 2" h, composition body,
metal feet, marked "Germany"   **15.00**
Cow, 4" h, celluloid, brown, Ja-
pan **10.00**
Donkey, 3" h, composition, hide
covering, wooden legs, Ger-
many **20.00**
Mary, 2" h, composition, kneel-
ing, Japan **2.00**
Ram, 2" h, celluloid, tan, USA . .   **7.00**
Sheep, 5" h, composition body,
white wool coat, wooden legs,
marked "Germany" on red rib-
bon collar **60.00**
Shepherd, $5\frac{1}{4}$" h, composition,
kneeling, Germany **9.00**
Ornament
Chromolithograph
Angel, resting on hands, tinsel
trim **10.00**
Father Christmas, 9" h, cotton
batting coat, flat **150.00**
Three Children, 4" h, winter
clothing, tinsel trim **15.00**
Cotton Batting
Bird on clip, 3" l, white **25.00**
Boy, 4" h, white, composition
face, brown cotton shoes,
Germany **120.00**
Carrot, orange and red, green
paper top **17.50**
Santa, 4" h, red suit, black trim,
legs, and boots **40.00**
Dresden
Doll Carriage, 3" h, three di-
mensional, gold **125.00**

Rooster, 6" h, flat, gold, red, and green **48.00**

Zeppelin, 3½" l, three dimensional, detailed trim **350.00**

Glass

Barrel, gold and white, wire wrap, unsilvered, Victorian **60.00**

Beads, garland string, red, Japan, 1950s **5.00**

Bell, 3" h, wire clapper, silvered, red, white, and blue stripe, 1930s. **12.00**

Bottle, red, wire wrap, unsilvered, Victorian **35.00**

Candle on clip, 3½" h, silver, 1940s **12.00**

Candy Cane, 7¼" l, red stripes on white **6.00**

Carrot, 3½" h, silvered, orange matte finish, green tucksheer leaf 1910s **50.00**

Fish, 5" h, blue, red trim **90.00**

House, elf peeking out door, gold, red trim **50.00**

Mushroom on clip, 3¼" h, red and white, unsilvered, 1920s **42.00**

Pine Cone, 2" h, red, early 1950s **10.00**

Windmill, blue, unsilvered . . . **8.00**

Metal, basket, 3" h, handle **35.00**

Plastic, Santa, 3" h, red and white, plastic hook on top of head **6.00**

Wax, angel, small **42.00**

Plaque, 14½" d, papier mache, center child portrait, holly berry leaf trail rim, buff ground, artist sgd, dated 1884 . . . . **90.00**

Roly Poly, 6" h, Santa, red, green belt. **250.00**

Santa

Celluloid

3/4" h, walking, holding staff **20.00**

1" h, standing in white mica covered cardboard sleigh, pulled by two brown reindeer. **45.00**

Rabbit, candy container, papier mache, pulling basket, pasteboard wheels, 9" l, $60.00.

Chenille, 2" h, green, composition face, Japan **18.00**

Composition, 19" h, doll, jointed, carrying toy sack, red cotton suit, black belt and boots, USA, 1930s **250.00**

Cotton Batting, 2" h, composition face, standing by paper house **65.00**

Papier Mache, 29" h, clock–work nodder, cotton beard, white trim on red flannel robe, basket attached to rope belt, holding feather tree, Germany, c1900 **1,200.00**

Stocking, 24" l, cotton, Victorian Christmas scenes both sides **175.00**

Tree

Brush, 2" h, green, snow, Japan **2.00**

Cellophane Needles, 19" h, green, multicolored bubble lights, white plastic base, 1950s **50.00**

Feather, 48" h, green, red berries, candle clips, holly stenciled on square white wooden base, Germany **400.00**

Paper, 8" h, green, USA **15.00**

Tree Fence

Cast Iron, 4" h, dark green, gate, 10 sections. **185.00**

Wood, 5" h, blue, picket gate, 4 sections **90.00**

Tree Stand, cast iron, painted black and gold, marked "North Bros, Mfg Co, Philadelphia, PA" **60.00**

Wreath, chenille, red, candle inside, late 1940s **20.00**

Easter

Basket

Metal, 8" d, yellow, rabbits and chicks illus, Chein Toy Co **15.00**

Wood, 6" d, painted flowers, paper label on base marked "Made in Germany," 10" handle **18.00**

Candy Container

Bunny, 6" h, composition, sailor shirt, holding yellow basket, marked "US Zone," Germany **90.00**

Duck, 4" h, composition, yellow, ribbon around neck, 3" d round cardboard base, Germany **35.00**

Egg, 4" l, papier mache, litho of boy golfer on front, separates in middle, marked "Germany" **15.00**

Farm House, bright colors, surrounded by brown wooden fence, composition chicks and rabbit in yard, roof comes off for candy, Germany **48.00**

Rabbit, papier mache, leather ears, glass eyes, Germany **70.00**

Rooster, 5" h, composition, bright

colors, fine detail, metal feet, removable head, marked "Germany"................. **60.00**

Chicken

Celluloid, lays eggs, c1910..... **80.00**

Composition, 4" h, hen on nest, straw nest, marked "Germany" **35.00**

Cotton Batting, 4" h, wire legs, glass eyes, chenille beak, marked "Japan".......... **40.00**

Egg

Celluloid, 5" l, purple, Japan.... **32.00**

Glass, 5" l, opaque, white, painted spring scene, "Happy Easter" painted in gold **25.00**

Rabbit

Celluloid, 4½" h, roly poly, dressed in purple, standing on ball, Japan.................... **25.00**

Chalk, 5" h, nodder, brown flocking, marked "USA," 1950s.... **12.00**

Cloth, 9" h, straw stuffed, wooden head **60.00**

Composition, 5½" h, white, pink golfing clothes, swinging golf club, marked "Germany" **38.00**

Hard Plastic, 7" h, rabbit pushing baby buggy, pink, blue trim ... **12.00**

Tin, 5" h, windup toy, fur covered, hops, marked "Japan" **55.00**

Fourth of July

Bunting, 23" w, red, white, and blue muslin, various lengths, per yard **5.00**

Candy Container

Box, 2¼ x 2½", shield shape, red, white, and blue............ **10.00**

Hat, Uncle Sam's, milk glass, painted red, white, and blue, slotted closure **50.00**

Flag, 10" h, 48 stars, wooden stick, **2.00**

Pencil, lead, red, white, and blue paper **3.00**

Post Card, Ground Hog Day, $20.00.

George Washington's Birthday

Axe, 7" h, wooden handle, "I cannot tell a lie" painted on blade **10.00**

Candy Container

Axe, 5" h, fabric over cardboard, plug in handle for candy, Germany.................. **25.00**

Hat, cardboard, tri-cornered, cloth cherries **30.00**

Tree Stump, 3" h, papier mache, surrounded by composition cherries, marked "Germany" **45.00**

Diecut, 2½" h, George Washington, hatchet with cherry, flanked by stump with hatchet, set of 3..... **8.00**

Halloween

Candy Container

Cat

Crepe Paper, 3" h, cup type, braided handle, black diecut cat on front, USA **10.00**

Hard Plastic, 4" h, orange and black, arched back, open area in back for candy, USA, 1950s **7.50**

Papier Mache, 5½" h, black, metal spring tail, removable head, Germany, 1930s **110.00**

Goblin, 3" h, orange pumpkin head, green suit, standing on round box, marked "Germany" **85.00**

Jack O'Lantern, 2½" h, clear pressed glass, melon ribbed, painted pumpkin yellow, red intaglio nose and mouth, raised white teeth, black ringed protruding pop eyeballs, wire bail handle, slotted metal screw on cap................. **300.00**

Owl, 8" h, papier mache, orange, opening in bottom for candy, USA **40.00**

Scarecrow, 8" h, hard plastic, pumpkin head, orange and black, open area in back for lollipops, USA, 1950s........ **15.00**

Witch, papier mache

5" h, red painted dress, straw broom, flax hair, removable head, Germany......... **250.00**

8" h, black and orange, sack on back for candy, Germany .. **95.00**

Diecut, 2½" h, witches on broom, set of forty on sheet, marked "Germany" **20.00**

Fan, fold-out, wooden stick, witch riding broom, black and orange, marked "Germany," 1920s **10.00**

Ghost, 9½" h, cardboard, stand-up, USA **15.00**

Lantern

Cardboard, 7" h, witch silhouette,

black, four sided, orange tissue paper background, wire bail handle, USA **42.00**

Glass, 3" h, pumpkin head, painted orange, brightly colored face, wire handle, candle holder in base, USA **40.00**

Papier Mache

Cat Head, 6" h, black, orig paper insert behind eyes and mouth, wire bail handle, marked "Germany" **150.00**

Devil Head, 7" h, two tone red, paper insert behind cut out eyes and mouth, wire bail handle, Germany **100.00**

Pumpkin Head, 5" h, orange, paper insert behind cut out eyes, "O"–shaped mouth, wire bail handle, USA **40.00**

Tin, 5" h, pumpkin on wooden pole, candleholder in base, orange and green, smiling face, marked "Germany" **125.00**

Noisemaker

Bell, litho tin, frying pan shape, wooden clappers, orange and black, marked "J. Chein" **15.00**

Clicker, 2½", metal, frog shape, orange and black, USA **10.00**

Horn

Cardboard, 9" h, black and orange, cat, witch, and moon figures, USA **7.00**

Paper, orange and black, wooden mouthpiece, Germany **5.00**

Wood, 4" h, black and orange, cat face, marked "Czecho–Slovakia" **18.00**

Rattle

Cardboard, 3½" d, round, orange and black tissue paper covering, wooden handle . .   **10.00**

Post Card, Halloween, bright orange pumpkin, artist signed "Ellen Clapsaddle," $8.00.

Tin, 3" d, wooden handle, orange, white, and green pumpkin and cats litho, USA   **7.50**

Squeaker, 3" d, cardboard and cloth, orange pumpkin face, marked "Germany" **20.00**

Tambourine, litho tin, with face, orange and black, marked "T Cohn, Inc" **10.00**

Pitcher, 1½" h, Halloween face, bisque **14.00**

St Patrick's Day

Candy Container

Irish boy, 4" h, composition, standing, green shamrock on gray fez, green jacket, red vest, yellow pants, purple socks, small oval wood box, Germany   **100.00**

Potato, 4" l, papier mache, green paper shamrock **45.00**

Top Hat, 3" h, cardboard, green, bisque pipe, cloth shamrock, Germany **25.00**

Corkscrew, Irish blackthorn handle, marked "Happy St Patrick's Day," green cloth ribbon attached to handle **10.00**

Diecut

Harp, 3" h, gold, entwined with shamrocks and green ribbon, marked "Germany" **1.50**

Leprechaun, green top hat, smoking clay pipe, set of 42, marked "Germany" **15.00**

Shamrock, Irish lass in center, set of 40, marked "Germany" . . .   **20.00**

Doll, 4½" h, composition, boy, green and white felt clothing, shamrock trim on white felt hat, marked "Japan" **35.00**

Shillelagh, wooden, carved **12.00**

Thanksgiving

Candy Container, turkey

Composition

5" h, fan tail, opening at base, marked "Japan" **35.00**

6" h, folded tail, glass eyes, metal feet, removable head, marked "Germany" **45.00**

12" h, fantail, horsehair beard, metal feet, marked "Germany" **85.00**

Papier Mache, 8" h, pale orange, opening in base, marked "Alco Co, USA" **30.00**

Figurine, 4" h, man and woman Pilgrims, composition, marked "Germany" **45.00**

Place Card, 3" h, turkey, emb cardboard, stand–up type, USA **5.00**

Sauce Tureen, china, figural turkey, top half lid, multicolored **20.00**

Turkey
  Celluloid, 4" h, white, pink, and
    blue, weighted bottom, marked
    "Irwin, USA" **25.00**
  Composition
    2" h, fan tail, metal feet,
      marked "Germany" **15.00**
    6" h, folded tail, green base,
      marked "Japan" **35.00**
    Pot Metal, 1¼" h, molded feet,
      marked "England" **10.00**
    Rubber, 1½" h, black, red and
      green trim, USA **7.50**
Valentine's Day
  Valentine
    Card Style
      4½" h, "Best Wishes," shades of
        blue, picture of bird in cen-
        ter, poem beneath, no greet-
        ing inside **5.00**
      6½" h, "To My Sweetheart,"
        small girl in green dress and
        hat, red wild rose border,
        verse inside **10.00**
      Easel Back, 8½", girl carrying red
        honeycomb paper parasol. . . .   **50.00**
    Fold Out
      5", "With Best Wishes," two
        cupids embracing, bordered
        by birds, marked "Germany"   **11.00**
      13 x 10", diecut, lady, lacy bor-
        der, c1890 . . . .   **25.00**
    Mechanical
      5", "To My Love," gray cat,
        movable eyes and mouth,
        stand–up, marked "Ger-
        many" **7.50**
      9", stand–up, chicken carrying
        a baby wrapped in blanket,
        blanket in beak, baby holds
        valentine, as baby swings,
        chicken's eyes move, marked
        "Germany" **15.00**
      Black boy and girl, chicken and
        duck pop out of watermelon
        with cards in beaks **25.00**
    Stand–Up
      4" h, "A Valentine Specially For
        You," delivery boy on motor-
        bike holding red hearts,
        marked "Germany" **7.00**
      6" h, "To My Sweetheart,"
        white dog, envelope in
        mouth, marked "Germany"   **3.50**
      6¾", diecut, girl holding doves,
        Germany **8.00**

HUNTING ITEMS

History: There is a strong linkage between the
country community and firearms. Almost every

farmer owns one or more rifles. These weapons
provide self preservation and sport.

Varmints from rats to groundhogs plague the
farmer. Some attack small domesticated animals,
eat harvested grain, or cause damage that can
lead to accidents. The standard means of ridding
the farm of varmints is to shoot them.

Hunting also plays an important role in the
agrarian community. In lean times, it provides all
important food for the table. In good times, it
provides sport and a means of escape from daily
chores.

The 15th century arquebus was the forerunner
of the modern firearm. The Germans refined the
wheel lock firing mechanism during the 16th and
17th centuries. English settlers arrived in America
with the smoothbore musket; German settlers had
rifled arms. Both used the new flintlock firing
mechanism.

A major advance was achieved when Whitney
introduced interchangeable parts into the manufacturing of rifles. The warfare of the 19th century
brought continued refinements in firearms. The
percussion ignition system was developed by the
1840s. Minie, a French military officer, produced
a viable projectile. By the end of the 19th century
cartridge weapons dominated the field.

Two factors control pricing firearms—
condition and rarity. The value of any particular
antique firearm covers a very wide range. For
instance, a Colt 1849 pocket model revolver with
a 5" barrel can be priced from $150.00 to
$750.00, depending on whether or not all the
component parts are original, whether some are
missing, how much of the original finish (bluing)
remains on the barrel and frame, how much silver
plating remains on the brass trigger guard and
back strap, and the condition and finish of the
walnut grips. Be careful to note any weapon's
negative qualities. Know the production run of a
firearm before buying it.

Muzzle loading weapons of the eighteenth and
early nineteenth centuries varied in caliber and
required the owner to carry a variety of equipment with him, including a powder horn or flask,
patches, flints or percussion caps, bullets, and
bullet molds. In addition, military personnel were
responsible for bayonets, slings, and miscellaneous cleaning equipment and spare parts.

In the mid–19th century, cartridge weapons
replaced their black powder ancestors. Collectors
seek anything associated with early ammunition
from the cartridges themselves to advertising material. Handling old ammunition can be extremely dangerous due to decomposition of com-
pounds. Seek advice from an experienced
collector before becoming involved in this area.

References: Ralf Coykendall, Jr., *Coykendall's
Sporting Collectilbes Price Guide*, Lyons & Bur-
ford, 1991; Norman Flayderman, *Flayderman's
Guide To Antique American Firearms. . .And
Their Values*, 5th ed., DBI Books, 1991; Joseph

Kindig, Jr., *Thoughts On The Kentucky Rifle In Its Golden Age*, 1960, available in reprint; Russell and Steve Quetermous, *Modern Guns: Identification & Values, Revised 8th Edition*, Collector Books, 1991.

Periodicals: *Gun List*, 700 East State Street, Iola, WI 54990; *Gun Week*, PO Box 488, Buffalo, NY 14209; *The Gun Report*, PO Box 38, Aldeo, IL 61231; *Shotgun News*, PO Box 669, Hastings, NE 68902.

Museums: National Firearms Museum, Washington, DC; Springfield Armory National Historic Site, Springfield, MA.

Reproduction Alert: The amount of reproduction and fake powder horns is large. Be very cautious!

Reproduction Craftspersons: *Firearms*—William J Cooey, 248 Van Horn Rd, Milton, FL 32570; Daniel Winkler, PO Box 255 DTS, Boone, NC 28607; *General*—Mark Odle, Rte 1, Box 40, Reedy, WV 25270; *Powderhorns*—Robert Miller, Golden Age Powderhorns, 100 Summer St, Kennebunk, ME 04043; Michelle Ochonicky, Stone Hollow Scrimshaw Studio, 4059 Toenges Ave, St Louis, MO 63116; Mark Odle, Rte 1, Box 40, Reedy, WV 25270; Scott & Cathy Sibley, Sibley's Engraved Powderhorns, 3224 Wyatt Rd, North Pole, AK 99705.

Reproduction Manufacturer: *Firearms*—Log Cabin Shop, Box 275, Lodi, OH 44254.

Clay Birds, Winchester, complete in orig box, marked "Pat May 29, 1917"	**100.00**
Powder Flask, copper, pear shape, hounds fighting bear illus emb both sides, brass top, script initials below illus, 7¾" h.	**90.00**
Powder Can	
Austin Powder Co, green can, tan paper label, ½ lb	**75.00**
Ditmar's Powder Co, New Sporting Powder, paper label, 1 lb	**90.00**
Eureka Powder Works, Imperial Gun Powder, orange label, 1 lb	**30.00**
Hercules Powder Co, Black Sporting Powder, orange and black label, 1 lb	**45.00**
Robin Hood Powder Co, green, Robin Hood in red on red and white label, 1 lb	**165.00**
Powder Horn	
5" l, three rings at tip	**125.00**
5⅜" l, Queen Anne style, tapered screw cap, flat butt plug	**115.00**
7⅞" l, brass trim and screw tip, butt plug missing	**950.00**
9" l, turned domed butt plug, turned tip, York County, PA	**250.00**
11¼" l, turned butt plug, well shaped screw tip	**700.00**
12¼" l, turned tip, dark patina	**175.00**

Powder Horn, engraved dec, inscribed "W. Carr, 1789," 12" l, $650.00.

Powder Keg	
American Powder Mills, black, green and black label, 25 lbs.	**60.00**
E I du Pont de Nemours Powder Co, green, dog on black and white label, 1 lb	**55.00**
Hazard Powder Co, Duck Shooting Gun Powder, red, 6 lbs.	**75.00**
King Powder Co, Quick Shot, red, paper label, 6 lbs	**50.00**
Rifle	
Colt Coltsman Standard, 30–06, bolt action, repeating, 5– shot box magazine, 22" blued barrel, ramp front sight, checkered walnut one-piece pistol grip stock & tapered forearm, swivels, late 1950s	**270.00**
Harrington & Richardson Pioneer 765, 22 caliber, long rifle, bolt action, single shot, 24" blued barrel, open rear and hooded bead front sights, wood Monte Carlo one–piece semi–grip stock and forearm, c1950	**45.00**
Iver Johnson Model X, 22 caliber, bolt action, single shot, 22" blued barrel, open rear and blade front sights, wood one–piece pistol grip stock and forearm, c1930.	**70.00**
Kentucky Long Rifle	
50¼" l, walnut half stock, percussion lock marked "Partridge, warranted"	**350.00**
52" l, converted to percussion, curly maple stock, powder horn and leather pouch, early 19th C	**700.00**
53" l, curly maple half stock, percussion lock, homemade brass lock plate marked "White," barrel marked "W. Cooper," brass patch box	**75.00**
Marlin Model 422 Varmint King, 222 caliber, bolt action, repeating, 3–shot detachable clip magazine, 24" barrel, peep sight rear and hooded ramp front sights,	

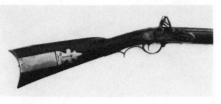

Rifle, Pennsylvania Long, marked "Peter Moll, Hellertown, Warranted No. 58," artificially striped stock, c1830, 55½" l, $1,500.00.

checkered Monte Carlo pistol grip stock and forearm, c1958 . . . . . .   **280.00**
Remington Model 141 Gamemaster, 30 caliber, slide action, hammerless, takedown model, 5–shot tubular magazine, 24" barrel, ramp front and adjustable rear sights, checkered walnut pistol grip stock, checkered semi–beavertail slide handle, c1940 . . . .   **265.00**
Winchester, model 56, 22 caliber, bolt action, repeating, 22" blued barrel, plain walnut one–piece semi–pistol grip stock, c1925 . . .   **180.00**
Rifle Bag, Kentucky, 9 x 7", leather, tarred fabric cov, homemade 6½" l knife in leather covered wooden scabbard attached to leather carrying strap, bag contains old flints and lead balls **175.00**
Shotgun
Browning Double Automatic Standard, 12 gauge, semi–automatic, hammerless, 2 shot, 28" full choke barrel, blued, checkered walnut pistol grip stock and forearm, late 1950s **290.00**
Harrington & Richardson Huntsman 351, 16 gauge, bolt action, repeating, 2–shot tubular magazine, 26" adjustable choke barrel, blued, plain Monte Carlo semi–pistol grip stock and forearm, recoil pad, c1955 . . . .   **70.00**
Ithaca Hammerless Double Field Grade, 20 gauge, box lock, top lever, break–open, double barrel, blued, checkered walnut pistol grip stock and short tapered forearm, c1930 . . . .   **400.00**
Iver Johnson Super Trap, 12 gauge, box lock, top lever, break–open, hammerless, 32" full choke double barrel, blued, checkered walnut pistol grip stock and forearm, recoil pad, standard grade, c1940   **410.00**
Marlin Model 410, 410 gauge, lever action, exposed hammer, 5–shot tubular magazine, 26" barrel, 2½" chamber, blued, walnut pistol grip stock and beavertail forearm, c1930 . . . .   **325.00**
Mossberg Model 83D, 410 gauge, bolt action, repeating, 2– shot top loading magazine, 23" barrel, blued, hardwood Monte Carlo semi–pistol grip one–piece stock and forearm, 1940s **65.00**
Remington Model 11 Sportsman, 16 gauge, semi–automatic, concealed hammer side ejection, repeating, 2–shot magazine, bottom load, blued barrel, wood semi–pistol grip stock, c1940 . . .   **250.00**
Richland Model 711 Long Range Waterfowl, 10 gauge, box lock, top lever, break–open, hammerless, double trigger, 32" full choke barrel, blued, checkered walnut pistol grip stock and tapered forearm, early 1960s **220.00**
Savage Model 220, 28 gauge, top lever, break–open, single shot, hammerless, automatic ejector, 30" full choke barrel, blued, plain wood pistol grip stock and forearm, c1935 . . . .   **65.00**
Stevens Model No 250, 12 gauge, top lever, break–open, exposed hammer, double trigger, 30" double barrel, blued, checkered walnut pistol grip stock and forearm, c1905 . . . .   **165.00**
Western Long Range, 20 gauge, box lock, top lever, break–open, hammerless, double trigger, double barrel, blued, plain walnut pistol grip stock and forearm, c1930 . . . .   **225.00**
Winchester Model 20, 410 gauge, top lever, break–open, box lock, exposed hammer, single shot, 26" full choke barrel, blued, checkered wood pistol grip stock and lipped forearm, early 1920s **190.00**
Target Ball
Amber, molded, raised sunburst on overall net pattern, ½" band around middle marked "BOGARDUS GLASS BALL PATd APRIL '10 1877," 2¾" d, chips at neck   **200.00**
Cobalt Blue, bands with squares pattern, smooth base, rough sheared lip, 2½" d, American, 1870–1880   **100.00**
Lavender, man shooting rifle illus on raised basketweave design, 2" d   **120.00**
Traps
Bear, Newhouse, hand–forged teeth, early **900.00**
Coyote and Fox, Verbail **100.00**

Kodiak Bear, Herter's #6, chain and swivel....................	**425.00**
Muskrat, Funsten Brothers, floating	**500.00**
Partridge, Davenport...........	**110.00**
Wolf, Newhouse #4½, chain and swivel....................	**160.00**
Trophy, mounted	
Antelope Stag Head, 12" w antlers	**40.00**
Black Bear Head, mouth open	**200.00**
Black Bear Rug, head and claws ...	**350.00**
Caribou Stag Head, full antlers, 56" w antlers..............	**225.00**
Deer Stag Head, four point antlers, 14" w antlers..............	**40.00**
Fox, red, standing, mounted on split log.....................	**145.00**
Moose Head.................	**900.00**
Squirrel, gray, poised on branched base....................	**40.00**

MUSICAL INSTRUMENTS

History: Music played an important role in rural life. A parlor organ and/or piano was found in most well–to–do homes. Family singing as a form of social interaction was common. In addition, farmers and housewives sang aloud, often to themselves, to pass the time of day.

Within the agrarian community, love of music enhanced social contact. Many individuals sang in church and secular choirs. "Barber Shop" harmonies were practiced informally.

Most individuals were proficient on a musical instrument. Community bands flourished. Most rural town parks had a band stand. Many fraternal associations, fire companies, and veteran organizations had their own bands to provide marching music for members during community and regional parades.

Brass instruments such as trumpet, trombone, and tuba were among the most popular. Many communities had an all brass band, albeit most had a few percussion players for marching purposes.

Live music was required for hoe–downs and community dances. The country fiddler enjoyed a prominent position. He was often joined on stage by a bass, guitar, and banjo player.

The more traditional musical instruments were often supplemented by a host of folk and improvised instruments, many of which were handmade. The best known of the folk instruments is the dulcimer. Improvised instruments range from the washboard to the boom–bas, a virtual one person band.

The most valuable antique instruments are those associated with the classical music period of 1650 to 1900, e.g., flutes, oboes, and violins. Few of these are found in the countryside. Most Country instruments, e.g., trumpets and guitars,

have more value on the "used" market than they do as antiques.

Reference: *The Official Price Guide To Music Collectibles, Sixth Edition,* House of Collectibles, 1986.

Collectors' Clubs: American Musical Instrument Society, 414 East Clark St, Vermillion, SD 57069; Fretted Instrument Guild of America, 2344 South Oakley Avenue, Chicago, IL 60608.

Periodical: *Concertina & Squeezebox,* PO Box 6706, Ithaca, NY 14851.

Museums: Yale University Collection of Musical Instruments, New Haven, CT; Smithsonian Museum, Division of Musical History, Washington, DC; The Musical Museum, Deansboro, NY; The Museum of the American Piano, New York, NY; The Shine to Music Museum, Vermillion, SD.

Reproduction Craftspersons: William J Cooey, 248 Van Horn Rd, Milton, FL 32570; Carl & Kathleen Gotzmer, June Apple Dulcimers, Rte 1, Box 709P, Accokeek, MD 20607; John C Hockett, Maiden Creek Dulcimers, 8 Gerstung Rd, Park Forest, IL 60466; Ken Ratcliff, Ratcliff String Instruments, 107 N Wilson Ave, Morehead, KY 40351; John & Ann Rawdon, Dulcimers by JR, Rte 1, CR 21, Newcomerstown, OH 43832.

Banjo	
Edwon C Dobson, New York City, c1900...................	**125.00**
Edgemere, nickel shell, wood lines, 17 nickel plated hexagon brackets, raised frets, imitation mahogany finish on birch neck, c1900...................	**325.00**
Unknown American Maker	
Calfskin Head, 10" d, nickel band on maple shell, imitation cherry finish on neck, six screw brackets, c1900...........	**225.00**
Homemade, skin stretched over barrel stave, hardwood neck, strings missing, skin broken, c1870.................	**150.00**
Trap Door style, snakehead, straight neck, 1920s........	**250.00**
Boom–Bas, one–man band, cymbals, bells, wood block, and tambourine attached to pogo stick type pole ...	**250.00**
Bugle, brass, American, Civil War ..	**400.00**
Drum, parade, polychrome dec, "Virginia" inscribed above panel depicting Washington and Mt Vernon, 16" d, 13" h, mid 19th C........	**850.00**
Dulcimer, violin shaped, heart shaped cutouts, whittled string keys, worn dark patina, 35½" l.............	**350.00**
Glockenspiel, carrying strap and case	**65.00**
Harmonica, Rol–Monica Player, bakelite, 1900s................	**165.00**

Ocarina, "Sweet Potato," wood, painted black, gold trim, 9" l, $35.00.

Horn, toleware, 14"	**20.00**
Sleigh Bells, 30 x 24" oak frame, six bells attached to each strap, eight straps, American, 1890s	**130.00**
Tambourine, hp, birds and bee on branch	**70.00**
Washboard, metal, wooden frame, thin chain with wooden stick at end attached to one side, Appalachia, c1890	**95.00**
Zither, J Schilt Solothurn, rosewood, 10 x 12½"	**50.00**

TOYS, DOLLS, AND GAMES

History: Toys, dolls, and games were favorite pastimes in rural America. Games that involved all members of the family were popular. Many of the toys found in the agrarian household were handmade.

The first manufactured toys in America were imported from Europe. The first toys manufactured in America were made of cast iron, appearing shortly after the Civil War. Leading 19th century manufacturers include Hubley, Dent, Kenton, and Schoenhut. In the first decades of the 20th century, Arcade, Buddy L, Marx, and Tootsie Toy joined the earlier firms.

The importation of toys never ceased. German toys dominated until World War I. After World War II, Japanese imports flooded the market. Today, many "American" toys are actually manufactured abroad.

During the 14th through the 18th centuries doll making was centered in Europe, mainly Germany and France. The French dolls produced in the era represented adults and were dressed in the latest couturier designs. They were not children's toys.

During the mid–19th century, child and baby dolls made in wax, cloth, bisque, and porcelain were introduced. Facial features were hand painted; wigs were made of mohair and human hair. They were dressed in baby or children's fashions.

Dollmaking in the United States began to flourish in the 1900s with names like Effanbee, Madame Alexander, Ideal, and others.

The first American board games have been traced back to the 1820s. Mass production of board games did not begin until after the Civil War. Firms such as Milton Bradley, McLoughlin Brothers, and Selchow and Righter were active in the 1860s. Parker Brothers began in 1883. Milton Bradley acquired McLoughlin Brothers in 1920.

Every toy, doll, and game is collectible. The key is condition and working order if mechanical.

References: There are a wealth of books devoted to the subject of toys, dolls, and games. A basic reference is Harry L. Rinker's *Collector's Guide to Toys, Games, and Puzzles* (Wallace–Homestead, 1991). The following references are merely starting points. Their bibliographies will point you in additional directions.

Toys: Richard Friz, *The Official Identification and Price Guide to Collectible Toys, Fifth Edition*, House of Collectibles, 1991; David Longest, *Toys: Antique & Collectible*, Collector Books, 1990; Richard O'Brien, *Collecting Toys: A Collectors Identification and Value Guide, 5th Edition*, Books Americana, 1990.

Dolls: Jan Foulke, *9th Blue Book Dolls and Values*, Hobby House Press, Inc., 1989; R. Lane Herron, *Herron's Price Guide to Dolls*, Wallace–Homestead, 1990.

Games: Lee Dennis, *Warman's Antique American Games, 1840-1940, Current Market Values*, Wallace–Homestead, 1991; Bruce Whitehill, *Games: American Games and Their Makers, 1822–1992, with Values*, Wallace-Homestead, 1992.

Periodicals: *The Antique Toy World*, PO Box 34509, Chicago, IL 60634; *Doll Reader*, Hobby House Press, 900 Frederick St., Cumberland, MD; *Dolls: The Collector's Magazine*, PO Box 1972, Marion, OH 43305; *Toy Shop*, 700 East State St, Iola, WI 54990.

Collectors' Clubs: American Game Collectors Association, 4628 Barlow Drive, Bartlesville, OK 74006; United Federation of Doll Clubs, PO Box 14146, Parkville, MO 64152.

Museums: Smithsonian Institution, Washington, DC; Museum of the City of New York, NY; Margaret Woodbury Strong Museum, Rochester, NY.

Reproduction Craftspersons: *Dolls*—Suzanne Berg, 1264 Estate Dr, West Chester, PA 19380; Sylvia June Brown, Hess Mill Rd, RD 2, Box 229 D, Landenberg, PA; Pat Broyles, Rte 1, Box 200, Grottoes, VA 24441; Jacquelyn Trone Butera, Colonial Yard, 500 S Park Ave, Audubon, PA 19403; Beth Cameron, 1000 Washington Ave, Oakmont, PA 15139; Nancy Coblentz, Timber Wool, 10040 Longs Mill Rd, Rocky Ridge, MD 21778; Maggie deYoung, Poppets, RR 1, PO Box 36, Beaverville, IL 60912; Jill R Lawrence, Dutch Hill Rd, RD 2, Union City, PA 16438; Jocelyn Mostrom, Corn Husk Crafts, 16311 Black Rock Rd, Darnestown, MD 20874; Lillian Prillaman

Folk Art, Rte 1, Box 148, Kearneysville, WV 25430; Lynne Robuccio, The Linen Bonnet, 29 Lantern Ln, Leominster, MA 01453; Diana Dale Simpkins, PO Box 143, Kemblesville, PA 19347; Judie Tasch Original Dolls, 3208 Clearview, Austin, TX 78703; *Doll House Furnishings*— Gary Sites, Doll Furniture by Jennifer's Dad, 2 Woodview Ln, Oxford, PA 19363.

Gameboards—Robin Lankford, Folk Hearts, 15005 Howe Rd, Portland, MI 48875; Barbara Strickland, 728 Hawthorne, El Cajon, CA 92020; C H Southwell, PO Box 484–B, Suttons Bay, MI 49682; Randy & Pam Tate, Knot in Vane, 805 N 11th St, DeKalb, IL 60115; Mary Thompson, Games People Played, PO Box 182, Cora, WY 28925.

General—Faith Allenby & Robert Kauffman, Allenby/Kauffman Wood Designs, RR 2, Box 325, Snake Meadow Rd, S Killingly, CT 06239; Nicolas D Cortes, Nicolas Cortes Gallery & Studio, 405 W 44th St, New York, NY 10036; Eleanor Meadowcroft, 25 Flint St, Salem, MA 01970; Lillian Prillaman, Lillian Prillaman Folk Art, Rte 1, Box 148, Kearneysville, WV 25430; Ken and Bobbie Ralphs, Our Family Toys, PO Box 262, Hatfield, PA 19440; Donna H Pierce, 522 Meadowpark La, Media, PA 19063; Randal A Smith Fine Toys & Fancy Goods, 207 Main St, Gilboa, OH 45847; Jay Trace, 1133 Manor Rd, Coatesville, PA 19320, Meg Whitney, 676 St Charles Ave, Warminster, PA 18974.

Kaleidoscopes—Anita Troisi, 286 N Hanover St, Pottstown, PA 19464; *Stuffed Animals*—Carri Landfield, Happily Ever After, 127 W Marquita St, San Clemente, CA 92672; *Teddy Bears*— Ginger Duemler, Designs by Ginger, Box 61, Hilltown, PA 18927.

Reproduction Manufacturers: *Dolls*—Anastasia's Collectibles, 6114 134th St W, Apple Valley, MN 55124; C J's Bailiwick, 6124 Walker Avenue, Lincoln, NE 68507; Cabin Fever, 5770 S Meridian, Laingsburg, MI 48848; Country Ritz, 1217 Moro, PO Box 875, Manhattan, KS 66502; Faith Mountain Country Fare, Main St, Box 199, Sperryville, VA 22740; Fernswood Strawwork, Box 26, RD 2, New London, OH 44851; Fitz and Friends, 1463 Rainbow Drive, NE, Lancaster, OH 43130; Lin Mac Dolls of Papier–Mache, 183 Glasgow St, Clyde, NY 14433; Pesta's Country Charm, 300 Standard Ave, Mingo Junction, OH 43938; Pieces of Olde, PO Box 65130, Baltimore, MD 21209; Ricyn: Country Collectables, PO Box 577, Twisp, WA 98856; *Doll Houses*— Little Lincoln's, 5373 W Houghton Lake Fr, Houghton Lake, MI 48629; *Doll House Furnishings*—Meadow Craft, PO Box 100, Rose Hill, NC 28458; Ohio Painted Furniture, Rte 4, Box 200, Athens, OH 45701; Pine Cone Primitives, PO Box 682, Troutman, NC 28166; The Storybook Collection of Miniatures, Inc, PO Box 13770, Richmond, VA 23225; *Doll Supplies*—Dollspart Supply Co, Inc, 5–15 49th Ave, Long Island City,

NY 11101; Mini–Magic, 3675 Reed Rd, Columbus, OH 43220; Pattern Plus, 21 Mountain View Avenue, New Milford, CT 06776.

Gameboards—The Prairie Stenciler, 7215 Nobel Court, Shawnee, KS 66218; *Teddy Bears*— Bear–in–Mind, 20 Beharrel St, Concord, MA 01742; Bullfrog Hollow, Keeny Rd, Lyme, CT 06371.

General—Cherry Tree Toys, Inc, PO Box 369–115, Belmont, OH 43718; Country Corner Collectibles, PO Box 422, Pitman, NJ 08071; Good Things, PO Box 2452, Chino, CA 91708; Knot in Vane, 805 N 11th St, DeKalb, IL 60115; Lace Wood 'N Tin Tyme, 6496 Summerton, Shepherd, MI 48883; Mill Pond Designs, PO Box 290, East Longmeadow, MA 01028; The Countryside, PO Box 722, Forsyth, MO 65653; Southern Manner, Inc, 106 North Trade St, PO Box 1706, Matthews, NC 28106; Woodbee's, RR #1, Poseyville, IN 47633.

Balancing Toy
  Circus Acrobats, wood, carved, painted, stylized and jointed figures, bald–headed acrobat standing on brown horse connected by balance bar to acrobat wearing red stockings and brown trunks, relief carved facial features, 13¼" h, late 19th C **600.00**
  Man wearing top hat, wood, carved, turned body and limbs, painted eyes, suspended from wire swing, two turned columns, turned ball counterweight, turned disc base, 7½" l, 19th C **600.00**
Bank, still
  Cast Iron
    Cow, walking, black finish, 4½" l **225.00**
    Dog, Boxer, seated, 4" h **265.00**
    Duck, squatty, painted, yellow, red, and black, 4" h **250.00**
    Hen on Nest, 3" h **75.00**

Bank, still, cast iron, seated pig, "The Wise Pig" and "Thrifty," copyright J.M.R, 6¾" h, $125.00.

Pig, "Invest in Pork," black, 7" h   **175.00**
Rooster, brass–look finish, 5" h   **200.00**
Chalkware, pig, 7" h **30.00**
Blocks
Animals, set of four, dressed as soldiers, paper litho over cardboard, oblong, c1890. . . . .   **65.00**
Hills Spelling Blocks, set of 20, orig box, multicolored chromolithographs on sliding lid, 9½" l. **135.00**
Illustrated Cubes, set of twelve, wood, painted and embossed, cube shaped, two emb painted letters, two painted illustrations, one printed letter, and one printed number each block, litho paper label on oblong cardboard box, boy at fence watching child pass in goat–pulled wagon illus, 1 1/16" cubed block, 4⅝" x 3½" box, Albany Embossing Co, Albany, NY, 1920–30. . . . .   **35.00**
Picture and Alphabets, set of twelve, paper litho on wood, oblong, c1890. . . . .   **175.00**
Read and Learn, set of 24, paper litho on wood, cylindrical, alphabet letters, simple verses, and children illus, 4" h, 1⅞" d, R Bliss Mfg Co, Pawtucket, RI, c1889. . .   **185.00**
Boat
Noah's Ark, pine, polychrome painted ark and figures, red hull and roof, blue windows, small bay window, and foliage scroll trim on cabin, Noah, his wife, and 29 animals **925.00**
Riverboat, pine, carved, painted, made from Van Houten cocoa box, red and yellow, landscape illus on sides, inscribed "Ohio River," swan neck prow, man seated in front, 4" h, 9" l, James Edington, Ross County, OH, late 19th C **1,325.00**
Sailboat, pine and metal, carved, painted, seated man wearing yellow top hat, navy blue frock coat, and yellow pants, metal sail, boat filled with kegs and barrels, fitted in box mechanism with raised waves, turn–key makes boat bob and roll on waves, 11½" h, 9½" l, early 19th C **3,575.00**
Building, warehouse, litho paper on wood, four stories, elevator, inside view of business activities, "Smith, Jones, & Green," 20" h, 12" w, 4" deep, c1890. . . . .   **650.00**
Clamp Toy, alligator, pine, carved, hand painted, stylized cross hatched figure, movable jaw and tail,

mounted on wood clamp, jaw and tail move when string is pulled, 4½" h, 6¾" l, 19th C. **275.00**
Cup and Ball, wood, varnished and stained finish, turned stick with wide shallow cup one end, short dowel other end, cord tied in middle connected to solid wooden ball, two holes in ball, 6⅝" l, 2¾" d ball, c1910   **20.00**
Doll
Apple Head, pr, man and woman, handmade black cloth costumes, jewelry, 7½" h **50.00**
Cloth
12", topsy–turvy
Babyland Rag, Horsman, muslin, mitt hands, pressed and painted facial features, black child has brown eyes, two rows of teeth in open smiling mouth, blue, brown, pink, and cream dress, white apron, and red bandanna, white child has blond hair, blue eyes, closed smiling mouth, pink cheeks, pink dress and bonnet, c1910 . . .   **550.00**
Bruckner, cotton stuffing, mitt hands, painted facial features on mask face, black child has brown eyes, two rows of teeth in open smiling mouth, red dress and bandanna, and white apron, white child has blond hair, blue eyes, closed mouth, red and white gingham dress and bonnet, white apron, early 1900s **300.00**
15", brown muslin, dimensional mask face, painted facial features, brown side–glancing eyes, short–stroke brows, accented nostrils, row of painted teeth in smiling mouth, one-piece firmly stuffed body, applied over–sized black shoes, wire armature supports cloth arms, blue polka dot dress and bandanna, white apron, bangle earrings, c1935 . . . .   **450.00**
16"
Chase, adult woman, dimensionally shaped, blush detail on oil painted facial features, stitched ears, brown painted hair, stippling around face, coiled bun at back of head, blue eyes, black and red eyeliner, single–stroke brows, accented nostrils and eye corners, closed mouth, cotton sateen body lining over

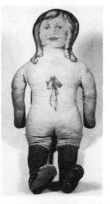

Rag Doll, painted, long curls, c1900, $85.00.

adult–modeled body, oil painted lower limbs, shaped fingers, calico frock and apron, c1900 . . . . **3,500.00**

Moravian Rag, cotton body, jointed hips, knees, and shoulders, stitched fingers, free standing thumbs, stub feet, hand drawn and painted facial features, no hair, lace ruffle sewn around face, blue and white gingham dress and bonnet, white apron, early 1900s **900.00**

17"

Muslin, bran stuffing, jointed shoulders, hips, and knees, oil painted mitt hands and shoes, oil painted facial features on flat face, smiling face, red dress, brown apron, white bonnet and under-clothes, c1900 . . . . **575.00**

Presbyterian Rag, unbleached cotton body, cotton stuffing, jointed shoulders and hips, stitched fingers, separate thumbs, long black stockings and black leather shoes on stub feet, flat head, oil painted facial features on flat face, ankle–length dress and matching prairie bonnet, white underclothes, late 1800s **950.00**

Unbleached Muslin, cotton and cloth stuffing, jointed hips and shoulders, stub hands and feet, vegetable dye facial features, flat head, no hair, lace trimmed brown and white polka dot dress, white bonnet, mid 1800s **225.00**

18"

Black, cotton body and stuffing, penciled facial features, four seam rounded head, no hair, separately stitched fingers, stub feet, blue and white dress, white bonnet and apron, late 1800s **300.00**

White, cotton body and stuff-ing, jointed hips and shoul-ders, stitched fingers, free standing thumbs, stitched–on velvet shoes, oil painted facial features, seam running down face center forms molded nose and chin, rounded head, no hair, early 1900s **150.00**

19"

Chase, hospital baby, cloth, molded face, painted facial features and hair, blue eyes, pierced nostrils and ears, white dress **325.00**

Columbian, heavy cotton body, jointed knees, hips, and shoulders, free standing thumbs, stitched fingers and toes, partially painted arms and legs, oil painted facial, curlicue nose, blue gingham dress and bonnet, hand–sewn kid slippers, rubber stamped "Columbian Doll/ Emma E. Adams/Oswego Center/N.Y.," on lower torso, c1900 . . . . **1,500.00**

22"

Alabama Baby, hard stuffed, painted extremities, jointed hips and shoulders, short painted shoes, applied sewn–on pate and ears, molded and painted facial features, "patent no. 2" marked on lower torso, early 1900s **1,000.00**

Unbleached Cotton, cotton bat-ting stuffing, stub hands, stitched facial features on flat face, mohair fabric hair sewn to rounded back of head, brown apron, brown and white polka dot dress, white underclothes, 19th C. **650.00**

23", Missionary Rag, Beecher, needle sculpted stockinet body, stitched fingers and toes, jointed knees, hips, and shoul-ders, needle sculpted and painted facial features, blue eyes, closed mouth, sparse wool yarn hair, white baby dress and bonnet, c1900 . . . . . **2,500.00**

24", unbleached cotton, cotton stuffing, jointed shoulders, knees, and hips, stub hands, stitched facial features, applied nose, stocking material hair sewn on head, blue, yellow, and white striped dress, white bonnet and shoes, c1900 . . . . **650.00**

30", cotton body and stuffing, jointed knees, hips, and shoulders, free standing thumbs on mitt hands, oil painted facial features on flat face, no ears, red, white, and blue plaid dress, white apron and bonnet, navy blue stockings, red slipper shoes, c1900 . . . . **1,500.00**

Raggedy Andy, Volland, 15", cotton body, printed facial features, shoe button eyes, sparse auburn wool yarn hair, white trim on green–blue pants and pointed hat, red, green, yellow, and white plaid shirt, black bow tie, c1918 . . . . . **500.00**

Raggedy Ann

Gruelle, 15", unbleached cotton, cotton stuffing, wooden heart hidden in chest, hand painted facial features, shoe button eyes, brown wool yarn hair, blue dress, white apron, 1915 **450.00**

Georgene Novelty Co, 15", cotton body, printed facial features, unlined nose, flat metal button eyes, light auburn hair, flowered dress, white apron, orig tag, c1945 . . . . **45.00**

Wood, carved

13$\frac{3}{4}$" h, painted, lady, blue eyes, brown hair, well defined facial features, orig clothing, 19th C **800.00**

15$\frac{1}{4}$" h, folk art, painted, black girl, smiling, linen cap and dress, movable arms, wood base, 19th C **325.00**

Doll Accessories

Bed, brass, 21$\frac{3}{4}$" h, 28$\frac{3}{4}$" l, 18" w, early 20th C **195.00**

Buggy, wood, painted, stake body construction, wooden wheels, 32$\frac{1}{2}$" l, 19th C **250.00**

Carriage

23" h, painted, bright green, black pinstriping, wooden handle, leather over material hood, iron wrapped wooden wheels, 1870–1880 . . . . **295.00**

34" l, wicker, open, parasol, brocade upholstery, early 20th C **385.00**

Rocker, armchair, 9$\frac{1}{4}$" h, blue repaint **165.00**

Doll House

Barn, wood, three stalls, litho paper sides, painted, two composition nodding pull toy horses, 16 x 20 x 12", c1900 . . . . **3,850.00**

Bliss

Two story, two rooms, Victorian style, litho paper on wood, high steeled roof, dormer windows, second floor balcony, spindled porch railing, 27 x 18 x 11" **900.00**

Three story, four rooms, paper litho on wood, metal, 25 x 20", c1910 . . . . **1,800.00**

Converse

Cottage, wood, hinged front, two rooms, 12" **250.00**

Red Robin Farm, double barn doors, six stalls, cupola on roof, nine orig animals, 19$\frac{1}{2}$ x 17", 1912 . . . . **425.00**

Folk Art, pitched roof, two chimneys, pierced glazed windows, shell dec, mounted on platform, 18 x 18 x 11", early 1900s **660.00**

Hacker, Christian, painted, 2$\frac{1}{2}$ story, five rooms, steeple roof, two chimneys, stuccoed front facade, bay window, wallpaper interior, FAO Schwartz label, 34" **500.00**

Handmade, wood, two rooms, includes three corn cob dolls, furniture, curtains, rugs, bedding, and accessories, 10$\frac{7}{8}$" h, 26$\frac{1}{2}$" l, 12$\frac{1}{2}$" deep, 19th C **250.00**

New England style, two story, removable roof, pierced glazed windows, turned columns and hand rails on front porch, two hinged doorways, 30 x 21 x 18$\frac{1}{2}$", c1900 . . . . **1,760.00**

Oklahoma style, one room, removable tiled gabled roof, clapboard sides, three pierced glazed windows, hinged door, two columns on front porch, 31 x 27 x 25", c1910 . . . . **500.00**

Schoenhut

Two story, two rooms, wood and pressed board, red shingled roof, green shutters, decal on base, 16 x 15 x 11" **275.00**

Eight rooms, attic, gray blocks, 28 x 23 x 23", c1917 . . . . **1,200.00**

Schwartz, FAO, cottage, five rooms, red painted mansard type roof,

Doll House, McLoughlin Folding Doll House, two rooms, decorated interiors, orig box, 17" l, 12" d, 16" h, $800.00.

Doll House Chair, hp, red and green floral dec, $55.00.

pierced multi–pane windows, hinged front door, includes 1920s furniture, 21 x 34 x 12", Germany, 1900.	**990.00**
Train Station, balustrade dec roof, two central arched doorways, elongated and round windows, gold painted pilasters, maroon, gold, and green finish, 17 x 16½ x 13", c1900	**610.00**
Tudor style, three story, thatched roofs, pierced glazed windows, includes furniture, 46 x 69 x 30", c1920.	**1,320.00**
Victorian style, litho paper on cardboard, one room, three sided, hinged, wood furniture, marked "Made in Germany," c1880. . . .	**250.00**
Whippany, wood, three story, nine rooms, pierced glazed windows, hinged front door, stairs, latticework, orig wallpaper, carpets, and lace curtains, includes furniture and accessories, electric lights and doorbell, 45 x 48 x 16", NJ, 1901	**8,250.00**
Doll House Furniture and Accessories	
Chest of Drawers, handmade, walnut, 4 x 6 x 7".	**48.00**
Cradle, wood	**25.00**
Cup and Saucer, ironstone, ⅝".	**5.00**
Desk, maple, slant front, royal blue and black interior, 3½ x 6"	**100.00**
Dining Room Suite, cast iron, white lacquer finish, two high backed benches, matching 4¾" l table, openwork legs, Curtis, 1936	**50.00**
Fernery, tin, painted, red and gold, two circular trays, fancy scrolled legs, 4¼" h	**175.00**
Floor Lamp, soft metal, black, gilded frame, glass beaded shade, 4" h	**100.00**
Foot Warmer, brass, working drawer, ¾"	**35.00**

Ice Cream Parlor Set, 3½" circular table, twisted metal legs, four matching chairs, heart shaped backs, four blue lemonade glasses, matching blown pitcher, 10 pcs.	**100.00**
Ironing Board, cast iron, folding, Kilgore, c1930.	**20.00**
Kitchen Set, finished hardwood, painted bright salmon, PA Dutch style hearts and flowers dec in red, yellow, and brown, 4¼" hutch, 4" l domed trunk, sq table, three chairs, cradle, bench, oven, orig box marked "Seit 1912, Kuhn Operboyeriche Heimathust," Germany.	**50.00**
Lady's Writing Desk, 5½" h, chair, c1875	**90.00**
Living Room Suite, cast iron, sofa and chair, deep pink, maroon trim, removable cushion, Arcade	**165.00**
Patio Set, litho tin, round table, four chairs, floral design	**35.00**
Piano, matching bench, Renwal . . .	**30.00**
Refrigerator, cast iron, white lacquer, gray trim, 5¾" h, marked "Leonard," Arcade	**35.00**
Rocking Chair, wood, carved arms, fabric seat and back	**25.00**
Rug, polar bear, white, royal purple velvet lining, glass bead eyes . . .	**25.00**
Settee, cast iron, Arcade	**80.00**
Sofa, metal, Tootsietoy	**35.00**
Stool, metal, Tootsietoy	**12.00**
Table, 4½" h, walnut, oval	**80.00**
Table Lamp, blue painted base, bulbous milk glass shade, 3" h	**42.00**
Tea Set	
Pewter, 3¾" h teapot	**45.00**
Porcelain, teapot, creamer, sugar, tray, and two lids	**50.00**
Washing Machine, cast iron, working rubber wringers, Sally Ann, c1920.	**48.00**

Dominoes, twenty–eight, ebony and
ivory, mahogany box, 6½" l **90.00**

Figures, wooden silhouettes, litho-
graphic printed surfaces of ponies,
hounds, and children in hunting at-
tire on horseback, detachable
wooden stands labeled "Wheil-
don," set of 13 . . . . **300.00**

Game Board

Checkerboard

Black squares on natural pine, 10½
x 14¾" **35.00**

Black and Brown squares, deep
yellow margins, inner molded
frame painted brown with yellow line, outer molded applied
lip painted black, late 19th C **1,100.00**

Black and Mustard Yellow
squares, red star and trim on
borders, edge molding, 16½ x
24¾" **500.00**

Black and Red squares, painted
pine, 13 x 13½", 19th C **225.00**

Black and White squares, rect, red
and green pretzel designs on
peach colored border, red and
green stars in corners, applied
molded lip, 17¼ x 15¾", 19th C **2,100.00**

Blue and White squares, painted
pine, rect, breadboard ends,
green ground, red, yellow,
blue, and white Masonic sym-
bols around border, late 19th/
early 20th C **935.00**

Maroon and Yellow squares,
elaborate gilt scrolling on black
ground border, green molded
lip, 16⅜" sq, late 19th C **1,425.00**

**Game, Milton Bradley Game of Scouting,
orig playing cards and instructions,
$75.00.**

Slate, incised, marble dec, green,
persimmon, black, and white,
22" sq, 19th C **1,000.00**

Walnut, folding, contrasting veneered squares, 13 x 16" open
size **45.00**

Parcheesi, painted, brilliant red,
green, yellow, and orange, neoclassical leaf motif dec in corners,
14" sq, late 19th/early 20th C . . . **1,100.00**

Two–Sided

Checkerboard/Backgammon,
wood, rect, folding, hinged,
red, green, mustard yellow,
and black geometric patterns,
pinstriped borders, and scrollwork and shield corners on outside checkerboard, interior
backgammon board painted
bright orange–red, green, and
yellow, holds maple checkers,
ivory dice, and leather dice
cups, 1½" h, 16½" l, late 19th C **1,750.00**

Checkerboard/Parcheesi, wood,
polychrome paint, raised
checkerboard, applied gallery,
18¼ x 18½" **425.00**

Checkerboard/Pinwheel, wood,
painted, red and black checkerboard one side, raised panel reverse with polychrome pinwheel on red ground, 15¾ x 16",
New England **1,600.00**

Hobby Horse, wood, carved, painted
24½" h, 51" l, dapple gray, green
saddle, heart shaped supports,
New England, early 19th C **1,200.00**

26½" h, 48½" l, solid head mounted
on bentwood frame, yellow pin-
striping, red ground, 19th C **10,500.00**

Hoop Toy, flat painted equestrian figure inside rolling hoop, 4½" d, 1870s **600.00**

Jack–in–the–Box, wood and fabric,
carved, painted, exaggerated stylized facial features, relief carved,
red and black on white ground,
turned wooden dunce cap, painted
cloth bag body, spring mounted,
gray pine box, hinged lid, hook clo-
sure, 12" h, 19th C **275.00**

Jumping Jack, wood, carved, monkey
on stick, front legs attached to slide,
21" l **420.00**

Jump Toy, black boxers, wood,
painted, black turned wood heads,
red and yellow bodies, cardboard
legs and arms, both fighters suspended from wire attached to central stick, figures bob and jab when
stick is twirled, 11" h, late 19th C . . **450.00**

Marble Toy, wood, carved, painted

red, series of descending ramps above stylized and articulated figure of man which catches marble at end of track, shaped wood base, 30½" h, 27" w, late 19th C **4,675.00**

Nodder, kitten, primitive, pine, carved, painted black, seated articulated figure, bobs head and tail when weighted string is pulled, 3½" h, 6" l, late 19th C **350.00**

Paddle Dancer, black man, composition head on wooden body, painted clothes and hat, jointed arms, hips, and knees, wire extends from back of dancer to upright post attached to paddle tapper and base, stamped "Pat'd Sept. 27, 1864" on base, 9½" h, 10¼" l **375.00**

Piano, upright, litho paper on painted wood, 10½" h, 14¼" l, Bliss **110.00**

Playing Cards, deck, heavy paper, leather case. **100.00**

Pull Toy

Alligator, pine, carved, painted, stylized, articulated tail, yellow, black, and red sponge painting, jaws move when toy is pulled, "Pat. App. for App. No. 5905/19" impressed on rolling platform, 9½" h, 29" l, late 19th/early 20th C. **3,250.00**

Angora Goat, white fur, painted wood base, cast iron wheels, 11" l **225.00**

Battleship, *New York*, cast iron, old worn yellow and white paint, red, blue, and black trim, 20" l **1,700.00**

Camel, flannel and wool, glass eyes, sheet metal wheels, 7⅞" l, early 20th C **300.00**

Carriage, open, horse–drawn, pine, carved, painted, three horses, passenger, driver, six wheels, 7" h, 13" l, late 19th C **775.00**

Cart, pine, painted, gray–white, two carved solid wheels, black, green, and red birds on three panels, back panel initialed "MMF," long wood handle, 34¼" l, 19th C **1,750.00**

Cow, composition, brown and white, wood base, 12" l **300.00**

Dachshund, wood, carved, painted, brown, black markings, leg mounted wheels, ears, neck, and tail move when dog is pulled, 7½" h, 16½" l, late 19th/early 20th C **825.00**

Dog, wood, carved, painted, wiggler, nine sections joined by string, black and white, wheels in paws, 6¼" h, 11½" l, c1890 . . . . **450.00**

Elephant, papier mache, gray, painted details, felt ears, wooden base, steel wheels, 8¾" l, Germany, early 20th C **140.00**

Goat, white goat skin, horns, glass eyes, red felt collar, bleats when head pushed down, painted wood platform, cast iron wheels, 9" h, 10½" l, Germany, 19th C. **550.00**

Goose, wood, 10" h, 1921. . . . . . . **125.00**

Hay Wagon, cast iron, painted blue, 16" l, 1910 . . . . **750.00**

Hen, mother with two chicks, composition, molded, painted, yellow, red, black, and white, spring legs, rolling base, 8½" h, 10" l, late 19th C **1,325.00**

Horse

Chestnut, carved, painted, stylized, horsehair tail, leather bridle and saddle, black and white stockings, shaped oak base, cast iron wheels, 24" h, 22" l, 19th C. **925.00**

Dapple Gray, carved, gesso, painted, stylized, black mane, horsehair tail, black leather saddle, glen plaid wool saddle blanket, shaped green base, wooden wheels, 26" h, 27¼" l, mid 19th C. **1,650.00**

Horse and Wagon, wood, worn black haircloth over papier mache and wood horse, leather harness, wood base, cast iron wheels, pulling two–wheeled wagon, orig red painted details, 29" l **350.00**

Pony Cart, litho paper on wood horse, red painted wooden cart, silver cast iron wheels, wires attached from axle to jointed legs

Pull Toy, 20" h, c1900, $550.00.

make horse walk as toy is pulled, 12" l, Gibbs, 1910s **225.00**

Railroad Hand Car, pine, carved, painted, four men, silhouette figures, litho paper on wool costumes, red four wheel hand car, long wood handle, men pump up and down when cart is pulled, 12½" h, 31" l, late 19th/early 20th C **1,650.00**

Sheep, sheepskin over wood, glass eyes, voice box, old red graining on pine base, cast iron wheels, 18½" l **900.00**

Soldier, pine, carved, cap, buttoned jacket, jointed arms and legs, seated on horse with jointed neck and tail, wheeled plank, 8¼" h, 6½" l, 1875–1900. . . . . **275.00**

Push Toy

American Eagle, perched on Uncle Sam's top hat, wood, carved, painted, stenciled, lithographed, crouched and stylized eagle with hinged wings stenciled as American flag, US shield shaped pedestal mounting inscribed "America," cast iron rolling wheels, eagle flaps wings as toy is pushed, maker's stamp on bottom, 11" h, 13" l, S A Smith Mfg Co, Brattleboro, VT, c1880 . . . . **2,310.00**

Bicycle, tandem, wire, fabric clad cyclers, painted faces, back rider plays metal shoe polish lid drum when toy is pushed, 30" h, 13" l, 20th C **700.00**

Hoop Toy, ash and maple, carved, painted, circular bent ash hoop, metal discs and turned and striped baluster spools on four wire spokes, maple handle centered on painted maple hub, 32¼" l, 19th C **1,200.00**

Mule Cart, pine, carved, painted, brown mule, leather and metal harness, green and red cart, metal banded wheels, black man driver, molded doll's head face, cloth clothed body, leather hat, 9½" h, late 19th C **1,325.00**

Wheelbarrow, "PMC" logo and black stenciled squirrel dec either side panel, red striping, red wheel, signed by Paris Manufacturing Co, South Paris, ME, natural varnished finish, 39" l **350.00**

Puzzle

Advertising

Armour, paper over cardboard, circus tent shape, crowds viewing animal exhibitions, 20 x 28" **190.00**

Hood's Sarsaparilla and Pills, A Wedding in Catland, cardboard, color, feline wedding party leaving church illus, 17 x 12", orig box **150.00**

Sherwin–Williams Paints, cardboard, two sided, house exterior illus one side, US map other side, 11¼ x 16" **75.00**

White Sewing Machines, paper covered wood, two sided, interior Victorian home one side, US map other side, 11 x 16". . . **130.00**

Map of Ohio, wood, litho, 12½" h, 16" w **185.00**

Rocking Horse

23" h, 45" l, wood, painted, gray, black mane and horsehair tail, leatherette saddle, brown stained rockers, 19th C **650.00**

23½" h, 41½" l, stylized, pine, carved, painted, incised eyes, sides form rockers, yellow, red, and black outline and feather painting, black leather bridle, black and white printed oil cloth cushioned saddle seat, c1840 . . . **1,325.00**

Push Toy, dog and cat bell toy, cast iron, Gong Bell Toy Company, Keene, NH, $850.00.

Puzzle, jigsaw, Santa Claus Puzzle Box, set of three puzzles in orig box, Milton Bradley, c1925, $175.00.

30½" h, 51" l, full figured, pine, carved, painted, white horse, leather star and shield stitched saddle and bridle, cast iron stirrups, brass button eyes, real horsehair tail, yellow pinstriping on red rockers, sailboat motif on platform, 1875–1900 . . . . **17,600.00**

See–Saw, wood and tin, carved, painted, seated boy and girl figures, painted tin, cloth bodies, yellow wooden see–saw, red, yellow, and black tin and wood base houses windup mechanism, 10" h, 19" l, Albert H Dean, Bridgeport, CT, c1873 . . . . **9,350.00**

Slide Toy

Fighting Gamecocks, pine, carved, fighting pen flanked by two stylized men holding gamecocks, each man straddles sliding wood rods, cocks trade pecks when slide and ratchet mechanism is pulled, 7" h, 17" l, late 19th/early 20th C **650.00**

Man, wood, carved, painted, stylized figure, bearded, wearing top hat and dark suit, carved facial features, peg doweled into torso slides on wrought iron stand, 8" h, late 19th C **450.00**

Squeak Toys

Blue Bird, felt composition, painted, red breast, turned thimble shaped wood stand on circular straw trimmed bellows base, 4½" h, 19th C **275.00**

Cats, mother and two kittens, felt composition, molded, painted, gray, black, and orange, bellows base, 4½" h, late 19th C **495.00**

Dog, composition, molded, painted, yellow body, white markings, black face, wearing boater hat, seated on bellows base, 5¼" h, late 19th C **1,200.00**

Duck, nesting, composition, painted, blue, white, orange, and red, flapping wings, bellows base, wings flap when base is squeezed, 6½" h, late 19th C **325.00**

Elephant, composition, painted, white body, red and blue trimmed saddle blanket, bellows base, 3½" h, late 19th C **275.00**

Goat, composition, molded, painted, white, black markings, leaping, 5" h, late 19th C **165.00**

Highlander on Donkey, composition and fabric, painted, young boy, stuffed fabric body, lace collared plaid jacket, astride small gray donkey, bellows base, 6¾" h, late 19th C **275.00**

Parrot, composition, molded, painted green, perched on rockwork, bellows base, 5½" h, late 19th C **135.00**

Peacock, composition and feather, painted, blue, green, orange, and black, standing, real tail feather, bellows base, late 19th C **450.00**

Rooster, composition, painted, white, blue, red, and black, iridescent bronze highlights, metal spring legs, bellows base, 6" h, late 19th C **165.00**

Stork, composition, molded, painted yellow, orange beak, black markings, spring legs, bellows base, 6" h, late 19th C . . **250.00**

Stuffed Animals

Beaver, brown mohair, Steiff **45.00**

Cat, mohair, green plastic eyes, movable head and legs, 5¼", Steiff, c1950 . . . . **45.00**

Cow, felt, brown and white, glass eyes, wooden wheels, 5½" **65.00**

Dog, plush, amber, swivel neck, over–sized head, milk glass and amber bead eyes, embroidered nose and mouth, stitched tail and ears, 8", early 20th C **75.00**

Goat, standing, white, brown felt horns, 6½", Steiff **50.00**

Hen, gold and black spotted feathers, yellow plush head, felt tail, black button eyes, 7", Steiff, c1949 . . . . **75.00**

Horse, amber hopsacking, straw stuffing, reinforced stitching, pale yellow underbelly, amber glass eyes, stitched smiling mouth, applied ears, black fur mane, horsehair tail, velvet and leather saddle and harness, 15", c1890 . . . . . . **85.00**

Rabbit, sitting up on haunches, brown tipped beige mohair, glass eyes, 32" h, Steiff, 1926–34 . . . . **330.00**

Teddy Bear

8½" h, yellow mohair, fully jointed, glass eyes, embroidered nose and mouth, ear button felt pads, Steiff, c1910 . . . . **450.00**

9" h, blonde plush, straw stuffed, shoulder hump, black button eyes, small tail, c1905 . . . . **165.00**

9½" h, brown wool, jointed limbs, swivel head, straw stuffed, shoe button eyes, black sewn nose and mouth, felt paws, c1900 **175.00**

12" h, long yellow mohair, fully jointed, glass eyes, embroidered nose, felt pads, 1916 . . . **190.00**

13" h, blonde mohair, fully jointed, shoe button eyes, horizontally stitched nose, stitched claws on four felt paws, excelsior stuffing, Steiff, 1903–10 **495.00**

14½" h, gold haircloth, articulated limbs, straw stuffed, glass eyes, felt paw pads and nose, embroidered detail, voice box **300.00**

15" h
  Brown Mohair, fully jointed, black shoe button eyes, black embroidered nose, mouth, and claws, "Bruin Mfg Co" label, c1907 . . . . **250.00**
  Yellow Mohair, excelsior stuffed, fully jointed, shoe button eyes, long nose, felt paws, pink vest, c1918 . . . . **275.00**

17" h, white mohair, growler, fully jointed, glass eyes, felt paws, horizontal nose stitching, three embroidered claws each foot, excelsior stuffing, c1932 **275.00**

19¾" h, yellow mohair, long fur, fully jointed, glass eyes, felt pads, excelsior stuffing, Twyford, England, c1915 . . . . . . **110.00**

20", brown mohair, fully jointed, flat face, Knickerbocker **100.00**

Train
  11¾" l, engine, steel, welded, homemade, old black paint, white trim **225.00**
  25½" l, steam locomotive, model, metal, old black repaint, incomplete cow catcher. **425.00**

LIGHTING

Country life cannot stop because the day is cloudy or the electric power fails. Daily chores need to be done daily. Rural America required cheap, dependable lighting.

The key concerns were utility and durability. Form did follow function—simple design, easy to service; fewer joints and edges, least likely to snag; and plain surface, less maintenance. Lighting devices, especially those used in barns and field, were expected to withstand rough treatment and last for years. The interchangeability of parts was essential. Repairs often had to be made on the spot.

Until the arrival of electricity, the kerosene lamp was king. Lamps burn fuel and generate heat. Heat attacks surfaces. This is why tin, which was painted and repainted to preserve it, and glass were favored. Fuel oil lamps also generate soot. To work effectively, they have to be cleaned regularly, a chore generally assigned to the children.

Decorative lighting was confined to the household with the best examples located in the dining room and parlor. Among the forms with the widest variety of pattern and color are miniature lamps and fluid lamps. They are important decorative accents in any Country setting.

The arrival of electricity changed life in rural America. Most initial electrical lighting and many appliances were purchased via mail order or at the general store. The arrival of a specialized electrical store in a rural community often was ten to fifteen years behind the arrival of electricity.

Because members of the agrarian community are "savers" by nature, rural basements, attics, sheds, and barns are major sources for early electrical lighting. There is a strong tendency to put an old lamp or appliance in storage just in case the new one breaks.

The current Country craze focuses heavily on the kerosene lamp era. However, change is in the wind. There is a growing interest in the rural farmstead of the 1920s through the 1950s. When this period becomes fashionable, electric lighting will play a major role in any decorating scheme.

LAMPS

History: An agrarian life means rising at first light and going to bed when the sun sets. While this is the ideal, many a farmer and small town merchant rose before the sun came up and went to bed long after it set. Lamps and lighting were cherished and well–cared–for possessions.

It was not until the late 1930s and in some areas the early 1950s that rural electrification was accomplished. As a result, the kerosene oil lamp survived in the countryside long after it was banished from urban America.

The kerosene oil lamp is an important decorative element in any Country decor. Variety was achieved through a wealth of glass patterns and colors as well as ornately decorated shades. The best, i.e., most decorative, lamps graced the parlor and dining room. Large lamps used in the kitchen and upstairs tended to be plain and highly utilitarian. On the other hand, miniature lamps were highly decorative, often adding a splash of color to a room.

Lighting devices have evolved from simple stone age oil lamps to the popular electrified models of today. Aimé Argand patented the first oil lamp in 1784. Around 1850 kerosene became a popular lamp burning fluid, replacing whale oil and other fluids.

References: J. W. Courter, *Aladdin, The Magic Name in Lamps*, Wallace–Homestead, 1980; J. W. Courter, *Aladdin Collectors Manual & Price Guide #13*, published by author, 1990; Robert De Falco, Carole Goldman Hibel, John Hibel, Larry Freeman, *New Light on Old Lamps*, American Life Foundation, 1984; Nadja Maril, *American Lighting: 1840–1940*, Schiffer Publishing, 1989; Jo Ann Thomas, *Early Twentieth Century Lighting Fixtures*, Collector Books, 1980; Catherine M. V. Thuro, *Oil Lamps*, Wallace–Homestead, 1976; Catherine M. V. Thuro, *Oil Lamps II*, Thorncliffe House, Inc., 1983.

Collectors' Clubs: Aladdin Knights of the Mystic Light, Route 1, Simpson, IL 62985; Historical Lighting Society of Canada, PO Box 561, Postal Station R, Toronto, ON M4G 4E1; The Incandescent Lamp Collectors Association, 717 Washington Place, Baltimore, MD 21201; Rushlight Club, Old Academy Library, 150 Main Street, Wethersfield, CT 06109.

Museum: Winchester Center Kerosene Lamp Museum, Winchester Center, CT.

Reproduction Craftspersons: Charles Baker Period Reproductions, 6890 N 700 E, Hope, IN 47246; David L Claggett, Artistry in Tin, PO Box 41, Weston, VT 05161; Karen Claggett, Tinsmith, RD #3, Box 330A, Quarryville, PA 17566; Jim W Darnell, Mill Creek Forge and Blacksmith Shop, Box 494, Rte 2, Seagrove, NC 27341; Jim DeCurtins, Tin Peddler, 203 E Main St, Troy, OH 45373; Charles Euston, Woodbury Blacksmith & Forge Co, PO Box 268, Woodbury, CT 06798; James W Faust, 488 Porters Mill Rd, Pottstown, PA 19464; Dawson Gillaspy, Tinsmith, Covered Bridge Rd, RD 2, Box 312, Oley, PA 19547; Robert and Anita Horwood, Horwood's Country House, 4037 Gotfredson Rd, Plymouth, MI 48170; Ronald Potts, Blacksmith, Chriswill

Forge, 2255 Manchester Rd, N Lawrence, OH 44666; Mark Rocheford, Thomas Savriol, Lighting by Hammerworks, 75 Webster St, Worcester, MA 01603; The Tin Man by Gerald Fellers, 2025 Seneca Dr, Troy, OH 45373; Barry Steierwald, Eagle Lantern, Rte 100, Eagle, PA 19480; Michael P Terragna, The Coppersmith, PO Box 755, Sturbridge, MA 01566; Stephen and Carolyn Waligurski, Hurley Patentee Lighting, RD 7, Box 98A, Kingston, NY 12401.

Reproduction Manufacturers: 18th Century Tinware, 1323 Twin Rd, West Alexandria, OH 45381; The Antique Hardware Store, 43 Bridge St, Frenchtown, NJ 08825; The Barn, PO Box 25, Market St, Lehman, PA 18627; Basye–Bomberger/Fabian House, PO Box 86, W Bowie, MD 20715; Briere Design, 229 North Race St, Statesville, NC 28677; Bullfrog Hollow, Keeny Rd, Lyme, CT 06371; Country Lighting and Accessories, PO Box 1279, New London, NH 03257; Country Store of Geneva, Inc, 28 James St, Geneva, IL 60134; Cumberland General Store, Rte 3, Crossville, TN 38555; Frombruche, 132 N Main St, Spring Valley, NY 10977; Independence Forge, Rt 1, Whitakers, NC 27891; Jori Handcast Pewter, 12681 Metro Parkway, Fort Myers, FL 33912; KML Enterprises, RR 1, Box 234L, Berne, IN 46711; Lt Moses Willard, Inc, 1156 State Route 50, Milford, OH 45150; Matthews Emporium, 157 N Trade St, PO Box 1038, Matthews, NC 28106; Mel–Nor, 303 Gulf Bank, Houston, TX 77037; Olde Mill House Shoppe, 105 Strasburg Pike, Lancaster, PA 17602; Period Lighting Fixtures, 1 West Main St, Chester, CT 06412; The Renovator's Supply, 7577 Renovator's Old Mill, Millers Falls, MA 01349; Sandi's, PO Box 170, Lake George, NY 12045, Sturbridge Yankee Workshop, Blueberry Rd, Westbrook, ME 04092; The Tinhorn, 1852 Forest Lane, Crown Point, IN 46307; Victorian Lightcrafters Ltd, PO Box 350, Slate Hill, NY 10973.

Early American

Baker's Lamp, 7" l, 9½" h, tin, rect, two burners, tin shade, wire hanger, hanger	**180.00**
Betty Lamp	
Iron, wrought iron hook and wick pick, mid 19th C	**40.00**
Tin, 6" h, wire and tin hanger . . .	**25.00**
Two Iron Lamps, 26" h, adjustable stand, 18th C	**700.00**
Chamber Lamp, 4" h, pewter, saucer base, ring handle	**75.00**
Chandelier	
Tin, punched design, six candle sockets on S shaped arms, PA, c1850	**550.00**
Wood and Tin, four candle sockets on S shaped arms, cut nail construction, PA, c1850	**500.00**

Lard, tin, 2 handles, skillet, $85.00.

Crusie, 11½" h, double, iron, handwrought hook, c1840 . . . .   **55.00**
Grease, 9" h, wrought iron, hang-
ing, large round pan with spout,
twisted hanger **105.00**
Hand Lamp, 2" h, 5½" d, tin, squatty,
saucer base, strap handle, orig
green paint, c1860 . . . .   **15.00**
Lecturer's, 10" h, bell in base, orig
black paint and gold striping,
pricket for candle **250.00**
Petticoat
4⅛" h, japanned tin, candlestick
peg, whale oil burner, 1850–
60 . . . .   **35.00**
5½" h, tin, brass whale oil burner,
handle, repainted flat black . . .   **35.00**
Rushlight, handwrought iron, can-
dle holder arm, three scrolled
feet, late 18th/early 19th C **350.00**
Whale Oil
6¼" h, tin, saucer base, old black
paint **55.00**
6⅝" h, pewter, saucer base, ring
handle. **150.00**
7⅛" h, pewter, baluster stem **175.00**
8" h, pewter, baluster stem, Israel
Trask, Beverly, MA, 1807–56   **125.00**
Fluid Lamp
Adams & Co, glass, clear, c1880
9", Corner Windows pattern, orig
artificial flower dec enclosed in
hollow stem, partial orig label   **65.00**

**Tavern, fat lamp, tin with brass caps, 5" l,
1¾" h, $115.00.**

9½", Plain Band pattern **25.00**
10¾", Ripley–Vogeley–Adams
patent lamp, orig artificial
flower dec enclosed in hollow
stem, ftd, most of orig label on
bottom **165.00**
Angle Lamp Co, 8", wall mount,
opaque white shade on clear
globular shade, orig black and
copper finish on emb font,
maker's name and patents marked
on clear shade and lamp, c1890   **325.00**
Atterbury & Co, glass, clear, c1870
3⅜", Atterbury Filley pattern. **30.00**
7½", Grecian pattern, paneled
milk glass base, patent date on
inside of base **175.00**
8¼", Atterbury Ex pattern **75.00**
8½", Atterbury Wave pattern, Tulip
pattern base **55.00**
9", Atterbury Heritage pattern . . .   **65.00**
9½", Atterbury Scroll pattern, Tulip
pattern base **55.00**
Boston & Sandwich Glass Co
3¾", clear, hand, Lyre pattern, ap-
plied handle, 1840–60 . . . . . .   **130.00**
9¾", clear, Sandwich Grapevine
pattern, c1860 . . . .   **250.00**
12", clear pear–shaped font, elab-
orately cut pattern, fluted brass
stem, stepped milk glass base,
orig burner, clear and frosted
cut globe and chimney, 21½" h
to top of chimney **950.00**
Bradley, 3⅜", marked "Bradley's Se-
curity Factory Lamp" in raised letters on font bottom and on brass
plate inside tin holder, yellow dec
on black ground, c1870 . . . .   **100.00**
Bradley & Hubbard
4¼", lemon shaped font, deep saucer base, ring handle, japanned
and gilt finish, alcohol burner,
c1900 . . . .   **220.00**

**Whale Oil, 8½" h, Loop pattern, peacock
blue, Boston & Sandwich Co., $950.00.**

12" to top of shade, miniature, nickel plated brass, marked "The B & H" on lamp and flame spreader, punched design around base, cased green shade, c1890 . . . .   **325.00**

15" to top of shade, vase lamp, nickel plated brass and iron, floral decorated opaque white shade, very ornate emb dec and handles, ftd, sgd three places, five patent dates, c1890 . . . . .   **300.00**

Bridgeport Brass Co
7½" to top of chimney, nickel plated brass, miniature bracket lamp, maker's name and address and "All Night" marked on shoulder, late 19th C **55.00**

14¾" to top of shade, student, nickel plated brass, opaque white shade, clear chimney, c1880 . . . .   **360.00**

Bryce Walker & Co, 3½", clear glass, hand, Diamond Sunburst pattern, applied handle, replacement collar, c1870. . . . .   **35.00**

Buckeye Glass Co, 15", bracket lamp, Optic Rib pattern on sapphire blue patent dated font with threaded exterior, Swirled Optic pattern on matching shade, orig black and gold finish on iron bracket and mount, J F Miller patent, c1880. . . . .   **685.00**

Central Glass Co, clear
5⅜", hand, Wheat in Shield pattern, applied handle, c1870 . .   **190.00**

9", Plain Band pattern, amethyst tint, c1870. . . . .   **55.00**

Consolidated Glass Co, 18" to top of shade, opaque light green lamp and shade, Prince Edward pattern, c1890 . . . .   **900.00**

Dalzell, Gilmore & Leighton, 9", glass, clear, Queen Heart pattern, hand painted flowers with green leaves and brown stems on frosted heart shaped panels, c1900 . . . .   **100.00**

Dietz Brothers & Co, NY, 9", clear blown font, brass stem and base, sgd on stem, heraldic eagle over name, c1860. . . . .   **875.00**

Dietz & Co, 9½", hand, tin, marked "Dietz Bestov Lamp" on shoulder, attached bracket for wall mount, brass side filler cap, old chimney marked "Rock Flint," c1890. . . . .   **245.00**

E Miller & Co
6", hand, Perkins type, brass, strap handle, c1880 . . . .   **75.00**

6¾", candle, tin, marked burner, 1890–1900 . . . .   **40.00**

11½" to top of shade, hand, brass, center draft, ornate Spelter handle, punched design around base, opaque white shade, marked "The Miller Lamp/ Made in/U.S.A." on shoulder, c1890 . . . .   **495.00**

F O Dewey, 3⅝", hand, Dillaway patent clear glass font made at Sandwich, brass plate on tin base marked "F.O. Dewey & Sons/ Makers, Boston.", strap handle, repainted black, c1870. . . . .   **28.00**

George Duncan & Sons, glass, clear
5½", hand, 8-panel font, Ripley–Duncan double handle, 1870–90. . . . .   **300.00**

10", Ribbed Band pattern, c1880   **145.00**

Glow Night Lamp Co, Inc, Boston, 4½", miniature, glass, swirled pattern on clear font, melon ribbed opaque white shade, c1890 . . . .   **110.00**

Hitchcock, 11⅞", brass, marked "Improved Hitchcock Lamp," side-winder motor stamped with patent dates ranging from Nov 30, 1880 to Feb 28, 1899, c1900 . . .   **165.00**

Hobbs, 8¼"
Clear, marked "Dyott's Patent Stand Lamp," c1870. . . . .   **65.00**

Clear and Colored, Snowdon pattern, clear font, cobalt blue base, c1880. . . . .   **190.00**

King Glass Co, 8", Double Arch pattern, circular base, 1880–90. . . .   **80.00**

LaBelle Glass Co, 8⅝", clear, Corn pattern, c1870. . . . .   **250.00**

New England Glass Co
3", clear, hand, blown, molded 10-panel, applied handle, pewter collar and whale oil burner. **250.00**

4¼", clear, sparking, globular blown font, circular stepped waterfall base, pot slag in base, pewter collar and whale oil burner. **225.00**

7⅜", sapphire blue, 3-Printie Block pattern, whale oil burner   **1,200.00**

8¼", canary yellow, Bull's-eye and Ellipse pattern font, pewter collar and whale oil burner . . .   **550.00**

9", clear, frosted bands on free-blown teardrop-shaped font, yellow flowers, brown vines, and green leaves dec on upper band, heavy pressed base, pewter collar, double drop whale oil burner. **375.00**

9¾"
Clear, Loop pattern font, heavy pressed base, pewter collar and whale oil burner **90.00**

Cobalt Blue, Loop pattern font, hexagonal base, pewter collar and whale oil burner, pr **1,700.00**

10", sapphire blue, Loop pattern, whale oil burner, pr **900.00**

Perkins & House, 10¾", brass font, iron stem and base, sgd, patent date, c1870. . . . . **130.00**

Pittsburgh Lamp Co, 10½" to top of prongs, nickel plated brass, cast iron foot, marked "The Pittsburgh," emb scrolled "S" designs around font, spiral design around foot, c1890 . . . . **55.00**

Richards & Hartley, 7¾", glass, medium yellow, Three Panel pattern, c1880. . . . . **250.00**

Riverside Glass Co, 8", glass, emerald green and clear, Riverside Panel pattern, emerald green font, clear stem and base, brass patent dated collar, c1880 . . . . **160.00**

Rochester Lamp Co, 28" to top of shade, brass and brass plated, New Rochester Banquet Lamp, acid cut Fleur-de-lis pattern on frosted globe, c1890 . . . . **495.00**

Sandwich Glass Co

4½", clear, hand, Waffle pattern, applied handle, c1850 . . . . . . **465.00**

8¼", clear, Heart and Thumbprint pattern, 1840-60. . . . . **190.00**

9¼", clear flint, Waffle pattern font, octagonal base, orig collar and whale oil burner. **125.00**

9¾", cobalt blue cut to clear, pear-shaped font, double cut overlay, fan-like cuttings, brass stem, square marble base **600.00**

9⅞", white cut to clear, partially

Student, 20¼" h, pewter and brass, glass font, patented June 14, 1870, $450.00.

frosted, pear-shaped font, double cut overlay, flower and leaf dec, opaque white base **200.00**

10⅛", white cut to cranberry, pear-shaped font, double cut overlay, fluted brass standard, square marble base. **250.00**

11¼", clear cylindrical font, cut and engraved dec, fluted brass stem, stepped marble base, mid 19th C. **125.00**

12", translucent jade green, pear-shaped font, fluted brass standard, stepped marble base, gold striping, kerosene burner **125.00**

T F Hammer, 4½", cast iron, marked "Convex" burner, bronze finish, c1870. . . . . **145.00**

Union Glass Co, c1870

5⅝", clear, hand, patterned Lomax font, ftd **175.00**

6⅜", clear, kitchen, Lomax font, patent date on underside **65.00**

Unknown Maker

2½", glass, clear, hand, miniature, blown three-mold body made from stopper mold, applied handle, tin "Patent" burner . . . **300.00**

3¼", jeweler's, amber glass font, tin egg cup shape base, alcohol burner, two patent dates on shoulder, 1880-90. . . . . **20.00**

3⅜", bracket lamp, shells and stars design on clear glass font, crudely cast brass bracket, 1870-80 . . . . **55.00**

3½", alcohol, brass, marked "Made in United States of America" on bottom. **12.00**

3¾", hand, tin, used with deodorizer burner, "Rauschenbergs/Formaldehyde/Deodorizer/Pat. May 1 1900" on brass label . . . **12.00**

4"

Glass, clear, sparking, miniature cup plate base, whale oil burner **425.00**

Tin, hand, strap handle, P & A burner, clear chimney, 1850-1900 . . . . **20.00**

4¾"

Brass, hand, sloping shoulder, strap handle, 1875-1900 . . **110.00**

Tin, squatty, brass burner, attached tank marked "Rainwater," Oakes patent dated Feb 17, 1903 . . . . **65.00**

5¼", hand, brass, emb handle, c1890 . . . . **75.00**

5½", glass, clear, marked "The Handy Night Lamp," tin burner and reflector, c1890 . . . . **28.00**

$6\frac{1}{4}''$

Glass

Amethyst font, brass saucer base, ring handle, acorn burner, patent date, c1870   **45.00**

Clear blown shield–shaped font, square waterfall base, whale oil burner, pr **400.00**

Emerald green font, cobalt blue globe, applied handle, c1880 . . . .   **165.00**

Tin, hand, center draft, patented, marked "The J.R. Rochester/Hotel Lamp/Pat. Sep. 14. 1886," 1889 and 1890 patent dates marked on flame spreader on brass burner, punched design around ftd base, tall tubular chimney, c1890 . . . .   **120.00**

$6\frac{3}{4}''$

Navigation Lamp, reflector, geared wick raisers, late 19th C **35.00**

Ship's, gimbaled, brass, standing or wall mount, glass font, lead weighted base, c1860   **75.00**

7", glass, clear, free blown cone–shaped font, square 5–step waterfall base, whale oil burner   **125.00**

$7\frac{1}{8}''$, flint glass, clear, rayed foot, brass collar **85.00**

$7\frac{3}{8}''$, double torch, cast iron, "PZL" in high relief both sides, remains of orig wicks inside, 19th C **120.00**

$7\frac{1}{2}''$, glass

Clear, free blown pear shaped font, crossed base, tin and cork whale oil burner **190.00**

Opaque Pink, onion–shaped font, translucent white base   **250.00**

$7\frac{5}{8}''$, glass, clear, partially fluted font, brass standard, marble base **90.00**

$7\frac{3}{4}''$, glass, medium purple–blue, 3–Printie Block pattern, unrecorded base, whale oil burner   **750.00**

$8\frac{1}{8}''$, glass, deep amethyst, Loop pattern, whale oil burner. **1,300.00**

$8\frac{1}{4}''$

Glass, clear, free blown teardrop–shaped font, circular lacy base, whale oil burner and wick, pr **450.00**

Tin, reflector, ribbed strikers on double fitted matchholders, removable tin reflector, blue japanned finish, c1880 . . . .   **45.00**

$8\frac{1}{2}''$ to top of tube, tin, tubular air intake, brass burner and filler cap, c1880 . . . .   **120.00**

9", clear glass Lomax font, iron base, dated **30.00**

$9\frac{1}{2}''$, nickel plated brass, bracket stand, weighted font and base, "September 14, 1880" patent date. **225.00**

$9\frac{5}{8}''$, flint glass, clear, pressed heart, sawtooth, and bull's–eye pattern font, hexagonal base, brass collar **125.00**

$9\frac{3}{4}''$, glass

Gothic Arch font, clear flint, hexagonal base, missing collar. **75.00**

Lacemaker's, globular blown font, fluted clear stem, scalloped diamond point base   **750.00**

10"

Brass, Victor wall lamp, silvered glass reflector, c1890   **300.00**

Glass, clear, Lutz–type, pear–shaped font, fine opaque white spiral threads, translucent blue base, double brass camphene burner, pewter caps. **150.00**

$10\frac{1}{8}''$, glass

Canary Yellow, Bull's–eye and Ellipse pattern font, monumental base, pewter collar and whale oil burner **650.00**

Cobalt Blue, Bigler pattern, square base, whale oil burner, pr. **4,250.00**

$10\frac{1}{4}''$

Brass font, June 7, 1881 patent date on cast iron bracket, $6\frac{1}{8}''$ d font **165.00**

Flint glass, clear, triangular fluted font, octagonal and triangular fluted base, pewter collar. **165.00**

11", glass, amethyst, 4–Printie Block pattern **600.00**

Miniature, ruby glass, $150.00.

11½", nickel plated brass, triangular punched design around base, kerosene burner, marked "Banner Electric Lamp" on flame spreader, c1880 ...... 135.00

12½", reflector wall lamp, tin, corrugated glass mirror reflectors, glass chimney, c1880 .... 130.00

15" to top of shade, stamped pattern on shoulder, punched design around base, marked "Royal Center Draft Lamp," patent dates on flame spreader, opaque white shade, c1890 .. 135.00

18" to top of shade, Paula pattern, opaque white dome shade and illuminator base, c1880 ..... 410.00

18¼" to top of shade, opaque white shade, clear glass support, brass font, stem, and base, c1880 .... 495.00

22", student, mercury, brass, font higher than reservoir, fuel level maintained by hydrostatic pressure, reservoir floats on mercury, burner marked "Waterbury," opaque white Vienna shade, c1880 .... 495.00

U S Glass Co, 10", King's Crown pattern, c1890 .... 90.00

Hanging, fluid
Adams & Westlake, 32" h, 30" w, railway car, double, cast bronze and brass, maker name marked on fonts, orig white enamel metal shades, c1890 .... 1,320.00

Bradley & Hubbard
52" h, 13⅝" d shade, emb brass font, company's mark stamped on shoulder and filler cap, opaque white shade, c1890 .. 600.00

58" h, 40" d, chandelier, cast iron openwork frame, 12–arm, clear glass fonts and crimped chimneys, brass burners, marked with May 26, 1868 patent date in openwork section at top row of arms and inside ceiling fitting, "January 31 1871" patent date marked inside bottom of four fonts, "January 31. 1871" patent date marked inside three fonts, and five fonts marked in ⅛" raised letters "Pat'd Jan. 31. 1871," c1870 1,210.00

Unknown Maker
25" h, 13⅝" d shade, library, patented, brass, cut and frosted glass font, brass shoulder and drip trough, brass frame and font holder, brass crown on wide conical shaped opaque

white shade, brass hanger with chain, c1880 .... 600.00

32" h, 26" w to edge of shades, cast iron, 2–arm, "January 31, 1871" patent date marked inside each font holder, clear bracket lamps, etched flowers and butterflies dec on frosted shades, black and gold finish, c1870 .... 825.00

Railway, Williams & Page Co, Boston, MA, 7" h, brass, bracket lamp, glass font, cast brass bracket, 1870–80 135.00

Safety, hand lamp
E Miller & Co, 5½", tin, c1890 ..... 45.00

Perkins & House, brass, custom made burner, early chimney, c1860 .... 385.00

Unknown Maker
4½", brass, strap handle, late 19th C 65.00

4⅞", sheet metal, side filler, patent dated cap, traces of old red paint, resoldered handle 5.00

LANTERNS

History: A lantern is an enclosed, portable light source, hand carried or attached to a bracket or pole to illuminate an area. Many lanterns can be used both indoors and outdoors and have a protected flame. Fuels used in early lanterns included candles, kerosene, whale oil, coal oil, and later gasoline, natural gas, and batteries.

Lanterns designed for use on the farm often had special safety features such as a filling cap lock or special base to prevent tipping. When collecting farm lanterns, do not overlook vehicle lanterns and the small hand held lanterns used to walk to the barn or necessary.

Reference: Anthony Hobson, *Lanterns That Lit Our World*, published by author, 1991.

Reproduction Craftspersons: Charles Baker Period Reproductions, 6890 N 700 E, Hope, IN 47246; John Kopas, Copper Antiquities, PO Box 153, Cummaquid, MA 02637; Mark Rocheford, Thomas Savriol, Lighting by Hammerworks, 75 Webster St, Worcester, MA 01603; Barry Steierwald, Eagle Lantern, Rte 100, Eagle, PA 19480; Stephen and Carolyn Waligurski, Hurley Patentee Lighting, RD 7, Box 98A, Kingston, NY 12401.

Reproduction Manufacturers: American Period Lighting, The Saltbox, 3004 Columbia Ave, Lancaster, PA 17603; Country Accents, RD 2, Box 293, Stockton, NJ 08559; KML Enterprises, RR 1, Box 234L, Berne, IN 46711; Lamb and Lanterns, 902 N Walnut St, Dover, OH 44622; Lt Moses Willard, Inc, 1156 State Rte 50, Milford, OH 45150; Olde Mill House Shoppe, 105 Strasburg

Pike, Lancaster, PA 17602; Period Lighting Fixtures, 1 West Main St, Chester, CT 06412.

Adams & Westlake Co, railroad
  Adlake Reliable, single horizontal wire guard, bellbottom frame, 5⅜" h, clear globe and frame marked "KCSRY," patent date May 9, 1922 . . . .   **160.00**
  The Adams, marked "C.P. RY." . . .   **30.00**
Armspear Mfg Co, NY, railroad, trouble lantern, red globe marked "B & O RR, Armspear Mfg. Co. New York 1925," two detonators attached to frame, weighted iron base, 10" bail handle **100.00**
Dietz & Co
  9" h, brass, square, four thick beveled glasses, turned wooden bail handle, late 19th C **80.00**
  11" h, inspector's lantern, New York Central System logo on globe, "Ideal Inspector Lamp" impressed on back and "B.R.&P.Ry" on front label, traces of silver paint on reflector, hanging ring, wire bail handle, late 19th C **70.00**
  15½" h, reflector, model #30, sgd, wire hanger, late 19th C **120.00**
  16" h, railroad, wire chimney protector, marked, waffle and flute patterned chimney, c1890 . . . . .   **220.00**
Eclipse, fireman's, green over clear globe, marked "American La France Fire Engine Company". **1,000.00**
E Miller & Co, 7¾" h, bicycle, nickel plated brass, Majestic model, carbide fueled, clear lens and reflector, faceted red and green side lights, c1900 . . . .   **160.00**
E T Wright & Co, 9" h, buggy, orig black paint, late 19th C **80.00**
Ham's, fireman's, brass and nickel, wire slide, water shield, distributed by Boston Woven Hose Co. **265.00**

Hawthorne Mfg Co, 6" h, bicycle, nickel plated, marked "Hawthorne Mfg Co, Old Sol Pat USA" **50.00**
Hurricane Lantern Co, 8⅞" h, brass, chain hanger, sgd, 1860–70 . . . . .   **465.00**
Kemp Mfg Co, 15" h, dashboard, spring clips, reflector, orig red paint, sgd brass label, c1900 . . . .   **150.00**
Keystone Lantern Co, railroad, The Casey, single horizontal wire guard, twist wick raiser, 5⅜" h amber globe, frame marked "NYP&N R CO," patent date Dec 30, 1902 . . . .   **850.00**
New England Glass Co, 12" h
  Glass, chimney shape globe, tin whale oil font **140.00**
  Tin, pierced, patent Oct 24, 1854   **175.00**
N L Piper Railway Supply Co Ltd, bulls–eye front lens, orig red and green side glasses, corrugated reflector lined door, Simplex burner   **200.00**
Perkins Marine Lamp Corp, 13" h, tin, S Sargent label, brass top, glass globe, patent dates 1861 and 1866   **150.00**
Unknown Maker
  5¾" h, pocket, folding, wire bail handle, ruby glass panel, black and gold litho illus of man seated on train, wearing top hat, lantern clipped to jacket pocket, reading newspaper, c1870 . . . .   **220.00**
  6" h, tin, box shaped, glass pane front, wire hanger, tin font **90.00**
  6½" h, skater's, brass, clear globe. . .   **45.00**
  7" h, skater's, brass, "Little Bobs" molded in shade, c1870. . . . . . .   **110.00**
  7¼" h, skaters, tin, clear globe **55.00**
  7¾" h, bicycle, Majestic model, nickel plated, clear lens, faceted red and green side lights, c1900   **160.00**
  8" h, miner, iron, chicken finial, wick pick **250.00**
  8⅛" h, marine, brass, Fresnel shade, bail handle, late 19th C **35.00**

Dietz & Co., Model #30, $120.00.

Miner's, "Patterson Lames, Ltd., Gateshead on Tyne," brass, $50.00.

Whale Oil, 10½" h, ftd, tin, glass on four sides, $100.00.

8¾" h, darkroom, triangular, tin, ruby glass panels, outside filler cap, brass label marked "The Challenge," 1850–1900 . . . . . .   **40.00**

8⅝" h, tin, A Ferguson patent with Thomas J Conroy agent on brass label, lens cover, c1880 . . . .   **28.00**

9" h, tin, clear blown bulbous shade, diamond and star cut–out air holes, traces of gold repaint, removable base, ring holder **150.00**

9½" h

    Miner, galvanized frame, wire hanger, late 19th C **25.00**

    Starboard, galvanized frame, cylindrical red globe, wire hanger, late 19th C **28.00**

10" h, railroad

    GTR, initials molded in glass shade, 1850–1900 . . . .   **135.00**

    Oxweld Railroad Lamp, calcium carbide operated, late 19th C   **35.00**

11" h, candle, tin, clear pressed globe, painted black, ring handle   **275.00**

12" h, wood frame, glass panes, barn, old red repaint **250.00**

12¼" h, tin, Revere type, punched circle designs, conical top, swing handle **130.00**

12½" h, railroad, tin and brass, pear–shaped chimney, wire hanger, late 19th C **45.00**

17" h, railroad, triangular, double lens, tin reflector, C&NW, 1880s   **230.00**

37¾" h, tin finial and frame, glass panels, wrought iron post bracket, cast iron wall bracket arms marked "New York U.S.A.," old black repaint, pr **450.00**

Wilcox, Crittendon & Co, Inc, Middletown, CT, 10½" h, marine, brass, wire chimney protectors, bail handle, late 19th C **220.00**

Williams & Page Co, Boston, MA, 7" h, railroad, 1870–80 . . . .   **125.00**

SHADES AND ACCESSORIES

History: Lamp shades were made to diffuse the harsh light produced by early gas lighting fixtures. This was achieved by a variety of methods–using an opaque glass such as milk glass, frosting the glass, painting the glass, or developing a mold pattern that scattered the light. In addition to being functional, lamp shades often were highly decorative.

During the "golden age" of American art glass in the last quarter of the nineteenth century and the first quarter of the twentieth century, many manufacturers including Durand, Quezal, Steuben, Tiffany, and others made shades for lamps and gas fixtures. Most shades are not marked. Examples did work their way into the countryside.

The popularity of these "high style" designs quickly led to the manufacturer of inexpensive copies. These copycats also are collectible. Lamp and gas shades can provide an important color highlight in a Country setting.

The most highly prized shades are those in stained glass. Beware of signed "Tiffany" examples. Over the years unscrupulous individuals have added Tiffany markings to many lesser quality shades.

One of the most overlooked collecting categories are electric lamp shades. The agrarian housewife was often a skilled handcrafter, especially in sewing. Many added a personal touch to their home by designing and making their own lamp shades. Shades were made to match draperies or furniture upholstery. The variety was endless. Often the frilliest examples were reserved for the guest bedroom.

Should you decide to take up lamp shade collecting, do not overlook the mass–produced shades. Many featured ornately printed designs and pattern on translucent material ranging from stiff paper to celluloid.

References: Dr. Larry Freeman, *New Lights on Old Lamps*, American Life Foundation, 1984; Jo Ann Thomas, *Early Twentieth Century Lighting Fixtures*, Collector Books, 1980.

Reproduction Craftperson: Larry Edelman, Applecore Creations, PO Box 29696, Columbus, OH 43229.

Reproduction Manufacturers: Anastasia's Collectibles, 6114 134th St W, Apple Valley, MN 55124; Carole Foy's Ruffled Curtains and Accessories, 331 E Durham Rd, Cary, NC 27511; Country Accents, RD 2, Box 293, Stockton, NJ 08559; Country Heart Homespun Collection, Inc, 1212 Westover Hills Blvd, Box 13358, Richmond, VA 23225; Country Lighting and Accessories, PO Box 1279, New London, NH 03257; Designs in Copper, 7541 Emery Rd, Portland, MI 48875; House of Vermillion/Heirloom Quality, PO Box 18642, Kearns, UT 84118; Lamplighter Antiques, 615 Silver Bluff Rd, Aiken, SC 29801; Lt Moses Willard, Inc, 1156 State Rte 50, Milford, OH 45150; Mak–A–Shade, 1340 W Strasburg Rd, West Chester, PA 19382; Mole Hill Pottery, 5011 Anderson Pike, Signal Mountain, TN 37377; Rowe Pottery Works, Inc, 404 England St, Cambridge, WI 53523; Victorian Lightcrafters, Ltd, PO Box 350, Slate Hill, NY 10973; Woodbee's, RR 1, Poseyville, IN 47633.

Blue, frosted glass, 2″ fitter, $3.00.

Burner and Chimney Sets, No. 0, 1, and 2, set of three	**75.00**
Chimney Top Heater, 6″ d, wire, loop holds cutling tongs, late 19th C. . . .	**45.00**
Hooks, hanging lamp or hall, cast iron, mounted on board, collection of 9, 1870s and 1880s	**440.00**
Lamp Mantle, orig box marked "Welsbach Junior J Mantle," early 20th C	**48.00**
Lantern Globe, 4½″ d, 5¾″ h, pale amber, fluted, 19th C	**10.00**

Oil Container
- Ohio Lantern Co, 12½″ h, clear blown glass jar, metal container, wire mesh guard marked "Made/by Ohio/Lantern Co./Tiffen" on one side, 1889 patent dates on other side, c1890 . . . . **135.00**
- Unknown Maker, 12½″ h, clear glass Princess Feather pattern jar, protective wire bands attached to metal banded container, metal filler cap, late 19th C **300.00**

Shade, glass
- Clear
  - 7¼″ d, 4½″ h, onion shaped, acid–etched floral pattern, late 19th C **60.00**
  - 7½″ d, 4″ fitter, pressed glass, scalloped sawtooth rim, imitates cut glass pattern, c1880, pr . . . **55.00**
  - 8½″ h, angle lamp shade, opalescent swirl pattern, c1890 . . . . **155.00**
- Clear and Frosted
  - 4¾″ d, 6″ h, chimney shaped, cut floral dec on frosted bands, fluted rim, c1900 . . . . **45.00**
  - 7″ d, 4½″ h, onion shaped, engraved flowers, late 19th C **45.00**
  - 7½″ d, 4″ h, slanting sides, acid etched flowers and berries design, late 19th C **15.00**
  - 8⅜″ d, 3¾″ h, flared rim, acid etched design, key–like double band, late 19th C **24.00**
  - 8½″ h, chimney shaped, Diamond pattern, folded scalloped top,

fitted to European brass burner, late 19th C.	**65.00**
Emerald Green, 3¼″ d, 2¾″ h, globe, late 19th C	**50.00**

Frosted
- 4½″ d
  - 6″ h, chimney shaped, turned–down rim, cut floral design, 1850–1900 . . . . **90.00**
  - 7¼″ h, chimney shaped, cut floral dec, early 20th C **45.00**
- 4⅝″ d, 3¼″ h, squat chimney shaped, cut floral design, c1900 . . . . **32.00**

Opalescent, 10″ d, 5¾″ h, squared . . **50.00**

Opaque White
- 6¼″ d, flat, crimped rim **38.00**
- 7¼″ d, 4¾″ h, onion shaped **32.00**
- 7½″ d, 5¾″ h, Vienna, c1900. . . . . **50.00**
- 7¾″ d
  - 5″ h, Vienna, clear glass illuminator base sgd "B. B. Schneider Illuminator Pat. Oct. 3. 1876" **110.00**
  - 5¾″ h, Vienna **78.00**
  - 6″ h, dome **55.00**
- 7⅝″ d, 3¼″ h, sloping sides, late 19th C. **25.00**
- 8¼″ d, 5½″ h, dome, clear illuminator base **75.00**

Carnival Glass, diamonds, 2″ fitter, $40.00.

9" d, 4½" h, gilt and gray bands,
    red line design separates bands **135.00**
9½" d, 2" h, flat, fluted, late 19th C **10.00**
9¾" d, 3½" h, shallow dome, late
    19th C **12.00**

10" d, 5½" h, slanting sides, dou-
    ble ring, late 19th C **85.00**
10⅛" d, 1½" h, flat, late 19th C . . . **28.00**
Ruby, 3¼" d, 1¾" fitter, globe, late
    19th C **45.00**

METALS

In a life filled with uncertainties, the agrarian community welcomed something associated with strength and permanence. Objects made of metal fit the bill. As a result, metal implements and household appliances were among the most treasured possessions.

Wrestled from the earth, metals symbolize man's ability to conquer and tame nature. Raw elements were transformed into useful products. Much of the success of working with metals during the eighteenth and nineteenth centuries was achieved through trial and error, a concept that stressed mankind's innovative nature.

The presence of an individual who could work metal was critical to a rural community's survival. In most cases, this task fell to the blacksmith who knew his own craft and dabbled in some of the other metal trades as well. The blacksmith worked at an anvil. His most important roles were the manufacture of tools and hardware along with keeping farm machinery operational.

The role of shoeing horses in agrarian America fell to the farrier. The farrier obtained his horseshoes from the blacksmith. Few farmers had the time or wished to incur the expense of bring their horses to the village smith. The farrier with his portable forge was a welcome visitor. Because he traveled a wide circuit, he was also a major source of "outside" news.

As a community grew, additional metal workers arrived. Some brought a combination of skills. The rural silversmith manufactured flatware and an occasional hollow piece. Often he acted as a jobber for a silversmith from a larger town or a silver plate manufacturer. A rural silversmith earned the bulk of his income as a jeweler and repairer of clocks, guns, and watches.

Tinsmiths tended to concentrate solely on their craft. Their products, ranging from dinner plates to coffeepots, were easily transportable and durable. Holes and cracks that did appear could be easily repaired. More difficult metal repairs were done by the tinker, a mobile sales and repair service specializing in brass, copper, and tin.

By the mid–19th century industrial production reached the point where most of the metal product needs of the rural community were not manufactured locally. The repair function far outweighed the production function of the local craftsman. A repair business was a viable business. Metal products were expected to last for generations provided they were well cared for and kept in good repair.

As times changed, so did the rural metal craftsperson. The blacksmith became the auto mechanic. Many silversmiths opened a jewelry store. Others, such as the tinsmith, entered the mercantile community. The farrier shifted his portable forge from the back of a wagon to a pickup truck.

Most of the metal products that are encountered in a Country setting are utilitarian in nature and found in a patinated finish. There was enough to do without having to spend time keeping an item polished. Of course, there were a few pieces that were "kept for nice," but these were brought out only on special occasions.

Most metal products in a Country setting are displayed out of context. Few individuals want to recreate a "shop" within their home environment. Shop settings along with individuals who have revived the old techniques are frequently found at farm museums.

The crafts revival of the 1970s and 1980s witnessed a rebirth of many of the metal crafts. Blacksmiths and tinsmiths abound. Their products often are exact duplicates of their historic counterparts. Most are unmarked. In time, the only way to distinguish them from period piece will be to analyze the metal content.

BRASS

History: Brass is a durable, malleable, and ductile metal alloy consisting mainly of copper and zinc. It achieved its greatest popularity for utilitarian and decorative art items in the eighteenth and nineteenth centuries.

When collecting brass, check to make certain that the object is not brass plated. This can be done with a magnet. A magnet will not stick to brass. If a magnet sticks to a "brass" item, it is plated.

References: Mary Frank Gaston, *Antique Brass and Copper Collectibles,* Collector Books, 1991; Mary Frank Gaston, *Antique Brass: Identification and Values,* Collector Books, 1985; Peter, Nancy, and Herbert Schiffer, *The Brass Book,* Schiffer Publishing, Ltd, 1978.

Reproduction Alert: Many modern reproductions of earlier brass forms are being made, especially in the areas of buckets, fireplace equipment, and kettles.

Reproduction Craftspersons: *General*—Michael Bonne, Coppersmith, RR 1, Box 177R, Carthage, IN 46115; James Chamberlain, Colony Brass, PO Box 266, Williamsburg, VA 23187; Christopher E Dunham, Brassfounder, PO Box 423, Worthington, MA 01098; *Hardware*—Steve Kayne, Kayne & Son Custom Forged Hardware, 76 Daniel Ridge Rd, Candler, NC 28715.

Reproduction Manufacturers: *General*—KML Enterprises, RR 1, Box 234L, Berne, IN 46711; Lemee's Fireplace Equipment, 815 Bedford St, Bridgewater, MA 02324; Olde Mill House Shoppe, 105 Strasburg Pike, Lancaster, PA 17602; *Hardware*—The Antique Hardware Store, 43 Bridge St, Frenchtown, NJ 08825; Bathroom Machineries, 495 Main St, PO Box 1020, Murphys, CA 95247; Bedlam Brass, 137 Rte 4 Westbound, Paramus, NJ 07652.

Bed Warmer, engraved
44" l, floral design, pierced, turned wooden handle, old dark finish	**200.00**
44½" l, floral pinwheel dec lid, turned wooden handle	**250.00**
45½" l, stylized bird and leaves dec lid, red and ochre grain painted ring–turned birch handle, late 18th C	**1,200.00**
48½" l, floral design, pierced lid, turned wooden handle	**325.00**

Bell
Door, metal netting hung with small spheres, larger center sphere, orig mounting bracket	**85.00**
School	
No 7, turned wooden handle	**40.00**
No 9, teak handle	**45.00**
Trolley Car	**125.00**
Candlestick	
5¼" h, capstan type	**415.00**
5½" d, pan, socket, 6½" long handle	**165.00**
6⅜" h, side pushup, saucer base	**100.00**
7¼" h, Queen Anne, petal base, late 18th, early 19th C, England, pr	**650.00**
7½" h, pushup, sgd "J T & Co"	**30.00**
8½" h, scalloped lip and base, detailed baluster stem, three hoof feet	**675.00**
9" h, baluster stem, square ftd base, no seam	**225.00**
9¾" h, Jack of Diamond pattern, pushups, pr	**125.00**
10" h, trumpet shape, pushups, 19th C, pr	**185.00**
Chamber Stick	
4" h, pushup	**150.00**
5½" h, pushup, holders for snuffer and wick trimmer	**75.00**
8" h, pushup, wick trimmer and snuffer	**275.00**
Coffee Pot, 3" h, miniature	**65.00**
Door Knocker	
Dog's Head, 7" h	**65.00**
Eagle, 8½"	**60.00**
Lion's Head, 5", ring knocker, c1880	**75.00**
Flagpole Finial, 7" w, spreadwinged eagle	**25.00**
Heater, 8¼" d, 7½" h, octagonal shape,	

Bed Warmer, 46" l, pine handle, $200.00.

pierced, four turned feet, ball handle, four inscribed "Dutch" script
lines on lid **300.00**
Inkwell, 5¼" l, 9" w, hinged well, sides
flaring to tray edges, etched stylized
tree motifs, sgd "WD," stamped
"709" **150.00**
Kettle
  7" d, cast, two pouring spouts,
    wrought iron bail handle **75.00**
  10" d, cast, wrought iron bail handle   **60.00**
  13" d, spun, wrought iron bail handle **65.00**
Kettle Stand, 8 x 9 x 10" h, reticulated
top, wrought iron base **115.00**
Letter Clip, 4½" h, cast, figural owl,
painted red, c1900 . . . .   **55.00**
Pail, 9½" d, 6" h, spun, iron bail handle, marked "Haydens Patent" **65.00**
Plate, 5½" d, hammered **5.00**
Stencil, 13½" square, rooster, marked
"HA&Co 56 Boston" **200.00**
Tea Kettle
  4" h, miniature, cast, wooden handle, wrought iron trivet **100.00**
  5½" h, sheet brass, wooden swivel
  handle **27.50**
  8" h, handmade, gooseneck spout,
    turned handle, polished **65.00**
  8¼" h, tin lined, copper rivet construction, gooseneck spout **150.00**
Trivet
  Rectangular, 4¾ x 6¼", pierced top,
    cast legs **45.00**
  Round, 7½" d, 5¼" h, reticulated top,
    worn tooling **95.00**
Warming Pan, orig turned wooden
handle **175.00**
Wick Trimmer
  6" l **30.00**
  9¼" l, includes tray **115.00**

COPPER

History: Copper objects, such as kettles, tea kettles, warming pans, measures, etc., played an
important part in the 19th century household.
Outdoors, the apple butter kettle and still were
the two principal copper items. Copper culinary
objects were lined with a thin protective coating
of tin to prevent poisoning. They were relined as
needed.

Great emphasis is placed by collectors on
signed pieces, especially those by American
craftsmen. Since copper objects were made
abroad as well, it is hard to identify unsigned
examples.

References: Mary Frank Gaston, *Antique Brass
and Copper Collectibles*, Collector Books, 1991;
—, *Antique Copper*, Collector Books, 1985;

Henry J. Kauffman, *Early American Copper, Tin,
and Brass*, Medill McBride Co., 1950.

Reproduction Alert: Reproductions, especially
those made thirty years ago and longer, are extremely difficult to distinguish from their historical counterparts without electrospectography
analysis.

Reproduction Craftspersons: *General*—Michael
Bonne, Copper Smith, RR 1, Box 177R, Carthage,
IN 46115; John Kopas, Copper Antiquities, PO
Box 153, Cummaquid, MA 02637; Peter Renzetti, 301 Brinton's Bridge Rd, West Chester, PA
19382; Kurt P Strehl, Orpheus Coppersmith, 52
Clematis Rd, Agawam, MA 01001; Michael P
Terragna, The Coppersmith, PO Box 755, Sturbridge, MA 01566; Galen Walters, Walters
Unique Metals, 140 Sandy Hill Rd, Denver, PA
17517; *Hardware*—Steve Kayne, Kayne & Son
Custom Forged Hardware, 76 Daniel Ridge Rd,
Candler, NC 28715.

Reproduction Manufacturers: The Calico Corner, 513 E Bowman St, South Bend, IN 46613;
Cape Cod Cupola Co, Inc, 78 State Rd, Rte 6, N
Dartmouth, MA 02747; Designs in Copper, 7641
Emery Rd, Portland, MI 48875; KML Enterprises,
RR 1, Box 234L, Berne, IN 46711; Rustique Designs, Rte 4, Box 295, Parsons, KS 67357.

Bed Warmer, engraved
  43" l, bird design on tooled lid,
    turned wooden handle **125.00**
  45" l, floral and bird design, turned
    wooden handle **375.00**
Bowl, 10" d, hammered, wrought copper handles **65.00**
Candleholder, four holders, sgd "W L
Fletcher" **25.00**
Chafing Dish, 11" h, dish supported by
three realistically modeled rabbits,
wooden base, marked "Black, Starr
& Forest" **450.00**
Coal Hod
  14¼" l, double ended **100.00**
  17" h, brass handles, 19th C **150.00**
Dipper, 80" l, orig wrought iron pole   **650.00**
Inkwell, 2" h, tapered cylinder, cov,
rivets around edge, glass liner, impressed Gustav Stickley mark **385.00**
Jar, 11¼" d, 9" h, hammered, dovetailed seams **35.00**
Kettle, apple butter, flat bottom, iron
handles, 40 gallons, 19th C **500.00**
Kettle on Stand, 11¾" h, sq, scroll cut
border, brass stud trim, spout, and
handles, open sq brass base,
scrolled feet and terminals, impressed Benham and Froud mark . .   **275.00**
Kettle Stand and Burner, 6" d, 6¼" h,
brass arms on circular base hold kettle, late 19th C **45.00**

Measure, 1 gallon, $75.00.

Letter File, 5" h, hammered copper, imp Gustav Stickley mark **165.00**

Measure

3⅞" h, 5" d, cylindrical, brass rim, labeled "Fairbanks & Co US Standard New York" **295.00**

7½" h, Fleming Apple Distillery, Fairmount, NJ **35.00**

8¼" h, haystack, dovetailed seams, flange base, handle marked "J. Sykes, Cin." **225.00**

Mitten Warmer, copper pan, brass ferule, turned wooden handle, 9" l . . . **105.00**

Mold, Turk's head, 8¼" d, tin lined . . . **85.00**

Pitcher, 9¼" h, tankard shape, marked "D Bentley & Sons, N 3rd St, Phila" **65.00**

Pot

8½" d, dovetailed, cylindrical, cast brass rim handles, marked "V Olac & Sons, Phila" **65.00**

9 x 13", oval, dovetailed seams, 12½" wrought iron handle **65.00**

10½" h, dovetailed, cov, iron handle **60.00**

11½" d, cast iron handle, marked "D H & M Co, NY" **55.00**

13¾" d, dovetailed, cast iron handle, marked "D N" **45.00**

Saucepan

5" d, dovetailed, 6¾" l handle **85.00**

7" d, dovetailed, cast iron handle **45.00**

9" d, dovetailed, wrought copper handle **75.00**

Sauce Pan, 8" d, 6¼" h, iron handle, 19th C, $65.00.

Tea Kettle

3¾" h, miniature **115.00**

6" h, brass trim, gooseneck spout, stamped monogram mark on bottom **55.00**

6½" h, dovetailed, swivel handle, stamped "4," polished, PA **265.00**

7" h, dovetailed, flap on gooseneck side spout, turned wooden handle, three wrought iron legs **100.00**

7½" h, dovetailed, gooseneck spout, swivel handle, stamped "W Morrison, NY 6 Q" **110.00**

11" h, dovetailed, acorn finial, gooseneck spout, brass trim **145.00**

Warming Pan, copper pan, engraved brass lid, turned wooden handle, late 18th/early 19th C **300.00**

Wash Boiler, cov, oval, turned wooden handle **65.00**

IRON

History: Iron, a metallic element that occurs abundantly in combined forms, has been known for centuries. Items made from iron range from the utilitarian to the decorative. Early hand–forged ironwares are of considerable interest to Country collectors.

The malleability of iron appealed to farmers. It could be shaped by hand into a wealth of useful products. When broken, it was easily repaired. It weathered well when properly cared for.

References: Frank T. Barnes, *Hooks, Rings & Other Things: An Illustrated Index of New England Iron, 1660–1860*, The Christopher Publishing House, 1988; Kathryn McNerney, *Antique Iron*, , Collector Books, 1984, 1991 value update; Herbert, Peter, and Nancy Schiffer, *Antique Iron*, Schiffer Publishing Ltd., 1979.

Reproduction Craftpersons: *General*—Michael Bonne, RR 1, Box 177R, Carthage, IN 46115; Michael Dutcher, 415 W Market St, West Chester, PA 19380; Ian Eddy, Blacksmith, RFD 1, Box 975, Putney, VT 05346; James W Faust, 488 Porters Mill Rd, Pottstown, PA 19464; Ernest Frederick, 340 Fairview Dr, Kutztown, PA 19530; Charles Keller, Forge and Anvil, PO Box 51, Newman, IL 61942; Thomas M Latane, T & C Latane, PO Box 62, Pepin, WI 54749; Greg Leavitt, 476 Valleybrook Rd, Wawa, PA 19063; Thomas Loose, Blacksmith, Rte 2, Box 2410, Leesport, PA 19533; Jonathan Marshall, The J Marshall Co, 1310 Westview, E Lansing, MI 48823; David Mathews, Stone County Ironworks, Rte 73, Box 427, Mountain View, AR 72560; C Leigh Morrell, West Village Forge, PO Box 2114, Marlboro Rd, W Brattleboro, VT 05301; Ronald Potts, Blacksmith, Chriswill

Forge, 2255 Manchester Rd, North Lawrence, OH 44666; Peter Renzetti, 301 Brinton's Bridge Rd, West Chester, PA 19382; Darold Rinedollar, Blacksmith, PO Box 365, Clarksville, MO 63336; Nick Vincent, Nathan's Forge, PO Box 72, Uniontown, MD 21157; *Hardware*—Jerry W Darnell, Mill Creek Forge and Blacksmith Shop, Box 494–B, Rte 2, Seagrove, NC 17341; Charles Euston, Woodbury Blacksmith & Forge Co, PO Box 268, Woodbury, CT 06798; Steve Kayne, Kayne & Son Custom Forged Hardware, 76 Daniel Ridge Rd, Candler, NC 28715; Elmer L Roush, Jr, Roush Forged Metals, Rte 2, Box 13, Cleveland, VA 24225.

Reproduction Manufacturers: *General*— Bullfrog Hollow, Keeny Rd, Lyme, CT 06371; Lancaster Collection, PO Box 6074, Lancaster, PA 17603; Lemee's Fireplace Equipment, 815 Bedford St, Bridgewater, MA 02324; Matthews Emporium, 157 N Trade St, PO Box 1038, Matthews, NC 28106; Town and Country, Main St, East Conway, NH 04037; The Vine and Cupboard, PO Box 309, George Wright Rd, Woolwich, ME 04579; *Hardware*—American Country House, PO Box 317, Davison, MI 48423; The Antique Hardware Store, 43 Bridge St, Frenchtown, NJ 08825; Antiques Americana, Box 19, North Abington, MA 02382; Old Smithy Shop, Box 336, Milford, NH 03055; South Bound Millworks, PO Box 349, Sandwich, MA 02563; Williamsburg Blacksmiths, Inc, Goshen Rd, Williamsburg, MA 01096.

Anchor, emb "Kaukauna, Wis, M16," heavy flukes, 14" l, 8" w.	35.00
Architectural Ornament, cast	
Eagle, outstretched wings, perched on sphere, 21" h, late 19th/early 20th C	700.00
Horse, prancing, molded, hollow, half round, painted silver, rear legs attached to incised disk, NY, 18" h, 26" l, late 19th C, pr	1,450.00
Bathtub, cast, ball and claw feet.	65.00
Bean Pot, cast, thimble finial on lid, three stubby feet, emb "Blue Valley Co. Kansas City, Mo.," 1920s	100.00
Bell, yoke, cast	
Church, 24" d, large clapper, emb "C.S. Bell & Co., Hillsboro, O.," c1900.	975.00
Plantation.	375.00
Book Ends, pr	
Oval, farmhouse, trees, and bridge over stream design, painted	55.00
Ship, three masts, black repaint . . .	45.00
Boot Jack, cast	
Beetle, 9¼", black paint	35.00
Closed Loop, large	70.00
Downs & Co.	85.00
Open Heart and Circle, 13" l, scalloped sides	220.00

Boot Jack, cast, eagle top, lyre base, 11½" l, $45.00.

Pheasants, 19" l, two birds, brushes	**225.00**
Scissor Action, marked "Pat 1877"	**85.00**
V-Shaped, ornate	**45.00**
Boot Scraper, cast	
Plain, emb "P&C Darain #33"	**35.00**
Rooster, pecking, molded, traces of polychrome paint, 9" h, 14" l, 19th C	**1,500.00**
Candlestick	
6¼", hog scraper, pushup, lip hanger	**150.00**
6⅜", hog scraper, pushup, lip hanger	**95.00**
7⅛", hog scraper, pushup, marked "Shaw's Birm"	**175.00**
7¾", wrought, spiral pushup, wood base	**200.00**
Chandelier, cast, made from crown shaped meat hook, four sockets, old chain, 21" d	**325.00**
Cigar Lighter, 7¾" h, cast, sheet metal arm, brass trim, "Gretchen Cigars, Louis Ash Co Makers, NY" adv and "The Brunhoff Mfg Co Cinti, O," patent date 1902–06	**350.00**
Coals Carrier, 31" l, wrought, sliding lid	**235.00**
Desk Set, 7⅝" h, closing inkwell, pen rack, and candle socket, varnished	**200.00**
Door Knocker, cast	
Flower Basket, openwork plate, oval	**45.00**

Door Knocker, cast, basket of flowers, 4" d, painted, $45.00.

Door Stop, Wild Roses, 7½" h, multi-colored flowers, Hubley No. 475, $125.00.

Fox Head, knocker ring hangs from
mouth, 5½" h head **85.00**
Doorstop, cast
Bellhop, 7½" h, black, carrying
satchel, facing sideways, orange–
red uniform and cap **350.00**
Bowl, 7 x 7", green–blue, natural
colored fruit, sgd "Hubley, 456"   **100.00**
Cat
7" h, kitten, 3 kittens in wicker
basket, sgd "M Rosenstein,
c1932, Lancaster, PA" **325.00**
8", black, red ribbon and bow
around neck, on pillow **125.00**
9½" h
Flat Silhouette, painted black   **235.00**
Full Figure, Persian, sitting,
gray, light markings, sgd
"Hubley" inside casting,
7" w **140.00**
10½" l, fireside, full figure, gray,
light markings, sgd "Hubley"
inside casting **140.00**
12½" h, full bodied, seated, black,
green eyes **125.00**
Cottage
6⅜" h, three-dimensional garden,
tan roof, 3 red chimneys, flowers, 2 pc casting, Ann Hatha-
way **250.00**
8⅝" l, 5¾" h, Cape type, blue roof,
flowers, fenced garden, path,
sgd "Eastern Specialty Mfg Co
14" **125.00**
Dog
Boston Terrier, 10" h, full bodied,
orig paint **65.00**
Boxer, 8½ x 9", full figure, facing
forward, brown, tan markings   **165.00**
Pekingese, 14½" l, 9" h, full figure,
life–like size and color, brown,
sgd "Hubley" **500.00**
Pointer, 15½" l, full bodied, worn
orig paint **95.00**

Police Dog, 9" h, full bodied,
worn orig paint **95.00**
Puppies, 7", three puppies in bas-
ket, natural colors, sgd "Copyright 1932 M Rosenstein, Lan-
caster, PA, USA" **275.00**
Terrier, 4½" h, sitting, full bodied,
red collar, black and white
body **115.00**
Wire Haired Fox Terrier, 9 x 8",
full figure, facing sideways, tan,
brown marking **90.00**
Duck, 7½", white, green bush and
grass **225.00**
Dutch Boy, 11" h, full figure, hands
in pocket, blue jump suit and hat,
red belt and collar, brown shoes,
blonde hair **375.00**
Fish, 9¾" h, three, fantail, orig paint,
sgd "Hubley 464" **135.00**
Fisherman, 6¼" h, standing at wheel,
hand blocking sun over eyes, rain
gear **140.00**
Flower
Goldenrods, 7⅛" h, natural color,
sgd "Hubley 268" **150.00**
Jonquil, 7", yellow flowers, red
and orange cups, sgd "Hubley
453" **150.00**
Mixed Flowers, polychrome paint   **65.00**
Tulips, 13" h, polychrome paint   **450.00**
Zinnias, 11⅝" h, multicolored
flowers, blue and black vase,
detailed casting, sgd "B & H"   **175.00**
Frog, 3", full figure, sitting, yellow
and green **50.00**
Girl, 13¾" h, 9¾" l, white hat, flowing
cape, holding orange jack–o-
lantern with red cut–out eyes,
nose, and mouth **650.00**
Horse, 7⅞" h, jumping fence,
jockey, sgd "Eastern Spec Co
#790" **185.00**
House
5½" h, 8¼" l, 2 story, attic, path to
door, shutters, sgd "Sophia
Smith House" **225.00**
6" h, woman walking up front
steps, grapevines, sgd "Eastern
Spec Co" **175.00**
Lighthouse, 7¾" h, 9" l, three-dimen-
sional buildings and lighthouse,
base, Highland **275.00**
Mammy
8½" h, full figure, red dress, white
apron, blue kerchief with white
spots, sgd inside "Hubley 327"   **125.00**
12", full figure, blue dress, white
apron, red kerchief with white
spots, sgd "copyright Hubley"
inside **300.00**
Parrot, 13¾" h, in ring, two sided,
heavy gold base, sgd "B & H" . . .   **210.00**

Pheasant, $8\frac{1}{2}''$, brown, bright markings, green grass, sgd "Fred Everett" front, sgd "Hubley" back . . . **200.00**

Quail, $7\frac{1}{4}''$ h, 2 brown, tan, and yellow birds, green, white, and yellow grass, sgd "Fred Everett" on front, sgd "Hubley 459" on back **225.00**

Rabbit
$8\frac{1}{2}''$ h, eating carrot, red sweater, brown pants **285.00**
$15\frac{1}{4}''$ h, sitting on hind legs, tan, green grass, detailed casting, sgd "B & H 7800" **400.00**

Rooster
7" h, standing, black, colorful detail **135.00**
12" h, full figure, black, red comb, yellow feet and beak . . .
13" h, red comb, black and brown tail and chest, yellow stomach **300.00**

Squirrel, 9" h, sitting on stump eating nut, brown and tan **175.00**

Woman
8" h, Colonial, sgd "Hubley" . . . **115.00**
12" h, carrying parasol and hat box in left hand, satchel with "Phoebe" in right hand, flowered hat **265.00**

Drip Pan, hall tree, oval, $8\frac{1}{2}''$ l, emb "M & H Schrenkeisen, New York," pr **45.00**

Figure, eagle, cast, $17\frac{1}{2}''$ h, $23\frac{1}{2}''$ wing span, detailed, old gold paint, modern wooden base **135.00**

Foot Warmer, sheet iron, 11" l, 8" w, 9" h, pierced both sides, double heart dec on top, brass turnip feet, handle, and maker's label, made by W O Dryer, Poughkeepsie, NY, dated 1864 . . . . **600.00**

Garden Stake, wrought, symmetrical sunburst, scrolled lyre shapes, and urns on center stake, 30" h **250.00**

Gate Post Finial, cast, horse head, flattened ears, open mouth, crenelated stylized mane, mounted on oval fluted columnar support, $15\frac{1}{4}''$ h, 20th C, pr **1,975.00**

Hat Rack, cast, painted, flower basket form, $40\frac{1}{2}''$ h, 33" w, late 19th C . . . **800.00**

Hinges, wrought, pr
$7\frac{1}{2}''$ l, ram's horn **75.00**
$10\frac{1}{2}''$ l, ram's horn **170.00**
32" l, barn door, shaped hinge section. **50.00**

Horse Anchor, round, c1870 . . . . **35.00**

Horseshoe, workhorse, imprinted "Patented July 23, 1912 Lockjaw #3F," snow and ice caulks, orig nails. **28.00**

Kettle, cast
Apple Butter, iron bail handle, ftd **125.00**

Hog Scalding, bulging bottom, ear handles for cradle, 27" d, 17" h **450.00**

Lard, sloping sides, iron bail handle, ftd, wrought stand, late 18th C . . **550.00**

Sugar Cane, wide flat rim, marked "Kelly Kettle," 19th C **350.00**

Lighting Device, wrought, primitive, adjustable rush light holder, candle socket counterbalance, and finial, $36\frac{3}{4}''$ h. **425.00**

Lock, wrought, simple decorative detail, 10" l **55.00**

Memo Clip, duck head shape, $5\frac{3}{8}''$ l, glass eyes, orig paint, cast **85.00**

Miniatures
Iron and Trivet, swan shape, $2\frac{3}{4}''$ h **65.00**
Puppy, cast, marked "Hines," traces of paint, $1\frac{3}{4}''$ h **35.00**
Tea Kettle, $3\frac{5}{8}''$, cast, gooseneck spout, wire bail handle, tin lid, black paint **155.00**

Mold, maple sugar, cast, eight fruit and vegetable sections, fluted handles **165.00**

Mortar and Pestle, cast, urn shape, 4" h, pedestal base, late 1800s **75.00**

Nutcracker, cast
Dog, 13" l, rect base **45.00**
Squirrel, $7\frac{1}{2}''$ h **200.00**

Padlock, wrought, decorative detail, key and fastening spikes **75.00**

Paper Spike, cast, wall mount, ornate **25.00**

Paperweight, 5" l, cast, frog, worn black paint **45.00**

Plaque, cast
Horse's Head, round, $18\frac{1}{2}''$ d, high relief, black repaint **100.00**
Owl, perched on quill pen, oval, $12\frac{1}{2}''$ h, $8\frac{1}{4}''$ w **150.00**

Plate Holder, 59" h, wrought, triangular tier, seven graduated shelves . . . **250.00**

Pump
Force, emb "Mast Foos & Company Springfield, Ohio," cut–out crisscross pattern on base, bucket bail spur on spout **85.00**
Pitcher, emb "Red Jacket Mfg. Co. Davenport, Iowa No. 1A" **55.00**

Trivet, cast, $9\frac{1}{4}''$ l, Gothic arch, filigree trumpet flowers insert, scroll handle, $25.00.

Sadiron, emb "Enterprise Mfg. Co., Phila. U.S.A./Star/Patd. October 1, '87," fluted handle **45.00**

Shutter Dogs, cast, girl's head, "Brevete SGDG" anchor mark, $8\frac{5}{8}$" l extended length, set of four **140.00**

Shelf Brackets, swivel, $5\frac{1}{2}$" h, pr **18.00**

Shoe Last, cobbler's, cast, 1850–90 **18.00**

Shoeshine Stand Foot Rest, cast, star design and bars, bolts to bench. . . . **25.00**

Shoe Stretcher, cast, emb "Patd. Oct. 12, 1891" one side, "Light–Fulton, Ill." other side. **28.00**

Skillet, cast

Griswold, No 7 . . . . **25.00**

Wagner, MiPet, No 3 . . . . **10.00**

Wapak Indian Head, No 9 . . . . **150.00**

Snowbirds, pr, cast, eagles, $5\frac{1}{4}$" h **130.00**

Spigot, maple sugar. **10.00**

Spittoon, 10" h, $9\frac{3}{4}$" d, granite lined inside rim **25.00**

Splint Holder, handwrought, $11\frac{1}{4}$" h, orig circular stepped wooden base **150.00**

Stove, cast

Burnside No. 20A, Enterprise, potbelly, name emb on door, 48" h **395.00**

Peoria, parlor, wood burning, round, emb stylized leaf and swirl designs, name on side **500.00**

Royal, gas, salesman's sample, name emb on front, includes skillet, griddle, and handled pot **145.00**

Station Agent, Union Stove Works, NY, potbelly, name emb on circular top rim, $25\frac{1}{2}$" d, $46\frac{1}{2}$" h **375.00**

Stove Lid Lifter, Jewel, emb name, openwork handle, c1890 . . . . **15.00**

Stove Plate, cast

5" d, emb wild turkey and trees design **35.00**

21" h, 23" w, arches and tulips, marked "S.F." and "1756". **425.00**

Sugar Nippers, wrought, $9\frac{1}{4}$" l. **35.00**

Tape Dispenser, cast, Victorian, ornate **125.00**

Target, cast, double, bird and star, 8" l **95.00**

Tea Kettle, cast, gooseneck spout, wrought handle

5" h, salesman's sample, lift lid, small bar finial, brass bail handle, marked "Baster Kyle & Co. #8, Louisville, KY. June 28, 1888" . . **150.00**

7" h, marked "No 1" **135.00**

$7\frac{1}{2}$" h **115.00**

$7\frac{3}{4}$" h, 12" w, flat lid emb "Terstegge, Gohmann & Co., New Albany, Ind. 1883," half–covered lip, wire bail handle **100.00**

9" h, marked "No 00 $4\frac{1}{2}$ Pints" **95.00**

Toaster, wrought, scrolled detail, 15" w, 28" handle. **175.00**

Trade Sign, 20 x 24", butcher's, saw, knife, meat cleaver, and bull, gold and silver paint. **400.00**

Trivet

$6\frac{1}{4}$" l, cast, four hearts in circle, heart shaped handle end. **85.00**

$7\frac{3}{4}$" d, round, marked "The Griswold Mfg. Co. Erie, PA., U.S.A./8/ Trivet/206" **25.00**

12" l, wrought, scrolled feet **195.00**

$21\frac{1}{2}$" h, wrought, adjustable roasting fork, wooden handle **200.00**

Utensil Rack, wrought, seven hooks, scrolled detail, 14" h, $19\frac{1}{4}$" w **225.00**

Wafer Iron, cast, circular design, wrought handles, 33" l. **85.00**

Waffle Iron, cast, wrought handles, 31" l. **55.00**

Washboiler, cast, oval, two handle bars, four short legs **35.00**

Washboiler Tray, cast, oval, pouring lip, handles. **30.00**

Weight, cotton scale, 4 lbs. **35.00**

PEWTER

History: Pewter is a metal alloy, consisting mostly of tin with small amounts of lead, copper, antimony, and bismuth added to improve malleability and hardness. The metal can be cast, formed around a mold, spun, easily cut, and soldered to form a wide variety of utilitarian articles.

Pewter ware was known to the ancient Chinese, Egyptians, and Romans. English pewter fulfilled most of the needs of the American colonies for nearly 150 years before the American Revolution. The Revolution ended the embargo on raw tin and allowed the small American pewter industry to flourish. This period lasted until the Civil War.

Pewter fits more easily into the early American decorative motif than it does in a Country decor. Wooden and tin utensils were far more common in the countryside than was pewter. However, since Country decorators like the patinated look of unpolished pewter, it is included in this book.

The listing concentrates on the American and English pewter forms most often encountered by the collector.

Reference: Donald L. Fennimore, *The Knopf Collectors' Guides to American Antiques, Silver & Pewter*, Alfred A. Knopf, Inc., 1984.

Collectors' Club: Pewter Collector's Club of America, 29 Chesterfield Road, Scarsdale, NY 10583.

Reproduction Craftpersons: S Barrie Cliff, Pewter Crafters of Cape Cod, 927 Main St, Yarmouthport, MA 02675; Fred Danforth, Danforth Pewterers, 52 Seymour St, Middlebury, VT 05753; Christopher E Dunham, PO Box 423, Worthington, MA 01098; Richard & Louise Graver, 504 W Lafayette St, West Chester, PA 19380; Stuart & Karen Helble, K & S Pewter, Rte 4, Box 591, Leesburg, VA 22075; Lydia Withington Holmes, Pewterer, Barton Hill, Stow, MA 01755; David & Sharon Jones, Three Feathers Pewter, Box 232, Shreve, OH 44676; William Melchior, 410 Swedesford Rd, North Wales, PA 19454; Don Miller, Spring Valley, Box 11, Charles Town, WV 25414; Donald W Reid, Plymouth Pewter Works, PO Box 1696, Plymouth, MA 02360; Peter Renzetti, 301 Brinton's Bridge Rd, West Chester, PA 19382; Jay Thomas Stauffer, Stauffer's Pewter Shop, 707 W Brubaker Valley Rd, Lititz, PA 17543; Barbara L Strode, The Pewter Spoon, Etc, 1033 Palm, Starke, FL 32091; David & Becky Weber, Village Pewter, 320 W Washington St, Medina, OH 44256; James W Wilson, Jori Handcast Pewter, 12681 Metro Pkwy, Ft Myers, FL 33912.

Reproduction Manufacturers: Homespun Crafts, Box 77, Grover, NC 28073; Ingrid's Handcraft Crossroads, 8 Randall Rd, Rochester, MA 02770; Lancaster Collection, PO Box 6074, Lancaster, PA 17603.

Basin
  American, angel touch mark,
    11¼" d, 2⅝" h **210.00**
  Austin, Nathaniel, Charlestown,
    MA, faint eagle touchmark, 8" d,
    2" h **135.00**
  Belcher, Joseph, faint touchmark,
    pitting and scratches, 8" d **650.00**
  Boardman, Thomas Danforth, faint
    eagle touchmark, 8" d **210.00**
  Danforth, Samuel, Hartford, CT,
    very faint touchmark, 6⅝" d,
    c1800. . . . .   **400.00**
  Ellis, Samuel, London, 9⅛" d, 18th C   **200.00**
  Hamlin, Samuel, partial touchmark,
    5¾" d, 2" h **250.00**
  Jones, Gershom, Providence, RI,
    minor pitting on inside, worn
    touchmark, 7¾" d, 1774–1809 . . **1,250.00**
  Lee, Richard, Springfield, VT, 5¾" d,
    1795–1815. . . . .   **300.00**

Basin, deep, 8" d, Richard Austin, $450.00.

Mabberley, Stephen, England, old
  repair in bottom, 9" l, c1670 . . . .   **75.00**
Rust, H N, 8" d **650.00**
Stafford, Spencer, Albany, NY,
  7¾" d, c1820 . . . .   **300.00**
Townsend & Compton, London,
  touchmarks, 11" d, 3" h **300.00**
Beaker
  American, unmarked, 3⅛" h **275.00**
  Woodbury, J B, Beverly, MA and
    Philadelphia, PA, good touch-
    mark, handle, 3" h, 1830–38 . . .   **400.00**
  Yale, Hiram, Wallingford, CT, cast
    dec handle, 2¾" h, 1822–31 . . . .   **150.00**
Bedpan, Thomas Danforth Boardman,
  Hartford, CT, triple touchmarks,
  10½" l, c1820 . . . .   **400.00**
Bowl, unmarked
  American, ftd, 6" d **250.00**
  England, ftd, 5⅛" d, 3⅝" h **55.00**
Candle Mold, twelve tube, pine frame,
  16 x 16 x 16¼" h **825.00**
Candlestick
  Calder, William, Providence, RI,
    minor pitting on base, 10" h,
    1817–56. . . . .   **325.00**
  Dunham, Rufus, Westbrook, ME,
    straight line touchmark, 6" h,
    c1840, pr **900.00**
  Endicott & Sumner, New York City,
    NY, 8⅜" h, 1846–51. . . . .   **350.00**
  Flagg & Homan, 7⅞" h, pr **420.00**
  Gleason, Roswell, Dorchester, MA,
    6½" h, c1840 . . . .   **250.00**
  Hopper, Henry, NY, straight line
    touchmark, 10" h. **275.00**
  Ostrander & Norris, New York City,
    saucer base, resoldered, 4" h,
    1848–50. . . . .   **150.00**
  Smith & Co, Boston, MA, curved
    line touchmark, 6⅛" h, mid 19th C   **150.00**
  Unmarked, pushup, 8" h, pr **150.00**
  Wildes, Thomas, Philadelphia, PA
    and New York City, NY, straight
    line touchmark, complete with
    bobeche, 10" h, 1829–40 . . . . .   **200.00**
Castor Set
  Dunham, Rufus, Westbrook, ME,
    five clear cut bottles, frame
    marked "R Dunham 200," 13¼" h   **285.00**
  Smith, Eben, Beverly, MA, four clear
    bottles, 1813–56. . . . .   **375.00**
  Trask, Israel, Beverly, MA, five clear
    Sandwich Glass "Gothic Arch"
    pattern bottles, three with orig
    pewter tops, 9½" h, 1807–56. . . .   **250.00**
Chalice, unmarked, dark patina, 6⅜" h   **105.00**
Chamberstick, Meriden Britannia Co.,
  saucer base, gadroon molding,
  4¼" h, 1850. . . . .   **225.00**
Charger
  Austin, Nathaniel, Charleston, MA,
    13½" d **450.00**

Badger, Thomas, Boston, MA, eagle touchmark, 13⅜" d **650.00**

Cloudsley, Nehemigh, England, multiple reed rim, 18¼" d, c1690 **600.00**

Danforth, Samuel, Hartford, CT, faint touchmark, wear and pitting, 13¼" d **225.00**

Eadem, Semper, Boston, MA, 12⅛" d **600.00**

Hamlin, Samuel, worn and pitted, knife scratches, touchmark, 11½" d **300.00**

Jones, Gersham, Providence, RI, 14½" d, late 18th C **725.00**

King, Richard, London, England, 16½" d **375.00**

Langworthy, Lawrence, Devonshire, England and Newport, RI, 15" d **400.00**

Leapidge, Thomas, London, 15" d, 1673–1725 . . . . **200.00**

Leigh, Charles White, London, England, 14¾" d **300.00**

Pierce, Samuel, Springfield, MA, pitting, knife marks, dent in rim, 11¼" d **210.00**

Coffee Pot

Boardman & Hart, NY, repair in bottom, touchmark, 10½" h **200.00**

Calder, William, Providence, RI, lighthouse, 11" h, c1839 . . . . . . **650.00**

Danforth, Josiah, Middletown, CT, dome lid, 11" h, early 19th C . . . **1,100.00**

Dunham, Rufus, Westbrook, ME, straight line touchmark, crude repair on bottom affecting small portion of mark, 11" h, 1836–61 **275.00**

Gleason, Roswell, Dorchester, MA, straight line touchmark, 11" h, 19th C **250.00**

Griswold, Ashbill, Meriden, CT, pyriform, 10½" h **350.00**

Homan & Co, Cincinnati, OH, cast foliage finial, engraved floral design, marked "H Homan," 10¼" h **235.00**

Lewis, Isaac C, Meriden, CT, 11½" h, 19th C **175.00**

Porter, Freeman, Westbrook, ME, pear shape, marked "F Porter No. 2/Westbrook," 10¾" h, c1840 . . . **250.00**

Richardson, George, Boston & Cranston, RI, "G Richardson, Warranted" touchmark, 11" h, 1818–45 . . . . **525.00**

Trask, Israel, Beverly, MA, lighthouse shape, bright cut engraved band, 11" h, c1830 . . . . **350.00**

Whitlock, John H, Troy, NY, marked "Whitlock, Troy, NY," 11½" h **325.00**

Communion Bowl, Hiram Yale & Co, Yalesville, CT, ftd, 10¼" d, 5¾" h, 1824–35 . . . . **600.00**

Communion Flagon, Eben Smith, Beverly, MA, lighthouse shape, straight line touchmark, 10½" h, 1814–56 **425.00**

Communion Plate, Thomas Boardman, Hartford, CT, eagle touchmark, 13⅛" d, 1805–50 . . . . **550.00**

Creamer

American, unmarked, 5⅛" h **95.00**

Joseph, Henry, English export, London, three small feet, marked "HJ," 1740–85 . . . . **2,500.00**

Cup

American, unmarked, ebonized handle, hinged lid, 5" h **100.00**

Birch & Villers, England, double handles, 1775–1820 . . . . **325.00**

Desk Set

Jars, three, ink well, sander, and seal jar, knob finials on lids, 2⅛" h . . . **115.00**

Rectangular, two hinged lids, divided compartments hold ink well and pull–out sander, hollow feet, 6¼" l **190.00**

Dish, deep

Calder, William, Providence, RI, 10⅜" d, c1830 . . . . **450.00**

Derby, Thomas S, Middletown, CT, Derby's General Jackson touchmark, 13¼" d, c1840 . . . . **600.00**

Hamlin, Samuel, Hartford, CT, late 18th C **600.00**

Egg Cup, American, unmarked **50.00**

Flagon

English, unmarked, 10¾" h, dated 1718 . . . . **160.00**

Boardman & Hart, New York, domed lid, shaped thumbpiece and handle, tapering sides, stepped circular base, Laughlin touch mark, 12½" h, c1835 . . . . . . **1,325.00**

Gleason, Roswell, Dorchester, MA, 10" h, mid 19th C **450.00**

Smith & Fletman, Albany, touchmark, 12" h **350.00**

Funnel, American, unmarked, ring hanger, 4⅜" d, 6⅜" l **125.00**

Gimbal Lamp, brass and pewter burner, pedestal base, bail handle, 8" h **175.00**

Spittoon, 7⅞" d base, 2½" h, D. Curtis, Albany, NY, $275.00.

Ice Cream Mold, spade playing card, 4" l **60.00**

Inkwell, American, unmarked, five quills, 6⅞" d **150.00**

Jardiniere, James Putnam, Malden, MA, three paw feet stand horizontally from the bottom, 7¾" d, c1840, pr **350.00**

Ladle
American, unmarked, engraved handle, 13¾" l **225.00**
Danforth, Josiah, Middletown, CT, 13¼" l **600.00**
Yates, John, Birmingham, England, minor pitting on bowl int., 13½" l, c1835 . . . . **80.00**

Measure
England
½ Gill to Quart, bellied, 2" to 6¼" h, set of six **270.00**
Tankard, engraved monogram and crown, interior touchmark, 7 size, 6" h **115.00**
Unmarked, attributed to Thomas Danforth III, tankard shape, 6" h **325.00**
Townsend & Compton, England, T & C touchmark, quart, tankard ¾" h **325.00**
Yates, James, England, quart, bellied, 6⅛" h **85.00**
Muffineer, 7½" h **200.00**

Mug
Eddon, William, London, pint, tulip shape, c1750 . . . . **150.00**
Unmarked, tankard, tulip shape, 3¾" h **55.00**
Whitmore, Jacob, Middletown, CT, quart, fair touchmark, 1758–90 **1,750.00**

Pitcher
American, unmarked, pigeon breasted, reverse "C" handle, removable lid, 5½" h **300.00**
Dunham, Rufus, Westbrook, ME, two quart size, cider type, 6½" h, c1845 . . . . **350.00**
Gleason, Roswell, Dorchester, MA, cov, 12" h, c1840 . . . . **650.00**
Homan & Co, Cincinnati, hinged lid, resoldered finial, touchmark, 12" h **110.00**
Richardson, George Sr, Boston, MA, cov, 10" h, 1818–28 . . . . **750.00**

Plate
American, unmarked, 8⅛" d **130.00**
Austin, Nathaniel, Charlestown, MA, eagle touchmark, 8" d **100.00**
Badger, Thomas, Boston, MA, 7¾" d, stamped initials on rim **300.00**
Barns, Blakeslee, Philadelphia, PA, eagle touchmark, 7⅞" d **300.00**
Billings, William, Providence, RI, touchmark, pitting, 8¼" d **45.00**

Boardman, Thomas, Hartford, CT, eagle touchmark, 7¾" d **300.00**
Calder, William, Providence, RI, 8⅜" d, eagle touchmark, c1840 . . **375.00**
Compton, Thomas, English export, single reed, 7⅝" d, 1802–17 . . . . **150.00**
Danforth, Josiah, Middletown, CT, rampant lion touchmark, 7⅞" d . . **275.00**
Danforth, Samuel, Hartford, CT, eagle touchmark, soldered repair near center, 7⅞" d **95.00**
Danforth, Thomas I, lion touchmark, 8" d **350.00**
Danforth, William, Middletown, CT, eagle touchmark, 8" d **225.00**
England, unidentified hallmarks, 8¼" d, 18th C **150.00**
Gleason, Roswell, Dorchester, MA, 9¼" d **275.00**
Griswold, Ashbill, Meriden, CT, eagle touchmark, 7⅞" d **1,330.00**
Havelin, Samuel, Hartford, CT, interior touchmark, 8⅛" d **375.00**
Jones, Gershom, Providence, RI, single reed, 8⅜" d, 1774–1808 . . **550.00**
Kilbourn, Samuel, Baltimore, MD, eagle touchmark, 7¾" d **155.00**
Lightner, George, Baltimore, MD, "G Lightner, Baltimore" touchmark, 7⅞" d **225.00**
Porter, James, Baltimore, MD, faint eagle touchmark, pitting, 8" d . . **35.00**
Swanson, Thomas, Ellis and Swanson touchmarks, 7⅞" d, c1770, pr **150.00**

Platter, England, "Made in London," engraved monogram and griffin, 14" l **245.00**

Porringer
American, unmarked, 5" d, cast crown handle, New England **175.00**
Boardman, Thomas Danforth, Hartford, CT, TD & SB touchmark on old English handle, 3¼" d **150.00**
Boardman, Thomas Danforth and Sherman Boardman, Hartford,

Plate, 8¾" d, Thomas Danforth, Philadelphia, $375.00.

CT, keyhole type crown handle, triangular bracket, 5" d, 1810–30 — **325.00**

Green, Samuel, Boston, MA, cast crown handle, 5½" d . . . . — **550.00**

Hamlin, Samuel Jr, Providence, RI, touchmark on flower handle, 5¼", 1801–56 . . . . — **500.00**

Unmarked, attributed to David Melville, Newport, RI, flowered handle initialed "FGW," 5" d, 1780–90 . . . . — **150.00**

Salt

Boyd, Parks, Philadelphia, PA, beaded rim and base, ftd, 1795–1819 . . . . — **950.00**

Unmarked

2" h, cast design on foot . . . . — **45.00**

2¼" h, molded leaf design, 18th C — **30.00**

Salt Spoon, marked "TW," 4⅛" l . . . . — **15.00**

Sauce Ladle, Yates, England, 7" l . . . . — **35.00**

Soapbox, American, unmarked, circular, hinged lid, 4⅜" . . . . — **125.00**

Soup Plate

Boardman & Co, NY, eagle touchmark, 9⅜" d . . . . — **375.00**

Boardman & Hart, NY, eagle touchmark, marked "Boardman Warranted," 9⅞" d . . . . — **250.00**

Spoon, William Bradford, New York City, NY, round bowl, 6⅝" l, 1719–85 . . . . — **1,600.00**

Sugar Bowl

Boardman & Hart, NY, orig lid, minor denting, 8" h, c1835 . . . . . — **350.00**

Hiram Yale & Co, Yalesville, CT, 5½" h, 1824–35 . . . . — **50.00**

Richardson, George, Boston, MA and Cranston, RI, 1818–45 . . . . . — **3,000.00**

Unmarked, attributed to Boyd Parks, Philadelphia, PA, beaded lid, rim, and foot, 1795–1819 . . . . — **7,500.00**

Syrup, American, unmarked, miniature lighthouse coffeepot shape, lid resoldered to hinge, 5½" h . . . . — **225.00**

Tall Pot

Dixon & Son, England, paneled, wooden handle, 12" h . . . . — **90.00**

Richardson, G, warranted, old soldered lid hinge repair, 10½" h . . . — **300.00**

Sellew & Co, Cincinnati, OH, 11½" h — **325.00**

Tankard

American, dome lid, heart in thumb tab, touchmark on bottom, 1 quart . . . . — **400.00**

IH, London, touchmark, hinged lid, resoldered hinge, 8" h . . . . — **150.00**

Teapot

American, unmarked, onion shaped, 3½" h . . . . — **110.00**

Boardman, NY, eagle touchmark, 7¼" . . . . — **400.00**

Boardman, Thomas D and Samuel, Hartford, CT, cast acorn finial,

Teapot, 6½" h, Morey & Ober, Boston, $325.00.

copper bottom marked "TD & SB," 8⅞" h . . . . — **100.00**

Gleason, Roswell, Dorchester, MA, inverted mold, minor pitting, 12" h, c1840 . . . . — **650.00**

Grenfell, griffin touchmark, individual size, pear shaped, old soldered repair, replaced wooden handle, 5½" h . . . . — **200.00**

Richardson, G, small eagle touchmark, marked "No A. Warranted," 7¾" h . . . . — **250.00**

Smith, Eben, Beverly, MA, bright cut engraved band, straight line touchmark, 7½" h, c1830 . . . . . . — **500.00**

Toddy Plate, unmarked, 5⅛" d . . . . . . — **80.00**

Vessel, H & I, flared lip, tapering to base, ftd, 8" h . . . . — **300.00**

SILVER AND SILVERPLATE

History: Sterling silver never enjoyed great popularity in the agrarian community. If a farmer or small town merchant hoarded anything, the preferred metal was gold. When a touch of class was needed, elaborately decorated silverplate was more than adequate.

Most pieces of silver and silverplate appeared only on special occasions. The rural housewife simply did not have the time or help to keep them polished. The best pieces were displayed on the dining room buffet when company came and then stored inside for the balance of the time.

The natural beauty of silver lends itself to the designs of artists and craftsmen, often pricing it out of reach for most members of the country community. Pure silver is too soft to be fashioned into strong, durable, and serviceable utensils. Alloys of copper, nickel, and other metals are added to give silver its required degree of hardness.

Plated silver production by an electrolytic method is credited to G. R. and H. Ekington, England, in 1838. In electroplating silver, the article is completely shaped and formed from a base metal, then coated with a thin layer of silver. In the late 19th century, the base metal was Britannia, an alloy of tin, copper, and antimony. Other bases are copper and brass. Today the base metal is nickel silver.

In 1847 the electroplating process was introduced in America by Rogers Bros., Hartford, Connecticut. By 1855, a number of firms were using the method to mass produce silver plated items.

The quality of plating is important. Extensive use or polishing can cause the base metal to show through. Silverplate has enjoyed a revival due to the Victorian decorating craze of the late 1980s.

References: Frederick Bradbury, *Bradbury's Book of Hallmarks*, J. W. Northend, Ltd, 1987; Rachael Feild, *Macdonald Guide To Buying Antique Silver and Sheffield Plate*, Macdonald & Co., 1988; Donald L. Fennimore, *Silver & Pewter*, Alfred A. Knopf *Knopf Collector's Guides To American Antiques*, 1984; *Jewelers' Circular Keystone Sterling Flatware Pattern Index, 2nd Edition*, Chilton Company, 1989; Dorothy T. Rainwater, *Encyclopedia of American Silver Manufacturers, 3rd Edition*, Schiffer Publishing Ltd., 1986; Dorothy T. and H. Ivan Rainwater, *American Silverplate*, Schiffer Publishing, Ltd., 1988; Jeri Schwartz, *The Official Identification And Price Guide To Silver and Silver–Plate, Sixth Edition*, House of Collectibles, 1989; Peter Waldon, *The Price Guide To Antique Silver, 2nd Edition*, Antique Collectors' Club, 1982 (price revision list 1988); Seymour B. Wyler, *The Book Of Old Silver, English, American, Foreign*, Crown Publishers, Inc., 1937 (available in reprint).

Periodical: *Silver*, PO Box 1243, Whittier, CA 90609.

Museums: Wadsworth Atheneum, Hartford, CT; Yale University Art Gallery, New Haven, CT; Boston Museum of Fine Arts, Boston, MA; The Bayou Bend Collection, Houston, TX.

Coin Silver
    Beaker, Joseph Anthony Jr, Philadelphia, PA, tapering cylindrical, double incised rim band, engraved script initials, marked twice on base, 2 oz, 1⅝" h, 1784–1814, pr **3,524.00**
    Bowl, Joseph Richardson Sr, Philadelphia, PA, circular, flaring sides, molded rim, molded circular foot, base engraved "IM," marked twice on base, 17 oz, 6¾" d, 3⅜" h, 1740–1775 . . . . . . **27,500.00**
    Brazier, Jacob Hurd, Boston, MA, circular, everted brim mounted with three scrolls, pierced foliate sides, circular pierced grate, turned wooden handle, three scrolled legs, turned wooden ball feet, side engraved crest, initials

Coin, Tablespoon, 9¾" l, marked "J. Brenise, York City, PA," $45.00

engraved on base, marked on base and grate, 16 oz, 10 dwt, 4" h, 12" l, 1740–58 . . . . **71,500.00**
Cann, Paul Revere II, Boston, MA, baluster, double scroll handle, acanthus grip, molded circular foot, front engraved foliate script initials in wreath, marked near rim, 18 oz, 6⅛" h, 1760–80 . . . . . **38,500.00**
Chatelaine Hook, Jacob Mytinger, Newtown, VA, heart shaped, roulettework border, engraved script initials, marked "J Mytinger," 10 dwt, 2" l, c1827 . . . . **1,100.00**
Coffeepot, William Hollingshead, Philadelphia, PA, inverted pyriform, domed, hinged lid, gadrooned finial and molding, carved wooden handle with foliate scrolled terminals, cast S-scrolled spout with ruffled cartouche, domed and molded circular foot, engraved foliate script initials "LP" within rococo cartouche, marked three times on base, 33 oz, 10 dwt, 12½" h, 1760–85 . . . . **52,800.00**
Pap Boat
    David, John, Philadelphia, PA, oval, everted brim with engraved border, marked twice on base, 1 oz, 10 dwt, 5" l, c1800 . . . . **825.00**
    Wishart, Hugh, NY, oval, curving spout, marked on base, 2 oz, 5" l, 1793–1824 . . . . **725.00**
Pepper Box
    Cooney, John, Boston, MA, cylindrical, low domed pierced lid, double molded rim, double scrolled and beaded handle, bottom engraved with contemporary initials, marked on side and base, repair to handle joins, 2 oz, 10 dwt, 2½" h, 1700–20 . . . . **9,350.00**
    Palletreau, Elias, Southampton, NY, octagonal, faceted domed pierced lid, baluster finial, S-scrolled handle, contemporary

engraved initials on base, marked on base, 3 oz, 10 dwt, 3⅞" h, c1760 . . . . **13,200.00**

Porringer

Boelen, Henricus, New York, NY, circular bowl, everted rim, pierced handle, marked on base with conjoined "HB" struck over center punch, 7 oz, 10 dwt, 5" d, 7⅝" l, 1661–91   **3,850.00**

Winslow, Edward, Boston, MA, circular, everted brim, pierced keyhole handle engraved "DRW," date "1760" engraved later in bowl, marked near rim, minor repairs to rim and base, 8 oz, 10 dwt, 5" d, 1725–53 . . . .   **1,750.00**

Punch Strainer, Daniel Parker, Boston, MA, circular bowl, decorative piercing, molded rim flanked by two open handles with stylized leafage and terminals, engraved on back, marked on back of handle, 4 oz, 10 dwt, 10⅜" l, 1755–75 . . . .   **6,600.00**

Salver, Chaundrons & Rasch, Philadelphia, PA, molded border, band of cast anthemia centering plain surface, three tapering legs, leaf dec, stippled ground, 11.2 oz, 8" d, early 19th C **600.00**

Sauceboat

Ball, William, Philadelphia, PA, oval, scalloped rim, scroll handle, acanthus grip, three scroll legs, shell dec, scalloped pad feet, marked twice on base, 11 oz, 4⅛" h, 7½" l, c1760 . . . . . .   **9,900.00**

Holland, Litteton, Baltimore, MD, oval, strap handle with bifurcated leaf terminal, oval molded foot, rim and foot with reeded molding, engraved monogram, marked on foot, 7 oz, 5½" h, 6½" l, c1805 . . . .   **3,520.00**

Spectacles, John Owen Jr, Philadelphia, PA, oval lens frame, hinged and sliding temple pieces, marked on one arm, 1 oz, 4⅝" w, 1804–31 . . . .   **550.00**

Sugar Sifter, Charles L Boehme, Baltimore, MD, pierced oval bowl, rounded end handle, engraved script monogram, 2 oz, 7" l, 1799–1812 . . . .   **825.00**

Sugar Urn, Daniel Dupuy, Philadelphia, PA, urn shape, tapering cylindrical lid, urn shaped finial, beaded borders, pierced gallery, flaring cylindrical stem, sq base, four ball feet, engraved foliate

script initials within bright cut reserve flanked by ribbons and wheat, marked twice on base, 10¾" h, 1785–1820 . . . . **10,500.00**

Tea Caddy, Joseph Richardson Jr, Philadelphia, PA, oval, flat hinged lid, urn finial, beaded borders, center keyhole, engraved oval cartouche with script initials, interior with later brass lock, marked on base, 12 oz, 10 dwt, 4¼" h, 5½" w, 1790–1810 . . . . . . **18,700.00**

Teapot

Aiken, George, Baltimore, MD, oval, domed lid, urn shaped finial, S-scrolled spout, borders on lid and body, engraved shield in wreath, script monogram, marked on base, 29 oz, 10 dwt, 6¾" h, 1790–1810 . . .   **1,650.00**

Barnet, Archibald, Baltimore, MD, oval, domed lid, acorn finial, molded shoulder, pierced gallery, straight spout, wood C-scroll handle, applied footrim, engraved script initial "F", marked four times on base, 29 oz, 10 dwt, 6½" h, c1790 . . . . .   **4,500.00**

Tea Service, Joel Sayre, NY, teapot, stand, cov sugar, creamer, and waste bowl, Neoclassical style, canoe form cross section, molded lid and cavetto engraved with bright cut floral bands, monogrammed wreath, 7" h, early 19th C **6,500.00**

Teaspoons, Myer Myers, New York, NY, oval bowl, downturned rounded end handle, midrib on back, front engraved "ICW," each marked "Myers," 2 oz, 4⅞" l, 1760–80, set of 4 . . . .   **3,500.00**

Water Pitcher

Gorham, Providence, RI, baluster, chased medallion, floral and shell design, 33 oz, 10⅛" h, 1848–65 . . . .   **1,000.00**

Richards, Thomas, New York, NY, baluster, squared handle, gadroon moldings at rim, shoulder, and footrim, engraved with later coat of arms, marked on base, 31 oz, 10 dwt, 9¼" h, c1810 . . . .   **3,850.00**

English

Beaker, Houle, Daniel & Charles, London, Victorian, tapered cylindrical, bright cut engraving, floral festoons between stylized foliate bands, gilt liners, 12 oz, 1865, pr   **1,320.00**

Candlestick, Story, J W, and W Elliott, London, Regency, nozzle with egg and dart, palmette moldings, gadrooned drip pan with intermittent shells, conical snuffer, engraved crest with motto, 23 oz, 4" h, 1812–13............. **1,900.00**

Castor, Boardman, Glossop & Co, Ltd, London, Edward VII, vase shape, pierced partly domed cov with baluster finial, rising circular base, three angular handles, two applied leaves, 8¼" h, 1904..... **350.00**

Coffee Set, marked "A E J," Birmingham, George V, after dinner, coffeepot, creamer, and sugar, classical form, olive branch band, hammered texture, maker's marks, 23 oz, 1929–30....... **600.00**

Dessert Basket, Comyns, William, London, Victorian, molded shaped oval, openwork scroll, flowerhead, and rocaille base, pierced sides at intervals below quatrefoils, chased large scrolls, tied ribbon and scrolls at each end, applied scrolls and flowersprays shaped rim, 17.5 oz, 12½" l, 1891............... **600.00**

Dresser Set, Dumenil, Charles, London, Victorian, silver gilt, hammer finish, oval silver cartouche within monogram, 1900, 17 pcs **900.00**

Mirror, Comyns, William, London, George V, oblong shape, openwork chased and engraved frame of flowers, scrolling foliage, and rocaille, worn velvet cov wood back with stand, 22½" l, 1910 ... **1,760.00**

Salver, Stevenson, William, London, Regency, molded circular rim shaped by scrolls with shells at intervals, four scroll feet, interior later chased scrolling foliage, engraved crest, 136 oz, 21½" d, 1815–16................. **5,500.00**

Sauce Tureen, Angell, Joseph, London, George IV, cov, molded oval, applied rocaille and foliate scroll rim, foliate ring handle with cast tied anchor finial, stylized leaf calyx and beaded border, two foliate capped upcurved loop handles, four lion's paw feet with acanthus joints, 35 oz, 9" l, 1835 **1,210.00**

Tankard, Shaw, William II & William Priest, London, George II, cylindrical, applied reeded band, double scroll monogrammed handle, heart shaped terminal, domed cov with openwork thumbpiece, short spreading foot, 25.5 oz, 8" h, 1732.......... **3,200.00**

Tea Set, Wakely & Wheeler, London, George I style, 6¼" h teapot, cream jug, sugar bowl, circular, molded spreading foot, wooden scroll handle, paneled curved spout, wooden button finial, 41 oz, 1946................. **990.00**

Water Pitcher, Atkin Brothers, Sheffield, Edward VII, urn finial over narrow waisted neck, globular body with stylized scroll and paw feet, monogram, handle dent, minor imperfections, 23 troy oz, 9" h, 1907–08............. **275.00**

Plated

Biscuit Box, book form hinged cov, engraved scrolling foliage within matting, applied tied gilt ribbon, molded spine engraved "Biscuits," engraved hinged hatch, gilt pages, interior with hinged pierced gilt grille, four bun feet, 8½" l **600.00**

Candelabra, Elkington & Co, Victorian, fluted campana shaped sockets with applied flowerheads and wave band, crystal pendants hung between three multi–scroll handles to vase shaped stem with Egyptian motifs, two beaded knobs, three winged sphinxes,

Plated, Creamer (6029), Sugar (6039), 6¼ x 9¾" Oval Tray, Inter. Silver Co., Camille, $85.00.

Plated, Mustache Cup and Saucer, trimmed loop handle, James W. Tufts, Boston, $95.00.

openwork palmette apron, three lion's legs with palmette foliage, stepped trefoil base with dentil band, 23½" h, pr............. **1,870.00**

Coffee and Tea Service, coffeepot, 16" h teakettle, stand, and lamp, two handled cov sugar, cream jug, and waste bowl, partly fluted vase shape, foliate scroll supports, elaborate scroll handles, high domed fluted cov with openwork bellflower finials, shaped 30⅜" l oblong tray on four bracket feet, gadroon and rocaille rim, engraved arabesques, conforming handles................. **500.00**

Compote, Derby Silver Co, Derby, CT, circular, fluted brim, applied frog, stem support, circular foot, dish and base with Japanese taste relief dec, 7" d, 5¾" h, late 19th C **200.00**

Flatware, luncheon service, twelve knives, eleven forks, two crumbers, serving knife and fork, engraved blades, ivory handles, English **125.00**

Inkstand, rect, two rect reeded bottle frames, cut glass bottles, cylindrical chamberstick holder, two pen trays, dentilated borders, wooden stand with drawer, plated ball handle, four ball feet, 9" l, c1810 **825.00**

Punch Bowl Set, 15½" d bowl with applied fruit and foliage within strapwork, 24 cups with flaring rims, foliage scroll handles **350.00**

Tea Service, Tufts, James W, Boston, MA, teapot, creamer, cov sugar, flaring square shape, bamboo form handles and spouts, cube finials, sides and cov chased and engraved with Japanese taste birds and ornaments, c1880 .... **650.00**

Tray, shaped oval, broad border applied and engraved with scrolling

Plated, Napkin Ring, 2⅞" h, 3¼" l, $265.00.

foliage, flowerheads, and rocaille, two upturned handles, stamped "Mounts stamped from the Original Boulton & Watt Dies, c1774," 30" l **275.00**

Waiter, Reed & Barton, oval, 26⅜" l **75.00**

Sterling

Ashtray, Unger Brothers, Newark, NJ, figural, Man in the Moon, smoking pipe, Art Nouveau woman's profile and curling smoke, 2 oz, 6⅞" w, 4" deep **800.00**

Bowl, James Wooley, Boston, MA, deep fluted, banded foot, impressed conjoined "JW" and "Sterling," 6 oz, 5½" d, 2½" h, early 20th C **325.00**

Cake Stand, J E Caldwell, Philadelphia, PA, oval, scrolling branch form loop handles, center molded cavetto, repousse continuous band of summer flowers enclosing diapered ground, monogrammed, 43 oz, 15" l, late 19th C, pr..... **1,500.00**

Candlesticks, Gale, Wood & Hughes, NY, shaped circular nozzle with cast applied flowers, scrolls, and shells, baluster shaped standard with acanthus

Plated, Sugar Bowl and Spooner, 10" h, bird finial, 1¼" emb border, mkd "R&R Mfg Co.," $135.00.

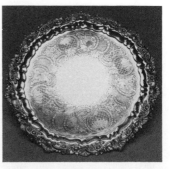

Sterling, Salver, 16" d, George IV, by J. E. Terry & Co. London, 1824, applied molded border of scrolls, flowers, shells, face engraved with like decor, 3 feet, headed with acanthus, $1,700.00.

leaves, scrolls, and flowers, domed shaped hexagonal foot with flowers, scrolls, and gadrooning, foot engraved with family crest, marked on nozzle and foot, 124 oz, 11" h, 1836–45, set of 4 . . . . **30,800.00**

Cigar Box, Tiffany & Co, New York, NY, rect, hinged domed cov, etched cactus and palm, center cast silver finial, sides etched with palm trees, applied cast elephants on four sides, four massive cast silver cactus legs with elephant feet, gilt cov interior, three part mahogany lined case, marked, attributed as presentation piece to Theodore Roosevelt, 13¼" w, 6¾" deep, 9" h **15,400.00**

Coffee Set, William B Durgin Co, Concord, NH, coffeepot with ivory finial, wooden handle, open sugar and creamer, hammered pattern, band of geometric devices, marked with logo and "Sterling," 3 pcs, 24 oz **700.00**

Compote, Dominick & Haff, NY, circular, spreading cylindrical foot, body and foot repousse and chased with flowers and leaves, matte ground, gilt interior, marked, 8 oz, 10 dwt, 7½" d, 6¾" h, c1880 . . . . **3,100.00**

Cup, Howard & Co, NY, baluster body, domed cov, repousse, spiral flutes and scrolling acanthus, scrolled handles, inscription, 77 oz, 16" h, 1899 . . . . **1,800.00**

Decanter, Shreve & Co, San Francisco, CA, hammered globular body, long neck, matching stopper, applied flowers, 11 oz, 8½" h **1,500.00**

Dish

Paval, Phillip Kran, rect rim on round bowl asymmetrically balanced on base, becoming large "C" curve handle attached to bowl rim, applied small strap handle, impressed "Paval Sterling," 5½ oz, 6⅜" l, 3" h **400.00**

Wood & Hughes, NY, oblong, wavy border, one end with sea form handle, etched center fish, repousse and wavy gilt interior, 3 oz, 10 dwt, c1885 . . . . **725.00**

Fruit Bowl, Black, Starr & Frost, NY, shaped and dec everted rim, low foot, 24 oz, 12¾" d **450.00**

Fruit Bowl and Tray, William Waldo Dodge Jr, Asheville, NC, flaring scallop edge on 13¾" d bowl, 14¼" d deep welled round tray, hand hammered and striated tex-

Sterling, Tea Set, 6 piece, Shreve & Co., San Francisco, 317 oz., $4,500.00.

tured dec, impressed logos and "Dodge/Sterling/By/Hand," 86 oz, early 19th C **1,200.00**

Ice Cream Spoons, Gorham, Providence, RI, Florentine pattern, gold washed bowls, monogrammed, 15 oz, 5¼" l, set of 12 **325.00**

Mug, Whiting Mfg Co, cylindrical, sides deeply repousse, chased with putti and scrolling acanthus, acanthus terminals on handles, base inscribed, 8 oz, 4⅛" h, dated 1892 . . . . **1,320.00**

Pitcher, William Wilson, Philadelphia, PA, baluster, curved handle, narrow circular footrim, repousse body, chased underwater scenery including octopus and stingray, 7½" h, c1885 . . . . **4,400.00**

Punch Bowl, Adelphi, NY, cut glass bowl, cut in star and crosshatch design, everted, beaded, and engraved silver rim, 13½" d, 6½" h, c1905 . . . . **1,000.00**

Salad Set, Arthur Stone, Gardner, MA, fork and spoon, engraved and pierced thistle dec, impressed shopmarks and craftsman's initial "B" for Charles W Brown, 7 oz, 9⅜" l, early 20th C **850.00**

Salt and Pepper Shakers, pr, Gorham, Providence, RI, square, trellis patterned sides, applied copper peacocks, butterfly, and foliage, pierced circular cap, Japanese taste, marked, 3 oz, 8⅞" h, c1880 **2,200.00**

Sauce Boat, Kirk, Baltimore, MD, repousse, chased floral dec, 9 oz, 8⅜" l, 1903–07 . . . . **400.00**

Stuffing Spoon, Kidney & Johnson, NY, Medallion pattern, Egyptian head, bright cut detail, 4 oz, 12⅝" h, c1848 . . . . **500.00**

Tray

Porter Blanchard, shallow round form, flared scalloped edge, stamped logo and "Sterling/ Porter Blanchard," 11" d **250.00**

Fisher, Jersey City, NJ, round corner rect, gadroon handles and rim, engraved center inscription, 61½ oz, 23¾" l, 13¾" w, c1930 . . . . **600.00**

Waiter, William Gale & Son, NY, oval, engraved bead molded rim, crest engraved on brim, marked on base, 17 oz, 12" l, 8⅛" w, 1856 **675.00**

Water Pitcher, Davis & Galt, Philadelphia, PA, repousse, overall chased garden flower dec, 21 oz, 7¾" h, late 19th C **650.00**

TIN

History: Beginning in the 1700s many utilitarian household objects were made of tin. Tin is nontoxic, rust resistant, and fairly durable. It can be used for storing food and often was plated to iron to provide strength. Because it was cheap, tinware and tin plated wares were within the price range of most people.

Almost every small town and hamlet had its own tinsmith, tinner, or whitesmith. Tinsmiths used patterns to make items. They cut out the pieces, hammered and shaped them, and soldered the parts. If a piece was to be used with heat, a copper bottom was added because of the low melting point of tin. The Industrial Revolution brought about machine made, mass produced tinware pieces. The handmade era ended by the late 19th century.

In addition to utilitarian tinware, the Country look also focuses on decorated tinware. Decorating sheet iron, tin, and tin–coated sheet iron dates back to the mid-18th century. The Welsh called the practice pontipool; the French, To'le Peinte. In America the center for tin–decorated wares was Berlin, Connecticut.

Several styles of decorating techniques were used—painting, japanning, and stenciling. Designs were created by both professionals and itinerants. English and Oriental motifs strongly influenced both form and design.

There were two periods of revival of handcrafted painted tin—1920–1940 and 1950 to the early 1960s. The easiest way to identify later painted pieces is by color tone and design.

Pennsylvania tinsmiths are noted for their punch work on unpainted tin. Forms include foot warmers, spice boxes, lanterns, and pie safe panels.

Reproduction Craftspersons: Charles Baker Period Reproductions, 6890 N 700 E, Hope, IN 47246; D James Barnette, The Tinner, PO Box 353, Spencer, NC 28159; David Claggett, Artistry in Tin, PO Box 41, Weston, VT 05161; Karen Claggett, Tinsmith, RD 3, Box 330A, Quarryville, PA 17566; Jim DeCurtins, Tin Peddler, 203 E Main St, Troy, OH 45373; Dawson Gillaspy, Tinsmith, Covered Bridge Rd, RD 2, Box 312, Oley, PA 19547; Robert and Anita Horwood, Horwood's Country House, 4037 Gotfredson Rd, Plymouth, MI 48170; Philip B Kelly, Colonial Tinware, 2389 New Holland Pike, Lancaster, PA 17601; Charles Messner, Colonial Lighting and Tinware Reproductions, 316 Franklin St, Denver, PA 17517; David & Marlene Moszak, Americana Today, 321 Wyndale Rd, Rochester, NY 14617; Peter Renzetti, 301 Brinton's Bridge Rd, West Chester, PA 19382; Reda Sypherd, RD 2, Phoenixville, PA 19460; The Tin Man by Gerald Fellers, 2025 Seneca Dr, Troy, OH 45373.

Reproduction Manufacturers: Applecore Creations, PO Box 29696, Columbus, OH 43229; Basye–Bomberger/Fabian House, PO Box 86, W Bowie, MD 20715; Bullfrog Hollow, Keeny Rd, Lyme, CT 06371; Clark Manufacturing Co, 1611 Southwind Dr, Raymore, MO 64083; Conewago Junction, 805 Oxford Rd, New Oxford, PA 17350; Country Accents, RD 2, Box 293, Stockton, NJ 08559; KML Enterprises, RR 1, Box 234L, Berne, IN 46711; Lamb and Lanterns, 902 N Walnut St, Dover, OH 44622; Lt Moses Willard, Inc, 1156 State Rte 50, Milford, OH 45150; Matthews Emporium, 157 N Trade St, PO Box 1038, Matthews, NC 28106; McClanahan Country, 217 Rockwell Rd, Wilmington, NC 18405; Olde Mill House Shoppe, 105 Strasburg Pike, Lancaster, PA 17602; The Tinhorn, 9610 W 190th, Lowell, IN 46356; The Vine and Cupboard, PO Box 309, George Wright Rd, Woolwich, ME 04579.

Basket, 8¼ x 16¼", open lattice weave, red paint traces **100.00**

Candle Box, 13 12", cylindrical **140.00**

Candle Mold
- 3 Tube, 10½" h, ear handle **145.00**
- 4 Tube, 11" h, double ear handles **75.00**
- 6 Tube
  - 4½" h, Miniature **500.00**
  - 10¼" h, Round **185.00**
- 8 Tube
  - 10¾" h, serpentine handle **70.00**
  - 11¼" h, double ear handles **125.00**
- 12 Tube
  - 12" h, round, pie plate base and top, conical finial, ring handle **300.00**
  - 20¾" h, 20" w, rectangular, tin tubes, pine frame, old gray paint **900.00**
- 24 Tube, 11½" h, double ear handles **200.00**
- 36 Tube, 11¾" h, 23½" w, double row **400.00**
- 72 Tube, 11¼" h, rect, missing handles **400.00**

Candle Mold Filler, 18" l, wooden handle **275.00**

Candlestick, 4" d, 3⅜" h, damper, flint, and steel in tinder lighter base, old patina. **350.00**

Fish Pan, oval, 13 x 11⅞ x 2½", $20.00.

Tole, Document Box, 4 x 3 x 4½", dome lid, black ground, white band trim with red flowers and green leaves, $195.00.

Chandelier, 22½" h, two tiers, "S"-curved wire arms, twelve crimped sockets, 19th C **1,300.00**

Coffeepot, 10¼" h, side spout, molded detail, turned handle, cast finial lid **145.00**

Comb Case, 9" h, 9" w, hanging, floral emb, old worn mirror **65.00**

Foot Warmer

8¾" w, 7¾" h, cherry frame, mortised, turned corner posts, punched tin panels **250.00**

9" w, 5⅞" h, wood frame, punched tin panels, concentric circles and hearts pattern, tin coal pan, 18th C **125.00**

Kitchen Display, 19" w, 11½" h, hanging utensils, stenciled dec, red, green, and black **475.00**

Sauce Pan, 3" d, miniature, brass lid, 4" l handle **65.00**

Tea Kettle, 4½" h, wooden knob **85.00**

Miniature coffee pot, 3⅜" h **65.00**

Plate, 7⅞" d, child's, ABC, emb "Who Killed Cock Robin?" **45.00**

Roaster, 27½" l, hemispherical hoppers, long wrought iron handles . . . **175.00**

Sconce

9" h, crimped edges, curved oval reflector, pr **1,400.00**

9½" h, punched diamond pattern backplate, New England, 19th C **475.00**

11½" h, candle, oval mirror backs, pr **190.00**

12" h, mirrored, New England, 19th C, pr **300.00**

13½" h, crimped semicircular top, rolled edges, stamped triple-ridge dec on back, 19th C, pr . . . **350.00**

17" h, cut and stamped leaf crest, painted black, New England, 19th C **950.00**

Spice Box, 9½" l, black, six 2" h cylindrical containers, stenciled labels **35.00**

Toleware

Bowl, 12" d, interior and exterior dec **70.00**

Box

3¾" d, 2¼" h, round, polychrome dec, red japanning **15.00**

6⅜" l, serpentine sides, conforming lid, polychrome and gilt dec, black ground **50.00**

Bread Tray, 7¾ x 12⅝", oval, brown crystalized center, white band, floral dec, dark brown japanning **900.00**

Canister, 6" h, lid, yellow, white, red, green, and black floral dec, brown japanning **300.00**

Coal Bin, 18½" h, rect hinged top, tapering case, trifid feet, marine motifs, Victorian **1,400.00**

Coffeepot

8" h, lid, straight spout, yellow, red, green, and white dec, asphaltum ground, 1800–50 . . . **900.00**

10½" h, dome lid, curved spout, collar base, yellow, red, black, and white floral dec, red ground, 1800–50 . . . . **3,300.00**

Colander, 9" d, 3¾" h, punched star on bottom **35.00**

Deed Box

6½" w, red striping, gold stenciled "Friendship" on lid, green ground **200.00**

7½" l, dome top, yellow striping, simple design on lid, red ground **125.00**

8" h, dome top, gold and black stenciled floral dec, yellow striping, red ground **150.00**

8½" l, emb lid, stenciled floral dec, yellow ground **100.00**

9" l, star dec lid, red ground, yellow, green, black, white, and red floral dec, gilded brass bail handle, paint flaking **500.00**

9¾" w, rect, loop handled dome lid, yellow, red, and white leaf and floral dec, asphaltum ground, 1800–50 . . . . **1,000.00**

Food Warmer, 8¼" h, orig brown japanning, stenciled gilded floral dec, double boiler top, font with whale oil burner **225.00**

Foot Warmer

$5\frac{1}{2}$ x $7\frac{3}{4}$ x $9\frac{1}{4}$", punched circle and heart design, mortised wooden case, turned corner posts. **200.00**

$7\frac{1}{4}$ x $8\frac{1}{2}$ x $5\frac{3}{4}$" h, punched heart design with curved tail, mortised wood frame, turned corner posts, worn red repaint **225.00**

Jack–O–Lantern, $6\frac{1}{2}$" d, yellow and black paint **310.00**

Lamp, $9\frac{3}{4}$" h, black striping, yellow ground, clear pressed font, pewter collar **200.00**

Miniature

Coffee Pot, $2\frac{3}{4}$" h, lid, ear handle, red paint **120.00**

Mug, 2" h, stenciled "My Girl," red ground. **35.00**

Tea Caddy, $2\frac{5}{8}$" h, lid, gold stenciled "Coffee," red paint. . . .   **150.00**

Tub, $3\frac{3}{8}$" d, ring handles, black striping, yellow ground **25.00**

Watering Can, 4" h, green paint   **85.00**

Mug, blue japanning, yellow scrolls and flowers, marked "Daisy" . . .   **50.00**

Painter's Box, 4" h, 13" l, rect, turned wooden handle, "A.F. Tait, Morrisania, N.Y." stenciled on hinged coffered lid, contains painter's palette, dry whisk, and dry paint tubes, 19th C **2,225.00**

Shaker, $2\frac{3}{4}$" h, green, red, and white floral dec, dark brown japanning   **95.00**

Spice Box, 11" l, six separate stencil labeled spice boxes, grater inside cover, gold striping on white ground exterior, bronze and gold interior **65.00**

Sugar Bowl, 4" h, cov, floral dec, dark brown japanning **110.00**

Syrup, 4" h, green, red, and yellow floral dec, asphaltum ground 1800–50. . . . .   **500.00**

Tall Pot, $8\frac{1}{2}$" h, yellow, red, white, and green floral dec, black japanning **1,900.00**

Tole, Milk Can, $8\frac{1}{2}$" h, black ground, stenciled, red and gold floral dec., $150.00.

Tea Caddy

$4\frac{1}{8}$" h

Floral dec, red, yellow, and green, white band, dark brown japanning. **175.00**

Stylized sunburst flower, red, yellow, and white, red ground **625.00**

$5\frac{7}{8}$" h, oval, green, red, and yellow floral dec, asphaltum ground, 1800–50 . . . .   **350.00**

Teapot, $5\frac{1}{2}$" h, orig brown japanning, red and green floral dec . . .   **105.00**

Tray

$8\frac{3}{4}$" l, octagonal, white band, red, green, and yellow floral dec, black ground **205.00**

$12\frac{5}{8}$" l, octagonal, brown crystalized center, white band, red and green apple dec **450.00**

$28\frac{1}{2}$" l, 21" w, rect, polychrome stenciled and painted peacock and swan scene, gilt, orig black paint **225.00**

Torch, $27\frac{1}{2}$" l, wide hooded reflector, horiz font, two burners, bail handle, ferrule for wooden pole, old black repaint, $27\frac{1}{2}$" l **135.00**

PAPER EPHEMERA

Maurice Rickards, author of *Collecting Paper Ephemera*, suggests that ephemera are the "minor transient documents of everyday life," material destined for the wastebasket but never quite making it. This definition is more fitting than traditional dictionary definitions that stress length of time, e.g., "lasting a very short time." A driver's license, which is used for a year or longer, is as much a piece of ephemera as is a ticket to a sporting event or music concert. The transient nature of the object is the key.

Collecting ephemera has a long and distinguished history. Among the English pioneers were John Seldon (1584–1654), Samuel Pepys (1633–1703), and John Bagford (1650–1716). Large American collections can be found at historical societies, libraries, and museums (e.g., Wadsworth Antheneum, Hartford, CT, and Museum of the City of New York) across the country.

When used by collectors, "ephemera" usually means paper objects, e.g., billheads and letterheads, book plates, documents, labels, stocks and bonds, tickets, valentines, etc. However, more and more ephemera collectors are recognizing the transient nature of some three–dimensional material, e.g., advertising tins and pinback buttons. Today's specialized paper shows include dealers selling both two– and three–dimensional material.

References: Anne F. Clapp, *Curatorial Care of Works of Art on Paper*, Nick Lyons Books, 1987; Joseph Raymond LeFontaine, *Turning Paper To Gold*, Betterway Publications, 1988; John Lewis, *Printed Ephemera*, Antique Collectors' Club, 1990; Maurice Rickards, *Collecting Paper Ephemera*, Abbeville Press, 1988; Demaris C. Smith, *Preserving Your Paper Collectibles*, Betterway Publications, 1989.

Periodicals: *The Check Collector*, PO Box 71892, Madison Heights, MI 48071; *PAC (Paper & Advertising Collector)*, PO Box 500, Mt. Joy, PA 17552; *PCM (Paper Collector's Marketplace)*, PO Box 127, Scandinavia, WI 54977.

Collectors' Club: Ephemera Society of America, Inc., PO Box 37, Schoharie, NY 12157.

BAND BOXES

History: Storage was a major problem in nineteenth and early twentieth century rural America. Most homes had limited closet space. Storage space was attics, basements, and sheds. Many bedrooms contained a trunk as well as a chest of drawers. Supplemental storage was provided by boxes, one version of which was the band box.

The name "band box" came from the utilitarian, lightweight pasteboard boxes used in England to store men's neckbands and lacebands. During their period of greatest popularity in America, 1820 to 1850, large band boxes were used to store hats and clothing while smaller boxes held gloves, handkerchiefs, powder, ribbons, and sewing materials.

Most band boxes were covered with highly decorative wallpaper. Floral, marble, and geometric designs were commonplace. The most desirable boxes are those covered with paper picturing an historical theme, e.g., the Erie Canal or a balloon ascent.

Individuals, such as Hannah Davis of East Jaffrey, New Hampshire, made a living as band box makers. A maker's label can double the value of a box. Band boxes also were sold as sets. A matching set commands a premium price.

Although the band box relates more to the early American rather than the Country look, Country collectors and decorators have found that they add a splash of color to several room decors. Before investing in a contemporary example, check the prices and availability of some of the more commonly found nineteenth century paper patterns. In many cases the historic examples will be cheaper and have a great deal more character.

Reproduction Craftspersons: Lindsay E Frost, Band Boxes, Box A, Campbell St, Avella, PA 15312; Virginia Kent, 340 S Russell St, York, PA 17402; Richard & Bess Leaf, Box 223, Rte 5, Jenkins Chapel Rd, Shelbyville, TN 37160; Elizabeth Mondress, 1045 Spring View Dr, Southampton, PA 18966; Eileen Sherrard, 2404 Lagonda Ave, Springfield, OH 45503; Michelle Worthing, Nancy Yeiser, The Band Box, 2173 Woodlawn Circle, Stow, OH 44224.

Reproduction Manufacturers: *General*—Bandboxes, Box AH, Avalla, PA 15312; Checkerberry Hill, 253 Westridge Ave, Daly City, CA 94015; *Kit*—Band Boxes by Irene, 480 Beechnut Dr, Blue Bell, PA 19422.

$10\frac{1}{2}$" l, 15" h, oval, rural country scene design, New England	**375.00**
$11\frac{1}{2}$" l, oblong, poplar, blue, green, and brown floral print on white ground	**115.00**
12" l, $6\frac{5}{8}$" h, oval, pink, green, and white peacocks and floral designs on light blue ground, interior lined with newspaper, c1834	**550.00**
$14\frac{1}{2}$" l, 11" h, squirrel pattern on top, blue, pink, green, and brown floral motif on sides, c1835	**950.00**
$15\frac{1}{2}$" l, oval, cardboard, brown, green, and pale blue deer, trees, and falls on white ground	**85.00**
16" l, oval, cardboard, white, tan,	

brown, black, and blue buildings and trees **500.00**
17" l, oblong, cardboard, white, black, and brown on pale yellow ground, blue band, bird–drawn chariot on lid, camels, drivers, and trees on base **500.00**
17¼" l
Oblong, bent cardboard, green, gray, black, and white harbor scene, eagle, and foliage scrolls   **275.00**
Oval, "Clayton's Ascension" pattern, two cows before castle, green, white, peach, and brown on blue ground, "S.M. Hurlbert's Paste Board Band Box Manufactory No. 25 Court Street, Boston" interior paper label, c1835 . . . . .   **1,430.00**
18½" l, oblong, poplar, faded blue and green floral print on white ground, interior lined with 1832 newspaper, "Band Boxes Manufactured by Hannah Davis, East Jeffrey, N.H." on paper label **300.00**
18¾" l, 12⅛" h, two dogs on top, sides covered with "Walking Beam Side Wheeler" pattern, labeled "Joseph S Tillinghast, Band Box Manufacturer, and Dealer in French and American Paper Hangings, one door west of the Post–Office, Union Street, New Bedford," MA, c1832 . . . .   **950.00**
19" l, bentwood, white, brown, blue, and green buildings and trees **400.00**
19¾" l, oblong, bentwood, purple, orange, olive, black, and yellow geometric floral design on cream colored ground **800.00**
21" l, 13" h, oblong, varnished wallpaper, red, white, and green on blue–green ground, Harvard College, clapboard houses, and stee-

20¼" l, 12¾" h, oblong, cardboard, black, brown, and white canal scenes and "Grand Canal" on teal ground, $700.00.

pled churches, cotton tape reinforced joints, "Joseph S Tillinghast, Band Box Manufacturer, and Dealer in French and American Paper Hangings, one door west of the Post–Office, Union Street, New Bedford" printed label on fitted lid, c1830 . . . .   **3,025.00**
23" l, 21½" h, oblong, blue, green, and white scenes of the French Revolution, interior lines with early 19th C newspaper mentioning NY and PA states, early 19th C **3,080.00**

BOOKS AND OTHER LITERATURE

History: The agrarian community enjoyed a relatively high reading level due in part to their desire to read almanacs, the Bible, and books. Every rural farmstead had a minimum of one bookcase filled with books. The family Bible was given a prominent place in the parlor or sitting room. Children's books were a means of education as well as enjoyment.

Practical books on subjects ranging from accounting to home medicine were prevalent, the latter serving as a reference in cases of emergency. Picture books also were found. The agrarian community did a great deal of traveling with their imaginations.

Most books were ordered through the mail. Literature sets were popular since many publishers sold them on a one–book–a–month basis.

Eighteenth and early 19th century almanacs contain astronomical data, weather forecasts, and agricultural information carefully calculated to the area of publication. They are a combination of things reasoned and things mystic, showing the dualistic nature of early rural America.

As important documents of early printing in the United States, their value increases when they contain woodcuts such as the astrological man, ships, exotic animals (elephants, tigers, etc.), and genre scenes. The Pennsylvania almanacs were among the first to label Washington as "Father" of this country and hence, are eagerly sought by collectors.

By the mid-19th century, almanacs became a compendia of useful information: stage coach routes, court schedules, business listings, humorous stories and jokes, health information, and feature articles. Their emphasis became strongly rural/agricultural. Businesses also began to issue almanacs to help advertise and promote their products.

The Bible, in its many early editions, versions, languages, and translations, is the most popular and widely published book in the world. Recently

Bible collecting has gained wider appreciation with a corresponding increase in prices.

King James Version English Bibles printed after 1800 are common, not eagerly sought, and command modest prices. Fine leather bindings and handsome illustrations add to value. Check for ownership information, family records, and other ephemera concealed within the pages of a Bible. These items may be worth more than the Bible itself.

References: *American Book Prices Current, Volume 96, 1990,* Bancroft–Parkman, Inc., 1991; Editors of Collector Books, *The Old Book Value Guide,* Collector Books, 1990.

Barbara Bader, *American Picture Books From Noah's Ark To The Beast Within,* Macmillan, 1976; E. Lee Baumgarten, *Price List for Children's and Illustrated Books for the Years 1880–1940, Sorted by Artist,* published by author, 1990; E. Lee Baumgarten, *Price List for Children's and Illustrated Books for the Years 1880–1940, Sorted by Author,* published by author, 1990; Margery Fisher, *Who's Who In Children's Books: A Treasury of the Familiar Characters of Childhood,* Holt, Rinehart and Winston, 1975; Virginia Haviland, *Children's Literature, A Guide To Reference Sources,* Library of Congress, 1966, first supplement 1972, second supplement 1977, third supplement 1982; Bettina Hurlimann, *Three Centuries Of Children's Books In Europe,* tr. and ed. by Brian W. Alderson, World, 1968; Cornelia L. Meigs, ed., *A Critical History of Children's Literature, Second Edition,* Macmillan, 1969.

Periodicals: *A. B. Bookman's Weekly,* PO Box AB, Clifton, NJ 07015; *Book Source Monthly,* PO Box 567, Cazenovia, NY 13035; *Martha's KidLit Newsletter,* PO Box 1488, Ames, IA 50010.

Collectors' Clubs: Antiquarian Booksellers Association of America, 50 Rockefeller Plaza, New York, NY 10020; National Book Collectors Society, Suite 349, 65 High Ridge Road, Stamford, CT 06095.

Reproduction Craftsperson: *Handmade Paper—* JoAnne Schiavone, Schiavone Books, 60 Itaska Place, Oceanport, NJ 07757.

Reproduction Manufacturers: *Children's—* Serenity Herbs, Box 42, Monterey Stage, Great Marrington, MA 01230; *General—* Amazon Vinegar & Pickling Works Drygoods, 2218 East 11th St, Davenport, IA 52803; Antiquity Reprints, PO Box 370, Rockville Centre, NY 11571.

Almanacs
   1750, Nathanial Ames, An Astronomical Diary: Or, Almanack. . . Calculated For The Meridian of Boston. . ., Boston, printed by J Draper, 16 pgs **70.00**
   1775, John Anderson's Almanack And Ephemeris. . .Calculated For

Newport, Rhode Island. . ., Newport, printed by Solomon Southwick, 28 pgs **85.00**
1779, Bickerstaff's New England Almanack. . .Referred To The Horizon of 41 Degrees, 35 Minutes, North Latitude and A Meridian of 4 Hours, 30 Minutes West. . ., Norwich, printed by L Trumbull, 22 pgs. **75.00**
1782, Thomas's Massachusetts, Connecticut, Rhode Island, New Hampshire, and Vermont Almanack for. . .1782, woodcut of astrological man, 36 pgs **50.00**
1796, Poor Will's Almanack for. . . 1796, Philadelphia, printed and sold by Joseph Crukshank, woodcut of the astrological man, 40 pgs. **40.00**
1807, The Farmer's Calendar or Utica Almanack for the Western District of the State of New York for. . .1807, Utica, Andrew Beers, printed by Asahel Seward   **28.00**
1818, Robert B Thomas, The Farmer's Almanack **25.00**
1822, David Young, Poor Richard's Almanac. . .New York, printed by S Marks for Daniel D Smith, 36 pgs **25.00**
1926, Dr Kilmer & Co, Binghamton, New York, Swamp–Root, 32 pgs   **12.00**
Bibles
1798, Thompson & Small, Philadelphia, *Bible,* two volumes in one, contemporary calf, 12 x 16" **65.00**
1805, Reading, PA, *Biblia, Das Ist: Die Ganze Gottliche Heilige Schrift. . .Erste Auflage,* Gottlob Jungmann, 8 x 10", 1,235 pgs,

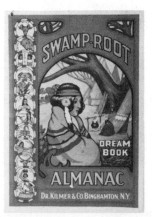

Swamp–Root Almanac, Dr. Kilmer & Co., **Binghamton, NY, 32 pgs, 8 $\frac{1}{4}$ x 5 $\frac{1}{2}$", $10.00.**

contemporary polished calf binding **125.00**

1846, New York, *The Illuminated Bible,* morocco gilt, two engraved titles, 1,600 plates, 8 x10" **250.00**

1850, Philadelphia, *Bible,* woodcut illus, English medical recipe (Pow–Wow) broadside on rear paste down, Petre family record **35.00**

Children's Books

Alcott, Louisa M, *An Old Fashioned Girl,* Clara Burd, illus, Winston, 1928, 1st ed, 342 pgs, dj **30.00**

Appleton, Victor, *Don Sturdy in the Land of Giants,* Grossett & Dunlap, 1930, 244 pgs, dj **6.00**

Bannerman, Helen, *Little Black Sambo,* Violet Lamont, illus, Whitman, 1959, unp **15.00**

Brandeis, Madeline, *Mitz and Fritz of Germany,* Grossett & Dunlap, 1933, 160 pgs **4.00**

Burd, Clara, illus, *Animals on the Farm,* Saalfield, 1836, unp, wraps **28.00**

Burgess, Thornton W, *Blacky the Cow,* Harrison Cady, illus, Grossett & Dunlap, 1922, 206 pgs, dj **8.00**

Carroll, Lewis, *Through the Looking Glass and What Alice Found There,* Boston and NY, 1872, 1st American ed, 50 illus by John Tenniel, orig green cloth **35.00**

Clinton, Althea L, adapted from Anna Sewell, *Black Beauty,* Saalfield Little Big Book, #1057, 1934, Park Sumner, artist, $4\frac{3}{4}$ x $5\frac{1}{4}$ x $\frac{7}{8}$", 160 pgs, hc **15.00**

Cyr, Ellen M, *The Children's Second Reader,* Ginn, 1894, 197 pgs **12.00**

Daniels, Leslie N Jr, *Jack Armstrong And The Ivory Treasure,* Whitman

Big Little Book, #1435, 1937, Henry E Vallely, artist, ss, 432 pgs, hc **30.00**

Elson, William H & William S Gray, *Elson–Gray Basic Readers–Book Two,* Scott, Foresman, 1936, 240 pgs **5.00**

Fassett, James H, *The Beacon First Reader,* Ginn, 1913, 160 pgs . . . **10.00**

Finlay, Edward, *Westward Ho,* John Wayne, Engel–Van Wiseman, Whitman Big Little Book, #18, 1935, Republic Pictures, $4\frac{1}{4}$ x $5\frac{1}{2}$ x $\frac{3}{4}$", 160 pgs, hc **36.00**

Garis, Howard R, *Uncle Wiggily's Airship,* Platt & Munk, 1939, 185 pgs **10.00**

Gruelle, Johnny, *Raggedy Ann's Alphabet Book,* Donohue, 1925, 40 pgs, dj **40.00**

Holling, Holling C, *The Book of Cowboys,* H C & Lucille Holling, illus, Platt & Munk, 1936, 1st ed, 126 pgs, dj **25.00**

Hope, Laura Lee, *Bobbsey Twins at Indian Hollow,* Marie Schubert, illus, Grossett & Dunlap, 1940, 214 pgs **4.00**

James, Will, *Sun Up, Tales of the Cow Camps,* Junior Literary Guild, 1931, 342 pgs **40.00**

Knerr, H H, *Katzenjammer Kids in the Mountains,* Saalfield Little Big Book, #1055, 1934, $7\frac{3}{4}$ x $3\frac{5}{8}$ x $\frac{7}{8}$", 160 pgs **35.00**

Mariana, *Miss Flora McFlimsey and Baby New Year,* Lothrop, Lee & Shepard, 1951, unp, dj. **22.00**

Packer, Eleanor, *Treasure Island,* Whitman Big Little Book, #1141, 1934, MGM Pictures, ms, 160 pgs, hc, softcover spine **35.00**

Petersham, Maud & Miska, *The Story Book of Food,* Winston, 1947, unp **7.00**

Pyle, Katherine, *The Christmas Angel,* Little, Brown, 1900, 1st ed, 136 pgs **40.00**

Thorne–Thomsen, Gudrun, *East O' the Sun and West O' the Moon,* Frederick Richardson, illus, Row, Peterson, 1912, 218 pgs **20.00**

White, Stewart Edward, *Daniel Boone: Wilderness Scout,* James Daugherty, illus, Garden City, 1922, 274 pgs **15.00**

Non–Fiction

Barber, John Warner, *Historical Collections. . .of Every Town in Massachusetts. . .Illustrated by 200 Engravings,* Worcester, 1839, 1st ed, 5 x 7", orig full leather, hand–colored map, scattered foxing . . . **60.00**

Under the Window, **Kate Greenaway, $65.00**

A Treatise on the Horse, Dr. B. J. Kendall Co., Publishing, rev. 1942, 80 pgs, 5⅛ x 7½", $5.00.

Bewick, Thomas, *A General History of Quadrupeds. The Figures Engraved on Wood By...,* Newcastle Upon Tyne, 1824, 8th ed, 526 pgs, 5 x 7", re-backed using orig leather covers **85.00**

Captain Back, *Narrative of the Arctic Land Expedition to the Mouth of the Great Fish River and along the Shores of the Arctic Ocean in the Years 1833, 1834, and 1835,* Philadelphia, 1836, 2nd ed, 456 pgs, 5 x 7", cloth backed boards, paper spine label, folding map, splitting hinges, darkened spine label, some foxing. **35.00**

Carvalho, S N, *Incidents of Travel and Adventure in the Far West with Colonel Fremont's Expedition across the Rocky Mountains: Including Three Months' Residence in Utah, and a Perilous Trip Across the Great American Desert to the Pacific,* NY, 1856, 2nd ed with frontis, 380 pgs, orig cloth. **88.00**

Davison, Gideon M, *Fashionable Tour in 1825. An Excursion to the Springs, Niagara, Quebec and Boston,* Saratoga Springs, 1825, 2nd ed, 169 pgs, 3 x 5", leather-backed marbled boards **38.00**

Eaton, Elon Howard, *Birds of New York,* Albany, 1910 and 1914, 2 vols, 1st ed, 8 x 10", orig green cloth, color plates **145.00**

Gilmor, Colonel Harry, *Four Years in the Saddle,* NY, 1866, 1st ed, 291 pgs, 4 x 6", engraved frontispiece, orig blue cloth with bevelled edges. **220.00**

Harris, A C, *Alaska and the Klondike Gold Fields. . . Routes Traversed by Miners: How to Find Gold: Camp Life at Klondike. Practical Instructions for Fortune Seekers,* pictorial cloth, Chicago, 1897, 556 pgs, illus, full color folded map of Alaska and the Klondike   **200.00**

House, Homer D, *Wild Flowers of New York,* Albany, 1923, 2nd printing, 2 vols, 8 x 10", orig green cloth, color plates **110.00**

Hurd, D Hamilton, comp, *History of New London County, Connecticut, with Biographical Sketches,* Philadelphia, 1882, 768 pgs, 8 x 10", leather-backed gilt-decorated cloth **70.00**

Marshall, John, *Life of George Washington,* Philadelphia, 1804-07, 1st ed, 5 vols, 5 x 7", full tree-calf, gilt spines, red leather spine labels, some foxing **165.00**

Neihardt, John G, *The Song of the Indian Wars,* illus by Allen True, NY, 1925, 1st ed, in publisher's slipcase, orig cloth backed boards, author sgd, limited to 500 numbered copies **45.00**

Oliphant, J. Orin, ed, *On the Arkansas Route to California in 1849. The Journal of Robert B Green of Lewisburg, Pennsylvania,* Bucknell U Press, 1955, 1st ed, orig boards, glassine wrapper   **100.00**

Periam, Jonathan and A H Baker, *American Farmer's Pictorial Cyclopedia of Live Stock... Including. . .Dogs and Feed; Being Also a Complete Stock Doctor,* NY & St Louis, 1888, 1232 pgs, 5 x 7", pictorial cloth, illus, chromo plates, 2 folding charts, back cov slightly warped, both inner hinges cracked, title page loose **55.00**

Pollard, Edward A, *The Lost Cause; A New Southern History of the War of the Confederates,* NY, 1867, 752 pgs, 5 x 7", 6 plates, orig cloth, faded spine, some wear, front blank flyleaf nearly detached, some foxing **935.00**

Roosevelt, Theodore, *Outdoor Pastimes of an American Hunter,* NY, 1905, 1st ed, 5 x 7", pictorial cloth.   **55.00**

Sachse, Julius F, *The German Pietists of Provincial Pennsylvania,* Philadelphia, for the author, 1895-1900, 3 vols, 8 x 10", limited to 500 copies, cloth, library numbers painted on spines **210.00**

Scudder, Horace E, *American Com-*

The Pronouncing Edition of the Holy Bible, A J Holman & Co, Philadelphia, 10 x 12¾", c1900, $35.00.

monwealths, Boston, 1888, 12 vols representing 11 states, cloth, frontis maps, ex–library **250.00**
Sewell, William, *A History of the Rise, Increase and Progress of the Christian People called Quakers intermixed with Several Remarkable Occurences. To Which is Prefixed a Brief Memoir of the Author Compiled From Various Sources,* Baker & Crane, NY, 1844, 1st ed, 2 vols bound as one, 422 pgs and 465 pgs including index, 5 x 7", full calf, black spine label, raised bands **1,350.00**
Tegetmeier, W B, *Pheasants: Their Natural History and Practical Management,* London, 1911, 5th ed, 276 pgs, 5 x 7", cloth, 6 color and 16 black and white plates . . .   **110.00**
Wheeler, Colonel Homer W, *Buffalo Days. Forty Years in the Old West: The Personal Narrative of a Cattleman, Indian Fighter and Army Officer,* Indianapolis, 1925, 1st ed, 18 plates, orig cloth **155.00**
Williams, Joseph, *Narrative of a Tour From the State of Indiana to the Oregon Territory in the Years 1841–2,* Eberstadt, 1921, 95 pgs, orig cloth, limited ed of 250 copies printed **50.00**
Sets
Complete Works of William Shakespeare, intro by Sidney Lee, Harper, NY, 1906–08, 20 vols, 5 x 7", paper labels **30.00**
Little Leather Library, Robert K Haas, NY, c1920, 32 different issues, one from early period, balance in red fabricoid covers **35.00**

Works of Charles Dickens, Collier, NY, 1911, 25 vols, cloth. **38.00**
The Writings of Mark Twain, Harper, NY, 1912, 25 vols, Author's National Edition, cloth . . .   **50.00**

CERTIFICATES

History: Carefully stored in a trunk or bureau drawer were the documents that chronicled the life of a member of the agrarian community— birth certificate, baptismal certificate, diploma, marriage certificate, professional appointments, and rewards of merit. Few were framed to hang on the wall. The major exception was an appointment document.

These certificates record the evolution of American printing. The woodblock certificates of the early nineteenth century were replaced by lithographed examples in the 1870s and 1880s. The presentation was often elaborate.

In addition, many of these certificates are very colorful and decorative. This is the feature that attracts the Country collector. Today these certificates are no longer hidden. They are framed and prominently displayed as major accent pieces.

Reproduction Craftspersons: Sally Green Bunce, 4826 Mays Ave, Reading, PA 19606; Meryl Griffiths, 1101 Gypsy Hill Rd, Lancaster, PA 17602; Joan Kopchik, 1335 Stephen Way, Southampton, PA 18966; Michael S Kreibel, 1756 Breneman Rd, Manheim, PA 17545.

Reproduction Manufacturers: The Evergreen Press, Inc, 3380 Vincent Rd, Pleasant Hill, CA 94523; Harwell Graphics, PO Box 8, Napoleon, IN 47034; Precious Memories, PO Box 313, Califon, NJ 07830.

Baptismal
1830, handcolored and printed, baptismal scene, 6 x 6" square, printed in Leipzig, Germany **10.00**
1925, Aldine May Sittler, PA, printed, pink dogwood flowers,

Birth and Baptism, 1873, 14 x 10", marked "Lith. and Pub. by Currier & Ives, 152 Nassau St. New York," $15.00.

white dove, baptismal font, background shades cream color to blue–green, 11½" w, 16" h, marked "The Abingdon Press, New–York Cincinnati/No. 60" **8.00**

Card of Honor, Diligency—One Hundred tokens of Merit, 1879, printed, mulitcolored chromolithograph front, writing on back, used **15.00**

Certificate of Honor, 60 Merits, 1877, George Jones, printed, red and white, used **20.00**

Confirmation
1877, Samuel W Gerhab, PA, black etching, gold printing, red and gold Bible verses, 8 x 11", tortoiseshell frame **12.00**
1926, Miriam Margaret Schroy, PA, white violets and roses, ribbons, dove, and church in shades of pink, purple, blue, and green, background shades blue–green to cream color, published by Abingdon Press, New York, Cincinnati, No. 80, 11½ x 16", framed **8.00**

Marriage, 1898, E A Strohl to Matilda C Hahn, PA, six vignettes of different stages of married life, Bible verses, multicolored on white ground, marked "No. 105/Published by Ernst Kaufmann, 330 Pearl Street, New York," 12¾" w, 17" l **15.00**

Membership
Association of Descendants of Edward Foulke, Martha Kinsey, 1898, commemorates 200th anniversary of landing of Edward and Eleanor Foulke, multicolored impressed coat of arms, white ground, 8¼ x 7", framed **8.00**
Trinity Reformed Church, 1898, Sarah Ann Fried, PA, hymn verse, decorative border, gold and red

Francis Scott Key Memorial Association certificate, framed, 14½ x 11¾", #43881, 1908, Chas. H. Weisgerber, $25.00.

lettering, published by Daniel Miller, Reading, PA, 8½ x 11½" ... **5.00**

Merit, pen and ink and watercolor on paper, floral border, "Miss Margaret Ann Matthews has been four days at the head of her class. . .July 8, 1829," green, yellow, black, and red, 6¼" h, 5⅜" w **165.00**

Music Award, printed, green, eight portrait vignettes, unused, Theodore Presser Co, Philadelphia **10.00**

Pupils Reading Circle, 1933, moth and butterflies illus, printed, color..... **10.00**

Reward of Merit
1872, "A Testimonial of Approbation," presented to Emma Clark, printed, black and white, 8½ x 10¼", used **12.00**
1893, "Excelsior, Fifty Merits," printed, color, copyright 1876, castle illus, used **8.00**

Stock
American Express Company, five shares, autographs of Henry Wells and William Fargo, 1860 ...... **525.00**
Baltimore and Ohio Railroad Company, Dutch revenue, vignette of a Tom Thumb engine and train, blue, 1914 .... **18.00**
Chicago and South Western Railroad of Iowa and Missouri, 100 shares, vignette of train, Union soldier with flag, and steamboat, green and black, 18-- (last two digits left blank to be inscribed by hand) **65.00**
Highway Bond, State of Arkansas, $10,000, vignette of the State House, green border, 1831..... **12.00**
Lump Gulch Silver Mines Company, eagle illus at top, ornate multicolored border, unissued **20.00**
Montana Phonograph Company, Helena, MT, two antique phonograph vignettes, black border, unissued, 1889 .... **8.00**
Pennsylvania Canal Company, $1,000 bone of 1870, vignette of a canal boat with a train passing over, black on white, blue $1,000 in field, sgd **150.00**
Visitor's, pen and ink calligraphy on laid paper, red and black ink, "To the honoured visitors of the school. . .Ebenezer Gilmans June 6 1786," verse and alphabet, 7¾ x 12¾" **175.00**

MAPS

History: Most agrarian libraries contained copies of world and county atlases. They provided a means of keeping in touch with the world and one's local community. County atlases from the 19th century often contained the names of individual property owners. When county directories arrived upon the scene in the mid-20th century, county atlases disappeared.

Maps provide one of the best ways to study the growth of a country or region. From the 16th to the early 20th centuries, maps were both informative and decorative. Engravers provided ornamental detailing which often took the form of bird's eye views, city maps, and ornate calligraphy and scrolling. Many maps were hand colored to enhance their beauty.

Maps generally were published in plate books. Many of the maps available today result from these books being cut apart and sheets sold separately.

In the last quarter of the 19th century, representatives from firms in Philadelphia, Chicago, and elsewhere traveled the United States preparing county atlases, often with a sheet for each township and a sheet for each major city or town. Although mass produced, they are eagerly sought by collectors. Individual sheets sell for $25 to $75. The atlases themselves can usually be purchased in the $200 to $400 range. Individual sheets should be viewed solely as decorative and not as investment material.

Collectors' Clubs: The Association of Map Memorabilia, 8 Amherst Road, Pelham, MA 01002; The Chicago Map Society, 60 West Walton St, Chicago, IL 60610.

America, engraved, shows California
   as an island, Allard, Amsterdam, 19
   x 23½", 1690–1710 . . . .   **1,000.00**
Atlas
   A New and Improved School Atlas,
      Robinson, Pratt & Co, NY, 1837,
      pictorial, 8 x 10" **40.00**
   A System of Geography for the Use
      of Schools Illustrated with More
      Than Fifty Cerographic Maps, and
      Numerous Wood–cut Engravings,
      Sidney E Morse, Harper, NY,
      1845, Texas shown as indepen-
      dent republic, leather backed pic-
      torial–printed boards, 72 pgs, 8 x
      10" **150.00**
   Mayo's Ancient Geography and His-
      tory, hand–tinted, nine maps,
      "Terra Veteribus, Romanum Im-
      perium, Orientis Tabula, Graecia
      Antique, Italia Antique, Books of
      Moses, Moriah, State of Na-
      tiona," and "Chronological Fall
      of Empires," complete, Philadel-
      phia, 1814 . . . .   **325.00**
   Mitchel's School Atlas, 17 hand–
      colored maps including "Map of
      North America," 1839, showing

Atlas Page, Delaware and Maryland, colored, J H Colton & Co, NY, 18½ x 15¾", 1855, $50.00.

upper California as separate en-
   tity, "Map of the United States,"
   1839, 2–pg map, "Map of the
   Chief Part of the Southern States,"
   1839, 2–pg map, "Map of the
   State of Texas," 1846, "Map of
   Oregon and Upper California,"
   1846, and three other US maps,
   Cowperthwait, Philadelphia,
   1848 . . . .   **22.00**
Official Topographical Atlas of Mas-
   sachusetts from Astronomical,
   Trigonometrical and Various Lo-
   cal Surveys, hand–colored maps,
   orig cloth covers, Stedman,
   Brown & Lyon, 1871, 12 x 16" . .   **20.00**
Chesapeake–Delaware Canal Routes,
   engraving, J Smithers after W
   Thomas Fisher, American Philo-
   sophical Society, Philadelphia, 12⅝
   x 17", 1771. . . . .   **950.00**
Connecticut, c1625, ink and water-
   color, Indian trails, villages, Sach-
   emdoms, The Connecticut Society
   of the Colonial Dames of America,
   sgd and dated "Hayden L Griswold
   C.E./1930," 20 x 25" **165.00**
Florida, chromolithograph, three
   colors, "US Dept of War, Topographical Study of Florida," Washington, DC, 16⅜ x 27½", 1891 . . . . .   **75.00**
Georgia, engraving, "A New And Ac-
   curate Map Of The Province Of
   Georgia In North America," published in *The Universal Magazine,* J
   Hinton, London, 12¾ x 10¾", 1779   **300.00**
Maine, New Hampshire, and Ver-
   mont, colored, A Finley, Philadel-
   phia, 18¾ x 25", 1826 . . . .   **200.00**
Missouri, State of Missouri and Terri-
   tory of Arkansas, colored, A Finley,
   Philadelphia, 18⅞ x 25", 1826 . . . . .   **150.00**
New England, "Map Showing The Pro-
   posed Rail Roads From Boston To

Burlington From Hale's Map of New England," four alternative routes with mileage charts, J H Bufford, Boston, 20 x 25", c1845 . . . .   **50.00**

New England and New York, uncolored, southwest to Chesapeake Bay, Thomas Basset and Richard Chiswell, London, 16½ x 21½", 1676   **650.00**

New York, "West Chester County," Stone and Clark, Ithaca, NY, 18½ x 13", 1839, framed **350.00**

Ohio, "Map of Ohio," engraving, hand colored, John Kilborne, published in Columbus, 31 x 32", 1822, barn siding frame. **650.00**

Pennsylvania, "Map of Carlisle," dowels for hanging at top and bottom, adv in corners, lists of merchants in lower and upper right quadrants, overall browning, 36 x 44", 1867 . . . .   **50.00**

Philadelphia, engraved, street plan, surrounding villages of Germantown, Derby, and Frankfort, and Quaker meetinghouses, Augusburg, Scull, and Heap, 18 x 23½", 1777 . .   **1,150.00**

Texas, "Map Of The State Of Texas From The Latest Authorities," multicolored, inset of Galveston City and Northern Texas, J H Young, published by Thomas, Cowperthwait, Philadelphia, 17 x 14", c1852 . . . .   **150.00**

United States

1819, hand drawn, pen and ink and watercolor on paper, eastern states from Maine to Georgia, west to Louisiana territory, "The United States drawn by Sally BL Ingell, aged 10 yrs, Saunton, August 23, 1819, Private School," 28¼" h, 34¼" w, matted, ogee bird's-eye frame **750.00**

1829, hand drawn, pen and ink and watercolor on paper, "The United States, drawn by Olive W. Bill, Eaton, July 4th 1829," 17½" h, 22¼" w, orig turned rod attached to modern frame **600.00**

1876, hand-colored, "Colton's Map of the United States of America," orig publisher's folding cloth case, NY, 28 x 17" **45.00**

World

1819, watercolor and ink, inscribed "sketched by Hannah P. Gilman under the direction of Miss Lucinda Gridley/Franklin Academy/Dover New Hampshire/1819," spread eagle surmounts views of Eastern and Western hemispheres above inscription, 44" w, 29" h **500.00**

1840, watercolor and ink, inscribed "Charlotte A. Rugg Groton Mass. 1840 aged 12," views of Eastern and Western hemispheres enclosed by colorful floral wreaths, 29½ x 21½", framed. **11,000.00**

PHOTOGRAPHS AND PHOTO ALBUMS

History: Next to the Bible, the most important book a rural family owned was the nucleated family photo album. Filled primarily with individual head and shoulder photographs, it provided a visual chronicle of the family's ancestry.

The chief problem is that most photographs are unidentified. The individual who received them knew who they were. This information was passed orally from generation to generation. Most was lost by the third and fourth generation.

The principal photographs are cartes de visite and cabinet cards. It is also common to find memorial cards and mass-produced photographs of important military and historical figures. Pictures that show a person in a working environment, identifiable building or street scene, or a special holiday, e.g., Christmas, are eagerly sought. Most studio shots have little value.

Many of the albums were ornately decorated in velvet and applied ormolu. Some covers contained celluloid pictures, ranging in theme from a beautiful young woman to the battleship *Maine*. The Victorian decorating craze drew attention to these albums in the late 1980s. Prices have risen significantly over the last several years.

Cartes de visite, or calling card, photographs were patented in France in 1854, flourished from 1857 to 1910, and survived into the 1920s. The most common cartes de visite was a 2¼ x 3¾" head and shoulder portrait printed on albumen paper and mounted on a 2½ x 4" card. Multi-lens cameras were used by the photographer to produce four to eight exposures on a single glass negative plate. A contact print was made from this which would yield four to eight identical photographs on one piece of photographic paper. The photographs would be cut apart and mounted on cards. These cards were put in albums or simply handed out when visiting, similar to today's business cards.

In 1866 the cabinet card was introduced in England and shortly thereafter in the United States. It was produced similar to cartes de visite, but could have utilized several styles of photographic processes. A cabinet card measured 4 x 5" and was mounted on a 4½ x 6½" card. Portraits in cabinet size were more appealing because of the larger facial detail and the fact that images could be retouched. By the 1880s the cabinet card was as popular as the carte de visite and by the 1890s was produced almost exclusively. Cabinet cards flourished until shortly after the turn of the century.

Tintypes, another photographic form, are also utilized in Country decor. Sometimes called ferrotypes, they are positive photographs made on a thin iron plate having a darkened surface.

References: Stuart Bennett, *How To Buy Photographs*, Salem House, 1987; William C. Darrah, *Cartes de Visite in Nineteenth Century Photography*, William C. Darrah, 1981; B. E. C. Howarth–Loomes, *Victorian Photography: An Introduction for Collectors and Connoisseurs*, St. Martin's Press, Inc., 1974; O. Henry Mace, *Collector's Guide To Early Photographs*, Wallace–Homestead, 1990; Lou W. McCulloch, *Card Photographs, A Guide To Their History and Value*, Schiffer Publishing, 1981; Floyd and Marion Rinhart, *American Miniature Case Art*, A. S. Barnes and Co., Inc., 1969.

Collectors' Clubs: American Photographical Historical Society, 520 West 44th Street, New York, NY 10036; Photographic Historical Society of New England, Inc., PO Box 189, West Newton Station, Boston, MA 02165; Western Photographic Collectors Association, PO Box 4294, Whittier, CA 90607.

Periodicals: *Photograph Collector*, 127 East 59th Street, New York, NY 10022; *The Photographic Historian*, Box B, Granby, MA 01033.

Museums: International Museum of Photography, George Eastman House, Rochester, NY; Smithsonian Institution, Washington, D.C.; University of Texas at Austin, Austin, TX.

Reproduction Alert: Excellent reproductions of Lincoln as well as other Civil War era figures on cartes de visite and cabinet cards have been made.

Note: Prices listed are for cards in excellent condition. Cards with soiling, staining, tears, or copy photographs are worth about half the prices listed. The categories on the list are for the most common or collectible types; other collecting categories do exist.

Reproduction Manufacturers: *Albums*—The Roos Collection, PO Box 20668, New York, NY 10025.

Album
10" w, 14" h, emb gold "Album" and floral design on cream colored front cov, orange and dark green floral pattern on crushed velvet back cov, emb brass clasp, gold–edged heavy cardboard pages **65.00**
10½" w, 14½" h, red velvet cov front and back, emb scroll design trim on front cov, emb brass clasp, gold–edged heavy cardboard pgs **55.00**

Cabinet Card, school, J. Notman, Boston, 5½ x 4¼", $3.00.

Booklet, "Logging in Wisconsin & Michigan," Chisolm Bros, Portland, ME, 2 pgs, 12 photos, different views, some lumber camps identified, printed, black and white, 1880s **25.00**
Cabinet Card, black and white
Boy, sitting on tricycle, Kansas **15.00**
Fireman, Chicago, 4¼ x 6½" **12.00**
Girl, standing with bicycle **12.00**
Tom Thumb and Wife, other unidentified man **20.00**
Two Women, holding violins, Springfield, NY **8.00**
Woman, seated, looking at her reflection in mirror, E W Lyon, Maple Rapids, MI **10.00**
Cartes De Visite
All Mine, child surrounded by toys, black and white **15.00**
Beating Grandpa, grandfather playing game with grandson, printed, hand colored, 1860s **8.00**
Christmas Tree, boy and girl carrying tree, printed, hand colored, 1860s **12.00**

Cartes de Visite, child with drum, 4 x 2⅜", $8.00.

His Only Pair, grandmother mending grandson's pants, printed, hand colored, 1860s **5.00**

Kittens at Peace, three kittens, black and white **6.00**

Red Riding Hood, in woods, printed, hand colored, 1860s . . .   **15.00**

Sinking the Alabama, boy urinating on boat, printed, black and white   **20.00**

The Little Barber, girl and cat, printed, hand colored, 1860s . . .   **10.00**

Untitled

Civil War Soldier, seated, black and white **10.00**

Post Mortem, deceased child in mother's arms, black and white   **20.00**

Young Dressmaker, three girls holding dolls, black and white **12.00**

Photograph, black and white

Baby, sitting in goat–drawn cart, $5\frac{1}{2}$ x 8".   **12.00**

Baseball Player, Kalkaska, MI, 6 x 9"   **10.00**

Boat, "Maid of the Mist," Niagara Falls, close–up, $5\frac{1}{2}$ x 6". **15.00**

Barryton Fair, entitled "The Fair at Barryton Mich., Oct. 11th 1909," Lyong photo, horses and buggies, 9 x 12" **40.00**

Charles Lindbergh, standing in front of Spirit of St Louis, close–up, 8 x 10" **20.00**

Christmas Tree, decorated branches, on table, gifts on table and floor, child sitting in rocker, 10 x 12" **25.00**

Fabric Store, interior, photographer Welsh, Cadillac, MI, 10 x 12" . . .   **20.00**

Family Reunion, large family posed

on lawn before large house, 8 x 10" **12.00**

Horse and Buggy, decorated for parade, close–up, 10 x 12". **10.00**

Lumber Camp, marked "Redy's Camp #2," 8 x 10". **25.00**

Lumberjacks, standing on mountain of cut logs, winter view, 7 x 9". . .   **12.00**

Memorial, "The Maine as she Lay in Havana Harbor," statistics on back, 5 x 7" **10.00**

Minstrels, nine men, six with black faces, 8 x $9\frac{3}{4}$". **20.00**

President and Mrs Harding, pr **8.00**

Railroad, marked "Railroad men at new Camp B. Oct., 21st 1909," 27 men posed outside building, 8 x 10" **12.00**

Road Crew, horse–drawn road graders, 7 x 9" **10.00**

School Children, standing in front of school, oak leaves cover bare feet, 8 x $9\frac{1}{2}$" **15.00**

Ship, Great Lakes ship "D.C. Kerr," glued to cardboard, 4 x 6". **8.00**

Steamboat, "The Quincy on Mississippi River," close–up, $5\frac{1}{2}$ x $6\frac{1}{2}$"   **15.00**

Street Car, conductors standing outside, $5\frac{1}{2}$ x $6\frac{1}{2}$" **10.00**

Theater Players, man and woman, Keene, NH, $5\frac{3}{4}$ x $7\frac{3}{4}$" **10.00**

US 4th Cavalry, men, wagon, horses, and tents, 11 x 13" **25.00**

Tintype, black and white

Boy on Tricycle. **10.00**

Girl, doll in doll bed, $2\frac{3}{4}$ x $3\frac{1}{4}$" **10.00**

Outdoor View, house and people, $3\frac{1}{2}$ x 5". **6.00**

Two Black Women **20.00**

Woman, Civil War, wearing fancy dress with stars on blouse, holding striped shield, 5 x 7" **85.00**

POST CARDS

History: America went post card crazy in the first decades of the twentieth century. Sending post cards to friends and relatives became a national pastime. "Postal" exchanges involving sending packs of unused cards were commonplace.

Special albums were developed to store and display post cards. These quickly found their way onto library shelves and parlor tables. A typical album held between 100 and 200 cards. In the past, collectors and dealers stripped the cards from these albums and discarded them. Now they are beginning to realize that there is value in the albums themselves as well as the insight that can be achieved from studying the post card groupings.

Photo Album, emb "Album" and floral dec on celluloid front cover, orange, red, and green velvet back cover, emb brass closure, 8 $\frac{1}{2}$ x 10$\frac{3}{4}$", $60.00.

The golden age of post cards dates from 1898 to 1918. While there are cards that were printed earlier, they are collected for their postal history. Post cards prior to 1898 are called "pioneer" cards.

European publishers, especially in England and Germany, produced the vast majority of cards during the golden age. The major post card publishers are Raphael Tuck (England); Paul Finkenrath of Berlin (PFB–German); and Whitney, Detroit Publishing Co., and John Winsch (United States). However, many American publishers had their stock produced in Europe, hence, "Made in Bavaria" imprints.

Styles changed rapidly, and manufacturers responded to every need. The linen post card which gained popularity in the 1940s was quickly replaced by the chrome cards of the post–1950 period.

The more common the holiday, the larger the city, or the more popular the tourist attraction, the easier it will be to find post cards about these subjects because of the millions of cards that still remain in these categories. The smaller runs of "real" photo post cards are the most desirable of the scenic cards. Photographic cards of families and individuals, unless they show occupations, unusual toys, dolls, or teddy bears, have little value.

Stamps and cancellation marks rarely affect the value of a card. When in doubt, consult a philatelic guide.

Post cards fall into two main categories: view cards and topics. View cards are easiest to sell in their local geographic region. European view cards, while very interesting, are difficult to sell in America.

It must be stressed that age alone does not determine price. A birthday post card from 1918 may sell for only ten cents, while a political campaign card from the 1950s may bring ten dollars. Every collectible is governed by supply and demand.

References: Many of the best books are out–of–print. However, they are available through libraries. Ask your library to utilize the inter–library loan system.

Diane Allmen, *The Official Price Guide to Postcards*, House of Collectibles, 1990; Frederic and Mary Megson, *American Advertising Postcards—Set and Series: 1890–1920*, published by authors, 1985; Dorothy B. Ryan, *Picture Postcards In The United States, 1893–1918*, Clarkson N. Potter, 1982, paperback edition; Jack H. Smith, *Postcard Companion: The Collector's Reference*, Wallace–Homestead Book Company, 1989; Jane Wood, *The Collector's Guide To Post Cards*, L–W Promotions, 1984, 1987 values updated.

Periodicals: *Barr's Postcard News*, 70 S. 6th Street, Lansing, IA 52151; *Postcard Collector*, Joe Jones Publishing, PO Box 337, Iola, WI 54945; *The Postcard Dealer*, PO Box 1765, Manassas, VA 22110.

Special Note: An up–to–date listing of books about and featuring post cards can be obtained from Gotham Book Mart & Gallery, Inc., 41 West 47th Street, New York, NY 10036.

Collectors' Clubs: *Barr's Postcard News* and the *Postcard Collector* publish lists of over fifty regional clubs in the United States and Canada. Two national groups are: Deltiologists of America (PO Box 8, Norwood, PA 19074) and International Postcard Association (Box 66, 1217 F.S.K. Highway, Keymar, MD 21757).

Reproduction Manufacturer: The Evergreen Press, Inc, 3380 Vincent Rd, Pleasant Hill, CA 94523.

Advertising

Allen Nursery Co, roses, printed, color	**6.00**
American Red Cross, Santa and Father Time, printed, red and silver, undivided back, 1901–07	**20.00**
Dinger & Conard Co, Leading Rose Growers of America, West Grove, PA, undivided back, 1901–07	**8.00**
Jack Dempsey's Restaurant, printed, black and white, white border	**10.00**
La Moreaux Nursery Co, seed catalog, printed, color, divided back, 1913	**9.00**
Lasha Bitters, view of lower New York from airship, printed, color, divided back, copyright 1911	**10.00**
Lexington Hotel, comic illus, George McManus, printed, color, white border	**15.00**
Lindsay Gas Lights and Gas Mantels, the Lindsay Girl, printed, color, divided back, 1907–15	**8.00**
Voights Milling Co Flour, uncut, printed, color, includes advertising sheet	**10.00**

Artist Signed

Boileau, Philip, R & N series, divided back, 1907–15	
A Little Devil, #295, printed, color, album marks	**8.00**
Miss Pat, #283	**6.00**
Peggy, printed, color	**12.00**
Clapsaddle, Ellen	
Halloween, mechanical, black child in white robe, pumpkin in arm moves, #1236, emb, divided back, 1907–15	**150.00**
St Patrick's Day, #1249, emb, divided back, 1907–15	**8.00**
Fidler, Alice Luella, Utah State Girl, printed, color, divided back, 1907–15	**12.00**

Artist Signed, A. Thiele, $5.00.

Gassaway, Katherine, "What are little boys...," printed, color, undivided back, 1901–07 . . . . **10.00**

Gibson, Charles Dana, "In Days to Come the Churches will be Fuller," #103, pictorial comedy, printed, black and white, divided back, 1907–15 . . . . **8.00**

Greiner, M, Christmas Bear under mistletoe, #791, emb, divided back, 1907–15 . . . . **8.00**

Kirchner, Raphael
  Girl, looking at butterfly on flower, Tuck Continental series 4025, printed, color, gilt trim, white border, undivided back, 1901–07 . . . . **50.00**
  Woman with insects, printed, color, gilt trim, undivided back, 1901–07 . . . . **45.00**

Leach, B K, San Francisco fire, comic, printed, color, undivided back, copyright 1906 . . . . **10.00**

McClure, "On the Golf Links," rabbits playing golf, printed, black and white, undivided back, 1901–07 . . . . **6.00**

O'Neill, Rose, Santa being lowered by Kewpies, Gibson #86180, printed, color, divided back, 1907–15 . . . . **45.00**

Outcault, R F
  "A Quiet Day in Town," #1, comic souvenir, printed, color, undivided back, P C Co, 1901–07 . . . . **10.00**
  Tige and Bees, "Don't Be Surprised," printed, color, undivided back, J Ottmann Lithograph, 1901–07 . . . . **8.00**

Price, Mary Evans, (M.E.P.), "Christmas Wishes," two stock-

ings, baby on pillow, series 875–C, emb, divided back, 1907–15 **8.00**

Twelvetrees, Charles, black girl, series 658, printed, color, divided back, 1907–15 . . . . **10.00**

Geographical
  Chicago, IL, "Century of Progress Expo," Donnelley, fold-out folder, printed, color, 1933. . . . . **5.00**
  Davenport, IA, "Night View Municipal Stadium," linen, printed, color. **15.00**
  Hot Springs, disaster, "Central Ave. looking South from Goddard Hotel after the fire, Sept. 6, 1913," black and white, divided back, 1907–15. . . . . **12.00**
  New York World's Fair, "The Royal Visitors, King George & Queen Elizabeth," Miller Art Co, linen **6.00**
  Tonapab, NV, The Bottle House, house made out of bottles, E Mitchell, Publisher, printed, black and white, divided back, 1907–15. . . . . **10.00**
  Virginia City, MN, bird's–eye view, Stern Publisher, printed, black and white, divided back, 1907–15 . . . . **6.00**

Holiday
  Christmas, Santa
    Brown Suit, carrying umbrella, snow storm, #254, emb, divided back. **10.00**
    Maroon Suit, walking in snow, emb, divided back **15.00**
    Red Suit, in car, emb, divided back, Winsch, 1913 . . . . **30.00**
  Halloween
    "A Joyful Halloween," three witches riding brooms, man in the moon, emb, divided back, Whitney **15.00**
    "May Halloween bring you a joy like this," boy and girl and jack–o–lanterns, series #188, emb, divided back, Tuck, 1907–15 . . . . **8.00**
    "The Halloween Spirit," cat and witch riding broom and bat in front of full moon, series 80, emb, divided back, 1909 . . . . **10.00**
  Thanksgiving, Indian couple with turkey, emb, dark green border, divided back, Winsch, 1907–15 **20.00**
  Valentine's Day, valentine
    Japanese Girl, with cupid, emb, divided back, Winsch, 1910 **20.00**
    Mushroom, large, one in installment set, #353, emb, divided back, 1907–15 . . . . **15.00**

Novelty
  Blarney Castle, woven silk, W H

Grant & Co, divided back, 1907–
15 . . . .   **6.00**

Copper Harbor, MI, copper, moose,
poem, divided back, 3 x 5¼", 1924   **8.00**

Empire State Building, card opens,
building rises from city, printed,
color, white border, Sherwin Baas
& Co, 1931 . . . .   **12.00**

Farmer, leather, printed, color, undivided back, 1901–07 . . . .   **6.00**

Magic Moving Pictures, pull tab,
man kisses woman, printed, black
and white, divided back, G Fel-
senthal & Co, Chicago, patented
Aug 1906 . . . .   **15.00**

Your Fortune Teller, Oracle, Charles
Gerlach, emb, divided back,
1910. . . . .   **8.00**

Photographic, black and white

Christmas Tree, child and toys, di-
vided back, 1915 . . . .   **20.00**

Colonel W F Cody and his group of
Sioux Indians, divided back, trim-
med on two ends, 1907–15 . . . .   **50.00**

Harvesting Tobacco, Weston, MO,
tobacco drying in field, undivided
back, 1901–07 . . . .   **6.00**

Indians, attacking white men,
staged, divided back, 1907–15   **8.00**

Masqueraders, five people cos-
tumed for Halloween, one with
black face, one woman dressed as
man, divided back, 1907–15 . .   **5.00**

Performing Bears, standing on hind
legs, Main St, divided back,
1907–15. . . . .   **35.00**

Pool Hall, interior, cigars, tables, divided back, 1907–15 . . . .   **25.00**

Surfing, Hawaii, divided back,
1907–15. . . . .   **8.00**

Political

Abraham Lincoln, "Log Cabins to
the White House," 1905, printed,
black and white, undivided back   **8.00**

Republican National Convention,
Chicago, June 7, 1916, no

women, black and white, divided
back **15.00**

Taft and Bryant, presidential election, "May the Best Man Win,"
Taft and Bryant in boxing ring,
Uncle Sam referee, world leaders
behind in stands, printed, color,
divided back, artist sgd, 1908 . . .   **65.00**

Woodrow Wilson, addressing Congress, Max Stein, sepia, divided
back, 1907–15 . . . .   **12.00**

Transportation

Airplane, "Lincoln Beachy, The
World's Greatest Aviator, Souvenir of Oakland–San Francisco
Aviation Meet, Feb 17 to 25,
1912," aeroplane station and aviation field, cancellation on back,
black and white, divided back. . .   **40.00**

Automobile, auto dealer card, 1936
Hudson Super Straight Eight,
printed, color, white border **10.00**

Great Lake Ship, Clarence A Black,
black and white, white border. . .   **10.00**

Lake Paddle Wheel, Mt Washington, on Lake Winnepesucker,
NH, black and white, divided
back, 1907–15 . . . .   **12.00**

Motor Car, "San Diego & La Jolla
Motor Car, San Diego, CA,"
printed, color, divided back **6.00**

Motorcycle, attached sidecar, black
and white, divided back **12.00**

Railroad Depot, Boyne City, Gay-
lord & Alpena Depot, Boyne City,
MI, printed, black and white, di-
vided back, 1907–15 . . . .   **10.00**

Sight–Seeing Car, "Seeing San-
dusky, OH," printed, color, di-
vided back, 1907–15 . . . .   **12.00**

Train, "The Denver Zephyrs,"
Chicago and Denver, schedule,
two–tone, white border **10.00**

PRINTS

History: Every room in a country home had several wall decorations, the vast majority of which
were prints. Several themes dominated—
historic, panoramic, nostalgic, patriotic, and religious. In almost every instance, color was the
key—the more colorful, the better.

Prints were inexpensive, meaning that they
could be changed every few years. Instead of
throwing them out, they went into storage. Most
prints were framed. In today's market, check the
frame. It could be more valuable than the print.

Prints serve many purposes. They can be reproductions of an artist's paintings, drawings, or designs, original art forms, or developed for mass
appeal as opposed to aesthetic statement. Much

**Photographic, Chemical and Hose Co.
No. 2, Johnstown, PA, $10.00.**

of the production of Currier & Ives fits this last category. Currier & Ives concentrated on genre, urban, patriotic, and nostalgic scenes.

References: Frederic A. Conningham and Colin Simkin, *Currier & Ives Prints, Revised Edition*, Crown Publishers, Inc., 1970; Victor J. W. Christie, *Bessie Pease Gutmann: Her Life and Works*, Wallace–Homestead, 1990; William P. Carl and William T. Currier, *Currier's Price Guide to American and European Prints at Auction, First Edition*, Currier Publications, 1989; Peter Falk, *Print Price Index 92: 1990–1991 Auction Season*, Sound View Press, 1991; Denis C. Jackson, *The Price & Identification Guide to J. C. Leyendecker & F. X. Leyendecker*, published by author, 1983; Denis C. Jackson, *The Price and Identification Guide to Maxfield Parrish, Eighth Edition*, published by author, 1992; W. D. & M. J. Keagy and C. G. & J. M. Rhoden, *Those Wonderful Yard–Long Prints and More*, published by authors, 1989; Robert Kipp and Robert Weiland, *Currier's Price Guide to Currier & Ives Prints, First Edition*, Currier Publications, 1989; Craig McClain, *Currier & Ives: An Illustrated Value Guide*, Wallace–Homestead, 1987; Rita C. Mortenson, *R. Atkinson Fox, His Life and Work*, revised, L–W Book Sales, 1991; Ruth M. Pollard, *The Official Price Guide To Collector Prints, 7th Edition*, House Of Collectibles, 1986.

Collectors' Clubs: American Antique Graphics Society, 5185 Windfall Rd, Medina, OH 44256; American Historical Print Collectors Society, Inc., PO Box 1532, Fairfield, CT 06430; Prang–Mark Society, Century House, PO Box 306, Old Irelandville, Watkins Glen, NY 14891.

Periodical: *The Illustrator Collector's News*, PO Box 1958, Sequim, WA 98392.

Reproduction Alert: Reproductions are a problem, especially Currier & Ives prints. Check the dimensions before buying a print.

Reproduction Craftsperson: Rose Brein Finkel, 11 Salem Way, Malvern, Pa 19355.

Reproduction Manufacturers: Adirondack Store and Gallery, 109 Saranac Ave, Lake Placid, NY 12946; The Americana Collection, 29 W 38th St, New York, NY 10018; Basye–Bomberger/Fabian House, PO Box 86, W Bowie, MD 20715; Cate Mandigo Editions, PO Box 221, Hadley, NY 12835; Country Artworks, PO Box 1043, Orem, UT 84057; Country Lady, PO Box 68, 201 E Main St, Larwill, IN 46764; The Fay Gallery, PO Box 749, 2155 Teton Village Rd, Wilson, WY 83014; Mt Nebo Gallery, RR, Box 243B, Grandma Moses Rd, Eagle Bridge, NY 12057; Southern Scribe, 515 E Taylor, Griffin, GA 30223.

Audubon, John James, Canada Otter, hand colored litho, printed by J T Bowen, Philadelphia, 1844, 27 x

Grant Wood, Seed Time and Harvest, artist sgd, dated 1937, $1,900.00.

32", matted and framed, damage to top right corner	200.00
Bartlett, William Henry, View from Mt Holyoke, hand colored litho, 6 x 8"	65.00
Beal, Reynolds, Cape Cod, etching, sgd and dated in pencil lower left "Reynolds Beal/1915," full margins, 7¾ x 9¾", matted and framed	275.00
Birch, William Russell, High Street from the Country Marketplace, Philadelphia–Procession of the Death of George Washington, engraving, 8¼ x 11"	225.00
Bowen, John T, after John Woodhouse Audubon, . . .Missouri Mouse, hand colored litho, typographical inscription below and above image, 1856, 21 x 27¼" sheet, unframed, minor soiling, nicks along edges	150.00
Calder, Alexander, Sun and Moon, hand colored litho, pencil sgd, inscribed "E A," 29¾ x 22"	450.00
Currier and Ives, publisher	
Scene of the Wissahickon/near Philadelphia, hand colored litho, titled in stone lower corner, 8½ x 12½", considerable foxing, framed	175.00
Western Farmer's Home, The, hand colored litho, 13½ x 17½", framed, stains	375.00
Currier, Nathaniel, publisher, American Winter Scenes, Evening, hand colored litho, 21 x 28", 1854, minor water stains along left margin	200.00
Fox, R Atkinson, Poppies	50.00
Gutmann, Bessie Pease, An Anxious Moment, hand colored litho, 18½ x 16", matted and framed	70.00
Havell, Robert Jr, Sharp–tailed Grouse, engraving, hand colored aquatint, 22½ x 34¾", dated 1735 on plate	550.00
Hazen, Bessie Ella, Ship of Fortune, color woodblock on laid tissue, sgd in pencil lower right, titled in pencil on reverse, 4¼ x 3¼" image, framed, tape on reverse upper left margin	125.00

Hyde, Helen, Cherry Blossoms Overhead, etching on paper, monogrammed in plate, laid down, 5 x
$3\frac{7}{8}''$, framed **100.00**
Kellogg, Double Fishing, litho, small
folio **165.00**
Klein, artist sgd, apples, multicolored,
6 x 9″ **15.00**
Norton, Elizabeth, Library Step, Stan-
ford University, color woodblock on
Japan paper, sgd and dated "E.
Norton 1922" in pencil lower right,
monogrammed in block lower right,
annotated "del. sc. et imp" in pencil
lower left, $5\frac{1}{2}$ x $4\frac{1}{2}''$, framed **500.00**
Parrish, Maxfield, "Dies Irae," multi-
colored, matted. **25.00**
Rachkam, "Unconquerable," multi-
colored, matted and framed **20.00**
Richert, Charles H, Manset Fish
Wharf, color woodblock, woven paper, sgd in pencil lower right, titled
in pencil lower left, annotated in
pencil on reverse, $4\frac{7}{8}$ x 7″ image,
framed **450.00**
Rideout, E G & Co, rabbits, multi-
colored, printed by Cadwell Litho-
graph, 5 x 7″ **8.00**
Steinlin, Theophile, Cat, litho, woven
paper, sgd in stone, 10 x 8″, framed,
faint buckling, few minor handling
creases **385.00**
Thayer & Co, Boston, Lithographers,
View of the Grand Mass Washingto-
nian Convention on Boston Common, on the 30th of May, 1844,
hand colored litho on paper, full ty-

**William Henry Bartlett, Harpers Ferry
(From the Potomac Side), hand colored
litho, marked "W. Radclyffe" lower right
corner and "London, Published for the
Proprietors, by Geo. Virtue, 26, Ivy Lane,
1838" along bottom margin, $10\frac{1}{2}$ x 8″,
$85.00.**

pographical inscription below im-
age, $8\frac{1}{2}$ x $13\frac{1}{3}''$ image, period burl
frame, staining and fading **150.00**
Watner, Charles, Return from Harvest-
ing, after Jules Adolphe Breton,
etching, proof on parchment, pencil
sgd by both artists, $16\frac{1}{4}$ x $32\frac{1}{2}''$,
framed **200.00**

SILHOUETTES

History: Silhouettes (shades) are shadow profiles,
produced by hollow cutting, mechanical tracing,
or painting. They were popular in the 18th and
19th centuries.

The name came from Etienne de Silhouette, a
French minister of finance, who tended to be tight
with money and cut shades as a pastime. In America the Peale family was one of the leading silhouette makers. An impressed stamp marked
"PEALE" or "Peale Museum" identifies their
work.

Silhouette portraiture lost popularity with the
introduction of the daguerreotype prior to the
Civil War. In the 1920s and 1930s a brief revival
occurred when tourists to Atlantic City and Paris
had their profiles cut as souvenirs.

Reference: Blume J. Rifken, *Silhouettes in America, 1790–1840, A Collectors' Guide,* Paradigm
Press, 1987.

Reproduction Craftpersons: Susan B Anderson,
SBA Silhouettes, 145 N Laurel St, Hazleton, PA
18201; Ellen Mischo, Profiles, PO Box 412, Leesburg, VA 22075.

Reproduction Manufacturers: Olde Virginea
Floorcloth and Trading Co, PO Box 3305, Ports-
mouth, VA 23707; *Silhouette Patterns*—Mill
Pond Designs, PO Box 390, East Longmeadow,
MA 01028.

Boy
  $4\frac{3}{4}''$ h, $3\frac{3}{4}''$ w, hollow cut, gilded mat
    in leatherized tintype case **125.00**
  $5\frac{1}{8}''$ h, $4\frac{1}{2}''$ w, ink, wearing cap, oval
    paper mat, framed **45.00**
Boy and Girl, $7\frac{7}{8}''$ h, $9\frac{1}{8}''$ w, hollow cut,
  full length, standing facing each
  other, gilt detail, bird's–eye veneer
  ogee frame **725.00**
Children and Lady, set of four, $3\frac{7}{8}''$ h,
  $2\frac{3}{4}''$ w, hollow cut, watercolor highlights, fabric backing, wooden
  frames, 19th C **600.00**
Duck Hunting Scene, 6 x $11\frac{3}{4}''$, cut
  black paper, pin pricked details,
  mounted on white paper, late 19th
  to early 20th C **225.00**
Family Portrait, 12″ h, 19″ w, hollow
  cut, full length, standing, father,

Lady and Gentleman, hollow cut, 4 x 3¼", $200.00.

mother, son, and two daughters, one daughter holding stick, others holding books, gilt wood frame, 19th C 825.00

Gentleman
- 3¾" h, 3¼" w, hollow cut, tintype case 35.00
- 5¼" h, 4½" w, hollow cut, pen and ink detail, attributed to William Chamberlain, framed 300.00
- 5⅝" h, 4¾" w, hollow cut, pencil detail, old gilt frame. 150.00
- 6¼" h, 5" w, ink, black lacquered gilt–trimmed frame 75.00
- 6⅜" h, 5¾" w, hollow cut, full length, gilded frame 250.00
- 7⅝" h, 6¼" w, hollow cut, gilt detail, "Your Oblided (sic) ser't J.W. Reddock," ink inscription, old black frame 55.00
- Reverse Painted, on convex glass, 4" d, eglomise silhouette, black, red, and gold, orig black and gilt frame 200.00

Girl
- 4⅞" h, 4⅛" w, hollow cut, pencil detail, emb battered brass frame, frame backing marked "Aliranda Hansing 1820" 425.00
- 5" h, 4⅝" w, ink and watercolor, wearing blue dress with white collar, gilded brass and ebonized wood frame. 325.00

Man and Woman, pr
- 5¼" h, 4½" w, hollow cut, ink detail, orig emb brass frames 900.00
- 5½" h, 4½" w, ink on paper, sgd "Trott Pinxt," eglomise mat, framed 700.00
- 7" h, 6" w, hollow cut, shadow box frames. 800.00
- 14¼" h, 12¼" w, Edwarts, orig labels "Mr. James Bruce Wallace" and "Mrs. Ths. Wharton, Birmingham, Coventry Road," dated 1838, oval pine frames, pr 350.00

Mother and Daughter, 6½" h, 6" w, painted, sgd "Adolphe," worn printed label "Mons Adolphe, Brighton," daughter identified as "S A Whitmore 1840 at 11 years old," orig frames, pr. 400.00

Reverend and Prayer Book, 9 x 8", free cut, black paper, gold foil, mounted on white paper ground, c1840 . . . . 825.00

Washington, George and Martha, 6¾" h, 5¾" w, rosewood veneer frames, gilded liners, pr 130.00

Woman
- 5¼" h, 4¼" w, old, hollow cut, old black reeded frame 150.00
- 6" h, 5" w, young, hollow cut, primitive, wearing large feathery hat, gilt frame. 200.00
- 8½" h, 6½" w, young, hollow cut, primitive, pencil detail, traces of faded ink inscription, molded frame 415.00
- 12⅜" h, 9½" w, young, hollow cut, holding bouquet, gold highlights, attributed to Hubbard, bird's–eye veneer ogee frame 350.00
- 15" h, 13" w, young, hollow cut, life–size head, old gilt frame. . . . 110.00
- 3⅝" h, 2½" w, young, three–quarter length, hollow cut head, applied printed paper dress, watercolor enhancement, framed, 19th C, pr 910.00
- 11¼" h, 7¾" w, young, ink, stylishly dressed, on paper, gold highlights, labeled "Miss Sophia Moore," framed. 175.00

POTTERY AND PORCELAIN

Rural housewives liked their pottery and porcelain to be decorative, functional, and durable. While the family may own a set of bone china to use on holidays and when special guests visit, their ordinary dinner service was a modestly priced set of American dinnerware.

Use was heavy, breakage inevitable. Replacement pieces had to be readily available. An everyday dinner service lasted between ten and fifteen years before it had to be replaced. When acquiring a new service, the rural housewife wanted the latest pattern.

American dinnerware manufacturers made patterns that appealed strongly to the rural family. Designs were simple and colorful. Bodies and glazes were thick. Fruits and animals often were part of the pattern. Colors were vivid, albeit several patterns stressed pastels and earth tones.

Occasionally sets were assembled through premium offers from a manufacturer, grocery store, or movie theater. The premiums normally provided only place setting pieces. Serving pieces were sold during the premium giveaway period.

Pottery storage vessels were common during the nineteenth century. Redware had to be glazed on the interior to prevent it from leaking. Pottery baking molds were an important kitchen utensil.

Every rural housewife kept a stash of pottery vases. Flower beds and gardens were a source of pride and accomplishment. Products from Roseville and Weller were highly favored. Occasionally an art pottery piece joined the stash.

Among the pottery in a rural homestead were family heirlooms, objects that belonged to grandparents and great grandparents. Most of these were English in origin since "English" pottery was perceived to be more valuable. English softpaste, especially pieces decorated in gaudy patterns, flow blue, historical Staffordshire, and Staffordshire chimney ornaments are a few of the most commonly found forms.

Finally, do not overlook the souvenir china, ranging in form from plates to vases. This category is still surprisingly affordable. Many pieces sell for under $25 despite the fact that they date from the turn of the century.

References: Susan and Al Bagdade, *Warman's English & Continental Pottery & Porcelain, Second Edition,* Wallace–Homestead Book, 1991; Jo Cunningham, *Collector's Encyclopedia of American Dinnerware,* Collector Books, 1982, 1991 value update; Harvey Duke, *The Official Identification and Price Guide to Pottery and Porcelain, Seventh Edition,* House of Collectibles, 1989; Paul Evans, *Art Pottery of the United States,* Feingold & Lewis Publishing Corp., 1987; Lois Lehner, *Lehner's Encyclopedia of US Marks on Pottery, Porcelain & Clay,* Collector Books, 1988.

Periodicals: *The Daze,* Box 57, Otisville, MI 48463; *The New Glaze,* PO Box 4782, Birmingham, AL 35206.

BAUER POTTERY

History: In 1909 John Andrew Bauer established the Bauer Pottery in Los Angeles, California, by relocating workers from the former family owned Paducah Pottery of Paducah, Kentucky. Train carloads of machinery were shipped from the Kentucky factory to the new plant.

Production included utilitarian items and an artware line. At one point Bauer was the only California pottery manufacturing red clay flowerpots, which accounted for half the company's sales. The Bauer family sold their interest before the incorporation of the firm in 1922–1923. The firm was sold to the Batchelder Tile Co around

1933. The plant closed in 1938 and reopened in 1948. The firm closed for the last time in 1962.

Colored dinnerware was introduced in 1930. A line of art pottery, mainly in Art Deco shapes featuring pastel matte glazes or dark high fired glazes, also was produced. The popularity of this dinnerware pattern kept Bauer alive. New patterns were added in the 1940s, including Monterey and La Linda, but they did not surpass the popularity of the original pattern, Ring.

The wares made in the art line were mostly molded and are usually found with molded marks. Other pieces of Bauer pottery have cobalt blue imprinted marks. Many items were not marked, or were simply stamped "Made In USA."

La Linda
   Ball Jug, blue, matte **38.00**

Carafe, chartreuse, glossy, wood
handle **20.00**
Casserole, cov, chartreuse, glossy,
1½ pint, copper frame **25.00**
Chop Plate, 13″ d
  Blue, matte **32.00**
  Turquoise, glossy **30.00**
Creamer, green, matte **10.00**
Cup
  Chartreuse, glossy **10.00**
  Pink, matte **8.00**
Custard, ivory, glossy **8.00**
Dish, 6″ d, gray, glossy **15.00**
Fruit Bowl, 5¼ d, pink, matte **7.00**
Gravy, pink, matte **15.00**
Mixing Bowls, #12 gray, #18 ivory,
  #30 orange, and #36 green,
  glossy, set of four **62.00**
Plate
  6½″ d
    Green, matte **8.00**
    Pink, matte **5.00**
  7½″ d, dark brown, glossy **12.00**
  9½″ d
    Ivory, glossy **10.00**
    Pink, matte **13.00**
Platter, oblong
  10″ l, blue, matte **15.00**
  12″ l, chartreuse, glossy **18.00**
Ramekin, pink, glossy **6.00**
Saucer
  Green, matte **4.50**
  Pink, matte **3.00**
Shaker
  Short, ivory, matte **5.00**
  Tall, turquoise, glossy **5.00**
Soup, 7″ d, olive green, glossy **15.00**
Sugar, green, matte **14.00**
Teapot
  4 Cup, light brown, glossy, Alad-
    din **18.00**
  8 Cup, olive green, glossy, Alad-
    din **35.00**
Tumbler, 8 oz, burgundy, glossy,
  metal handle **20.00**
Vegetable
  8″ l, oval, ivory, matte **20.00**
  9½″ d, round, pink, glossy **25.00**
  10″ l, oval, chartreuse, glossy . . .   **28.00**
Monterey Moderne
Butter Dish, ivory **48.00**
Cake Plate, green, pedestal **80.00**
Candleholder, canary yellow **30.00**
Casserole, cov, 2 quart, chartreuse,
  metal frame, crazed lid **35.00**
Chop Plate, 13″ d, California or-
  ange–red **45.00**
Console Set, 3 pc, Monterey blue   **245.00**
Creamer, midget, turquoise **18.00**
Cup
  Jade green **12.00**
  Olive green **12.00**

Turquoise **15.00**
Fruit Bowl, ftd
  9″ d, ivory **32.00**
  12″ d, canary yellow **55.00**
Gravy
  Burgundy **35.00**
  California orange–red **42.00**
Pitcher, 2 quart, green **42.00**
Plate
  6″ d, Monterey blue **8.00**
  7½″ d, white **15.00**
  9½″ d
    Canary yellow **10.00**
    Turquoise **12.00**
  10½″ d, green **25.00**
Platter, oval
  12″ l, red–brown **30.00**
  17″ l, canary yellow **38.00**
Sauce Boat, turquoise **40.00**
Shaker, California orange–red **10.00**
Soup Plate, 7″ d
  Green **12.00**
  White, crazed **12.00**
Sugar, green **22.00**
Teapot, 6 cup, burgundy **60.00**
Tumbler, 8 oz, ivory **15.00**
Vegetable Bowl
  Oval, divided, Monterey blue . . .   **40.00**
  Round, 9½″ l, oval, canary yellow   **28.00**
Ring
  Ashtray, 2″ l, gray **20.00**
  Baking Dish, cov, 4″ d, orange–red   **25.00**
  Barrel Jug, red–brown **135.00**
  Batter Bowl, orange–red **75.00**
  Butter, ¼ lb, light brown **85.00**
  Candlestick, spool, ivory **42.00**
  Carafe, Chinese yellow, metal han-
    dle **40.00**
  Casserole, 7½″, turquoise, metal
    holder **50.00**
  Cereal Bowl, 4½″ d, light blue **20.00**
  Chop Plate
    12″ d, Chinese yellow **30.00**
    17″ d, orange–red **68.00**
  Coffee Pot, orange–red **40.00**
  Coffee Server, 8 cup, ivory, wood
    handle **50.00**

Mixing Bowls, Ring pattern, nesting, set of four, impressed "Bauer" and 12, 18, 24, and 36, $115.00.

Creamer

Jade green................	**15.00**
Orange–red	**15.00**
Custard, white	**12.00**
Egg Cup, turquoise	**75.00**
Gravy Bowl, chartreuse	**42.00**

Mixing Bowl

#12, olive green	**28.00**
#24, Chinese yellow	**15.00**
#30, black	**35.00**

Pitcher

1½ pint, orange–red	**30.00**
2 quart, ice lip, ivory, metal handle	**85.00**

Plate

6" d

Burgundy................	**12.00**
Chinese yellow	**8.00**

7½" d

Chinese yellow	**15.00**
Dark blue	**18.00**
9" d, orange–red..............	**17.50**
10½" d, light blue..............	**35.00**
Platter, 12" l, oval, orange–red....	**28.00**
Punch Cup, dark blue	**22.00**
Ramekin, 4" d, orange–red	**12.00**
Salt and Pepper Shakers, pr, jade green, low................	**12.00**
Saucer, turquoise	**3.00**
Sherbet, ivory	**35.00**
Soup Plate, 7½" d, olive green	**25.00**
Tea Cup, light blue	**30.00**

Teapot

2 cup, black	**100.00**
6 cup, chartreuse, wood handle	**80.00**

Tumbler

3 oz, Chinese yellow, wood handle	**15.00**
6 oz, gray	**12.00**
12 oz, light blue.............	**22.00**
Vegetable Bowl, oval, divided, burgundy	**62.00**

BENNINGTON AND BENNINGTON–TYPE POTTERY

History: In 1845 Christopher Webber Fenton joined Julius Norton, his brother–in–law, in the manufacture of stoneware pottery in Bennington, Vermont. Fenton sought to expand the company's products and glazes; Norton wanted to concentrate solely on stoneware. In 1847 Fenton broke away and established his own factory.

Fenton introduced the famous Rockingham glaze, developed in England and named after the Marquis of Rockingham, to America. In 1849 he patented a flint enamel glaze, "Fenton's

Enamel," which added flecks, spots, or streaks of color (usually blues, greens, yellows, and oranges) to the brown Rockingham glaze. Forms included candlesticks, coachman bottles, cow creamers, poodles, sugar bowls, and toby pitchers.

Fenton produced the little known scroddled ware, commonly called lava or agate ware. Scroddled ware is composed of different colored clays, mixed with cream colored clay, molded, turned on a potter's wheel, coated with feldspar and flint, and fired. It was not produced in quantity, as there was little demand for it.

Fenton also introduced Parian ware to America. Parian was developed in England in 1842 and known as "Statuary ware." Parian is a translucent porcelain which has no glaze and resembles marble. Bennington made the blue and white variety in the form of vases, cologne bottles, and trinkets.

Five different marks were used, with many variations. Only about twenty percent of the pieces carried any mark; some forms were almost always marked, others never. Marks: (a) 1849 mark (4 variations) for flint enamel and Rockingham; (b) E. Fenton's Works, 1845–1847, on Parian and occasionally on scroddled ware; (c) U. S. Pottery Co., ribbon mark, 1852–1858, on Parian and blue and white porcelain; (d) U. S. Pottery Co., lozenge mark, 1852–1858, on Parian; and (e) U. S. Pottery, oval mark, 1853–1858, mainly on scroddled ware.

The hound handled pitcher is probably the best known Bennington piece. Hound handled pitchers also were made by some 30 potteries in over 55 different variations. Rockingham glaze was used by over 150 potteries in 11 states, mainly the Mid–West, between 1830 and 1900.

References: Richard Carter Barret, *How To Identify Bennington Pottery*, Stephen Greene Press, 1964; Laura Woodside Watkins, *Early New England Potters And Their Wares*, Harvard University Press, 1950.

Museums: Bennington Museum, W Main St, Bennington, VT 05201; Museum of Ceramics at East Liverpool, 400 E 5th Street, East Liverpool, OH 43920.

Bowl, 11⅞" d, flint enamel, impressed 1849 mark	**100.00**
Bust, 5" h, parian, girl with bird on shoulder...................	**50.00**

Candlestick

6¾" h, columnar, yellow–brown, flint enamel, blue glaze	**400.00**
9" h, Rockingham glaze........	**300.00**
Chamber Pot, 9⅛" d, flint enamel, Scalloped Rib pattern.............	**600.00**

Coffee Pot, flint enamel

12" h, Scalloped Rib pattern, crack in base	**650.00**

Bennington, creamer, 4″ h, flint enamel, blue, green, and brown, $125.00.

12¾″ h, olive and mottled amber glaze, fluted finial, 1849–58. . . . **1,700.00**

Commode Set, washbowl and pitcher, 13 x 4⅜″ bowl, 10½″ h pitcher, Diamond pattern, flint enamel, orange, yellow, and green, 1849 mark **950.00**

Creamer, 5½″ h, figural, cow, Rockingham glaze, imp "N" **300.00**

Curtain Tiebacks, 4½″ l, flint enamel, 1849–58, pr **250.00**

Cuspidor
  8½″ d, brown and yellow flint enamel, Diamond pattern **275.00**
  9½″ d, flint enamel, rare 1849 mark **450.00**

Dish, 9¼″ d, flint enamel, marked "Fenton Co," 1849 . . . . **400.00**

Ewer, 7″ h, parian, raised grapevines **150.00**

Figure, 9½″ l, 8¼″ h, poodles, flint enamel, one leg repaired, one half of basket handle missing, pr **5,500.00**

Flask, book type
  'Hermit's Companion," 1849 mark **850.00**
  Untitled, marked "L. F. & Co/Patent" on spine, Lyman Fenton Co circular mark **500.00**

Foot Bath, 19½″ l, flint enamel, brown and cream mottled glaze, blue and amber highlights, Scalloped Rib pattern, crack beside handle **700.00**

Goblet, 4½″ h, Rockingham glaze **275.00**

Jar, 4⅜″ h, 4¼″ d, parian, blue and

white, Acanthus Leaf pattern, lid missing. **70.00**

Nameplate
  7⅞″ l, white, numerals "702" **100.00**
  8″ l, Rockingham glaze **125.00**

Paperweight, 5 x 3 x 2¾″, flint enamel, imp 1849 mark **350.00**

Picture Frame, 8¾ x 9¾″, opening size 3⅜ x 4¼″, oval, Rockingham glaze, old repairs, pr **325.00**

Pie Plate, 8¼″ d, imp 1849 mark **160.00**

Pipkin, 9″ h, flint enamel, lid **2,600.00**

Pitcher
  6¼″ h, brown, scroddled, Alternate Rib pattern, oval U S Pottery mark, age cracks **400.00**
  6¾″ h, Diamond pattern, Rockingham glaze **175.00**
  8¾″ h, white, tulip and sunflower, U S Pottery ribbon mark **1,300.00**
  8⅞″ h, white, cascade pattern, highly glazed, U S Pottery raised lozenge mark. **300.00**
  9″ h, molded hunt scenes and vintage, hound handle, Rockingham glaze, c1850 . . . . **175.00**
  9⅞″ h, parian, Wild Rose pattern . . . **235.00**
  10″ h, parian, Cascade pattern, imp label "United States Pottery Co. Bennington, VT." **150.00**
  10½″ h, flint enamel, octagonal paneled, imp 1849 mark **300.00**

Relish Dish, 10″ l, Rockingham glaze **350.00**

Snuff Jar, 4″, toby hat, Rockingham glaze, Fenton, 1849 mark **400.00**

Soap Dish, 5¼″, flint enamel, olive brown and cream, glazed, green flecks, dated "1849" on bottom . . . **125.00**

Sugar Bowl, 3¾″ h, parian, blue and white, Repeated Oak Leaves pattern, raised grapevine dec lid **125.00**

Syrup Jug, 8½″ h, Spinning Wheel pattern **70.00**

Teapot, flint enamel, Alternate Rib pat-

Bennington-type Cuspidor, 3¾ x 7¼″ d, brown glaze, yellow ground, $75.00.

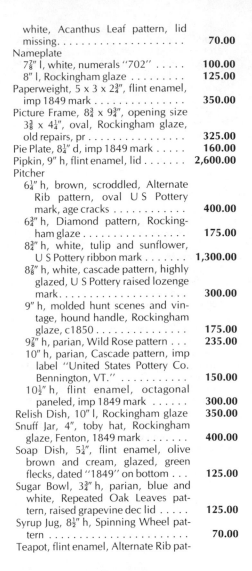

Bennington, pitcher, 9″ h, seated hunter and hounds, Fenton, $175.00.

tern, pierced pouring spout, period
lid **400.00**
Toby Jar, Rockingham glaze, 1849
mark **175.00**
Toby Jug
Coachman, 10⅜" h, Rockingham
glaze, honey colored, 1849 mark **475.00**
General Stark, Rockingham glaze **1,200.00**
Toothbrush Holder, flint enamel, Alter-
nate Rib pattern, lid **500.00**
Vase
7⅞" h, parian, eagle, blue and red
enamel, gilt. **145.00**
9¾" h, tulip, scroddled, variegated
brown clays **1,500.00**

BLUE RIDGE POTTERY

History: Blue Ridge dinnerware was produced by
Southern Potteries of Erwin, Tennessee, from the
late 1930s until 1956. The company used eight
shapes and over 400 different patterns. Reasons
for the company's success included cheap labor,
easily changed and decorated patterns, and the
use of dinnerware as premiums. Many a set of
Blue Ridge china was accumulated by going to
the theater or using a particular brand of gasoline.
Sales of this popular dinnerware were through
Sears and Montgomery Ward in the 1950s.

Blue Ridge Pottery is especially appealing to
the Country decorator and collectors because of
its simple designs. Flowers, roosters, and similar
designs grace the patterns. Bright, cheery colors
predominate.

Southern Potteries products, including the Blue
Ridge patterns, are identified by a variety of
marks, ranging from simple script names to elaborate marks featuring rocky landscapes and trees.

References: Winnie Keillor, *Dishes, What Else?
Blue Ridge of Course!*, privately printed, 1983;
Betty Newbound, *Southern Potteries, Inc. Blue
Ridge Dinnerware, 3rd Edition,* Collector Books,
1989.

Periodical: *National Blue Ridge Newsletter,* 144
Highland Dr, Blountville, TN 37617.

Arlington Apple, Skyline blank
Cup, rope handle **3.00**
Plate, 9½" d **5.00**
Saucer **2.50**
Beaded Apple
Cup **2.00**
Plate, 10½" d **5.00**
Saucer **2.00**
Bluebell Bouquet
Bowl, 9" d, oval **12.00**
Carafe, cov **25.00**
Cup **3.50**

Fruit Bowl **3.00**
Plate
6" d, bread and butter **2.50**
7" d, luncheon **3.50**
9¼" d, dinner **6.00**
Saucer **3.50**
Sugar, no lid **5.00**
Carnival, Candlewick blank
Bowl, 9" d, round **14.00**
Cereal Bowl **8.00**
Creamer **8.00**
Cup and Saucer . . . .' **7.00**
Fruit Bowl, 5¼" d **3.50**
Plate
6" d **3.00**
9½" d, dinner **7.50**
Platter, 13" l **14.00**
Sugar, lid **11.00**
Cherry Bounce, dinner service, 45 pcs **200.00**
Cherry Tree Glen
Bowl
5½" d **5.00**
6¼" d **6.00**
9½" d **12.00**
Creamer **7.00**
Plate
6" d **3.00**
7½" sq **15.00**
9½" d **8.00**
Vegetable Bowl, 9¼" l, oval **15.00**
Cherokee Rose, plate, 8" d **5.00**
Chick, pitcher **50.00**
Chintz
Bonbon **37.00**
Cake Plate, maple leaf **45.00**
Celery **30.00**
Children's Set, complete **250.00**
Cigarette Box, four ashtrays **100.00**
Creamer, pedestal **25.00**
Chrysanthemum
Plate
6" d **2.50**
7" d **5.00**
9½" d **6.00**
Platter, 12" l **12.00**
Colonial
Cake Knife **9.50**
Cake Plate **12.00**

**Creamer and Sugar, Colonial, yellow
flower, $18.00.**

Soup Plate, 8" d, blue and yellow flowers, $8.00.

Cereal Bowl	4.00
Coaster	8.00
Cup	2.00
Demitasse Cup and Saucer	14.00
Fruit Bowl	3.50
Gravy Boat	15.00
Plate	
6" d, bread and butter	4.00
7" d, luncheon	5.00
9¼" d, dinner	9.00
Relish, divided	18.00
Salt and Pepper Shakers, pr	14.00
Saucer	2.00
Vegetable Bowl	10.00
Country Rose, plate, 8" d	5.00
Crab Apple	
Cereal Bowl, 6" d	4.00
Creamer	20.00
Cup	3.00
Plate	
6" d	5.00
8½" d	8.00
9½" d	9.00
Platter, 13½" l, oval	8.00
Saucer	3.00
Sugar	25.00
Vegetable Bowl, oval	10.00
Cumberland	
Cup	2.75
Platter, 13½" l	15.00
Saucer	2.50
Daffodil, plate, 10½" d	12.00
Dazzle, plate, 6" d	3.00
Double Sunday Best, egg cup	25.00
Emalee, demitasse cup and saucer	8.00
Evening Flower, cake plate, 10½" d	14.00
Fantasia, Skyline blank, salt and pepper shakers, pr	10.00
French Peasant	
Cake Tray, maple leaf shape	85.00
Celery	100.00
Ramekin, 5" d, red base	10.00
Salad Bowl	125.00
Salt and Pepper Shakers, pr	150.00
Vase, handle	70.00

Green Briar, Piecrust blank	
Cup	5.00
Gravy Boat	22.00
Green Eyes	
Plate	
6" d	2.50
9½" d	6.00
Sugar, cov	6.50
Hornbeak, bowl, 9½" d	12.00
Ivy Vine #6, bowl, 9" d	10.00
John's Plaid, dinner service, 35 pcs	65.00
Julie, pie baker	25.00
June Bouquet, Colonial black, cereal bowl, tab handle	6.00
Katherine, candy box	110.00
Leaf, celery	24.00
Mardi Gras	
Creamer	2.50
Cup	5.00
Fruit Bowl	4.00
Gravy Boat, underplate	18.00
Plate	
6½" d, bread and butter	1.50
7" d, luncheon	2.50
9½" d, dinner	4.00
Saucer	1.00
Vegetable Bowl, 9" d	8.00
Mirror Image	
Cup and Saucer	6.50
Plate, 6" d	3.00
9½" d	8.00
Modern Tulip, plate, 9½" d	6.00
Mountain Crab Apple	
Cereal Bowl, 6" d	6.00
Creamer	7.00
Cream Soup, 6" d, tab handle	9.00
Platter, 15" l	12.00
Mountain Ivy	
Cup	2.50
Plate	
6" d	2.50
10" d	10.00
Saucer	2.50
Muriel, demitasse cup and saucer	20.00
Petunia, gravy boat	22.00
Pink Daisy, cigarette box, four ashtrays	50.00
Pinke	
Bowl, 5¼" d	4.00
Plate, 9½" d	6.00
Pink Petticoat, creamer	7.00
Plantation Ivy	
Creamer and Sugar	7.00
Cup	2.50
Gravy Boat	14.00
Plate, 6" d	2.50
Saucer	2.00
Poinsettia	
Creamer	7.50
Cup	6.00
Plate	
6¼" d	3.00
9¼" d	8.00

Saucer	1.00	Wild Cherry #3	
Sugar	7.50	Plate	
Tumbler	7.00	6" d	3.50
Quaker Apple		9½" d	7.50
Bowl, 6" d	6.00	Saucer	2.50
Dinner Service, service for four	130.00	Wildflower, creamer	5.00
Platter, 11" l	12.50	Wild Rose, demitasse cup and saucer	12.00
Soup, 8" d, flat	11.00	Wild Strawberry, plate, 8" d	10.00
Red Apple, ashtray	12.00	Yellow Nocturne, Colonial blank	
Ridge Daisy, Colonial blank		Bowl	
Bowl, 6" d	6.00	5¼" d	5.00
Plate		6" d	3.50
6" d	2.00	Creamer and Sugar	18.00
9½" d	8.00	Cup and Saucer	4.50
Rose Marie, sugar, pedestal	25.00	Demitasse Cup and Saucer	22.00
Rustic Plaid		Dinner Service, for eight	150.00
Casserole, open	10.00	Gravy	20.00
Creamer	6.00	Plate	
Cup	2.50	6¼" d, bread and butter	3.00
Dinner Service, includes salt and pepper shakers, butter, creamer and sugar, gravy, and serving platters, 69 pcs	145.00	6½" sq	3.50
		8" d	7.00
		9½" d, dinner	8.00
Pepper Shaker	8.00	Platter, 11½" l, oval	12.00
Saucer	2.00	Vegetable Bowl, 9½" d	9.00
Shadow Fruit			
Cup	5.00		
Plate, 7" d	4.50		

CHALKWARE

History: William Hutchinson, an Englishman, invented chalkware in 1848. It was a substance used by sculptors to imitate marble. It was also used to harden plaster of Paris, creating a confusion between the two products.

Chalkware often was used to copy many of the popular Staffordshire items of the 1820 to 1870 period. It was cheap, gayly decorated, and sold by vendors. The Pennsylvania German "folk art" pieces are from this period.

Carnivals, circuses, fairs, and amusement parks awarded chalkware pieces as prizes during the late 19th and early 20th centuries. They were often poorly made and gaudy. Don't confuse them with the earlier pieces. Prices for these chalkware items range from ten to fifty dollars.

Reference: Thomas G. Morris, *Carnival Chalk Prize*, Prize Publishers, 1985.

Reproduction Manufacturers: *General*—Basye–Bomberger/Fabian House, PO Box 86, W Bowie, MD 20715; *Santas*—The Painted Pony, 8392 West M–72, Traverse City, MI 49684; Vaillancourt Folk Art, PO Box 582, Millbury, MA 01527.

Stanhome Ivy		
Bowl, 5¼" d	4.00	
Cup	5.00	
Dinner Service, 69 pcs	150.00	
Plate, 6" d	2.50	
Strawberry Sundae, Colonial blank, vegetable bowl, round	6.00	
Sun Bouquet, plate		
6" d	3.00	
9½" d	8.00	
Sunfire, dinner service, 42 pcs	200.00	
Sungold #2, bowl, 5¼" d	4.00	
Symphony, plate, 9½" d	6.00	
Tulip, saucer	2.50	
Whirligig		
Fruit Bowl, 5¼" d	2.00	
Saucer	2.00	

Bird, 6" h, on plinth, polychrome paint	205.00
Cat, polychrome paint	
4" h, reclining, oval pillow base, mouse in mouth	375.00
5⅜" h, seated	425.00
6" h, nodder, red and black	325.00
9½" h, seated, polychrome paint	1,250.00
10¼" h, pipe in mouth	235.00

Vegetable Dish, Dogwood, 9¼ x 7", yellow and brown, $10.00.

Church, $9\frac{1}{2}$ x 18", molded, white, decorative pierced pattern, colored glass insert window, PA, 19th C . . .   **1,050.00**
Compote, 9" h, fruit, polychrome paint, pr
  Basket shaped compote **550.00**
  Urn shaped compote **850.00**
Deer, 10" h, antlered, reclining, orig polychrome paint, glued repair to one antler, pr **500.00**
Dog, polychrome paint
  $5\frac{1}{2}$" h, seated, black, yellow, and red   **150.00**
  $6\frac{7}{8}$" h, standing, red and black **165.00**
  $7\frac{3}{4}$" h, standing, red, black, and green **100.00**
  $8\frac{3}{8}$" h, seated, red and black on smoked yellow varnish **100.00**
Dove, 11" h, polychrome paint
  Bank **350.00**
  Standing on base, pr **750.00**
Garniture, polychrome paint
  $7\frac{3}{4}$" h, fruit basket, pair of lovebirds, yellow, red, and black **400.00**
  $12\frac{1}{2}$" h, fruit and foliage, name and "1857" date incised inscription on back **2,600.00**
Horse, $10\frac{3}{8}$" h, brown and green polychrome paint **900.00**
Horse and Rider, $6\frac{7}{8}$" h, red, black, and blue–green polychrome paint **450.00**
Horse Head, plaque, 9" h, $9\frac{1}{2}$" w, orig polychrome paint **100.00**
Lamb, $4\frac{1}{8}$" h, reclining, polychrome paint, old repair on one ear **155.00**
Lovebirds, 5" h, kissing, polychrome paint **300.00**
Old Woman, $9\frac{1}{2}$" h, holding parasol, orig polychrome paint **225.00**
Parrot, polychrome paint
  $7\frac{3}{4}$" h, ball base, yellow, green, and black, emb feather detail **270.00**
  $8\frac{1}{4}$" h, standing on plinth. **250.00**
Rabbit, polychrome paint
  $5\frac{1}{4}$" h, sitting, green, red, and black, pinpoint hole in one ear **425.00**

Chalkware ewe and lamb, 4 x $7\frac{1}{4}$ x $8\frac{5}{8}$", $300.00.

$5\frac{3}{4}$" l, nodder, reclining, black and red, neck chip **950.00**
Rooster, polychrome paint
  $5\frac{1}{4}$" h, yellow, black, and red, worn   **675.00**
  $6\frac{5}{8}$" h, red, black, and green on deep yellow **550.00**
Squirrel, polychrome paint
  $6\frac{1}{4}$" h **300.00**
  7" h, holding nut, white, yellow, red, black, and brown **285.00**
Stag
  $5\frac{3}{8}$", reclining, black stripes on olive amber, red and black features, oblong base **300.00**
  6 x $9\frac{1}{2}$", polychrome paint and smoke dec, PA, c1850 . . . .   **400.00**
Watch Hutch
  $11\frac{1}{2}$" h, architectural, arch over two pillars, cherub, polychrome paint   **200.00**
  $13\frac{3}{4}$" h, $8\frac{1}{4}$" w, figural, woman, blue shawl, spotted dress, red apron, carved leaves on bottom, glass enclosure **550.00**
Young Girl, 11" h, bust, pedestal base, polychrome paint, old touch up . . .   **200.00**

CHILDREN'S FEEDING DISHES

History: Unlike toy dishes meant for play, children's feeding dishes are the items actually used in the feeding of a child. Their colorful designs of animals, nursery rhymes, and children's activities are meant to appeal to the child and make meal times fun. Many plates have a unit to hold hot water, thus keeping the food warm.

Although glass and porcelain examples from the late 19th and early 20th centuries are most popular, collectors are beginning to seek some of the plastic examples from the 1920s to 1940s, especially those with Disney and other character designs on them.

References: Doris Lechler, *Children's Glass Dishes, China and Furniture*, Collector Books, 1983 values updated 1991; Doris Lechler, *Children's Glass Dishes, China, Furniture, Volume II*, Collector Books, 1986; Lorraine May Punchard, *Child's Play*, published by author, 1982; Margaret & Kenn Whitmyer, *Children's Dishes*, Collector Books, 1984.

Collectors' Club: Children's Things Collectors Society, *CTCS Newsletter*, Linda Martin, PO Box 983, Durant, IA 52747.

Bowl, $8\frac{1}{2}$" d, ABC, multicolored transfer, doctor examining little girl, gold alphabet, scalloped edge **70.00**
Chamber Pot
  $5\frac{1}{2}$" d, medium blue transfer, Athens, H H & M **150.00**

$8\frac{3}{4}''$ d, multicolored transfer, garden scene, gilt trim, white ground, Royal Staffordshire Pottery Dickinsen Ltd, England **60.00**

Creamer, $3\frac{1}{4}''$ h, blue spatterware, green, black, and red Fort pattern   **1,450.00**

Cup, spatterware

Peafowl pattern, red, blue, green, and black peafowl, blue–green spatter. **95.00**

Tree, black and green, purple spatter   **125.00**

Cup and Saucer

Spatterware

Fort pattern, blue spatter, green, black, and red fort, handleless   **350.00**

Peafowl pattern, blue, red, and green spatter, red, yellow, and blue peafowl **100.00**

Transfer, multicolored, children marching with infant, "One Foot Up and One Foot Down, That's the Way to London Town," Germany **75.00**

Dinner Service, transfer, partial

15 pcs, blue, "Humphrey's Clock," Ridgway **395.00**

22 pcs, purple, floral design, Morley, c1860. . . . .   **550.00**

26 pcs, black leaves and vines pattern, pink, green, and yellow accents, pink rims, Dimmock, c1860. . . . .   **550.00**

36 pcs, green, Maidenhair Fern, white ground **275.00**

38 pcs, black Gooseberry pattern, includes tureens with underplates, sauce boats, platters, plates, and soup plates, incomplete **400.00**

Feeding Dish, $7\frac{1}{2}''$ d, blue transfer, five children at fence, green "BABY'S DISH" on green rim, Royal Doulton   **85.00**

Mug

$2\frac{1}{8}''$ h, creamware, black transfer, two girls and "A Present for my dear Girl," red border. **247.00**

$2\frac{1}{4}''$ h, blue–gray transfer, "Boys at Play" **60.00**

$2\frac{3}{8}''$ h, transfer

Black, ABC, G for goose, H for horse, red and green accents, 19th C **175.00**

Red, child with lion, "PEACEABLE KINGDOM" and biblical saying **100.00**

$2\frac{1}{2}''$ h

Ironstone, Tea Leaf, England **250.00**

Transfer

Blue, maxim, "None are wise or safe but they who are honest," c1840 . . . .   **137.00**

Brown, two children, cat, and dog **33.00**

Red, ABC, N and n, nest of eggs, c1840 . . . .   **165.00**

Rust, boy riding a dog, "He who rides may fall," pink luster border **132.00**

$2\frac{5}{8}''$ h

Decal, multicolored, Humpty Dumpty on wall, gold "Humpty Dumpty Sat on a Wall, Humpty Dumpty Had a Great Fall". **42.00**

Transfer, black, maxim, "Keep thy shop. . .," two Franklin Maxims **121.00**

$2\frac{3}{4}''$ h, transfer

Black, girl and puppy, "Playing With Pompey," red, yellow, and green enamel accents **120.00**

Red, ABC, P and p for pigeon, H and h for horse **145.00**

3" h, transfer

Black, floral pattern, polychrome enamel accents, Staffordshire   **55.00**

Green, "Poultry Feeding," c1840   **135.00**

Iron–red, ABC, printed alphabet, three scenes of children at play   **125.00**

Plate

4" d, Blue Willow **8.00**

$4\frac{1}{2}''$ d, multicolored transfer, ABC, farmer, cow, and sheep illus, raised alphabet border, J & G Meakin **150.00**

$4\frac{3}{4}''$ d, brown transfer, "Hey Diddle Diddle" nursery rhyme, Hanley, Great Britain **30.00**

$4\frac{7}{8}''$ d, ironstone, Columbia shape, Joseph Goodwin, Ironstone China, 1855 . . . .   **28.00**

5" d, red, blue, green, and yellow transfer, ABC, Harvest Home, raised alphabet border **50.00**

$5\frac{1}{8}''$ d, black transfer, ABC, boy sailing boat on pond, mother and farmhouse in background, polychrome accents, raised alphabet border. **135.00**

$5\frac{1}{4}''$ d, black transfer, ABC, sheep and cow, "Everybody Bids. . ."

Tea Set, spatterware, Peafowl, PA, $1,550.00.

around scene, polychrome accents, raised alphabet border, red line rim . . . **85.00**

$5\frac{3}{8}$" d, multicolored transfer, maxim, "Constant Dropping Wears Away Stones" and "Little Strokes Fall Great Oaks," raised floral border **145.00**

$5\frac{1}{2}$" d, brown transfer, ABC, "Old Mother Hubbard," with dog at cupboard, polychrome accents, printed alphabet border . . . **145.00**

6" d, blue transfer, ABC, boys playing banjo, blue transfer, raised alphabet border . . . **45.00**

$6\frac{1}{8}$" d, black transfer, ABC, zebra, polychrome enamels, raised alphabet border "Powell and Bishop" mark, stains . . . **94.00**

$6\frac{3}{16}$" d, multicolored transfer, ABC, boy and two girls fishing, "The First Nibble," raised alphabet border . . . **135.00**

$6\frac{3}{8}$" d, blue transfer, ABC, Miss Muffet, printed alphabet . . . **75.00**

$6\frac{1}{2}$" d, black transfer, ABC, three children playing leapfrog, polychrome accents, raised alphabet border . . . **145.00**

$6\frac{9}{16}$" d, green transfer, ABC, two men working at hearth, raised alphabet border on stippled ground . . . **175.00**

$6\frac{5}{8}$" d, brown transfer, knight on horseback, polychrome enamel accents, emb daisy rim, Staffordshire . . . **25.00**

$6\frac{3}{4}$" d, brown transfer, ABC, seated bulldog, "My face is my forturne," raised alphabet border **125.00**

$6\frac{7}{8}$" d, pink transfer, ABC, boy and girl on brick wall, raised alphabet border, Staffordshire, England . . . **95.00**

7" d, transfer

Dark Red, ABC, boys playing cricket, raised alphabet border **55.00**

Green, Franklin's Maxim, "Want of Care Does Us More Damage than Want of Knowledge," raised animal border, green rim **150.00**

$7\frac{1}{16}$" d, blue, brown, red, green, and black transfer, ABC, girl sitting on mother's knee, "Mother & Daughter Dear to Each With a Love Surpassing Speech," raised alphabet border, Ellsmore & Forster . . . **195.00**

$7\frac{1}{8}$" d, black and white transfer, Franklin's Proverbs, "Make Hay While the Sun Shines," raised floral and leaf border . . . **185.00**

$7\frac{3}{16}$" d, multicolored transfer, ABC, children drawing caricature of seated soldier, raised alphabet border . . . **145.00**

$7\frac{1}{4}$" d, pink transfer, ABC, Punch and Judy, raised alphabet border . . . **185.00**

$7\frac{5}{16}$" d, blue transfer, ABC, bird and flowers, polychrome accents, raised and printed alphabet border . . . **145.00**

$7\frac{3}{8}$" d, multicolored transfer, ABC, boys playing baseball, raised alphabet border . . . **42.00**

$7\frac{1}{2}$" d, blue transfer, ABC, man and boy on donkey, blue transfer, raised alphabet border, C A & Sons, England . . . **125.00**

$7\frac{5}{8}$" d, pink transfer, ABC, clock face with Roman numerals, months and days around border, printed alphabet border . . . **100.00**

8" d, red, brown, green, and blue transfer, ABC, Brighton Beach Bathing Pavilion, raised alphabet border . . . **95.00**

$8\frac{1}{4}$" d, brown transfer, ABC, Crusoe and his pets, yellow, blue, and green accents, printed alphabet border . . . **70.00**

$8\frac{1}{2}$" d, black transfer, maxim, "They Took It Away to the end of the Field," raised wreath border . . . **145.00**

$8\frac{5}{8}$" d, brown transfer, ABC, man falling in river, polychrome enamel accents, Staffordshire . . . **85.00**

Platter, $15\frac{1}{2}$" d, brown transfer, "Fox and Sick Lion" Aesop's Fable, Copeland and Garrett, 1833 . . . **85.00**

Saucer, spatterware, red, green, yellow ochre, and black Peafowl pattern, blue spatter

$4\frac{1}{2}$" d . . . **75.00**

$5\frac{1}{2}$" d . . . **100.00**

Sugar

$3\frac{3}{4}$" h, Gaudy Staffordshire, black stripe, red, green, and blue floral band . . . **75.00**

4" h, spatterware, green, black, and red Fort pattern, blue spatter . . . **625.00**

$4\frac{7}{8}$" h, spatterware, paneled, blue, green, red, and black Peafowl pattern, blue spatter . . . **450.00**

Teapot, $4\frac{3}{8}$" h, spatterware, green, black, and red Fort pattern, blue spatter . . . **1,050.00**

Tea Service

Ironstone

Chelsea type, 5" h teapot, $3\frac{3}{4}$" h sugar, $2\frac{5}{8}$" h creamer, 3" d waste bowl, six $4\frac{7}{8}$" d plates, four 2" h handled cups, three $4\frac{1}{2}$" d saucers, sprays of lavender violets, gold luster trim, 1880s . . . **185.00**

Floral pattern transfers, teapot, creamer, sugar, six 5" d plates, six cups, and five saucers . . . **200.00**

Vegetable Tureen, cov, 8½" l, "This is the Cow" and "This is the Cat" decals, white ground, England, $32.00.

Tracery type, 4½" h teapot, sugar bowl, creamer, and four cups and saucers, bulbous body style, emb scallops, 1890s. . . .	**195.00**
Spatterware	
Brown, stick spatter, teapot, creamer, cov sugar, waste bowl, six plates, and six cups and saucers, brown bands, white ground, England	**485.00**
Brown and White, teapot, creamer, sugar, and five cups and saucers, Staffordshire	**260.00**
Staffordshire, Sprig pattern, teapot, creamer, sugar, and six cups and saucers, imp "Davenport" mark	**400.00**
Transfer	
Blue, 4¾" h teapot, creamer, cov sugar, waste bowl, 5" d plate, and five cups and saucers, Stag	**325.00**
Pink, teapot, creamer, sugar, and cup and saucer, Stag	**90.00**
Red	
Oriental pattern, 2⅞" h teapot, creamer, sugar, and two cups and saucers, polychrome enamel accents, purple luster trim, Staffordshire	**275.00**
Star pattern, 4¼" h teapot, sugar bowl, and two cups and saucers, Staffordshire	**170.00**
Tea Set, Blue Willow, teapot, creamer, and sugar	**30.00**

COORS POTTERY
COORS ROSEBUD U.S.A.

History: Coors Pottery was manufactured in Golden, Colorado. Adolph Coors founded both the Coors Porcelain Company and the Coors Brewing Company. By 1914, the war and Prohibition caused the Coors family to concentrate on pottery production. A close alliance with the Herold China and Pottery Company was established. In 1920, the Herold Company became part of the Coors Porcelain Company. The demand for good-quality American-made pottery

continued after the war. Coors eagerly tried to fill the need.

Coors produced high gloss, brightly colored dinnerware several years before Fiesta became the rage. Dinnerware lines contained standard table settings as well as casseroles, teapots, coffeepots, waffle sets, and other essentials for the homemakers of the 1930s and 1940s. Rosebud is the most widely collected Coors pattern.

Government orders caused the factory to discontinue dinnerware production during World War II. Expansion of other lines caused large quantities of dinnerware to be given to major customers who often used it as premiums. After World War II, a variety of wares, including ovenware, teapots, beer mugs, ashtrays, and vases were made. By the 1980s, all tableware and ovenware lines had been discontinued.

Coors' glazes and colors were industry leaders. Because of this, many companies hired Coors for commemorative pieces. Limited edition items served as employee gifts or giveaways. These are eagerly sought by collectors.

The Coors Porcelain Company continues, but no longer produces the vibrant dinnerware known to Country collectors.

Reference: Robert H. Schneider, *Coors Rosebud Pottery*, Busche–Waugh–Henry Publications, 1984.

Periodical: *Coors Pottery Newsletter*, Robert Schneider, 3808 Carr Pl N, Seattle, WA 98103-8126.

Rosebud	
Baking Pan, 12¼ x 8¼ x 2¼".	**20.00**
Bean Pot, cov, yellow	**18.00**
Cake Knife, 10" l, maroon, yellow rosebud, three green leaves	**20.00**
Cake Plate, yellow.	**18.00**
Casserole, cov, 3½ pint, green	**35.00**
Cereal Bowl, 6" d, yellow	**10.00**
Cookie Jar, cov, yellow	**25.00**
Cream Soup, 4" d, blue	**12.00**
Cup and Saucer, green.	**7.50**
Custard Cup, blue	**9.00**
Fruit Bowl, 5" d, maroon, handle . .	**10.00**
Honey Pot, cov, maroon	**20.00**
Mixing Bowl, handle, orange	**24.00**
Pie Baker, yellow	**13.00**
Plate	
6" d, bread and butter, rose.	**10.00**
7" d, salad, yellow	**10.00**
9½" d, dinner	
Cobalt blue	**12.00**
Green	**12.00**
Yellow.	**12.00**
Salt and Pepper Shakers, pr, blue . .	**18.50**
Soup Plate, 8" d, green.	**15.00**
Teapot, large, rose.	**50.00**
Utility Jar, cov, yellow	**25.00**
Vase, 8" h, yellow	**15.00**

CROOKSVILLE CHINA COMPANY

CROOKSVILLE U.S.A. C·U

History: The Crooksville China Company, Crooksville, Ohio, was founded in 1902 for the manufacture of artware such as vases, flowerpots and novelties. Dinnerware soon became its stock in trade. Crooksville made a good grade of semi–porcelain that rivaled more expensive vitrified ware. The factory continued until 1959 and employed over 300 people for many years.

Crooksville China produced several patterns. The decoration of their wares was primarily through the use of decals. These detailed decals are very colorful and durable. Silhouette was one of the most popular patterns. The Silhouette decal is in black on a yellow glaze ground and shows two men sitting at a table with a dog looking up at them, waiting for food. Other patterns feature country–type decorations.

Crooksville answered the need for practical, attractive, utilitarian pieces. Earliest production included teapots, waffle sets, jugs, spice jars, and covered baking sets. Dinnerware followed this line of interestingly shaped pieces.

The Crooksville China Company used over fifteen different marks. Some contain pattern names and dates, others were simply the company name.

Autumn		
Batter Jug		**22.00**
Casserole, 8" d		**15.00**
Coaster, 4" d		**5.00**
Coffee Pot		**25.00**
Cup		**4.00**
Pie Baker, 10" d		**7.50**
Plate		
6" d		**1.50**
$9\frac{3}{4}$" d		**4.00**

Apple Blossom, pie baker, 10" d, mkd "Pantry–Bak–In," $15.00; bean pot, 2 handles, $25.00; casserole, cov, 8" d, mkd "Pantry–Bak–In," $18.00.

Silhouette, pitcher, $18.00.

Platter, $11\frac{1}{2}$" l, rect		**5.00**
Saucer		**1.00**
Sugar		**10.00**
Vegetable Dish, $9\frac{1}{4}$" l, rect		**9.00**
Petit Point House		
Bowl		
5" d		**3.50**
6" d		**4.50**
Cup		**4.00**
Pie Baker		**15.00**
Plate		
6" d		**2.50**
9" d		**6.00**
Platter, 11" l		**10.00**
Saucer		**1.25**
Soup Bowl, $7\frac{1}{4}$" d		**4.00**
Teapot		**25.00**
Utility Jar, cov		**45.00**
Vegetable Bowl, 9" d		**7.50**
Silhouette		
Batter Jug, cov		**45.00**
Casserole, cov		**28.00**
Creamer		**7.50**
Cup		**6.00**
Juice Pitcher, large		**15.00**
Pie Baker		**18.00**
Plate, dinner		**8.00**
Saucer		**3.50**
Teapot		**20.00**
Tumbler		**15.00**
Spring Blossom, soup, flat		**6.00**
Vegetable Medley		
Casserole, 8" d		**15.00**
Coffee Pot		**25.00**
Creamer		**6.00**
Cup		**3.50**
Custard Cup		**3.00**
Plate		
6" d		**2.00**
9" d		**4.00**
$9\frac{3}{4}$" d		**5.00**
Platter, $15\frac{1}{2}$" l, rect		**10.00**
Saucer		**1.00**
Sugar		**10.00**
Syrup Pitcher		**18.00**
Vegetable Dish, $9\frac{1}{4}$" l, rect		**12.00**

DEDHAM POTTERY

History: Alexander W. Robertson established the Chelsea Pottery in Chelsea, Massachusetts, in 1860. In 1872 it was known as the Chelsea Keramic Art Works.

In 1895 the pottery moved to Dedham, and the name was changed to Dedham Pottery. Their principal product was gray crackleware dinnerware with a blue decoration, the rabbit pattern being the most popular. The factory closed in 1943.

The following marks help determine the approximate age of items: (1) Chelsea Keramic Art Works, "Robertson" impressed, 1876–1889; (2) C.P.U.S. impressed in a cloverleaf, 1891–1895; (3) foreshortened rabbit, 1895–1896; (4) conventional rabbit with "Dedham Pottery" stamped in blue, 1897; (5) rabbit mark with "Registered", 1929–1943.

References: Paul Evans, *Art Pottery of the United States,* Feingold & Lewis Publishing Corp, 1987; Lloyd E. Hawes, *The Dedham Pottery And The Earlier Robertson's Chelsea Potteries,* Dedham Historical Society, 1968.

Reproduction Manufacturers: Country Loft, 1506 South Shore Park, Hingham, MA 02043; The Potting Shed, 43 Bradford St, Box 1287, Concord, MA 01742.

Bowl
   5¼" d, rabbit border, blue rabbit stamp on bottom and Davenport mark **55.00**
   5¾" d, cov, rabbit border, blue rabbit stamp on bottom **165.00**
   5⅞" d, rabbit border, blue stamp on bottom **90.00**

Bowl, 9" d, 3½" h, rabbit border, inscribed mark "Dedham Pottery," dated 1898, $850.00.

6⅞" d, rabbit border, blue registered mark on bottom **140.00**
7" d, 3¼" h, grape border, "Dedham Pottery" **225.00**
7½" d, flared rim, rabbit border, blue rabbit stamp on bottom **140.00**
8" sq, rabbit border **300.00**
9¼" d, 2¼" h, azalea border, cut edge, "Dedham Pottery, Registered," two imp rabbits **935.00**
10⅝" d, flared rim, rabbit border, blue registered mark on bottom **110.00**
Candle Holders, pr
   1⅜" h, rabbit border, blue rabbit registered mark on bottom **330.00**
   1½" h, blue rabbit border around base, blue bands around socket and rim, blue "Dedham Pottery, Registered" **385.00**
Celery Tray, 10" l, rabbit border **300.00**
Charger, 12" d, elephant border, stamped and impressed marks, early 20th C **1,540.00**
Coaster, 4" d, single elephant medallion, "Dedham Pottery, Registered, Dedham Tercentenary" **1,320.00**
Coffee Pot, 8" h, rabbit border, blue rabbit stamp on bottom **165.00**
Creamer, rabbit border
   2¼" h **55.00**
   3½" h, stamped mark, early 20th C **95.00**
   4⅝" h, blue registered mark on bottom **140.00**
Creamer and Covered Sugar, repeating elephants border, stamped mark on 2" h creamer, 2¾" h sugar, early 20th C **250.00**
Cup, 3½" h, rabbit border, double handles, ftd, stamped mark, early 20th C, pr **325.00**
Cup and Saucer
   Azalea border, blue rabbit stamp . . **50.00**
   Rabbit border, 3¾" h, handle, blue, "Dedham Pottery, Registered" and 1931 stamp on both **253.00**
Demitasse Cup and Saucer, 2½" h, blue rabbit borders, blue "Dedham Pottery, Registered" and two imp rabbits on saucer bottom. **412.50**
Egg Cup, 2½" h, set of 6, blue rabbit stamp on bottom **360.00**
Flower Holder
   4⅝" d, blue rabbit stamp on bottom **30.00**
   6¼" h, standing rabbit dec, applied blue facial features, fifteen holes, "Dedham Pottery, Registered" . . **1,980.00**
Mug, 6" h, rabbit border, incised and stamped marks **330.00**
Pickle Dish, 5½" l, 1¾" h, azalea border, oval, "Dedham Pottery, Registered" **550.00**
Pitcher
   2¾" h, rabbit border, miniature, blue

Plate, 6⅛" d, bread and butter, horse chestnut, $95.00.

band around rim and base, blue "Dedham Pottery, Registered"   **1,040.00**
4½" h, standing rabbit dec, blue ink "Dedham Pottery" **2,035.00**
5" h
Day/Night, blue on white, stamped mark, early 20th C. . .   **400.00**
Elephant border, baby elephant, "Dedham Pottery, Registered"   **2,090.00**
6¾" h, rabbit border, cylindrical form, angular handle, stamped mark, early 20th C **150.00**
Plate
6" d
Rabbit border, "Dedham Pottery" and lightly imp rabbit **130.00**
Snow Tree border, slightly raised, blue rabbit stamp on bottom . .   **70.00**
6⅛" d, swan border, blue rabbit stamp and two incised rabbits mark **250.00**
6¼" d
Lotus Water Lily border, "Dedham Pottery, Registered" **200.00**
Rabbit border, blue stamp on bottom **50.00**
6½" d, iris border, blue rabbit stamp   **45.00**
7½" d
Horse Chestnut border, stamped mark, two imp marks, base chip, early 20th C. **125.00**
Swan border, blue rabbit stamp and two incised rabbits **255.00**
7⅝" d, rabbit border, blue rabbit stamp **75.00**
8¼" d, horse chestnut border, blue rabbit stamp **50.00**
8⅜" d
Magnolia border, blue rabbit stamp and one incised rabbit mark **25.00**
Poppy Pod border, blue rabbit stamp, incised rabbit and underlined X mark **45.00**

8½" d
Flying Woodcock border, stamped mark, early 20th C. . .   **250.00**
Iris border, "Dedham Pottery" and imp rabbit **150.00**
Poppy Pod border, painted poppy center, blue and white, incised mark and painted mark **660.00**
Rabbit border, raised, incised mark **45.00**
Swan border , repeating swan and cat-o-nine tails within border, imp double rabbit mark, stamped mark, early 20th C . . .   **275.00**
Swimming Ducks border, blue and white, raised border, incised mark **165.00**
Tapestry Lion border, stamped and impressed marks, Dedham, MA, early 20th C **880.00**
Turkey border, stamped and imp marks, minor imperfections, 20th C **135.00**
8⅝" d, raised rabbit border, incised rabbit mark **55.00**
8¾" d, butterfly border, blue ink mark, one imp bunny **415.00**
8⅞" d, magnolia border, blue rabbit stamp and two imp mark. **70.00**
9¾" d
Azalea border, blue rabbit mark   **40.00**
Cherry border, stamped mark, 20th C **130.00**
Duck border, stamped and imp mark, early 20th C **225.00**
Grape border, stamped and imp rabbit mark, early 20th C **70.00**
Rabbit border, blue rabbit stamp on bottom **40.00**
9⅞" d
Rabbit border, blue mark and two incised rabbits on bottom **80.00**
Turkey border, blue rabbit mark   **35.00**
10" d
Grape border, blue grape clusters, ink mark with rabbit **275.00**

Plate, 9⅞" d, butterfly border, $285.00.

Iris border, stamped mark, 20th C **150.00**
Moth border, blue rabbit mark on
bottom **40.00**
Tufted Duck border, "Dedham
Pottery" and imp rabbit. **200.00**
Turkey border, partial Maude
Davenport "O" rebus, "Ded-
ham Pottery" and imp rabbit **200.00**
10⅛" d, iris border, stamped and imp
rabbit mark, early 20th C **130.00**
10¼" d, azalea border, "Dedham
Pottery," blue "X," and imp rab-
bit **120.00**
Tapestry Lion border, moon and
Kings Crown inner border, four
Maude Davenport "O" rebus signatures, blue "Dedham Pottery,"
imp rabbit **2,200.00**
Rasher, 9⅞ x 6¼", rabbit border, "Ded-
ham Pottery, Registered" **250.00**
Salt and Pepper Shakers, pr, 2¾" h, rab-
bit border, early 20th C **300.00**
Saucer
4⅜" d, rabbit border, blue rabbit
stamp on bottom **140.00**
6¼" d, dolphin border, "Dedham
Pottery, Registered" **325.00**
Stein, 4¼" h, 3½" d, rabbit border, cylindrical form, imp and ink stamped
marks, early 20th C **225.00**
Sugar Bowl, cov, 4¼" h, blue rabbit
mark on bottom **55.00**
Teapot, 6" h, 7" wide from handle to
spout, lid, blue rabbit border, blue
band around lid and rim, blue ink
"Dedham Pottery". **1,870.00**
Tea Stand, 6" d, rabbit border,
stamped, early 20th C **165.00**
Tile, 5½" sq, rabbit border **250.00**
Tumbler, 3⅜" h, rabbit border, blue
stamp on bottom **30.00**
Vase
8" h, blue jay resting on branch,
short neck, swollen cylindrical
form, dated, stamped registered
mark, 1931 . . . . **1,100.00**
9 x 8½", bulbous shoulder, multi-
colored volcanic glaze, incised
"HCR," ink mark "DP37C" **1,320.00**
10½" h, experimental, short neck,
swollen cylindrical body,
semigloss tan glaze, incised "BW,
Dedham Pottery HCR," late
19th C **275.00**
12½" h, pillow, rect neck, flattened
ovoid body, two lion faces, rect
foot, blue–green glossy glaze,
stamped "Chelsea Keramic Works
Robertson & Sons". **450.00**
13¼" h, pillow shape ovoid, flaring
rect foot, blue glaze, small loop
handles, imp "Chelsea Keramic

Art Works Robertson & Sons,"
wear to glaze at handles **165.00**

DORCHESTER POTTERY

History: Dorchester Pottery was a contemporary
of Dedham Pottery. George Henderson made this
stoneware type pottery in Dorchester, Connecticut. Production began in 1895 and continued
until the 1980s.

One of the most popular lines began in the
1940s. The motif is blue and white and uses a
New Jersey clay base. Complete dinner services
were made. The decoration varied from a painted
cobalt blue decoration to a sgraffito–type decoration. Some pieces are almost totally glazed with
cobalt blue and then have portions scraped away
to reveal the light body below. Both molded and
thrown pieces are known. Traditional New England designs of codfish, pinecones, scrolls,
stripes, lace, blueberries, and even pussy willows
are common. Some special order patterns have a
bayberry green or gold glaze.

Like many other pottery companies, Dorchester Pottery also made commercial items.
Their high–fired stoneware was excellent for acid
proof applications and was used widely in the
medical and food preparation industries. It is the
hand decorated and hand thrown pieces that attract the attention of the Country decorators and
collectors.

Most pieces of Dorchester Pottery are signed by
the decorators and potters. Each bears the pottery
name. A lead stamped mark was used until 1941.

Bird Bath, 21¾" d, 27½" h, shallow
rimmed bowl, columnar pedestal,
cobalt blue painted S–scrolling foliage dec, five petaled center flower,
horizontal base bands, artist sgd "N
Ricci," potter's initials **770.00**
Bowl
5¾" d, cobalt blue clown face dec,
white ground. **110.00**
6" d, cobalt blue painted blueberry
dec, marked "CAH," set of 7 . . . **315.00**
8" d, Bicentennial, blue plum dec **165.00**

**Cup, 2" h, 2¾" d, blue dec., stamp mark,
$25.00.**

Candy Dish, starfish shape, marked "JM"	**75.00**
Casserole, cov, 8½" d, Blueberry pattern	**125.00**
Chowder Bowl, cobalt blue whale dec, marked "CAH"	**100.00**
Cup, handle, Blueberry pattern, marked "CAH," set of 3	**65.00**
Foot Warmer, 9½" h, brown glaze, attached wood back rest	**75.00**
Mug	
Advertising, 4⅝" h, Tuft's Dental, 1933–1958, ochre and blue striped glazes, white ground	**75.00**
Bicentennial, grapes dec	**145.00**
Pitcher, Blueberry pattern, marked "N Ricci, CAH"	**100.00**
Shell Dish, ochre	**65.00**
Soup Bowl, cov, 5¾" d, double handles, blue glaze, orig paper labels, set of 8	**200.00**
Syrup pitcher, cov, sgraffito dec, blue glaze	**85.00**

FIESTA

History: The Homer Laughlin China Company introduced Fiesta dinnerware in January 1936 at the Pottery and Glass Show in Pittsburgh, Pennsylvania. Fredrick Rhead designed the pattern; Arthur Kraft and Bill Bensford molded it. Dr. A. V. Blenininiger and H. W. Thiemecke developed the glazes.

The original five colors were red, dark blue, light green (with a trace of blue), brilliant yellow, and ivory. A vigorous marketing campaign took place between 1939 and 1943. In 1938 turquoise was added; red was removed in 1943 because of the war effort and did not reappear until 1959. In 1951 light green, dark blue, and ivory were retired and forest green, rose, chartreuse, and gray were added to the line. Other color changes took place in the late 1950s, including the addition of a medium green.

Fiesta ware was redesigned in 1969 and discontinued in 1972–1973. In 1986 Fiesta was reintroduced by Homer Laughlin China Company. The new china body shrinks more than the old semi–vitreous and ironstone pieces, thus making the new pieces slightly smaller than the earlier pieces. The modern colors also differ in tone. The cobalt blue is darker than the old blue. Other modern colors are black, white, apricot, and rose.

Fiesta is one of the most widely recognized dinnerware patterns. During its heyday it was probably the most popular dinnerware made in America. Original production began with fifty–four items. Several specialized pieces and sets were made in the 1940s as sales stimulators. These limited production items, such as handled chop plates, covered refrigerator jars, and French casseroles are highly prized today. Millions of pieces of Fiesta ware were manufactured during its forty years of production.

The molds used originally had the name molded into the base of the piece. The new 1986 line is made from original molds but also carries a stamped mark making them easily recognizable.

There is some concern today over the red glaze. Uranium oxide was used as a base for this bright glaze. During World War II this glaze was suspended and the popular color did not reappear until May of 1959. Production of this uranium oxide glaze continued until 1972. Some radiation can be detected on the red glazed pieces and these should not be used. Care should be taken when storing and displaying them as well.

References: Linda D. Farmer, *The Farmer's Wife Fiesta Inventory and Price Guide*, published by author, 1984; Sharon and Bob Huxford, *The Collectors Encyclopedia of Fiesta, Seventh Edition*, Collector Books, 1992.

Ashtray	
Gray	**60.00**
Green.	**25.00**
Red	**35.00**
Turquoise.	**25.00**
Yellow	**25.00**
Bowl, 8½" d	
Cobalt blue.	**30.00**
Gray	**30.00**
Green.	**20.00**
Ivory	**20.00**
Rose.	**30.00**
Turquoise.	**20.00**
Yellow	**20.00**
Bud Vase, ivory	**48.00**
Cake Plate, yellow, Kitchen Kraft	**30.00**
Candlesticks, pr	
Bulbous	
Cobalt blue	**65.00**
Ivory.	**45.00**
Red.	**75.00**
Turquoise	**60.00**
Yellow	**40.00**
Tripod, pink, pr	**85.00**
Carafe	
Cobalt blue.	**165.00**
Green.	**225.00**
Turquoise.	**140.00**
Yellow	**125.00**
Casserole, cov, 8½"	
Cobalt blue, Kitchen Kraft	**95.00**

Ivory	90.00
Turquoise	90.00
Chop Plate, 13"d	
Cobalt blue	20.00
Gray	30.00
Ivory	17.00
Light green	20.00
Rose	35.90
Yellow	20.00
Coffee Pot, cov	
Chartreuse	235.00
Cobalt blue	145.00
Green	130.00
Red	140.00
Yellow	75.00
Compote, 12"	
Cobalt blue	135.00
Turquoise	110.00
Creamer	
Cobalt blue, side handle	22.00
Medium green	60.00
Red, individual	120.00
Red, stick handled	29.00
Turquoise	15.00
Yellow, individual	50.00
Cream Soup	
Cobalt blue, lid	35.00
Red	40.00
Turquoise	32.00
Yellow	30.00
Cup	
Chartreuse	25.00
Cobalt blue	18.00
Light blue	12.00
Light green	12.00
Turquoise	18.00
Yellow	16.00
Cup and Saucer	
Chartreuse	30.00
Green	14.00
Medium green	35.00
Rose	30.00
Turquoise	14.00
Yellow	14.00
Deep Plate	
Chartreuse	22.00
Cobalt blue	22.00
Dark green	30.00
Gray	30.00
Green	18.00
Ivory	18.00
Light green	20.00
Medium green	45.00
Red	22.00
Rose	30.00
Turquoise	20.00
Yellow	20.00
Dessert Bowl, 6" d	
Cobalt blue	25.00
Ivory	28.00
Light green	25.00
Red	38.00
Turquoise	28.00
Yellow	28.00
Egg Cup	
Chartreuse	70.00
Light green	50.00
Red	40.00
Rose	70.00
Turquoise	45.00
Fruit Bowl, 4¾" d	
Chartreuse	28.00
Cobalt blue	25.00
Dark green	16.00
Green	14.00
Ivory	15.00
Medium green	53.00
Red	25.00
Rose	18.00
Turquoise	12.00
Yellow	12.00
Gravy Boat	
Green	20.00
Light blue	32.00
Red	50.00
Jar, cov, large, cobalt blue, Kitchen Kraft	260.00
Jug	
2 pint	
Green	48.00
Ivory	35.00
Light green	39.00
Turquoise	39.00
3 pint, ivory	48.00
Juicer, cobalt	20.00
Lid, coffeepot, green	15.00
Marmalade	
Green	150.00
Turquoise	160.00
Mixing Bowl	
#1	
Red	90.00
Turquoise	95.00
#2	
Cobalt blue	70.00
Green	69.00
Turquoise	60.00
#3	
Cobalt blue	65.00
Ivory	65.00
#4	
Red	80.00
Turquoise	60.00
#5, cobalt blue	85.00
#6, turquoise	80.00
#7, green	150.00
Mug	
Chartreuse	65.00
Cobalt blue	60.00
Forest green	40.00
Gray	50.00
Red	50.00
Rose	40.00
Turquoise	45.00

Yellow	45.00
Mug, Tom and Jerry	
Chartreuse	65.00
Cobalt blue	55.00
Forest green	60.00
Gray	65.00
Ivory	28.00
Medium green	70.00
Red	60.00
Yellow	28.00
Mustard, cov	
Light green	50.00
Red	145.00
Nappy, 8½" d	
Chartreuse	52.00
Forest green	32.00
Gray	32.00
Ivory	30.00
Red	32.00
Turquoise	18.00
Yellow	26.00
Pitcher	
Disc, juice, yellow	27.00
Disc, water	
Chartreuse	175.00
Ivory	70.00
Light green	58.00
Red	75.00
Yellow	40.00
Ice Lip, red	100.00
Plate	
6" d, dessert	
Chartreuse	7.00
Cobalt blue	5.00
Gray	7.00
Green	4.00
Ivory	5.00
Light green	4.00
Red	6.00
Turquoise	4.00
Yellow	4.00
7" d	
Cobalt blue	8.00
Ivory	8.00
Light green	6.00
9" d, luncheon	
Chartreuse	15.00
Cobalt blue	10.00
Ivory	12.00
Red	13.00
Yellow	8.00
10" d, dinner	
Cobalt blue	28.00
Gray	45.00
Ivory	20.00
Light green	17.00
Red	25.00
Rose	30.00
Yellow	22.00
10" d, grill	
Chartreuse	45.00
Cobalt blue	25.00

Gray	45.00
Ivory	23.00
Light green	22.00
Red	27.00
Rose	45.00
Turquoise	22.00
Yellow	22.00
12" d, grill	
Cobalt blue	32.00
Ivory	32.00
Light green	30.00
Red	32.00
Yellow	30.00
13" d, grill	
Cobalt blue	25.00
Yellow	21.00
15" d, grill, turquoise	26.00
Platter, 12" l, oval	
Chartreuse	35.00
Dark green	20.00
Forest green	28.00
Green	16.00
Ivory	20.00
Medium green	45.00
Turquoise	15.00
Yellow	16.00
Refrigerator Dish, lid, Kitchen Kraft,	
round, blue	75.00
Relish Tray, light blue	18.00
Salad Bowl	
Footed, green	190.00
Individual	
Medium green	80.00
Red	60.00
Yellow	60.00
Salt and Pepper Shakers, pr	
Medium green	45.00
Red–orange	15.00
Turquoise	18.00
Yellow	12.00
Saucer	
Chartreuse	6.00
Cobalt blue	4.00
Green	3.00
Red	4.00

Salad Bowl, 9½" l, yellow, $60.00.

Rose	6.00
Turquoise	5.00
Yellow	3.00
Shaker, Kitchen Kraft	
Green	40.00
Yellow	40.00
Stack Set	
Cobalt blue	22.00
Green	22.00
Sugar	
Medium green	75.00
Red, cov	40.00
Turquoise, cov	18.00
Yellow, individual	70.00
Syrup	
Light green	210.00
Yellow	125.00
Tea Cup	
Cobalt blue	16.00
Red	20.00
Yellow	16.00
Tea Cup and Saucer	
Chartreuse	35.00
Cobalt blue	25.00
Gray	35.00
Ivory	23.00
Light green	21.00
Medium green	43.00
Red	28.00
Rose	35.00
Turquoise	24.00
Yellow	21.00
Teapot	
Large	
Green	125.00
Red	70.00
Medium	
Cobalt blue	125.00
Red	85.00
Turquoise	85.00
Tidbit Tray	
Medium green, 3 tiered	175.00
Rose	65.00
Tray, figure eight, cobalt blue	55.00
Tumbler	
Juice	
Cobalt blue	30.00
Green	15.00
Red	32.00
Rose	35.00
Yellow	15.00

Water	
Cobalt blue	45.00
Green	28.00
Red	48.00
Yellow	38.00
Utility Tray	
Cobalt blue	30.00
Green	16.00
Ivory	30.00
Light green	25.00
Red	30.00
Turquoise	25.00
Yellow	25.00
Vase	
$6\frac{1}{2}''$ h, red	25.00
8" h, yellow	360.00
10" h, cobalt blue	395.00
12" h, green	565.00
Vegetable Bowl, medium green	65.00

Utility Tray, turquoise, $25.00.

FLOW BLUE

History: Flow blue, or flowing blue, is the name applied to a cobalt blue and white china, whose color, when fired in a kiln, produced a flowing or smudged effect. The blue varies in color from dark cobalt to a grayish or steel blue. The flow varies from very slight to a heavy blur where the pattern cannot be easily recognized. The blue color does not permeate through the china.

Flow blue was first produced around 1835 in the Staffordshire district of England by a large number of potters including Alcock, Davenport, J. Wedgwood, Grindley, New Wharf, and Johnson Brothers. Most early flow blue, 1830s to 1870s, was ironstone. The late patterns, 1880s to 1910s, and modern patterns, after 1910, were usually a more delicate semi–porcelain variety. Approximately 95 percent of the flow blue was made in England, with the remaining 5 percent made in Germany, Holland, France, Belgium, and the United States. American manufacturers included Mercer, Warwick, and Wheeling Pottery companies.

References: Susan and Al Bagdade, *Warman's English & Continental Pottery & Porcelain, 2nd Edition,* Wallace–Homestead, 1991; Mary F. Gaston, *The Collector's Encyclopedia Of Flow Blue China,* Collector Books, 1983, 1989 value update; Petra Williams, *Flow Blue China—An Aid To Identification, Revised Edition,* Fountain House East, 1981; —, *Flow Blue China II, Revised Edition,* Fountain House East, 1981; —, *Flow Blue China and Mulberry Ware–Similarity and Value Guide, Revised Edition,* Fountain House East, 1981.

Collectors' Club: Flow Blue International Collectors' Club, 28 Irene St, Brooksville, FL 34601.

Museum: Hershey Museum of American Life, 170 West Hershey Park Drive, Hershey, PA 17033.

Beaker, 4" h, Watteau, Doulton **65.00**
Berry Dish
- Georgia, Johnson Bros **30.00**
- Hudson, $5\frac{1}{4}$" d, J C Meakin **27.50**
- Touraine. **45.00**

Bone Dish
- Linda **60.00**
- Lorraina **25.00**
- Marguerite, W H Grindley **65.00**
- Tulip **40.00**

Bowl
- 6" d, Abbey, ftd, Petrus Regout, Holland **55.00**
- 6" l, oval
  - Florida, W H Grindley **35.00**
  - Janette, W H Grindley **30.00**
- $7\frac{1}{2}$" d, Jenny Lind, Wilkinson, c1895 **165.00**
- $7\frac{3}{4}$" d, Clover. **35.00**
- $8\frac{1}{2}$" d, LaFrancais. **20.00**

Butter Pat
- Aldine, W H Grindley **12.00**
- Byzantine, Wood & Sons **30.00**
- Clarence. **30.00**
- Constance **20.00**
- Kelvin, Alfred Meakin **30.00**
- Virginia, John Maddock, set of 10 **110.00**

Cake Plate
- 10" l, Richmond, handles, Alfred Meakin, c1900 . . . . **245.00**
- 11" l, Non Pariel, gilt trim, handles, Burgess & Leigh, c1891 . . . . **185.00**

Cake Stand, 10" d, Pearl, ftd **245.00**
Casserole, cov, 11" l, Turin, Johnson Bros **150.00**
Cereal Bowl, $6\frac{1}{4}$" d, Watteau, NWP . . **35.00**
Chamber Pot
- $8\frac{1}{2}$" d
  - Glenwood. **170.00**
  - Watteau, Doulton **125.00**
- $9\frac{1}{2}$" d, $5\frac{1}{2}$" h, Gainsborough, cov, fancy finial, Ridgways **275.00**

Chamber Set, pitcher, bowl, soap dish, chamber pot, Alhambra, Meakin . . **975.00**
Charger
- $11\frac{1}{2}$" d, pierced for hanging, Hanley, Meakin **135.00**
- $12\frac{1}{2}$" d, Camellia, Wedgwood. **395.00**

Coffee Pot, 9" h, Lily **125.00**
Compote
- $4\frac{3}{4}$" h, $9\frac{3}{4}$" d, fruit, Watteau, pedestal, double handles, Doulton . . . **300.00**
- $6\frac{1}{4}$" h, 10" d, Chusan, Morley **550.00**
- 9" h, octagonal, two handles, Formosa, Ridgway **950.00**
- 12" l, Bluebell, Ridgway **95.00**

Creamer, $3\frac{1}{2}$" h, Alton, W H Grindley **95.00**
Creamer and Sugar, Glentine, W H Grindley. **175.00**

Cup and Saucer
- Abbey **45.00**
- Albany, gold trim **55.00**
- Canton, James Edwards **140.00**
- Celeste, handleless **60.00**
- Gironde, W H Grindley **110.00**
- Hops, Royal Bonn **25.00**
- Kenworth, Johnson Bros. **60.00**

Demitasse
- Clayton **55.00**
- Roseville **55.00**
- Vermont, Burgess & Leigh, set of 6 **275.00**

Dessert Stand, Poppea. **165.00**
Dish, 11" l, 8" w, heart shape, cut–out handle, Crossed Bands, Ridgway . . **225.00**
Dresser Set, Petunia, $12\frac{1}{2}$ x 9" tray, 4 x $2\frac{3}{8}$" pin tray, $3\frac{1}{2}$" l oval handled trinket box, $6\frac{7}{8}$" h candlestick. **375.00**
Dresser Tray, 11" l, 8" w, Claremont, Johnson Bros. **75.00**
Egg Cup
- Dainty **100.00**
- Holland **50.00**

Gravy Boat
- Albany. **75.00**
- Argyle, 8" l, underplate **150.00**
- Dundee, Ridgways **95.00**
- Osborne, c1905 . . . . **90.00**
- York, undertray, Meakin **120.00**

Honey Dish, 6" d, hexagonal, Kyber, Adams, set of 6 . . . . **245.00**
Jardiniere, 12" h, $12\frac{1}{2}$" d, double handles, gold trim, Dog Rose, Ridgways **350.00**
Ladle, 9" l, Corey Hill **250.00**
Meat Server, $12\frac{3}{4}$" l, oval, Watteau, meat well, two cut–out handles, domed lid **395.00**
Mug, $4\frac{1}{8}$" h
- Spinach, ale, crazing, 1890s **195.00**
- Whampoa **295.00**

Pickle Dish, $8\frac{1}{2}$" l, 5" w, Verona, Ridgway **50.00**
Pitcher
- $5\frac{3}{8}$" h, melon ribbed, Candia, Cauldon. **165.00**
- 6" h
  - Beauty Rose **95.00**
  - Grace, W H Grindley **170.00**

Mug, Singa pattern, 8" handle to handle, marked "C.E.& M.," c1865, $150.00.

Norbury **55.00**
7½" h, Nankin, Doulton **175.00**
8" h, milk, Madras, Doulton. **345.00**
8½" h, corset shape, Basket, Swin-
nerton.   **95.00**
Pitcher and Bowl, Coburg **1,750.00**
Plate
5" d, bread and butter, Belmont . . .   **45.00**
6" d, Marquis **65.00**
7" d
Amoy, 12 sided **75.00**
Ayr, W & E Corn **45.00**
7⅞" d, Manhattan, c1900 . . . .   **45.00**
8" d
Albion **50.00**
Colonial, Meakin. **25.00**
Manilla. **50.00**
Marie, W H Grindley **40.00**
8½" d
Delft, Minton. **50.00**
Lahore, Phillips & Sons. **120.00**
8¾" d, Raleigh, Burgess & Leigh. . . .   **30.00**
9" d
Amoy **95.00**
Chapoo. **90.00**
Hampton Spray, W H Grindley   **30.00**
9⅛" d, Melrose, gilt rim, Doulton,
c1891. . . . .   **65.00**
9½" d, Meissen, Tidgway **25.00**
9¾" d
Corinthian Flute, c1905 . . . .   **72.00**
Gladys, scalloped edge **45.00**
Marlborough. **65.00**
10" d
Brooklyn, semi–porcelain, gold
trim, Johnson Bros **45.00**
Fairy Villas II, W Adams & Co . . .   **75.00**
Melbourne **35.00**
10¼" d, Chusan, Royal Doulton. . . .   **125.00**
10½" d
Abbey. **28.00**
Amoy, Davenport **83.00**
Arabesque. **95.00**
Platter
10" l, Amoy **150.00**

10½" l, 7¾" w, scalloped edge, Con-
way, NWP, c1891 . . . .   **135.00**
12" l, Delmar **50.00**
14" l
Abbey. **125.00**
Albany, W H Grindley **100.00**
Dresden, Villeroy & Boch **85.00**
15½" l, 12" w, Carlton, Samuel
Alcock **225.00**
16" l, Chusan, P W & Co **350.00**
16¼" l, Gem, Hammersley **165.00**
18" l, 18" w, Aldine, W H Grindley   **225.00**
18½" l, 14½" w, Indiana, Wedgwood
& Co Tunstall. **75.00**
Relish Dish
7½" l, Clover **65.00**
8½" l, Argyle **35.00**
Sauce Boat, Halford, Burgess and
Leigh **20.00**
Sauce Dish, Lancaster. **30.00**
Sauce Tureen
Amerilla, ladle and undertray, P W
& Co. **735.00**
Chinese, shell finial, Dimmock. . . .   **395.00**
Fleur–De–Lis, undertray **250.00**
Scinde, ladle and undertray, Alcock   **1,195.00**
Soup Plate
9½" d, Oregon **100.00**
10¼" d, France, Brown, Westhead,
c1868.   **45.00**
10½" d
Canton, Maddock **145.00**
Indian.   **110.00**
Soup Tureen, cov
Erie, 9" d **70.00**
Hague, 8¼" l, 6½" h, underplate,
Johnson Bros **245.00**
LePavot, 12" l, W H Grindley **265.00**
Melsary, 8" l, underplate and ladle,
Booth **150.00**
Morning Glory, 9" d, 9" h, scalloped

Sugar Bowl, Tonquin pattern, 8" h, c1850, $195.00.

Platter, Scroll pattern, 14¾" l, 12" w, marked "F.M.," $250.00.

rim and cov, gold trim, scalloped
raised base, fancy handles, Wood
& Hughes **295.00**
Sugar Bowl
  Circassia. **150.00**
  Lobelia. **125.00**
  Olympia, W H Grindley **90.00**
  Temple, 8" h, cov **250.00**
Syrup, 6½" h, pewter top, Claremont   **95.00**
Teapot
  Chapoo, 9½" h, chips on base **325.00**
  Tivoli **625.00**
Tea Tile, 7" d, Warwick, raised gold
  gadrooned border **110.00**
Tooth Brush Holder
  Cyprus, Booth. **250.00**
  Venice, 5⅜" h, Grimwades **80.00**
Tray, 10" l, 8" w, Lonsdale, Samuel
  Ford & Co, England **85.00**
Vase
  8½" h, hexagonal, Venetia, Barker
    Bros Ltd, Meir Works, Longton . .   **235.00**
  9½" h, Iris, Doulton Burslem **195.00**
  12" h, Cavandish. **325.00**
Vegetable Bowl
  9" d, Rose, W H Grindley. **85.00**
  9½" d, gold trim, Del Monte, Johnson
    Bros **55.00**
  10" d, Beaufort **90.00**
  10" l, 7" w, Florida, W H Grindley   **65.00**
  10¼" l, 7½" w, Blue Willow, scal-
    loped edge, Minton, c1891 . . . .   **145.00**
  10½" d, Alhambra **48.00**
  10¾" l, 8¾" w, oval, Cashmere. **495.00**
  11" d, Abbey, George Jones **68.00**
  12½" l, 10" w, 7½" h, cov, double
    handles, ftd, Fairy Villas, Adams   **350.00**
Vegetable Tureen
  Celtic, cov, W H Grindley **225.00**
  Weir, 11" l, 7" w, Ford & Sons **110.00**
  Yeddo, cov, 11⅝" l, 6" h, pedestal
    base, Ashworth, c1862. . . . .   **235.00**
Waffle Cup, 6½" h, Watteau, three han-
  dles, Royal Doulton. **395.00**
Warming Dish, 10½" d, Pekin, stopper,
  scalloped rim, Davenport, c1844   **440.00**
Waste Bowl, 5¾" d, 3" h, Gironde, W
  H Grindley **95.00**

FRANCISCAN WARE

History: Franciscan Ware was manufactured by
Gladding, McBean and Company, located in
Glendale and Los Angeles, California. Charles
Gladding, Peter McBean and George Chambers
organized the firm in 1875. Early products in-
cluded sewer pipes and architectural items.

Production of dinnerware and art pottery began
in 1943. The dinnerware was marketed under the
trademark Franciscan and first appeared in plain

shapes and bright colors. Soon, skillfully molded
underglaze patterns were developed. Patterns
like Desert Rose, Ivy, Autumn, and Apple are
eagerly sought by Country collectors. Numerous
setting and service pieces allow collectors to assemble large collections. More pieces are seen at
flea markets and antiques shows.

Franciscan Ware has been marked with over
eighty different marks. Many contain the pattern
name, patent numbers or dates.

Reference: Delleen Enge, *Franciscan Ware*, Collector Books, 1981.

Apple
  Ashtray, 9", oval **25.00**
  Bowl
    7½" d. **25.00**
    8½" d. **22.00**
  Butter Dish, cov **17.50**
  Casserole, cov, 1½ quart. **40.00**
  Cereal Bowl, 6" d **12.00**
  Creamer. **8.50**
  Creamer and Sugar, cov **20.00**
  Cup and Saucer. **25.00**
  Fruit Bowl, 5" d **7.00**
  Gravy. **30.00**
  Jumbo Cup and Saucer. **15.00**
  Plate
    6½" d **6.00**
    7½" d **7.00**
    9½" d **8.00**
    10½" d **10.00**
    12½" d **25.00**
  Platter, 14" l **32.00**
  Salad Bowl **10.00**
  Salt and Pepper Shakers, pr **30.00**
  Sherbet, underplate. **22.00**
  Soup Bowl **12.00**
  Sugar, cov **12.00**
  Tumbler, large **22.00**
  Vegetable Bowl
    9" **20.00**
    11", oval, divided **37.00**
Autumn
  Coffee Pot. **24.00**
  Creamer. **5.00**
  Cup **8.00**
  Mug. **15.00**
  Pickle Dish, 12" l. **16.00**
  Pitcher
    6" h **8.00**
    8" h **10.00**
  Plate
    Bread and Butter **4.00**
    Dinner **6.00**
  Salt Shaker, individual **8.00**
  Tray, three part **15.00**
  Vegetable, divided, tab handle. . . .   **15.00**
Coronado
  After Dinner
    Coffee Set, coffee pot, creamer,

Desert Rose, pink rose buds, green leaves, 2¾" h, $15.00.

cov sugar, four cups and saucers, coral, satin	**75.00**
Cup and Saucer, maroon, glossy	**18.00**
Bowl	
5¾" d, coral, satin	**4.00**
7½" d, coral, satin	**9.00**
Chop Plate, 12" d, turquoise	
Glossy	**15.00**
Satin	**4.00**
Cup, coral, satin	**4.00**
Gravy, underplate	
Apple Green, glossy	**14.00**
Turquoise, satin	**18.00**
Plate	
6" d, turquoise, glossy	**2.00**
7½" d, coral, satin	**4.00**
8" d, turquoise, glossy	**5.00**
9½" d, coral, satin	**6.00**
10" d, turquoise, glossy	**8.00**
Platter, 13" l, oval	
Apple Green, glossy	**12.00**
Coral, satin	**17.00**
Saucer, coral, satin	**1.50**
Sugar, cov, coral, satin	**12.00**
Teapot, turquoise, satin	**35.00**
Vegetable Bowl, oval, yellow, satin	**10.00**
Desert Rose	
Bell	**45.00**
Bowl	
7¾" d, low	**25.00**
8" d, deep	**22.00**
9" d, salad	**30.00**
Butter, ¼ lb	**28.00**
Candle Holders, pr	**82.00**
Celery, oval	**18.00**
Cereal Bowl	**9.00**
Creamer and Sugar, cov	**25.00**
Cup and Saucer	**9.00**
Fruit Bowl, 6"	**5.00**
Gravy	**25.00**
Mug, large	**25.00**
Plate	
6" d	**4.50**
8" d, luncheon	**5.50**
9½" d	**9.00**
10½" d	**10.00**

Platter	
12½" d	**25.00**
14" d	**32.00**
Shakers, pr, rosebud	**15.00**
Sherbet, ftd	**18.00**
Soup, flat	**18.00**
Soup Tureen, cov	**95.00**
Teapot	**70.00**
Tumbler, large	**25.00**
Vegetable Bowl	
Divided	**40.00**
Round, 8¾"	**13.00**
Duet Rose	
Baby Dish, divided	**45.00**
Butter Dish, cov	**25.00**
Casserole, cov	**35.00**
Chop Plate, 13" d	**18.00**
Creamer	**6.00**
Cup, green rim	**2.00**
Gravy, liner	**15.00**
Party Platter	**18.00**
Plate	
6" d, bread and butter	**2.00**
9" d, dinner	**8.00**
Platter, 15" l	**16.00**
Salt and Pepper Shakers, pr	**12.00**
Saucer	**1.50**
Sugar, cov	**8.00**
Teapot	**25.00**
TV Plate, indent	**20.00**
El Patio	
Cereal Bowl, yellow, glossy	**5.00**
Creamer, Redwood Brown	**8.00**
Cup, Redwood Brown	**5.00**
Fruit Bowl, 5", gray, satin	**3.50**
Gravy, yellow, glossy	**20.00**
Saucer, Redwood Brown	**2.00**
Vegetable Bowl, divided, green, glossy	**15.00**
Ivy	
Jumbo Cup and Saucer, 7" d saucer	**9.50**
Nappy, 5½"	**3.00**
Relish, 10½", oval	**15.00**
Tumbler	**9.00**
Oasis	
Bowl, 4¾" d	**5.00**
Chop Plate, 13" d	**22.00**
Cup	**8.00**
Plate, 10" d	**7.00**
Platter, 13" l	**10.00**
Saucer	**4.00**
Sierra Sand	
Bowl, 6⅜" d	**7.00**
Butter Dish, cov	**35.00**
Cup	**9.00**
Plate	
6⅝" d	**7.00**
8⅜" d	**8.00**
10½" d	**10.00**
Saucer	**2.00**
Starburst	
Berry Bowl	**9.00**

Bowl, 4¾" d	**7.00**
Butter Dish, cov	**48.00**
Candy Dish, loop handle	**15.00**
Child's plate	**50.00**
Creamer	**8.00**
Cup	**8.00**
Egg Cup	**7.50**
Plate	
6" d	**6.00**
8" d	**8.00**
10" d	**12.00**
Saucer	**3.00**
Soup, flat	**12.00**
Vegetable Bowl, oval, divided	**20.00**
Tiempo	
Bowl, 4½", tan	**4.00**
Creamer, gray	**3.50**
Cup	
Gray	**3.00**
Tan	**3.00**
Plate	
5⅞" d, tan	**4.00**
7¾" d, tan	**4.00**
9½" d	
Gray	**1.00**
Tan	**5.00**
Saucer, tan	**1.50**
Tumbler, gray	**6.50**
Wheat Brown	
Ashtray	**12.00**
Bread Tray	**35.00**
Butter, open	**25.00**
Creamer	**20.00**
Cup	**4.50**
Pitcher	**45.00**
Plate	
6½" d	**10.00**
8½" d	**15.00**
10½" d	**18.00**
Salt and Pepper Shakers, pr	**20.00**
Saucer	**3.00**
Soup, lug	**18.00**
Sugar	**22.00**
Vegetable Bowl, round, large	**30.00**

GAUDY WARES

History: Gaudy Ware is the name used by many collectors and dealers to describe a particular type of pottery. This white bodied ware usually sports stylized floral, luster, and enamel under-the-glaze decorations. Gaudy Ware is made up of three basic types—Gaudy Dutch, Gaudy Ironstone, and Gaudy Welsh.

Gaudy Dutch is an opaque, soft-paste ware made between 1790 and 1825 in England's Staffordshire district. Most pieces are unmarked; marks of various potters, including the impressed marks of Riley and Wood, have been found.

Pieces were first hand decorated in an underglaze blue, then fired, and finally they received additional decoration over the glaze. This overglaze decoration is extensively worn on many of today's examples pieces. Gaudy Dutch found a ready market within the Pennsylvania German community because it was inexpensive and intense with color. It had little appeal in England.

Gaudy Ironstone was made in England around 1850. Most pieces are impressed "Ironstone" and bear a registry mark. Ironstone is an opaque, heavy-bodied earthenware which contains large proportions of flint and slag. Gaudy Ironstone is decorated in patterns and colors similar to Gaudy Welsh.

Gaudy Welsh is a translucent porcelain that was originally made in the Swansea area of England from 1830 to 1845. Although the designs resemble Gaudy Dutch, the body texture and weight differ. One distinguishing factor is the gold luster on top of the glaze.

All of the Gaudy Wares are welcomed additions in a Country setting. Their brightly colored decorations add an interesting dash to cupboards and shelves. The patterns are fun to identify. Variety can also be achieved through shapes and sizes.

References: Susan and Al Bagdade, *Warman's English & Continental Pottery & Porcelain, 2nd Edition,* Wallace-Homestead, 1991; Eleanor and Edward Fox, *Gaudy Dutch,* published by author, 1970, out-of-print; John A. Shuman, III, *The Collector's Encyclopedia of Gaudy Dutch & Welsh,* Collector Books, 1990, 1991 value update; Howard Y. Williams, *Gaudy Welsh China,* Wallace-Homestead, out-of-print.

Reproduction Alert: Gaudy Dutch cup plates, bearing the impressed mark "CYBRIS," have been reproduced and are collectible in their own right. The Henry Ford Museum has issued pieces in the Single Rose pattern, although they are porcelain rather than soft-paste.

Gaudy Dutch	
Bowl	
6¼" d, Dahlia	**350.00**
6½" d, Grape, lustered rim	**375.00**
Coffee Pot	
9½" h, Sunflower	**1,650.00**
11½" h, Oyster, domed cov	**2,090.00**
Creamer	
3½" h, Butterfly	**660.00**
4⅜" h, War Bonnet	**450.00**
4½" h, Urn	**880.00**
4⅞" h, Dove	**450.00**
5¼" h, Double Rose	**630.00**
Dish, deep well	
7⅜" d, Single Rose	**350.00**
9½" d, War Bonnet	**825.00**
9⅞" d, Butterfly	**990.00**

Gaudy Dutch, cup and saucer, handleless, Dove pattern, $525.00.

Gaudy Ironstone, soup, 7⅝" d, unmarked, $40.00.

10⅛" d, Single Rose, imp "RILEY" mark	**660.00**
Jug, 6¼" h, Double Rose, mask spout with light beard	**550.00**
Pitcher	
8" h, Grape	**2,420.00**
8¼" h, Double Rose	**1,430.00**
Plate	
4¾" d, Primrose	**410.00**
5⁵⁄₁₆" d, Urn Variant.	**380.00**
5½" d	
Straw Flower	**370.00**
Urn	**775.00**
6⅜" d, Zinnia	**550.00**
6½" d	
Oyster	**450.00**
Sunflower	**750.00**
7¼" d, Butterfly.	**775.00**
8¼" d	
Dove	**675.00**
War Bonnet	**675.00**
8⅜" d, Dahlia, double border. . . .	**1,200.00**
8½" d	
Oyster	**525.00**
Single Rose	**220.00**
Zinnia	**575.00**
8¾" d	
Double Rose	**1,200.00**
Primrose, imp "RILEY"	**650.00**
9¼" d, Straw Flower	**750.00**
9¾" d	
Carnation	**565.00**
Grape	**525.00**
Sunflower	**1,150.00**
War Bonnet	**425.00**
9⅞" d	
Oyster	**630.00**
Primrose	**2,640.00**
10" d	
Double Rose	**715.00**
Urn	**600.00**
Zinnia, imp "RILEY" mark. . . .	**660.00**
Platter	
14" l, Butterfly, oval	**1,800.00**
15" l, Double Rose.	**3,630.00**

Soup Plate	
8⅜" d, Carnation.	**425.00**
8¾" d, Grape	**675.00**
Sugar Bowl, cov	
5" h, Double Rose, sq shape	**1,100.00**
5¼" h, Dove	**630.00**
Tea Bowl and Saucer	
Carnation	**600.00**
Leaf	**775.00**
Oyster.	**425.00**
Single Rose	**250.00**
Urn.	**400.00**
War Bonnet.	**550.00**
Teapot	
5¾" h, Butterfly, rect	**1,320.00**
6¼" h, Double Rose, rect	**1,980.00**
6½" h, Carnation.	**660.00**
6½" h, War Bonnet	**2,500.00**
Gaudy Ironstone	
Bowl, 10" l, 7½" w, Strawberry	**385.00**
Creamer	
3¼" h, floral dec, red, blue, green, and black.	**45.00**
5¾" h, molded floral design, polychrome enamel, blue underglaze.	**125.00**
Cup and Saucer, handleless	
Floral dec, red, blue, black, and two shades of green, imp mark	**65.00**
Morning Glory, blue underglaze, polychrome enamels, hairline	**85.00**
Strawberry	**150.00**
Demitasse Cup and Saucer, floral dec, red and blue, green rim, handleless	**65.00**
Coffee Pot, 10" h, Strawberry	**575.00**
Creamer, 6½" h, Morning Glory, paneled, foliage handle	**150.00**
Jug, 7½" h, tulips dec, yellow, red, white, and blue, light blue pebble ground, luster trim and rim	**295.00**
Pitcher	
4¼" h, floral dec, luster trim, minor chips	**65.00**

8" h
Floral dec, red, blue, green,
and black **100.00**
Morning Glory, paneled, blue
underglaze **210.00**
Rose, blue underglaze, blue,
red, and green enamels, mi-
nor edge flakes **225.00**

Plate
$6\frac{1}{4}$" d, Morning Glory, blue underglaze, polychrome enamel and
luster dec **60.00**
$6\frac{3}{4}$" d, Sunflower, yellow, green,
and black **40.00**
$6\frac{5}{8}$" d, floral dec, red, green, yellow, purple, and black **50.00**
$7\frac{1}{8}$" d, Urn **65.00**
$7\frac{3}{4}$" d, Sunflower, red, yellow,
black, green, and blue **60.00**
$7\frac{7}{8}$" d, floral dec, red and green . .   **50.00**
8" d
Floral dec, red, blue, green,
and black, set of six **75.00**
Pansies and vines dec, blue,
yellow, green, red, and
black, scalloped edge **85.00**
Urn, multicolor **110.00**
$8\frac{1}{2}$" d
Floral dec, blue underglaze,
polychrome and purple luster
dec **100.00**
Strawberry, twelve sided **95.00**
$8\frac{3}{4}$" d, Strawberry, red, purple,
green, and black, scalloped
edge **85.00**
$8\frac{7}{8}$" d, floral border, red, blue,
green, and black, scalloped
and beaded rim **60.00**
$9\frac{1}{4}$" d
Blackberry, twelve sided,
1850s **165.00**
Rose, red, green, black, and
yellow **45.00**
$9\frac{3}{8}$" d, Morning Glory, blue underglaze, red and two–tone green
enamels **120.00**
$9\frac{1}{2}$" d
Rose, red, blue, green, and
black **85.00**
Urn **125.00**
$10\frac{1}{2}$" d, floral dec, red, blue, and
green, green and red stripes on
emb scalloped border **50.00**

Platter
$11\frac{3}{4}$" l, Oriental, blue underglaze,
orange and yellow enamels . . .   **65.00**
$12\frac{3}{8}$" l, floral dec, blue underglaze, red, purple and blue en-
amels **145.00**
$15\frac{1}{8}$" l, Strawberry **525.00**
$15\frac{1}{2}$" l, 12" w, floral dec, yellow,
green, brown, red, and gold,

wide cobalt blue border,
marked "Ashworth" **15.00**
Soup Plate, $9\frac{1}{4}$" d, floral dec, red,
black, and teal green **45.00**
Sugar Bowl
4" h, floral dec, red, blue, and
green, striped rim **70.00**
$4\frac{7}{8}$" h, floral dec, cov, red, blue,
and green, emb shell handles   **70.00**
$7\frac{3}{4}$" h, floral dec, red, green, blue,
and black **110.00**
8" h, Morning Glory, cov, pan-
eled, blue underglaze, foliage
handles **150.00**
$8\frac{1}{2}$" h, Strawberry, cov **400.00**
Teapot
5" h, floral dec, red, black, blue,
and green **115.00**
$8\frac{3}{4}$" h, floral dec, paneled, polychrome enamels **95.00**
$9\frac{1}{2}$" h, floral dec, luster trim, fruit
finial, marked "Walley," and
English registry mark **235.00**
Waste Bowl
$3\frac{3}{8}$" h, $6\frac{5}{8}$" d, floral dec, red, purple, black, and two shades of
green **65.00**
$5\frac{3}{8}$" h, Strawberry **150.00**
Gaudy Welsh
Bowl
$5\frac{1}{4}$" d, Grape **50.00**
6" d, Oyster **80.00**
$6\frac{1}{4}$" d, Tulip **45.00**
10" d, Columbine, ftd, blue un-
derglaze, polychrome enamel
floral dec **400.00**
$10\frac{1}{2}$" d, Flower Basket **185.00**
Cake Plate, 10" d, Tulip, molded
handles **100.00**
Compote, $8\frac{1}{8}$" d, Aberystwyth, ftd,
blue, burnt orange, green, and
luster **375.00**
Creamer
3" h, Oyster, wide dark blue neck
band, ovoid body **100.00**
$5\frac{1}{4}$" h, Tulip **80.00**
Creamer and Sugar, floral dec, hair-
line in creamer **130.00**

Gaudy Welsh, creamer, $3\frac{1}{4}$" h, $75.00.

Cup, Wagon Wheel.	60.00
Cup and Saucer	
Buckle	85.00
Drape	75.00
Honeysuckle	100.00
Tulip, set of six.	210.00
Egg Cup, 2$\frac{1}{2}$" h, Tulip, c1840	145.00
Jug, Oyster	
2$\frac{1}{4}$" h, c1800	75.00
5$\frac{3}{4}$" h, c1820	80.00
Mug	
2" h, Grape, c1840	145.00
2$\frac{1}{2}$" h, Wagon Wheel	65.00
4" h, Flower Basket	85.00
4$\frac{1}{8}$" h	
Oyster	225.00
Strawberry	125.00
Pitcher	
3" h, Sunflower, c1840.	115.00
4$\frac{1}{4}$" h, Anglesey	90.00
5$\frac{1}{2}$" h, Sunflower, marked "Aller-	
ton"	65.00
7$\frac{1}{2}$" h, Hanging Basket, small	
crack, c1825	225.00
8$\frac{1}{2}$" h, Wagon Wheel	175.00
Plate	
5$\frac{1}{4}$" d, Grape	55.00
5$\frac{1}{2}$" d, Columbine.	50.00
8$\frac{1}{4}$" d, Strawberry	140.00
8$\frac{1}{2}$" d, Grape	55.00
8$\frac{3}{4}$" d	
Flower Basket.	65.00
Wagon Wheel	75.00
9" d, Urn, c1840	80.00
10" d, Oyster, marked "Allerton"	65.00
Soup Plate	
9" d, Strawberry.	115.00
10" d, Oyster, flange rim.	85.00
Sugar, cov	
Daisy and Chain	200.00
Flower Basket, lion's head han-	
dles, luster trim.	150.00
Tulip, 6$\frac{3}{4}$" h	115.00
Teapot	
Daisy and Chain	200.00
Flower Basket, 7$\frac{1}{4}$" h.	325.00
Grape, dome cov, boat shaped	
body, wide flaring rim, curved	
spout, angular handle, blue un-	
derglaze, polychrome enamels,	
pink luster trim, small filled	
spout flakes	325.00
Tulip, 7$\frac{1}{4}$" h	150.00
Waste Bowl, 5$\frac{1}{4}$" d, Columbine	85.00

HALL CHINA COMPANY

History: Robert Hall founded the Hall China Company in 1903 in East Liverpool, Ohio. He died in 1904 and was succeeded by his son, Robert Taggart Hall. After years of experimentation, Robert T. Hall developed a leadless glaze in 1911, opening the way for production of glazed household products.

The Hall China Company made many types of kitchenware, refrigerator sets, and dinnerware in a wide variety of patterns. Some patterns were exclusive, such as Heather Rose for Sears.

One of the most popular patterns was Autumn Leaf, an exclusive premium designed in 1933 for the Jewel Tea Company by Arden Richards. Still a Jewel Tea property, Autumn Leaf has not been listed in catalogs since 1978 but is produced on a replacement basis with the date stamped on the back.

References: Harvey Duke, *Superior Quality Hall China*, ELO Books, 1977; —, *Hall 2*, ELO Books, 1985; —, *The Official Price Guide to Pottery And Porcelain*, Collector Books, 1989; Margaret and Kenn Whitmyer, *The Collector's Encyclopedia of Hall China*, Collector Books, 1989, 1992 value update.

Autumn Leaf	
Bud Vase	165.00
Butter, 1 lb	185.00
Cake Plate	17.50
Creamer	5.00
Cream Soup	20.00
Cup	5.00

Autumn Leaf, tidbit tray, 3 tiers, 11$\frac{1}{2}$" h, $35.00.

Custard	7.00
Drip Jar.	15.00
Fruit Bowl, 5½" d	4.00
Gravy, underplate	14.00
Marmalade, 3 pcs	45.00
Mixing Bowl, #9.	14.00
Pickle Dish	24.00
Pie Baker	14.00
Plate	
6" d	3.50
7¼" d	5.00
10" d	12.50
Platter, 13½" l	14.00
Salt and Pepper Shakers, pr	12.00
Saucer	2.00
Sugar, cov	7.50
Tea Cup	4.00
Vegetable Bowl	
Divided	52.00
Oval	17.50
Blue Blossom, bean pot	125.00
Blue Bouquet	
Pitcher, 5" h	14.00
Platter	5.00
Salt Shaker, range	12.00
Cameo Rose	
Bowl, 5¼" d	2.00
Butter Dish, quarter pound	28.00
Casserole	25.00
Creamer	5.00
Cream Soup, 6" d	7.00
Cup	4.00
Gravy.	12.00
Pickle Dish, 9" l	9.00
Plate	
6½" d	2.00
8" d	2.50
10" d	4.00
Saucer	1.00
Sugar, cov	12.00
Teapot, six cups	35.00
Tidbit Tray	28.00
Vegetable, oval	10.00
Heather Rose	
Bowl	
5" d	3.00
6" d	3.50
Coffee Pot.	27.50
Creamer and Sugar, cov	12.00
Cup and Saucer	4.50
Fruit Bowl, 5½" d	4.00
Gravy Boat, underplate	10.00
Pie Plate	22.00
Pitcher	12.00
Plate	
6" d, bread and butter	1.25
7½" d, salad	3.00
10" d, dinner	4.00
Platter, 13½" l	9.00
Salad Bowl, 9" d	10.00
Sugar, cov	7.00
Tureen, cov	18.00

Red Poppy, range salt and pepper shakers, red and black dec., 5" h, $20.00.

Vegetable Bowl	
9" d, round	8.00
10½" l, oval	7.00
Mt Vernon	
Berry Bowl	2.50
Creamer, ftd	4.00
Cup	3.25
Fruit Bowl, 5¼" d	2.00
Gravy Boat	6.00
Plate	
6½" d	2.00
10" d, dinner	4.00
Platter, 13¼" l	9.50
Saucer	1.25
Soup Bowl, 8" d, flat	6.50
Sugar, cov, ftd	6.50
Vegetable Bowl, 9¼" l, oval	9.50
Peach Blossom	
Butter Dish	9.00
Creamer	4.50
Gravy Basket, orig ladle	20.00
Jug, large	35.00
Ladle	5.00
Plate, 7" d	2.50
Salt Shaker	5.00
Sugar, cov	7.50
Teapot	40.00
Poppy and Wheat	
Baker	15.00
Bean Pot	50.00
Bowl Set, 3 pcs	30.00
Canister	60.00
Casserole, cov	25.00
Creamer	7.00
Custard	5.00
Pitcher	35.00
Plate	
7¼" d	5.00
8¼" d	5.00
9⅛" d	7.00
Platter, 13¼" l	18.00
Salt and Pepper Shakers, pr	25.00
Soup, 8½" d	15.00
Sugar, cov	10.00
Teapot	45.00
Tea Tile, 6" sq	30.00

- Tidbit Server 35.00

Red Poppy
- Baker, French, fluted 15.00
- Bowl
  - $5\frac{1}{2}''$ d, fruit 4.25
  - $9''$ d, salad 14.00
- Cake Plate 16.00
- Cake Server 65.00
- Casserole, cov 25.00
- Cereal Bowl, 6″ d 7.00
- Coffee Pot 10.00
- Creamer 7.50
- Cup 4.00
- Drip Jar, cov 12.00
- Jug 18.00
- Mixing Bowl, set of 3 . . . . . . 35.00
- Mustard, 3 pcs 45.00
- Pitcher 18.50
- Plate, 9″ d, dinner 6.00
- Salad Bowl, 9″ d 14.00
- Salt and Pepper Shakers, pr 20.00
- Saucer 2.00
- Souffle Dish 14.00
- Sugar 8.00
- Teapot, Aladdin 50.00
- Vegetable Bowl, $9\frac{1}{8}''$ d 14.00

Rose Parade
- Bean Pot 35.00
- Casserole 25.00
- Drip Jar, cov 16.00
- Salad Bowl 16.00
- Vegetable Bowl, 9″ d 15.00

Silhouette
- Baker, French 14.00
- Bean Pot 50.00
- Bowl, $7\frac{7}{8}''$ d 20.00
- Coffee Pot 30.00
- Jug 24.00
- Mug 32.00
- Pretzel Jar 75.00
- Salt Shaker, red handle 8.00

Springtime
- Bowl, $5\frac{1}{2}''$ d 5.00
- Butter Dish 9.00
- Cake Plate 12.00
- Casserole, sunken knob 25.00
- Creamer 5.00
- Cup 3.00

Teapot, Chinese red, 3 cup, $30.00.

- Fruit Dish 2.00
- Gravy 8.00
- Jug, 6″ h 25.00
- Pie Plate 22.00
- Plate
  - $6\frac{1}{8}''$ d 1.00
  - $9''$ d 4.50
- Platter, oval 15.00
- Saucer 1.00
- Sugar, cov 6.00
- Vegetable, oval 6.00

Taverne
- Coffee Pot, china, drip 110.00
- Leftover, rect. 20.00
- Mug 30.00
- Tea Tile, 6″ sq, round 90.00

Wildfire
- Bowl
  - $5\frac{1}{2}''$ d 5.00
  - $6''$ d 6.00
  - $9''$ d 9.25
- Cup and Saucer 8.00
- Egg Cup 30.00
- Gravy Boat 15.00
- Pie Baker 15.00
- Plate, 9″ d 7.00
- Platter, 11″ l 10.00
- Shaker, handled, "S" 10.00
- Soup Bowl 10.00

Teapots
- Aladdin, maroon swag 30.00
- Apple, sky blue and gold 225.00
- Baltimore
  - Emerald 35.00
  - Maroon, gold label 42.00
- Basket, canary yellow, silver trim 95.00
- Bird Cage, canary yellow, gold trim 40.00
- Boston, chartreuse, gold trim, eight cups 26.00
- Buchanan, dark green 35.00
- Cleveland, yellow, gold trim, six cups 45.00
- Crest 20.00
- Daffodil, gold trim, cosy 25.00
- French Ivory, gold trim, six cups . . . 18.00
- Gold Label, two cups, yellow, all–over gold flowers, French shape, round 25.00
- Hollywood, ivory 18.00
- McCormick, turquoise, infuser 17.50
- Nautilus, six cup, yellow, gold trim 65.00
- New York, cobalt blue, gold trim, six cups 35.00
- Panel Dripolator, potted flower . . . 25.00
- Parade, canary 18.00
- Philadelphia, turquoise, gold trim, six cups 18.00
- Polka Dot, windshield, ivory gold label 25.00
- Saf–Handle, six cup, cobalt blue . . 65.00
- Terrace Dripolator, floral 42.50
- Twin Spout, ivory 35.00

HULL POTTERY

History: In 1905 Addis E. Hull purchased the Acme Pottery Company, Crooksville, Ohio. In 1917 the A. E. Hull Pottery Company began making a line of art pottery, novelties, stoneware, and kitchenware, later introducing the famous Little Red Riding Hood line. Most items had a matte finish with shades of pink and blue or brown.

After a disastrous flood and fire in 1950, J. Brandon Hull reopened the factory in 1952 as the Hull Pottery Company. Newer, more modern styles, mostly with glossy finish, were introduced. The company currently produces pieces, e.g. the Regal and Floraline lines, for sale to florists.

Hull pottery molds and patterns are easily identified. Pre–1950 vases are marked "Hull USA" or "Hull Art USA" on the bottom. Many also retain their paper labels. Post–1950 pieces are marked "Hull" in large script or "HULL" in block letters.

Each pattern has a distinctive number, e.g., Wildflower with a "W" and number, Water Lily with an "L" and number, Poppy with "600" numbers, and Orchid with "300" numbers. Early stoneware pieces have an "H."

References: Brenda Roberts, *The Collectors Encyclopedia Of Hull Pottery*, Collector Books, 1980, 1991 value update; Joan Hull, *Hull: The Heavenly Pottery*, published by author, 1990; Mark E. Supnick, *Collecting Hull Pottery's "Little Red Riding Hood": A Pictorial Reference and Price Guide*, L–W Book Sales, 1989.

PRE–1950s PATTERNS

Bow Knot
B–1, 5½", pitcher................	**95.00**
B–5, 6½", cornucopia............	**95.00**
B–10, 10¼", vase...............	**350.00**
B–17, candleholders, pr	**75.00**
B–18, 5¾", jardiniere...........	**70.00**
B–25, 6½", basket	**225.00**
B–27, wall pocket, whisk broom shape	**65.00**

Dogwood (Wild Rose)
503, 8½", vase	**75.00**
510, 10½", vase	**135.00**
514, 4", jardiniere............	**42.00**
517, 4¾", vase	**45.00**
521, 7", bowl, shallow..........	**48.00**
522, 4", cornucopia...........	**25.00**

Iris (Narcissus)
401, 8", pitcher..............	**125.00**
407, 7", vase................	**75.00**
413, 9", jardiniere............	**135.00**
414, 10½", vase	**165.00**

Jack–in–the–Pulpit (Calla Lily)
500–32, 10", bowl	**75.00**
501–33, 6", vase..............	**55.00**
510–33, 8", vase..............	**90.00**
590–33, 13", console bowl	**150.00**

Vase, 9¼" h, floral dec., blue base shading to cream to pink, $25.00.

Little Red Riding Hood
Batter Jug, 5½"	**95.00**
Canister, cereal...............	**385.00**
Casserole, red handle	**650.00**
Grease Jar, Wolf	**350.00**
Mustard jar, spoon, 5½"	**200.00**
Salt and Pepper Shakers, pr, 5½" ...	**85.00**
Spice Jar	**300.00**
Wall Pocket	**265.00**

Magnolia (Glossy)
H–8, 8½"...................	**38.00**
H–15, 12", cornucopia, double ...	**48.00**
H–22, sugar	**20.00**
H–23, console bowl	**65.00**
H–24, candleholders	**50.00**

Magnolia (Matte)
1, 8½", vase	**60.00**
6, 12", double cornucopia	**85.00**
10, 10½", basket.............	**145.00**
13, 4¾", vase	**30.00**
17, 12½", winged vase	**125.00**
21, 12½", vase, open handles	**85.00**
24, creamer	**24.00**

Open Rose (Camellia)
102, 8½", vase	**75.00**
105, 7", ewer	**75.00**
110, 111, 112, tea set	**250.00**
116, 12", console bowl	**125.00**
117, 6½", candleholders, dove–shaped, pr.................	**80.00**
120, 6¼", vase	**45.00**
129, 7", bud vase	**40.00**
139, 10½", lamp vase	**200.00**
140, 10½", basket............	**275.00**

Orchid
302, 4¾"	**45.00**
303, 6½"	**60.00**
306, 6¾", bud vase...........	**45.00**
307, 8"....................	**95.00**
308, 10"	**225.00**
314, 13", console bowl	**165.00**
316, 7", bookends, pr	**275.00**

Poppy
601, 12", basket	**425.00**

602, 6½", planter **100.00**
605, 4¾", vase **95.00**
610, 13", pitcher **450.00**
Rosella
R–2, 5", vase **25.00**
R–4, 5½", creamer **22.00**
R–6, 6½" **40.00**
R–10, wall pocket **48.00**
R–13, 8½", cornucopia **50.00**
Stoneware
39, H, 8", vase **40.00**
536, H, jardiniere **70.00**
Thistle, 52, 6½" **65.00**
Tile (Hull Cushion)
Designed **50.00**
Plain **20.00**
Tulip (Sueno)
100–33, 6½", vase **55.00**
102–33, 6", basket **125.00**
107–33, 8", vase **60.00**
109–33, 13", ewer **160.00**
116–33, 4¾", flower pot, saucer . . . **38.00**
117–30, 5", jardiniere **50.00**
Water Lily
L–3, 5½", pitcher **40.00**
L–11, 9½", vase **85.00**
L–22, 4½", candleholder, pr **50.00**
L–24, 8½", jardiniere **150.00**
L–25, 5½", flower pot, saucer **55.00**
L–27, 12", double cornucopia **75.00**
Wildflower
52, 5½", vase **75.00**
65, 7", low basket **350.00**
69, double candleholder **45.00**
70, 12", console bowl **115.00**
71, 12", vase **175.00**
74, sugar, open **42.00**
Woodland (Matte)
W–4, 6½", vase **45.00**
W–9, 8¾", basket **75.00**
W–13, 7½", shell wall pocket **60.00**
W–17, 7½", suspended vase **115.00**
W–19, 10½", window box **48.00**
W–31, 5¾", hanging planter **80.00**

POST–1950 PATTERNS

Blossom Flite
T–4, 8½", basket **60.00**
T–7, 10½", vase **50.00**
T–14, 15, 16, tea set **125.00**
Butterfly
B–1, bud vase, pitcher–shaped,
    matte **20.00**
B–6, 5½", candy dish **35.00**
B–9, 9", vase **40.00**
B–18, teapot **65.00**
B–21, console bowl, ftd **40.00**
B–24/B–25, 16", lavabo set **90.00**
Capri
C–47, 5¼ x 8", round flower bowl **35.00**
C–81, twin swan planter **65.00**

Continental
C–53, 8½", vase **35.00**
C–54, 12½", vase **50.00**
Ebbtide
E–2, 7", twin fish vase **45.00**
E–9, 11¾", cornucopia **38.00**
E–10, 14", pitcher vase **115.00**
E–11, 16½", basket **135.00**
Figural Planters
24, Madonna planter **25.00**
46, 6½", strawberries, yellow, white,
    and red, glossy, ftd **9.00**
62, 12", deer planter **45.00**
80, 7½", swan, shaded green, high
    glossy, sgd **75.00**
98, 10", unicorn base **35.00**
Parchment & Pine
S–4, 10", vase **70.00**
S–7, 13½", ewer **90.00**
S–9, 16", console bowl **45.00**
S–11, 10½", scroll planter **40.00**
S–14, ashtray **75.00**
Serenade (Birds)
S–2, 6", pitcher **25.00**
S–4, 7¼", hat vase **30.00**
S–9, 12½", window box **28.00**
S–11, 10½", vase **65.00**
S–19, sugar **18.00**
S–21, beverage pitcher **55.00**
Sunglow (Kitchenware)
54, salt and pepper shakers, pr **20.00**
55, 7½", pitcher **50.00**
82, whisk broom wall pocket **30.00**
85, 8¾", flamingo vase **25.00**
91, 6½", vase **30.00**
99, 7", hanging planter **35.00**
Tokay/Tuscany
1, 6½", cornucopia **25.00**
5, 5½", urn **18.00**
7, 9½", fruit bowl **68.00**
8, 10", vase **75.00**
9–C, 8½", candy dish, cov **35.00**
14, 15¾", consolette **65.00**
15, 12", basket **95.00**

Vase, 6½" h, White Lily, cream ground, $35.00.

Tropicana
  51, 15½", flower bowl. **175.00**
  52, 10", ashtray. **160.00**
  56, 13½", pitcher **275.00**
  57, 14½", planter vase. **225.00**
Woodland
  W–3, 5½", pitcher **35.00**
  W–8, 7½", vase **35.00**
  W–10, 11", cornucopia. **40.00**

IRONSTONE, WHITE PATTERNED

History: White patterned ironstone is a heavy earthenware, first patented in 1813 by Charles Mason, Staffordshire, England, using the name "Patent Ironstone China." Other English potters soon began copying this opaque, feldspathic, white china.

White ironstone dishes first became available in the American market in the early 1840s. The first patterns had simple Gothic lines similar to the shapes used in transfer wares. Pattern shapes, such as New York, Union, and Atlantic, were designed to appeal to the American housewife. Embossed designs, inspired by the American western prairie, included wheat, corn, oats, and poppy motifs. Eventually over 200 shapes and patterns, with variations of finials and handles, were made.

White patterned ironstone is identified by shape names and pattern names. Many potters named only the shape in their catalogs. Pattern names usually refer to the decoration motif.

There is something elegant about these all white ironstone pieces. Country collectors and decorators alike eagerly seek this ware. Large, crisp, white tureens look quite at home in the Country setting.

References: Susan and Al Bagdade, *Warman's English & Continental Pottery and Porcelain, 2nd Edition,* Wallace-Homestead, 1991; Jean Wetherbee, *A Look At White Ironstone,* Wallace–Homestead, 1980; Jean Wetherbee, *A Second Look At White Ironstone,* Wallace–Homestead, 1985.

Reproduction Manufacturer: Homespun Crafts, Box 77, Grover, NC 28073.

Baking Dish, 13" l, 10⅛" w, 3" d, Gothic shape, eight sided rect, imp "J. Edwards, Dale Hall, Opaque China" mark, c1850 . . . .   **45.00**
Cake Plate, 12" l, Cable and Ring, reticulated handles, Anthony Shaw and Son, England **10.00**
Chamber Pot, Corn and Oats, cov, imp "Ironstone China, Wedgwood," 1863 . . . .   **130.00**

Coffee Pot, Grape Medallion, $200.00.

Coffee Pot, Wheat and Blackberry, Clementson Bros **100.00**
Compote
  Gothic shape, 7½" h, pedestal, ten sided, handled, black "Ironstone China, I. Meir & Son" mark, c1850 . . . .   **95.00**
  Pearly Sydenham, ftd, Meakin **175.00**
Creamer
  Cable and Ring, 5½" h, bulbous shape, black "Stone China, H. Burgess, Burslem" mark **35.00**
  Fuchsia, 5¼" h **30.00**
  Wheat and Clover, Turner & Tomkinson. **60.00**
Cup and Saucer
  Acorn and Tiny Oak, Pankhurst . . .   **25.00**
  Grape and Medallion, Challinor . . .   **35.00**
  Wheat, black "Robert Cochran & Co., Glasglow, Imperial Ironstone China" mark, 1860s. **30.00**
Ewer, 12¾" h, Corn and Oats, Wedgwood **150.00**
Gravy Boat
  Fuchsia, 5¼" h, bulbous, 1860s. . . .   **25.00**
  Vintage **25.00**
  Wheat and Blackberry, 5" h, 1860s   **40.00**
Nappy, Prairie Flowers, Livesley Powell **15.00**

Gravy Boat and Saucer, 9" l, 4½" h, 5 x 8½" oval underplate, marked "Royal Ironstone China, Johnson Bros., England," $75.00.

- Pancake Server, octagonal, Botte, 1851 . . . . **40.00**
- Pitcher
  - 5" h, Paneled Columbia, 1850s **60.00**
  - $8\frac{1}{2}$" h, Wheat, ribbed **30.00**
  - 9" h
    - Embossed Civil War scenes, eagle with serpent, and "Union and the Constitution," commemorates Colonel Ellsworth's death, crazing and hairlines **550.00**
    - Wheat and Blackberry, marked "Taylor and Hanley" **65.00**
  - 11" h, Ceres, ewer body style, imp "Elsmore & Forster, Ceres shape, Tunstall" mark, 1859 . . . . **250.00**
- Plate
  - $6\frac{5}{8}$" d, Prairie shape, imp "Clementson, Hanley" mark, 1862 . . . . **10.00**
  - $7\frac{1}{4}$" d, Sydenham shape, round, imp "T & R Boote, Sydenham Shape" mark, 1853–54 . . . . **18.00**
  - 7" d, Wheat and Clover, Turner & Tomkinson **15.00**
  - $8\frac{3}{4}$" d, Corn and Oats, Wedgwood, 1863 . . . . **20.00**
  - 9" d, Ceres, Elsmore & Forster **20.00**
  - $9\frac{1}{4}$" d, Scalloped Decagon, imp "Davenport, Ironstone China" mark, 1852 . . . . **2.00**
  - $9\frac{1}{2}$" d, Fluted Pearl, twenty sides, imp "Registered October 9, 1845, J. Wedgwood" and black "Ironstone China, Pearl, J. Wedgwood" marks, 1847 . . . . **15.00**
  - $9\frac{3}{4}$" d, Bell Flower, imp "J & J Edwards, Manufacturers, Fenton" mark, 1860s **15.00**
  - $10\frac{1}{2}$" d, Corn, Davenport **20.00**
- Platter
  - $14\frac{1}{2}$" l, Lily of the Valley, Alfred Meakin **40.00**
  - 16" l
    - Ceres, Elsmore & Forster **55.00**
    - Sydenham shape, oval, 1853–54 **50.00**
- Relish Dish
  - Parish shape, Alcock **20.00**
  - Wheat, $8\frac{1}{4}$" l, $5\frac{1}{8}$" d, 1860s **20.00**
- Sauce Dish
  - Baltic shape, 4" l, cov, ladle, imp "T. Hulme, Baltic Shape," mark, 1855 . . . . **85.00**
  - Cable and Ring, $6\frac{7}{8}$" l, $2\frac{7}{8}$" d, ladle, 1870s **45.00**
- Sauce Tureen
  - Columbia shape, $7\frac{7}{8}$" l, cov, underplate, imp "Joseph Goodwin, Ironstone China" mark, 1855 . . . **110.00**
  - Fluted Pearl, undertray, J Wedgwood **100.00**
  - Prize Bloom, 8" h, eight sided round shape, black "Prize Medal 1851, T.J.& J. Mayer, Dale Hall Pottery, Longport, Improved Berlin Ironstone" mark **220.00**
  - Ribbed Bud, $6\frac{11}{16}$" h, oval shape, 1860s **220.00**
  - Wheat and Blackberry, Clementson Bros **60.00**
- Shaving Mug
  - $3\frac{1}{4}$" h, Athens shape, 1842 . . . . **70.00**
  - $3\frac{3}{8}$" h, Wild Flower, 1860s **85.00**
- Soap Dish, $4\frac{1}{4}$" h, Bordered Hyacinth, cov, insert, marked "W. Baker & Co.," 1860s **140.00**
- Soup Plate
  - $8\frac{7}{8}$" d, Paneled Grape, JF **18.00**
  - 9" d, Wheat and Clover, Turner & Tomkinson **25.00**
  - $9\frac{1}{2}$" d, Fig, ten sided, imp "Davenport, Ironstone China" mark, 1856 . . . . **25.00**
- Soup Tureen, Wheat, cov, underplate, orig ladle, marked "R Froster, England," mid 19th C **325.00**
- Sugar Bowl, Fuchsia, Meakin **40.00**
- Syllabub Cup, Trumpet Vine **20.00**
- Teapot, $8\frac{7}{8}$" h, Forget–Me–Not, Wood, Rathbone and Co, Cobridge, Staffordshire **80.00**
- Toothbrush Holder
  - Hyacinth, lid, Wedgwood **60.00**
  - Wheat and Blackberry, $8\frac{1}{8}$" l, $2\frac{5}{8}$" d, lid, 1860s **70.00**
  - Wheat and Clover, underplate, Turner and Tomkinson **50.00**

MAJOLICA

History: Majolica, an opaque, tin–glazed pottery, has been produced by many countries for centuries. It originally took its name from the Spanish Island of Majorca, where figuline (a potter's clay) is found. Today majolica denotes a type of pottery which was made during the last half of the 19th century in Europe and America.

Majolica designs frequently depict elements in nature: leaves, flowers, birds, and fish. Human figures were rare. Designs were painted on the soft clay body using vitreous colors and then fired under a clear lead glaze to impart the characteristically rich, brilliant colors.

English majolica manufacturers who marked their works include Wedgwood, George Jones, Holdcraft, and Minton. Most of their pieces can be identified through the English Registry mark and/or the potter–designer's mark. Sarreguemines in France and Villeroy and Boch in Baden, Germany, produced majolica that compared favorably with the finer English majolica. Most Continental pieces had an incised number on the base.

Although 600 plus American potteries produced majolica between 1850 and 1900, only a handful chose to identify their wares. Among these manufacturers were George Morely, Edwin Bennett, the Chesapeake Pottery Company, the New Milford–Wannoppee Pottery Company, and the firm of Griffen, Smith, and Hill. The others hoped their unmarked pieces would be taken for English examples.

References: Susan and Al Bagdade, *Warman's English & Continental Pottery & Porcelain, 2nd Edition,* Wallace–Homestead,1991; Nicholas M. Dawes, *Majolica,* Crown Publishers, 1990; Marilyn G. Karmason with Joan B. Stacke, *Majolica: A Complete History And Illustrated Survey,* Abrams, 1989; Mariann K. Marks, *Majolica Pottery: An Identification And Value Guide,* Collector Books, 1983; M. Charles Rebert, *American Majolica 1850–1900,* Wallace–Homestead, 1981; Mike Schneider, *Majolica,* Schiffer Publishing, 1990.

Collectors' Clubs: Majolica Collectors Association, PO Box 332, Wolcotville, IN 46795; *Majolica International Society,* Michael G Strawser, Pres, Suite 103, 1275 First Ave, New York, NY 10021.

Reproduction Craftsperson: Marlene Humberd, 2314 Guthrie Ave, NW, Cleveland, TN 37311.

Bowl
  $2\frac{3}{4}''$ d, $3\frac{1}{4}''$ h, raised basket design, green shading to brown **50.00**
  10" l, $5\frac{1}{2}''$ h, molded design, pink lilies, green leaves, tan and brown ground, blue interior **225.00**
Bread Plate
  $12\frac{1}{4}''$ l, Oak Leaf with Acorns pattern   **115.00**
  13" l, yellow wheat on green and brown rim, cobalt blue center, emb "Eat thy bread with joy and thankfulness" **150.00**
Compote, 9" d, $5\frac{1}{4}''$ h, Daisy pattern, light pink int., Griffin, Smith, & Hill, imp GSH monogram **375.00**
Dish
  $3\frac{1}{4}''$ d, yellow butterfly, olive green trim **90.00**
  7" l, Begonia Leaf, Griffin, Smith, & Hill, imp GSH monogram. **185.00**

Mayonnaise, 5" bowl, $6\frac{3}{4}''$ underplate, green cabbage, $60.00

Pitcher, $6\frac{5}{8}''$ h, Sunflower, purple interior, sgd, $165.00.

  $11\frac{1}{4}''$ d, $1\frac{1}{4}''$ h, wide molded rim, variegated light green–blue scrolls and flowers, variegated olive center, scene of gnomes and leaves, birds in flight **125.00**
Pitcher
  $5\frac{1}{2}''$ h, squatty, mottled brown and yellow, raised flowers and leaves   **125.00**
  $6\frac{1}{2}''$ h, figural, frog, mauve spots on green back, yellow belly and feet, mauve twist handle, green lily pad base **150.00**
  7" h, figural, fish **155.00**
Planter, 10" h, figural tree trunk, central well surrounded by three smaller wells, molded leaves, central bird's nest flanked by two bird figures, imp mark on base, Taft, Keene, NH, late 19th C **300.00**
Platter, 11" l, Wild Rose and Rope pattern, aqua ground, cobalt blue center **115.00**
Spittoon
  $6\frac{3}{4}''$ d, yellow glaze, raised water lilies, soft pink interior **80.00**
  7" d
    Blue Glaze, pink, yellow, and white raised flowers, soft pink interior **65.00**
    Flint Enamel Glaze, raised flower band **25.00**
Tray, 20" l, figural, fish **110.00**
Vase, $6\frac{1}{2}''$ h, emb morning glories, stem handles, green, blue, pink, and lavender **75.00**

McCOY POTTERY

History: The J. W. McCoy Pottery Co. was established in Roseville, Ohio, in September 1899. The early McCoy Company produced both stoneware and some art pottery lines, including Rosewood. In October 1911, three potteries merged, creating the Brush–McCoy Pottery Company This company continued to produce the original McCoy lines and added several new art lines. Many early pieces are not marked.

In 1910, Nelson McCoy and his father, J. W. McCoy, founded the Nelson McCoy Sanitary Stoneware Company. In 1925, the McCoy family sold their interest in the Brush–McCoy Pottery Company and concentrated on expanding and improving the Nelson McCoy Company. The new company produced stoneware, earthenware specialities, and artware. Most pottery marked McCoy was made by the Nelson McCoy Company.

McCoy Pottery is best known for its cookie jars, kitchenwares, tablewares, and florist pieces. Bright colors and country motifs abound. Several types of glazes were used. The highly glazed utilitarian wares are valued as they stand the test of time and hard use. One of the most widely recognized McCoy pieces is a small brown glazed mustard jar which was made for the Heinz Company.

Over twenty different marks have been identified.

References: Sharon and Bob Huxford, *The Collectors Encyclopedia of McCoy Pottery,* Collector Books, 1991 value update; Harold Nichols, *McCoy Cookie Jars: From The First To The Latest,* Nichols Publishing, 1987.

Periodical: *Our McCoy Matters,* 12704 Lockleven Lane, Woodbridge, VA 22192.

Ashtray	
Hands, leaf dec, yellow, 1941	**6.50**
Square, brown, white dappled edges, 1964	**3.75**
Baby Planter	
Cradle, pink	**7.50**
Lamb, white, blue bow	**8.00**
Stork, green	**7.00**
Bank, Happy Face	**20.00**
Basket, oak leaf and acorns, cream, brown highlights, 1952	**15.00**
Bookends, pr, jumping horses, marked "Nu–Art".	**18.50**
Bowl, 5 x 6½", ftd, drippy green over onyx glaze	**35.00**
Cat Dish.	**55.00**
Centerpiece Bowl, 8¾" d, blue, tulips dec	**7.50**
Cornucopia	**18.00**
Creamer, Elsie The Cow adv	**15.00**
Custard Cup, light blue, beaded edge, c1953	**3.00**
Dresser Caddy, figural, buffalo.	**12.50**
Flower Pot, attached base	
Embossed flowers, pink glaze, 1940	**5.00**
Plain, matte blue glaze.	**4.00**
Smiley Face	**4.50**
Gravy Boat, rooster on nest	**55.00**

Planter, 7¼ x 4⅛ x 6⅜", "Down by the Old Mill Stream," Bennington style glaze, double well in back, $12.00.

Grease Jar, cov, cabbage, 1954	**17.50**
Jardiniere, white, applied bud, 1947	**8.50**
Lamp, cowboy boots.	**34.00**
Mug	
Corn pattern, pale yellow kernels, green husk, c1910	**65.00**
Happy Face	**8.00**
Pet Dish, 5" d, rust on ivory	**2.50**
Pitcher	
Ball Jug, yellow, c1950	**15.00**
Old Crow	**17.50**
Planter	
Blossom Time, yellow	**5.00**
Frog.	**8.50**
Rabbit, ivory.	**7.00**
Springwood, white flowers, pink matte, ftd	**6.00**
Sprinkling Can, white, rose decal	**6.50**
Turtle	**14.00**
Uncle Sam	**15.00**
Wagon, green, yellow wheels, umbrella	**55.00**
Wishing Well, green–brown	**9.50**
Reamer, Ivy	**14.00**
Salt and Pepper Shakers, pr, cabbage, 1954	**10.00**

Tea Set, English Ivy pattern, vine handles, $35.00.

Snack Dish, three leaves, rustic glaze, 1952 . . . . **8.50**
Spoon Rest, penguin, 1953 . . . . **15.00**
Teapot
- Daisies on white ground, #140 . . . **12.50**
- Grecian pattern **25.00**
- Pine Cone **20.00**

Tumble Up, blue and white spatter, 1975 . . . . **4.00**
Vase
- $5\frac{1}{2}''$ h, matte green **20.00**
- $7''$ h, ripple ware, green, bright pink rim trim, 1950 . . . . **5.00**
- $7\frac{1}{2}''$ h, mottled green, marked "Brush, #709" **18.00**
- $8''$ h, pink hyacinth **13.00**
- $9''$ h, sq, light green, stylized floral sculpting, 1941 . . . . **8.00**
- $10''$ h, light green, straight ribbed sides, 1957 . . . . **6.50**

Vegetable Dish, divided, brown and cream drip **8.00**
Wall Pocket
- Flower, rustic glaze, 1946 . . . . **10.00**
- Umbrella, yellow, 1955 . . . . **12.50**

Wash Bowl and Pitcher, white, blue trim, 1967 . . . . **12.00**

MOCHA

History: Mocha decoration usually is found on utilitarian creamware and stoneware pieces and is produced through a simple chemical action. A color pigment of brown, blue, green, or black is made acidic by an infusion of tobacco or hops. When the acidic colorant is applied in blobs to an alkaline ground, it reacts by spreading in feathery, seaweed–like designs. This type of decoration usually is supplemented with bands of light colored slip.

Types of decoration vary greatly, from those done in a combination of motifs, such as "Cat's Eye" and "Earthworm," to a plain pink mug decorated with green ribbed bands. Most forms of mocha are hollow, e.g., mugs, jugs, bowls, and shakers.

English potters made the vast majority of the pieces. Marked pieces are extremely rare. Collectors group the ware into three chronological periods: 1780–1820, 1820–1840, and 1840–1880.

Country collectors treasure mocha ware. Warm colors and interesting designs lend themselves well to Country collections.

Reference: Susan and Al Bagdade, *Warman's English & Continental Pottery & Porcelain, 2nd Edition,* Wallace–Homestead, 1991.

Bowl
- $4\frac{1}{8}''$ d, medium blue glaze, black and white checkered band on rim, foot **70.00**
- $4\frac{3}{4}''$ d, $2\frac{1}{4}''$ h, marbleized black, white, blue, and orange dec on emb green band **650.00**
- $5\frac{1}{8}''$ d, $3\frac{1}{8}''$ h, white, brown, and blue cat's eye dec on orange band, black stripes **200.00**
- $5\frac{5}{8}''$ d, $3''$ h, white wavy lines on dark brown band, tan ground **375.00**
- $8\frac{1}{2}''$ d, $4''$ h, tooled rim, pale blue and black earthworm dec on orange–tan band, black and green stripes **600.00**

Bowl, $5\frac{1}{2}''$ d, $2\frac{3}{4}''$ h, blue band, \$175.00.

Chamber Pot
- $2\frac{1}{4}''$ h, miniature, yellow ware, blue seaweed dec on white band **110.00**
- $9''$ d, $8''$ h
  - Cat's Eye and Leaf dec, tan, olive, dark brown, and white on emb green band, lid, emb leaf handle **500.00**
  - Seaweed dec, blue on white band, brown stripes **250.00**

Creamer
- $3\frac{1}{2}''$ h, emb green band, brown and light blue stripes, emb spout and leaf handle **175.00**
- $5\frac{1}{4}''$ h, medium blue glaze, black and white checkered band around shoulder **200.00**

Cup and Saucer
- Black seaweed design on beige ground, white interior on cup and saucer **400.00**
- Black seaweed design on orange ground, emb blue rim, handleless **1,300.00**
- Medium blue glaze, black and white checkered band at top, white fluted band at bottom, handleless, matching saucer **125.00**

Jar, $5\frac{1}{2}''$ d, $3\frac{3}{4}''$ h, yellow ware, blue stripes on sanded bands, air hole in lid **155.00**

Jug

6⅝" h, blue and white raised earth-worm designs on two blue bands **675.00**

8¼" h, one gallon size, dark brown seaweed dec on gray band, enclosed by upper and lower blue bands **350.00**

8½" h, Liverpool shape, medium blue glaze, two black and white checkered bands, foliate handle and spout **325.00**

Mug

2¾" h, medium blue glaze, black and white checkered band at top, white fluted band at bottom **100.00**

3½" h, blue, white, and brown earth-worm design on yellow ochre and chocolate brown bands, black stripes, leaf handle **350.00**

3½" h, medium blue glaze, band of white vertical bars around center, black and white checkered bands above and below **170.00**

3¾" h

Cat's Eye and Seaweed dec, emb green rim, gray band, orange stripes, emb leaf handle **850.00**

Checkered bands, black and white, barrel shape, medium blue glaze **175.00**

4¼" h, earthworm dec on gray band, dark brown stripes, emb leaf han-dle **300.00**

4⅜" h

Black seaweed on orange band, brown and black stripes, emb leaf handle. **700.00**

Marbleized blue, brown, and white band, blue and black stripes, leaf handle **675.00**

4¾" h

Checkered body, black and white, blue rings top and bottom. **225.00**

Seaweed dec, green on orange–tan band, emb green rim, dark brown stripes, leaf handle **350.00**

5" h, wide brown band, blue stripe

Mug, half pint, tree design, wide blue band, black stripes, $325.00.

top and bottom, emb leaf handle, some crazing. **125.00**

5⅝" h, blue, white, and black rope design on emb bands, green, black, brown, and tan stripes, emb leaf handle, hairline **800.00**

6" h, interlocking white circles on wide orange–yellow band, green, black, white, blue, and gray–green stripes, emb leaf handle. . . **525.00**

Mustard Pot, cov, 3¼" d, 2¼" h, earth-worm dec on blue band, dark brown and orange stripes, emb leaf handle **375.00**

Pepper Pot

3½" h, scroddled pattern, pale blue, brown, and yellow on white ground **525.00**

4" h, geometric pattern, brown, black, and cream, engine turned **650.00**

4¾" h, incised geometric design, me-dium blue and brown **700.00**

Pitcher

4½" h, green seaweed dec on white band, dark brown stripes **65.00**

4¾" h, emb green bands, blue, brown, and dark brown stripes, emb leaf handle **325.00**

4⅞" h, ironstone, seaweed dec on blue bands, black stripes, marked "Pint". **125.00**

5¾" h, rope design on wide orange–tan band, black, blue, and white stripes, emb leaf handle, hairline at handle **525.00**

5⅞" h, blue, brown, and dark brown earthworm design, purple rimmed band, small chip **600.00**

6¼" h

Cat's Eye design, black and white on blue bands, black stripes, emb leaf handle **400.00**

Seaweed design, black, blue band, blue and black stripes . . **300.00**

6½" h, circular brown and white dots with green incised loop band . . . **800.00**

7" h

Earthworm design, brown and white on blue band, green and black stripes, molded band and leaf handle. **925.00**

Twig design, tobacco, dark brown, and tan. **800.00**

7⅛" h, brown, blue, olive, tan, and white cat's eye and earthworm dec and herringbone bands, emb leaf handle **1,450.00**

7¼" h, blue, brown, and white earth-worm dec, gray–green ground, blue bands, slight loss of glaze . . **500.00**

7½" h

Foliage design, blue, tan, and

dark brown, white wavy lines,
blue, dark brown, and white
stripes and bands **2,050.00**
Stripes, black and white, blue
bands **55.00**
8" h, medium blue glaze, black and
white checkered band around
middle, white fluted band around
bottom **100.00**
8¼" h, brown, blue, and gold cat's
eye and earthworm dec **1,300.00**
8½" h, wide blue bands, black and
white stripes, emb leaf handle,
ironstone. **350.00**
Salt, 3¼" d, black seaweed dec on gray
band, black stripes **200.00**
Shaker
4" h, foliage design on deep orange
band, emb green band, blue,
white, and brown stripes **800.00**
4⅛" h, herringbone design, black
and blue stripes, machine tooled
surface **700.00**
4⅞" h, medium blue speckled glaze,
black and white checkered band
around center, pedestal base. . . . **75.00**
5" h, seaweed dec on brown band,
black stripes, blue finial and stripe **725.00**
Sugar Bowl, cov, 4⅛" d, medium blue
glaze, black and white checkered
band on cover, acorn finial. **425.00**
Tankard, 7" h, black seaweed design
on wide orange band, white, green,
and black stripes, emb leaf handle,
pewter lid, soldered repair to lid at
thumb piece **675.00**
Tea Caddy
4" h, medium blue glaze, blue,
black, and white band on shoulder, white fluted band around bot-
tom, no lid **70.00**
4¼" h, medium blue speckled glaze,
black and white checkered band
on shoulder, no lid. **80.00**
4⅞" h, lid, black, tan, and blue geo-
metric dec. **525.00**
5¼" h, lid, marbleized brown,
sienna, and white, small nicks. . . **1,600.00**
Teapot
4½" h, marbleized brown, sienna,
and white, green Leeds rim, minor
nicks on cov and base. **2,000.00**
4⅞" h, marbleized brown, emb blue
ribs. **1,025.00**
5½" h, globular, medium blue glaze,
acorn finial cov, black and white
checkered band around shoulder **200.00**
5⅞" h, oval, medium blue glaze,
acorn finial cov, black and white
checkered band on top, white

fluted band on bottom, straight
spout **550.00**
Waste Bowl
5" d, 2¾" h, black and white earth-
worm dec on blue band **175.00**
5½" d, 2⅞" h, brown and white cat's
eye dec on pale orange band, light
blue stripes, hairline. **105.00**
6⅜" d, 3¼" h, brown and white earth-
worm dec on gray–green band,
blue stripes, hairline. **125.00**

MORTON POTTERIES

History: Pottery was produced in Morton, Illinois, for 99 years. In 1877 six Rapp brothers, who
emigrated from Germany, established the first
pottery, Morton Pottery Works. Over the years
sons, cousins, and nephews became involved in
the production of pottery. Other Morton pottery
operations were spin–offs from the original.
When it was taken over in 1915 by second generation Rapps, Morton Pottery Works became the
Morton Earthenware Company. Work at that pottery was terminated by World War I.

The Cliftwood Art Potteries, Inc., operated
from 1920 to 1940. One of the original founders
of the Morton Pottery Works and his four sons
organized it. They sold out in 1940, and the
operation continued for four more years as the
Midwest Potteries, Inc. A disastrous fire brought
an end to that operation in March 1944. These
two potteries produced figurines, lamps, novelties and vases.

In 1922 the Morton Pottery Company, which
had the longest existence of all of the Morton's
potteries, was organized by the same brothers
who had operated the Morton Earthenware Company. The Morton Pottery Company specialized
in beer steins, kitchenwares, and novelty items
for chain stores and gift shops. They also produced some of the Vincent Price National Treasures reproductions for Sears Roebuck and Company in the mid–1960s. The Morton Pottery
closed in 1976, thus ending the 99 years of pottery production in Morton.

By 1947 the brothers who had operated the
Cliftwood Art Potteries, Inc., came back into the
pottery business. They established the short–
lived American Art Potteries. The American Art
Potteries made flower bowls, lamps, planters,
some unusual flower frogs, and vases. Their
wares were marketed by florists and gift shops.
Production at American Art Potteries was halted
in 1961. Of all the wares of the Morton potteries,
the products of the American Art Potteries are the
most elusive.

The potteries of Morton, Illinois, used local clay until 1940. The clay fired out to a golden ecru color which is quite easy to recognize. After 1940 southern and eastern clays were shipped to Morton. These clays fired out white. Thus, later period wares are sharply distinguished from the earlier wares.

Few pieces were marked by the potteries. Incised and raised marks for the Morton Pottery Works, the Cliftwood Art Potteries, Inc., and the Morton Pottery Company do surface at times. The Cliftwood, Midwest, Morton Pottery Company, and American Art Pottery all used paper labels in limited amounts. Some of these have survived, and collectors do find them.

Glazes from the early period, 1877–1920, usually were Rockingham types, both mottled and solid. Yellow ware also was standard during the early period. Occasionally a dark cobalt blue was produced, but this color is rare. Colorful drip glazes and solid colors came into use after 1920.

Reference: Doris and Burdell Hall, *Morton's Potteries: 99 Years,* published by author, 1982.

Museums: Illinois State Museum, Springfield, IL; Morton Public Library (permanent exhibit), Morton, IL.

Baker, 1¾" h, 5½" d, brown Rockingham mottled glaze.	**35.00**
Bank	
Hen, 4 x 3", white	**20.00**
Pig, 5½ x 7", black	**25.00**
Uncle Sam, 4 x 2", white	**12.00**
Bookends, pr, 6", eagles, brown.	**30.00**
Casserole, metal frame, Woodland . .	**78.00**
Coffee Pot	
¾ pt, individual, dark brown glaze	**25.00**
5 pt, brown Rockingham, ornate emb top and bottom	**90.00**
Cookie Jar	
Basket of Fruit	**25.00**
Hen, chick finial on lid	**50.00**
Custard, Woodland	**30.00**
Figurine	
Cat, 4 x 6", reclining, gray	**10.00**

Wall Plaque, Shoe House, 9½" h, yellow shoe, green roof, door, and sole, $12.00.

Oxen with Yoke, 3¼", brown, pr . . .	**30.00**
Woman, 7¾", wearing bonnet, holding baskets of flowers, pink	**15.00**
Grease Jar, 4", Woodland	**40.00**
Grease Pitcher, 2¾"	**38.00**
Jar, stoneware, Albany slip glaze, marked on side, 2 gal.	**65.00**
Lamp Base, 7½" h, Davy Crockett	**25.00**
Miniature	
Coffee Pot, 3" h, brown glaze, 4 pcs	**75.00**
Pitcher	
1¾" h, bulbous	
Brown glaze.	**20.00**
Green glaze	**25.00**
3¼" h, cobalt blue glaze	**55.00**
Mixing Bowl, 12½" d, yellow ware, wide white band, narrow blue stripes top and bottom	**45.00**
Pie Plate	
9" d, brown Rockingham mottled glaze	**100.00**
11" d, yellow ware	**80.00**
Pitcher, Woodland	
Milk, double spout	**60.00**
Water, 7", ice lip	**90.00**
Planter	
Bird Dog with Pheasant, 9".	**40.00**
Buffalo, on rocky cliff, 11"	**50.00**
Horse with Colt, brown and tan, 9½"	**38.00**
Turkey, 5".	**10.00**
Salt and Pepper Shakers, pr, Woodland	**110.00**
Spittoon, 15" d, scalloped dec top and bottom, brown Rockingham mottled glaze	**55.00**
Teapot	
1 Cup, 4½" h, individual, brown Rockingham glaze	
Acorn shape	**30.00**
Pear shape.	**35.00**
4 Cup, Woodland	**65.00**
Vase, 10¾" h, bulbous	**130.00**
Water Dispenser, cov, 4" h, refrigerator, flat, Woodland	**85.00**

Spittoon, 15" d, scalloped dec top and bottom, brown Rockingham mottled glaze, $55.00.

PAUL REVERE POTTERY

History: Paul Revere Pottery, Boston, Massachusetts, was an outgrowth of a club known as "The Saturday Evening Girls." The S.E.G. was a group of young female immigrants who met on Saturday nights for reading and crafts such as ceramics.

Regular production began in 1908. The name Paul Revere was adopted because the pottery was located near the Old North Church. In 1915 the firm moved to Brighton, Massachusetts. Known as the "Bowl Shop," the pottery grew steadily. In spite of popular acceptance and technical advancements, the pottery required continual subsidies. It finally closed in January 1942.

Items produced range from plain and decorated vases to tablewares to illustrated tiles. Many decorated wares were incised and glazed either in an Art Nouveau matte finish or an occasional high glaze.

In addition to the impressed mark, paper "Bowl Shop" labels were used prior to 1915. Pieces also can be found dated with P.R.P. or S.E.G. painted on the base.

References: Paul Evans, *Art Pottery of the United States, Second Edition,* Feingold & Lewis Publishing Corp, 1987; Ralph and Terry Kovel, *The Kovels' Collector's Guide to American Art Pottery,* Crown Publishers, Inc., 1974.

Collectors' Club: American Art Pottery Association, 9825 Upton Circle, Bloomington, MN 55431.

Bookends, pr, 4" h, 4¾" l, sloping blue blocks, pastoral riverview scenes, impressed Revere circular mark, sgd "F2 24" **825.00**

Bowl
4¾" d, green and beige landscape border, blue ground, indistinctly sgd "S. E. G. . .17. . ." **150.00**
5½" d, 2¼" h, incised and painted border design, swans and flowers, white and green on teal blue ground, painted marks "F.L. 196–5–11 S.E.G.," paper label "Bowl. Shop/S.E.G./18 Hull St./ Boston, Mass," executed by Fanny Levine, 1911 . . . . **700.00**
6" d, incised motto "The.Best. Laid.Schemes.O'.Mice.An'.Men. Gang.Aft.Agley," alternating bands of olive green, yellow, and

cream glaze, painted marks "S.E.G./113–6–09/F.L.," executed by Fanny Levine, Boston, MA, 1909 . . . . **400.00**
6¼" d, 2½" h, bulbous, incised and painted band, lotus flower dec, white, blue ground, painted marks "S.E.G./5.7," artist's initials "SG," executed by Sara Galner, Boston, MA, 1907 . . . . **450.00**
6½" d
Central design, chick, pale yellow, blue, and white, deep yellow ground, impressed circular mark "Paul Revere Pottery/Boston," painted marks "FL. 2–26," executed by Fanny Levine, 1926 . . . . **200.00**
Rolled Rim, shallow, matte slate blue glaze, faintly sgd **165.00**
9" d, flared rim, matte turquoise glaze, sgd, dated, artist's initials **175.00**
Creamer, 4⅜" h, cylindrical, painted goose dec, blue and white, yellow ground, impressed circular mark "Paul Revere Pottery/Boston," painted marks "10–23" and crossed circle, 1923 . . . . **225.00**
Cup and Saucer, 3¼" h cup, 7¾" d saucer, yellow–green and blue landscape with center yellow chick, turquoise ground, imp, sgd "016," artist's initials "E. M.," Edith Brown monogram **375.00**
Dish, 5⅜" d, shallow, incised band, five mice, cream glaze, black outlines, painted marks "S.E.G./7–09/ 204/TB," Boston, 1909 . . . . **350.00**
Lamp Base, 10¾" h, cylindrical form, light blue and white drip glaze, speckled grave blue ground, partial paper label, drilled at base and side, Boston, MA, early 20th C **275.00**
Mug, 5" h, motto, flaring cylindrical,

Bowl, child's, 5½" d, 2¼" h, blue tones, yellow and green center design, marked "Johan," $325.00.

applied loop handle, incised and painted roosters and motto, teal ground, sgd, paper label, chip **550.00**

Mush Set, 5½" d bowl, matching pitcher, green and yellow highlights, central goose medallion, medium blue ground, Brighton, MA, c1925 . . . .   **400.00**

Pitcher

4½" h, cylindrical, incised and painted, tulips, yellow, green and light blue, navy ground, imp circular mark "Paul Revere Pottery/ Boston," painted marks "11–23," 1923 . . . .   **225.00**

9¾" h, ovoid, incised and painted band, roosters above "Oh. Up. In. The. Morning. Early. That. Is The Way. Quite. Clearly," black and white, turquoise ground, painted marks "103. . .S.E.G.," indistinct artist's initials, Boston, MA, early 20th C **2,200.00**

Plate, 8½" d, brown and white landscape border, sgd "S. E. G. 10–13," artist's initials "FL" **200.00**

Tile

5¼" d, incised and painted band, landscape design, shades of brown and cream, yellow ground, painted marks "S.E.G./FL/5.18," executed by Fanny Levine, Boston, 1918 . . . .   **200.00**

5⅝" d, central landscape design, green, yellow, and blue, navy blue ground, impressed circular mark and paper label "Paul Revere Pottery/Boston," painted marks "FL/4–2," executed by Fanny Levine, c1925 . . . .   **250.00**

Vase

4¼" h, bulbous, incised and painted band, trees, blue, green, brown, and tan, teal ground, painted marks ". . .S.E.G.," artist's initials "AM," Boston, MA, early 20th C. **950.00**

4¾" h, ovoid, wide mouth, incised and painted band, lotus flowers, ochre, blue, and brown, sky blue ground, impressed circular mark and paper label "Paul Revere Pottery/Boston," early 20th C **200.00**

6¾" h, ovoid, incised and painted band, tulips, yellow–green, blue, and white, teal ground, painted marks "S.E.G./12–22" and crossed circle, Boston, MA, 1922   **325.00**

8½" h

Ovoid, wide mouth, incised and painted band, trees, hills, and sky, green, brown, and blue, yellow ground, painted marks "P.R.P./11–26," traces of paper label **775.00**

Swollen cylindrical, deep blue glaze, painted marks "S.E.G. 1–16," artist's monogram "LS," 1916 . . . .   **175.00**

10" h, swollen cylindrical, wide mouth, rolled lip, sea blue glaze, painted mark "S. E. G. 1–2. . .," initial P **250.00**

10½" h, cylindrical, incised and painted band, birds in flight, green and white, yellow ground, imp circular mark "Paul Revere Pottery," painted marks "8.25/ JMD," Boston, MA, 1925 . . . . . .   **850.00**

PENNSBURY POTTERY

History: Henry and Lee Below established Pennsbury Pottery in 1950. Named for its close proximity to William Penn's estate "Pennsbury," the pottery is three miles west of Morrisville, Pennsylvania. Henry, a ceramic engineer and mold maker, and Lee, a designer and modeler, had previously worked for Stangl Pottery in Trenton, New Jersey.

Many of Pennsbury's forms, motifs, and manufacturing techniques have Stangl roots. A line of birds similar to those produced by Stangl were among the earliest Pennsbury products. The carved design technique is also Stangl in origin.

Pennsbury products are easily identified by their brown wash background. The company also made pieces featuring other background colors. Do not make the mistake of assuming that a piece is not Pennsbury because it does not have a brown wash.

Pennsbury motifs are heavily nostalgia, farm, and Pennsylvania German related. Among the

Plate, 7½" d, "The.Best.Laid.Schemes. O'.Mice.An'.Men.Gang.Aft.A'Gley.," teal blue glaze, $125.00.

most popular lines were Amish, Black Rooster, Delft Toleware, Eagle, Family, Folkart, Gay Ninety, Harvest, Hex, Quartet, Red Barn, Red Rooster, Slick–Chick, and Christmas plates (1960–1970). The pottery made a large number of commemorative, novelty, and special order pieces.

In the late 1950s the company had 16 employees, mostly local housewives and young girls. In 1963 employees numbered 46, the company's peak. By the late 1960s, the company had just over 20 employees. Cheap foreign imports cut deeply into the pottery's profits.

Marks differ from piece to piece depending on the person who signed the piece or the artist who sculptured the mold. The identity for some initials has still not been determined.

Henry Below died on December 21, 1959, leaving the pottery in trust for his wife and three children with instructions that it be sold upon the death of his wife. Lee Below died on December 12, 1968. In October 1970 the Pennsbury Pottery filed for bankruptcy. The contents of the company were auctioned on December 18, 1970. On May 18, 1971, a fire destroyed the pottery and support buildings.

Since the pieces were hand carved, aesthetic quality differs from piece to piece. Look for pieces with a strong design sense and a high quality of execution. Buy only clearly marked pieces. Look for decorator and designer initials that can be easily identified.

Pennsbury collectors are concentrated in the Middle Atlantic states. Many of the company's commemorative and novelty pieces relate to local businesses and events, thus commanding their highest prices within this region.

Reference: Lucile Henzke, *Pennsbury Pottery*, Schiffer Publishing, 1990.

Ashtray
Amish Couple	**25.00**
Don't be so Doppich, 5"	**25.00**
Such Schmootzers	**20.00**

Beer and Pretzel Set, Sweet Adeline, 9 pcs **120.00**

Bird Figurine, cream body, brown trim
Hen, 11" h	**225.00**
Rooster, 12" h	**225.00**

Bread Tray, Wheat pattern	**25.00**
Candleholder, pr, Rooster	**110.00**
Coaster, Sweet Adeline	**10.00**
Cookie Jar, Rooster	**75.00**
Creamer, Red Rooster, 4" h	**30.00**
Cruet, pr, oil and vinegar, Amish, figural head stoppers	**110.00**
Cup, hex	**8.00**
Desk Basket, B & O RR	**45.00**

Mug
Eagle, 5" h	**35.00**
Red Barn, 4½" h	**40.00**

Pie Plate, 9½" d, PA German motif, double eagle, $50.00. $12.00.

Rooster, red	**27.50**
Sweet Adeline	**25.00**
Valentine, brick company anniversary	**19.00**
Pie Plate, apple tree dec	**85.00**

Pitcher
Amish Woman, miniature	**15.00**
Eagle, 6¼" h	**50.00**
Hex, 6½" h	**39.00**
Red Rooster, 6¼" h	**70.00**

Plaque
B & O Railroad	**30.00**
Walking to Homestead, 6"	**35.00**

Plate
Angel	**20.00**
Christmas, 1970 Yuletide, first edition, sgd	**28.00**
Leaf pattern, 6½" d	**8.00**
Mother's Day, 1971	**32.00**
Pretzel Bowl, Sweet Adeline	**45.00**

Snack Tray
Hex	**8.00**
Rooster	**8.00**
Sugar, cov, rooster	**20.00**

Tile, 4" sq
Dutch Couple	**25.00**
Outen Light	**25.00**
Skunk, round	**15.00**
Tray, NEA Centennial, 1857–1957 . .	**10.00**

PURINTON POTTERY

Purinton
SLIP WARE

History: Bernard Purinton founded Purinton Pottery in 1936 in Wellsville, Ohio. In 1941 the pottery relocated to Shippenville, Pennsylvania. The plant ceased operations around 1959. William H. Blair and Dorothy Purinton were the chief designers.

Purinton Pottery did not use decals as did many of its competitors. All slipware was cast. Greenware was hand painted by locally trained decorators who then dipped the decorated pieces into glaze. This demanded a specially formulated body and a more expensive manufacturing process. Hand painting also allowed for some of the variations in technique and colors found on Purinton ware today.

Reference: Pat Dole, *Purinton Pottery, Book I* (1985) and *Book II* (1990), Denton Publishing.

Apple

Bowl	6.50
Butter, $\frac{1}{4}$ lb	45.00
Cereal Bowl	6.75
Chop Plate, 12″ d	18.00
Creamer and Sugar, cov	30.00
Cup and Saucer	12.00
Dutch Jug	25.00
Fruit Bowl, 12″ d	20.00
Honey Pot	10.00
Marmalade	15.00
Mug	25.00
Pitcher, 5 pint	45.00
Plate	
$8\frac{1}{2}$″ d	8.00
$9\frac{1}{4}$″ d, dinner	12.00
Platter, 12″ l	18.00
Relish, divided	20.00
Salad, ftd, 11″ d	28.00
Salt and Pepper Shakers, pr, jug shape	15.00
Sugar, cov	17.50
Tea and Toast Set	15.00
Teapot, 2 cup	12.00
Tumbler, juice	8.00
Vegetable Bowl, $8\frac{1}{2}$″ d	15.00
Water Set, pitcher and six tumblers	80.00

Fruit

Coffee Pot	25.00
Creamer and Sugar	18.00
Lazy Susan, triangular canister set	85.00
Salt and Pepper Shakers, pr, range top	12.00
Teapot, 2 cup	20.00

Plate, Apple, $6\frac{7}{8}$″ d, $5.00.

Heather Plaid

Bean Pot	22.00
Beer Mug	40.00
Casserole, 9″ d	28.00
Coffee Pot, 8 cup	45.00
Creamer, individual	9.00
Fruit Bowl	6.50
Party Plate, $8\frac{1}{2}$″ d	15.00
Plate	
$6\frac{3}{4}$″ d	6.50
$8\frac{1}{2}$″ d	9.00
$9\frac{3}{4}$″ d	12.50
Platter, 11″ l	16.50
Relish Dish, 3 pcs	24.00
Salad Bowl, 11″ d	24.00
Sugar	12.00
Teapot, 6 cup	34.00
Tumbler	
6 oz	13.00
12 oz	15.00
Vegetable Bowl, divided	25.00

Intaglio, brown

Cup and Saucer	8.00
Plate	
Dinner	10.00
Salad	5.00
Platter	15.00
Tea and Toast Set	15.00
Tumbler, juice	15.00

Ivy, yellow flower

Drip Jar, cov	20.00
Honey Jug	15.00
Jug, 1 pint	10.00
Teapot	20.00
Tumbler, juice	8.00

Normandy Plaid

Beer Mug	25.00
Fruit Bowl	15.00
Grease Jar, cov	37.00
Marmalade, cov	17.00
Mug, jug shape	12.00
Pepper Shaker, jug shape	4.00
Plate, dinner	6.00
Salt and Pepper Shakers, pr	20.00
Tea and Toast Set	15.00

Pennsylvania Dutch

Bread Tray	36.00
Butter, $\frac{1}{4}$ lb	32.00
Casserole, 9″ d	38.00
Cereal Bowl	8.00
Chop Plate, 12″ d	28.00
Creamer, individual	10.00
Marmalade	24.00
Pickle Dish, 6″	8.00
Plate	
$8\frac{1}{2}$″ d	12.00
$9\frac{3}{4}$″ d	18.00
Platter	
11″ l	22.00
12″ l	28.00
Salad Bowl, 11″ d, ftd	38.00
Spaghetti Bowl, $14\frac{1}{2}$″ l, rect	72.00

Sugar, individual **9.00**
Teapot, 2 cup **24.00**
Vegetable Bowl, divided **30.00**

REDWARE

History: The availability of clay, the same used to make bricks and roof tiles, accounted for the great production of red earthenware pottery in the American colonies. Redware pieces are mainly utilitarian—bowls, crocks, jugs, etc.

Lead glazed redware retained its reddish color, but a variety of colored glazes were obtained by the addition of metals to the basic glaze. Streaks and mottled splotches in redware items resulted from impurities in the clay and/or uneven firing temperatures.

"Slipware" is a term used to describe redwares decorated by the application of slip, a semi–liquid paste made of clay. Slipwares were made in England, Germany, and elsewhere in Europe for decades before becoming popular in the Pennsylvania German region and elsewhere in colonial America.

"Sgraffito" is a term used to describe redware that has a unique decoration. The entire surface is covered with a thick yellow glaze and the design is scratched into it, removing thin lines to create stylized decorations. Other colors may be added as highlights. Sgraffito ware is time consuming to produce and the glaze often flakes. Pieces in good condition command high prices. Sgraffito ware makes an excellent display piece and new reproductions should not be overlooked.

Reference: Kevin McConnell, *Redware: America's Folk Art Pottery,* Schiffer Publishing, 1988.

Reproduction Craftspersons: *Figures*—James J Nyeste, RD 1, Green Valley Rd, Seven Valleys, PA 17360; *General*—Lester Breininger, Breininger Pottery, 476 S Church St, Robesonia, PA 19551; Susan Campbell, 32 S Merion Ave, Bryn Mawr, PA 19010; David & Mary Farrell, Westmoore Pottery, Rte 2, Box 494, Seagrove, NC 27341; C Ned Foltz, The Foltz Pottery, 225 N Peartown Rd, Reinholds, PA 17569; Gris Pottery, 111 W Main St, Dundee, IL 60118; Richard L Hamelin, The Pied Potter Hamelin, PO Box 1082, Warren, MA 01083; Debra & Joel Huntley, Wisconsin Pottery, W3199 Hwy 16, Columbus, WI 53925; Scott R Jones, 1005 Oak Ln, New Cumberland, PA 17070; The Long Family Potters, Old Eagle Studios, 237 Bridge St, Phoenixville, PA 19460; Becky Mummert, 30 Fish and Game Rd, East Berlin, PA 17316; Stephen Nutt, Yankee Redware Pottery, 25 Ellicott Place, Staten Island, NY 10301; Jeff White, Hephaestus Pottery Studio, 2012 Penn St, Lebanon, PA 17042; Gerald Yoder & William Logan, Oley Valley Redware, RD 5, Box 5–095, Fleetwood, PA 19522.

Reproduction Manufacturers: Basye–Bomberger/Fabian House, PO Box 86, W Bowie, MD 20715; Country Lighting and Accessories, PO Box 1279, New London, NH 03257; Country Loft, 1506 South Shore Park, Hingham, MA 02043; Faith Mountain Country Fare, Main St, Box 199, Sperryville, VA 22740; Gooseberry Patch, PO Box 634, Delaware, OH 43015; Turtlecreek Potters, 3600 Shawhan Rd, Morrow, OH 45152; The Vinery, 103 Alta Vista, Waterloo, IA 40703.

Bank
- 6″ h, ovoid, knob finial, mottled brown glaze, black slashes **145.00**
- 7¼″ w, 4″ deep, 8″ h, figural, chest of drawers, marked "Savings Bank," marbleized yellow stripes, molded detail, ftd. **75.00**

Bean Pot, 7″ h, ovoid, tooled shoulder line, side spout, ribbed strap handle, clear glaze, dark brown sponging **250.00**

Bowl
- 6⅛″ d, 3⅛″ h, ftd, dark brown sponging **75.00**
- 7¼″ d
  - 2″ h, yellow slip wavy lines and dot dec, reddish glaze **325.00**
  - 2¼″ h, white slip stripes, green and running brown glaze. **425.00**
  - 3½″ h, open rim handles, brown glaze **50.00**
- 8¼″ d, 2¾″ h, yellow slip spiral stripe, dark brown wide stripe and dots **85.00**
- 9½″ d, tooled band, dark brown sponging, deep orange ground, rim spout, ribbed handle **175.00**
- 9¾″ d, orange glazed interior. **45.00**
- 15½″ d, wheel turned, lengthwise cut, glazed interior. **50.00**

Bread Tray, rect, 13¼″ l, slip dec, stylized speckled and striped bird figure, early 19th C **1,750.00**

Bust, 4¾″ h, black man, dark brown glaze, beaded necklace, yarn hair and beard **200.00**

Bowl, 8″ d, 3½″ h, $70.00.

Butter Mold, 4⅛" d, stylized tulip design, unglazed **450.00**
Candle Sconce, 6½" h, wheel turned, socket in base **350.00**
Candlestick, 2¾" h, dark brown glaze   **30.00**
Charger
    12¼" d, coggeled rim, yellow slip dec **700.00**
    14" d, white, green, and brown slip dec, wavy lines and crossed tulips   **300.00**
    15" d, yellow and green slip dec, scrolled calligraphic circular designs, PA, early 19th C **3,575.00**
Coffee Pot
    4¾" h, miniature, lid, dark brown glaze **175.00**
    11¼" h, dome top, tooled dec, emb leaf handle, mismatched lid, English **150.00**
Creamer, 4½" h, side spout, ribbed strap handle, bottom impressed . . .   **35.00**
Cup
    2¾" h, brown splotches **50.00**
    3⅝" h, two ribbed strap handles, mottled green glaze, brown highlights **125.00**
Dish
    3½" d, miniature, yellow slip dec, two crossed wavy lines, PA, early 19th C **450.00**
    4½" d, crimped edge, yellow slip stylized leaf dec, reddish brown ground, PA, early 19th C **2,750.00**
    6¼" d, 3" h, applied rim handles, brown splotched glaze **325.00**
    7" d, brown sponged glaze, flecks   **225.00**
    7⅜" d, 1⅝" h, yellow slip wavy lines dec **175.00**
    7¾" d, white slip, sgraffito pinwheels, green and brown sponging, coggeled rim, black back . . .   **1,300.00**
    8" d, sgraffito bird on branch and vine border dec, mottled brown, yellow, and green ground glaze, Medinger Potteries, 20th C **1,425.00**
Figure
    Dog, 8¾" h, seated, open front legs, unglazed, tooled coat **450.00**
    Eagle, 4½" h, standing on conical

Cup, 3¾" d, 1⅞" h, green mottled glaze, Thomas Stahl, $55.00.

plinth, tooled detail, mottled brown glaze, yellow beak, Shenandoah **525.00**
Flask, 4⅛" h, commemorative, yellow slip stenciled inscription "The Best is not to good for you, Job Funnel 1774," and impressed mark "The Dicker, UC & N Sussex" **175.00**
Flower Pot
    4⅞" h, attached saucer base, tooling, green glaze and white slip on red ground, all over clear glaze **200.00**
    6" h, attached saucer base, "John Bell, Waynesboro" impressed label on bottom **300.00**
    8¼" h, saucer, finger crimped rims, unglazed, Galena **45.00**
Food Mold
    5⅞" d, 1¾" h, jelly, impressed "John Bell, Waynesboro" **550.00**
    6½" d, 2⅝" h, hexagonal, mottled amber glaze **40.00**
    7" d, 3⅛" h, turk's head, two–tone green glaze, emb ribs, small handle **65.00**
    7½" d, turk's head, sponged rim **30.00**
    9" d, turk's head, brown sponging, chips **25.00**
    9⅞" d, 3" h, smooth round rim, yellow amber glaze with brown flecks **185.00**
    11¼" d, 10½" h, coiled fish, greenish amber glaze **225.00**
    11¾" d, turk's head, clear glaze, brown and green **75.00**
Grotesque Jug, 6" h, ash glazed, grimacing face, bulging eyes, prominent ears, and broken porcelain bits for teeth on front, pulled handle on back, NC, 20th C **3,850.00**
Harvest Ring, 11½" d, green and yellow slip dec, zigzag and wavy lines, glazed ground, PA, early 19th C . . .   **9,925.00**
Jar
    2½" h, miniature, slightly flared rim, tapered sides, Manganese–decorated, black splotches, reddish ground, New England, 1800–1850 . . . .   **275.00**
    4⅜" h, ovoid, flared rim, deep orange and green **115.00**
    6¾" h, flared lip, tooled straight and wavy lines, brushed brown swags, clear glaze **225.00**
    8" h, shiny dark brown glaze **25.00**
    8½" h, ovoid, tooled shoulder band, protruding handles, clear glaze, dark brown splotches **275.00**
    9½" h, ovoid, applied twisted handles, mottled green and brown glaze, incised bird and numerals, incised band inscribed "Wm. Mc-

Carter's Property, July 3, 1835,"
David Mandeville, Mandeville
Pottery, Circleville, NY. **7,150.00**
9$\frac{3}{4}$" h, ovoid, tooled lines at shoulder, applied handles, dark brown
splotches, clear glaze **200.00**

Jug
4$\frac{3}{8}$" h, miniature, ovoid, tooled
lines, ribbed strap handle, brown
brush dec, clear glaze **225.00**
4$\frac{1}{2}$" h, ovoid, strap handle, green
and brown slip dec, incised cog-
gle wheel design at neck, PA,
early 19th C **1,425.00**
6" h, flared lip, applied handle,
brown fleck glaze, Galena **55.00**
6$\frac{1}{4}$" h, sloping shoulders, tooled
lines at shoulder and lip, applied
handle, mottled greenish orange
glaze, Galena **150.00**
6$\frac{1}{2}$" h, oversize strap handle, amber–greenish glaze **35.00**
7$\frac{1}{4}$" h, ovoid, strap handle, dark
glaze, Lyndeboro Pottery, old pa-
per label **350.00**
8$\frac{5}{8}$" h, tooled lip, applied handle,
greenish mottled glaze, two white
slip circles, Galena **400.00**

Lamp, 3$\frac{3}{8}$" h, flared base, open font
with wick support, clear glaze with
running brown **1,000.00**

Loaf Tray
8" l, miniature, brown slipware hyacinth dec in center, PA, early
19th C **5,225.00**
14" l, rect, yellow slip inscription
"St Nicholas Bishop of Mira," CT,
mid 19th C **4,125.00**
16$\frac{3}{4}$" l, 3" h, coggeled rim, three line
yellow slip dec. **1,400.00**
17" l, 3$\frac{1}{2}$" h, yellow slip dec **485.00**

Milk Bowl
10$\frac{1}{4}$" d, 3$\frac{3}{8}$" h, tooled lid, mottled
green glaze, orange spots, Galena   **160.00**
11$\frac{1}{2}$" d, brown spots, exterior glaze   **125.00**
12$\frac{1}{4}$" d, brown sponged interior
glaze **55.00**
12$\frac{1}{2}$" d, white and bluish green
combed slip dec **60.00**

Mixing Bowl, 9$\frac{1}{2}$" d, 6$\frac{1}{4}$" h, stacking
rim, dark green, orange spots, Ga-
lena **150.00**

Mug
3$\frac{1}{4}$" h, strap handle, mottled brown
and green glaze **350.00**
6$\frac{1}{2}$" h, sponged brown, ribbed strap
handle **800.00**

Mustache Cup, 4$\frac{5}{8}$" h, dark brown
glaze, impressed "George Bol-
linger" **115.00**

Pie Plate
7$\frac{5}{8}$" d, coggeled rim, brown slip design, dark glaze **90.00**

8" d, three line yellow slip dec,
coggeled rim **350.00**
9$\frac{1}{4}$" d, coggeled rim, four line yellow
slip dec **750.00**
9$\frac{1}{2}$" d, coggeled rim, yellow slip
crow's–foot dec. **400.00**
10$\frac{3}{4}$" d, coggeled rim, three line yellow slip dec. **150.00**

Pitcher
4$\frac{1}{4}$" h, mottled amber and brown
glaze **125.00**
5$\frac{1}{2}$" h, side spout, tooled shoulder
line, applied strap handle, mot-
tled greenish–orange glaze, Ga-
lena **230.00**
5$\frac{3}{4}$" h, brown sponging, strap handle   **95.00**
7$\frac{1}{2}$" h, brown splashes on yellow
slip, applied rib handle. **355.00**
8" h, ribbed strap handle, brown
fleck glaze. **90.00**
10$\frac{1}{4}$" h, thick bluish–green mottled
glaze **150.00**
10$\frac{1}{2}$" h, white slip, clear glaze, running green and brown, strap han-
dle, applied ornaments, Shenan-
doah.   **1,350.00**

Plate
7$\frac{1}{4}$" d, crimped edge, slip dec, all–
over yellow scroddle–agate de-
sign over brown glaze, NY, early
19th C **2,225.00**
8$\frac{3}{8}$" d, coggeled rim, sixteen dot yellow slip. **250.00**
11" d, serrated border, yellow slip
dec, one continous looping line,
red ground, New England, c1830   **650.00**
12" d, serrated border, yellow slip
dec, two sets of triple straight lines
alternating with triple wavy lines,
red ground, New England, c1830   **775.00**
14$\frac{1}{4}$"
Oval, crimped edge, slip dec, yellow and brown–black dab-
bings, PA, early 19th C **5,000.00**

**Flower Pot, attached saucer, 4$\frac{1}{2}$" d, 2$\frac{1}{4}$" h,
crimped edges, green and brown glaze, I.
S. Stahl, 1938, $85.00.**

Plate, 9$\frac{1}{2}$" d, yellow four line slip dec, reddish brown glaze, $150.00.

Round, yellow slip dec "St Justin the Apologist," PA **800.00**
16" l, oval, crimped edge, slip dec, alternating groups of three yellow and three green wavy lines, groups divided by straight brown lines, PA, early 19th C **5,775.00**
Pot, 4$\frac{1}{2}$" h, ruffled rim, strap handles, attributed to Schofield Potteryworks, Chester County, PA, early 20th C **175.00**
Preserving Jar, 7$\frac{1}{4}$" h, ridge at flared lip, greenish glaze, orange spots, brown flecks, Galena **225.00**
Rundlet, 7$\frac{1}{2}$" l, spotted green glaze, attributed to Moravian Potters, NC, early 19th C **300.00**
Salt, 11$\frac{3}{4}$" h, white slip floral dec, "Salt" on rim opening, dark green glaze **65.00**
Stove Leveler, 2$\frac{3}{4}$" h. **10.00**
Sugar Bowl
4$\frac{3}{4}$" h, dark glaze, white and red slip dec, mid to late 19th C **45.00**
5$\frac{3}{4}$" h, rope twist handles, tooling, dark brown fleck glaze **175.00**
Trencher, 21" l, rect, yellow slip dec, three triple wavy lines running lengthwise alternating with triple dashes, PA, 19th C **13,750.00**
Washboard, 7 x 13$\frac{1}{2}$", poplar frame. . . **325.00**

ROCKINGHAM WARE

History: Rockingham ware can be divided into two categories. The first consists of the fine china and porcelain pieces made between 1826 and 1842 by the Rockingham Company of Swinton, Yorkshire, England, and its predecessor firms: Swinton, Bingley, Don, Leeds, and Brameld.

The second category of Rockingham ware includes pieces produced in the famous Rockingham brown glaze, that became an intense and vivid purple–brown when fired. It had a dark, mottled tortoiseshell appearance. The glaze was copied by many English and American potteries. American manufacturers who used Rockingham glaze include D. & J. Henderson of Jersey City, New Jersey, United States Pottery in Bennington, Vermont, potteries in East Liverpool, Ohio, and several potteres in Indiana and Illinois.

Rockingham glazed pieces are eagerly sought by Country collectors and decorators. The warm brown glazes blend with earth tones and similar color palettes. Rockingham ware is also found in unusual forms, such as foot warmers, bedpans, and spittoons.

Reference: Susan and Al Bagdade, *Warman's English & Continental Pottery & Porcelain, 2nd Edition,* Wallace–Homestead, 1991.

Bedpan, 17" l **10.00**
Bowl
8$\frac{1}{2}$" d, 3$\frac{1}{4}$" h **65.00**
8$\frac{3}{4}$" d, 2$\frac{1}{2}$" h **25.00**
10$\frac{1}{4}$" d, 4$\frac{3}{4}$" h, molded exterior ribs, scalloped band **45.00**
10$\frac{1}{2}$" d, 4$\frac{1}{2}$" h **30.00**
11$\frac{1}{2}$" d, 3" h, emb leaf design exterior, impressed "Fire Proof, J.E. Jeffords & Co., Phila." **175.00**
12$\frac{3}{8}$" d, 4$\frac{1}{2}$" h **115.00**
12$\frac{3}{4}$" d, 5$\frac{3}{4}$" h **125.00**
13" d, 3$\frac{7}{8}$" h. **30.00**
14" d, 3$\frac{1}{2}$" h. **75.00**
Canning Jar
5$\frac{1}{2}$" h, keg shape **20.00**
6$\frac{1}{4}$" h **95.00**
Creamer
2$\frac{5}{8}$" h **45.00**
3$\frac{7}{8}$" h, glued handle **25.00**
Crock, 6$\frac{1}{2}$" d, 5" h, cov, emb peacocks **65.00**
Dish
7" d, 2" h **30.00**
8" sq, glazed **125.00**
9" sq, emb rim. **45.00**
Figure
Cat, 11" h, seated, chipped ears, reglued to base **95.00**
Dog, 10" h, seated, open front legs **125.00**
Flask
7$\frac{1}{4}$" h, emb morning glory, eagle, and flag. **100.00**
8" h, molded floral dec, band **35.00**
Flower Pot, 2 pc
8$\frac{3}{4}$" h, emb tulips, East Liverpool . . . **165.00**
10$\frac{1}{4}$" h, emb acanthus leaves. **45.00**
Food Mold, turk's head
9$\frac{1}{4}$" d, spiraled flutes. **45.00**
10$\frac{1}{2}$" d, 4" h, straight tapering sides, blue flecks in glaze. **145.00**
Foot Warmer **70.00**
Frame, 8$\frac{1}{4}$ x 9$\frac{1}{2}$", cherubs, naked ladies, and foliate scrolls dec **850.00**
Ink Well, shoe shape, 4$\frac{1}{8}$" l. **55.00**

Toby Jug, 6″ h, basketweave body, tricorn hat, Rockingham glaze, $225.00.

Spittoon, $7\frac{1}{2}$″ d, $3\frac{7}{8}$″ h, brown Rockingham glaze, beaded rim, raised medallion sides, impressed "R" in bottom, early 20th C, $45.00.

Jar, cov
- 8″ h, 8″ d, leaf handles . . . **85.00**
- $9\frac{1}{4}$″ h, 8″ d, cov . . . **150.00**
- 12″ h . . . **175.00**

Jug, figural, man's head, two-tone green and brown glaze, 8″ h . . . **35.00**

Mug
- 3″ h . . . **45.00**
- $3\frac{1}{2}$″ h . . . **105.00**

Nesting Bowls, emb exterior design, set of 3 . . . **75.00**

Pie Plate
- $8\frac{3}{4}$″ d . . . **55.00**
- $9\frac{5}{8}$″ d . . . **75.00**
- $10\frac{7}{8}$″ d . . . **85.00**

Pitcher
- 7″ h, emb hunt scenes . . . **150.00**
- $7\frac{1}{4}$″ h, ovoid, flared foot . . . **155.00**
- $8\frac{1}{4}$″ h, molded peacock . . . **65.00**
- 9″ h, molded tulips . . . **55.00**
- $9\frac{3}{8}$″ h, molded swan . . . **25.00**
- $9\frac{5}{8}$″ h, emb hunter . . . **115.00**
- $10\frac{1}{4}$″ h, molded panels . . . **45.00**
- 11″ h, emb hunt scenes and vintage design, hound handle, William Bromley, Zanesville, eagle mark **1,700.00**
- $11\frac{1}{4}$″ h, rings at shoulder, strap handle . . . **125.00**

Plate
- $9\frac{5}{8}$″ d . . . **55.00**
- $10\frac{1}{2}$″ d . . . **105.00**

Platter, $13\frac{3}{4}$″ l, oval . . . **95.00**

Presentation Pitcher, 10″ h, medallion portraits on sides, glaze frog figure on bottom interior, marked "Mrs. John Webb" . . . **225.00**

Punch Pot, $7\frac{1}{2}$″ h, inset lid, knob finial, 2 quart . . . **230.00**

Ramekin, $2\frac{3}{8}$″ h . . . **15.00**

Salt, 6″ d, emb peacocks, crest, hanging hole . . . **45.00**

Serving Dish, 10″ l, oval . . . **25.00**

Soap Dish
- $4\frac{1}{8}$″ d, round . . . **50.00**
- $4\frac{3}{4}$″ l, oval . . . **55.00**
- 6″ l, molded leaf design . . . **45.00**

Spittoon
- $6\frac{1}{2}$″ sq, emb American eagles . . . **65.00**
- $7\frac{1}{2}$″ d, raised medallion sides . . . **45.00**
- $8\frac{1}{2}$″ d, shell form . . . **45.00**
- $9\frac{3}{4}$″ d . . . **1,250.00**

Sugar Bowl, cov, $5\frac{7}{8}$″ h . . . **285.00**

Teapot, cov
- 6″ h, marked "Rebekah at the Well" **65.00**
- $7\frac{3}{4}$″ h, emb ribs and acanthus leaves **120.00**
- $8\frac{3}{8}$″ h, molded fern and foliage designs . . . **75.00**

Toby Pitcher, $8\frac{1}{4}$″ h, man's head . . . **75.00**

Tray, $8\frac{1}{2}$ x 11″, scalloped rim . . . **100.00**

Tumbler, $6\frac{1}{4}$″ h, applied tavern scene **65.00**

Vegetable Dish, octagonal, spotted glaze, $11\frac{1}{2}$″ l . . . **175.00**

Washboard, $12\frac{3}{4}$ x $25\frac{1}{2}$″, pine frame, Rockingham insert . . . **525.00**

ROSEVILLE POTTERY

Roseville U.S.A.

History: In the late 1880s a group of investors purchased the J. B. Owens Pottery in Roseville, Ohio, and made utilitarian stoneware items. In 1892 the firm was incorporated and joined by George F. Young, who became general manager. Four generations of Youngs controlled Roseville until the early 1950s.

A series of acquisitions began: Midland Pottery of Roseville in 1898, Clark Stoneware Plant in Zanesville (formerly used by Peters and Reed), and Muskingum Stoneware (Mosaic Tile Company) in Zanesville. In 1898 the offices moved from Roseville to Zanesville.

In 1900 Roseville introduced its art pottery—Rozane. Rozane became a trade name to cover a large series of lines. The art lines were made in limited amounts after 1919.

The success of Roseville depended on its commercial lines, first developed by John J. Herald and Frederick Rhead in the first decades of the 1900s. In 1918 Frank Ferrell became art director and developed over 80 lines of pottery. The economic depression of the 1930s brought more lines, including Pine Cone.

In the 1940s a series of high gloss glazes were tried to revive certain lines. In 1952 Raymor dinnerware was produced. None of these changes brought economic success. In November 1954 Roseville was bought by the Mosaic Tile Company.

Country collectors are fond of Roseville pottery. Large collections of interesting patterns, shapes, and colors may be easily acquired. Baskets, urns, and vases readily lend themselves to Country settings as accent pieces. Because most Roseville pieces are marked, identification is easy and accurate.

References: Sharon and Bob Huxford, *The Collectors Encyclopedia Of Roseville Pottery*, Collector Books, 1976, 1991 value update; —, *The Collectors Encyclopedia Of Roseville Pottery, Second Series*, Collector Books, 1980, 1991 value update.

Collectors' Clubs: American Art Pottery Association, 9825 Upton Circle, Bloomington, MN 55431; Roseville's of the Past, PO Box 1018, Apopka, FL 32704–1018.

Ashtray
  Pine Cone
    Blue, 4"................... **120.00**
    Brown................... **135.00**
  Snowberry, pink.............. **45.00**
Basket
  Bittersweet, green, marked #810–
    10..................... **175.00**
  Bleeding Heart, hanging........ **175.00**

Columbine, brown, 10"......... **145.00**
Foxglove................... **85.00**
Freesia
  Blue, #391–8.............. **95.00**
  Brown, #390–7............. **75.00**
Gardenia, 10", #609........... **120.00**
Imperial I.................... **80.00**
Magnolia, brown, #384–8...... **75.00**
Peony, hanging............... **135.00**
Snowberry, green, 10".......... **95.00**
Zephyr Lily, brown............ **87.50**
Bookends, pr
  Freesia, green............... **70.00**
  Wincraft, blue............... **45.00**
Bowl
  Baneda, pink............... **180.00**
  Bleeding Heart, pink, #380–8.... **60.00**
  Clematis, brown, #459–10...... **75.00**
  Columbine, blue, #402........ **75.00**
  Imperial I
    Ftd..................... **55.00**
    Shallow, 10".............. **58.00**
  Ivory II, 4", cupped geometric pattern, matte, silver paper label... **22.00**
  Jonquil, #621............... **55.00**
  Mostique
    6", ivory, low.............. **20.00**
    7"...................... **38.00**
  Pine Cone, green, 4½", #457–7... **155.00**
  Snowberry, handle........... **60.00**
  Sunflower, 4"................ **180.00**
  Topeo, blue................. **145.00**
  Tuscany, pink, 4 x 10".......... **135.00**
Box, Wincraft, rect, chartreuse, 4½".. **65.00**
Candleholder
  Cosmos, pr................. **55.00**
  Lily, #1162–2, pr............. **40.00**
  Panel, brown, pr............. **48.00**
  Pine Cone, triple, green........ **95.00**
Candlestick, pr
  Dahlrose, 3½"............... **105.00**
  Magnolia, brown, 5" h, #1157.... **55.00**
Compote, Florentine............ **30.00**

Basket, Cosmos, 10" h, #397, $115.00.

Bowl, Peony, 6½" d, 4" h, white flowers, green ground, marked "Roseville USA," $45.00.

Console Bowl
Apple Blossom, blue, #331–12 . . . **80.00**
Baneda, green, 9" **275.00**
Bittersweet, green, #830–14 . . . . . **50.00**
Columbine, rose to green, #405–12 **95.00**
Ferrella, rose, frogs, 9½" **350.00**
Gardenia, gray, #627–8 . . . . **80.00**
Iris, #361–8 . . . . **95.00**
Magnolia, brown **95.00**
Zephyr Lily, dark blue, #478–12 **90.00**
Console Set, Thorn Apple, one piece
double candlestick and bowl **140.00**
Cookie Jar, cov, Magnolia, blue **165.00**
Cornucopia
Bushberry, brown, #155–8 . . . . . . **70.00**
Cosmos, blue, #136–6 . . . . **75.00**
Gardenia, #621–6 . . . . **35.00**
Creamer and Sugar, Zephyr Lily,
brown **90.00**
Ewer
Freesia, #19–6 . . . . **70.00**
Silhouette, #717–10 . . . . **48.00**
Wincraft, blue, #217–6 . . . . **30.00**
Flower Frog
Imperial II **32.00**
Peony, green. **28.00**
Flower Pot and Saucer
Donatello, 4½" **75.00**
Pine Cone, brown **125.00**
Ginger Jar, Rosecraft, black, 8" **150.00**
Gravy, Raymor, terra cotta. **15.00**
Jardiniere
Clematis, #667–4. . . . . **50.00**
Corinthian, 9 x 12" **160.00**
Donatello, 22", pedestal **595.00**
Foxglove, #659–3 . . . . **50.00**
LaRose, 6½" **35.00**
Moss, pink, 4". **70.00**
Mostique, 8" **90.00**
Normandy, 7" **65.00**
Pine Cone, #632–5 . . . . **100.00**
Poppy **67.50**
Snowberry, green, 4". **50.00**
Sunflower, 4" **75.00**

**Ewer, Foxglove, 15½" h, green, pink, and
white, $95.00.**

Water Lily, pink, pedestal **700.00**
White Rose, sea blue, 7" **45.00**
Loving Cup, Crystalis, orange matte **1,950.00**
Match Holder, #498–3 . . . . **150.00**
Mug
Bushberry, brown **50.00**
Magnolia, #3 . . . . **45.00**
Pitcher
Pine Cone, brown, #485–10 . . . . . **250.00**
Tulip **65.00**
White Rose, green and rust, #1234 **75.00**
Planter, hanging
Apple Blossom **110.00**
Silhouette, burgundy **75.00**
Water Lily, brown **155.00**
Zephyr Lily **115.00**
Urn
Foxglove, #161–6 . . . . **75.00**
Ivory II, Tourmaline shape, 5½" **32.00**
Magnolia, blue, #446–6 . . . . **90.00**
Topeo, blue, 6" **130.00**
Wisteria, blue, 5" **195.00**
Vase
Apple Blossom
7", #382. . . . . **50.00**
10", green, #388. . . . . **95.00**
Baneda, pink, 4½" **160.00**
Blackberry, beehive, 5½" **235.00**
Bleeding Heart, blue, #964–6 . . . . **95.00**
Bushberry, brown, 12½" **225.00**
Cherry Blossom, 5" **150.00**
Clematis
5", double, brown tones, #194 **35.00**
6", #188 . . . . **65.00**
7", #105 . . . . **55.00**
Dahlrose, 6" **65.00**
Dogwood, 8" **48.00**
Donatello, 10" **82.00**
Foxglove, 6½", bulbous, side han-
dles, relief flowers **49.00**
Freesia, blue, #124–9 . . . . **100.00**
Fuschia
Blue, 7", #895. . . . . **115.00**
Brown, 9" **155.00**
Futura, blue, fan shape, 6" **380.00**
Imperial I, bud, #31–9 . . . . **75.00**
Iris, #917–6 . . . . **75.00**
Jonquil, 4" **70.00**
Laurel, 6½" **50.00**
Mostique, gray, spearhead dec, 10" **35.00**
Pine Cone
Blue, #709–10 . . . . **260.00**
Green, #839–6 . . . . **85.00**
Tan gloss, fan shape, #272–6 . . . **65.00**
Primrose, brown, #767–8 . . . . **70.00**
Snowberry, blue, #IV–6 . . . . **55.00**
Thorn Apple, blue, #810–6 . . . . . . **65.00**
White Rose, blue, #979–6 . . . . . . **45.00**
Wincraft. **28.00**
Wall Pocket
Clematis, brown **90.00**
Dahlrose, 8" **115.00**

Fuchsia, blue	**250.00**
Imperial I	**75.00**
Peony, yellow.	**130.00**
Rosecraft Vintage	**100.00**
Snowberry, pink	**65.00**
Tuscany, orig sticker	**110.00**
White Rose, brown, 6½"	**110.00**
Wall Shelf, Pine Cone, brown	**280.00**
Window Box	
Apple Blossom, green, 4 x 13"	**145.00**
Bushberry, green, #383–6	**45.00**
Freesia, brown	**45.00**
Gardenia, green	**45.00**
Magnolia, brown	**45.00**

RUSSEL WRIGHT

History: Russel Wright was an American industrial engineer with a design passion for domestic
efficiency through simple lines. His streamlined
influence is found in all aspects of living. Wright
and his wife, Mary Small Einstein, wrote *A Guide
to Easier Living* to explain the concepts.

Russel Wright was born in 1904 in Lebanon,
Ohio. His first job was as a set designer and stage
manager under the direction of Norman Bel Geddes. He later used this theatrical flair for his industrial designs. Wright received awards from the
Museum of Modern Art in 1950 and 1953.

Russel Wright did design work for Chase Brass
and Copper, General Electric, Imperial Glass,
National Silver Co., Shenango, and Steubenville
Pottery Company. In 1983 major exhibitions of
his designs were held at the Hudson River Museum in Yonkers, New York, and the Smithsonian's Renwick Gallery in Washington, D.C.

In addition to working for other companies,
Wright created material under his own label,
American Way. Wright's contracts often called
for the redesign of pieces that did not produce or
sell well. As a result, several lines contain various
forms of the same item.

Wright's American Modern dinnerware was an
instant success. Production by the Steubenville
Pottery began in 1939 after the Wrights agreed to
finance the venture. Due to its affordability and
innovation of design, reaction to this new line
was overwhelming. The muted rainbow hues fit
well in a Country decor.

The original colors were Seafoam Blue, Granite
Gray, Chartreuse Curry, Coral, Bean Brown, and
White. After World War II Wright discontinued
use of the less popular Bean Brown and replaced
it with Black Chutney. The addition of Cedar
Green, Canteloupe, and Glacier Blue further enhanced the pattern. Production of Seafoam Blue
was discontinued during World War II due to
shortage of cobalt, but resumed on a limited basis
at war's end.

In 1946 Wright designed a new line of dinnerware, Iroquois Casual. This dinnerware had special thermal properties. Again, Wright was innovative in both design and marketing. This ware
was heavily advertised for its dual usage pieces.
The carafe could double as a vase, the large platter was also the underplate of the coffee service.
Today's collectors are finding additional uses for
this colorful and versatile dinnerware.

Early Iroquois glazes were mottled, later pieces
had a polished look. Collectors should be cautious when dating by color or glaze because new
production closely resembles the original.

Iroquois is found in twelve colors, including
Avocado Yellow, Lettuce Green, Nutmeg, Pars-
ley, and Ripe Apricot. Two–color combinations
for saucers, lids, and liners offer collectors endless ways to display this dinnerware.

Russel Wright also designed restaurant and
commercial dinnerware lines. Don't overlook a
piece that has the right design appearance.
Watch for advertising pieces and even railroad
and airline china with a Russel Wright back-
stamp.

Reference: Ann Kerr, *The Collector's Encyclopedia of Russel Wright Designs*, Collector Books,
1990.

American Modern

Ashtray, Seafoam Blue.	**8.00**
Baker, 8" l, oval, Bean Brown.	**15.00**
Butter, cov, Granite Gray.	**150.00**
Casserole, cov, stick handle	
Cantaloupe.	**110.00**
Coral	**30.00**
Seafoam Blue	**42.00**
Celery Dish, 13" l	
Chartreuse Curry	**20.00**
Granite Gray	**25.00**
Child's plate, Coral	**95.00**
Chop Plate	
Chartreuse Curry	**20.00**
Granite Gray	**18.00**
Coffee Pot, Chartreuse Curry	**120.00**
Creamer	
Chartreuse Curry	**7.00**
Granite Gray	**9.50**
Seafoam Blue	**8.00**
Cup and Saucer	
Black Chutney.	**6.50**
Cedar Green	**6.00**

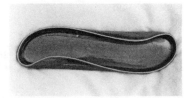

**American Modern, celery, Chartreuse
Curry, $20.00.**

American Modern, creamer, Granite Gray, $9.50.

Chartreuse Curry	6.00
Granite Gray	5.00
Seafoam Blue	6.00
Demitasse Cup and Saucer, Coral	9.00
Fruit Bowl, Chartreuse Curry	5.00
Gravy Bowl, underplate	
Coral	13.00
Granite Gray	18.00
Hostess Plate	
Coral	40.00
Granite Gray	40.00
Mug	
Black Chutney	40.00
Chartreuse Curry	35.00
Granite Gray	40.00
Pickle Dish, Granite Gray	10.00
Pitcher, water	
Bean Brown	150.00
Chartreuse Curry	35.00
Plate	
6" d	
Cedar Green	3.00
Granite Gray	2.50
8" d, salad, Granite Gray	7.00
10" d	
Black Chutney	7.00
Chartreuse Curry	5.00
Coral	8.00
Platter, 13¾" l, Granite Gray	25.00
Salad Bowl	
Chartreuse Curry	38.00
Coral	30.00
Ramekin, cov, Glacier Blue	110.00
Refrigerator Dish, cov, Granite Gray	150.00
Salt and Pepper Shakers, pr	
Chartreuse Curry	12.00
Granite Gray	8.00
Soup, Granite Gray, lug handle . . .	9.00
Stack Set, Coral	125.00
Sugar, cov	
Chartreuse Curry	7.00
Seafoam Blue	7.50
Teapot, Cantaloupe	65.00
Vegetable, oval	
Chartreuse Curry, cov	28.00
Granite Gray	14.00
Iroquois	
Bowl	
5" d, Avocado Yellow	5.00
5½" d, Avocado Yellow	4.00

Casserole, 2 quart, Lemon Yellow	35.00
Creamer, stacking	
Avocado Yellow	7.00
Ice Blue	7.00
Cup and Saucer	
Avocado Yellow	6.00
Cantaloupe	6.00
Nutmeg Brown	6.50
Pink Sherbet	8.00
Sugar White	6.50
Gravy Bowl, 5¼" d, Ice Blue, 12 oz	5.00
Plate	
6" d	
Avocado Yellow	3.00
Nutmeg Brown	3.00
7½" d	
Lemon Yellow	4.00
Sugar White	4.00
9" d	
Avocado Yellow	5.00
Sugar White	5.00
9¾" d, Ice Blue	5.50
10" d, Avocado Yellow	5.00
Platter	
12½" l, Ice Blue	14.00
14" l, Avocado Yellow	17.00
Soup, 8" d, flat, Ice Blue	12.00
Vegetable Bowl, cov, 10" l, Avocado Yellow, divided	25.00
Residential	
Bowl	
4½" d, Gray	5.00
5" d, handles, Gray	6.00
Creamer, Copper Penny	9.50
Cup	
Gray	3.00
Lemon Ice	3.50
Fruit Bowl, Sea Mist	5.00
Onion Soup, cov, Blue	20.00
Plate	
6" d	
Gray	1.00
Lemon Ice	4.00
Salmon	4.00
10" d	
Aqua	4.00
Gray	3.50
Platter, Black Velvet	15.00
Saucer, Gray	1.00
Tumbler, Sea Mist	8.50
Vegetable Bowl, Lemon Ice, divided	10.00

SEWER TILE ART

History: The sewer tile factories in the area of eastern Ohio, near Akron, produced utilitarian objects made of clay. These companies made a number of advertising giveaways featuring miniature examples of their products or decorative items such as plaques, paperweights, and horseshoes. At day's end workers fashioned leftover clay into myriad objects for personal enjoyment. Molds also were available, and miscellaneous figures from cats to pigs were made.

Although sewer tile materials date from the 1800s to the 1950s, the golden age of this folk art forms dates from 1900 to 1940. Emphasize the hand sculpted pieces. Research has identified many of the artisans who produced these materials.

Since pieces are highly individualistic, artistic consideration is a large factor in determining price. Damage causes serious problems for the collector. One-of-a-kind items need to be carefully restored if damaged. Collectors prefer items in very good or better condition. Prices do fluctuate; the market is still seeking a level of stability. Whenever a collecting category attracts the folk art collectors, it is difficult to find an accurate pricing level. Design, style, and even the whimsical nature of the piece determine the price, as well as how much the collector is willing to pay.

Reference: Jack E. Adamson, *Illustrated Handbook of Ohio Sewer Pipe Folk Art,* privately printed, 1973.

Bank, 10" h, bust of man on cylinder, incised inscription "Green's Bank"	**900.00**
Birdhouse, 10" h, tooled detail	**195.00**
Desk Set, 8¼" w, 5¼" h, fireplace shape, repaired chimney	**90.00**
Figure	
Cat, 9" l, reclining, yellow slip facial dec, tooled detail	**235.00**
Dog, seated	
4¾" h, solid body, primitive hand tooling.	**85.00**
10½" h, flat headed, bold hand tooling.	**450.00**
11" h, tooled detail	**280.00**
11¼" h, tooled detail	**275.00**
Frog, 7½" h, marked "Superior"	**175.00**
Lion, 7" l, tooled detail, rect stepped base	**350.00**

Cat, 8" h, by W. A. Baker, $300.00.

Lion, 13½ x 9", unglazed terra cotta, OH, c1830–1840, $175.00.

Pig, 6¾" l, freestanding legs, "1927" date incised on bottom	**165.00**
Turtle, 7¼" l, incised detail, sgd and dated 1921	**200.00**
Flower Pot, tree stump	
6" h	**15.00**
6¼" h	**20.00**
Lamp Base, 9½" h, tree trunk shape	**25.00**
Mask, 12½" h	**85.00**
Paperweight	
Dog, 3¾" h, seated, base inscribed "Nobody Loves Me"	**175.00**
Frog, 2¼ x 4¼", incised detail, round base	**85.00**
Planter, tree stump, T–shaped horizontal log on log pedestal, tooled bark	**55.00**
Slipper, 4" l, miniature	**40.00**

SPATTERWARE

History: Spatterware is made of common earthenware, although occasionally creamware was used. The earliest English examples were made about 1780. The peak period of production was 1810–1840. Marked pieces are rare. Firms known to have made spatterware are Adams, Barlow, and Harvey and Cotton.

The amount of spatter decoration varies from piece to piece. Some objects simply have decorated borders. These often are decorated with a brush, requiring several hundred touches per square inch to achieve the spatter effect. Other pieces have the entire surface covered with spatter. Aesthetics of the final product is a key to value.

Collectors today focus on the patterns: Cannon, Castle, Fort, Peafowl, Rainbow, Rose, Thistle, Schoolhouse, etc. On flat ware the decoration is in the center. On hollow pieces it occurs on both sides.

Color of spatter is another price key. Blue and red are most common. Green, purple, and brown are in a middle group. Black and yellow are scarce.

Like any soft paste, spatterware was easily broken or chipped. Prices are for pieces in very good to mint condition.

References: Susan and Al Bagdade, *Warman's English & Continental Pottery & Porcelain, 2nd Edition,* Wallace–Homestead, 1991; Kevin McConnell, *Spongeware and Spatterware,* Schiffer Publishing, 1990; Carl and Ada Robacker, *Spatterware and Sponge,* A. S. Barnes & Co., 1978.

Reproduction Manufacturer: The Vine and Cupboard, PO Box 309, George Wright Rd, Woolwich, ME 04579.

Child's Cup and Saucer, Peafowl, handleless, blue, yellow, red, and black, red and green rainbow spatter ... **275.00**
Creamer
  $2\frac{1}{2}$" h, miniature, red stripes, floral design green spatter band, black handle stripe, pinpoint spout chips **75.00**
  $3\frac{1}{2}$" h, Columbine with rose bud and thistle, red, green, blue, purple, and black, red border stripe, green spatter floral design border **150.00**
  $3\frac{5}{8}$" h, Rainbow, red and blue spatter **95.00**
  $3\frac{3}{4}$" h, blue spatter, emb leaf handle **85.00**
  $4\frac{1}{4}$" h, green, yellow, black, and purple violet–like flower, red border stripe, green spatter floral design border.................. **70.00**
  $5\frac{3}{4}$" h, Rose, red, black, and green, blue spatter, paneled **270.00**
Cup and Saucer
  Handle
    Gaudy Floral design, stick spatter, red, blue, and green, oversize, flake on saucer........... **105.00**
    Purple spatter, glaze chips on cup rim **145.00**
  Handleless
    Flower, stick spatter, red, green, and black, miniature........ **75.00**
    Fort, blue spatter, miniature **550.00**
    Geometric design, green, yellow, and black, stick spatter, ironstone................. **85.00**
    Molded Panels, blue spatter, miniature **85.00**
    Peafowl, red, blue, ochre yellow, and black
      Green spatter............ **450.00**
      Red spatter, miniature....... **325.00**
    Primrose, red, green, and black, red border stripe, ribbon design blue spatter border **200.00**
    Rainbow, red and blue spatter... **375.00**

Schoolhouse, red, yellow, black, and green, blue spatter **625.00**
Sponge spatter, blue, miniature **60.00**
Thistle
  Blue, green, and black, red spatter **75.00**
  Red and green, yellow spatter **250.00**
Cup Plate, $4\frac{1}{8}$" d
  Peafowl, red, yellow, green, and black, blue spatter, imp "Stoneware, E.W. & Co.".......... **625.00**
  Rose, red, black, and green, yellow spatter.................. **600.00**
Dinner Service, 27 pcs, gaudy stick spatter, ironstone, red, blue, and green, molded basket weave border, Adams Tunstall **325.00**
Mug
  $2\frac{1}{2}$" h, Peafowl, blue, green, red, and black, blue spatter **425.00**
  $2\frac{3}{4}$" h, blue and green spatter...... **250.00**
  $3\frac{1}{8}$" h, blue spatter **55.00**
Plate
  $6\frac{1}{2}$" d, Columbine, rose bud and thistle, red, green, blue, purple, and black, red border stripe, floral design green spatter border....... **100.00**
  8" d, Rooster, yellow ochre, red, blue, and black, red spatter..... **210.00**
  $8\frac{1}{8}$" d, Peafowl, green, blue, yellow, and black, red spatter **400.00**
  $8\frac{1}{4}$" d, Vine and Berry, red and yellow, green spatter **350.00**
  $8\frac{1}{2}$" d, Pomegranate, red, blue, green, and black, blue spatter, imp "Meakin".............. **105.00**
  $8\frac{5}{8}$" d
    Geometric design, stick spatter, ironstone, polychrome **25.00**
    Primrose, red, green, black, and yellow ochre, blue spatter **70.00**
  $8\frac{3}{4}$" d
    Rose, red, green, and black, blue

Pitcher, $6\frac{1}{2}$" h, Rainbow, green and red spatter, $450.00.

and green design border, pinpoint flakes **180.00**
Rose and Bird, red, blue, green, and black, blue border stripe, ribbon design blue spatter border **75.00**
9¼" d, Peafowl, blue, yellow ochre, green, and black, red spatter **450.00**
9⅜" d
  Acorn and Oak Leaf, green, black, teal, and yellow, blue spatter **550.00**
  Peafowl, black, green, red, and blue
    Blue spatter, molded rim **500.00**
    Red spatter **200.00**
9½" d
  Bull's Eye, red and green rainbow spatter **250.00**
  Cowboy and Horse, red transfer and spatter **100.00**
  Flower, red, green, and black, red and green sponge spatter rim   **175.00**
  Fort, green, yellow, red, and black, blue spatter, paneled rim   **75.00**
  10" d, violet–like flower, green, yellow, black, and purple, blue border stripe, ribbon design red spatter border **55.00**
  10¼" d, blue eagle transfer and spatter **125.00**
  9¼" d, Star, blue spatter, paneled rim   **85.00**
  9⅜" d, Tulip, red, green, blue, and black, purple spatter **450.00**
Platter
  13⅜" l, red and purple center design, rainbow spatter **950.00**
  14⅜" l, green, yellow, black, and purple violet–like flower, red border stripe, floral design blue spatter border, small glaze flakes **150.00**
  15½" l, blue eagle and shield transfer, purple spatter **250.00**
Salt, 3¼" d, 2" h, ftd, ironstone, blue and white stick spatter **50.00**
Sugar Bowl
  Blue and White, Leeds **80.00**

Sugar Bowl, Thistle, red and black rainbow spatter, $400.00.

Columbine with rose bud and thistle, 4⅛" h, red, green, blue, purple, and black, red border stripe, floral design green spatter border, pinpoint flakes on inner flange, chip on lid **100.00**
Thistle, 6⅝" h, red and green, yellow spatter, lid, paneled **500.00**
Violet–like flower, green, yellow, black, and purple, red border stripe, floral design green spatter border, dome top **90.00**
Teapot
  5" h, Roseate, blue floral centers, chips on lid and spout. **200.00**
  5½" h, lid, blue and white **205.00**
  8⅜" h, green, yellow, black, and purple violet–like flower, blue border stripe, floral design red spatter border, dome top, hairlines in lid   **300.00**
Tea Set, child's, 5⅜" h teapot, creamer, open sugar, two cups and saucers, two plates, ironstone, blue stick spatter dec **175.00**
Waste Bowl, 5¾" d, 3½" h, Columbine, rose bud and thistle, red, green, blue, purple, and black, red border stripe, floral design green spatter border, paneled, pinpoint flakes on table ring **175.00**

SPONGEWARE

History: Spongeware is a specific type of decoration, not a type of pottery or glaze.

Spongeware decoration is found on many types of pottery bodies—ironstone, redware, stoneware, yellow ware, etc. It was made in both England and the United States. Marked pieces indicate a starting date of 1815, with manufacturing extending to the 1880s.

Decoration is varied. In some pieces the sponging is minimal with the white underglaze dominant. Other pieces appear to be sponged solidly on both sides. Pieces from 1840–1860 have sponging which appears in either a circular movement or a streaked horizontal technique.

Examples are found in blue and white, the most common colors. Other prevalent colors are browns, greens, ochres, and greenish–blues. The greenish–blue results from blue sponging which has been overglazed in a pale yellow. A red overglaze produces a black or navy color.

Other colors are blue and red (found on English creamware and American earthenware of the 1880s), gray, grayish–green, red, dark green on stark white, dark green on mellow yellow, and purple.

References: Susan and Al Bagdade, *Warman's English & Continental Pottery & Porcelain, 2nd*

Edition, Wallace–Homestead, 1991; Kevin McConnell, *Spongeware and Spatterware,* Schiffer Publishing, 1990; Earl F. and Ada Robacker, *Spatterware and Sponge,* A. S. Barnes & Co., 1978.

Reproduction Manufacturer: Wesson Trading Co, PO Box 669984, Marietta, GA 30066.

Bank, $5\frac{7}{8}$" l, figural, pig, brown and blue sponging **115.00**
Bean Pot, $4\frac{7}{8}$" h, blue and white sponging **450.00**
Bowl
- 6" d, blue sponging, white ground **55.00**
- $6\frac{1}{2}$" d, blue and rust sponging, cream ground, Iowa adv **50.00**
- $6\frac{3}{4}$" d, 3" h, brown and green sponging, cream ground **40.00**
- 7" d, tan and blue sponging, light gray ground **65.00**
- $10\frac{3}{4}$" d, $4\frac{1}{8}$" h, light blue sponging, tan ground, arch molded sides . . **210.00**
- $13\frac{3}{4}$" d, blue and white sponging . . . **275.00**

Bread Plate, 10" l, blue sponging, double open handles **100.00**
Cookie Jar, green, brown, and ochre sponging, gold trim **300.00**
Creamer, 4" h, green sponging, corset shape **65.00**
Cup and Saucer
- Blue and white sponging, handleless, set of six **195.00**
- Blue sponging, earthenware, c1840 **130.00**

Cup Plate, $3\frac{1}{8}$" d, blue sponging, white ground **60.00**
Cuspidor, $7\frac{1}{2}$" d, blue sponging and bands, white ground **90.00**
Inkwell, green sponging **180.00**
Jar, cov, 6" h, blue sponging, cream ground, wire handle **215.00**
Jardiniere, 11 x $8\frac{1}{4}$", blue sponging, gold flecked green rim, white ground **100.00**

Coffee Pot, blue and white sponging, c1830, $275.00.

Jug
- 3" h, green, brown, and ochre sponging **125.00**
- $7\frac{1}{4}$" h, flared top, blue sponged bands, cream ground, applied handle **125.00**

Mixing Bowl, $12\frac{1}{4}$" d, blue sponging, molded design, white ground **125.00**
Mug
- $1\frac{3}{4}$" h, miniature, red sponging, cream ground **125.00**
- $4\frac{1}{4}$" h, brown sponging, yellow ground **70.00**

Nappy, $8\frac{1}{2}$" l, rect, blue interior sponging, white ground **175.00**
Pie Plate, 9" d, brown and green sponging, cream ground **50.00**
Pitcher
- $4\frac{1}{2}$" h, brown and green sponging, yellow ground **65.00**
- 5" h, brown, blue, red, and white sponging, cream ground **125.00**
- $7\frac{3}{8}$" h, blue and white sponging, gold trim, hairlines and rim chips **120.00**
- $8\frac{7}{8}$" h, blue and white sponging **325.00**
- 9" h, blue and white sponging, stoneware, molded floral design, chips and hairlines **110.00**
- $9\frac{5}{8}$" h, blue and white sponging **425.00**
- 10" h, beige and blue sponging, white ground, edge chips and hairlines **125.00**

Plate, $10\frac{1}{4}$" d, blue sponging, white ground, emb scalloped edge **175.00**
Platter
- $11\frac{1}{2}$" l, blue and white sponging, rim hairlines **35.00**
- 12" l, blue sponging, white ground, Trenton, NJ, c1865 . . . . **210.00**
- $13\frac{3}{4}$" l, blue and white sponging . . . **110.00**

Salt and Pepper Shakers, pr, hand thrown, white, green, and amber sponging **100.00**
Soap Dish, blue sponging, cream ground **60.00**
Sugar, blue and red sponging, cream ground **175.00**
Toddy Plate, $4\frac{3}{4}$" d, blue and white sponging, marked "Burford Bros" **40.00**
Wash Bowl and Pitcher, blue and olive green sponging, blue bands, white ground **325.00**

STAFFORDSHIRE

History: The Staffordshire district of England is the center of the English pottery industry. There were eighty different potteries operating there in 1786, with the number increasing to 179 by 1802. The district includes Burslem, Cobridge,

Etruria, Fenton, Foley, Hanley, Lane Delph, Lane End, Longport, Shelton, Stoke, and Tunstall. Among the many famous potters were Adams, Davenport, Spode, Stevenson, Wedgwood, and Wood.

In historical Staffordshire the view is the most critical element. American collectors pay much less for non–American views. Dark blue pieces are favored. Light views continue to remain undervalued. Among the forms, soup tureens have shown the highest price increases.

A wide variety of ornamental pottery items originated in England's Staffordshire district, beginning in the 17th century and extending to the present. The height of production was from 1820 to 1890.

These naive pieces are considered folk art by many collectors. Most items were not made carefully; some were even made and decorated by children.

The types of objects varied, e.g., animals, cottages, and figurines (chimney ornaments). The key to price is age and condition. Generally, the older the piece, the higher the price.

References: David and Linda Arman, *Historical Staffordshire: An Illustrated Check List,* published by author, 1974, out–of–print; David and Linda Arman, *First Supplement, Historical Staffordshire: An Illustrated Check List,* published by author, 1977, out–of–print; Susan and Al Bagdade, *Warman's English & Continental Pottery & Porcelain, 2nd Edition,* Wallace–Homestead, 1991; Ada Walker Camehl, *The Blue China Book,* Tudor Publishing Co., 1946, (Dover, reprint); A. W. Coysh and R. K. Henrywood, *The Dictionary Of Blue And White Printed Pottery, 1780–1880,* Antique Collectors' Club, 1982; Pat Halfpenny, *English Earthenware Figures, 1740–1840,* Antique Collectors' Club; P. D. Gordon Pugh, *Staffordshire Portrait Figures Of The Victorian Era,* Antique Collectors' Club; Charles Kenyon Kies, *Collecting Victorian Staffordshire Pottery Figures,* Antique Publications, 1989; Ellouise Larsen, *American Historical Views On Staffordshire China, 3rd Edition,* Dover Publications, 1975; Dennis G. Rice, *English Porcelain Animals Of The 19th Century,* Antique Collectors' Club; 1989.

Museum: Hershey Museum of American Life, 170 West Hershey Park Drive, Hershey, PA 17033.

Dinnerware
  Creamer
    4" h, Lafayette at Franklin Tomb, dark blue, chip on spout **425.00**
    6" h, flowers and bird, dark blue, impressed "Wood" **230.00**
  Cup and Saucer
    City Hall, New York, medium blue, unmarked **275.00**

    Landing of General Lafayette, dark blue, Clews **300.00**
    New Orleans, Lace border, dark blue, Stevenson **100.00**
  Cup Plate
    3½" d, kite flying, light blue **85.00**
    3⅝" d, feather edge, blue **85.00**
    3⅞" d, View Near Sandy Hill, Hudson River Series, dark brown, unmarked Clews **85.00**
    4" d
      Broadlands, Hampshire, dark blue, R Hall **175.00**
      Fair Mount, Hudson River Series, pink, Adams **80.00**
    4⅝" d, two sailboats and rowboat scene, dark blue, shell border, impressed "Wood & Sons," hairline **165.00**
  Mug, 2½" h
    Black, "A present for a good girl, faith," polychrome enameling, luster border, leaf handle **65.00**
    Brown, "Be you to others kind and true. . ." **65.00**
  Pitcher
    6½" h, Utica and The Grand Erie Canal, dark blue, hairline at spout. **775.00**
    8" h, Schenectady on Mohawk River, J & J Jackson **275.00**
  Plate
    5¼" d, Fort Edwards, Hudson River, Hudson River Series, pink, Adams **60.00**
    6½" d, City Hall, New York, Spread Eagle border, dark blue, Stubbs **200.00**
    6⅞" d, Peace, Plenty, dark blue, impressed "Clews," short rim hairline **200.00**

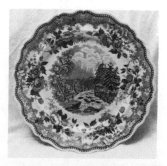

Plate, 10½" d, View of the Canal, Little Falls, Mohawk River, American Scenery Series, medium blue, J & J Jackson, $125.00.

7" d

Deaf and Dumb Asylum, Philadelphia, American Scenery Series, blue, J & J Jackson . . . **70.00**

Near Hudson, Hudson River, Picturesque Views Series, brown, Clews **60.00**

8" d, Hancock House Boston, dark brown, edge chips, hairline **75.00**

8½" d

City Hotel, New York, medium blue, hairline **30.00**

Fulham Church, Middlesex, R Hall's Picturesque Scenery, dark blue **85.00**

Nahant Hotel Near Boston, dark blue **150.00**

8⅝" d, Warleigh House, Somersetshire, R Hall's Select Views, dark blue **85.00**

8¾" d

State House, Boston, medium blue, impressed "Enoch Wood & Sons," pinpoint glaze flakes **150.00**

Upper Ferry Bridge over the River Schuylkill, Spread Eagle border, dark blue **150.00**

8⅞" d, Kingsweston, Gloucestershire, impressed "Riley," dark blue **25.00**

9" d

English Landscape, fisherman in foreground, dark blue, impressed "Adams" **65.00**

Picturesque Views, Baker's Falls, Hudson River, dark brown **65.00**

9⅛" d, Commodore MacDonnough's Victory, dark blue, impressed "E. Wood," minor surface damage **275.00**

9¼" d, Marine Hospital, Louisville, Kentucky, dark blue, impressed "E. Wood," pinpoint glaze flakes **300.00**

9½" d, Meredith, Catskill Moss series, light blue, Ridgway **60.00**

10" d

Fairmount Near Philadelphia, Spread Eagle border, dark blue, Stubbs **200.00**

Feather edge, blue, emb rim designs **55.00**

Llanarth Court, Monmouthshire, dark blue, R Hall **45.00**

Park Theater, New York, Acorn and Oak Leaves border, dark blue, Stevenson **270.00**

State House, Boston, medium blue, impressed "Rogers" . . **200.00**

10⅛" d

Bank of the United States, Philadelphia, dark blue **500.00**

City of Albany, State of New York, dark blue, impressed "E. Wood" **800.00**

Pine Orchard House, Catskill Mountains, dark blue, impressed "E. Wood" **550.00**

Table Rock Niagara, dark blue, impressed "E. Wood" **600.00**

10¼" d

Fairmount near Philadelphia, medium dark blue, impressed "Stubbs," chip on table ring **200.00**

La Grange, the Residence of Marquis de LaFayette, blue, grape border, impressed "Enoch Wood & Sons," 1825–50 . . . . **100.00**

10⅜" d

Picturesque View Near Fishkill, Hudson River, dark brown, impressed "Clews" **95.00**

Valencia, blue and black, crazing **55.00**

10½" d

Canova, red and green **45.00**

State House, Boston, American Scenery Series, blue, J & J Jackson **60.00**

Three–story Building with One–story Wing, states series, dark blue, impressed "Clews," 1825–50 . . . . **200.00**

View of the Canal, Little Falls, Mohawk River, American Scenery Series, blue, J & J Jackson **125.00**

10¾" d, Columbus, light blue, impressed "Adams" **65.00**

Platter

15¼" l, Landing of General Lafayette, dark blue, impressed "Clews" **1,100.00**

Platter, 15½" l, The Residence of the Late Richard Jordan, New Jersey, lavender, Joseph Heath & Co., $250.00.

17" l, New York, Select Sketches Series, J & J Jackson **400.00**

20¼" l, Canova, purple, T Mayer **225.00**

21½" l, oblong, sea battle scene, medium blue **925.00**

Soup Plate

8¾" d, Landing of General Lafayette, dark blue, Clews **200.00**

9⅞" d

Feather edge, green **45.00**

Lady of the Lake, Carey's, light blue **85.00**

10" d

Guy's Cliff, Warwickshire, medium blue transfer **60.00**

Kosciusko's Tomb, Catskill Moss series, light blue, Ridgway **70.00**

10¼" d, Catskill Mountain House, U S Views, light blue **75.00**

10½" d, Hudson, Hudson River, Picturesque Views Series, brown, Clews **60.00**

Sugar Bowl, 6¾" h, horse–drawn sleigh, dark blue, impressed "E. Wood," mismatched lid **175.00**

Teapot, 7½" h, lake scene, shell borders, dark blue, hairlines **575.00**

Tea Set, partial, child size, red star transfer, two cups and saucers, 4¼" h teapot, sugar **155.00**

Toby Shaker, 5⅝" h, polychrome enameling **10.00**

Toddy Plate

5⅝" d, Landing of General Lafayette, dark blue, Clews **160.00**

6" d, English boating scene, dark blue, impressed "Adams" **65.00**

6⅛" d, Remains of the Church Thornton Abbey, dark blue, impressed "Clews" **75.00**

6¼" d, Atheneum, Boston, medium blue, Ridgway, hairline **150.00**

6½" d

Family of sheep, medium blue, impressed "Enoch Wood & Sons" **200.00**

Maison de Raphael, dark blue, impressed "Wood" **85.00**

6⅝" d, R Hall's Select Views, The Hospital Near Poissy France, dark blue, hairline **35.00**

Tray, President's House, Catskill Moss series, light blue, Ridgway **100.00**

Vegetable Dish

9¾" l, 2⅛" h, Catskill Moss series, Little Falls, NY, railroad scene, light blue, Ridgway, mid 19th C **175.00**

11" l, America and Independence, states border, dark blue, impressed "Clews," hairlines **825.00**

Blacksmith, 16¼" h, yellow apron, striped shirt, $165.00.

Waste Bowl, Log Cabin, medallions of General Harrison on border, brown, Adams **250.00**

Figure

Cat, 7" h, seated, white, black markings, wearing copper luster collar, 19th C **200.00**

Country Couple, 10" h **275.00**

Couple, 10" h, man holding sheaf of wheat, woman holding ewer. . . . **265.00**

Ewe, 3⅞" h, reclining, relief textured, pale blue eyes, green glazed base, c1780–90 . . . . **300.00**

Hound, 10¼" h, chasing hare, multicolored **300.00**

Huntsman, Horse, and Dog, 4¼" h, miniature, polychrome enamel **75.00**

Old Woman, 6½" h, pearlware, polychrome enameling, black base **90.00**

Two Girls and Dog, 9½" h **350.00**

STANGL POTTERY

History: The Stangl Pottery, located in Trenton and Flemington, New Jersey, was founded in 1930 by J. M. Stangl, formerly of Fulper Pottery. In 1978 it was purchased by the Pfaltzgraff Company. The Flemington factory currently serves as a Pfaltzgraff factory outlet. One of the original kilns remains intact to exemplify the hard work and high temperatures involved in the production of pottery.

Stangl Pottery produced several lines of highly collectible dinnerware and decorative accessories, including the famed Stangl birds. The red bodied dinnerware was produced in distinctive shapes and patterns. Shapes were designated by numbers. Pattern names include: Country Garden, Fruit, Tulip, Thistle, and Wild Rose. Special Christmas, advertising and commemorative wares were also produced.

Bright colors and bold simplistic patterns have made Stangl pottery a favorite with Country collectors. Stangl's factory sold seconds from its factory store long before outlet malls became popular. Large sets of Stangl dinnerware currently command high prices at auctions, flea markets, and even antiques shops.

Stangl's ceramic birds were produced from 1940 until 1972. The birds were produced at Stangl's Trenton plant, then shipped to the Flemington plant for hand painting.

During World War II the demand for these birds and Stangl pottery was so great that 40 to 60 decorators could not keep up with the demand. Orders were contracted out to private homes. These pieces were then returned for firing and finishing. Colors used to decorate these birds varied according to the artist.

As many as ten different trademarks were used. Dinnerware was marked and often signed by the decorator. Most birds are numbered; many are artist signed. However, signatures are useful for dating purposes only and add little to values.

Several birds were reissued between 1972 and 1977. These reissues are dated on the bottom and worth approximately one half the value of the older birds.

References: Joan Dworkin and Martha Horman, *A Guide To Stangl Pottery Birds,* Willow Pond Books, Inc., 1973; Norma Rehl, *The Collectors Handbook of Stangl Pottery,* Democrat Press, 1982.

Ashtray
  Antique Gold
    #3972 . . . .   **12.50**
    #5060 . . . .   **9.00**
    #5067 . . . .   **6.50**
  Granada Gold
    #5173 . . . .   **5.50**
    #5174 . . . .   **9.50**
Birds
  Allen Hummingbird, $3\frac{1}{2}$" h, 3634 . .   **40.00**
  Bobolink, $4\frac{3}{4}$" h, 3595 . . . .   **125.00**
  Cardinal, $6\frac{1}{2}$" h, 3444 . . . .   **55.00**
  Cockatoo, $11\frac{3}{8}$" h, 3484 . . . .   **190.00**
  Cock Pheasant, $6\frac{1}{4}$ x 11", 3492 . . . .   **150.00**
  Hen Pheasant, $6\frac{1}{4}$ x 11", 3491 . . . .   **155.00**
  Hummingbird, 8 x $10\frac{1}{2}$", 3599D, pr   **240.00**
  Indigo Bunting, $3\frac{1}{4}$" h, 3589 . . . . . .   **35.00**
  Kentucky Warbler, 3" h, orig tag, 3598. . . . .   **40.00**
  Kingfisher, $3\frac{1}{2}$" h, 3406S **50.00**
  Love Bird, 4" h, 3400 . . . .   **50.00**
  Oriole, $3\frac{1}{4}$" h, orig tag, 3402S **40.00**
  Parakeets, pr, 3582D **145.00**
  Parula Warbler, $4\frac{1}{4}$" h, orig tag, 3583   **50.00**

  Red–Faced Warbler, 3" h, 3594 . . .   **55.00**
  Rieffers Hummingbird, $4\frac{1}{2}$" h, 3628   **125.00**
  Rufous Hummingbird, 3" h, 3585 . . .   **50.00**
  Wilson Warbler, $3\frac{1}{2}$" h, 3597 . . . . .   **45.00**
  Wren, pr, 8" h, 3401D **90.00**
  Yellow Warbler, 5" h, 3447 . . . . . .   **50.00**
Dinnerware
  Antique Gold
    Bowl, #4084 . . . .   **28.00**
    Bud Vase, #4050 . . . .   **17.00**
    Shell Bowl, #4019 . . . .   **18.00**
  Blueberry
    Cereal Bowl **4.50**
    Coffee Pot **60.00**
    Cup **8.00**
    Plate, dinner **12.50**
    Saucer **4.00**
  Blue Daisy
    Cup and Saucer **5.50**
    Plate
      8" d **6.00**
      10" d **9.50**
    Snack Plate and Cup **13.50**
  Corn, butter dish, green **15.00**
  Country Garden
    Mug, pink flowers **12.50**
    Vegetable Bowl, divided **22.50**
  Fruit and Flowers
    Cup **6.00**
    Fruit Bowl **5.00**
    Plate
      6" d **4.00**
      8" d **5.00**
    Vegetable Bowl, divided **15.00**
  Fruits
    Bean Pot **48.00**
    Cereal Bowl **7.50**
    Cup and Saucer **7.50**
    Dinner Service, 40 pcs **425.00**
    Plate, 6" d **4.50**
    Teapot, individual size **12.00**
  Garden Flower, coaster **5.50**
  Garland
    Creamer **6.00**

Colonial Rose, $10\frac{1}{2}$" d, pink dec, scalloped edge, $8.50.

Cup and Saucer	7.50
Plate, dinner	8.00
Salad Bowl, 12" d	28.00
Sugar	6.00

Golden Blossom

Gravy Boat, stand	7.00
Server, center handle	12.50
Vegetable Bowl, 8" d	9.00

Golden Harvest

Candlestick, green	14.00
Chop Plate, 12½" d	20.00
Coffee Warmer	18.00
Creamer, green	6.50
Holly, punch mug	22.00

Granada Gold

Flower Bowl, #5139	20.00

Magnolia

Cream Soup, lug handle	10.00
Egg Cup	12.50
Plate, 6" d	5.00

Orchard Song

Candle Holders, pr, round	20.00
Coffee Warmer	25.00
Dinner Service, service for four, seven serving pcs	90.00
Plate, 10" d	5.00
Server, center handle	15.00
Red Cherry, casserole, handle	9.00

Star Flower

Cream Soup, lug handle	10.00
Salad Bowl, 10" d	32.00

Terra Rose

Creamer and Sugar.	18.50
Pitcher	
1 pint.	12.50
1 quart.	18.00
Plate, 8" d	9.50
Server, center handle	17.50
Teapot	48.00

Thistle

Cereal Bowl	5.00
Coaster	6.50
Creamer	13.00
Cup and Saucer	9.50
Fruit Bowl	5.00

Sunflower, 11¼" d, $9.00.

Plate, 9" d	8.75
Sherbet	15.00
Sugar, cov.	17.00
Town and Country, server, 10" d, center handle, green speckled. . .	20.00

Tulip, yellow

Flower Pot	
4" d	5.00
5" d	7.00
Plate, 9¼" d	6.00
Platter, 12½" d, round	20.00
White Dogwood, cup and saucer	10.00

TAYLOR, SMITH, AND TAYLOR

History: C. A. Smith and Colonel John N. Taylor founded Taylor, Smith, and Taylor in Chester, West Virginia, in 1899. In 1903 the firm reorganized and the Taylor interests were purchased by the Smith family. The firm remained in the family's control until it was purchased by Anchor Hocking in 1973. The tableware division closed in 1981.

Taylor, Smith, and Taylor started production with a nine–kiln pottery. Local clays were used initially. Later only southern clays were used. Both earthenware and fine china bodies were produced. Several underglaze print patterns, e.g. Dogwood and Spring Bouquet, were made. These prints, made from the copper engravings of ceramic artist J. Palin Thorley, were designed exclusively for the company.

Taylor, Smith, and Taylor also made Lu Ray, produced from the 1930s through the early 1950s. Available in Windsor Blue, Persian Cream, Sharon Pink, Surf Green, and Chatham Gray, their coordinating colors encourage collectors to mix and match sets.

Competition for a portion of the dinnerware market of the 1930s through the 1950s was intense. Lu Ray was designed to compete with Russel Wright's American Modern. Vistosa was Taylor, Smith, and Taylor's answer to Homer Laughlin's Fiesta.

Taylor, Smith, and Taylor used several different backstamps and marks. Many contain the company name as well as the pattern and shape names.

Periodical: *The New Glaze*, PO Box 4782, Birmingham, AL 35206.

Autumn Harvest

Butter, cov	15.00

Casserole, cov	16.00
Cup	3.00
Plate, bread and butter	2.00
Platter	
11" l	8.00
13½" l	12.00
Salt and Pepper Shakers, pr	8.50
Saucer	1.50

Lu Ray

After Dinner	
Creamer, Sharon Pink	40.00
Coffee Pot, Windsor Blue	80.00
Sugar, Sharon Pink	45.00
Bud Vase, Surf Green	115.00
Cake Plate, 11", lug handle, Windsor Blue	28.00
Calendar Plate, Windsor Blue	45.00
Casserole Cov, Sharon Pink	38.00
Chocolate Pot, Persian Cream	135.00
Chop Plate, 14", Surf Green	24.00
Creamer, Chatham Gray	6.00
Cream Soup, tab handle, Windsor Blue	10.00
Cup	
Persian Cream	6.50
Sharon Pink	5.00
Egg Cup, Sharon Pink	10.00
Epergne, Surf Green	70.00
Fruit Bowl, Windsor Blue	4.00
Gravy, Persian Cream	18.00
Mixing Bowl	
6¾" d, Sharon Pink	55.00
10" d, Windsor Blue	70.00
Nut Dish, Surf Green	65.00
Pitcher	
Juice, Sharon Pink, 38 oz	72.00
Water, ftd, Persian Cream, 76 oz	45.00
Plate	
6½" d	
Persian Cream	3.00
Windsor Blue	2.00
7¼" d, Windsor Blue	4.00
9" d	
Sharon Pink	5.00
Surf Green	5.00
10" d, Windsor Blue	12.00
Platter, oval	
11½" l, Persian Cream	10.00
13¼" l, Windsor Blue	10.00
Relish, 4 part	
Persian Cream	80.00
Windsor Blue	85.00
Salad Bowl, 9¾" d, Sharon Pink	35.00
Sauce Boat, Windsor Blue	20.00
Saucer, Windsor Blue	1.50
Chatham Gray	10.00
Windsor Blue	8.00
Soup Plate, 7¾" d, Persian Cream	10.00
Sugar, Chatham Gray	7.50
Teapot, Sharon Pink	50.00
Tumbler, juice, 5 oz, Windsor Blue	24.00
Vegetable Dish, oval, Chatham Gray	27.00

Vistosa

Bowl	
5¾" d, red	8.00
8½" d, two handles, green	20.00
Chop Plate	
11" d, yellow	20.00
14" d, blue	24.00
Creamer, blue	12.00
Cup and Saucer, green	15.00
Egg Cup, yellow	25.00
Gravy Boat, red	135.00
Pitcher, yellow	25.00
Plate	
6" d, green	3.00
7" d, blue	8.50
9" d, yellow	8.00
10" d, green	12.00
Salad Bowl, ftd, blue	140.00
Salt and Pepper Shakers, pr, green	14.00
Salver, 12", green	16.00
Soup Plate, 6½" d, lug handle, green	28.00
Sugar, cov, green	15.00
Teapot, red	125.00
Vegetable Bowl, 8½" d, blue	95.00

WATTS POTTERY

History: Watts Pottery, founded in 1922 in Crooksville, Ohio, was well known for its stoneware. The pottery occupied the site of the former Globe Stoneware Company (1901–1919) and the Zane W. Burley Pottery (1919–1922). Local Crooksville clay was used. Kitchenware production began in 1935. The plant was destroyed by fire in 1965 and never rebuilt.

It is the color tones and patterns of Watt Pottery that appeal to Country collectors and decorators. The background consists of earth tones of off–white and light tan. It is similar in feel to many patterns from Pennsbury, Pfaltzgraff, and Purinton as well as the English Torquay pieces.

Most Watts pottery features an underglaze decoration. The Red Apple pattern was introduced in 1950, the Cherry pattern in 1955, and the Star Flower in 1956. Other popular patterns include Pennsylvania Dutch Tulip and Rooster. Examples with advertising are highly collectible.

Reproduction Alert: A Japanese copy of a large spaghetti bowl marked simply "U.S.A." is known. The Watt example bears a "Peedeeco" and "U.S.A." marks.

Apple	
Baking Dish, oblong, 1 quart, #85	55.00
Bowl, deep	
4 pint, #64	35.00
6 pint, #65	45.00
Canister	
5" h, #82	70.00
6" h, #81	75.00
Casserole	
1½ quart, oval, #86	65.00

2 quart, #110	**75.00**
2½ quart, square, #84	**85.00**
Creamer, adv	**45.00**
Cup, small	**60.00**
Drip Jar, #01	**55.00**
Mixing Bowl	
#5	**15.00**
#8	**65.00**
Mug, #121	**95.00**
Nesting Bowls, round, #04, 05, 06, and 07	**125.00**
Pitcher	
1 pint, #15	**50.00**
2 pint, #16	**60.00**
5 pint, ice lip, #17	**95.00**
Pizza Plate, 14½" d, #105	**115.00**
Plate	
8½" d	**20.00**
12" d	**50.00**
Salt and Pepper Shakers, pr, hour- glass shape, #117 and #118	**75.00**
Saucer	**18.00**
Sugar, cov, #98	**85.00**
Teapot, 1½ quart, #112	**300.00**
Pansy, plate	
7" d	**50.00**
10" d	**65.00**
Starflower	
Baker	
6¼" d, #60	**15.00**
7¼" d, #95	**22.00**
Berry Bowl, 5½" d, #4	**10.00**
Bowl	
6" d, low, banded, #06	**20.00**
7½" d, low, banded, #07	**25.00**
Casserole, 1½ quart, oval, #86	**55.00**
Cup	**15.00**
Mixing Bowl	
4" d, horizontal lined, #4	**20.00**
8" d, adv, #8	**30.00**
Mug, 16 oz, barrel, #501	**95.00**
Plate	
6½" d	**16.00**
8½" d	**20.00**
9¾" d	**40.00**
Salad Bowl, 11" d, #106	**80.00**
Spaghetti Bowl, 13" d, #39	**70.00**
Salt and Pepper Shakers, pr, cylinder	**50.00**
Saucer, large	**20.00**

WELLER POTTERY

History: In 1872 Samuel A. Weller opened a small factory in Fultonham, Ohio, to produce utilitarian stoneware, e.g. milk pans and sewer tile. In 1882 he moved his facilities to Zanesville. In 1890 Weller built a new plant in the Putnam section of Zanesville along the tracks of the Cincinnati and Miskingum Railway. Additions followed in 1892 and 1894.

In 1894 Weller entered into an agreement with William A. Long to purchase the Lonhuda Faience Company, which had developed an art pottery line under the guidance of Laura A. Fry, formerly of Rookwood. Long left the company in 1895 and this line was renamed Louwelsa. Charles Babcock Upjohn became the new art director. He, along with Jacques Sicard, Frederick Hurten Rhead, and Gazo Fudji, developed Weller's art pottery lines.

At the end of World War I, many high prestige lines were discontinued and Weller concentrated on commercial wares. Rudolph Lorber joined the staff and designed the Roma, Forest, and Knifewood lines. In 1920 Weller acquired Zanesville Art Pottery and claimed to be the largest pottery in the country.

Art pottery enjoyed a revival in the 1920s and 1930s with the introduction of the Hudson, Coppertone, and Graystone Garden lines. However, the Depression forced the closing of the Putnam and Marietta Street plants in Zanesville. Following World War II, cheap Japanese imports took over Weller's market. In 1947 Essex Wire Company of Detroit bought the controlling stock. Early in 1948 operations ceased.

References: Sharon and Bob Huxford, *The Collectors Encyclopedia Of Weller Pottery*, Collector Book, 1979; values updated 1992; Ann Gilbert McDonald, *All About Weller: A History And Collectors Guide To Weller Pottery*, Zanesville, OH, Antique Publications, 1989.

Collectors' Club: American Art Pottery Association, 125 E Rose Ave, St. Louis, MO 63119.

Ashtray	
Roma, 2½" d	**25.00**
Woodcraft, 3" d	**65.00**
Basket	
Cameo, 7½" d, blue	**25.00**
Roba, brown to tan	**45.00**
Wild Rose, 6" d, peach	**31.00**
Bowl	
Bonito, underplate	**110.00**
Cornish	**35.00**
Marbleized, 5½" d	**30.00**
Pierre, 8" d, seafoam	**20.00**
Square, 8" d	**65.00**
Squirrel, glossy	**82.00**
Candlesticks, pr, Glendale	**150.00**
Centerpiece Bowl, Wild Rose, 7½" d	**30.00**
Child's Mug	**29.00**
Compote, Bonito, 4" h	**55.00**
Console Bowl, 16" d, 7" h, handled, orig liner, roses, leaves, stems	**195.00**
Console Set, Blossom, bowl and two candlesticks	**50.00**

Cornucopia
Softone, 10" d, light blue **20.00**
Wild Rose. **25.00**
Creamer and Sugar, Pierre, seafoam   **35.00**
Ewer
Cameo, 10" h, blue **30.00**
Floretta, 12½" h **260.00**
Louwelsa, iris **200.00**
Figure
Boy Fishing, Muskota **215.00**
Chicken, 10" full bodied, rose, cream, green, and brown, inscribed "Weller Pottery" on base   **245.00**
Frog, Coppertone, 2" h **75.00**
Flower Frog, Cameo **50.00**
Ginger Jar
Golden Glow, pr. **125.00**
Greora **175.00**
Hanging Basket
Creamware, 11½" d, reticulated pattern.   **45.00**
Forest, 10" d, chains **225.00**
Scenic Green, chains. **95.00**
Jardiniere
Claywood, 8" d, cherries and trees   **75.00**
Dragonflies, 8¾" d, 4½" h, relief dec, matte green glaze. **245.00**
Turada, 8½" **125.00**
Jug, currants, 6½" h **160.00**
Lamp Base
Dickensware I, oil lamp **125.00**
LaSa.   **425.00**
Pelican, multicolored **195.00**
Turada **550.00**
Mug
Claywood, star shaped flowers **50.00**
Dickensware
Dolphin handle and band, sgraffito ducks **250.00**
Stag Deer, green **450.00**
Pitcher
Bouquet, 6" h, ruffled top, lavender flower, white ground, artist sgd "M" **30.00**
Louwelsa, 14", artist sgd, #750 . . .   **600.00**
Pansy, 6½" h **85.00**
Planter
Dachshund, 8½" h **60.00**

Woodcraft, 5" h, 11" d, log **50.00**
Plate, 9½" d, dinner, Zona **20.00**
Teapot, 6" h, pumpkin **75.00**
Vase
Baldin, red apples, green leaves, gold ground. **65.00**
Blossom, 9" h **39.00**
Blossomtime, 6½" h, green, double bud.   **36.00**
Bronzeware, 10½" h **200.00**
Cameo, 7" h, blue **20.00**
Darsie, 5½" h, pale blue **32.00**
Delsa **58.00**
Florenzo, 5½" h **90.00**
Floretta, 6½" h, tri–cornered, grape clusters **125.00**
Forest, 4½" h **90.00**
Fox Hunt Scene, 7" h, white, deep blue ground. **165.00**
Greora, 8", double handled, baluster form, mottled orange–brown and green glaze, incised "Weller Pottery," Zanesville, OH, c1930   **55.00**
Hudson
7" h, sgd "Pillsbury" **350.00**
8" h, yellow roses, dark blue to pink, light green, and dark green, sgd "HP" **450.00**
13" h, Timberlake **475.00**
Knifewood, 7" h, low relief molded daisies **75.00**
LaSa, 11¼" h **325.00**
Louwelsa
4½" h, pansies, green to brown, artist sgd **150.00**
5½" h, buttercups, squat, artist sgd   **155.00**
6" h, pansies, brown, three handles, ftd **195.00**
Manhattan, 6½" h **40.00**
Oak Leaf. **28.00**
Patricia, white. **60.00**
Roma, 8" h **50.00**
Sabrinian, 9½" h. **140.00**

Flower Pot and Saucer, Bonito, 5" d, 4½" h, stamped mark, artist sgd, $70.00.

Vase, 11¼" h, duck dec., shades of green, matte glaze, marked "X357," impressed "Dickensware," $675.00.

Sicard, 6" h.	**650.00**
Silvertone	**130.00**
Wild Rose, 6" h, double bud	**30.00**
Woodcraft, double bud	**45.00**
Wall Pocket	
Glendale	**215.00**
Owl	**160.00**
Squirrel	**120.00**
Wood Rose	**75.00**
Woodcraft, squirrel	**120.00**
Woodland, azaleas	**135.00**
Window Box, Wood Rose	**85.00**

Bowl, 6¼" d, 2¾" h, brown bands, $28.00.

YELLOW WARE

History: Yellow ware is a heavy earthenware of differing weight and strength. Yellow ware varies in color from a rich pumpkin to lighter shades which are more tan than yellow. Although plates, nappies, and custard cups are found, kitchen bowls and other cooking utensils are most prevalent.

The first American yellow ware was produced at Bennington, Vermont. English yellow ware has additional ingredients which make its body much harder. Derbyshire and Sharp's were foremost among the English manufacturers.

Yellow ware has long been a favorite of Country collectors. Large bowls, unusual molds, and other household items are cornerstone collection pieces and desirable decorative accents.

References: John Gallo, *Nineteenth and Twentieth Century Yellow Ware*, Heritage Press, 1985; Joan Leibowitz, *Yellow Ware: The Transitional Ceramic*, Schiffer Publishing, 1985.

Baking Dish, 12" l, oval, unglazed, applied vintage and cauliflower handle, impressed "Wedgwood"	**175.00**
Bank, 3¾" h, pig, black and brown sponging, amber glaze	**100.00**
Bowl	
8⅜" d, 4¼" h, blue and brown sponging	**65.00**
8¾" d, oval, brown sponging	**25.00**
9¾" d, brown and blue sponging, marked "Red Wing Saffron Ware"	**30.00**
13" d, 3⅜" h, impressed "Sharpe's Warranted Fire Proof"	**70.00**
Box, 15½" l, rect, emb vintage and urns of fruit dec, clear glaze, running brown and green glaze	**200.00**
Butter Tub	
4¾" d, 4" h, pale blue glaze on molded staves	**185.00**
7¼" d, dark blue stripes, ribbed bottom.	**100.00**
Casserole, cov, 7¼" d, brown sponging	**50.00**
Colander, yellow bands, white interior	**175.00**

Creamer	
3¼" h, blue bands	**85.00**
4¼" h, molded tavern scenes, brown running Rockingham glaze	**15.00**
4½" h, green and brown sponging . .	**75.00**
Creamer and Sugar, 3⅛" h creamer, 4⅝" h sugar, molded floral design, classical figures	**300.00**
Crock, 5" d, three brown bands	**30.00**
Cuspidor, 5 x 7½", green, blue, and tan sponging	**60.00**
Custard Cup, brown sponging	**10.00**
Dish, 4½" d, brown sponging	**35.00**
Figure, 11⅜" h, seated cat, oval base, brown and bluish–green running glaze	**2,000.00**
Food Mold	
Corn	**90.00**
Heart	**85.00**
Pinwheel	**100.00**
Turk's Head, 9" d, brown sponging	**105.00**
Foot Warmer, wedge shaped, cork plug	**100.00**
Grease Lamp, 14½" h, bluish–green running glaze, rayed circle with "W"	**55.00**
Jar	
8¾" h, brown slip dec	**525.00**
12¼" h, brown running glaze, chipped lid	**85.00**
Milk Pan, 11½" d	**60.00**

Food Mold, corn, 5 3/16 x 3⅜ x 2⅛", $90.00.

Mixing Bowl Set, nested set
  Set of Three, 7 to 9½" d, molded
    ridges, brown and green spatter
    dec.................... 165.00
  Set of Four, 10 to 14" d, white band 260.00
Mug
  1/2 quart, brown sponge dec pattern 125.00
  2¾" h, white stripes 175.00
  3¼" h, brown polka dots 675.00
  3⅞" h, white band, brown stripes... 115.00
Pepper Pot, 4½" h, blue and white
  bands.................... 250.00
Pie Plate, 11½" d 75.00
Pitcher
  4½" h, adv, green and brown spong-
    ing, emb ribs, rect area with trans-
    fer label "Equity Elev. & Trading
    Co. Whitman, ND".......... 45.00
  6¼" h, molded shoulder and neck,
    blue spotted glaze 40.00

8½" h, brown band, dark brown
  stripes, repaired handle 210.00
10" h
  Blue and white bands........ 400.00
  Paneled, emb floral designs, am-
    ber glaze, impressed "Norton &
    Fenton, East Bennington Vt.,"
    hairlines, old spout and rim re-
    pair.................... 250.00
Preserving Jar, 6" h, 8" d, tan and
  white stripes, chipped lid 35.00
Rolling Pin, wood handles........ 175.00
Vegetable Dish, open, 9⅜ x 12¾ x 2",
  octagonal, impressed "Bennett &
  Brothers, Liverpool, Ohio" 475.00
Wash Bowl, 12" d, plain, 1865 ..... 75.00
Wash Bowl and Pitcher, black, tan,
  and blue stripes, marked "T.G.
  Green & Co. England".......... 225.00

SHAKER

When looking for an elegant handcrafted look, Country collectors and decorators turn to Shaker. The look has a natural and utilitarian emphasis. Warm earth tones dominate.

Because the Shakers were self–sufficient, they developed products for all aspects of daily living. Individuals who are only familiar with Shaker furniture are missing much of the picture.

The Shakers, so named because of a dance used in worship, are one of the oldest communal organizations in the United States. This religious group was founded by Mother Ann Lee, who emigrated from England and established the first Shaker community near Albany, New York, in 1784. The Shakers reached their peak in 1850 with 6,000 members.

Shakers lived celibate and self–sufficient lives. Their philosophy stressed cleanliness, order, simplicity, and economy. Highly inventive and motivated, the Shakers created many utilitarian household forms and objects. Their furniture reflected a striving for quality and purity in design.

In the early 19th century, the Shakers produced many items for commercial purposes. Chair making and the packaged herb and seed business thrived. In every endeavor and enterprise, the members followed Mother Ann's advice: "Put your hands to work and give your heart to God."

References: Charles R. Muller and Timothy D. Rieman, *The Shaker Chair,* The Canal Press, 1984; Don and Carol Raycraft, *Shaker, A Collector's Source Book II,* Wallace–Homestead, 1985; June Sprigg and David Larkin, *Shaker Life, Work, and Art,* Stewart, Tabori & Chang, 1987.

Periodicals: *Shaker Spirit,* PO Box 1309, Point Pleasant, NJ 08742; *The Shaker Messenger,* PO Box 1645, Holland, MI 49422.

Museums: Hancock Shaker Village, PO Box 898, Pittsfield, MA 01202; Shaker Historical Museum, 16740 S Park Blvd, Shaker Heights, OH 44120; The Shaker Museum, Shaker Museum Rd, Old Chatham, NY 12136.

Reproduction Craftspersons: *Baskets*—Darryl & Karen Arawjo, PO Box 477, Bushkill, PA 18324; John E McGuire, Baskets & Bears, 398 S Main St, Geneva, NY 14456; Gary A O'Brien, Meadow Farm, Ruggles Hill Rd, Hardwick, MA 01037; Martha Wetherbee, Martha

Wetherbee Basket Shop, HCR 69, Basket St, Sanbornton, NH 03269; Stephen Zeh, Basket-maker, PO Box 381, Temple, ME 04984; *Boxes*—Donald Butler, 402 Lombard St, Philadelphia, PA 19147; Charles Harvey, Simple Gifts, 201C N Broadway, Berea, KY 40403; *Furniture*—Dan Backenstose, Jr, Spring House Classics, PO Box 541, Schaefferstown, PA 17088; Gene Cosloy, Great Meadows Joinery, PO Box 392, Wayland, MA 01778; Lenore Howe & Brian Braskie, North Woods Chair Shop, 237 Old Tilton Rd, Canterbury, NH 03224; Ian Ingersoll Cabinetmakers, Main St, W Cornwall, CT 06796; Paul & Bonnie Rung, Llewellyn House, 2198 Mont Alto Rd, Chambersburg, PA 17201; Gregory Vasileff Reproductions, 740 North St, Greenwich, CT 06831.

Reproduction Manufacturers: *General*—C H Southwell, PO Box 484, Suttons Bay, MI 49682; Country Loft, 1506 South Shore Park, Hingham, MA 02043; The Country Stippler, Rte 2, Box 1540, Pine Mountain, GA 31822; David T Smith & Co, 3600 Shawhan Rd, Morrow, OH 45152; Faith Mountain Country Fare, Main St, Box 199, Sperryville, VA 22740; Five Trails Antiques and Country Accents, 116 E Water St, Circleville, OH 43113; Hammermark Associates, 10 Jericho Turnpike, Floral Park, NY 11001; J T Nicholas & Son, 704 N Michigan Ave, Howell, MI 48843; McClanahan Country, 217 Rockwell Rd, Wilmington, NC 28405; Mulberry Magic, PO Box 62, Ruckersville, VA 22968; Olde Virginea Floorcloth and Trading Co, PO Box 3305, Portsmouth, VA 23707; Our Home, Articles of Wood, 666 Perry St, Vermilion, OH 44089; Shaker Accents, PO Box 425, 4 Martin Ave, Lee, MA 01238; Shaker Carpenter Shop, 8267 Oswego Rd, Liverpool, NY 13090; Shaker Shops West, Five Inverness Way, Inverness, CA 94937; Spring House Classics, PO Box 541, Schaefferstown, PA 17088; Traditions, RD 4, Box 191, Hudson, NY 12534.

Basket
Berry, 6½" l, Sabbathday Lake Community **150.00**
Gathering, black ash, 24" sq, sgd ''Seed Shop, N.F.'' and ''N.F.L.S.'' **605.00**
Rect, two handled, sgd ''By J.A. May, 1890'' **770.00**
Round, 6" d, swing handle **770.00**
Sewing
Heart shaped, woven splint and raffia, faded painted floral dec on lid, 4" l **105.00**
Square, finely woven poplar splint, worn green satin lining and exterior ribbons, stamped label ''Sabbath Day Lake Shakers,'' accessories included, 4½" sq **180.00**
Bed, cherry and pine, on wheels, 6 feet 1" long, 38" w, Mount Lebanon, NY **990.00**
Bench
Cobbler's, orig blue paint, 54½" w, Canterbury, NH **4,125.00**
Wash, pine, mortised legs, gray paint, 6 feet long **400.00**
Blanket, wool, handwoven, initialed ''LMF 68,'' Canterbury, NH, slight moth damage **440.00**
Blanket Box, lift lid, dovetailed case, orig red paint, dated 1801 . . . . **5,500.00**

Blanket Chest
1 Drawer, refinished, 38" w, Enfield, NH **11,980.00**
2 Drawers, pine, painted, lift lid well, graduated thumb molded drawers, old red wash, orig wooden pulls, replaced lock and mortise, 39¼" w, 19¼" deep, 36¾" h, Canterbury, NH, c1820 **1,210.00**
3 Drawers, pine, bracket base, older finish **4,125.00**

Butter Churn, strap hinges, old red paint, $365.00.

Bonnet Mold, poplar, woven, white glaze exterior, paper label "8" **135.00**
Bottle, Shaker Digestive Cordial **150.00**
Bowl, turned, mustard wash, 9" d, Harvard, MA, late 19th C **8,250.00**
Box
Cutlery, rect, three sections **770.00**
Document, pine, dovetailed, $5\frac{1}{2}$ x $13\frac{1}{2}$ x 8", Copley–Lyman Family, Enfield, NH **300.00**
Mail, pine, hinged lid, natural finish, 20 x 24 x 11", Enfield **500.00**
Oval, lid
3" l, miniature, double hinged rotating top, attributed to Thomas Fisher, Enfield, CT, late 19th C **330.00**
$3\frac{1}{4}$" l, three finger construction, labels inside inscribed "Shaker Village" and "Hancock, Mass.," orig varnish finish **1,210.00**
$3\frac{5}{16}$" l, $1\frac{1}{4}$" h, miniature, oval, bentwood sides, pine top and bottom, two finger construction, polychrome yellow stain, c1875 .... **10,500.00**
$4\frac{5}{8}$" l, four finger construction, orig varnish finish, New Lebanon, NY, c1830 .... **1,540.00**
$5\frac{1}{4}$" l, $2\frac{1}{2}$" h, pine and maple, three finger construction, orig green paint, New Lebanon, NY, 1820–30 .... **4,675.00**
$5\frac{3}{4}$" l, pine and maple, three finger construction, orig light chrome yellow stain, attached card inscribed "Once owned by Sister Ann Buckingham (Shakers Watervliet, Made at Lebanon Shaker Village, 1827)" **6,050.00**
7" l, three finger construction, plaid fabric fitted interior, old red lipstick paint **5,500.00**
$11\frac{1}{2}$" l, $4\frac{1}{4}$" h, five finger construction, orig chrome yellow paint **7,500.00**
Seed, "Shakers' Choice Vegetable Seeds," cov, pine and poplar, six section interior, 22" l, Mount Lebanon, NY **1,210.00**
Sewing
Heart shaped, poplar, tomato pincushion top, blue satin ribbons, $4\frac{1}{4}$ x $4\frac{5}{8}$" top, $2\frac{1}{4}$" h, New Lebanon, NY, c1890 .... **2,860.00**
Oval, pine and maple, light brown wool covered pincushion, red and black tape border, copper tacks and points, three finger construction, orig chrome yellow finish, $3\frac{5}{8}$" l, $2\frac{1}{4}$" w, $2\frac{1}{2}$" h, c1830 .... **8,800.00**
Storage, pine, breadboard hinged lid, dovetailed case, orig orange shellac finish, $11\frac{1}{4}$ x $13\frac{1}{2}$ x $17\frac{1}{2}$", sgd "Sadie A. Neale, her box" .. **990.00**
Wood
Maple, lift lid, dovetailed case, traces of mustard paint, $35\frac{3}{4}$" h **2,530.00**
Pine, molded one–board top, dovetailed case, orig chrome yellow paint, 31" l, 20" deep, 21" h, South Family, New Lebanon, NY, c1830 .... **22,500.00**
Brush
$10\frac{1}{2}$" l, horsehair bristles, turned maple handle, painted black, stamped "44," 19th C **195.00**
14" l, dusting, worn gray paint **75.00**
Bucket, yellow wash, carved "A.D.56" and pressed "D.H." in bottom **550.00**
Can, paint, tin, Canterbury, NH **1,375.00**
Candlestand, cherry, round top
$14\frac{1}{4}$" d, 25" h, shaped metal plate, tripod base, snake legs, orig finish on base, Mount Lebanon, NY ... **11,000.00**
$14\frac{3}{8}$" d, $24\frac{1}{2}$" h, turned tapering stand, arched tripod base, snake feet, mahoganized surface with red–brown stain, New Lebanon, NY, 1800–50 .... **9,900.00**
18" d, $25\frac{1}{4}$" h, chamfered cherry cleat held with inset screws, turned shaft, shaped iron plate, tripod base, tapered spider legs, attributed to Samuel Turner, Church Family, New Lebanon, NY, c1837 .... **55,000.00**
Carrier
Berry, holds four berry boxes **440.00**
Herb, fixed handle, orig finish, 13 x $9\frac{1}{2}$ x 4" **1,210.00**
Oval, bentwood, maple and ash sides and handle, pine bottom, four finger construction, stained red and varnished, $11\frac{1}{4}$" l, $10\frac{1}{2}$" h, New England, c1875 .... **1,925.00**
Sewing, nest of four, Mount Lebanon, NY **2,475.00**
Chair
Arm, presentation, maple, turned finials, five shaped slats, from William Perkins to Lillian Barlow, 1910–20 .... **9,350.00**
Dining, birch back, pine seat, Canterbury, NH, 25" h **880.00**
Side
$37\frac{3}{4}$" h, maple, tilter, turned finials, three shaped slats, orig cane seat, Harvard, MA, c1840 **1,980.00**
$40\frac{1}{2}$" h, tilter, steam–bent back posts, Enfield, NH **2,200.00**
41" h, maple, rush seat, old refinish, Canterbury, NH **4,675.00**
$41\frac{1}{2}$" h, maple, turned finials and backposts, three beveled edge

Chair, ladderback, hardwood, splint seat, sgd "Sick, 1840," $1,200.00.

slats, old painted rush seat, Harvard, MA, 1840–60 . . . . . **1,045.00**

Cheese Drainer, tin, pierced sides and bottom, 18 x 6" **325.00**

Chest

Apothecary, grain painted, nine drawers, cut–out feet **2,200.00**

Spice, poplar, nine drawers, walnut pulls, natural finish, 7 x 13 x 6" **300.00**

Work, pine and poplar, three drawers, square tapering legs **2,750.00**

Chest of Drawers, pine, five drawers, paneled ends, orig finish, Watervliet, NY. **6,050.00**

Churn, cylinder type, Canterbury Community, Londonderry, NH, 19th C **650.00**

Clothing

Bonnet, straw, insert, black neck cape, in hat box **1,320.00**

Dorothy Cloak, Sabbathday Lake, ME **550.00**

Dress, purple, labeled "M.A.W." **880.00**

Shirt, brethren, work, homespun, initials "J.C.", Copley–Lyman Family **400.00**

Coffeepot, tin, handle at right angle, 11" h, Sabbathday Lake **250.00**

Counter, tailoring, pine and poplar, overhanging top, eight drawers, pumpkin orange and chrome yellow stained, marked "February 1844" in pencil on two drawers, 65¾" l **8,800.00**

Cricket, pine, upholstered, hooked floral motif on black ground, oneboard mustard washed plank top, incised turned legs, button feet, 12" w, 7" deep, 7¼" h, Enfield, CT, early 19th C **375.00**

Cupboard

Hanging, one door, two drawers, orig red paint, 15¾" w **5,775.00**

Wall

72" h, 34¼" w, 17¾" deep, pine, two doors over four drawers over two doors, paneled doors, orig red wash, c1830 . . . . **55,000.00**

74" h, 36" w, 15¼" deep, pine, two door, inset molded panels, mortised and diagonally pinned, canted foot, six interior shelves, orig yellow wash and knobs, New Lebanon, NY, c1820 . . . . **11,000.00**

84" h, cupboard door over five graduated drawers, refinished **5,500.00**

Desk

School, double, mixed woods, lift lids, trestle base, shoe feet, refinished **2,860.00**

Sewing

Double, butternut, flame birch, pine, and cherrywood, upper case has split paneled cupboard door and bank of four drawers on each side and paneled front and back, butternut and wavy birch door panels, bright red wash on cupboard interiors, 4" overhang on upper case supported by two brackets and board at back, overhanging work surface, cherry breadboard ends on pine slides extend from both sides for added work space, lower case has two banks of four wide drawers alternating with two banks of four narrow drawers, nailed drawers, cleat locking devices on six drawers, two key locking bottom drawers, and paneled ends, ball feet, mellow old finish, 44" h, sgd "B.H. Smith 1862, N.F. 1862," Canterbury, NH . . **33,000.00**

Single, six over six drawers, 29 x 26¾" work surface, attributed to Elder William Briggs, Canterbury, NH **7,425.00**

Trustee's, butternut and pine, 3 pcs, dovetailed cases, three paneled cupboard doors upper section, two paneled doors and sixteen drawers mid section, desk lift lid on slide and two paneled cupboard doors in base, turned and figured knobs, turned feet, light varnish, refinished, Enfield, CT, c1850 . . . . **22,000.00**

Writing, pine, pigeon hole interior, birch tapered and chamfered legs, refinished, 31" w, attributed to Sabbathday Lake, ME **2,970.00**

Dipper, maple, turned handle, 6" d bowl, 19th C. **500.00**

Doll Bonnet, red neck cape, some damage **250.00**

Drying Rack, oak frame, mortise, tenon, and peg construction, splint weavers, 65 x 32", Alfred Maine community **600.00**

Dust Mop, blue wool, 65" l handle, Enfield, NH **330.00**

Dust Pan, tin, handle ring, 12" l, 19th C **125.00**

Fireplace Tongs, iron, 24" l, late 19th C **375.00**

Hanger, wood, carved design, 13" l, paper printed label "EJ" **150.00**

Hatchet/Hammer, handmade, sgd "I.Y.," Canterbury, NH **495.00**

Iron, coat sleeve, Canterbury, NH . . . **25.00**

Kerchief, silk, maroon, striped borders, framed, woven in KY or OH, pre–1860 . . . . **1,870.00**

Loom, sgd "Sister Sarah Neale," New Lebanon, CT **3,575.00**

Neck Yoke, green paint, Canterbury, NH **330.00**

Painting, oil, birch trees by the water, 30 x 22", attributed to Cora Helena Sarle **880.00**

Peg Board, 24 pegs, 62 x 14" **1,100.00**

Pickle Jar, yellow/amber color, barrel shaped, emb "Shaker Brand/FD Petterngill & Co/Portland/ME," smooth base, applied mouth, 5" h, 1870–1880 . . . . **745.00**

Rocker

Arm

44" h, four slats, painted polychrome yellow, replaced tape seat, New Lebanon, NY, c1830 . . . . **12,100.00**

Side

36" h, no. "4" on top slat, cushion rail, replaced twill tape seat, orig dark varnished finish, R.M. Wagan, Mt. Lebanon, NY, c1875 . . . . **450.00**

41" h, maple, three slats, no. "2" on reverse of center slat, old rush seat, orig a straight chair with tilters, Harvard, MA, mid 19th C **440.00**

Rug

Hooked, round, knitted background **1,210.00**

Rag, wool, square, alternating blue, green, and red stripes, S and Z twists, woven tape binding, 36 x 36", Canterbury, NH **4,675.00**

Rule, brass inlays, 36" l, dated "1841" **880.00**

Sander, turned, yellow wash, remnants of orig green paper label at base, $3\frac{7}{16}$" h, late 19th C **140.00**

Settee

58" l, 38" h, birch and pine, nineteen spindles, varnished, Enfield, NH **5,000.00**

10 feet long, meeting house, spindle back, six legs, arched metal braces, orig finish, Enfield, NH . . **11,100.00**

Spinning Wheel, wool, stamped "D.M.," c1800 . . . . **990.00**

Spool Holder Rack, tiger maple, peg legs, three rows, seven spool holders each row, 7" h, mid to late 19th C **635.00**

Stand

Sewing, pine and butternut, two drawer, South Family, New Lebanon, NY **7,425.00**

Tailoring, round top, four legs, 24" d, 13" h, orig red paint **1,870.00**

Wash

16" w, one drawer, NH **2,200.00**

$31\frac{1}{2}$" h, gallery, single paneled door, red wash under varnish, c1830 . . . . **6,600.00**

36" w, 16" deep, $36\frac{1}{2}$" h, pine, painted, hinged lid on dovetailed storage compartment over paneled cupboard door, two interior half–shelves, orig red wash, Harvard, MA, 19th C **11,000.00**

Work, pine top, cherry base, one drawer, shelf, tapering legs, $28\frac{1}{2}$" w, $16\frac{1}{2}$" deep **7,975.00**

Stool

Production, maple, mahogany stain, varnished, orig black and gold cotton tape, Shaker production decal, 14" w, 14" deep, 17" h, New Lebanon, NY, 1900–25 . . . **660.00**

Sewing, two–step, pine, painted, upholstered, hooked red and yellow floral motif on gray ground, red washed sides, stretcher, 14" w, $13\frac{3}{4}$" deep, $12\frac{1}{4}$" h, Eastern Community, 1800–50 . . . . **450.00**

Stove, iron, lift lid, canted cornered base, cabriole legs, wrought penny feet, $21\frac{3}{4}$" w, $22\frac{1}{2}$" deep, 26" h, Harvard, MA, c1800 . . . . **4,275.00**

Swift, Hancock, MA **275.00**

Table

Dining, ministry, cherry two–board scrubbed top, arched maple base, carved maple feet, orig red wash, "45" and "4" die–stamped on legs, 84" l, $34\frac{1}{4}$" deep, $26\frac{3}{4}$" h, New England, 1800–50 . . . . **82,500.00**

Work, butternut and cherry, overhanging top, one drawer, square tapering legs **4,400.00**

Tall Chest, pine, two over six drawers, dovetailed case and base, thumbnail molded, old gray paint over red paint, c1820 . . . . **23,100.00**

STONEWARE

Slip and sgraffito decorated redware dominate the early American look. The pottery of choice for the Country collector and decorator is stoneware.

Made from dense kaolin clay and commonly salt–glazed, stonewares were hand–thrown and high–fired to produce a simple, bold vitreous pottery. Stoneware crocks, jugs, and jars were produced for storage and utility purposes. This use dictated shape and design—solid, thick–walled forms with heavy rims, necks, and handles with little or no embellishment. When decorated, the designs were simple: brushed cobalt oxide, incised, slip trailed, stamped, or tooled.

Stoneware has been made for centuries. Initially, early American settlers imported stoneware items but soon began producing their own. Two major North American traditions emerged based only on the location or type of clay. North Jersey and parts of New York comprise the first area; the second was eastern Pennsylvania spreading westward and into Maryland, Virginia, and West Virginia. These two distinct locations, style of decoration, and shape are discernible factors in classifying and dating early stoneware.

By the late 18th century, stoneware was manufactured in all sections of the country. During the 19th century, this vigorous industry flourished until glass "fruit jars" appeared and the widespread use of refrigeration began. By 1910, commercial production of salt–glazed stoneware came to an end.

References: Georgeanna H. Greer, *American Stoneware: The Art and Craft of Utilitarian Potters*, Schiffer Publishing, Ltd., 1981; Don and Carol Raycraft, *Country Stoneware And Pottery*, Collector Books, 1985; Don and Carol Raycraft, *Collector's Guide To Country Stoneware & Pottery*, 2nd Series, Collector Books, 1990.

Museums: Museum of Ceramics at East Liverpool, East Liverpool, OH; The Bennington Museum, Bennington, VT.

Reproduction Craftspersons: Bastine Pottery, RR 3, Box 111, Noblesville, IN 46060; Heather & Jack Beauchamp, Salt O' Thee Earth Pottery, 71456 Bates Rd, Guernsey, OH 43741; Gerald T Beaumont, Beaumont Pottery, 293 Beech Ridge Rd, York, ME 03909; Al & Barbara Blumberg, Bon Aqua Pottery, Rte 1, Box 396–10, Bon Aqua, TN 37025; Wendy Cotton, RR 1, Box 528, Avondale, PA 19311; David Eldreth, Eldreth Pottery, 902 Hart Rd, Oxford, PA 19363; David & Mary Farrell, Potters, Westmoore Pottery, Rte 2, Box 494, Seagrove, NC 27341; Tim Galligan & Kathy Kellagher, Cooksburg Pottery, Star Rte, Box 155, Marienville, PA 16239; Lee Gilbert, The Studio in Swarthmore, 14 Park Ave, Swarthmore, PA 19081; Joel & Debra Huntley, Wisconsin Pottery, Inc, W3199 Hwy 16, Columbus, WI 53925; Jean Lehman, 103 Dickinson Ave, Lancaster, PA 17603; David C Meixner, Buffalo Pottery Co, Rte 6, Box 108, Menomonie, WI 54751; Linda Milliner, 49 Bluestone Dr, Chadds Ford, PA 19317; Becky Mummert, 30 Fish and Game Rd, East Berlin, PA 17316; Rowe Pottery Works, Inc, 404 England St, Cambridge, WI 53523; Yvonne Snead, Plantation Days Dinnerware by Yvonne, 327 Magnolia St, Raeford, NC 28376; Stebner Studios, 3933 Smith–Kramer St, Hartville, OH 44632; Sid & Eileen Vernon, Vernon Pottery, 1537 Quail Pt Rd, Virginia Beach, VA 23454; Jonathan & Jan Wright & Rick Fitzsimmons, Crocker & Springer, PO Box 212, Elsah, IL 62028.

Reproduction Manufacturers: Adirondack Store and Gallery, 109 Saranac Ave, Lake Placid, NY 12946; Anastasia's Collectibles, 6114 134th St W, Apple Valley, MN 55124; The Barn, PO Box 25, Market St, Lehman, PA 18627; Bastine Pottery, RR 3, Box 111, Noblesville, IN 46060; Basye–Bomberger/Fabian House, PO Box 86, W Bowie, MD 20715; Bathroom Machineries, 495 Main St, PO Box 1020, Murphys, CA 95247; Chinaberry General Store, 1846 Winfield Dunn Highway, Sevierville, TN 38762; Country Loft, 1506 South Shore Park,

Hingham, MA 02043; Crazy Crow Trading Post, PO Box 314B, Denison, TX 75020; Cumberland General Store, Rte 3, Crossville, TN 38555; Eldreth Pottery, 4351 Forge Rd, Nottingham, PA 19362; Faith Mountain Country Fare, Main St, Box 199, Sperryville, VA 22740; Georgia Folk Pottery, 2579 W Fontainebleau Court, Doraville, GA 30360; Gooseberry Patch, PO Box 634, Delaware, OH 43015; Lamb and Lanterns, 902 N Walnut St, Dover, OH 44622; Log Cabin Shop, Box 275, Lodi, OH 44254; Mole Hill Pottery, 5011 Anderson Pike, Signal Mountain, TN 37377; Pure and Simple, PO Box 535, 117 W Hempstead, Nashville, AR 71852; Rowe Pottery Works, Inc, 404 England St, Cambridge, WI 53523; Southern Manner, Inc, 106 North Trade St, PO Box 1706, Matthews, NC 28106.

Bank
4½" h, inverted top shape, incised and cobalt blue dec, fleur–de–lis one side, coin slot and stylized flower other side, attributed to David Morgan, New York, c1800 ... **3,000.00**
6½" h, conical top, sloping shoulders, flared base, incised bands at shoulder, cobalt blue floral and leaf dec, "Mary Warren 1866" inscribed along coin slot, attributed to Remmey Family, Philadelphia ... **4,675.00**

Batter Jug
3 Quart, W Roberts, Binghamton, NY, brown Albany slip covered ... **50.00**
1 Gallon
Unknown Maker, imp "4," dark brown Albany slip, wire bail and wooden handle ... **25.00**
Whites, Binghamton, imp label, cobalt blue at ears, spout, and label, 7⅞" h, hairlines, small chips ... **155.00**
1 ½ Gallon
Evan R Jones, Pittston, PA, ovoid, flower dec, cobalt blue at spout and ears ... **635.00**
F H Cowden, Harrisburg, PA, triple stencil dec, brushed cobalt blue at spout, ears, and handle ... **990.00**

Bottle, 1 quart
C G Sawyer, cobalt blue highlights at imp label, 9¾" h, lip chip ... **15.00**
J F Thompson, cobalt blue imp label, salt glaze, golden highlights, 9⅞" h ... **85.00**

Butter Crock
2 Quart
A P Donaghho, Parkersburg, W VA, stenciled ... **185.00**
1 Gallon
Jas Hamilton & Co, Greensboro, PA, stenciled rose and lettering ... **385.00**
Sipe Nichols & Co, Williamsport, PA, handles, brushed cobalt blue dec ... **150.00**
Unknown Maker, lid, handles, cobalt blue leaf dec around crock and lid ... **250.00**

1½ Gallon, lid, leafy cobalt blue dec all around and at handles ... **465.00**

Cake Crock, 2 gallon
Evan R Jones, Pittston, PA, handles, drooping tulip dec ... **385.00**
Sipe Nichols & Co, Williamsport, PA, handles, large cobalt blue brushed dec ... **350.00**
Unknown Maker, handles, cobalt blue floral dec around crock ... **250.00**

Chicken Fountain
2 quart
A L Hyssong, Bloomsburg, PA, brown Albany slip ... **85.00**
Unknown Maker, marked "Fountain, Pat'd Apr. 7, 1885," brown Albany slip, 7½" l, chips on foot ... **55.00**
W R & Co, Akron, OH, brownish–black Albany slip, emb label, patented Apr 7, 1885, 6½" d, 6" l, glued lip ... **80.00**
1 Gallon, hooded, cobalt blue floral dec ... **330.00**

Churn
1½ Gallon, imp "1½," brushed cobalt blue floral dec, 13½" h ... **125.00**
3 Gallon, unknown maker, brushed cobalt blue floral dec, marked "3," 14¾" h, short hairline in base ... **100.00**
4 Gallon
Haxton Ottman & Co, Fort Edward, NY, ovoid, cobalt blue slip stylized floral dec, 16½" h ... **275.00**
Unknown Maker
15¾" h, cobalt blue brushed floral dec ... **325.00**
16½" h, cobalt blue slip stylized floral design, lid and dasher ... **275.00**
5 Gallon
C Hart & Son, Sherburne, NY, handles, triple slip dec ... **330.00**
E & L P Norton, Bennington, VT, cobalt blue flower and leaves dec ... **400.00**
Haxstun & Co, Fort Edward, NY, handles, cobalt blue swirl dec, dasher ... **275.00**
J Burger Jr, Rochester, NY, han-

dles, cobalt blue floral dec, dasher **300.00**

Unknown Maker, handles, cobalt blue bird on branch dec, Canadian **415.00**

6 Gallon, Whites, Utica, handles, fantail bird in floral and fern dec, cracked **1,045.00**

8 Gallon, J Burger, Rochester, NY, applied black dec, large numeral 8 enclosed by two–leaf wreath **900.00**

Cooler

3 Gallon, handles, unknown maker, cobalt blue floral and rings dec . . **360.00**

4 Gallon, barrel design, spigot, no dec **95.00**

5 Gallon

Fulper Pottery Co, Flemington, NJ, barrel shaped, marked "Ice Water," cobalt blue banded dec **95.00**

J Armstrong, NY, barrel shape, incised cobalt blue hand, small fish, and two bands, imp "V," spigot hole at base, 15¾" h, c1830 . . . . **2,425.00**

8 Gallon, unknown maker, barrel shaped, brushed cobalt blue slip "1861, 8g," 19" h, hairlines **260.00**

10 Gallon, unknown maker

20" h, ovoid, salt glazed, double handled, spout at base, deeply incised and cobalt blue dec, baskets of flowers, imp numeral "10" and "1847" date, hole for spigot at base **5,500.00**

21¾" l, keg shaped, cobalt blue brushed floral dec, wooden stand **750.00**

Crock

1 Gallon

Jacob Henry & Co, Albany, NY, imp label, dark brown Albany slip, 6" h, small chips, hairline **15.00**

Lyons, lid, brushed floral dec, cobalt blue at handles **295.00**

T Reppert, Greensboro, PA, semi–ovoid, stenciled rose and lettering **250.00**

Unknown Maker, handles, cobalt blue jay dec **325.00**

Whites, Utica, handles, cobalt blue dec fantail roadrunner . . . **550.00**

Williams & Reppert, Greensboro, PA, semi–ovoid, stenciled dec **220.00**

1 ½ Gallon

E & L P Norton, Bennington, VT, imp label, brushed cobalt blue leaf, 7¼" h, minor chips **140.00**

E Norton & Co, Bennington, VT, cobalt blue slip leaf, 8½" d, 7¼" h, chips, glaze flaked **125.00**

Crock, H J Heinz Co, impressed label and dec, straight sides, 6¼" d, 5¼" h, $250.00.

G Myers, adv, marked "Dealer in dry goods, groceries, etc. Batesville, Ohio.," stenciled cobalt blue label, 10½" d, 7½" h **500.00**

N A White & Son, Utica, NY, handles

6½" h, floral slip dec **275.00**

6¾" h, imp label, cobalt blue brushed leaf design, hairlines **175.00**

New York Stoneware Co, imp label, cobalt blue slip floral dec, 7⅞" h, stains, hairline **90.00**

Ottoman Bro's & Co, Fort Edward, NY, imp label, cobalt blue slip bird on branch dec, 8" h, missing one handle **90.00**

Unknown Maker

7¼" h, semi–ovoid, handles, outlined profile of woman dec **1,430.00**

7½" h, handles, brushed cobalt blue dec **65.00**

White, Utica, NY, imp label, cobalt blue slip backwards–looking bird, 7" h, hairlines . . . **365.00**

2 Gallon

A K Ballard, Burlington, VT, handles, cobalt blue stylized flower dec **100.00**

Cowden & Wilcox, Harrisburg, PA, semi–ovoid, cobalt blue floral dec, cobalt blue at handles **150.00**

E & L P Norton, Bennington, VT, imp label and "2," cobalt blue quill work stylized floral design, 9" h, chips, hairlines **100.00**

F B Norton & Co, Worcester, MA, handles, cobalt blue slip stylized floral dec, 9" h **105.00**

Geo H Swearingen, Dry Goods, Notions and General Mdse,

Crock, 1½ gallon, J Norton & Co, Bennington, VT, handled, impressed label, cobalt blue bird on branch, 10" d, 6⅞" h, 1859–1861, $395.00.

Dunbar, PA, adv, semi–ovoid, stencil and freehand dec, western PA	330.00
Hamilton & Jones, Greensboro, PA, stenciled and freehand soaring dove dec	550.00
John Waugh, Jr, Lowell, MA, imp label, cobalt blue dec, 11½" h	350.00
N A White & Son, Utica, NY, handles, straight sided, bold floral dec	185.00
Somerset Potters Works, handles, cobalt blue dandelion gone to seed dec	375.00

Unknown Maker

9½" h, imp "2," cobalt blue slip pecking chicken, chips and glaze flakes	385.00
10" h, imp "2," cobalt blue quill work pecking chicken	225.00
W Roberts, Binghamton, NY, semi–ovoid, handles, cobalt blue bird dec	385.00

White, Utica, NY

9" h, ovoid, imp label, cobalt blue slip bird on branch, hairlines	285.00
9½" h, imp label and "2," cobalt blue slip long–tailed bird on branch, large rim chip	195.00

3 Gallon

E & L P Norton, Bennington, VT, handles, cobalt blue slip dec

10" h, stylized floral design	325.00
10½" h, feather dec	275.00
F Young, ovoid, imp label, incised lines at shoulder, 12" h	70.00
Hart Bros, Fulton, NY, handles, brushed cobalt blue floral dec	155.00
J M Pruden, Elizabeth, NJ, handles, stick flower dec	170.00

N A White & Son, Utica, NY, cobalt blue floral dec	120.00
Norton & Fenton, East Bennington, VT, small cobalt blue slip floral dec, 10½" h	135.00
Savage & Rogers, Havana, NY, semi–ovoid, handles, large cobalt blue double floral dec	385.00
T Harrington, Lyons, semi–ovoid, bull's–eye starburst dec	2,970.00

Unknown Maker

10¾" h, handles, simple cobalt blue slip floral dec and "3," stains and hairlines	65.00
10½" h, brushed cobalt blue "3" and simple design	175.00
White & Wood, Binghamton, NY, imp label, cobalt blue dec, 11¼" h	750.00

4 Gallon

A O Whittemore, Havana, NY, handles, cobalt blue house, flag, and tree dec	11,500.00
Evan R Jones, Pittstown, PA, handles, cobalt blue polka dot bird on leaf dec	165.00
Gardner Stoneware Manufactory of Gardner, ME, handles, eagle carrying draped flag, flying over two swimming swans, incised and light blue highlighted dec	125.00
Haxstun & Co, Fort Edward, NY, handles, cobalt blue slip stylized floral dec, 11½" h	350.00
T S Balsley, Manufacturer, Detroit, MI, handles, cobalt blue floral dec, cobalt blue at handles	330.00
Unknown Maker, OH, cobalt blue inscription "Hurrah for Abe Lincoln," c1860	4,400.00

Crock, 2 gallon, unknown maker, cobalt blue running bird decoration, incised "2", 10¾" d, 7¾" h, $245.00.

Whites, Utica, handles, fantail
bird looking back dec **495.00**
5 Gallon
Evan R Jones, Pittston, PA, semi–
ovoid, handles, large floral dec
on front, beehive and bees on
back, script writing "Shupps
Bee Hive, Plymouth, PA" **1,980.00**
J Burger Jr, Rochester, NY, ovoid,
cobalt blue slip bird and plant,
imp label, 14" h **1,650.00**
J Norton & Co, Bennington, VT,
handles, large flower basket
dec, early Norton stamp **1,430.00**
S Hart, Fulton, handles, brushed
floral dec **145.00**
Unknown Maker, cinnamon col-
ored, handles, wreath and dot-
ted anchor dec, NY **775.00**
6 Gallon
E & L P Norton, Bennington, VT,
handles, stylized cobalt blue
slip floral dec, 13" h **405.00**
N A White & Son, Utica, NY,
bright blue slip dec, large–
tailed bird on branch, 13½" h **1,250.00**
Unknown Maker
13½" h, cobalt blue slip flower
and "6," stains, hairlines,
and rim chip **55.00**
14" h, cobalt blue quill work
bouquet of flowers and "6" **225.00**
8 Gallon, Boughner, Greensboro,
PA, ovoid, imp label, cobalt blue
brushed dec, three bands, three
rows of stylized foliage dec,
18" h, bad crack in base **775.00**
Cucumber, figural, 11¾" l, green and
cream colored mottled glaze,
c1860–80 . . . . **85.00**
Double Jug, 7" h, Stedman, Seymour,
New Haven, ovoid, incised and cobalt blue singing birds dec, joined
from shoulder to base, single strap
handle at center, early 19th C **1,750.00**
Flask, ovoid
7" h, cobalt blue outlined man's
head dec, early 19th C **4,500.00**
8" h, incised bands below tooled lip,
incised and cobalt blue filled
flower dec front, incised and cobalt blue floral dec reverse, attributed to Crolius Family, New York
City, c1800 . . . . **2,425.00**
Flower Pot
3⅞" h, attached saucer, molded flo-
ral surface, brown glaze **35.00**
9" h, attached saucer, gray salt glaze **95.00**
Foot Warmer, cylindrical, imp label
"Logan Pottery Co. Logan, O. O.K.
Foot Warmer," blue and white, 12" l **55.00**
Funnel, 5" h, brown Albany slip **155.00**

Ink Well
2½" h, reddish–brown Albany slip,
paneled base **45.00**
3⅝" d, gray salt glaze, minor edge
flakes **55.00**
Jar
1 Pint, greenish–black glaze, 4⅞" h,
small edge chips **5.00**
1 Quart
Anchovisch, incised label, cobalt
blue bands **115.00**
E S G, ovoid, lid, two handles,
dark brown Albany slip sgraffito
initials, 7" h, handles repaired **115.00**
Unknown Maker
7¼" h, cov, applied handles,
molded foliage design on lid,
tan glaze, black highlights,
hairline, small edge chips . . **25.00**
7⅜" h, ovoid, applied handles,
tooled band, attributed to
Boscowin Pottery, no lid . . . **25.00**
7⅞" h, stenciled rose, western
PA **155.00**
2 Quart
S L Pewtress & Co, New Haven,
CT, ovoid, strap handle, tan Al-
bany slip, 8⅜" h **30.00**
Unknown Maker
8½" h, cobalt blue brushed foliage at shoulder, firing hair-
lines in bottom **65.00**
8¾" h, lid, brushed cobalt blue
design at shoulder, indistinct
imp label, hairline **145.00**
1 Gallon
N Clark & Co, ovoid, imp label,
cobalt blue and label and handles, 9¾" h, minor chips, short
rim hairline **70.00**

**Jar, canning, Jas Hamilton & Co,
Greensboro, PA, cobalt blue stenciled label, $85.00.**

Penn Yan, tulip dec, cobalt
at handles **195.00**
Roberts, Binghamton, NY, ovoid,
imp label, applied handles, cobalt blue slip polka dot bird on
branch, 7¼" h, blurred dec, rim
chip **300.00**
Sipe & Sons, Williamsport, PA,
sloping shoulders, brush dec,
cobalt blue at handle **300.00**
T M Mead & Co, ovoid, imp label,
cobalt blue at label and handles, 9¾" h, minor chips, hair-
line **95.00**
Unknown Maker
7" h, applied handle, cobalt
blue at handle, minor hair-
lines. **65.00**
8" h, ovoid, applied handles,
cobalt blue floral dec, chips
on lip and one handle **250.00**
1½ Gallon, unknown maker, ovoid,
applied handles, brushed cobalt
blue vining floral design, imp
"1½," 11½" h, rim chip **270.00**
2 Gallon
C Hart & Son, Sherburne, NY,
handles, no dec **45.00**
Cortland, cobalt blue slip floral
dec and "2," 10½" h **375.00**
Fred Kampfer, Gen Store, Claring-
ton, OH, adv, freehand and
stenciled dec **275.00**
Fulper Bros, Flemington, NJ, han-
dles, brushed cobalt blue floral
dec **215.00**
Hamilton & Jones, Greensboro,
PA, cobalt blue stenciled and
freehand label and "2," 12¼" h,
rim chips **125.00**

**Jar, 1½ gallon, E & L P Norton, Bennington,
VT, impressed label, cobalt blue slip stylized floral dec, $165.00.**

John Burger, Rochester, handles,
lid, cobalt blue floral dec **660.00**
Julius Norton, Bennington, VT
10⅜" h, semi–ovoid, imp label **45.00**
10½" h, ovoid, imp label and
"2," cobalt blue label high-
lights, minor rim chips **55.00**
S Hart
Fulton, handles, cobalt blue
polka dot bird dec **135.00**
Oswego Falls, ovoid, handles,
imp label, brushed cobalt
blue "2," golden highlights,
10½" h, minor chips, short rim
hairline **125.00**
Sipe & Sons, Williamsport, PA,
sloping shoulders, double
flower, cobalt blue at handles **165.00**
S James McGee, Winfield, NY,
handles, floral slip dec **190.00**
Unknown Maker
10¼" h, ovoid, cobalt blue quill
work flourish and "2," edge
chips **55.00**
11½" h, ovoid, cobalt blue
brushed floral design **100.00**
12¼" h, ovoid, applied handles,
brushed cobalt blue vining
floral design, small edge
chips **275.00**
13" h, ovoid, cobalt blue slip
dec flower one side, "1851"
and "2" in balloon–like outline other side, old edge
chips and paint traces **275.00**
Whites, Utica, handles, fantail
roadrunner **410.00**
Williams and Reppert, Greens-
boro, PA, cobalt blue stenciled
and freehand dec, 11¾" h. **275.00**
3 Gallon
A P Donaghho, Parkersburg, WV,
ovoid, cobalt blue stenciled label, "3," and geometric dec,
14½" h, small chips **375.00**
Hamilton & Jones, Greensboro,
PA, semi–ovoid, cobalt blue
stenciled and freehand label
and eagle, 13½" h **700.00**
I M Mead & Co, ovoid, imp label
and "3," cobalt blue at label
and handles, 12½" h, firing hairlines in one handle, chip on
base **80.00**
James Hamilton & Co, Greens-
boro, PA, handles, stencil and
brush dec. **495.00**
J F Hart, Ogdensburg, ovoid, imp
label, cobalt blue brushed floral
design and label highlights,
12¾" h, hairlines, chipped han-
dles. **250.00**

Jordon, ovoid, imp label and "3," brushed cobalt blue floral dec, gray salt glaze, golden highlights, 13¼" h, chips, minor hairlines, mismatched lid **115.00**

McDonald–Benjamin, imp label, simple brushed cobalt blue flower, 14¼" h, hairlines and rim chip. **65.00**

Unknown Maker

13" h, brushed cobalt blue floral design entire front. **235.00**

13¼" h, ovoid, applied handles, brushed cobalt blue fruit and flowers dec, large "3" at each handle, lip chip, hairline in bottom **150.00**

13¾" h, ovoid, imp "3," brushed cobalt blue floral and foliage designs all sides **475.00**

14" h, imp "3," brushed cobalt blue floral dec both sides and at applied handles, rim chip **95.00**

15" h, indistinct incised label, cobalt blue brushed design **95.00**

4 Gallon

J Swank & Co, Johnstown, PA, ovoid, cobalt blue brushed floral design **175.00**

Kampfer & Muhleman, Clarington, OH, ovoid, applied handles, cobalt blue stenciled and freehand label and "4," 14¾" h, stains, hairlines **200.00**

Liminier, imp label and "4," brushed cobalt blue tulip dec, 13¼" h, rough and bubbled glaze, small chips. **150.00**

Jar, 2 gallon, Richard C Remmey, Philadelphia, PA, impressed label, cobalt blue feather dec, $400.00.

Unknown Maker

14" h, semi–ovoid, handles, cobalt blue brushed foliage dec, tooled lines at shoulder, imp "4" **450.00**

14½" h, ovoid, brushed cobalt blue floral band, hairlines and chips **115.00**

14¾" h, ovoid, tooled lines, applied handles, brushed cobalt blue floral dec, minor stains and rim chips. **250.00**

Western PA, handles, freehand bands and feather dec **385.00**

5 Gallon

A Conrad, New Geneva, PA, handles, cobalt blue stenciled eagle and brush dec, western PA **350.00**

C L Williams & Co, cobalt blue stenciled and freehand label "C.L. Williams & Co., Successors to R.T. Williams, Manufacturers of Stoneware, New Geneva, Pa.5.," 15½" h, hairlines, small chips. **200.00**

Hamilton & Jones, Greensboro, PA, ovoid, applied handles, cobalt blue stenciled and freehand label and "5," 16" h, chip, some wear. **225.00**

Williams and Reppert, Greensboro, PA, cobalt blue stenciled and freehand label, eagle and "20," 25½" h **1,850.00**

6 Gallon

J I Ambright, Newport, OH, ovoid, tooled lines at shoulder, double ear handles, cobalt blue quill work label, reverse flourish, and "6," 19" h **145.00**

Unknown Maker, ovoid, imp "6," grayish–yellow glaze, 15½" h **40.00**

8 Gallon, T F Reppert, Greensboro, PA, ovoid, stenciled and freehand cobalt blue label, eagle, and "8," 19¾" h **1,075.00**

Jug

1 Quart, unknown maker, ovoid, ribbed strap handle, blue paint traces, 7¼" h. **70.00**

2 Quart, Fred Schwartz & Bro, Plymouth, PA, script **200.00**

1 Gallon

Adams, Jeff County, NY, ovoid, imp label "Made Expressly for R.B. Doxtater & Co," brushed cobalt blue design and "1," 11¾" h **130.00**

C Crolius, Manufacturer Manhattan–Wells, NY, ovoid, cobalt blue dec **1,100.00**

Dean Foster & Co, 14 Blackstone St, Boston, cobalt blue flower dec **125.00**

S Blair, Cortland, ovoid **330.00**

S Hart

8" h, squatty, simple cobalt blue flower **190.00**

10¾" h, ovoid, imp label, simple cobalt blue brushed design, short hairline in handle base **95.00**

Sibb J Beighel, Pleasant Unity, PA, ovoid, cobalt blue star shaped leaves and "1," stenciled label, 11¼" h **275.00**

Sipe & Sons, Williamsport, PA, cobalt blue brushed double floral dec, cobalt blue at handles **300.00**

Unknown Maker

9¼" h, imp label "E.G.Scovil, Maratime Agents for Pelee Island Wine Co., St. John N.B.," old varnish, stains . . **45.00**

11½" h, ovoid, ribbed strap handle, brushed cobalt blue foliage design, chips on lip and bottom edge **135.00**

Whites, Utica, pine tree dec **220.00**

1½ Gallon

Brewer & Holm, Havana, NY, ovoid, cobalt blue brushed floral dec, 10¾" h, lip chips, handle glued **105.00**

Campbell & Morion, Penn Yan, ovoid, cobalt blue at handle and label, 11½" h **225.00**

Gilson & Co, Reading, PA, ovoid, imp label, brushed cobalt blue at handle and label, 11" h **150.00**

Goodwin & Webster, ovoid, cobalt blue daubs at label and handle, 11¼" h, short hairlines and crazing **100.00**

Jug, 2 gallon, unknown maker, cobalt blue bird on branch dec, $275.00.

Hamilton & Jones, Greensboro, PA, cobalt blue stenciled label, 11¾" h **175.00**

Hopkins & M'Elveney, 612 Market St, brushed dec around name **210.00**

I Seymour, Troy, ovoid, incised flower, cobalt blue highlights on label and dec, 11" h **650.00**

J H Dipple, imp label, shiny dark brown Albany slip, 9½" h, minor wear and surface firing chips **25.00**

J Norton & Co, Bennington, VT, cobalt blue slip parrot on branch, 11¼" h **450.00**

L B Billiner, New Geneva, PA, cobalt blue stenciled label, 11¾" h, lip chip **145.00**

N White, Utica, NY, ovoid, imp label, simple brushed cobalt blue design, 11½" h, minor chips **200.00**

Orcutt & Croft, Portland, ovoid, imp label, 10¾" h, small chips, firing crack in side **75.00**

T F Reppert, Greensboro, PA, adv, cobalt blue stenciled label "Geo. A. Kelly & Co. Wholesale Druggists. . .Pittsburgh.," 11½" h **500.00**

Thompson & Co, Gardiner, ovoid, imp label, cobalt blue at base of handle, 11½" h **105.00**

T Shepard Jr, Geddes, NY, ovoid, imp label, cobalt blue brushed feather design, 11¼" h **110.00**

Unknown Maker

11" h, ovoid, imp label "Boston," two–tone gray salt glaze, brownish–amber pebble finish top half, three tooled lines under label, applied tooled handle, chip on lip, hairlines **225.00**

11¼" h, ovoid, cobalt blue brushed floral dec, lip chip **75.00**

2 Gallon

A Gay, Utica, ovoid, cobalt blue dec **300.00**

A K Ballard, Burlington, VT, pouring spout lip, cobalt blue vintage design, 12" h **500.00**

A P Donaghho, Parkersburg, WV, cobalt blue stenciled label, 13" h **100.00**

C Hart, Sherburne, semi–ovoid, slip flower dec **415.00**

Clark & Co, Mount Morris, ovoid, brushed cobalt blue dec **330.00**

Cowden & Wilcox, Harrisburg, PA, sloping shoulders, brushed drooping flower, cobalt blue at handle **385.00**

C Pharis & Co, Geddes, NY, semi–ovoid, dark cobalt blue floral dec **495.00**

Darwin E Reid, Fort Plain, NY, cobalt blue dec, cobalt blue wash at name **310.00**

E & A K Ballard, Burlington, VT, imp label and "2," brushed cobalt blue slip stylized floral design, 14" h **195.00**

E & L P Norton, Bennington, VT, cobalt blue slip stylized floral design, 13¼" h **150.00**

Evan R Jones, Pittston, PA, three brushed flowers, cobalt blue wash in name **385.00**

F B Norton & Co, Worcester, MA 13½" h, cobalt blue slip stylized floral dec **200.00**

13¾" h, imp label and "2," cobalt blue floral design, pebbly glaze **350.00**

Hastings & Belding, brushed cobalt blue dec **300.00**

Honesdale, PA, handled, blooming poppy leaves dec, blue and gray glaze **350.00**

I Seymour, Troy, ovoid, cobalt blue floral dec **275.00**

James Hamilton & Co, Greensboro, PA, ovoid, cobalt blue dec bands, brushed swirls, and striped inverted triangles, stenciled and freehand label **525.00**

J C Waelde, North Bay, imp label, cobalt blue dec, sponged and stenciled running rabbit and trees, quill work "2," polka dots, brushed cobalt blue at label, 13¾" h, minor edge chips, short hairlines in base **1,550.00**

J Fisher, Lyons, NY, imp maker's label, cobalt blue slip label "Aug Boetzhold, 567 to 571 Michigan St., Buffalo, N.Y.," 13¾" h, chips **155.00**

J Norton & Co, Bennington, VT, semi–ovoid, brushed cobalt blue stylized plant, imp label, 13" h **225.00**

Julius Norton, Bennington, VT, cobalt blue slip floral design, 14" h **27500**

N Clark & Co, Lyons, ovoid, imp label, brushed cobalt blue design and "2," 13¾" h **155.00**

N White & Co, Binghamton, cobalt blue poppy dec **220.00**

Ottman Bro's & Co, Fort Edward, NY, cobalt blue bird dec **400.00**

Rich, ovoid, tooled lines at shoulder, imp script label and "2," 14½" h **85.00**

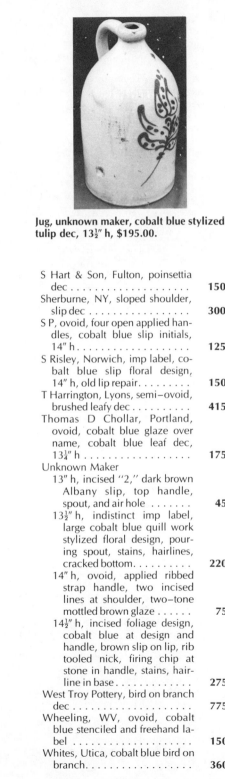

Jug, unknown maker, cobalt blue stylized tulip dec, 13½" h, $195.00.

S Hart & Son, Fulton, poinsettia dec **150.00**

Sherburne, NY, sloped shoulder, slip dec **300.00**

S P, ovoid, four open applied handles, cobalt blue slip initials, 14" h **125.00**

S Risley, Norwich, imp label, cobalt blue slip floral design, 14" h, old lip repair. **150.00**

T Harrington, Lyons, semi–ovoid, brushed leafy dec **415.00**

Thomas D Chollar, Portland, ovoid, cobalt blue glaze over name, cobalt blue leaf dec, 13¼" h **175.00**

Unknown Maker

13" h, incised "2," dark brown Albany slip, top handle, spout, and air hole **45.00**

13½" h, indistinct imp label, large cobalt blue quill work stylized floral design, pouring spout, stains, hairlines, cracked bottom. **220.00**

14" h, ovoid, applied ribbed strap handle, two incised lines at shoulder, two–tone mottled brown glaze **75.00**

14½" h, incised foliage design, cobalt blue at design and handle, brown slip on lip, rib tooled nick, firing chip at stone in handle, stains, hairline in base **275.00**

West Troy Pottery, bird on branch dec **775.00**

Wheeling, WV, ovoid, cobalt blue stenciled and freehand label **150.00**

Whites, Utica, cobalt blue bird on branch. **360.00**

W Roberts, Binghamton, NY, sloping shoulders, cobalt blue bird dec............... 525.00

3 Gallon

B L Fahnestock & Co, Pittsburgh, PA, adv, freehand and stencil dec, cobalt blue at handle 330.00

C Hart & Son, Sherburne, cobalt blue tentacle design 185.00

Clark & Co, Rochester, NY, ovoid, imp label and "3," cobalt blue highlights, 16½" h, minor chips, short hairline 100.00

E & L P Norton, Bennington, VT, cobalt blue bird dec 175.00

J Shepard Jr, Geddes, NY, cobalt blue quill and brush work, stylized floral dec, 15½" h 200.00

Norton & M'Burney, Jordan, ovoid, brushed palm–like flowers, cobalt blue at handle 330.00

Ottman Bro's & Co, Fort Edward, NY, imp label and "3," simple cobalt blue floral design, 15½" h, hairline at handle 325.00

Thomas Commeraw, Manhattan, NY, ovoid, strap handle, incised rings below lip, imp cobalt blue–filled half moons above "Commeraw.s Stoneware N. York" inscription, 15" h, 1800–25 . . . . 1,200.00

Unknown Maker, cinnamon colored, cobalt blue flower 190.00

4 Gallon

A O Whittemore, Havana, NY, semi–ovoid, cobalt blue bird dec 330.00

Cowden & Wilcox, Harrisburg, PA, cinnamon color, quadruple floral dec, cobalt blue at handle 715.00

James Collins, 133 Beach and 78, 80 & 82 South St, Boston, cobalt blue quill work, stylized four bloom flower, 18" h 450.00

J Norton, Bennington, VT, imp label and "4," cobalt blue slip stylized floral dec, pebbly glaze, 18" h 495.00

Unknown Maker

15" h, cobalt blue quill work flourish and "4" 85.00

17" h, ovoid, imp "4," brushed cobalt blue at strap handle 115.00

5 Gallon

N A White & Son, Utica, NY, dark cobalt blue dec. 350.00

R A Power, 347 Grand St, sloping shoulders, cobalt blue script writing. 138.00

Unknown Maker, double handle, imp "5," brown Albany slip, 17½" h 30.00

W Hart, Ogdensburgh, sloping shoulders, brush flower dec. . . 135.00

Kiln Separator, 5" d, gray salt glaze, edge chips 45.00

Match Holder, 2⅝" h, cone shaped, molded serrated striking surface, cobalt blue highlights on decorative band on base 20.00

Measure, 3¾" h, cobalt blue floral dec, incised numerals, 19th C 1,425.00

Meat Tenderizer, 9" l, wooden handle, marked "Pat'd Dec. 25, 1877". . . . 70.00

Milk Pan

1 gallon, AGC Dipple, Lewistown, PA 45.00

.9" d, unknown maker, rim spout, cobalt blue brushed rim design, hairlines 150.00

11" d, applied handles and rim spout, brown Albany slip interior 100.00

17" d, brown glaze on imp floral design exterior, cobalt blue dec on gray glazed interior, 19th C 550.00

Milk Pitcher, green glaze 35.00

Miniature

Double Jug, 3" h, New England, ovoid, cobalt blue lip, strap handle, and flower on each jug, joined at waist, early 19th C 3,575.00

Flask, 3½" h, New Jersey, barrel shaped, incised bands, cobalt blue dec, marked "S. King, South Amboy," dated 1823 . . . . 4,500.00

Jar

4¼" h, sgraffito bird, flowers, and border, brown Albany slip, small edge chips. 245.00

4½" h, ovoid, applied handles, incised and cobalt blue–filled tulips and leaves dec both sides, early 19th C 1,750.00

5" h, ovoid, pulled handles, cobalt blue splotch dec, incised bands at shoulder and "Joseph Morgan" around waist, c1800 1,975.00

Jug

3" h, ovoid, strap handle, incised cobalt blue inscription "Mrs.

Mug, 4⅜" h, barrel shaped, cobalt blue bands, salt glaze, $40.00.

S.G. Hazard, Taunton," early
19th C **775.00**
3⅝" h, ovoid, cobalt blue dec,
incised bird on branch,
"M.E.", and basket and star. . .   **3,300.00**
Pitcher, 3¾" h, incised and cobalt
blue floral dec and band, cobalt
blue at strap handle, tooled base,
1830–60 . . . .   **2,525.00**
Mug
Barrel shape, cobalt blue bands,
coggle wheel dec, stamped #20
on bottom **38.00**
Straight sided, swirl and banded
dec **60.00**
Pitcher
5⅞" h, adv, marked "Compliments of
Hirsch Bros., & Co. Celebrated
Pure Vinegars, Louisville, Ky.,"
small chips, hairline in base of
handle **150.00**
7¾" h, John Fowler, dark brown Al-
bany slip, incised zigzag band,
"Made by John Fowler, Dec 20th,
1867" sgraffito inscription on bot-
tom **65.00**
8" h, brown Albany slip **65.00**
8¼" h, W Roberts, Binghamton, NY,
light brown Albany slip, unusual
shape, molded screw heads on
spout, imp label, small chips. . . .   **75.00**
8½" h, light tan and ivory glaze,
hound handles **50.00**
9" h, ovoid, brushed cobalt blue flo-
ral dec **425.00**
9⅛" h, blue glazed, bird, rose, and
maple tree in relief, tree stump
handle, 1880–1900 . . . .   **120.00**
9½" h, ovoid, tooled lines, ribbed
strap handle, brown streaks, edge
chips **95.00**
11" h, dark brown Albany slip, edge
chips **25.00**
13" h, Williams & Reppert, Greens-
boro, PA, stenciled and freehand
cobalt blue label and "2," iron
band around base **1,400.00**
13½" h, W E Howe, Worcester, MA,
cobalt blue flower dec, age cracks   **100.00**
2 Quart, unknown maker, large co-
balt blue floral dec, no handle. . .   **440.00**
1 Gallon, F H Cowden, Harrisburg,
cobalt blue stencil dec **990.00**
1½ Gallon, Reiss & Parr, Richmond,
VA, leafy cobalt blue dec all
around **600.00**
2 Gallon, Sipe Nichols & Co, Wil-
liamsport, PA, semi–ovoid,
brushed cobalt blue floral dec at
center and under lip, 12¾" h **1,000.00**
Preserving Jar
1 Quart
A P Donaghho, Parkersburg, WV,

stenciled cobalt blue label,
7½" h, edge chips **85.00**
Jas Hamilton & Co, Greensboro,
PA, stenciled shield dec **285.00**
2 Quart
Hamilton & Jones, Greensboro,
PA, stenciled **120.00**
Unknown Maker
8⅜" h, three brushed cobalt blue
bands **105.00**
8⅝" h, cinnamon colored, co-
balt blue floral dec **285.00**
1 Gallon
A M Curdy, General Store, Laincs,
OH, wax seal, stencil dec **165.00**
A P Donaghho, Parkersburg, WV,
cobalt blue stenciled label,
8" h, small flakes **95.00**
Hamilton & Jones, Greensboro,
PA, stenciled dec **195.00**
J C Pickett & Bro, cobalt blue sten-
ciled label "Dealers in Groceries & C. . .Wheeling, Va,"
10¼" h **400.00**
L B Dilliner, New Geneva, PA,
wax seal, stencil and freehand
dec **210.00**
Lyons, brushed cobalt blue
flower, 10" h, hairlines and
chips **105.00**
Unknown Maker
8¼" h, cobalt blue straight and
wavy bands, small lip chip   **325.00**
8⅜" h, wax seal, freehand dec,
western PA **160.00**
1½ Gallon
A Conrad, New Geneva, PA, cobalt blue stenciled label, 9½" h,
rim wear **250.00**
A P Donaghho, cobalt blue
stenciled label, 9½" h, small
chips **130.00**
2 Gallon
S Bell & Son, simple cobalt blue
dec around shoulder **300.00**
Unknown Maker
11" h, imp "2," brushed cobalt
blue flower **110.00**
12" h, blurred stenciled cobalt
blue label, two shields, and
"2" **125.00**
Salt, 2⅝" h, cobalt blue dec, two rim
chips **500.00**
Snuff Jar
1 Quart, brushed Albany slip dec all
around **165.00**
1 Gallon, "Fine Maccoboy" sten-
ciled on front **105.00**
Spittoon
Cowden & Wilcox, brushed cobalt
blue dec all around **260.00**
M Woodruff, Cortland, cobalt blue
dec and "2" **425.00**

Unknown Maker
9" d, brushed cobalt blue dec all
around, PA **195.00**
9½" d, cobalt blue long–stemmed
flower dec **95.00**
Squirrel, figural, molded, cobalt blue
dec, standing on cobalt blue tree
stump, 4½" h, 19th C **2,750.00**
Syrup Jug, C H Freeman, Corning, NY,
brown Albany slip glaze, incised let-
tering **65.00**
Water Filter, 4 gallon, imp label "West

Troy, N.Y. Pottery, 4," 16¾" h, bung
hole in base, punched drainage
holes in bottom **35.00**
Wine Cooler, barrel form, salt glazed,
incised and cobalt blue dec, bands,
"WINE" flanked by two hearts, central flower and holly leaf motif,
13" h, early 19th C **2,225.00**
Wine Jug, wooden cradle, 1 gallon,
marked "A A Co, Pat Apld For,"
incised cobalt blue band dec **150.00**

TEXTILES

Thrift was a way of life in agrarian America. Few had money to waste. Textiles were purchased that would wear well. When something did "wear out," it was recycled. Patch-work quilts and hooked rugs are the final resting place for many a shirt and dress. Feed bags wound up as dresses and shirts when times were lean.

Textiles are cloth or fabric items, especially anything woven or knitted. Those that survive usually represent the best since these were the objects that were used carefully and stored by the housewife.

Textiles helped brighten life in rural America. Red and blue are dominant colors with block, circle, and star pattern motifs the most common. Colorful window curtains were changed seasonally. The same held true for bedspreads. A party dress or shirt was a welcome respite from the pastel colors of daily work clothes.

Textiles are collected for many reasons—to study fabrics, understand the elegance of a historical period, and for decorative and modern use. The renewed interest in clothing has sparked a revived interest in textiles of all forms.

References: Suzy Anderson, *Collector's Guide to Quilts,* Wallace–Homestead Book Co, 1991; Alda Homer, *The Official Guide to Linens, Lace, and Other Fabrics,* House of Collectibles, 1991; Florence Montgomery, *Textiles in America: 1650–1870,* W. W. Norton & Co, 1984; Betty Ring, ed, *Needlework: An Historical Survey,* revised edition, The Main Street Press, 1984; Carlton Safford and Robert Bishop, *America's Quilts and Coverlets,* reprint, Bonanza Books, 1985.

Collectors' Club: Costume Society of America, PO Box 761, Elizabethtown, NJ 07726.

Museums: The Textile Museum, Washington, DC; Museum of American Textile History, North Andover, MA.

CLOTHING AND ACCESSORIES

History: Farm clothing can be divided into two groups—workday and Sunday. Within each group, clothing is further divided into manufac-tured and homemade. The agrarian housewife was usually an expert seamstress.

Most collectors of vintage clothing and acces-sories have focused on high style items. Only in the last few years have some collectors begun to focus on clothing used in rural America. While Country decorators have used clothing as decora-tive highlights within room settings for years, em-phasis has fallen largely on accessories such as aprons and infant wear.

"Vintage clothing" is a broad term used to describe clothing manufactured from the late Vic-torian era (1880s) to the end of the psychedelic era (1970s). While purists would prefer a cutoff date of 1940, clothing from World War II, the fifties, and sixties is also highly collectible. In reality, vintage clothing is defined by what is available and current collecting trends.

A few clues to dating clothing are: (1) do not depend on style alone; (2) check labels; (3) learn which fabrics and print patterns were popular in each historical period; and, (4) examine decorative elements.

Clothing is collected and studied as a reference source in learning about fashion, construction and types of materials used. Collecting vintage clothing appears to have reached a plateau. Although there are still dedicated collectors, the category is no longer attracting a rash of new collectors annually.

The hot part of the clothing market in the 1990s is accessories. Clothing collectors acquire everything from hats and shoes to handbags and jewelry to accessorize their garments. However, because many clothing accessories are collectibles in their own right (compacts, hatpins, purses, etc.), collectors of clothing often find themselves competing with these specialized collectors.

Country auctions are usually rich in clothing accessories. Hand–me–down was a way of life. However, many items in the hand–me–down pile never made it to their next owner, winding up in long–time storage instead.

References: Maryanne Dolan, *Vintage Clothing, 1880–1960, Second Edition,* Books Americana, 1988; Ellen Gehret, *Rural Pennsylvania Clothing,* Liberty Cap Books, 1976; Tina Irick–Nauer, *The First Price Guide to Antique and Vintage Clothes,* E. P. Dutton, 1983; Sheila Malouff, *Collectible Clothing With Prices,* Wallace–Homestead, 1983; Terry McCormick, *The Consumer's Guide To Vintage Clothing,* Dembner Books, 1987; Diane McGee, *A Passion For Fashion,* Simmons–Boardman Books, Inc, 1987.

Periodical: *Vintage Clothing Newsletter,* PO Box 1422, Corvallis, OR 97339.

Collectors' Club: The Costume Society of America, PO Box 761, Englishtown, NJ 07726.

Museums: Metropolitan Museum of Art, New York, NY; the Costume and Textile Department of the Los Angeles County Museum of Art, Los Angeles, CA; Philadelphia Museum of Art, Philadelphia, PA.

Reproduction Craftsperson: *Children's—* Barbara Lawn, Tomorrow's Heirlooms, Main Line–Berwyn, C–303, Berwyn, PA 19312.

Reproduction Manufacturers: *Aprons—* Olde Virginea Floorcloth and Trading Co, PO Box 3305, Portsmouth, VA 23707; *General—* Amazon Vinegar & Pickling Works Drygoods, 2218 East 11th St, Davenport, IA 52803; The Calico Corner, 513 E Bowman St, South Bend, IN 46613; Campbell's, RD 1, Box 1444, Herndon, PA 17830; Country Heart Homespun Collection, Inc, 1212 Westover Hills Blvd, Box 13358, Richmond, VA 23225; The Cover Up Handweaving Studio, Rte 1, Box 216, Rabun Gap, GA 30568; Cumberland General Store, Rte 3, Crossville, TN

38555; Lamb and Lanterns, 902 N Walnut St, Dover, OH 44622; Log Cabin Shop, Box 275, Lodi, OH 44254; Pesta's Country Charm, 300 Standard Ave, Mingo Junction, OH 43938; *Patterns—* Amazon Vinegar & Pickling Works Drygoods, 2218 East 11th St, Davenport, IA 52803; Campbell's, RD 1, Box 1444, Herndon, PA 17830; Crazy Crow Trading Post, PO Box 314B, Denison, TX 75020; Old World Sewing Pattern Co, Rte 2, Box 103, Cold Spring, MN 56320; Past Patterns, 2017 Eastern, Grand Rapids, MI 49507; *Restoration—* Mountain Shadow Studio, PO Box 619, Nederland, CO 80466.

Apron
Calico, red and white	**25.00**
Cotton, hand sewn, patchwork design, waist length, ties	**25.00**
Baby Bonnet, cotton, tatted, ribbon rosettes	**15.00**
Baby Booties, wool, cream colored, red braid trim, c1850	**85.00**
Baby Coat, cotton, gathered yoke and capelet, embroidery, flannel lining	**25.00**
Baby Dress, cotton, tucked, eyelet trimmed yoke, sleeves, skirt, 3½" open work, scalloped hem, 38" l . . .	**20.00**
Baby Shoes, leather, high top, 1930s	**20.00**
Bloomers, wool, cream colored	**25.00**
Blouse, cotton, white, crocheted accents on large collar, fitted at waist	**35.00**
Christening Gown, cutwork embroidery bodice, tuck pleats around ruffled skirt	**65.00**

Dress
Calico, blue, 2 pc, matching bonnet, c1900	**165.00**
Gingham, child's, blue and white, hand and machine sewn, white embroidery trim, 25" h	**50.00**
Homespun Linen, child's, blue, yellow, and white plaid, drawstring neck, high waist, long set–in	

Child's Dress, matching cape, cotton, white, $85.00.

Sun Bonnet, calico, Pennsylvania Dutch, $25.00.

sleeves, c1830, minor discoloration.	300.00
Muslin, embroidered stripes, long sleeves, tucking edges, c1820.	135.00
Wool, Amish, dark green, c1830	45.00
Gloves, man's, clipped buffalo and leather, medium	50.00
Lap Robe, wool, embroidered, leather binding	50.00
Nightgown, cotton, white, leg of mutton sleeves, high collar, handmade eyelet lace trim	285.00
Nightshirt, man's, cotton, white, long	25.00
Petticoat	
Cotton, white, crocheted insert, wide crocheted hem.	45.00
Muslin, white, deep laced edge flounce, 24" waist	18.00
Shawl	
Lace, black, flowers, scalloped hem, 112" w, 54" l.	36.00
Wool, green, beige, and olive green plaid, fringed.	25.00
Shirt, man's, homespun linen, natural color, button closure.	50.00
Shoes, lady's, brown leather, high button top	40.00
Skirt	
Felt, gray, velvet embroidered border, c1880	40.00
Muslin, white, full length, deep tucks, ruffled flounce, hand embroidered.	40.00
Skirt and Top, homespun, black lace bodice and cuffs, high neck	125.00
Slip, cotton	
Full, white, rows of tucks and lace inserts, crocheted top and flowers	25.00
Half, string waist, lace bottom	35.00
Suit, boy's, wool, Amish, herringbone, lined, c1920.	40.00

COVERLETS

History: A loom in every country home is a myth. Most coverlets were woven by a semi-professional (e.g., a farmer who supplemented his income by weaving in the winter months) or a professional weaver.

A coverlet is made by weaving yarns together on a loom. A quilt, made by sewing together layers of fabric, is an entirely different textile.

The earliest coverlets are overshot. The double weave dates from 1725 to 1825. Single weave, double face coverlets (winter/summer) were popular in the first quarter of the 19th century.

The Jacquard loom arrived upon the scene in the early 1820s. It allowed the manufacture of wide, single piece coverlets. However, the pieced coverlet tradition continued well into mid–century.

Natural dyes in soft hues were made from animal, mineral, and plant matter and used prior to 1820. Mineral dyes made between 1820 and 1860 are harsher in color. Synthetic dyes, which retain a bright, permanent color, were in use by the early 1860s.

By the 1860s, commercially made blankets replaced coverlets and quilts as the principal bedcovering. While quilt making survived, coverlet production ceased.

References: Harold and Dorothy Burnham, *"Keep Me Warm One Night": Early Handweaving in Eastern Canada*, Toronto Press, 1972; John W. Heisey, *A Checklist of American Coverlet Weavers*, The Colonial Williamsburg Foundation, 1978; Carleton Safford and Robert Bishop, *America's Quilts and Coverlets*, Bonanza Books, 1985.

Reproduction Craftspersons: *General*—Ieva Ersts, Rosemary Hill Farm, PO Box 196, Church Hill, MD 21623; Kathy & Bob Harman, Old Abingdon Weavers, PO Box 786, Abingdon, VA 24210; Maggie Kennedy, Ozark Weaving Studio, PO Box 286, Cane Hill, AR 72717; William A Leinbach, The Itinerant Weaver, 356 Royers Rd, Myerstown, PA 17067; Dotty Lewis, 9 Indian Hill Rd, Conestoga, PA 17516; Donna Nedeeisky, Handweaver, The Coverlet Co, PO Box 02–616, Portland, OR 97202; Jacki Schell, Jacki's Handwoven Originals, RD 4, Box 352, Lewistown, PA 17044; Mary Worley, Traditional Textiles, RD 2, Box 3120, Middlebury, VT 05735; *Jacquard*—Gabrielle & Robert Black, Jr, Black's Handweaving Shop, 497 Main St, W Barnstable, MA 02668; David & Carole Kline, Family Heir–Loom Weavers, RD 3, Box 59E, Red Lion, PA 17356; *Overshot*—Susan Eikenberry, 611 N Van Buren St, Batavia, IL 60510; Julia A Lindsey, Lindsey Woolseys of Ohio, 275 N Main St, Germantown, OH 45327.

Reproduction Manufacturers: *General*—Goodwin Guild Weavers, Blowing Rock Crafts, Inc, Box H–314, Blowing Rock, NC 28604; Homespun Crafts, Box 77, Grover, NC 28073; Winters Textile Mill, 9110 Winters Rd, PO Box

614, Winters, CA 95694; *Restoration—* Mountain Shadow Studio, PO Box 619, Nederland, CO 80466.

Double Weave, two–piece

60 x 74", snowflake and pine tree pattern, navy blue and natural white, cotton side puckered, wear, minor stains, top edge damage **275.00**

70 x 84", navy blue, tomato red, and natural white, stains, some wear, holes **450.00**

74 x 90", optical pattern, soft red, navy blue, and natural white, minor stains, some wear, moth damage, small holes **175.00**

74 x 94", snowflake and pine tree pattern, blue and black, minor wear, small holes **350.00**

Embroidered, wool, ivory, gray–blue "chenille" embroidery, one piece weaving, 66 x 90" **475.00**

Jacquard

24 x 36", miniature, one pc, double weave, flower and star central design, vintage borders, sgd "Piqua," blue and white, worn, hand repairs **300.00**

64 x 88", two pc, single weave, rose in urn and hearts floral design, bottom edge labeled "Fancy Weaving by G. Heilbronn, Lancaster, O," blue and white, worn, holes **150.00**

64 x 94", two pc, double weave, turkeys, peacocks, and houses,

Jacquard, floral medallions, bird and tree border, corners labeled "Made by J Lutz, E Hempfield Township, for Rebacca Hershey, 1839," 99 x 77" with 4½" fringe, $650.00

corners labeled "Cadiz, Ohio," red, blue, and natural white **300.00**

67 x 88", two pc, single weave, floral design, vintage border, corners labeled "E.A.P. 1860," navy blue, salmon red, and white **125.00**

68 x 74", two pc, double weave, snowflake and pine tree pattern, navy blue and natural white, cotton side puckered, wear, minor stains, top edge damage **275.00**

68 x 87", two pc, single weave, bold floral pattern, navy blue and natural white **165.00**

68 x 90", two pc, single weave, floral design on stripe ground, bird border, corners labeled "Mary R. Stoker Fancy Coverlet, Wove by G. Heibronn Basil, Ohio 1844," red, blue–green, and natural white **750.00**

69 x 88", two pc, double weave, floral design, tulip borders, corners labeled "Elisabeth Ann Nigher 1853," navy blue and natural white, incomplete fringe . . . **950.00**

70 x 76", two pc, single weave, floral medallions, bird borders, corners labeled "Gabriel Rausher, Delaware County, Ohio 1845," red, blue, and natural white, worn, minor stains, no fringe . . . **200.00**

70 x 84", two pc, double weave, floral medallions, eagle, tree, and "Liberty" borders, corners labeled "Maria Rose, Milford, Pa. 1840, J. Stiff Weaver," navy blue and natural white, stains **550.00**

70 x 90", two pc, single weave, large floral medallions, corners labeled "Sarah A. Smith 1870," red, blue, and natural white **400.00**

71 x 86", two pc, double weave, four rose medallions, star and double bird border, dark navy blue and white **350.00**

72 x 88", two pc, single weave, floral wreaths, floral vining border, navy blue and natural white, two separate halves never sewn together, fringe wear, moth damage, small stains **300.00**

72 x 94", two pc, single weave, floral wreaths, pots of flowers in borders, peacocks in corners, red, green, navy blue, and natural white, minor wear, minor fringe wear **275.00**

73 x 78", two pc, single weave, floral medallions, bird borders, corners sgd "Woven by A. Wolf, Ohio, AD. 1850 for Gerttrud

Rogers," red, navy blue, and natural white, wear, stains, some edge damage **150.00**

73 x 84", two pc, double weave, bold floral medallions, meandering floral border, medium blue and natural white **150.00**

73 x 85", two pc, double weave, floral design, chickens and eagles on borders, dark navy blue and natural white, sgd "J. R. Van Houten 1834" **2,300.00**

73 x 93", one pc, double weave, floral medallions in square grid, bird in tree and house border, corners labeled "Sold by S. Kater and manufactor'd for. . .1839," red, deep yellow, and natural white, minor small dark stains **600.00**

74 x 84", two pc, single weave, vase of flowers, medallions, and rose, Christian and heathen borders, eagle corners, red, blue, green, and natural white, minor wear . .   **550.00**

74 x 86", two pc, single weave, floral design, bird borders, corners labeled "Made by W. Fasig, U.S. 1855," red, pale yellow, blue, and natural white, worn, faded   **175.00**

74 x 88", two pc, single weave, floral design, vintage border, corners labeled "Benjamin–Lichty, Bristol, Ohio 1840," red, navy blue, teal green, and natural white   **325.00**

74 x 90", two pc, double weave, peacocks feeding young, Christian and heathen borders, navy blue and natural white **250.00**

74 x 94", two pc, double weave, snowflake and pine tree pattern, blue and black, minor wear, small holes **350.00**

75 x 80", two pc, double weave, floral design, Hempfield Railroad border, blue, faded red, and white   **1,250.00**

75 x 86", two pc, single weave, large foliage medallions, vintage border, red, blue, and natural white **125.00**

76 x 78", two pc, single weave, floral medallions and stars, vintage and eagle border, corners labeled "John Long, Holmes County, Ohio 1853," teal and navy blue, soft salmon red, and natural white, minor wear **550.00**

76 x 90", two pc
Double Weave, roses and stars, pots of roses border, corner eagles and "Sena Edwards, Darien, Genesee Co. N.Y.," navy blue and natural white, no

fringe, some wear, edge damage, small repairs **450.00**

Single Weave, floral design, potted flower border, corner dated "1862," maroon, green, and natural white **450.00**

77 x 89", two pc, double weave, Penelope flower basket design with compotes of fruit and peacock feeding young, Christian and heathen border, navy blue and white, wear, small holes, frayed areas along edge **750.00**

77 x 90", two pc, single weave, floral design, star flower and bird border, corners labeled "Peter Lorentz 1839," magenta, olive, two shades of brown, gray–green, deep green–black, and natural white **300.00**

78 x 82", two pc, single weave, floral design, vintage borders, corner sgd "W. in Mt. Vernon, Knox County, Ohio by Jacob and Michael Ardner 1852," navy blue, green, red, and natural white . . .   **500.00**

78 x 85", two pc, double weave, floral design, Capitol buildings, and "Capitol in Washington, 1846," floral borders, red, blue, and natural white, wear, damage, small holes, incomplete fringe . .   **550.00**

78 x 90", two pc, single weave, four rose medallions, meandering and star border, corners labeled "Sarah Cooper 1851," red, two shades of blue, green, and natural white, wear, moth damage, small holes, and fringe wear **350.00**

78 x 92", one pc, double weave, geometric floral medallions, vining rose border, corners labeled "Manufactured by Fehr & Keck, Emaus, 1845," red, green, and natural white, minor stains, PA   **340.00**

79 x 92", one pc, double weave
Flags and "Liberty" coins in center medallion, vining flowers, floral and urn borders, eagle and "1849" each corner, one edge labeled "Barbara Harris woven at Palmyra, N.Y. by J. Van Ness," tomato red and natural white **1,500.00**

Star center, eagles in corners, red, green, blue, and natural white, minor stains **450.00**

80 x 82", two pc, single weave, floral design, eagle borders, blue and white, worn, no fringe **115.00**

80 x 84", two pc, double weave, urns of fruit and flowers and pea-

cocks feeding young, red, blue, green, and natural white, minor stains **550.00**

80 x 86", two pc, single weave, floral design on stripes, corners labeled "Peter Lorenz 1845," black, red, green, and natural white **950.00**

80 x 88", two pc, single weave, floral design, bird border, corners labeled "Manufactured by C.K. Hinkel, Shippensburg, Pa. 1856, S. Dael Housen," red, blue, light green, and natural white, wear, fringe loss, edge damage **375.00**

80 x 91", two pc, single weave, pots of flowers, floral borders, corners labeled "Agnes Clunk," deep pink, navy blue, and natural white, attributed to Mathias Mann, Hanover, PA, wear, moth damage. **250.00**

80 x 94", two pc, double weave, floral medallions, eagle borders, corners labeled "Fanny Tous Teffot 1833," navy blue and white, stains, no fringe **475.00**

80 x 96", two pc, single weave, bold floral design, peacocks in corners, red, blue, olive green, and natural white, stains, fringe wear **225.00**

82 x 84", one pc, double weave, floral design, bird border, corners labeled "Made by Samuel Dornback, Sugarloaf, Luzerne Co. Penn. 1846 for. . .," red, green, blue, and natural white, wear, fringe incomplete, top edge frayed **250.00**

82 x 98", two pc, single weave, rose design, triple bird border, labeled "E. Fordenback 1843," two shades of blue, red, and olive, top edge has wear **1,000.00**

82 x 99", two pc, single weave, floral and border designs, red, two shades of blue, and natural white, edge labeled "E. Longanecker 1845," minor stains **625.00**

84 x 88", two pc, double weave, birds and floral design, double floral border, red, teal blue, and natural white **300.00**

86 x 92, two pc, double weave, floral medallions, double vine border, four part label on corners "Manufactured by D. Pursell, Portsmouth, Ohio, Liberty," navy blue, tomato red, and natural white, minor stains and edge wear **1,800.00**

89 x 95½", two pc, double weave, snowball pattern, pine tree border, blue wool and cream cotton yarns, cut corners, fringed on three sides, c1830 . . . . **375.00**

92 x 104", one pc, double weave, center medallion and floral design, vintage border, long tailed birds and "1851" in corners, tomato red wool and natural linen **350.00**

Overshot, two piece

64 x 78", blue wool and cream cotton yarns, woven inscription "AP 1795" **325.00**

66 x 94", blue, red, and natural white, worn. **125.00**

70 x 84", navy blue, tomato red, and natural white, stains, some wear, holes **450.00**

72 x 88", diamonds and half diamonds, blue, red, and natural white, minor wear **235.00**

73 x 94", rust and navy cotton and wool yarns, 19th C. **250.00**

74 x 90", optical pattern, soft red, navy blue, and natural white, minor stains, some wear, moth damage, small holes **175.00**

76 x 84", optical diamond and star pattern, blue, red, olive green, and natural white **225.00**

76 x 86", navy blue and natural, some wear. **135.00**

78 x 92", white on white, minor stains, faded label one corner . . . **125.00**

80 x 96", optical pattern, woven and tied fringe, round corners one end, blue and white, minor wear and stains **225.00**

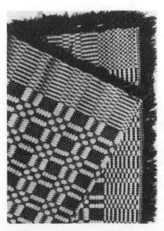

Overshot, two pc, red, white, and blue geometric design, 72 x 94" with 3¾" applied fringe, $240.00.

Woven, two piece
  69 x 93", plaid pattern, blue and
    white **50.00**
  74 x 82", cotton, plaid pattern, pale
    blue and white, loosely woven . .   **115.00**
  74 x 84", cotton and wool, plaid pat-
    tern, blue and white, stains **215.00**
  82 x 92", wool, plaid pattern,
    salmon red and blue **175.00**

FEED AND GRAIN BAGS

History: The first cotton grain bags appeared in the early 1800s and were used as an alternative to the barrel. They were handmade and not widely used.

The invention of the sewing machine and machines expressly designed to manufacture flour sacks opened the door to the daily use of textile bags in areas such as the packaging of feed, grain, sugar, and fertilizer. Feed bags reached the peak of their popularity from the 1930s through the 1950s.

The original sizes of bags corresponded to barrel measurements. One barrel of flour weighed 96 lbs, a half barrel weighed 48 lbs, and so forth down to $\frac{1}{8}$ barrel at 12 lbs. In 1943 the War Production Board standardized weights at 100, 50, 25, 10, 5, and 2 lb sizes.

The first manufactured bags were solid colors, usually white. Labels were either printed directly on the bag or paper labels were sewn or pasted to the front. Bags printed with floral or striped designs or doll and clothing patterns were introduced during the late 1920s and early 1930s. The rural housewife made clothing, dish towels, quilts, and toys from them.

Reference: Anna Lue Cook, *Textile Bags*, Books Americana Inc, 1990.

Reproduction Manufacturers: Country Heart Homespun Collection, Inc, 1212 Westover Hills Blvd, Box 13358, Richmond, VA 23225; Lamb and Lanterns, 902 N Walnut St, Dover, OH 44622.

Airlight All Purpose Flour, H C Cole
  Milling Co, Chester, IL, 10 lbs, 18 x
  10½", Werthan Bag Co, Nashville,
  TN, striped floral print **14.00**
Always A–Head Scratch Feed, Black &
  White Milling Co, East St Louis, IL,
  Bemis Bros Bag Co, 100 lbs, 38 x
  19½", large chicken head in circle,
  rows of smaller chicken heads illus,
  red and blue on white **24.00**

Ascension Self Rising Flour, Pinckney-
  ville Milling Co, Pinckneyville, IL,
  12 lbs, 17½ x 11", Bemis Brother Bag
  Co, woman holding staff, mountains
  in background, white **28.00**
Aunt Jemima, Quaker Oats Co, 100
  lbs, 37 x 23", Aunt Jemima illus,
  white **60.00**
Bannock Chief Flour, Peavey Flour Co,
  MO, 25 lbs, 26½ x 12½", Hutchinson
  Bag Corp, narrow stripes on white   **18.00**
Bell's Brand Seeds, American Seed Co,
  Fort Worth, TX, 24 x 14", Fulton
  Bags, Dallas, TX, bell in wreath
  illus, white **18.00**
Birchmont Flour, St Cloud Milling Co,
  St Cloud, MN, 98 lbs, 36 x 20",
  Fulton Bag Co, building illus front,
  eagle over "Fulton seamless A junior
  size" in circle on back, white **75.00**
Blackhawk Wheat Bran, International
  Milling Co, Minneapolis, MN, 100
  lbs, 38 x 23", blackhawk illus, white   **42.00**
Blair's Certified Flour, Blair Milling Co,
  Atchison KS, 98 lbs, 34 x 16", script
  "Certified" on sunburst front, pig
  doll pattern back, white **30.00**
Buffalo Alfalfa Seed, 60 lbs, 28 x 14½",
  buffalo illus, white. **20.00**
Bull Brand Dairy Rations, Maritime
  Milling Co, Inc, Buffalo, NY, 100
  lbs, 38 x 25", center bull illus, "BB"
  printed overall in rows **40.00**
Chippewa Medium Salt, Ohio Salt Co,
  Wadsworth, OH, 50 lbs, 28 x 14½",
  Indian head illus, white **40.00**
Clover Hill Hybrid Seed Corn, Clover
  Hill Hybrid Seed Corn Co, Audu-
  bon, IA, 56 lbs, 32 x 17", Hutchin-
  son Bag Corp, Hutchinson, KS, four
  ears of corn illus, white **12.00**
Colonial Pure Cane Sugar, Colonial
  Sugars Co, New Orleans, LA, 100

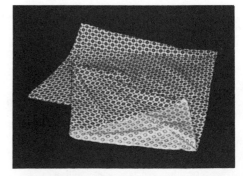

Feed Bag, 100 lbs, 35¼ x 17½", red, brown, and black print on white, no label, $15.00.

lbs, 34 x 18", two narrow bands vertical red and blue stripes on white   30.00

Dekalb Seed Corn, Dekalb Agricultural Assoc, Inc, Dekalb, IL, 56 lbs, 30 x 18", Bemis Bros Bag Co, winged ear of corn over banner "More Farmers Plant Dekalb Than Any Other Brand" illus, white 25.00

Deltapine 15 Cotton Seed, Delta & Pine Land Co, Scot, MS, 100 lbs, 38 x 23", Fulton Bags, New Orleans, LA, pine tree illus, white 22.00

Double Diamond Feed, Daily Mills, Inc, Olean, NY, 100 lbs, 38 x 23", large floral print. 48.00

Eclipse Hog Supplement, Eclipse Feed Mills, Inc, Highland, IL, 100 lbs, 39 x 20", Werthan Bag Corp, Nashville, TN, solar eclipse illus, white 15.00

Happy Dog Food, Happy Mills, Memphis, TN, 25 lbs, 25 x 13", Bemis Bros Bag Co, dog head illus, white   15.00

Heard's Best Flour, Raymond Heard Inc, Ruston, LA, 24 lbs, 24 x 12$\frac{1}{2}$", Percy Kent Bag Co, shield illus front, printed quilt block patterns back, white 42.00

Jockey Oats, M J Pritchard, Inc, Minneapolis, MN, 96 lbs, 38 x 21", horse and jockey illus, white 28.00

Merit Poultry Feed, Clark–Burkle and Co, Memphis, TN, 100 lbs, 33 x 17$\frac{1}{2}$", rooster, hen, and chick illus, white 40.00

Plowman Seed, W L Crawford Seed Co, Mayfield, KY, 1 bushel, 29 x 16", Werthan Bag Co, Nashville, TN, farmer plowing field illus, white   32.00

Purina Flock Chow, Purina Co, 100 lbs, 38 x 22", checkerboard print . .   15.00

Quaker Oats Poultry Feed, Quaker Oats Co, Chicago, IL, 100 lbs, 38 x 18", chicken and clock illus, white   35.00

Quaker Pure Cane Sugar, Pennsylvania Sugar Co, Philadelphia, PA, 10 lbs, 16 x 9", woman wearing bonnet illus, white, copyright 1930 . . . . . .   20.00

Red Head White Corn Meal, Shreveport Grain and Elevator Co, Shreveport, LA, 25 lbs, 26 x 13", Central Bag Co, Kansas City, MO, woodpecker and ear of corn illus, white   30.00

Revere Granulated Cane Sugar, Revere Sugar Refinery, Boston, MA, 10 lbs, 16 x 9", Paul Revere illus, white . . .   25.00

Sea Island Sugar, Western Sugar Refinery, San Francisco, CA, 10 lbs, 16 x 10$\frac{1}{2}$", doll pattern back, white, copyright 1936. . . . .   42.00

Self Action Self–Rising Flour, Cadick Milling Co, Grand View, IN, 2 lbs, 9 x 6", pistol illus, white 15.00

LINENS AND DOILIES

History: Homespun is a loosely hand–woven fabric, usually of handspun linen or wool yarns. Flax was an important secondary crop on many agrarian farmsteads of the eighteenth and first half of the nineteenth centuries. During this period, the rural housewife often spun her own linen thread. However, once spun, the housewife took the thread to a semi–professional or professional weaver to have it woven into cloth.

The mass–production of inexpensive cloth by the 1840s and 1850s meant that the rural housewife could store the spinning wheel up in the attic for good. Time devoted to spinning was rechanneled into sewing and handcrafting decorative textile pieces.

In Pennsylvania a unique textile form known as the show towel developed. These long, narrow towels of white homespun linen were gaudily decorated with colorful embroidery and drawn–thread panels. They were generally worked by adolescent girls for pastime and pleasure. They hung on the door between the sitting room and kitchen in the Pennsylvania German household. The golden age of the show towel was between 1820 and 1850.

The literature explosion, especially in the first quarter of the 20th century, included a number of magazines devoted to sewing and needlework. The rural housewife was an eager subscriber. Among the most popular handcrafted needlework was crocheting.

Most fine crochet was done during the period between 1850 and 1950, almost exclusively by women. Crochet is done by hand using a crochet hook and varying sizes of cotton thread. Occasionally linen or wool threads are used. The thread came in a variety of colors. The most widely used were white, cream, and ecru. Among the most popular patterns are filet work, pineapple, and Irish.

The country wife believed in the adage of "waste not, want not." Textiles used for one purpose were recycled for something else. The rural housewife was decades ahead of her time.

References: Ellen J. Gehret, *This Is the Way I Pass My Time: A Book about Pennsylvania German Decorated Hand Towels*, The Pennsylvania German Society, 1985.; Frances Johnson, *Collecting Antique Linens, Lace, & Needlework: Identification, Restoration, and Prices*, Wallace–Homestead, 1991.

Reproduction Craftspersons: Gabrielle & Robert Black, Jr, Black's Handweaving Shop, 497 Main St, W Barnstable, MA 02668; Nancy Borden, PO Box 4381, Portsmouth, NH 03801; Betsy Bourdon, Weaver, Scribner Hill, Wolcott, VT 05680; Elsie Carter, Carter Canopies, PO Box 808, Troutman, NC 28166; Andrea Cesari, Handweaver, PO Box 123, Nobleboro, ME 04555; Connie Sue Davenport, 1293 Goshentown Rd, Hendersonville, TN 37075; Helen Deuel, 2020 Kensington, Ocean Springs, MS 39564; Janice L Ebert, Traditional Handweaver, 4375 S Kessler–Frederick Rd, West Milton, OH 45383; Ieva Ersts, Rosemary Hill Farm, PO Box 196, Church Hill, MD 21623; Lynn Garringer, Rte 2, Box 253, Lewisburg, WV 24901; Kathy & Bob Harman, Old Abingdon Weavers, PO Box 786, Abingdon, VA 24210; Jeanne M Henderson, Woven Concepts, 10 Chestnut Rd, Newburg, PA 17240; Maggie Kennedy, Ozark Weaving Studio, PO Box 286, Cane Hill, AR 72717; David & Carole Kline, Family Heir–Loom Weavers, RD 3, Box 59E, Red Lion, PA 17356; Thomas E Knisely, Handweaver, 1785 York Rd, Dover, PA 17315; Sandra H Lambiotte, Crabapple Woolens & Textiles, 3864 Dawley Rd, Virginia Beach, VA 23456; Ellen Leone, Plain and Fancy, RD 2, Box 450, Bristol, VT 05443; Julia A Lindsey, Lindsey Woolseys of Ohio, 275 N Main St, Germantown, OH 45327; Judy Robinson's Country Textiles, 3350 Chickencoop Hill Rd, Lancaster, OH 43130; Jacki Schell, Jacki's Handwoven Originals, RD 4, Box 352, Lewistown, PA 17044.

Reproduction Manufacturers: American Country House, PO Box 317, Davison, MI 48423; Basye–Bomberger/Fabian House, PO Box 86, W Bowie, MD 20715; Bullfrog Hollow, Keeny Rd, Lyme, CT 06371; Carole Foy's Ruffled Curtains and Accessories, 331 E Durham Rd, Cary, NC 27511; Carter Canopies, PO Box 808, Troutman, NC 28166; Checkerberry Hill, 253 Westridge Ave, Daly City, CA 94015; Country Curtains, Stockbridge, MA 01262; Country Heart Homespun Collection, Inc, 1212 Westover Hills Blvd, Box 13358, Richmond, VA 23225; The Cover Up Handweaving Studio, Rte 1, Box 216, Rabun Gap, GA 30568; Custom Crochet House Granny Square Inc, 336 Woodcrest, Sulphur Springs, TX 75482; Das Federbett, 961 Gapter Rd, Boulder, CO; Donna's Custom Hand–Made Canopies, Rte 1, Box 456, Banner Elk, NC 28604; Especially Lace, 120½ Fifth St, West Des Moines, IA 50265; The Examplarery, PO Box 2554, Dearborn, MI 48123; Five Trails Antiques and Country Accents, 116 E Water St, Circleville, OH 43113; The Flower Patch & Herbal Co, Inc, RD 2, Box 21, Mifflintown, PA 17059; Goodwin Guild Weavers, Blowing Rock Crafts, Inc, Box H–314, Blowing Rock, NC 28604; Gooseberry Patch, PO Box 634, Delaware, OH 43015; Great Coverups, 484 New Park Ave, W Hartford, CT 06110; Homespun Crafts, Box 77, Grover, NC 28073; House of Vermillion/Heirloom Quality, PO Box 18642, Kearns, UT 84118; Ingrid's Handcraft Crossroads, 8 Randall Rd, Rochester, MA 02770; Lace Wood 'N Tin Tyme, 6496 Summerton, Shepherd, MI 48883; Legendary Folk Art, 342 East St, Pittsford, NY 14534; Olde Mill House

Shoppe, 105 Strasburg Pike, Lancaster, PA 17602; Pesta's Country Charm, 300 Standard Ave, Mingo Junction, OH 43938; South Bound Millworks, PO Box 349, Sandwich, MA 02563; Southern Manner, Inc, 106 North Trade St, PO Box 1706, Matthews, NC 28106; Sturbridge Lace Co, 559 Main St, Sturbridge, MA 01518; Traditions, RD 4, Box 191, Hudson, NY 12534; The Vine and Cupboard, PO Box 309, George Wright Rd, Woolwich, ME 04579; *Restoration*—Mountain Shadow Studio, PO Box 619, Nederland, CO 80466.

Antimacassar, 12 x 15", filet crochet, cream colored, reclining cat design, scrollwork around border, three pc set **35.00**

Bread Tray Cover, 12½" l, filet crochet, white, "Staff of Life," c1925 . . . . . **5.00**

Clothespin Apron, 16 x 18", feed bag, floral print, rounded bottom edge **10.00**

Clothespin Bag
   10 x 11½", homespun, worn around waist, brown, blue, and natural white ticking stripe, hand sewn, worn tape tie **95.00**
   35 x 15", bushel size feed bag **8.00**

Dish Towel, 38 x 18", white textile bag, embroidered designs and day of week on each towel, set of seven **25.00**

Doily
   8" d, white cotton center, crocheted edging **5.00**
   18" d, crocheted twine cotton thread, pineapple pattern **12.00**
   24 x 24", quatrefoil shape, formed filet crochet with roses, white, late 19th C **35.00**

Laundry Bag, 28 x 22", cotton, printed textile bag **10.00**

Mattress Cover, homespun
   52 x 68", blue and white plaid, white backing **150.00**
   60 x 104", blue and white, one seam, white homespun backing, minor wear and age stains **115.00**

Doily, crochet, pineapple pattern, cotton thread, 18" d, $12.00.

Napkin, 18 x 19½", homespun, blue and white, hand sewn hem. **55.00**

Pillow Case

17 x 28", white 25 lb flour bag, pr **15.00**

19¼ x 33", pieced, red and white, pr **55.00**

30 x 30", woven, red, blue, and white plaid, machine sewn, button closure **65.00**

Pot Holder, 8" sq, white textile bag, embroidered, face on flower surrounded by leaves **4.00**

Sheet

54 x 40", crib size, cotton textile bags, white **10.00**

64 x 92", homespun, two pc, hand sewn seam and hem, ink corner signatures **40.00**

76 x 100", homespun linen, two pc, hand hemmed, Ephrata, PA **45.00**

77 x 78", cotton homespun, two piece, center seam, hand sewn hem **65.00**

80 x 90", homespun, two pc, hand sewn hems and seams, red embroidered initials **65.00**

Show Towel

10 x 10", homespun, cross stitch and cutwork, tied fringe, gray and several shades of brown embroidery floss, fringe, framed **475.00**

13½ x 51", homespun, linen and cotton cutwork, floral embroidery, sgd "C.L.," minor stains **100.00**

15 x 60", linen, pink embroidered stars, flowerheads, birds, reindeer, dogs, potted flowering shrubs, zigzag crochet panel, fringed bottom, sgd "Anna Marie Nies, 1816" **350.00**

18½ x 51", white, pink embroidered

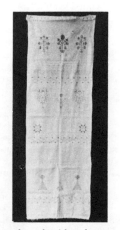

Show Towel, embroidered, rose ground, 16¼ x 50½", $185.00.

stars, pots of flowers, and two chairs, sgd "Lea Sartham 1834," fringed bottom **195.00**

Tablecloth, homespun

33 x 52", blue and white plaid check, minor stains, small holes **85.00**

38 x 71", white on white **35.00**

39 x 55", linen, gold and white check, unhemmed **125.00**

40 x 60", blue and white check, machine woven, hand sewn hem one end, unhemmed other end **55.00**

54 x 76", two piece, gold and white plaid, hand sewn hem one edge, basted selvage other **125.00**

58 x 72", blue and white plaid, hand sewn hem, off center seams **90.00**

58 x 72", two piece, cotton and linen, white, woven diamond design, center seam **25.00**

60 x 74", two piece, white on white design, red embroidered initials and date "1862," hand sewn seam. **25.00**

60 x 76", two piece, blue and white plaid, off center seam, hand sewn hem **165.00**

76 x 116", linen, cutwork and filet lace inserts, twelve matching napkins **310.00**

Towel, homespun

11½ x 32", natural linen, natural and white embroidery **20.00**

13½ x 40", natural linen, coarsely woven, hand sewn hem **20.00**

14 x 39", linen, red embroidered initials, hand hemmed **7.50**

15 x 39", woven diamond pattern, red embroidered initials, hand hemmed, hanging tabs **30.00**

16 x 46", brown embroidered initials, hand sewn hem, tab hanger **15.00**

16½ x 51", woven overshot bands, red embroidered initials "B.M." **25.00**

17 x 26", brown and white check, three sides hand hemmed, wear, small holes and thin spots **65.00**

17 x 52", red initials and date "1851" on white, tab hanger . . . **30.00**

18 x 56", white on white design, tab hanger **12.00**

19 x 49½", red embroidered initials, hand hemmed, hanging tabs **40.00**

NEEDLEWORK AND SAMPLERS

History: Finding time to do needlework in rural America was a luxury. It was an art form that was centered along the eastern seaboard, primarily in urban areas. Needlework is found in many forms:

clothing, embroidered pictures, fire screens, pocketbooks, samplers, and seat coverings.

Country collectors and decorators have romanticized needlework. They have formulated an idyllic image of a woman sitting in front of a blazing fireplace at the end of day, happily doing needlework as a means of relaxation. If this were true, tens of thousands more examples would have survived. Executing a needlework picture was time consuming and required great skill. Few were trained and capable of doing it.

English needlework has flooded the American market. The following clues will help you distinguish American examples from their English counterparts. Identify the maker and check vital statistic records in the region of the needlework's origins. Do not rely on town names. Many English and American town names are identical. By 1750 American needlework was more naturalistic in style and often contained a greater variety of stitches than its English counterpart. British samplers are usually more balanced and possess brighter colors because of better dyes. By 1800 Americans favored the pictorial approach to the more formal, horizontal band style. When doubt exists, assume the piece is English.

Samplers, a needlework form, served many purposes. For a young child they were a practice exercise and permanent reminder of stitches and patterns. For a young woman they demonstrated her skills in a "gentle" art and preserved key elements of family genealogy. For the mature woman they were a useful occupation and functioned as gifts or remembrances, e.g., mourning pieces.

Schools for young ladies of the early 19th century prided themselves on the needlework skills they taught. The Westtown School in Chester County, Pennsylvania, and the Young Ladies Seminary in Bethlehem, Pennsylvania, are two examples. These schools changed their teaching as styles changed. Berlin work was introduced by the mid–19th century.

Examples of samplers date back to the 1700s. The earliest ones were long and narrow, usually done only with the alphabet and numerals. Later examples were square. At the end of the 19th century, the shape tended to be rectangular.

The same motifs were used throughout the country. The name is a key element in determining the region. Samplers are assumed to be on linen unless otherwise indicated.

References: Tandy and Charles Hersh, *Samplers of the Pennsylvania Germans*, The Pennsylvania German Society, 1991; Glee Krueger, *A Gallery of American Samplers: The Theodore H. Kapnek Collection*, Bonanza Books, 1984 edition; Betty Ring, *American Needlework Treasures; Samplers and Silk Embroideries From The Collection of Betty Ring*, E. P. Dutton, 1987; Anne Sebba, *Samplers: Five Centuries of a Gentle Craft*, Thames and Hudson, 1979.

Reproduction Craftspersons: *Samplers*—Liz Chronister & Kathleen Brock, Country Baskets and Collectables, RD 2, Dillsburg, PA 17019; Virginia Colby, Samplers by Virginia Colby, 205 Richmond Ave, Amityville, NY 11701; Elizabeth Creeden, The Sampler, 12 N Park Ave, Plymouth, MA 02360; Susan R Diefenderfer, 12 Esther Circle, Sinking Spring, PA 19608; Jean Hipp, Kitnit Needlecrafts, 20 Valley Rd, Neffsville, PA 17601; Alyce Schroth, Sampler Recreations, 3598 Buttonwood Dr, Doylestown, PA 18901.

Reproduction Manufacturers: *Kits, Patterns, and Supplies*—The Examplarery, PO Box 2554, Dearborn, MI 48123; Folk Art Emporium, 3591 Forest Haven Ln, Chesapeake, VA 23321; Ginny's Stitchins, 106 Braddock Rd, Williamsburg, VA 23185; Mill Pond Designs, PO Box 390, East Longmeadow, MA 01028; Mini-Magic, 3675 Reed Rd, Columbus, OH 43220; Ramsgate Limited, PO Box 143, Okemos, MI 48864; T & N Designs, Inc, 901 Brookshire Dr, Evansville, IN 47715; *Restoration*—Mountain Shadow Studio, PO Box 619, Nederland, CO 80466; *Samplers*—The Americana Collection, 29 W 38th St, New York, NY 10018; Pure and Simple, PO Box 535, 117 W Hempstead, Nashville, AR 71852; Ramsgate Limited, PO Box 143, Okemos, MI 48864.

Family Register
22 x 24", homespun, alphabets, Lilly family listings, dark olive brown on natural linen **325.00**
$22\frac{1}{4}$ x 20", "A record of the family of Mr. Robert and Mrs. Hannah Fosgate," homespun, multicolored floss, geometric border, dated 1831, modern bird's–eye frame, date added later, stains, some color fading and bleeding **150.00**
$22\frac{1}{2}$ x $22\frac{1}{2}$", "Louisa Webb, Nov. 16, 1827," homespun, verse, family record, and inscription, vining bud border, blue, faded red, and white, modern bird's–eye frame   **375.00**
Memorial
$8\frac{3}{4}$ x $10\frac{3}{4}$", satin, German inscription, dated "1801," woman laying flowers at tomb, framed **110.00**
17 x $21\frac{1}{2}$", "Sacred to the Memory of Hiram Bemis who was born July 20, 1806 died May 20 1809" and "Wrought by Harriet Bemis Aged 11 years Southborough June 26, 1820," linen, alphabets, numerals, urn, verse, inscriptions, wreaths with family names and dates, houses, trees, and picket fence, floral border, blue, cream, and gold threads, framed **900.00**
$17\frac{1}{4}$ x 18", needlework on linen, verse, family genealogy, memo-

rial inscription, alphabets, trees, floral border, green, blue, white, and pink silk threads, sgd and dated, Clarissa Squire, 1827 .... **2,200.00**

23½ x 23½", "Can a woman's tender care cease toward the child she bare yes she may forgetful be yet will I remember thee" and "Watch and Pray," ladies, birds, flowers, and angels, sgd and dated, Catharine Booth, 1839, framed **300.00**

26 x 24", "Caroline Webbs Work 1854," wool and silk threads on linen, signature, verse, and trumpeting angels over tomb flanked by weeping willows **200.00**

Needlepoint Panel

19¼ x 16¼", satin, three central figures, worn paper faces, arms, and legs, framed, faded colors...... **125.00**

19¾ x 18¾", dog on cushion, shades of brown, blue, white, olive, orange, and yellow, sgd and dated "H. 1885," framed **475.00**

22¾ x 18", shepherd girl and dog seated under trees, warm colors, framed, old white repaint on sky area **325.00**

28½ x 28½", intricate floral design, multicolored on black ground, white border, early 20th C, framed **210.00**

Sampler

6 x 13¾", alphabets and numerals, natural linen homespun, blue and gold, wear, holes **160.00**

9½ x 7¼", "M.P. 1811," multicolored silk threads, stylized flowers, stars, parrot, signature and date, framed, holes, deteriorated edges **300.00**

11¾ x 16", "Ida Basset 1835," homespun, alphabets, simple floral designs.................... **245.00**

12 x 9", "'Emma Arnold, September 18, 1873," rows of alphabets ... **225.00**

12¼ x 10⅞", "Isabella Brooks age 14 years Badminton School 1808," religious verse, potted flower, flowering and pine trees, birds, and inscription, meandering floral border................... **750.00**

12½ x 12¾", "Lydia Mitchell, Nine Partners 1810" and "The Rule to mark napkins," green dyed linen homespun, white threads, alphabets and inscriptions, framed, small holes **2,550.00**

13 x 9, "Janet Fisher's work aged 12 years 1839...Mrs. Chamberlain teacher," homespun, vining flowers, verse, and inscription, shades of green and gold, wide rosewood

1809, M L, multicolored threads on linen, Tree of Life, Adam and Eve, stylized flowers, birds, animals, people, and buildings, 17½ x 23", Philadelphia, PA, $950.00.

veneer frame, gilded liner, small holes **375.00**

13⅝ x 16¾", "Eliza P. Freeman, born Nov. 19th 1828, aged 10 years, China 1838. This needlework of mine doth tell my name, my age and where I dwell, when friends are dead and money spent, Learning is most excellent," homespun, beige, blue, and green on natural white, framed, small hole in bottom border **255.00**

13¾ x 12¼", "Edith Mary Crabtree, aged 9 years 1895," wool, bright colors on white ground **200.00**

13¾ x 18¾", "Mary L Montaqu, A.D. 1828 AE 11 yrs," silk threads, alphabets, numbers, stylized trees and flowers, black, green, blue, and tan **150.00**

14 x 14", "Marion McDonald, Finished August 1873," wool threads on homespun, alphabets, numbers, trees, birds, and people, framed **400.00**

14 x 15½", "Winchester, Mass" label, alphabets, angel, crucifixion, Adam and Eve, animals, and flowers **350.00**

15 x 12½"

1838, "This I have done for you to see, the care my parents took of me. Jane Harris, August 8,

1823, "Elisheba Edwards Sampler, made in the 12 year of her age, Franklin, June 11, 1823," ivory, light green, and teal silk threads on linen ground, alphabet bands, potted flowers, house, tree, and inscription, diamond borders, 16 x 17½", $475.00.

1838, aged 12 years," linen, silk stitches, stylized trees, potted flowers, animals, and birds, floral border, framed **750.00**

1856, homespun, alphabet, numerals, stylized birds and flowers, hearts, and date, red, blue, green, and yellow, framed **270.00**

15 x 15", "A. Jackson 1835," homespun, cottage scene, dog, girl, trees, flowers, verse "Religion," and inscription, shades of green, brown, gold, and black, gilt frame, hole at bottom corner **700.00**

15¼ x 15", "Margaret Tyson Ham work'd this sampler in the year of our Lord 1808 and in the ninth year of her age," two religious verse, bells, flowers, lady with parasol, roosters, stylized trees and potted flowers, and inscription, meandering floral border, mahogany veneered frame **700.00**

15½ x 10", "Christian Niell, 1799," homespun, alphabets, flowers, birds, and crowns **550.00**

15¾ x 14⅜", "Mercy Ratt aged 11 years," finely woven homespun, stylized flowers, animals, parrots, angels, Adam and Eve, verse, and inscription, vining border, shades of brown and green, minor wear, small holes **725.00**

16¼ x 14", "Mary Ann Daileys work in the 12 yr. of her age, 1831," homespun, Adam and Eve with serpent, shepherd, animals, flowers, verse, and inscription, soft colors, framed, small holes, minor fading **850.00**

16¼ x 22½", "Burmela Morgan, Sampler, July 1, 1812, aged 12 years," homespun, alphabets, numbers, verse, and inscription, framed, stains, faded colors **225.00**

17 x 17", "Betsy Patten born September 1802, aged 11 A.D. 1812 Mary Cummings instructress," silk threads on linen, alphabets, numbers, trees, house, birds, and inscription, floral border, green, yellow, blue, cream, and brown, Westford, MA, "Betsy Patten– Richardson (September 1, 1800– December 25, 1835) Trekked to Quincy, Illinois 1834" label inscription on frame **450.00**

17¼ x 13½", homespun, alphabets and verse, faded shades of brown and green, framed, wear, some damage, stains **95.00**

17⅜ x 10¼", "September 182–, Louisa Eastes, born December 18th 1812," homespun, alphabets, two trees, dog, and inscription, framed, faded colors, date partially obscured by frame **275.00**

17⅜ x 14¼", "By Abigail Haines at Betsy Pickering's School in North Hampton, July the 20th in the 14th year of her age AD 1814," homespun, alphabets, pot of flowers, verse, and inscription, floral border, soft colors, framed **1,750.00**

18 x 14", "Catharine Forgall, aged 11," homespun, alphabets, house, trees, animals, sets of initials, and inscription, framed, wear, stains, small holes, missing some floss **500.00**

18 x 15½", "Abigail Bush's sampler wrought in the 10th yr. of her age, Grt. Barrington, Novbr 6th AD 1807. . .," linen homespun, rows of alphabets, numbers, and inscription on top inside panel, leaves, cornucopia, basket of flowers, black handlebar mustache shape, and further inscriptions on white satin stitch ground lower panel, multicolored and multistitched floral design on dark brown applique cotton inner border, vining flowers, bows in corners, and birds and berries on bot-

tom edge, sawtooth outer border, framed **10,000.00**

18 x 18", "Eliza Ann Petrs, 8 years of age, Poughkeepsie, January. . .," homespun, alphabets, birds, stylized flowers, verse, and inscription, vining border, blue, green, yellow, brown, and black, framed, faded colors, embroidered year removed, minor stains **300.00**

$18\frac{1}{4}$ x $9\frac{3}{4}$", "Lydia Clark, Mendon, Mass, Waterford March 3, 1832," linen homespun, alphabets, house, numbers, and inscription, red, brown, and two shades of green, framed **425.00**

$18\frac{3}{8}$ x $14\frac{1}{2}$", "Sarah Ann Cooper, Sherborne, Dorset 1850," silk on finely woven linen, pots of flowers and verse, stylized floral border **500.00**

$18\frac{1}{2}$ x $9\frac{1}{4}$", homespun, alphabets in several styles, illegible name, dated "1750," framed, small dark stains **500.00**

$18\frac{1}{2}$ x 13", "Fanny Brett aged twelve years, March sixth day 1822," silk on linen homespun, stylized house, flowers, trees, and verse "The Rose. . ." **450.00**

$18\frac{1}{2}$ x $14\frac{3}{4}$", "Mary Day work this sampler in the year of our Lord 1799, 8 yrs," homespun, Adam and Eve, angels, flowers, verse, and inscription, vining border, framed **300.00**

$18\frac{1}{2}$ x 18", "Wrought by Hannah Wilder, Aged 13, 1820," homespun, alphabets, verse, yellow house, birds in two trees, and inscription, stylized floral border, multicolored, gilt frame, holes . . **675.00**

$18\frac{1}{2}$ x $19\frac{1}{2}$", "Hannah Bond, her work 1837," finely woven linen homespun, flowers, birds, cherubs, hearts, swans, detailed red house, trees, picket fence, verse, and inscription, vining strawberry border, framed **1,750.00**

$18\frac{5}{8}$ x $15\frac{3}{4}$", "Julia Mary Newton, November 26, 1835," homespun, alphabets, verse, stylized foliage designs, and inscription, red floss, framed, wear, small holes. **450.00**

$18\frac{5}{8}$ x 18 $\frac{1}{8}$", "Sarah Gill Bedale, October 17, 1800, aged 9 year old," homespun, alphabet and numbers, stylized flowers, trees, and animals, verse, two shades of green, olive gold, and shades of ivory, minor stains, bird's-eye veneer frame. **700.00**

$18\frac{3}{4}$ x $14\frac{3}{4}$", "Mary Tongate aged 12 years, May 1822," homespun, stylized birds, flowers, buildings, trees, two large quail, verse, and inscription, vining border, soft colors, framed **1,500.00**

$19\frac{1}{4}$ x $15\frac{3}{4}$", homespun, alphabets, verse, flowers, and birds, vining floral border, red, green, gold, blue, and white, bird's-eye veneer ogee frame, moth damage, holes **350.00**

$19\frac{1}{2}$ x 14", "To Virgins all to you I call. . .Mary Pollard is my name at nine and half I mark'd the same, 1740," homespun, long verse, blue and blue-green threads, minor damage, small holes, shadow box frame **325.00**

$19\frac{1}{2}$ x 20", "Elizabeth Batten Aged 9 years 1836," homespun, verse, stylized flowers, dogs, and inscription, vining border, framed, wear, damage, old repaired holes **375.00**

20 x 16", "M.S. age 12, 1797," homespun, alphabets, verse, stylized flowers, deer, birds, people, and inscription, soft colors, framed, fragile and worn homespun, holes **600.00**

20 x $16\frac{1}{2}$", "Abigail Dana Seaver, age 9, 1819," alphabets, Lord's Prayer, four line verse, flowering bushes, spruce trees **450.00**

$20\frac{3}{8}$ x $20\frac{3}{8}$", "Ann Forde, March 13, 1848, aged 9 years," homespun, black floss alphabets, verse, and inscription, red, pink, and green vining bud border, modern bird's-eye ogee frame **450.00**

$20\frac{3}{4}$ x $21\frac{1}{2}$", "Margaret Johnston," homespun, wool needlepoint,

1836, H Croll, red and blue threads on natural linen, alphabet bands, verse, and inscription, 15 x $15\frac{1}{2}$", unfinished, $250.00.

stylized flowers, animals, birds, verse, building, and inscription, old beveled frame **1,000.00**

21¼ x 23¾", "Anne Lindemuth, Sampler made in the year of our Lord 1853," wool and silk, flowers, building, and alphabets **450.00**

21½ x 16", "Lydia Hall Noyes, Born November 5, 1773, AE 10 years," silk threads on linen, bands of alphabets above pious verse with inner borders of hearts and oak leaves on upper register, pairs of pine trees, sprays of strawberries, birds, lambs, and baskets of fruit and flowers, green on lower register, white, pink, brown, and blue, Newbury, MA **1,300.00**

21¾ x 8", homespun, alphabets, flowers, and birds, framed, worn, holes, missing stitches **275.00**

22 x 14", "Hanna Headher Sampler the year 1801," linen homespun, alphabets, yellow house **180.00**

22¼ x 17½", "Clarkson School, Louiza Thompson, George Ward 1819," homespun, alphabets, stylized flowers, birds, verse, and inscription, framed, incomplete stitching on two names, worn, dark stains, faded colors **550.00**

22½ x 18⅞", "Eliza Griswold wrought this sampler, August 1826, AE 9 years," homespun, alphabets, verse and inscription, black, green, and white, stains, minor edge damage **575.00**

22¾ x 18¾", "Harriet R. Trumbo, Feb-

ruary 7," homespun, wool embroidery, verse, pot of flowers, and inscription, vining border, framed, small holes and stains. . . **475.00**

23 x 17", "Hannah Closson daughter of Stephen and Lydia Closson born Cambridge, Dec. th. 29, 1812. Aged 13 years AD 1825," American eagle in oval wreath, family record information, house, and flowers, vining border, shades of blue, green, salmon, purple, tan, and white, minor stains **1,550.00**

25 x 19", "Marianne Thompson 1849," wool and silk on linen, bowl of flowers, verse, and inscription, vining border, framed, stains **450.00**

25¾ x 25½", animals, flowers, and train, cross stitch, multicolored on black cloth, late 19th C **775.00**

26 x 24", "Esther Beaulah her work aged 11 years, 1842," homespun, parrot, dog, swans, flowers, other birds, verse, flowering border . . . **1,250.00**

29 x 24", "Lou Vosmeck Work 1844," homespun, wool needlepoint, flowers, trees, birds, horse, buildings, and inscription, framed, minor selvage damage, stains, small holes **1,100.00**

1801, "Elizabeth Shade, Her Work 1801," silk threads on loosely woven linen, large basket of fruits between bands of alphabet, large brick building on stepped lawn terrace flanked by potted tulips and trees, paired birds perched on steeples, white dog and recumbent antlered stag on lawn, stylized vine and flower border, yellow bird in each corner. **3,300.00**

QUILTS

History: In the agrarian household a quilt combined beauty with function. Most were not show pieces. They were used. Quilts varied in weight. It was customary to change quilts with the season.

The quilting bee, a group of women working together to quilt a pieced top to its backing, was an important form of social interaction. Almost every rural farmstead, especially in the nineteenth century, had a quilting frame set up in a room corner. When another woman came to call, it was common for them to spend some time talking over the quilting frame.

1837, Sarah Jane Rest, multicolored threads, potted flowers, birds, buildings, trees, verse, and inscription, vining border, $525.00.

Quilts have been passed down as family heirlooms for many generations. Each is an individual expression. The same pattern may have hundreds of variations in both color and design.

The advent of the sewing machine increased, not decreased the number of quilts being made. Quilts are still being sewn today.

The key considerations for price are age, condition, aesthetic beauty, and design. Prices are now at a level position. The exceptions are the very finest examples which continue to bring record prices.

References: Suzy Anderson, *Collector's Guide to Quilts*, Wallace–Homestead, 1991; American Quilter's Society, *Gallery of American Quilts, 1849–1988*, Collector Books, 1988; Barbara Brackman, *Clues in the Calico: A Guide To Identifying and Dating Antique Quilts*, EPM Publications, 1989; Barbara Brackman, *Encyclopedia of Pieced Patterns, Volume* , Prairie Flower Publications, 1984; William C. Ketchum, Jr., *The Knopf Collectors' Guides to American Antiques: Quilts*, Alfred A. Knopf, Inc., 1982; Jean Ray Laury and California Heritage Quilt Project, *Ho For California: Pioneer Women and Their Quilts*, E. P. Dutton, 1990; Lisa Turner Oshins, *Quilt Collections: A Directory For The United States And Canada*, Acropolis Books, Ltd., 1987; Rachel and Kenneth Pellman, *The World of Amish Quilts*, Good Books, 1984; Schnuppe von Gwinner, *The History of the Patchwork Quilt*, Schiffer Publishing Ltd., 1988; Carleton L Safford and Robert Bishop, *America's Quilts and Coverlets*, Bonanza Books, 1985.

Collectors' Clubs: The American Quilter's Society, PO Box 3290, Paducah, KY 42002; National Quilting Association, PO Box 393, Ellicott City, MD 21043.

Periodicals: *Quilter's Newsletter*, Box 394, Wheat Ridge, CO 80033; *Vintage Quilt Newsletter*, 311 West 6th, Alice, TX 78332.

Reproduction Craftspersons: June Blackburn, 4148 S Norfolk Ave, Tulsa, OK 74105; Arlinka Blair, 2301 N Grant Ave, Wilmington, DE 19803; Jane Blair, 504 Dogwood Ln, Conshohocken, PA 19428; Sherri Dunbar, 105 Hewett Rd, Wyncote, PA 19095; Molly Fish, The Garden Patch, 1228 N W Dixon St, Corvallis, OR 97330; R C Pirrone, 107 E Chestnut St, West Chester, PA 19380.

Reproduction Manufacturers: *Amish*—Amish Country Collection, RD 5, Sunset Valley Rd, New Castle, PA 16105; Pure and Simple, PO Box 535, 117 W Hempstead, Nashville, AR 71852; *Baby*—The Roos Collection, PO Box 20668, New York, NY 10025; *General*—Apple Tree Quilts, Box 335–E, Berlin, OH 44610; Basye-Bomberger/Fabian House, PO Box 86, W Bowie, MD 20715; Country Loft, 1506 South Shore Park, Hingham, MA 02043; Donna's Custom Hand–Made Canopies, Rte 1, Box 456, Banner Elk, NC 28604; Faith Mountain Country Fare, Main St, Box 199, Sperryville, VA 22740; Gooseberry Patch, PO Box 634, Delaware, OH 43015; Great Expectations Quilts, 155 Town & Country Village, Houston, TX 77024; Hands All Around, Inc, 971 Lexington Ave, New York, NY 10021; Hearthside Quilts, Box 429, Rte 7, Shelburne, VT 05482; Judy's of Cape Cod, PO Box 677, Osterville, MA 02655; Quilted Selections, Rte 1, Box 137, Luthersville, GA 30251; The Quiltery, Box 337, RD 4, Boyertown, PA 19512; Quilts Unlimited, 124 W Washington, PO Box 1210, Lewisburg, WV 24901; Strunk, Box 77, Main St, Virginville, PA 19564; *Kit*—Cotton Exchange, 105 Silverwood Ln, Cary, NC 27511; Folk Art Emporium, 3591 Forest Haven Ln, Chesapeake, VA 23321; Hearthside Quilts, Box 429, Rte 7, Shelburne, VT 05482; Judy's of Cape Cod, PO Box 677, Osterville, MA 02655; *Restoration*—Mountain Shadow Studio, PO Box 619, Nederland, CO 80466; *Quilt Stencils*—Olde Mill House Shoppe, 105 Strasburg Pike, Lancaster, PA 17602.

Crib Size

28½ x 31½", pieced, Star of Bethlehem pattern, corner stars, pink calico on white, conforming quilting	375.00
34 x 49", pieced, Nine Patch variant, black and five shades of blue	250.00
36 x 47", pieced, Tumbling Blocks pattern, silk, multicolored, minor wear...................	225.00
41 x 40", pieced, Star of Bethlehem pattern, printed cotton patches, conforming quilting, 19th C	300.00
41 x 41", appliqued, single feathered pinwheel, red and green on white.............	160.00
42½ x 48", pieced, Nine Patch variant, multicolored prints and pink and white calico, navy blue and white polka dot grid..........	375.00
43 x 45", appliqued, trefoil and diamond design, red and yellow-green calico on white, geometric quilting..................	145.00
43 x 47", pieced and appliqued, central stylized floral medallion, red, yellow, and olive calicoes on blue calico ground, sawtooth border.....................	250.00
44 x 52", diamond and square design, multicolored prints and goldenrod, minor wear........	175.00
47½ x 49", five central blue and maroon bands, meandering, sunbursts, and floral quilting, green print backing, minor stains, Amish	1,025.00

Doll Size

14¼ x 15", pieced, diamond design, multicolored patches, green stripe, beige borders, gray binding, Amish, framed **325.00**

17 x 22", pieced, black and white gingham, blue, and goldenrod . .   **120.00**

17 x 26½", pieced, Nine Patch variant, colorful prints, pink binding, corner cut–outs **85.00**

20 x 23", pieced, checkerboard design, maroon and white calico, minor age stains **225.00**

24 x 26½", pieced, Nine Patch variant, pastel colors, diagonal quilting **150.00**

25½ x 25½", pieced, single star variant, navy blue and white print on white, pencil quilt pattern intact, minor age stains **400.00**

Full Size

60 x 76", pieced, twelve linked stylized floral medallions, name embroidered in red in each medallion, faded red and ivory on white, worn **125.00**

62 x 78", pieced, silk, satin, and velvet, multicolored bars, maroon velvet border, hot pink satin back, worn **70.00**

62 x 82", pieced, silk, satin, and velvet, Tumbling Blocks, multicolored **475.00**

64 x 79", appliqued, tulip medallions, red, goldenrod, and ecru, red and ecru grid and alternating borders **275.00**

65 x 77", pieced, Drunkard's Path pattern, olive on white, printed roosters on white, red floral print on olive, olive border, red print backing, diagonal quilting **165.00**

66 x 72", white on white, diamond in square center and meandering border quilting, machine sewn edge **350.00**

66 x 74", pieced, Star pattern, multicolored prints and solid red on beige print ground, stains, wear   **95.00**

66 x 78", pieced, Basket pattern, multicolored prints on white ground, red grid **175.00**

66 x 82", pieced, Nine Patch variant, multicolored prints on white ground, maroon calico zigzag border, minor stains **125.00**

68 x 70", pieced, Log Cabin pattern, simple quilting **245.00**

68 x 74", pieced and embroidered, Crazy Quilt, silk, velvet, and printed baseball player tobacco silks patches, embroidered verses,

border motifs, floral, and figural designs, early 20th C **700.00**

68 x 78", pieced, circle and grid design, alternately reversing pink and white **225.00**

69 x 75", pieced, Monkey Wrench pattern, solid red, beige floral print, and faded blue, overlapping concentric ring quilting, lavender, olive, and white homespun backing, post cut–outs **125.00**

70 x 70", white on white, round center medallion, scrolls, shells, and floral design quilting. **400.00**

70 x 78", pieced, Cactus Baskets pattern, pink and green calico and prints **125.00**

70 x 80", pieced

Crazy quilt comforter, velvet, knotted **100.00**

Four–point star flowers, multicolored prints on blue check squares on white ground **225.00**

70 x 86", pieced, twelve eight–point stars in blue, green, and maroon on black ground, blue border . . .   **700.00**

70 x 88"

Appliqued, baskets of tulips, red, green, and goldenrod, feather quilting, corners embroidered "Mrs. Saiddie Ford age 67 years, Sept 15, 1882, West Hope, Henry Co., Ohio," minor wear and fading **550.00**

Pieced, Log Cabin pattern, multicolored prints and solid red center squares **600.00**

72 x 72", pieced, Diamond in the Square pattern, cotton, light blue, maroon, and navy blue patches, concentric nine–point star quilting on central diamond, rose sprays and feathers quilting on borders, Amish, early 20th C . . .   **5,225.00**

72 x 73", pieced, appliqued, and embroidered, Crazy Quilt, silk and velvet, silk backing, initialed "LAS 1885" **700.00**

72 x 76", pieced, "X" design, pink and white, minor wear and fading   **300.00**

72 x 79", pieced and appliqued, Carolina Lily pattern, goldenrod and green calico on white, small stamped ink maker's label on back, cut–out corners **275.00**

72 x 80"

Pieced, pink and white calico four patch alternating with brown calico squares, machine sewn binding **400.00**

Pieced and Appliqued, President's Wreath with Buds pat-

**Diamond, pieced, multicolored, 86 x 86",
$250.00.**

tern, cotton, red and gray–blue patches, white ground, running diamond chain inner border, blossoms and leaves chain outer border, diagonal channel line quilting, Columbus County, OH, c1860 . . . . **2,225.00**

72 x 82", pieced, Log Cabin pattern, multicolored prints and calico, sawtooth edge, worn binding . . . **675.00**

72 x 84", pieced, Nine Patch variant, cotton, mulberry, light blue, green, olive green, navy blue, sapphire blue, and lavender patches, cube quilting on central field, blossom and leaves quilting on wide border, bronze colored backing, Amish, c1930 . . . . **2,530.00**

73 x 78", appliqued, nine stylized floral medallions, vining border, blue, red, pink calico, and goldenrod on white, faded, minor stains, replaced binding **225.00**

73 x 87", pieced

Drunkard's Path pattern, solid red and green calico, bar design in alternating dark brown prints on back **150.00**

Triangle and sawtooth design, red and ecru on white ground **175.00**

74 x 74", appliqued, sixteen pots of flowers, green calico and solid red **350.00**

74 x 84", Irish Chain pattern, pink and green calico **200.00**

74 x 86"

Appliqued, twelve pink and green flowers, swag border, minor stains. **575.00**

Pieced, pinwheels and squares, pink and white, worn, stained **150.00**

74 x 87", pieced, cotton, black, black sateen, and green, stars and foliage scroll border quilting, Amish **550.00**

74 x 88", pieced, pink and white, pencil quilting pattern intact, age stains **500.00**

74 x 90", pieced, Wild Goose Chase pattern, pink and white, machine sewn binding. **200.00**

75 x 82", pieced, Flying Geese pattern one side, bars other side, red and white **600.00**

75 x 82½", appliqued, stylized floral design, red, green, and goldenrod on white ground, white homespun back **975.00**

75 x 87", pieced, Diamond pattern, two shades of blue and black, solid brown back, Amish **875.00**

76 x 76"

Linsey Woolsey, solid red wool, blue linsey woolsey on reverse, circle pattern quilting, c1840 **700.00**

Pieced, Sunshine and Shadow pattern, multicolored prints and solids, machine sewn binding **240.00**

76 x 77", pieced, Diamond pattern, black, yellow, white, and multicolored prints **480.00**

76 x 78", pieced, Pineapple pattern, blue and white calico, hand pieced, machine quilted. **300.00**

76 x 80"

Appliqued, Double Fleur–de–Lis pattern, cotton, printed navy blue and white patches on white field, double sawtooth border, feather wreath and diamond quilting, Michigan, 1860–1870 . . . . **2,000.00**

**Log Cabin, pieced, multicolored, 82 x 82",
$350.00.**

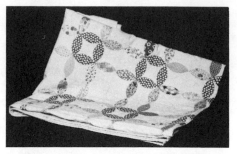

Melon Patch, appliqué, multicolored on natural ground, vining and floral border quilting, pencil quilting pattern intact, 80 x 92", early 20th C, $250.00.

Embroidered, red central floral design, corner sprays, and borders on white ground **400.00**

76 x 82", Rob Peter to Pay Paul pattern, multicolored prints and solids **105.00**

76 x 84", pieced, Sawtooth Cross pattern, cotton, red and green on brown ground, leaf and diagonal line quilting on field, diagonal line and meandering vine quilting on border, Amish, late 19th C . . . **5,225.00**

76 x 87", pieced, multicolored eight–point stars on white squares, goldenrod grid, one corner embroidered "1935" **325.00**

76 x 89", appliqued, Tulip pattern, meandering floral border, red and green calico and solid yellow–green, OH **400.00**

77 x 88", Monkey Wrench pattern, lemon yellow and white, pencil quilting pattern intact, machine sewn edge **350.00**

77 x 90", appliqued, diamonds in circles design, red and green calico, won blue ribbon for 1955 Kentucky State Fair **1,300.00**

78 x 61", pieced, Bow Tie pattern, geometric quilting, never used, Mennonite, 20th C **250.00**

78 x 78"
   Carolina Lily pattern, pieced and appliqued, cotton, green calico, solid goldenrod, machine sewn binding **395.00**
   Sunlight and Shadow pattern, pieced, wool and cotton, multicolored, deep purple and blue borders, blue binding, sewn printed label one corner "Verna Mae Beiler," Amish **700.00**

79 x 80", pieced, Irish Chain variant, multicolored prints and navy blue on white **90.00**

79 x 88", pieced, pinwheel design, shades of blue on gray ground, bluish–green sateen back, minor wear, stains, small holes **300.00**

80 x 76", pieced, appliqued, and printed, Harrison–Morton Campaign theme, cotton, red, white, and blue printed and solid patches, four printed bust portraits of candidates flanking stars and stripes and "Protection" slogan on center banner, field of pieced stars mounted on navy blue and white calico, three borders of red, white, and navy blue calico, c1889 . . . . **7,500.00**

80 x 80", pieced, Open Bar pattern, navy blue and maroon patches, cube quilting on central area, undulating leaves and grape clusters quilting on wide border, Amish, c1930 . . . . **5,725.00**

80 x 82"
   Pieced, single star design, medium blue and white, feather quilted circles, machine and hand sewn **400.00**
   Pieced and embroidered, Crazy Quilt, mostly solid colors, embroidered names, dates, "Ohio," "1885," and "1905," minor wear **200.00**

80 x 88", pieced, Baskets pattern, multicolored print baskets on white squares, alternating patches of small white stars on navy blue, new backing and quilting **300.00**

80 x 94", appliqued, Album, cotton, white blocks, red designs and grid, florals, moon and stars, animals, church, anchor, horseshoes, and basket designs, quilt top, Ephrata, PA. **2,200.00**

81 x 90¼", pieced, Flower Garden pattern, red floral roller printed border, printed cottons, cut corners, mid 19th C **300.00**

81½ x 98", appliqued, four trees with red berries, yellow birds, green leaves, and mauve branches, vining border, 20th C **1,300.00**

82 x 82", appliqued, nine Mariner's Compass designs, red, green, and yellow on white, green sawtooth and red scalloped borders, red binding frayed **600.00**

82 x 90", pieced, triangular designs, blue and white calico on white ground, minor wear **550.00**

82 x 97", pieced and appliqued, triangle block center, stylized birds and trees border, blue polka dot star print on white **575.00**

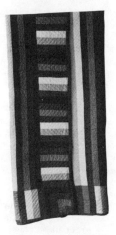

Rainbow, pieced, 86 x 84", $950.00.

83 x 68", appliqued, Baskets pattern, gold on white **175.00**

84 x 86", pieced and appliqued, sunflower stars, navy blue calico and white, vining floral border, red centers in border flowers, minor stains **3,600.00**

84 x 90", trapunto, knotted lace fringe, pinwheel designs, cut-out corners **850.00**

85 x 85", appliqued, nine stylized potted flower medallions, red, yellow, and olive green on white, red zigzag border, minor stains **500.00**

86 x 86", pieced
  Album, sampler type, multicolored prints, ink signatures, quilt top, minor stains **225.00**
  Star of Bethlehem pattern, pastel shades of peach, yellow, and white. **300.00**

86 x 100", pieced and appliqued, Baskets pattern, red print and medium solid green baskets and edge stripes on white, trapunto baskets and circles. **500.00**

86 x 102"
  Appliqued, flower in squares, tree and flower borders, red and green calico on white ground, flower and leaf design quilting **825.00**
  White on White, star center with cherries, birds, meandering border, and pair of birds in corners quilted designs, ball fringe, pencil quilt pattern intact, minor age stains, 20th C **550.00**

87 x 70", appliqued, Rose Wreath pattern, yellow, pink, and green, geometric quilting, scalloped edges **300.00**

88 x 90", pieced, album, teal blue grid, multicolored prints, white center squares, signed in ink, presentation inscription reads "J.T. Foster, Salem (N.H.) December 6th, 1845," later paper label reads "Quilt given to Israel Thorndike Foster when he was married to Lydia Cluff in Sept. 1847," post cut-outs **350.00**

88 x 93", pieced, Irish Chain pattern, navy blue and pink calico **500.00**

90 x 90", appliqued, Wild Rose pattern, meandering rose bud and leaf border, dark teal green, kelly green, and red, floral and diagonal quilting, partially intact pencil pattern, cloth label reads "Pieced by Sarah Pierce, owned by Eliza E. Matteson" **600.00**

90 x 92", appliqued, Tulip and Oak Leaf pattern, teal blue and red on white, meandering tulips in scalloped border **1,700.00**

91 x 91", pieced, Irish Chain pattern, medium blue on deep mustard gold ground, blue back **300.00**

92 x 92", pieced, Blazing Star pattern, bright yellow, green, rose, maroon, blue, and pink calico patches, wide border of yellow, rose, green, and red fruit and flower printed polished chintz, diagonal line quilting, mid 19th C **2,750.00**

99 x 79", appliqued, Whig Rose pattern, deep pink, light pink, and green, geometric quilting **300.00**

100 x 108", pieced, Delectable Mountain pattern, cotton, printed navy blue and white calico on white field, flower, feather, and cube quilting, mid 19th C **2,225.00**

Star of the East, pieced, navy blue and white print stars and border, red and white print ground and backing, geometric quilting, $275.00.

100 x 112", pieced, Four Patch variant, red, white, brown, and blue
floral and geometric printed calico patches, deep spiking sawtooth border, diagonal line quilting, printed chintz stripe back,
post cut–outs, 19th C **1,325.00**

101 x 101", pieced, Bethlehem Star
pattern, suns and rising suns,
green and red calico and beige
and brown floral print, feather
quilted circles and half circles,
meandering floral border quilting,
attributed to Ephrata, PA **2,300.00**

103 x 106", pieced, triangular
patches, square inside diamond
inside square, stripe and sawtooth
borders, predominately brown
and pink on white ground **750.00**

104 x 92", pieced, Sunflower pattern, red, yellow, brown, navy
blue, and green calico flowers on
white ground, red and blue
printed sashings, batting, PA,
19th C **2,650.00**

106 x 86", pieced and appliqued,
Tulips pattern, red tulips and lat-
ticework frame on white ground,
green tree and stylized trefoil border, red back, Hudson Valley,
NY, 19th C **1,200.00**

RUGS

History: Although American mass–produced
rugs were available as early as 1830, many agrarian families made do with handmade examples
during much of the nineteenth century. Yarn–
sewn rugs, constructed with two–ply yarn on a
homespun linen backing or grain sack, were popular between 1800 and 1840. Popular patterns
were patriotic, nautical, animal, floral, and geometric motifs.

The importation of burlap to America in the
1850s opened the door for the hooked rug. The
hooked rug tradition began in New England and
quickly spread throughout the country. The rug
was made by pulling narrow stripes of fabric up
through holes in the burlap. Most of the early
designs were free–form. By 1900 preprinted patterns were available from Diamond Dye Co. and
Montgomery Ward Co.

Rug hooking enjoyed a revival in the 1920s and
1930s when the early American decorating craze
dominated. In the 1970s the folk art community
discovered hooked rugs and turned them into an
art form. Design motif and artwork was stressed.
Many collectors and dealers failed to realize that
factory production of hooked rugs was well established by the 1930s. Examples that can be easily

confused with handworked pieces have been
found marked "MADE IN OCCUPIED JAPAN."

Three other types of rugs also appeared in the
rural homestead—woven, braided, and penny.
Woven rugs, also called rag rugs, were done on
simple wooden hand looms. Braided rugs became popular in the 1830s and have continued
ever since. Penny rugs date from the 1880 to
1915 period.

Prosperous members of the agrarian community liked to demonstrate their wealth and good
taste by placing an Oriental rug in their parlor
and/or dining room. Hall runners were another
favorite way of introducing Oriental rugs to a
rural home.

Oriental rugs first appeared in the West in the
16th century. The rugs originated in the regions of
Central Asia, Iran (Persia), Caucasus, and
Anatolia. Early rugs can be classified into basic
categories: Iranian, Caucasian, Turkoman, Turk-
ish, and Chinese. Later, India, Pakistan, and Iraq
produced rugs in the Oriental style.

The pattern name is derived from the tribe
which produced the rug, e.g., Iran is the source
for Hamadan, Herez, Sarouk, Tabriz, and others.

When evaluating an Oriental rug, age, design,
color, weave, knots per square inch, and condition determine the final value. Silk rugs and
prayer rugs bring higher prices.

Native American Indian rugs are also commonly found in country settings. Many examples
of these colorful woven rugs have been brought
back east by visiting tourists. Others were purchased and used as accent rugs to brighten country homes. Today these rugs can be identified by
tribes or region and may command high prices.

References: Murray Eiland, *Oriental Rugs: A
New Comprehensive Guide*, Little, Brown and
Company, 1981; H L James, *Rugs And Posts*,
Schiffer Publishing, 1988; Linda Kline,
Beginner's Guide To Oriental Rugs, Ross Books,
1980; Ivan C. Neff and Carol V. Maggs,
Dictionary of Oriental Rugs, Van Nostrand Rein-
hold Company, 1979; Marian Rodee, *Weaving
Of The Southwest*, Schiffer Publishing 1987; Hel-
ene Von Rosenstiel, *American Rugs and Carpets:
From the Seventeenth Century to Modern Times*,
William Morrow and Company, 1978; Jessie A.
Turbayne, *Hooked Rugs: History and the Contin-
uing Tradition*, Schiffer Publishing, 1991.

Periodical: *Oriental Rug Review*, Beech Hill
Road, RFD 2, Meredith, NH 03253.

Reproduction Craftspersons: *Braided*—Pat
Nolan, The Rug House, 1437 Herschel Ave, Cin-
cinnati, OH 45208; *General*—Elizabeth Black
Designs, PO Box 28, Bentonville, VA 22610;
Julia A Lindsey, Lindsey Woolseys of Ohio, 275
N Main St, Germantown, OH 45327; Judy Robin-
son's Country Textiles, 3350 Chickencoop Hill
Rd, Lancaster, OH 43130; *Hooked*—Betsy Bour-

don, Weaver, Scribner Hill, Wolcott, VT 05680; Pat Hornafius, 113 Meadowbrook Ln, Elizabethtown, PA 17022; Suzanne C & Cleland E Shelby, Aged Ram, PO Box 201, Essex, VT 05451; *Penny*—Jo Morton, Prairie Hands, 1801 Central Ave, Nebraska City, NE 68410; *Rag*—Rebecca Francis, Weaver, Box 307, Dillsburg, PA 17019; Martha Richard, The Weaver's Corner, 1406 E Spring St, New Albany, IN 47150.

Reproduction Manufacturers: *Braided*—Braid-Aid, 466 Washington St, Rte 53, Pembroke, MA 02359; Chinaberry General Store, 1846 Winfield Dunn Highway, Sevierville, TN 38762; Jugtown Mountain Rugs, 791 Tower Rd, Enola, PA 17025; Olde Mill House Shoppe, 105 Strasburg Pike, Lancaster, PA 17602; The Rug Factory Store, PO Box 249, 560 Mineral Spring Ave, Pawtucket, RI 02860; *General*—Country Loft, 1506 South Shore Park, Hingham, MA 02043; The Cover Up Handweaving Studio, Rte 1, Box 216, Rabun Gap, GA 30568; *Hooked Rug Kit*—The Hooking Room, 1840 House, 237 Pine Point Rd, Scarborough, ME 04074; National Carpet Co, 1384 Coney Island Ave, Brooklyn, NY 11320.

Indian—Crazy Crow Trading Post, PO Box 314B, Denison, TX 75020; *Kit*—Folk Art Emporium, 3591 Forest Haven Ln, Chesapeake, VA 23321; *Oriental*—National Carpet Co, 1384 Coney Island Ave, Brooklyn, NY 11320; *Rag*—Checkerberry Hill, 253 Westridge Ave, Daly City, CA 94015; Country Rugs, Box 99 H, RD 1, Kintnersville, PA 18930; Faith Mountain Country Fare, Main St, Box 199, Sperryville, VA 22740; Folkheart Rag Rugs, 18 Main St, Bristol, VT 05443; Heritage Rugs, PO Box 404, Street Rd, Lahaska, PA 18931; Jugtown Mountain Rugs, 791 Tower Rd, Enola, PA 17025; Lancaster Collection, PO Box 6074, Lancaster, PA 17603; Mulberry Magic, PO Box 62, Ruckersville, VA 22968; *Stenciled*—Adirondack Store and Gallery, 109 Saranac Ave, Lake Placid, NY 12946; The Barn, PO Box 25, Market St, Lehman, PA 18627; Legendary Folk Art, 342 East St, Pittsford, NY 14534; The Vine and Cupboard, PO Box 309, George Wright Rd, Woolwich, ME 04579.

Braided Patchwork, $127\frac{1}{2}$" x 68", Crazy Quilt design, polychrome wool yarns, early 20th C 800.00
Embroidered
   19 x 46", floral design on red felt, black wool fish scale border 200.00
   48 x 72", floral design, pastel colors on light green ground, 20th C . . . 125.00
   Wool, multicolored, pot of flowers on black center field, fish scale borders, cotton tape and embroidery binding 125.00
Hooked
   $12\frac{1}{2}$ x 24", floral design, brown ground 65.00

14 x $37\frac{1}{2}$", reclining dog, multicolored floral frame–type border 275.00
17 x $33\frac{1}{2}$", diamond design, multicolored, minor wear. 95.00
18 x 36", winter scene, two people riding horse–drawn sleigh, pine trees in background, c1900 . . . . 150.00
18 x 70", geometric diamond design, red, white, blue, and green, minor wear 550.00
$18\frac{1}{2}$ x 24", "Welcome" and floral design on black ground 70.00
$18\frac{1}{2}$ x 35", fox and stork, soft colors, minor wear and fading 195.00
19 x 36", yarn details, Indian in canoe, teepees in background, multicolored 125.00
19 x $40\frac{1}{2}$", stylized landscape, dog, two fawns, birds, and trees, multicolored 175.00
19 x 129", runner, dark triangles on red ground, black and olive borders 900.00
20 x 32", black and brown Airedale dog, stylized background, maroon trees, partially sheared, worn, repaired. 95.00
$21\frac{1}{2}$ x 35", rose design and "You Are Going Home Sunday Arn't You?," shades of red and green on two–tone gray ground, red inscription, blue border, several rows of stitches missing from border 255.00
22 x $38\frac{1}{2}$", three cat–like animals, brown on yellow ochre ground 200.00
$22\frac{1}{2}$ x $34\frac{1}{2}$", oval, bird and stylized flowers, shades of olive green, red, white, and blue, braided and crocheted oval border, worn, rebacked 125.00
23 x 35", hens, chicks, squirrels, and owls, multicolored. 345.00

Hooked, brown and black cat, pastel flowers, black border, yellow ground, 16 x $12\frac{1}{2}$", $165.00.

23 x 44½", plush wool, reclining dog lying on rug, three borders, pattern maker Edward Sands, ME, burlap backing **400.00**

23¾ x 39½", room interior, broom, chair, and spinning wheel, curtained window in background, gray walls, olive floor boards, red, blue, white, and black **150.00**

24 x 35", cattails and floral design on large oval, floral designs in spandrels on brown border, burlap backing **85.00**

24 x 38", geometric design, maroon ground **70.00**

25 x 38", landscape, dog sled and two men wearing parkas, labeled "Grenfell Labrador Industries" . .   **500.00**

25 x 39", stag in oval landscape, striped border, faded **95.00**

26 x 48½", central floral design on gray ground, stylized maroon leaf border, burlap backing **115.00**

26½ x 51", sheared, stagecoach and four horses, brown border, rounded corners **125.00**

27 x 34", dog, standing, surrounded by tulips, flowerheads, kitten, puppy, and "Old Shep," striped border, cotton and wool, red, yellow, blue, pink, magenta, and black on burlap ground, early 20th C **900.00**

28 x 52", tulips, striped ground, bright colors, crocheted yarn edge   **65.00**

28 x 61", stylized floral center on oblong beige ground, leaf border, burlap backing, overall edge wear, small repairs **115.00**

28½ x 45", two squirrels and bluejays, oak leaf border, shades of brown, black, gray, rust, and blue on gray and beige ground, cloth binding tape worn **125.00**

28½ x 51", oval landscape, cottage and pier on lake, floral border on dark brown ground, frayed edges   **100.00**

28½ x 52", stag in landscape, multicolored stylized floral border, pattern maker Edward Sands Frost, ME, burlap backing **200.00**

29 x 45", basket of flowers, Waldoboro–type, scatter rug, Maine, 19th C **500.00**

29 x 57", multicolored horizontal inside zigzag stripes, red and olive striped border **725.00**

29 x 64", two stylized floral medallions enclosed by abstract leaf designs, wear and fading, old rebinding **85.00**

29 x 90", multicolored jumbled rain-

bow designs, rebacked, old rebinding **525.00**

30 x 39", two Scotties, one brown, one white, red collars, black background, unused **400.00**

32 x 80", three flowers on confetti center, multicolored ripple design border. **450.00**

33 x 47", beaver on log, encircled by maple leaves, Grenfell type, late 19th, early 20th C **325.00**

33 x 52", two birds in center, facing same direction, black beaks, spindly legs, red, brown, black, beige, green, and orange fabric, large stylized leaves on dark brown border, 20th C **2,300.00**

33 x 65", two bluejays in stylized floral design, deep shades of red, blue, green, black, and olive brown, Greek key border, worn   **500.00**

34 x 54", stylized floral design on beige ground **250.00**

35½ x 65¼", two horned goats, facing each other in shaped reserve, maroon, gray, green, beige, and black fabric, meandering floral vine on gray border, c1930 . . . . .   **2,225.00**

40" l, Star of Bethlehem pattern, octagonal, multicolored. **350.00**

43¼ x 60", floral, red, beige, pale green, yellow, brown, black, and white spray of spring blossoms in shaped and scalloped reserve, key and knot pattern on green, red, and brown border, late 19th, early 20th C **825.00**

48 x 72", American flag, shirred wool, red, white, and blue, 20th C **3,300.00**

50 x 84", multicolored central floral design in scroll–edged oval on beige ground, leaf border, cloth backing. **850.00**

55 x 65", striped ground, solid dark colors, diamond borders, rebacked, pair originally one long carpet **900.00**

72 x 80", steam–powered ship, black and beige, flying red pennants, green and yellow seas, yellow chain inner border, rose chain on broad brown border, Waldoboro, ME, late 19th, early 20th C **9,900.00**

86" d, round, sailing ship, zodiac signs, mariner's compass, blue, maroon, yellow, beige, and white yarns, 20th C **250.00**

108 x 144", farm and garden motif, fruit, flowers, vegetables, animals, wheelbarrow, sheaf of

wheat, butter churn, corn crib, and other different designs on 108 individual squares, rect, c1940   **4,125.00**

134 x 29", runner, circles, multi-colored, three rows of fifteen 8½" d circles, black ground **650.00**

Machine Woven, 37 x 19", kittens on fence, red poppies in foreground . .   **415.00**

Navajo

30 x 62", Corral and "T" designs, old style dark warp, tan, red, and dark brown on natural white ground, c1900, selvage breaks, bleeding **125.00**

31 x 60", Ganado design, stepped terrace design, red, dark brown, and natural white on arbrush tan ground, worn, repaired **250.00**

32½ x 55", traditional geometric diamond design, faded red, brown, natural dye green, tan, black, and white, c1910, repaired ends, minor selvage breaks **250.00**

33 x 38", Toadlena area, natural tan, black, and white wool, minor edge wear **55.00**

34½ x 69", transitional period, natural brown, arbrush tan, tan, and natural white, repaired **175.00**

36 x 17", Saltillo design, stylized, red, dark brown, and carded brown on white ground **150.00**

36 x 48", geometric diamond and hourglass design, light brown and black on white ground, red binding **200.00**

36 x 56", Ganado/Klagetoh feather pictorial design, dark brown, arbrush tan, natural white, and faded aniline red, small breaks in wool.   **375.00**

36 x 59", early West Reservation geometric stripe pattern, dark brown, natural white, tan, and gray, faded aniline red stripe. . . .   **200.00**

38 x 19", Ganado design, red, black, and white banded St Andrew's Cross, stripe ends **245.00**

38 x 55", Ganado with Tees–nos–Pas border design, red, dark brown, tan, and natural white hand spun wool **500.00**

38 x 66", classic geometric design, red, gold, gray, and dark brown on natural white ground, c1940   **405.00**

38 x 70", transitional period, serrate design, cross center, dark brown, arbrush tan, and faded red on natural white ground, c1900, wear, broken selvage threads **200.00**

39 x 60", West reservation stylized

corn stalk design, feather edge, natural brown, small repair. **200.00**

40 x 59", early Modified Storm pattern, tan, black, and white on aniline red ground, c1915, removable bleeding, small holes, selvage breaks **325.00**

46 x 74", serrate diamond design, red, russet, tan, black, and gray on natural white ground, c1930, weft selvage cord broken **300.00**

47 x 44", Diamond Stripe pattern, white, gray, brown, orange, and red, black stripes **100.00**

50 x 37", Wide Ruins design, feather and stripe design, natural dye colors, dark brown ground **300.00**

52 x 70", diamond design, bright aniline dyed colors, black hand-spun wool, cotton warp, 2" damaged area one end, 1880–90 . . .   **1,400.00**

55 x 36", J B Moore design, tan terraced diamonds, orange and dark brown outlining, natural carded ground **125.00**

55 x 88", transitional period, natural color wool, dark brown, carded tan, and white, weft breakage . . .   **400.00**

63 x 41", Diamond pattern, red, black, and gray, white ground. . .   **225.00**

Oriental

53 x 41", Perepedil, Northeast Caucasus, ram's horn motifs, red, navy blue, ivory, and deep gold small medallions and bird figures on midnight blue field, red flower-head and vine border, late 19th C   **2,000.00**

53 x 50", Kula Prayer, West Anatolia, star flower decorated royal blue field, sky blue spandrels, narrow black cross panels, ivory and black shobokli border, 1850–1900. . . . .   **825.00**

54 x 40", Yagcibedir Prayer, West Anatolia, rows of red and ivory stars on midnight blue field, red spandrels, midnight blue cross panel within red indented flower-head border, late 19th C. **925.00**

54 x 52", Bessarabian Corridor Kelim, three roundrels with identical scene of a man and woman surrounded by foliage, rose, blue, gold, tan, green, and teal on dark brown field, summer blossoms and leaves border, dated 1877 . .   **9,900.00**

56 x 46", Marasali Prayer, East Caucasus, staggered rows of red, sky blue, gold, and light green rayed boteh, midnight blue field, ivory striped boteh border, 1870–1900   **2,250.00**

Oriental, Heriz rug, midnight blue water bug, palmette, and vine border, red field, large angular medallion anchored in fan palmettes, extending to stylized flowers, leaves, ivory and red spandrels, 8' 4" x 11' 1", $3,500.00.

57 x 43", Kashan, Central Persia, circular lobed royal blue and rose medallion, blossoming vines, and royal blue spandrels on red field, midnight blue palmette and arabesque vine border, early 20th C   **650.00**

58 x 34", Baluch, Northeast Persia, sawtooth diamond lattice of navy blue, dark brown, and rust hooked hexagonal medallions, camel field, apricot geometric border, 1875–1900 . . . .   **825.00**

58 x 48", Chi–Chi, Northeast Caucasus, red, royal blue, gold, green, and teal octagons and hooked polygons in alternating rows, black rosette and diagonal bar border, 1870–1900 . . . .   **2,225.00**

64 x 38", Shirvan, East Caucasus, three red and gold indented diamond medallions flanked by four aubergine cruciform medallions and other geometric motifs on abrashed navy blue field, ivory flowerhead and vine border, late 19th C **1,750.00**

85 x 57", Kazak, Southwest Caucasus, three hooked diamond medallions in navy and royal blue, pale gold, aubergine, and teal, red field, ivory crab border, late 19th C **2,300.00**

104 x 63", Qashqai Kelim, Southwest Persia, narrow horizontal bands of small stepped diamonds in shades of red, gold, royal blue, ivory, and dark brown, stepped reciprocal border, late 19th C . . .   **1,975.00**

116 x 96", Ersari, West Turkestan, three columns of seven blue, apricot, and ivory gulli–guls with starburst secondaries on deep red field, red concentric diamond border, multicolored compartmented leaf motif elems, mid 19th C **5,500.00**

120 x 53", Uzbek Jajim, West Turkestan, geometric motifs on horizontal bands alternating with small rosettes, dark red, blue, and green, early 20th C **450.00**

120 x 59", Malayer Sarouk, West Persia, red, rose, blue, tan–gold, and teal rosettes and floral sprays on abrashed navy blue field, dark red palmette and flowering vine border, early 20th C **2,750.00**

124 x 57", Gendje, South Central Caucasus, columns of five stepped diamond medallions in shades of dark red, royal blue, gold, ivory, and dark teal, abrashed navy blue field, ivory wine cup and serrated leaf border, late 19th C **2,750.00**

126 x 88", Mahal, West Persia, blue, rose, gold, ivory, and teal rosettes and small blossoming vines on abrashed terra cotta red field, midnight blue rosette and flowerhead border, early 20th C **3,250.00**

138 x 110", Soumak, Northeast Caucasus, four large concentric navy and royal blue, rust, rose, and dark teal diamond medallions flanked by eight mustard octagons and other small medallions on rust red field, narrow black leaf and vine meander border, early 20th C **3,500.00**

144 x 57", Konya Kelim, Central Anatolia, rows of rose, blue, gold, aubergine, and teal double wing-like motifs, ivory field, red–rose eli–belinde border, dark brown elems, c1850. . . . .   **2,425.00**

146 x 108", Kashan, West Persia, realistically drawn floral sprays with slender curved leaves in red, rose, sky blue, camel, soft brown, and teal, midnight blue field, red palmette and blossoming vine border, c1925 . . . .   **4,500.00**

148 x 106", Serapi, Northwest Persia, navy blue, camel, and rose gabled square medallion with navy palmette pendants on abrashed terra cotta red field, camel and navy blue spandrels, navy blue rosette and serrated leaf border, late 19th C **4,675.00**

154 x 120", Tabriz, Northwest Per-

sia, ogival lattice of curving red vertical bands enclosing red, sky blue, tan–gold, and gray–green boteh and small blossoms, ivory field, ivory triple flowerhead and leafy vine border, c1925. . . . . . . **1,500.00**

160 x 98″, Fereghan Sarouk, West Persia, small ivory and teal pendanted diamond medallion surrounded by palmettes, cloud bands, and floral sprays, blue, tan, beige, and teal, abrashed rust–red field, midnight blue palmette and indented leaf border, early 20th C **6,500.00**

Penny Rug

19 x 120″, runner, diamond design, wool, dark solid colors and black on pale green ground **375.00**

$27\frac{1}{2}$ x 61″, six–sided, multicolored wool felt on blue denim ground, green felt border **205.00**

30 x 34″, hexagonal, applique wool, star design, multicolored, worn, faded **150.00**

Woven Rag, 27″ w, 13′ long, multicolored, three strips make one large carpet. **175.00**

SEWING AND WEAVING IMPLEMENTS

History: A wide variety of sewing items were found in almost every rural home. Necessity required that rural housewives were skilled in dress making, sewing, and sewing repairs. Just as the farmer valued his tools, the rural housewife treasured her favorite sewing implements.

Many implements served special functions. Sewing birds, an interesting convenience item, were used to hold cloth (in the bird's beak) while sewing. Made of iron or brass, they could be attached to table or shelf with a screw–type fixture. Later models featured a pin cushion.

Sewing implements were frequently received as gifts and passed down from generation to generation. Many manufacturers used sewing implements as giveaway premiums. Advertising needle threaders and needle holders are two examples.

Although large–size weaving was left to professionals, many rural housewives did have small tape and ribbon looms. Also found along with sewing implements are tools associated with carding and spinning. Although no longer used, they tended to be saved for nostalgic reasons.

References: Joyce Clement, *The Official Price Guide To Sewing Collectibles,* House of Collectibles, 1987; Victor Houart, *Sewing Accessories: An Illustrated History,* Souvenir Press (London),

1984; Gay Ann Rogers, *American Silver Thimbles,* Haggerston Press, 1989; Gay Ann Rogers, *An Illustrated History of Needlework Tools,* John Murray (London), 1983; Estelle Zalkin, *Zalkin's Handbook Of Thimbles & Sewing Implements,* First Edition, Warman Publishing Co., 1988.

Collectors' Club: Thimble Collectors International, PO Box 2311, Des Moines, IA 50310.

Periodical: *Thimbletter,* 93 Walnut Hill Road, Highlands, MA 02161.

Museums: Fabric Hall, Historic Deerfield, Deerfield, MA; Museum of American History, Smithsonian Institution, Washington, D.C.; Shelburne Museum, Shelburne, VT.

Reproduction Manufacturers: *General*—Braid–Aid, 466 Washington St, Rte 53, Pembroke, MA 02359; The Examplarery, PO Box 2554, Dearborn, MI 48123; Hearthside Quilts, Box 429, Rte 7, Shelburne, VT 05482; The Hooking Room, 1840 House, 237 Pine Point Rd, Scarborough, ME 04074; *Old Spools, Bobbins, and Shuttles*—Joel S Perkins & Son–Vt, Inc, PO Box 76, South Strafford, VT 05070; *Spinning Wheels and Supplies*—Log Cabin Shop, Box 275, Lodi, OH 44254; The Coverlet Co, PO Box 02–616, Portland, OR 97202; *Weaving*—The Golden Lamb, 9 Meadow Ln, Lancaster, PA 17601.

Bobbins, lace maker's, wooden, turned, orig box **45.00**

Box

$6\frac{3}{4}$″ d, 3″ h, round, cov, Shaker, bentwood, swivel handle, orig pale blue silk damask lining, old varnish finish **400.00**

7″ h, Shaker, hardwood, one drawer, thread compartment, pin cushion finial, old red varnish stain finish **75.00**

$7\frac{1}{4}$″ l, oval, cov, Shaker, bentwood, three finger construction base, one finger construction lid, copper tacks, bentwood swivel handle, worn silk lining, accessories, natural finish **250.00**

10″ l, rect, cov, rosewood veneer, inlaid brass and wood floral designs, fitted red satin and gold star–patterned red paper interior **125.00**

$11\frac{1}{2}$″ l, cov, Lehneware, pine, red, black, and yellow striping, gilded transfer designs, floral decoupage, and "1875" date on brown ground, turned feet, lift–out fitted interior tray, orig lock and key . . . **350.00**

12″ h, primitive, hardwood and pine, one drawer, tiered thread caddy, wooden pins, traces of old finish **25.00**

13" l, 4½" h, cov, pine, rect, deco-
rated, grain painted **80.00**
13½" d, cov, bentwood, natural
smoked finish, gold and silver
stenciled dec **100.00**
Crochet Thread Holder, figural, apple,
thread through stem, 4 x 3½" **25.00**
Darner, ebony, emb floral handle
marked "Sterling" **40.00**
Distaff, chip carved designs, 42" l . . .   **85.00**
Emery, cat head, black **18.00**
Hatchel, flax comb, primitive, hard-
wood and pine, one fine and one
coarse group of iron spikes, 23½" l   **45.00**
Loom, pine, mortised and pinned construction, wrought iron fittings, two
replaced treadles, 27 x 37½ x 49" h   **275.00**
Loom Light, wrought iron, hanging,
candle arm on adjustable trammel,
adjusts from 33" h **150.00**
Needle Case, toleware, dark brown ja-
panning, red and yellow stylized fo-
liage dec, 9" l **105.00**
Niddy–Noddy
9" l, cherry, turned detail, old dark
finish **195.00**
18½" l, wood, turned, bentwood
brace is old replacement **25.00**
Pin Cushion
Cossack, 4½" h, stuffed cloth, worn   **10.00**
Dog, 5¼" h, stuffed velvet, embroi-
dered features, glass eyes, orange
ribbon bow, worn and faded **15.00**
Heart, 6¼" h, red satin, colored–
head pins dec **45.00**
Strawberry, 8" h, folk art, red and
green, large inverted strawberry
on pressed glass base, four smaller
hanging needle–sharpener straw-
berries **200.00**
Quilt Rack, primitive, old blue paint
on 33" l oak tapered and chamfered
legs, adjustment holes in four pine
bars, 95 x 111" largest size, missing
fastening wedges **25.00**
Rug Hook, wood, cast iron, and steel,
marked "Jewel," block and floral
dec, dated 1886 . . . .   **105.00**
Sewing Bird
4" h, cast and wrought iron, heart
shaped thumb screw **150.00**
4¼" h, iron, heart shaped thumb
screw **135.00**
4¾" h, brass, old worn pin cushion,
heart shaped thumb screw **160.00**
5" h, brass, two worn pin cushions,
table clamp **165.00**
5¼" h, silver plated brass, large and
small pin cushions, table clamp   **125.00**
Shuttle, wood **60.00**
Spinning Wheel
19¼" l, cast iron, table clamp, hand

**Sewing Bird, silver plated, patent dated
1853, 3⅝" l bird, 5¼" h, $125.00.**

crank, orig yellow striping on
black paint, old welded repair . . .   **85.00**
23½" h, wood, slender turnings, chip
carving, damaged **130.00**
30" h, wood, chair frame type, gray
weathered finish, old repairs and
replacements, new distaff **50.00**
32½" h, wood, two spindles, turned
members, old patina, age cracks
in wheel **150.00**
35" h, wood, hardwood, two spin-
dles, three turned legs, chip
carved detail, stamped "S.B.,"
old brown finish **150.00**
39" h, hardwood, chair frame type,
old refinish **175.00**
39½" h, hardwoods, turned and chip
carved detail, old dark patina . . .   **200.00**
45½" h, wood, chair frame type,
hardwood, old brown patina. . . .   **300.00**
32" h, hard and soft woods, 19" d
wheel, replaced distaff **325.00**
46" h, vertical, hardwoods, turned
details, double bobbins and
spinners, old dark finish **245.00**
Stretcher Frame, 23½" w, 30" h, ma-
hogany, turned, adjustable, worn
finish **275.00**
Swift
17" h, wood, table clamp, needs re-
stringing **55.00**

**Swift, umbrella style, walnut with pine
standard, Shaker, $150.00.**

23½" h, wood, orig yellow varnish
finish **100.00**
24" h, umbrella type, wood, accordion folding slats, table clamp, orig yellow varnish. **125.00**
39½" h, hardwood and pine, four squirrel cages, vertical adjustable post, old patina **45.00**
47" h, hard and soft woods, two squirrel cages, adjustable reel, four legs, old dark patina, 47" h **105.00**

Table Clamp
3½" l, cast bronze. **35.00**
4" l, cast iron, table screw clamp, set of four. **100.00**

Tape Loom
14¾" l, oak, spatula shaped, fish tail handle, old patina **155.00**
19¼" l, poplar, old gray–blue paint **125.00**
20¾" l, 8" w, paddle shaped, old patina. **115.00**
21½" l, 12½" w, hard and soft woods, leather and metal fittings, two heddles. **150.00**
22" l, wood, two heddles, old patina **250.00**
25½" l, primitive, pine, wrought iron nails, old patina. **40.00**
27¾" l, vertical, hardwood, paddle shaped, ftd base. **55.00**
28" l, primitive, paddle shaped, oak, old worn patina **45.00**

Tape Measure, pig in red shoe, celluloid **35.00**

Tatting Shuttle
Celluloid, adv, Lydia Pinkham, portrait top, adv bottom. **100.00**
Sterling Silver, marked "1912". . . . **65.00**

Thimble
Advertising
Clark's O.N.T., "Our New Thread," brass **20.00**
Domestic Sewing Machine, silver **50.00**
Scenic Band, silver, early 20th C . . **25.00**
Thimble Holder, 3" l, ivory, acorn shaped, allover sinuous leaf carving **85.00**

Thread Caddy
9½" h, turned hardwood, ebonized trim, flanged base **90.00**
9⅝" h, mahogany, turned, two tiers, flanged base **150.00**

Yarn Winder
12" h, turned hardwood, tripod base, snake feet, old finish **250.00**
25½" h, 22" l, hardwoods, old blue paint. **160.00**

Yarn Winder, turned hardwood, six spokes, $95.00.

30" h, 29" d reel, six turned spokes, old red repaint. **105.00**
31½" h, 26½" d reel, geared counting mechanism, four turned spokes, gray weathered finish, age cracks, handle missing from reel. **90.00**
32" h, 26" d reel, hardwood, geared counting mechanism, good patina **75.00**
34½" h, 30" d reel, turned hardwoods, six spokes, chip carved base stamped "A. Love," refinished **95.00**
35" h, 27" d reel, horizontal shaft, geared counting mechanism, four splayed legs, old worn patina, age cracks in reel **110.00**
36" h, 25" d reel, turned detail, box base, four splayed legs, geared counting mechanism with "click," old red paint **90.00**
36½" h, 30" d reel, floor standing, turned hard and soft woods, geared counting mechanism with "click," old brown patina. **75.00**
37" h, primitive, pine, turned post, four part interior in dovetailed box base, scalloped dividers **150.00**
38¾" h, vertical type, hardwood frame, pine staves, old natural patina, some staves replaced **50.00**
42" h, 26½" d reel, hardwoods, four spokes, four splayed legs, geared counter mechanism, wooden hand, scored face. **100.00**
47" h, hardwoods, turned, six spokes, chip carved base, four splayed legs, traces of old red finish, turned reel handle missing . . **75.00**

VEHICLES AND ACCESSORIES

While Country collectors and decorators emphasize the vehicles and accessories from the horse–drawn vehicle era, there is a growing collector interest in steam and gasoline powered equipment. Country collecting is focusing more and more on twentieth century rural America. The following is the first listing in a general Country price guide to blend old with new.

The decorating community views vehicles and vehicle accessories primarily as accent pieces. They frequently can be found in department store window displays. Favorite forms include sleighs and surreys. Animal–drawn children's carts are also popular. Since decorators want the vehicles for effect, they are willing to accept defects.

Individuals who collect and restore vehicles for display or use are much more demanding. They want the vehicles in working order with as many original parts as possible. Just as in the automobile field, there is a strong tendency to over-restore, i.e., make the vehicle look as though it just left the carriage shop or factory.

The formation of collectors' clubs contributed significantly to the preservation of farm equipment. These clubs, along with specialized periodicals, allowed a network to be established for the exchange of information and parts. You will find them exhibiting at most farm shows and state agricultural fairs.

Within the paper collecting community, farm equipment advertising and catalogs enjoy strong collecting interest. Again, the principal emphasis is on horse–drawn vehicles, albeit the interest in steam and gasoline powered vehicle material is growing.

Periodicals: *Antique Power*, PO Box 838, Yellow Springs, OH 45387; *The Belt Pulley*, PO Box 83, Nokomis, IL 62075; *The Country Wagon Journal*, PO Box 331, West Milford, NJ 07480; *Farm Antique News*, PO Box 96, Tarkio, MO 64491; *Iron Man Album*, PO Box 328, Lancaster, PA 17603; *Red Power Newsletter*, Box 277, Battle Creek, IA 51006; *Rusty Iron Monthly*, PO Box 342, Sandwich, IL 60548.

Collectors' Clubs: Antique Engine, Tractor & Toy Club, Rt 1, Box 385, Slatington, PA 18080; J. I. Case Collectors' Association, Inc., Rt 2, Box 242, Vinton, OH 45686; Early American Steam Engine & Old Equipment Society, PO Box 652, Red Lion, PA 17356; International Harvester Collectors, RR 2, Box 286, Winamac, IN 46996; The M–M Collectors Club, 409 Sheridan Drive, Eldridge, IA 52748; Midwest Old Settlers & Threshers Association, Rt 1, Threshers Rd, Mt. Pleasant, IA 52641; Rough & Tumble Engineers' Historical Association, Box 9, Kinzers, PA 17535.

Reproduction Manufacturers: *Horse–Drawn Vehicles*—Cumberland General Store, Rte 3, Crossville, TN 38555; J T Nicholas & Son, 704 N Michigan Ave, Howell, MI 48843; *Miniature Vehicle Kits*—Criss–Cross Creations, Box 324, Wayne, NJ 07470; *Sleigh Bells*—Conewago Junction, 805 Oxford Rd, New Oxford, PA 17350.

Accessories
  Conestoga Wagon Box, pine, slant top, wrought iron strap hinges and decorative hardware
    17" w, 21" h, traces of old paint **300.00**
    18½" w, 17½" h, old blue repaint **1,000.00**
  Lamps, pr, Brewster & Co', NY, sgd **1,800.00**
Seats
  Buggy, child size, 27½" l, wooden plank seat and back, wrought iron frame **375.00**
  Conestoga Wagon, 30½" w, hard and soft woods, cutout ends, chamfered edges, shoe feet, old worn red repaint over black . . . **575.00**
Sleigh, 33" w, hardwood, bench style **70.00**
Wagon
  22¼" h, double, ladder back, pointed finials, turned, woven splint seat, old finish . . . **650.00**
  32¼" h, 33½" w, double, ladder back, turned front legs, replaced woven splint seats . . **550.00**
  40" w, pine, bootjack ends, old refinishing **240.00**

Sleigh Bells, graduated, 29 bells, 90" l, c1870, $225.00.

Sleigh Bells, 8 feet long, twenty 2½" h numbered brass bells, wide leather strap, orig red paint, geometric dec, 1880 . . . .   135.00

Step

    Buggy, cast iron, rect foot plate attached to angled support, ornamental treads, pr. 28.00

    Carriage, cast iron, cut–out plate on U–shaped support, c1870   25.00

    Tool Box, wagon, 16 feet long, 5¼" w, 8½" h to top of spout, wooden, cast iron oil spout dome and cut–out end panels, marked "Whitely". 145.00

    Trim, from horse–drawn carriage, cast iron, ornamental, cross designs, 19th C 24.00

    Wagon Wheel Hub, hickory, iron axle throats and bands 10.00

Horse–Drawn Vehicles

Brougham

    Demarest & Co, dark blue body, blue suede upholstery, wheels on rubber, orig front wheel brakes, pole, restored 4,100.00

    Healey & Co, NY, ¾ size, equipped with brakes, wheels on rubber, serial #2590 . . . . .   5,700.00

    Henry Killam, Broadway, NY, serial #3259, marked on hubcaps   1,075.00

Buckboard

    J J Haydock Carriage Co, Cincinnati, OH, natural wood body, burgundy wheels and shafts, stick seat, shafts 1,650.00

    Unknown Maker, stick seat, black body, burgundy running gear and upholstery, brass trim, cargo rack on back, removable back seat, wheels on rubber, shafts. 2,800.00

Buggy

    Concord type, W A Patterson, Flint, MI, folding top, side springs, wheels on rubber, shafts, restored 1,800.00

Doctor's

    Unknown Maker, 50" wheels, painted, gold leaf trim, shafts   1,800.00

    W F Whiton & Co, Bangor, ME, pneumatic tires, shafts 325.00

    Pony, unknown maker, pony size, wicker sides, fenders, wheels on rubber, shafts, pole, restored 3,000.00

    Road, A P Stevens, Athens, PA, midnight blue, white stick seat, leather sides, pole, shafts, restored 2,300.00

    Side Bar, H H Babcock Co, dark green body, white stick seat, gold trim, wire spoke wheels   900.00

    Side Spring, Clarence Lowell, New Bedford, MA, black, top, shafts. 750.00

Carriage

    Amish, unknown maker, brakes, lights, shafts 285.00

    Child's, C L Stone & Sons, Harford, CT, black, red and green striping, red striped wheels, fold–down top, black tufted upholstery, maker's name stamped under seat 1,000.00

Cart

Governess

    Van Tassell and Kearney, NY, four wheels, black body, yellow wicker basket, wheels on rubber 700.00

    Unknown Maker, pony size, maroon and black body, wicker basket, gray upholstery, wheels on rubber, restored 2,900.00

    Horse, Brewster & Co, Broome St, NY, marked on brass wheel caps, small horse size 400.00

    Pony, D & J Furniture Co 775.00

    Road, unknown maker, storage under seat, orig leather harness   200.00

    Tandem, Columbia Buggy Co, Detroit, MI, black and maroon, ivory wicker sides and back, drivers wedge, wheels on rubber, two sets of shafts, product #976 marked under seat, restored 3,100.00

    Village, Van Tassell & Kearney, NY, burgundy body, yellow running gear, black upholstery, wood hub, wheels on rubber, Dennet 3–spring suspension, wooden dash and fenders, fulcrum shafts, height adjustment at rear, two rear steps, c1905, restored 1,100.00

Coach

Pall Bearer's, Cunningham, maroon and black body, beveled glass windows, wheels on rubber, pole **10,000.00**

Pony, unknown maker, black and yellow body, black striping, red running gear, brakes, crab end pole, leader bars. **15,500.00**

Road, Brewster & Co, New York, NY, The Outlaw, black and yellow body, yellow striping, wheels on rubber, brakes, boxes in rear boot, crab end pole, serial #22800 . . . . **49,500.00**

Stage, Abbott & Downing, red body, yellow gear, leather slung, side curtains, brakes, pole, serial #339 . . . . **11,200.00**

Gig

Brewster & Co, NY, Stanhope, Brewster green and black, leather dash and fenders, wheel wrench, shaft stand, serial #24788, marked on brass wheel hub **5,000.00**

Unknown Maker, wicker body and dash, woven diamond design on sides, c–spring **2,700.00**

Hansom Cab, unknown maker, black body, red tufted upholstered interior **400.00**

Hearse

C P Kimball & Co, Chicago, IL, black, ornately carved wood, lamps, shafts, hub wrench, plated cross, wheels on rubber, removable sleigh runners, funeral establishment name painted both sides. **5,800.00**

Unknown Maker, bowed front, full fifth wheel cut under, wheels on steel, pole **2,400.00**

Jenny Lind, unknown maker, side springs, stick seat, side curtains **850.00**

Phaeton

American Stanhope, unknown maker, folding top, royal blue, camel hair cloth upholstery, cut under with reach, wheels on rubber, shafts **3,500.00**

Doctor's, Ferd F French & Co, Ltd, Boston, MA, folding top **1,400.00**

Drop Front, Brewster & Co, NY, burgundy and natural wood finish,. black folding top, wheels on rubber, shafts, serial #18301. . . . . **5,500.00**

Folding Top, Kimball, Boston, MA, wheels on rubber, shafts, old restoration **2,150.00**

Gentleman's

Studebaker, black body, carmine gear, tuckaway groom's seat, cut under with reach, wheels on rubber, shafts, restored **7,700.00**

Unknown Maker, green, yellow striping, wicker seat, dash, and groom's seat, cut under, wheels on rubber, shafts **6,600.00**

Lady's

J E Guyer, Waverly, NY, parasol top, burgundy, black, and wicker body, wicker dash, fenders, and groom's seat, wheels on rubber, tan Bedford cord upholstery, shafts, shaft stand, pole, yoke, serial #3711, tag located under toeboard, restored. **7,200.00**

J M Quimby, Newark, NJ, parasol top, Webster green, yellow striping, wicker seat, groom's seat, and dash, whipcord cushioned seats, shafts with patent leather, restored **5,700.00**

T W Lane Carriage Co, Amesbury, MA, drop front, blue and black, auto folding top, fenders, shafts, wrench **2,900.00**

William R Bishop, 36 Warren St, NY, wicker, natural finish, shafts **1,900.00**

Rockaway

Coupe, H H Babcock Co, Watertown, NY, black, red, and natural body, natural finish wheels, wheels on rubber, shafts, whipple tree, old restoration **2,500.00**

Curtain, S E Bailey Co, Lancaster, PA, dark green and wine, leather upholstery, cut under with reach, pole, shafts, c1910 . . . . **2,600.00**

Runabout

Columbus Carriage & Harness Co, Columbus, OH, spindle seat, shafts, bicycle axle **1,225.00**

John Moore & Co, Warrent St, NY, pony size, wheels on rubber, shafts **540.00**

Unknown Maker, tulip seat, black body, restored black upholstery, yellow wheels, wheels on rubber, shafts **900.00**

Van Tassell & Kearny, 130–132 E 13th St, NY, pony size, natural wood finish, cut under with reach, wheels on rubber, shafts and pole **3,600.00**

Sleighs
Albany Cutter
Charles Schlosser, 03 Loch St, Syracuse, NY, black, maroon panels and runners, striping, burgundy upholstery, shafts, restored **2,100.00**
C T Nevens, Auburn, ME, striping, artist sgd paint "G. Gisgen, Pntr.," shafts, c1865 . . .   **1,000.00**
Flandrau & Co, NY, four passenger, black body, red runners, gold striping, decorative plumes attached to dash, shafts **1,400.00**
H Murray, Niles, MI, burgundy, green, and black, striping, shafts **2,500.00**
R Millers Son, Kutztown, PA, Brewster green and burgundy body, tufted upholstered seat, shafts with shaft bells **2,000.00**
Unknown Maker, four passenger, dark green and maroon, brushed striping and scroll work, scene on back, triple striping, maroon mohair upholstery, pole, restored **3,100.00**
William Winter, Schoharie, NY, carved eagle heads on dash ironwork, orig paint and striping. **1,450.00**
Basket, unknown maker, wicker body **290.00**
Bob
J Colyer & Co, Newark NJ, pony size, four passenger, black body, red bob runners. **2,100.00**
Unknown Maker, black, red trim and runners, collapsible driver's seat swings both directions, brakes, pole, 12 volt headlight **750.00**
Box, T C Sawyer, South Amesbury, MA, red and black body, black leatherette upholstery, shafts, restored **400.00**
Butcher's, unknown maker, painted "E. L. Whitcomb" on sides, bob runners, canvas sides, orig butcher block and tools **3,400.00**
Cabriolet, unknown maker, black body, gold striping, ornate ironwork **1,550.00**
Country Cutter, unknown maker, red body, gray tufted upholstered seat, rein rail, restored   **550.00**
Hearse, unknown maker, bob runners **850.00**
Pony, unknown maker, "Manu-

factured for Wise Bros., Lewisberry, PA" tag, removable sleigh body, shafts **700.00**
Portland Cutter
Blackhall & Co, Troy, NY, black and red body, red runners **700.00**
S B Wise & Sons, Orrstown, PA, shafts, late 1800s **450.00**
Sturtevant & Larrabee Co, Binghamton, NY, Welsh pony size, black, red runners and shafts, lambs wool seat cover   **575.00**
Racing, unknown maker, black body, maroon undercarriage, gold striping, maroon tufted upholstery, restored **2,200.00**
Squareback Cutter
Charles Childs & Co, Utica, NY, black body, tan upholstery, yellow runners **625.00**
John S Wilber, Sandy Hill, NY,, black body, gold striping, red upholstery **550.00**
Unknown Maker, green, red upholstery, shafts, maker's tag. . .   **400.00**
Surrey, unknown maker, four passenger, bob runners **550.00**
Swell Body Cutter, unknown maker, dark green and maroon, striping, maroon mohair upholstery, shafts, restored **3,000.00**
Trap, unknown maker, oak, burgundy body, striping, gray wool upholstery, spindled sides, front seat moves back and forth for easy entry, folddown back seat, shafts **3,400.00**
Victoria, panel boot, Brewster & Co, Broome St, NY, pole **3,400.00**
Vis–A–Vis
Heiko Wurhmann, six to eight passenger, burgundy, navy upholstery, hand carved lion heads both sides, brass trim, hand crank brake, brass heads on pole, restored **2,900.00**
Unknown Maker, black body, yellow runners, two screens in front of coachman's seat, doors on both sides of passenger's seats **3,300.00**
Wicker Cutter, unknown maker, dark green and yellow platform and runners, wicker body, restored **400.00**
Sulky, unknown maker, cob size, natural finish, cane seat, shaft irons, black hickory shafts, c1891   **425.00**
Surrey
Michigan Buggy Co, pony size,

four passenger, cut under with reach, canopy fringe top, whip holder, shafts **1,600.00**

Studebaker, four passenger, auto top, black body, maroon wheels, striping on side enclosures, shafts, marked on step treads, new top and sides **2,050.00**

Unknown Maker, four passenger, canopy fringe top, side spring, natural wood finish, tan upholstery, brakes, wheels on rubber, shafts **1,500.00**

Trap

A T Demarest, side bar, natural wood finish, beige upholstery, rear seat reverses to face forward or backward, wheels on rubber, pole, yoke, restored . .   **2,800.00**

Unknown Maker, back to back seating, black body, maroon undercarriage, natural wicker sides, striping on siding, cut under with reach, wheels on rubber, shafts, restored **3,200.00**

Viceroy, unknown maker, natural wood finish, stick seat, wire spoke pneumatic wheels, two sets of shafts **300.00**

Wagon

Amish, Harper, sliding doors, 1920s **2,500.00**

Bronson

Clark Coach Co, black and maroon, ivory striping, maroon upholstery, cut under with reach, wheels on rubber, pole, shafts, lamps, restored   **3,500.00**

Unknown Maker, natural wood finish, cut under with reach, drivers wedge seat, wheels on rubber, shafts **2,500.00**

Calliope, Gus Kelting, Germany, pony size, 114" long, 69" wide hub to hub, 91" h to top of flare board, carved and painted, circle gear, tongue pole, body pole for six–up hitch, red sunburst wheels. **1,600.00**

Democrat, unknown maker, natural wood finish, oak shadow box side panels, adjustable seats, five sets of springs, new foam rubber cushions, c1870, restored **2,100.00**

Explosives, unknown maker, parasol top, black body, red running gear, side springs, brakes, wheels on steel, "Explosives" painted on sides **2,300.00**

Express, C Eastman & Sons, West Concord, NH, former fire

wagon from South Berwick, ME, brass rails on sides of body, gold striping, pole, shafts **3,500.00**

Farm

Studebaker, green, red gear, spring seats, brakes, pole . . .   **575.00**

Unknown Maker, high box body, stenciled sideboards, metal wheels, handset brake, cast iron step. **225.00**

Hay

Gruber Wagon Works, 1$\frac{3}{4}$" axle, 14 foot hay bed, pole, hay rack, serial #1116 running gear. **4,500.00**

Unknown Maker, stake body, rect hardwood bed, iron–rimmed wheels. **135.00**

Hitch, unknown maker, red, white wheels, gold trim, full fifth wheel cut under, brakes, brass trim, pole, restored. **1,850.00**

Huckster, unknown maker, "W. Steigerwalt, Bowmanstown, PA" painted on sides, brakes, pole, lamps **5,200.00**

Ice, unknown maker, stenciled sideboards. **550.00**

Mail, unknown maker, red and blue body, red running gear, shafts, "Rural Delivery Route No. 2, U. S. Mail" and American flag painted on sides, restored **725.00**

Popcorn, Cretors, cut under, advertising painted on sides **2,000.00**

Showman's, Smith & Sons Carriage Co, Barnesville, GA, louvered racks on back hold circus tent, brakes, c1880 . . . .   **2,100.00**

Spray Rig, unknown maker, NY, cast iron axles, cast iron and forged spoked wheels, wood plank platform, 1890–1900 . .   **145.00**

Spring

Studebaker, six passenger, brakes, pole **1,800.00**

Unknown Maker, upholstered seats, steel leaf springs, cast iron steps, painted, faded stenciling **450.00**

Wright Bros, Deckertown, NJ, four passenger, canopy top, Brewster green body, red gear, wheels on rubber, brakes, pole, shafts, c1890, restored **2,700.00**

Water, Studebaker, yellow, black trim, wheels on steel, brakes, full fifth wheel cut under, meter on top of tank, sprinkler on rear, restored **7,500.00**

Tractors
Case
   1921, 10–18 . . . . **2,000.00**
   1925, Cross motor, restored **6,000.00**
   1935, model C, rubber, spokes **2,400.00**
   1937, model L, on steel, runs . . . **825.00**
   1950, model SC **675.00**
Farmall
   1930, Regular **900.00**
   1938, model F–14, rubber **1,750.00**
   1940, model B, mower **1,900.00**
   1946, model M, restored **2,300.00**
   1949, model MD, complete, runs **600.00**
Ford, 1953, model NAA **2,250.00**
Fordson
   1923, on steel, runs **2,300.00**
   1936, rubber, runs **1,100.00**
Gray, 1916, three wheel **15,000.00**
Hart–Parr, 1925, 28–50 . . . . **2,500.00**
John Deere
   1931, model GPWT, restored . . . **8,000.00**

1935, model A, factory round
   spokes **1,300.00**
1936, model B, on steel **2,200.00**
1941, model AR **1,350.00**
1951, model AR **1,950.00**
1952, model 50 . . . . **1,075.00**
1953, model 50 . . . . **2,000.00**
1955, model 80 . . . . **4,200.00**
Lawson, 1925, full jeweled **1,500.00**
Mc–Deering
   1936, model O–12, rubber, runs **2,500.00**
   1952, model WD–6 . . . . **600.00**
M–H, 1936, Challenger, steel **2,200.00**
M–M
   1938, model KTA **1,200.00**
   1947, model GTA **1,025.00**
   1953, model UT **400.00**
Oliver, 99 GM **3,400.00**
Silver King, 1946, runs **1,800.00**

WOOD AND NATURAL MATERIALS

Rural America used wood because it was inexpensive and readily available. As land was cleared for settlement and farming, the wood from trees became fuel for heat or lumber for building or the manufacture of a host of products ranging from barrels to furniture.

Grain and tone explain the appeal of natural wood. Each piece exhibits individual characteristics. This aspect was understood and admired in an agrarian society. Natural wood has an earthy tone, strong yet subdued.

Over the years wood patinates and oxidates. These two forces create a feel to wood that is impossible to duplicate. Only time can accomplish the effect.

Many wooden forms were grained, painted, or stenciled. Because this was done by hand, they also exhibit strong individual characteristics. In the 1950s it was common practice to strip painted pieces and refinish them to expose the natural wood grains. The folk art revival of the late 1960s through the early 1980s focused interest on painted pieces, showing that the painting is an integral part of the piece.

Painted pieces now have strong appeal among Country collectors as well. Tastes range from ornately decorated blanket chests to the warm milk paint tones often found on pie safes. Painted wooden pieces have found a permanent home in Country.

BASKETS

History: The Country look focuses on baskets made of splint, rye, straw, or willow. Emphasis is placed on handmade examples. Nails or staples, wide splints which are thin and evenly cut, or wire bail handles denote factory construction which can date to the mid–19th century. Painted or woven decorated baskets rarely are handmade, unless American Indian.

Baskets are collected by (a) type—berry, egg, or field, (b) region–Nantucket or Shaker, and (c) composition—splint, rye, or willow. Stick to ex-

amples in very good condition; damaged baskets are a poor investment even at low prices.

References: Frances Johnson, *Wallace–Homestead Price Guide To Baskets, Second Edition*, Wallace–Homestead, 1989; Martha Wetherbee and Nathan Taylor, *Legend of the Bushwhacker Basket*, published by author, 1986; Christoph Will, *International Basketry For Weavers and Collectors*, Schiffer Publishing, Ltd., 1985.

Reproduction Craftspersons: *General*—Darryl & Karen Arawjo, PO Box 477, Bushkill, PA 18324; Cheryl I Boyer, Berkshire Ash Baskets, PO Box

144, Lanesborough, MA 01237; Mr & Mrs J H Durham, Rte 2, Box 60, Cherokee, AL 35616; Richard & Christine Foster, Stannard Mountain Basketry, RD 1, Box 1385, East Hardwick, VT 05836; Bonnie & Jeffrey Gale, RFD 1, Box 124A, South New Berlin, NY 13843; Ross A Gibson, Day Basket Co, 110 W High St, North East, MD 21901 Barbara & Norbert Hala, 1641 Etta Kable Dr, Beavercreek, OH 45432; Sue Hahn, Old Times–Baskets, 41547 S R 558, Leetonia, OH 44431; Jonathan Kline, Black Ash Baskets, 5066 Mott Evans Rd, Trumansburg, NY 14886; Susan Kolvereid, 834 Old State Rd, Berwyn, PA 19312; Dave Lewis Basketry, RD 2, Box 684, Bedford, PA 15522; Martha Watson Lorentzen, 2 Jared Ln, Yarmouthport, MA 02675; Richard & Jodi McAllister, Red Bird Mission Crafts, HC–69, Box 15, Queen Dale Center, Beverly, KY 40913; John E McGuire, Baskets & Bears, 398 S Main St, Geneva, NY 14456; Carol Nelson, Walnut Creek Baskets, 12018 217th St W, PO Box 84, Illinois City, IL 61259; Susi Nuss, Basketmaker, 5 Steele Crossing Rd, Bolton, CT 06043; Gary A O'Brien, Meadow Farm, Ruggles Hill Rd, Hardwick, MA 01037; Gwynne Ormsby, 415 W Market St, West Chester, PA 19382; Beth Peterson & Mark Kelz, Splintworks, PO Box 858, Cave Junction, OR 97523; Joyce Schaum Basketry, 2212 Reifsnider Rd, Keymar, MD 21757; Alvin & Trevle Wood, 2415 E Main St, Murfreesboro, TN 37130; Aaron Yakim, Rte 2, Box 314A, West Union, WV 26456; Stephen Zeh, Basketmaker, PO Box 381, Temple, ME 04984.

Indian—Donna Rohkohl, The Basket Barn, PO Box 138, Howell, MI 48844; *Nantucket Lightship*—Barbette & Richard Behm, Maine Island Baskets, 112 Euclid Ave, Portland, ME 04103; Barbara Bonfanti, 112 Oxford Dr, Lititz, PA 17543; Sue Gruebel, Log House Primitives, PO Box 206, Circleville, OH 43113; John & Holiday Hays, Holiday and Garshwiller, Rte 1, Box 34, Bloomingdale, IN 47832; Joe & Sylvia Hemphill, Heritage Baskets, PO Box 305, Britton, MI 49229; Virginia S Knight, PO Box 39575, Ft Lauderdale, FL 33339, Kathy & Robert Loring, Heirloom Baskets of Chatham, PO Box 1145, S Chatham, MA 02659; Carol S Lasnier, Country Companions, 35 Chittenden Rd, Hebron, CT 06231; Jack Nichols, 392 Schuylkill Rd, Birdsboro, PA 19508; Leslie Marshall Nutting, 32 Forest Hill Dr, Simsbury, CT 06070; Bill & Marilyn Rosenquist, Lightship Baskets, 342 Moose Hill Rd, Guilford, CT 06437; Ronald J Wilson, 1600 Westbrook Ave, Apt 633, Richmond, VA 23227; *Rye Straw*—Marie Stotler, 23 Frame Ave, Malvern, PA 19355.

Reproduction Manufacturers: *General*—Adirondack Store and Gallery, 109 Saranac Ave, Lake Placid, NY 12946; American Folklore, 330 W Pleasant, Freeport, IL 61032; Anastasia's Collectibles, 6114 134th St W, Apple Valley, MN 55124; Bullfrog Hollow, Keeny Rd, Lyme, CT 06371; Checkerberry Hill, 253 Westridge Ave, Daly City, CA 94015; Chinaberry General Store, 1846 Winfield Dunn Highway, Sevierville, TN 38762; Country Loft, 1506 South Shore Park, Hingham, MA 02043; The Country Stippler, Rte 2, Box 1540, Pine Mountain, GA 31822; Country Wicker, 2238D Bluemound Rd, Waukesha, WI 53186; Faith Mountain Country Fare, Main St, Box 199, Sperryville, VA 22740; Flying Pig Artworks, PO Box 474, Milford, MI 48042; Folk Art Emporium, 3591 Forest Haven Ln, Chesapeake, VA 23321; Gooseberry Patch, PO Box 634, Delaware, OH 43015; The Herb Cottage, Lincoln Way East, RD 2, Box 130, Fayetteville, PA 17222; Ingrid's Handcraft Crossroads, 8 Randall Rd, Rochester, MA 02770; J M Brel, Rte 8, Box 246, Fairmont, WV 26554; Matthews Emporium, 157 N Trade St, PO Box 1038, Matthews, NC 28106; McClanahan Country, 217 Rockwell Rd, Wilmington, NC 28405; Mulberry Magic, PO Box 62, Ruckersville, VA 22968; Pure and Simple, PO Box 535, 117 W Hempstead, Nashville, AR 71852; Southern Manner, Inc, 106 North Trade St, PO Box 1706, Matthews, NC 28106; A Special Blend of Country, RD 1, Box 56, Fabius, NY 13063; The Vine and Cupboard, PO Box 309, George Wright Rd, Woolwich, ME 04579; The Vinery, 103 Alta Vista, Waterloo, IA 40703; West Rindge Baskets, West Main St, Rindge, NH 03461.

Kits and Supplies—The Back Door–Country Baskets, 10 Batchellor Dr, North Brookfield, MA 01535; The Basket Barn, PO Box 138, Howell, MI 48844; Cane Bottom, 1 Park Dr, Roxana, IL 62084; The Country Seat, RD 2, Box 24, Kempton, PA 19529; Frank's Cane and Rush Supply, 7252 Heil Ave, Huntington Beach, CA 92647.

Apple
    15″ d, 9″ h, oak staves, solid turned pine bottom, bentwood bail handle, overlapping rim strip, wire reinforcement around lower section   **150.00**
    16″ d, split wood, rounded bottom, bentwood swivel handle, hanging strap and hook, c1915 . . . . **68.00**

Berry, split wood
    5″ d, $2\frac{7}{8}$″ h, tin edging **75.00**
    7″ d, $5\frac{3}{4}$″ h, crisscross bands **45.00**
    8 x $9\frac{1}{2}$″, 5″ h, woven splint, melon rib, old red paint and natural **200.00**
    10 x $10\frac{1}{2}$, 6″ h, woven splint, buttocks, good age and color, bentwood handle **80.00**
    $10\frac{3}{4}$ x $11\frac{1}{2}$″, $5\frac{1}{2}$″ h, woven splint, buttocks, bentwood handle **125.00**

Berry Carrier, turned handle, square tray, four stapled machine–cut softwood berry baskets **24.00**

Berry, 8¼ x 6¼", 8½" h, woven splint, carved handle, $135.00.

Field, 23" d, 15" h, oak splint, carved rim handles, $125.00.

Burden, 14" sq, 16" h, woven splint, square bottom, round rim, old patina **45.00**

Bushel, 18 x 11", stave construction, wrapped with wire bands, wooden rim, bentwood rim handles, old varnish finish **150.00**

Cheese, hexagonal weave
14" d, woven splint, dark brown stain exterior **55.00**
21½" d, 7½" h, woven splint **275.00**
24" d, woven splint, gray scrubbed finish, blue paint traces **475.00**

Clothespin, 14¼ x 12½", willow, early 20th C **85.00**

Cotton Gathering, splint, 22" d, 20" h **115.00**

Dough Rising, 23" d, shallow, rye straw, hickory splint binding, PA, late 19th C **115.00**

Drying
11 x 15, 6¼" h, woven splint, open work bottom, open rim handles **55.00**
14½ x 15", woven splint, open weave wire bottom, bentwood handle branded "Dr. Webb" **70.00**

Egg
6½ x 9", 4" h, woven splint, buttocks, Eye of God design at bentwood handle **95.00**
7¼" d, 4½" h, woven splint, bentwood handle sgd "Haver," good patina **250.00**
7½ x 8", 4" h, woven splint, buttocks, bentwood handle **85.00**
8 x 10¾", 5" h, woven splint, radiating ribs, bentwood handle . . . **135.00**
8½" d, woven splint, old green paint **225.00**
9 x 11", 4½" h, woven splint, melon rib, Eye of God design at handle **35.00**
10½ x 12", 6" h, woven splint, radiating ribs, bentwood handle, old varnish finish **60.00**
11 x 12", 6½" h, woven splint, buttocks, bentwood handle **75.00**

15 x 17, woven splint, bentwood handle, weathered gray scrubbed finish **55.00**

Feather
20" d, 26" h, ash splint, New England, early 19th C **275.00**
21" d, 25" h, sliding lid, Shaker, New England, 19th C **425.00**

Field
28 x 17", 12" h, oval, oak splint, bow handles, ftd, carved oak runners reinforce bottom, c1875 **135.00**
29" d, ash and hickory splint, loosely woven, c1900 . . . . **325.00**
29½ x 17", oak splint, rib construction, wrapped bentwood handle, 19th C **265.00**
30" d, 15¾" h, oak splint, rib construction, carved handles, c1880 **225.00**
32" d, 16½" h, woven splint, rib construction, bow handles, New England, c1850 . . . . **275.00**
42 x 26", 12" h, rect, ash splint, CT, 19th C **350.00**

Flower
6" h, woven splint, bentwood handle **85.00**
10½" d, ash splint, tightly woven, extra long carved handle, 1800s, New England **110.00**

Game, 21" h, woven splint, two part, loom crest, hanging **195.00**

Garden, 11½" d, 6½" h, woven splint, carved handle continues to bottom, VA, 19th C **190.00**

Gathering
9½" d, woven splint, flat tray, bentwood handle, old green paint . . . **145.00**
12 x 18½", rect, woven splint, boat shaped, shallow, high bentwood handle **55.00**
12¼" d, 5½" h, woven splint, bentwood handle **50.00**
14 x 22½", 6" h, woven splint, bent-

Gathering, cov, 17 x 12½", 17" h, wicker, $55.00.

Indian, storage, 11" d, 7¾" h, grass, $150.00.

wood handle, sun bleached, minor damage **45.00**
15 x 19½", 6" h, woven splint, bentwood handle, rim repair. . . . **45.00**
15½ x 20½", 10" h, woven splint, two bentwood rim handles, one perpendicular handle **145.00**
16 x 27", 11" h, woven splint, buttocks, wrapped bent sapling handle **60.00**
17 x 23", 7¾" h, oblong, woven splint, built up rim handles, good age and color, minor rim wear . . **70.00**
19 x 27", oval, splint, plaited rim, bentwood handles **120.00**
Goose Feather, 16" d, 24" h, lid, woven splint, bentwood handles **95.00**
Half, 11½ x 7", 5" h, woven splint, bentwood handle, good detail **175.00**
Herb Drying, rect
15½ x 24", 2¼" h, woven splint **135.00**
20½ x 21", woven splint **355.00**
Hourglass Shaped
10½" d, 12" h, woven splint **50.00**
12" d, 22" h, splint, two part **70.00**
Indian
Achumawi, Pitt River, 8¼" d, 5¼" h, jar shaped, redbud wrapped rim, geometric step design, old paper label, loose rim, repaired breaks **275.00**
Algonquin, storage, 16½ x 24½", 13" h, birch bark, negative scraped leaf designs, wear and breaks in bottom **200.00**
Astugewi, Hot Creek, northern CA, 6½" d, 5" h, turned base changes to full twist overlay of beargrass and redbud, lattice twined band, checkerboard design **250.00**
Cahvilla, southern CA, 11½" d, 3¾" h, natural and dyed juncus design, rim wear **215.00**
Chemehuevi, 5¾" d, 4¾" h, polychrome basketry olla, brown and

purple geometric design on natural ground, attributed to Ann Land, c1900 . . . . **3,500.00**
Eskimo, 7¼" d, 7¾" h, knobbed lid, grass, polychrome design, c1900 **115.00**
Hupa, acorn storage, 10" d, 7½" h, half and full twist twined beargrass and woodwardia design, heavy reinforced rim, two holes at base, one warp break at top spacing **75.00**
Macha, 3" d, 2" h, lid, twined, whaling ships and birds, minor rim damage **115.00**
Makah, storage
8½" d, 5½" h, brown, green, and natural stripes, wire supported rewrapped rim **25.00**
10 x 12", 4¾" h, leaf design between double bands **105.00**
Mission, 9½" d, 2¾" h, juncus design, rim damage **175.00**
Papago, 8" d, 5½" h, geometric and bird designs, wear and damage **25.00**
Pima, 7½" d, 4½" h, prehistoric type braid rim **325.00**
Piute, seed storage, 9½" d, 6½" h, twined, jar shaped, plant cordage lugs **350.00**
Salishan, berry, 6" d, 4½" h, bowl shaped, braided rim, beargrass spot design, loose rim end **85.00**
Woodland, 18½" d, 18½" h, lid, woven splint, potato print designs, faded red, yellow, green, and natural **275.00**
Kitchen, 12 x 14, 6½" h, woven splint, buttocks, woven in three shades of splint **150.00**
Knife, 9 x 12", 3½" h, woven splint, divided interior, polychrome watercolor floral design, bentwood handle **225.00**

Laundry
   18½" d, 12" h, round, woven splint, bentwood rim handles, marked "OHW" **55.00**
   19" d, 11¾" h, round, woven splint, rim hand holds, copper wire woven in bottom **95.00**
   19 x 31", 13½" h, woven splint, bentwood rim handles **100.00**
   21" d, 10" h, round, woven splint, bentwood rim handles **65.00**
   22 x 27", 12½" h, oval, woven splint, rim hand holds. **100.00**
   24 x 19", 10" h, rect, woven splint, bentwood rim handles **115.00**
Loom
   7½" w, 6¾" h, hanging, cane, faded curliqued ribbon, and string dec **35.00**
   9½" w, 9½" h, woven splint, faded green and yellow **65.00**
   10½" w, 17" h, hanging, woven splint, two section, traces of yellow paint. **375.00**
   12" w, 13" h, hanging, woven splint, crest **100.00**
Lunch, 8 x 6", oval, woven splint, ash wrapped handle, two lift lids on crosspieces, tightly woven, 1800s **165.00**
Market
   8½ x 14½", 6¼" h, woven splint, natural, red, and black woven design, bentwood handle. **85.00**
   9 x 15", 8" h, rect, woven splint, bentwood handle. **65.00**
   11 x 20", 9" h, lid, woven splint, bentwood handle, damaged **75.00**
   12" d, 7½" h, round, woven splint, wooden bottom, swivel handle **125.00**
   12½ x 17½", 6½" h, rect, woven splint, double swing handles. **120.00**
   16 x 23", 11¾" h, woven splint, woven center brace, faded green bands, bentwood handle **195.00**
Miniature
   3" l, 3½" h, woven splint, buttocks, "one egg" size. **350.00**
   3¼" d, 1⅝" h, woven splint, square base, round rim, old patina **85.00**
   3½ x 7⅞", 2" h, rect, woven splint, old patina, minor damage **115.00**
   4 x 4½", 2" h, woven splint, buttocks, bentwood handle, old patina, minor damage **250.00**
   4¼" h, melon rib, late 19th, early 20th C **330.00**
   5 x 5¼", 2¾" h, woven splint, buttocks, bentwood handle **165.00**
Nantucket
   5¾" d, 6⅜" h, shaped handle, brass ears, late 19th C. **660.00**
   6¼ x 7", 5" h, oval, woven cane and splint sides, wooden bottom,

bentwood swing handle, worn dark brown repaint, handle stamped "E.A.S." **300.00**
   8¾" d, woven cane and splint, turned wooden bottom, bentwood swing handle, old patina, out of round **250.00**
   10½" d, shaped handle, maker's and owner's names burnished in base, PB and BS Heywood, Nantucket Island, MA, dated 1950 .... **300.00**
   11 x 7¾", lightship, label "Alfred D Williams," 18th C **1,100.00**
   12" d, incised turned base, shaped swing handle, paper label "Lightship Basket made by William D Appleton, Nantucket, Mass," early 20th C **1,700.00**
   13 x 15½", 8" h, oval, splint staves, woven cane, cane lashed rim, wooden base, bentwood swing handle, old printed paper label "Mitchell Ray, Starbuck Court, Nantucket Island, Mass" **475.00**
Peanut Gathering, 19¾" l, 3¼" h, factory made, machine-cut wide splint, painted white, VA **75.00**
Pea Picking, 16" l, 11" w, 6" h, oval, wide overlapping split wood, attached feet, full circular bentwood handle **75.00**
Picnic
   7¾ x 15", 7" h, splint, double hinged lid, green and natural colored interior design, faded exterior, bentwood handle **100.00**
   9¾ x 15", 7" h, woven splint, red paint over earlier black paint, swivel handle **65.00**
   16" l, 12½" w, lid, woven splint, bentwood swivel handle. **85.00**
Potato, round, ash splint **35.00**
Sower's, 12 x 14½", 7" h, woven splint, bentwood handle **50.00**
Storage
   10" h, oval, rye straw.......... **50.00**

Storage, 18½" d, rye straw, $175.00.

12 x 15", 9½" h, rect, woven splint, red, black, and green painted dec **105.00**

12 x 16¼", 6½" h, woven splint, bentwood rim handles, dark patina .. **75.00**

13 x 15", 10½" h, woven splint, bentwood handle, minor damage ... **75.00**

14" d, 15¾" h, woven splint, twill pattern, square base, round rim, old patina, c1910............ **145.00**

15 x 19", 12" h, rect, lid, woven splint, teal blue and pink watercolor designs, worn.......... **135.00**

16" d, 8½" h, rye straw, rim handles **85.00**

17" d, 9" h, woven splint, bentwood handle, misshapen........... **95.00**

17 x 18", 9" h, woven splint, bentwood swing handle, old mustard yellow paint **1,300.00**

17¼" l, rect, lid, woven splint, alternating red potato print design and yellow paint, minor damage **250.00**

19 x 20", 11" h, rect, lid, woven splint, red, blue, and yellow watercolor designs, worn **170.00**

21" d, 14½" h, woven splint, rim hand holds, minor damage **145.00**

Table, 14" d, white oak splint, loosely woven **45.00**

Tobacco, 38" l, splint, open weave, shallow **75.00**

Utility

5¾" d, round, woven splint, bentwood handle, old worn dark varnish....................... **75.00**

7½ x 12½", 4½" h, oblong, bentwood handle **75.00**

8" d, 5" h, woven splint, hickory handle, weathered **105.00**

8½ x 9½", 4¼" h, woven splint, buttocks, bentwood handle **135.00**

9" d, 5" h, round, woven splint, bentwood rim handles, old patina **175.00**

9¾" d, 5½" h, round, woven splint, faded red woven design **150.00**

10" d, 4" h, round, woven splint, scalloped rim, bentwood handle **250.00**

10½ x 12", 7¼" h, boat shaped, woven handle **55.00**

11 x 22", 7" h, rect, woven splint, buttocks, bentwood handle **25.00**

11½" d, 6½" h, woven splint, bentwood handle, old varnish **105.00**

12 x 12", 6¾" h, square, woven splint, radiating ribs, bentwood handle **20.00**

13" d, 6¼" h, woven splint, curlique band, bentwood handle **155.00**

13 x 17", 7½" h, oblong, woven splint, radiating ribs, bentwood handle, old patina **65.00**

13½" d, 8" h, woven splint, bentwood handle.............. **110.00**

13½ x 15½", 9½" h, woven splint, polka dot designs on red and black watercolor and natural ground, worn rim........... **85.00**

14 x 15½", 9½" h, oval, woven splint, horizontal ribs in sides, incomplete rim binding **55.00**

15 x 17", 8½" h, woven splint, bentwood swing handle, out of round, old varnish, old repair in bottom **130.00**

16½ x 18½, 8½" h, woven splint, buttocks, old patina, bentwood handle **65.00**

Vegetable, 18 x 14½", 7¾" h, rect, woven splint, bentwood handle attached lengthwise, c1880 .... **120.00**

Wall

8 x 6", 5" h, oak splint, c1900..... **65.00**

12 x 9", 6" h, poplar splint, New England, c1850............. **95.00**

Wine, 21¾" l, willow, divided interior holds twelve bottles, factory made, early 20th C **65.00**

Work, 11½ x 18", woven splint, bentwood rim handle, attached small woven oval basket interior corner, light blue paint **110.00**

BOXES

History: Boxed storage was commonplace in the rural American home. Although pasteboard boxes (see Band Boxes) were available, most rural individuals preferred boxes made from wood. There simply was something sturdy and lasting about a wood box.

Boxes were designed for specific tasks. Among the most commonly found forms are candle boxes, document boxes, jewelry, and knife boxes. Everything imaginable was stored in boxes—clothing, salt, spices, and trinkets, just to name a few. Often the family Bible was kept in a Bible box.

The folk art collecting craze of the 1970s and 1980s drew attention to the painted box. A grain painting revival occurred among contemporary craftspersons. The Country movement became enamored with "primitives," i.e., crudely constructed boxes. Completely overlooked were the high style and better constructed boxes, many of which were imported from abroad.

During the early American revival from the 1930s through the 1950s, a great hoopla was raised over bride's boxes, ornately painted oval bentwood boxes, many of which featured a picture of bride and groom. Many were passed as American in origin. Research has proven that almost all originated in Europe.

In fact, there is a strong painted furniture tradition in a number of European countries—Norway, southwest Germany, and many Slavic countries. Although different in color tone and design, many novice collectors buy these items believing them to be American in origin.

Reproduction Craftspersons: *Bentwood and Pantry*—Donald Butler, 402 Lombard St, Philadelphia, PA 19147; E B Frye and Son, Inc, Frye's Measure Mill, Wilton, NH 03086; Charles Harvey, Simple Gifts, 201 C N Broadway, Berea, KY 40403; Bill Scherer, Shaker Carpenter Shop, 8267 Oswego Rd, Liverpool, NY 13088; Eric Taylor & Betty Grondin, Northern Swallow Tails, 13A High St, Danbury, NH 03230; Mary Travis, RR 1, Box 96, Fairbury, IL 61739.

Decorated—Donna W Albro, Strawberry Vine, 6677 Hayhurst St, Worthington, OH 43085; Carol Fankhauser, Heartwood, PO Box 458, Canfield, OH 44406; Petra & Thomas Haas, PO Box 20, Oley, PA 19547; *General*—Gary S Adriance, Adriance Heritage Collection, 5 N Pleasant St, South Dartmouth, MA 02748; Richard and Bess Leaf, Box 223, Rte 5, Jenkins Chapel Rd, Shelbyville, TN 37160; Jan Switzer, Painted Pony Folk Art, 8392 M–72 West, Traverse City, MI 49684; *Wall*—Tom Douglass, RD 1, Box 38, Hopwood, PA 15445.

Reproduction Manufacturers: *Bentwood and Pantry*—Chinaberry General Store, 1846 Winfield Dunn Highway, Sevierville, TN 38762; Country Lighting and Accessories, PO Box 1279, New London, NH 03257; Hofcraft, PO Box 1791, Grand Rapids, MI 49501; The Friends, Box 464, Frederick, MD 21701; Unfinished Business, PO Box 246X, Wingate, NC 28174; *Bible*—Conewago Junction, 805 Oxford Rd, New Oxford, PA 17350.

General—Classics in Wood, 82 Lisbon Rd, Canterbury, CT 06331, The Colonial Keeping Room 16 Ridge Rd, RFD 1, Box 704, Fairfield, ME 04937; Country House, 5939 Trails End, Three Oaks, MI 49128; Country Loft, 1506 South Shore Park, Hingham, MA 02043; KML Enterprises, RR 1, Box 234L, Berne, IN 46711; The Ohlinger's, PO Box 462, Gurnee, IL 60031; Our Home, Articles of Wood, 666 Perry St, Vermilion, OH 44089; Out of the Woods, 38 Pinehurst Rd, Marshfield, MA 02050; Pine Cone Primitives, PO Box 682, Troutman, NC 28166; South Bound Millworks, PO Box 349, Sandwich, MA 02563; Ye Olde Wood Smith, Box 300, Alliance, NE 69301; *Jewelry*—Honeybrook Woods, RD 2, Box 102, Honey Brook, PA 19344; *Pipe*—Five Trails Antiques and Country Accents, 116 E Water St, Circleville, OH 43113; *Salt*—Log Cabin Shop, Box 275, Lodi, OH 44254; Mulberry Magic, PO Box 62, Ruckersville, VA 22968.

Apple
11½" l, 5½" h, 7½" deep, pine, dovetailed, short pyramidal feet, old red stain **200.00**
11¾" l, pine, orig green paint. **195.00**

Ballot
6" l, poplar, decorated, red and black graining, polychrome bronze powder stenciled eagle, shield, and vintage on lid, bird and foliage on front, gold striping, ballot slot in lid and bottom. **160.00**
14¼" l, walnut, dovetailed case, slot in lid, orig lock, red stained interior, refinished exterior. **125.00**
Bible, 17¼" l, pine, chip carved design on facade, rose head wrought iron nail construction, old dark patina, age cracks, replaced hinges **120.00**
Book, 12" l, walnut, interior slide out compartment, green gilt and red trimmed emb paper covering **200.00**
Bride's, pine, bentwood, oval, decorated, laced seams
16½" l, polychrome floral dec, red paint. **500.00**
18" l, polychrome house dec on sides, old repainted houses, trees, and couple walking dog illus on lid **625.00**
19" l, polychrome floral dec on red ground sides, man and woman illus and German inscription around edge of lid **900.00**
21" l, orange paint and polychrome floral dec and striping on sides, decoupage children in goat cart print on lid **750.00**
Bugle, 19¼" l, decorated, hard and soft woods, old black repaint over earlier blue, red striping, gold stenciled designs, initials, and polychrome bugle, repaired bottom board, missing handle **300.00**
Burl, 9½" l, locking **235.00**
Candle
6½" l, sliding lid with thumb notch, four applied hand fashioned round feet, orig finish, c1825 . . . **100.00**
6⅞" h, pine, sliding raised panel lid,

Bride's Box, pine, bentwood, oval, 22 x 14¾", $200.00.

Candle, beveled sliding cov, 7½ x 4 x 2½", $85.00.

eagle on lid, stars and shield side dec, date "1823" on front, shield on back, painted green, 1790–1830. . . . . **1,500.00**

9" l, birch, dovetailed, finger grips on beveled sliding lid, red stain   **175.00**

9½" l, pine, sliding lid, square nail construction, circular saw marks, orig blue paint **375.00**

11½" l, pine, sliding lid, old green paint, white letters, "G.M.D. 1858". **150.00**

14" w, 15" h, hanging, poplar, cut–out crest, drawer, nail construction, old finish **145.00**

15" l, poplar, sliding paneled lid, old red paint **175.00**

16¼" l, cherry, dovetailed, finger grips and lock on sliding lid, old worn finish **300.00**

Carved

3½" l, allover chip carving, sliding lid, made from one pc of wood . . **100.00**

7¾" d, 5" h, round, cork, chip carved designs, leather trim, worn brown patina **55.00**

9" l

Mahogany, relief carved flower and foliage dec. **85.00**

Pine, relief carved designs four sides and lid, four different eagles, foliage, crossed flags, and "U.S.A. Fort Hancock," homemade locking mechanism, old varnish finish, 7¾" h **325.00**

12¼" l, walnut, dovetailed case, geometric chip carved and stamped designs, line inlay in base and lid molding, brass bail handle, old finish **400.00**

18" l, walnut, dovetailed, allover chip carving, engraved metal plate on lid inscribed "Desmond Fitzgerald 1877," ftd, lift–out interior tray, age cracks **225.00**

Decorated

7" l, poplar, lock and key, orig red flame graining **110.00**

8½" d, 8¼" h, round, poplar, red sponging on yellow ground, replaced lid finial **700.00**

9⅝" l, poplar, orig tan paint and gold stenciled designs on beveled edge lid **75.00**

10" l, 9" deep, 3" h, pine, gold stenciled floral dec and fruit compote on black ground, ftd, marbleized paper–lined interior. **130.00**

10¼" l, pine, book shaped, wood graining, brown striping and red roses on lid **100.00**

11¼" l, tulip wood, imitation exotic wood graining, inlaid striping . . . **105.00**

14" l, pine, red and black graining, applied base and lid moldings, brass handle and latch **205.00**

14⅝" l, poplar, white striping and black edging, red stain, bluish–green interior, brass bail handle, alligatored finish **275.00**

14¾" l, pine, red and brown graining on yellow ground, paneled sides and lid, small porcelain button feet. **95.00**

19¾" l, poplar, dovetailed, brown vinegar graining, wrought iron handles and lock, thistle design on emb brass handle, missing hasp and escutcheon **350.00**

24" l, pine and poplar, iron lock and hasp, brass keyhole cover, orig black and white graining **1,450.00**

Desk, 12¼" w, 10" deep, 7⅓" h, table top, pine, slant top lid, orig lock, emb brass escutcheon, dovetailed case, old refinish **200.00**

Document

12" w, 6¼" deep, 5" h, mahogany veneer, inlaid bird's–eye maple, 19th C **350.00**

18" w, 9" h, pine, painted to resemble iron–bound trunk, black and yellow paint, natural finish, c1830. . . . . **200.00**

Dome Top

9¾" l, pine, staple hinges, orig blue paint, white striping, polychrome floral dec. **425.00**

12¼" l, mahogany, dovetailed, ogee feet, old varnish finish, replaced brass lock and hasp and staple hinges, age cracks **350.00**

14" l, poplar, decorated, black and yellow polka dots, red ground, "This trunk was made by mother's great grandfather guild" paper label inside lid **825.00**

19¼" l, pine and poplar, dovetailed, red vinegar graining, orig iron lock and hasp **1,150.00**

Hanging, hinged lid, square nail construction, weathered finish, 6 x 6½ x 13", $55.00.

Hanging
  14¼" h, 9" w, 8" deep, pine, carved, painted, pierced stylized figures crest, sloping lid on well above one drawer, polychrome stylized pinwheels and stellate design on sides and back, dark blue–green ground, Connecticut River Valley, New England, 1750–1800 . . . . . **8,750.00**
  17½" h, 11" w, 5½" deep, poplar, two compartments, old orange paint **350.00**
  20½" h, walnut, inlaid dec, fiddle-back crest, shaped apron **245.00**
  21" h, 10" w, 10¼" deep, poplar, weathered blue repaint **280.00**
Inlaid, 13" w, 8¾" deep, 5¼" h, herring-bone patterned sides, star dec on lid, 19th C **150.00**
Jewelry
  8" l, two drawers, gold painted cut-out design with red cloth backing, white porcelain pulls, cigar box back board **35.00**
  11¼" h, tramp art, miniature chest of drawers shape, traces of gold paint **100.00**
  14" l, tramp art, mirror and drawer in blue velvet–lined interior, old varnish finish **195.00**
Knife
  2¼" l, miniature, mahogany, dove-tailed, cut-out handle, early 19th C **200.00**
  11¾" l, bentwood, cut-outs and wooden knob fasteners on lami-nate sides, old varnish finish **45.00**
  13" l
    Decorated, yellow striping, floral dec, and "Lizzie" on orig brown finish **200.00**
    Pine, square nail construction,

    old natural yellow finish, 19th C **50.00**
  Poplar, scalloped edge and di-vider, orig red interior, old green overpaint exterior **90.00**
  Walnut, spurred cut–out handle, old finish **135.00**
13½" h
  Hardwood, turned handle, refin-ished, age crack **55.00**
  Mahogany Veneer, upright, slanted lid, silver plated bail handles, tooled silver escutch-eon, replaced interior **450.00**
14" l, walnut and ash, inlaid, chev-ron herringbone pattern, varnish finish **125.00**
14¼" l, mahogany, dovetailed, incised scrollwork, heart handle, early 19th C **350.00**
16¼" l, poplar and pine, dovetailed, hinged lids, cut–out handle, old dark finish **250.00**
17¼" l, mahogany, dovetailed, scal-loped ends, cut–out handle, 19th C **225.00**
Pantry, bentwood
  3" d, round, single finger construc-tion, old patina, lid **45.00**
  4⅞" l, oval, single finger construc-tion, iron tacks, old red and black handwritten label "Copoons" . . . **200.00**
  5¾" l, oval, single finger construc-tion, pine and beech, chip carv-ing, old green repaint, lid **200.00**
  5⅞" l, oval, two finger construction, copper tacks, old blue paint, poly-chrome decoration and fold art rooster on lid **200.00**
  6½" d, round, straight seam, copper rivets, orig green paint **45.00**
  6½" d, 3" h, round, straight seam, riveted, branded label "S. Short," old finish **95.00**
  8¾" d, 5½" h, round, bentwood swivel handle fastened by wooden knobs, old patina **195.00**
  9½" d, round, straight seam, wire bail handle, worn red repaint **175.00**
  10" l, oval, string laced straight seam, old red paint, lid **275.00**
  11½" l, oval, straight seam, deco-rated, orig red, white, and blue floral dec, brown ground **325.00**
Perfume, 5" l, copper inlay, mirror and blue velvet lined fitted interior holds four cut glass perfume bottles **45.00**
Pipe, hanging
  12" h, 6½" w, 3½" deep, pine and hardwood, scalloped edge, dove-tailed drawer, square nail con-struction **150.00**

16" h, pine, cut-out top rim and crest, dovetailed drawer, old black repaint **2,200.00**

16½" h, oak, old green over red paint, 1720–50 . . . . **275.00**

17½" h, mahogany, replaced leather hinge, old finish, 19th C **100.00**

20" h, cherry, scalloped top edge, single drawer, brass knob, old refinish **220.00**

22¾" h, curly maple, shaped crest, rect body, shaped sloping sides, small molded drawer, molded base, New England, 1770–90 . . . **1,650.00**

Salt, 10" h, wall hanging, chip carved hex sign–type dec, wire nail construction **150.00**

Scouring

12" l, walnut, old finish **55.00**

19" h, 9" w, hanging, pine, old finish, age crack in backboard **115.00**

Slant Lid

10" l, pine and poplar, staple hinges, orig red paint, black stenciled dec on four sides and lid . . . **475.00**

14½" l, poplar, dovetailed, blue wallpaper lined interior, traces of orig red finish **275.00**

Spice, 16" h, walnut, shaped crest, two columns of four drawers, wooden pulls, wire nail construction **250.00**

Storage, 13" l, 13" h, poplar, primitive, old grayish–green paint **60.00**

Trinket

4½" l, dovetailed, pegged base, cotter pin hinges, orig paint, red ground, blue, white, and black enameled motif, 1780–1830 . . . **350.00**

6¼" l, walnut, dovetailed, bracket feet, old finish, replaced hinges **250.00**

BUCKETS, BARRELS, AND BOWLS

History: Wooden buckets, barrels, and bowls, were a necessity in rural America. Barrels were used to store a wide variety of materials ranging from fruits to flour to whiskey. Every medium-size village along a major transportation route had a cooper in residence.

Burl bowls were prized possessions. The individuality of the grain captivated the owners. They wore like iron. Their major problem is that they were subject to cracking.

Like many other wooden objects, a number of specialized bucket forms developed. The pail is one example. However, the ones most sought by Country collectors and decorators are sugar buckets and firkins. Many sugar buckets eventu-

ally wound up inside the rural home as sewing baskets or storage containers for objects such as cookie cutters. Buckets with a manufacturer's mark or period paint bring a premium.

If not properly cared for, wooden barrels, bowls, and buckets will crack and fall apart. Keep them away from areas of high heat and low humidity. Barrels that were meant to hold liquid should be filled for a few days several times each year to keep the joints swollen tight. Do not oil bowls. Simply wipe them clean with a damp cloth.

Reproduction Craftspersons: *Bowls*—Carl Desko, PO Box 201, Willow Grove, PA 19090; Rip and Tammi Mann, Handhewn Bowls, PO Box 1584; Etowah, NC 28729; Don Mounter, Rte 1, Box 54, Fayette, MO 65248; John D Sadler, Wooden Bowls by John Sadler, Rte 1, Box 81, Bradyville, TN 37026.

Reproduction Manufacturers: *Bowl*—Lace Wood 'N Tin Tyme, 6496 Summerton, Shepherd, MI 48883; The Painted Pony, 8392 West M–72, Traverse City, MI 49684; Southern Manner, Inc, 106 North Trade St, PO Box 1706, Matthews, NC 28106; Unfinished Business, PO Box 246X, Wingate, NC 28174; *Buckets*—Chinaberry General Store, 1846 Winfield Dunn Highway, Sevierville, TN 38762; Conewago Junction, 805 Oxford Rd, New Oxford, PA 17350; Country Loft, 1506 South Shore Park, Hingham, MA 02043; Log Cabin Shop, Box 275, Lodi, OH 44254.

Barrel, 19" h, stave constructed, laced wood bands, refinished **100.00**

Bowl

6" d, round

2⅞" h, burl, old soft finish **725.00**

4½" h, cov, burl, painted black stripe on foot and shoulder . . . **1,400.00**

7" d, 2¾" h, burl, simple turned detail, old soft finish **375.00**

8¼" d, 3" h, burl, soft scrubbed finish, minor rim crack **600.00**

10¼" d, 3¼" h, burl, old soft finish . . . **900.00**

Bowl, burl, 16¾" d, 5¾" h, early 19th C, $600.00.

13½" d, 6" h, round, burl, white
scrubbed finish **550.00**
15" d, 5" h, burl, tightly grained fig-
ure throughout, thin sides, flared
lip, old dark worn patina. **4,500.00**
19" l, 12" w, 4¼" h, oblong, burl,
protruding end handles. **125.00**
20½" l, 7" h, oval, burl, iron handle,
wear, cracks, damage in bottom   **1,150.00**
21" l, 14¼" w, 6" h, oval, burl, simple cut–out handles, tight grained
figure, old finish. **2,750.00**
22½" l, walnut, burl, carved handles
both ends, Hudson Valley, late
18th, early 19th C **350.00**
25" d, 9¼" h, scrubbed interior, red
repainted exterior, old repair in
bottom **450.00**
Bucket
3¾" h, miniature, stave constructed,
alternating light and dark wood,
wood bands, old worn patina . . .   **40.00**
7½" h, 9¾" d, stave constructed, old
brown graining, black painted
bands, diamond fasteners, wire
bail and wooden handle, un-
painted inset lid **175.00**
10½" d, lid, iron–bound, locking
peg, orig red paint **55.00**
11" h, stave constructed, laced
wooden bands, swivel bentwood
handle, handle **150.00**
Keg, 13" h, stave constructed, split
sapling bands, worn paper label "Rifle Powder, Rustin Powder Co.,
Cleveland, Ohio" **125.00**
Piggin, 6¾" h, 9¼" d, stave constructed,
bottom stamped "N. Corthell," old
worn finish **160.00**
Sugar Bucket
3½" h, 4¾" d, miniature, stave constructed, tin bands, wire bail and
wooden handle, painted pale
pink **220.00**
4¼" h, 5¼" d, miniature, stave con-
structed, tin bands, wire bail and
wooden handle, old red paint . . .   **250.00**
5¼" h, stave constructed, sapling
bands, swivel handle, green over-
paint.   **240.00**
5¾" h, 6½" d, stave constructed, iron
bands, swivel handle, old dark
finish, bands pitted, replaced pins   **95.00**
6⅝" h, stave constructed, single finger construction lid, wire bail and
wooden handle, old red repaint
over gray. **300.00**
8" h, old green repaint, wire bail
handle **185.00**
9½" h, stave constructed, lid branded
"Wilder P. Clark," wooden pins
hold handle, refinished. **70.00**

Sugar Bucket, 9½" d, 9" h, marked "C. S. Hershey," $75.00.

9¾" h, lid, stave constructed,
branded label "F Lane & Son
Marlboro Depot, NH," old refin-
ishing **85.00**
10" h, stave constructed, mustard
color over blue paint, alligatored
finish **185.00**
11¾" h, lid, stave constructed, bent-
wood swivel handle, old varnish
finish **45.00**

WOODENWARE

History: Many utilitarian household objects and farm implements were made of wood. Although they were used heavily, these implements were made of the strongest woods and well taken care of by their owners.

One of the elements that attracts collectors and decorators to woodenware is the patinated and oxidated finish on unpainted pieces. The wood develops a mellowness and smoothness that is impossible to duplicate.

Lehneware is a favorite with folk art collectors because of its polychrome decorations. It blends nicely with the stencil-decorated pieces of the mid–19th century. These collectors have chosen to ignore the fact that most of the pieces are mass–produced.

This category serves as a catch–all for wood objects that do not fit into other categories.

Reproduction Craftspersons: *General*—Carl Desko, PO Box 201, Willow Grove, PA 19090; Tom Douglass, RD 1, Box 38, Hopwood, PA 15445; Robert P Emory, 115 Hickory Ln, Rosemont, PA 19010; Kevin Riddle, Mountainman Woodshop, PO Box 40, Eagle Rock, VA 24085; John D Sadler, Rte 1, Box 81, Bradyville, TN 37026; *Ladles, Scoops, and Spoons*—Virginia

Petty, Whistlin' Whittler, 1684 Three Forks–Flatrock Rd, Oakland, KY 42159.

Reproduction Manufacturers: *Butter Churn*—Chinaberry General Store, 1846 Winfield Dunn Highway, Sevierville, TN 38762; *General*—Conewago Junction, 805 Oxford Rd, New Oxford, PA 17350; McClanahan Country, 217 Rockwell Rd, Wilmington, NC 28405; *Sock Stretchers*—Sock Stretchers, 112 SE Roza Vista Dr, Yakima, WA 98901.

Barber Pole, $30\frac{3}{4}$" l, turned, old black, white, and red repaint, iron hanging brackets **325.00**

Barn Vent, 42" h, pine, open cut nine point star in triangle, traces of red, white, and blue paint on triangle, traces of gilt on star, wrought iron hinges and hasp on back **700.00**

Busk, $13\frac{1}{2}$" l, chip carved heart and diamond dec, old worn patina **125.00**

Candle Drying Rack, 32" d, 40" h, hardwood and pine, wire hooks on eight removable disks, old patina . .   **575.00**

Churn, $22\frac{1}{2}$" l, 39" h, keg–shaped, small round top door, metal bands, wrought iron fittings, hand crank, dasher, sawbuck base **60.00**

Compote, 5" h, $6\frac{1}{4}$" d, burl, varnish. . .   **250.00**

Crane, 94" l, wall bracket, soft brown finish **425.00**

Dipper, $10\frac{1}{2}$" l, burl, well–shaped curly handle, curved hook and drilled hole for hanging, worn patina   **250.00**

Drying Rack
  50" h, 24" w, pine, three mortised and pinned bars, shoe feet, old brown patina. **175.00**

Lehneware, saffron jar, cov, $5\frac{1}{4}$" h, hp, pink ground, stem with leaves, applied rose and fruit decals, pedestal foot, $315.00.

57" h, vertical pole, tripod base, five accordion arms **25.00**

Grain Measures, nesting, set of four, graduated $8\frac{3}{4}$" d to 15" d, bentwood, old gray repaint **160.00**

Ink Well, $2\frac{1}{2}$" d, turned, gold trim on black ground, glass liner printed paper label "S. Silliman & Co. Chester, Conn." **20.00**

Jar, lid
  4" h, orig varnish finish **135.00**
  $5\frac{1}{4}$" h, ftd, worn varnish finish **75.00**
  $6\frac{1}{2}$" h, $7\frac{1}{4}$" d, turned, wire bail and wooden handle, old varnish finish, minor age crack in base, glued crack in lid, Pease **375.00**
  $6\frac{3}{4}$" h, turned, finial on lid, old varnish **205.00**
  $8\frac{1}{2}$" h, $9\frac{3}{4}$" d, turned, finial on lid, wire bail and wooden handle, old repair in base, scorched bottom, Pease **150.00**

Lehneware
  Cup, $3\frac{1}{8}$" h, ftd, orig polychrome floral dec on blue ground **925.00**
  Egg Cup, turned, ftd
    $2\frac{3}{4}$" h, orig red, green, black, and yellow strawberry dec on salmon pink ground **525.00**
    $3\frac{3}{8}$" h, orig polychrome floral dec and decals, glued break on foot   **205.00**
  Jar
    $2\frac{3}{4}$" h, ftd, polychrome floral dec on salmon ground. **225.00**
    9" h, stave constructed, porcelain knob on turned lid, metal bands, orig red graining, yellow, green, white, and red floral vines painted on black bands, alligatored surface **2,000.00**
  Saffron Jar, lid, ftd
    $4\frac{3}{4}$" h, polychrome flowers and strawberries on yellow ground, chips on foot **350.00**
    5" h, polychrome flowers and strawberries on lavender ground, paint wear on lid, chip on foot. **400.00**
  Salt, $2\frac{7}{8}$" h, ftd, polychrome floral dec on pink ground, chip on foot   **275.00**

Shoe Lasts, Century, size 10D, pr, $30.00.

Mortar, 7" h, burl, worn surface **125.00**
Mortar and Pestle
  $3\frac{1}{4}$" h, miniature, turned, Lignum
    vitae, worn **110.00**
  $6\frac{1}{4}$" h, burl mortar, chestnut pestle,
    old finish **200.00**
  7" h, turned hardwood, age cracks
    in mortar **35.00**
  $7\frac{1}{4}$" h, burl, ftd **320.00**
  8" h, turned, old red finish **80.00**
Noggin, $7\frac{3}{4}$" h, chamfered sides, old
  patina **150.00**
Sock Stretcher, $14\frac{1}{2}$" l **12.00**
Treenware
  Bowl, 19" l, oval, orig seafoam
    green paint, Hudson Valley, NY,
    early 19th C **175.00**
  Canister, 13" h, lid, maple, barrel
    shaped, lathe turned, early 19th C   **275.00**
  Jar
    3" h, lid, wire bail and wooden
      handle, varnish finish, Pease   **75.00**

    $4\frac{1}{2}$" h, turned hourglass shape,
      emb brass button in lid, varnish
      finish **25.00**
    $5\frac{3}{4}$" h, ftd, bottom stamped "Hand
      Turned, J. C. Brown, Paines-
      ville, Ohio," varnish finish . . .   **175.00**
Match Holder
  3" h, beehive shaped, tartan de-
    coupage, ivory top socket holds
    burning match **75.00**
  $3\frac{1}{2}$" h, wine glass shaped, two free
    turned rings, black striping . . .   **55.00**
Plate
  $7\frac{1}{2}$" d, worn patina **225.00**
  $9\frac{1}{4}$" d, deep rim, scrubbed finish   **250.00**
Spoon, $8\frac{1}{8}$" l, rope twist handle,
  turned ivory finial **40.00**
Wall Pocket, 24" h, 18" w, $7\frac{1}{2}$" deep,
  poplar, old blue repaint over green
  and gold, serrated and scalloped
  edges, wire nail construction **150.00**

INDEX